The British Establishment

1760–1784

II

Volume II

I - Z

The
British
Establishment
1760-1784

An Eighteenth-Century
Biographical Dictionary
by ALAN VALENTINE

UNIVERSITY OF OKLAHOMA PRESS : NORMAN

International Standard Book Number 0-8061-0877-0

Library of Congress Catalog Card Number: 69-16734

Copyright 1970 by the University of Oklahoma Press, Publishing Division of the University. Composed and printed at Norman, Oklahoma, U.S.A., by the University of Oklahoma Press. First edition.

The British Establishment

1760–1784

II

I - Z

I

Ilchester, 2d Earl. See **Henry Thomas Fox-Strangways**

Impey, Elijah. 1732–1809

Youngest son of Elijah Impey (wealthy East India merchant of London). Westminster from 1739; Cambridge from 1751; B.A., 1756; fellow from 1757; M.A., 1759; barrister of Lincoln's Inn in 1756; grand tour with John Dunning, 1766–67. He was recorder of Basingstoke in 1766 and counsel for the East India Company before Parliament in 1772. In 1774 he was knighted and served in India as a member of the new Council for Bengal, 1774–80. As chief justice of Bengal he ruled favoring Warren Hastings on the question of Hastings' resigning from the post of governor general in 1777. He was opposed and hampered by Philip Francis (*q.v.*), against whom he was awarded damages in 1779. In 1783 he was recalled to England to answer charges of illegal actions preferred by Francis and others, and successfully defended himself against impeachment. But thereafter he had less influence in the company and in politics. M.P. for New Romney, 1790–96.

Inchiquin, 5th Earl. See **Murrough O'Brien**

Ingestre, 1st Viscount. See **John Chetwynd-Talbot (Talbot)**

Inglefield, John Nicholson. 1748–1828

Of unknown parentage. He married ca. 1775 a daughter of Sir Thomas Slade. He entered the navy in 1759 and became able seaman in 1766 and lieutenant in 1768, when he saw service under Samuel Hood and was with Alexander Hood off Ushant. He was flag captain and second-in-command under Samuel Hood in the action in the West Indies, 1781–82, and survived the wreck of the *Centaur* in 1782. He was a captain in the Mediterranean in 1794 and in that year declined the rank of rear admiral but was commissioner of the navy, 1795–1811.

Inglis, Charles. ca.1731–91

Younger son of Sir John Inglis (of Cramond, Edinburgh). He entered the navy in 1745 and saw service under Hawke from 1747. He commanded a sloop under Howe in the raid on Rochefort in 1757 and was with Rodney at Havre in 1759, with Howe at the relief of Gibraltar in 1781–82, and with Hood in the West Indies in 1782. He became rear admiral in 1790.

Ingram, Charles. 1727–78

Of Templenewsam, near Leeds, Yorkshire; oldest son of General Charles Ingram (1696–1748; M.P.); in 1763 succeeded his uncle George Ingram as 9th Viscount Irvine and Baron Ingram (both Scottish). Westminster, 1737–43. In 1758 he married Frances Gibson of Whitehall, "a considerable heiress." He was groom of the bedchamber to the Prince of Wales, 1756–60, and continued in that office when the prince became king, 1760–63. His family had supported the Pelhams, but he deserted Newcastle for Bute in late 1762. He controlled the borough of Horsham for which he sat, and he served as Scottish representative peer, 1768–78. One of his daughters married Francis Ingram Seymour Conway (*q.v.*); another married William Gordon (1744–1823) (*q.v.*). M.P. for Horsham, 1747–63.

Innes, William. ca.1719–95

Of London and Blackheath, Kent; son of Alexander Innes (of Cathlaw, West Lothian; merchant-banker of Edinburgh). During his brief membership in the House of Commons he made only one speech, in November, 1775, urging conciliation of the colonies and offering a detailed plan to that end. There is no record of any vote by him in the House. M.P. for Ilchester, 1774–75.

Irby, William. 1707–75

Of Whaplode, in Holland, Lincolnshire; in 1718 succeeded his father,

Sir William Irby (of Boston, Lincolnshire), as 2d baronet; in 1761 created Baron Boston. Westminster, 1719–22. He was page of honor to the king, 1724–28; equerry to the Prince of Wales, 1728–36; vice chamberlain and chamberlain to the Princess of Wales, 1736–72. He was considered a Tory. In 1760 he offered Bute his controlling interest in elections in Cornwall and Lincolnshire. At Bute's request he secured certain elections to Bute's nominees and was shortly afterward made a peer. He was chairman of committees in the House of Lords, 1770–75, and appears to have supported the North ministry. M.P. for Launceston, 1735–47; Bodmin, 1747–61.

Irnham, 1st Baron. See **Simon Luttrell**

Irvine, 9th Viscount. See **Charles Ingram**

Irving, Paulus Aemilius. 1751–1828

Son of Paulus Aemilius Irving (governor of Upnor Castle, on River Medway, Kent); created baronet in 1809. In 1786 he married Elizabeth, daughter of Thomas St. Lawrence (1st Earl of Howth, Scottish). He served with the 47th Foot in Canada and the colonies, and was made prisoner of war with Burgoyne at Saratoga in 1777. Exchanged, he commanded the 47th Foot, 1783–94, and as major general captured LaVigre at St. Vincent in 1795. He was made general in 1812.

Irwin (or Irvin or Irvine), John. 1728–88

Of Cavendish Square, London; only son of Lieutenant General Alexander Irwin. He was educated chiefly in Ireland, and then made the grand tour. He became a protégé of Lionel Sackville (1st Duke of Dorset), who, when lord lieutenant of Ireland, appointed him a page of honor, ca. 1735. He became a close lifetime friend and disciple of the duke's 3d son and private secretary, Lord George Sackville (later Germain). He became ensign in 1736, lieutenant in 1737, and captain in 1745. He served as lieutenant colonel of the 5th Foot under Prince Ferdinand in Germany in 1760, and was made major general in 1762. He served as governor of Gibraltar, 1766–68. Probably through the influence of Germain, he was commander of the British forces in Ireland, 1775–82, and was made Knight of the Bath in 1779 and general in 1783. In January, 1770, he voted against unseating Wilkes. His seat for East Grinstead was a pocket borough of the Sackville family, and he usually voted accordingly. He was extremely extravagant, and in 1783 was obliged by his debts to retreat to the Continent. He died at Parma. He was considered a good-humored, well-intentioned fop. M.P. for East Grinstead, 1762–83.

Isham, Edmund. 1690–1772

Of Lamport, near Northampton, Northamptonshire; 4th son of Sir Justinian Isham (1687–1737; 4th baronet; M.P.); in 1737 succeeded his brother as 6th baronet. Rugby, 1699–1707; Oxford from 1707; fellow, 1720–35. He was judge advocate for the Admiralty Court, 1731–41. He was an avowed Tory in the general elections of 1754. He did not vote on Bute's peace preliminaries in 1762, on the cider tax in 1763, or on general warrants in 1764 but voted against repeal of the Stamp Act in 1766. He cast no recorded vote, 1768–72, and apparently never addressed the House of Commons. M.P. for Northamptonshire, 1737–72.

J

Jackson, George (Duckett). 1725–1822

Of Upper Grosvenor Street, London, and Hartham House, near Corsham, Wiltshire; oldest surviving son of George Jackson (of Richmond, Yorkshire); created baronet in 1791. He entered the navy office ca.1743, and was secretary to the Navy Board in 1758, judge advocate for the fleet in 1766, and 2d secretary to the Admiralty Board, 1766–82. He served in the courts-martial of Keppel and Palliser in 1779. He added the surname Duckett upon inheriting from his wife's uncle in 1797. Portrait by Nathaniel Dance; miniature by Copley. M.P. for Weymouth and Melcombe Regis, 1786–88; Colchester, 1788–89 and 1790–96.

Jackson, Richard. 1722–87

Of Weasenham, near Fakenham, Norfolk; only son of Richard Jackson (ca.1700–82; merchant of London and deputy governor of the South Sea Company, 1764–68). Cambridge from 1739, Lincoln's Inn from 1740, barrister in 1744, bencher of Inner Temple from 1770, reader from 1779, and treasurer in 1780. He was king's counsel from 1762;

secretary to the chancellor of the exchequer and to George Grenville, 1763–65; and briefly an undersecretary of state. He was counsel for Cambridge University, 1771–87; to the South Sea Company, 1764–67 (while his father was deputy governor); and to the Board of Trade and Plantations, 1770–82. He was agent for Massachusetts Bay Colony, 1765–70; and for Connecticut, 1760–70. It was probably chiefly through those positions that in 1765 he and Benjamin Franklin developed a cautious friendship. In that year he warned the House of Commons against passage of the Stamp Act. In 1778 he accepted a place on Lord North's peace commission, conditional upon its membership, measures, and powers, but withdrew from the mission before it left England. He opposed the North ministry on its belligerent American policy but supported it on most other issues, voting against the Dunning resolution of April 6, 1780. After the fall of the North ministry and the death of Rockingham in 1782, he was appointed by Shelburne a member of the Treasury Board, and voted for Shelburne's peace terms in 1783. He was competent and well-intentioned, but the pomposity of his erudition made him known as "Omniscient Jackson." He was a fellow of the Society of Arts from 1781. M.P. for Weymouth and Melcombe Regis, 1762–68; New Romney, 1768–84.

James, William. ca.1721–83

Of Park Farm Place, near Eltham, Kent; said to have been the son of a miller and to have been born in Pembrokeshire; created baronet in 1778. He entered the service of the East India Company as chief mate in 1747, became commander in chief of the Company's marines in 1751, and in 1755 and 1756 led expeditions which destroyed pirate strongholds in the East. In 1759 he returned to England with a fortune acquired more discreetly than by open piracy and allied himself with the Earl of Sandwich in politics and as a director of the East India Company, 1768–83. He supported the North ministry (of which Sandwich was a member) until its fall, voted against Shelburne's peace terms, and did not vote on Fox's India Bill in 1783. M.P. for West Looe, 1774–83.

Jannsen, Stephen. d. 1777

Son of Sir Theodore Jannsen (ca.1658–1748; a Dutchman born in France who became a director of the South Sea Company); in 1766 he succeeded his brother Sir Henry Jannsen as 4th baronet. He was a successful merchant of London; was alderman of London, 1748–65; sheriff, 1749–50; and lord mayor, 1754–55. He became bankrupt in 1756 but paid off all his debts with interest and thereby gained increased respect as a man of almost unexampled integrity. He was chamberlain of London, 1765–76. M.P. for London, 1747–54.

Jebb, John. 1736–86

Born in Ireland; oldest son of John Jebb (dean of Cashel, County Tipperary); nephew of Samuel Jebb (ca.1694–1772; dissenter, physician, and scholar; 1st baronet). Trinity College, Dublin, from 1753; Cambridge from 1754; B.A., 1757; M.A., 1760; fellow from 1761. He was first groomed for the church and was rector of Ovington in Norfolk, 1764–75, but while serving as a lecturer on the Greek Testament he expressed Unitarian and other views that did not entirely please some of his ecclesiastical associates and may have suggested to them, as well as to himself, that perhaps a career in the Established Church was not his happiest choice. He opposed the current limitations on dissenters and in 1774 urged open public examinations at Cambridge to determine acceptable entering students. He turned to medicine, became M.D. of St. Andrews in 1777, and briefly practiced medicine in London in 1778. Meanwhile, he had also become an Oriental scholar of distinction, an ardent supporter of Charles James Fox and the reform of Parliament, and a leader of the Wyvill Yorkshire Association movement in London, until he broke with Wyvill. He canvassed for the election of Charles Fox in 1780. He was a fellow of the Royal Society from 1779, and his selected works were published in 1786. It was said that during his last illness he devoted himself to the study of Anglo-Saxon philology.

Jebb, Richard. 1729–87

Of Trent Park, near Barnet, Middlesex; son of Samuel Jebb (ca. 1694–1772; dissenter, physician, and scholar; 1st baronet); cousin of John Jebb (q.v.); created baronet in 1778. Oxford from 1747; M.D., Aberdeen, 1751. He was a member of the London College of Physicians from 1755 and its censor in 1772, 1776, and 1781. He was Harveian orator in 1774; physician at Westminster Hospital, 1754–62; physician at St. George's Hospital, 1762–68; and fellow of the Society of Arts from 1765 and of the Royal Society from 1778. He accompanied the

Duke of Gloucester to Italy and was rewarded with a baronetcy. He was physician to the Prince of Wales from 1780 and to the king from 1786. His fees from private practice, 1779–81, were recorded as £21,000. He was a friend and supporter of John Wilkes. He was buried in Westminster Abbey. Portrait by Zoffany.

Jedburgh, Lords. See **William Henry Ker** (or **Kerr**) and **William John Ker** (or **Kerr**)

Jeffreys, John. ca.1706–66

Of The Priory, Breconshire, and Skeen, Surrey; oldest surviving son of John Jeffreys (M.P.). He was joint secretary in the treasury, 1742–46; secretary to the chancellor of the exchequer, 1752–54; warden of the mint, 1754–66; deputy ranger of St. James's and Hyde Parks, 1757–66. In 1761 he held both a placeman's post and a pension but deserted Newcastle for Bute in December, 1762. The move did not enhance his later standing or his influence. He was an intimate of Lord Lincoln and with him gambled heavily at White's Club until he had dissipated his fortune; thereafter he sought further government support. M.P. for Breconshire, 1734–47; Dartmouth, 1747–66.

Jenkinson, Charles. 1729–1808 (*DNB* says 1727–1808)

Of Addiscombe, near Croydon, Surrey; oldest son of Charles Jenkinson (d. 1750; colonel of horse guards); created Baron Hawkesbury in 1786; succeeded his cousin as baronet in 1790; created Earl of Liverpool in 1796, Charterhouse, to Oxford in 1746; B.A., 1749; M.A., 1752; D.C.L., 1773; Lincoln's Inn from 1747. He was private secretary to Lord Holderness (or Holdernesse) (1756–58). In 1758 he asked for a sinecure position, and was supported by George Grenville and Henry Bilson Legge. After 18 months of promising, Newcastle provided him with £250 a year. He was private secretary to Bute, 1760–61; in December, 1762, he helped Bute prepare a list of officeholders to be dismissed for failing to support him. Under Bute he was an undersecretary of state, northern department, and then treasurer of ordnance. He continued in office under Grenville, and later said that he had been more devoted to Grenville than to any other chief. He was joint secretary in the treasury, 1763–65, and became a leading King's Friend, but was out of office during the Rockingham administration, 1765–66. He was a member of the Admiralty Board,

1766–67, and the Treasury Board, 1767–73, when Lord North developed a high opinion of his financial judgment and later called him the man best qualified to head the Exchequer. He remained steadily in office during the North ministry: as privy councillor and vice treasurer of Ireland, 1772–75; as clerk of the pells for Ireland, 1775–1808; as master of the mint from 1775, and as secretary at war, 1778–82. In the years 1777–82 his influence over the king, Lord North, and his fellow ministers greatly exceeded that due merely his official position. He corresponded frequently, intimately, and directly with the king at the king's request and with the king's other confidential adviser, John Robinson, especially on the subject of Lord North's state of mind, current measures, and capacity. He opposed the Dunning resolution of April 6, 1780, and indeed was thought to be a chief source of that "secret influence" upon the king which the opposition repeatedly condemned. After the fall of the North ministry he allied with Pitt, and was president of the Board of Trade, 1786–1804, and chancellor of the Duchy of Lancaster, 1786–1803. In 1785 he published *A Collection of Treaties 1648–1743*. His published study of *Coins of the Realm* was reprinted by the Bank of England as late as 1880. He was competent and loyal, a public servant of the type which developed into the permanent undersecretariat of the following century, but his abilities exceeded those of the mere bureaucrat. M.P. for Cockermouth, 1761–66; Appleby, 1767–72; Harwich, 1772–74; Hastings, 1774–80; Saltash, 1781–86.

Jenkinson, John. 1734–1805

3d son of Colonel Charles Jenkinson (d. 1750); brother of Charles Jenkinson (*q.v.*). He was schooled at Charterhouse. In 1778 he married Fanny, daughter of Admiral John Barker. He was gentleman usher to the queen, 1761–1815. He was cornet of horse in 1752, captain in 1765, and retired from military service in 1773. In the House of Commons he voted with his influential brother, through whom he gained government favors, such as appointment as 2d secretary to the lord lieutenant of Ireland in 1775. He naturally supported the North ministry, voting against the Dunning resolution of April 6, 1780. M.P. for Corfe Castle, 1768–80.

Jennings, George. ca.1720–90

Of Newsells, near Barkway, Hertfordshire; only son of Admiral Sir

John Jennings (of Barkway, Hertfordshire). Westminster from 1730, Cambridge from 1737. In 1741 he married Mary, daughter of Michael Burke (10th Earl of Clanricard, Irish). He became comptroller general of the army. In the House of Commons he voted against Bute's peace preliminaries in 1762; against Grenville on Wilkes and general warrants, 1763–64; with the Rockingham ministry, 1765–66; for Chatham's land tax in 1767; against the Grafton ministry for Savile's *Nullum Tempus* Bill in 1768; and with the North ministry, 1770–74. M.P. for Whitchurch, 1757–68; St. Germans, 1768–74; Thetford, 1784–90.

Jennings-Clerke, Philip. 1722–88

Of Lyndhurst, in New Forest, Hampshire, and Duddleston Hall, Somerset; oldest son of Philip Jennings (ca.1680–1742; of Duddleston Hall). In 1774 he added the surname Clerke upon inheriting estates as 6th baronet from his uncle Sir Talbot Clerke. Westminster from 1733, Oxford from 1739. He was army lieutenant in 1741, captain in 1749, and lieutenant colonel in 1761, but retired from military service in 1770. In Parliament he was a consistent opponent of the North ministry. In 1770 he voted against unseating Wilkes and in 1771 against finding printers Wheble and Thompson in contempt. In 1778 he presented a bill to exclude holders of government contracts from seats in Parliament. His bill was defeated, but after repeated efforts he finally secured passage of a similar bill in 1782 and compelled several important members of the House to abandon lucrative contracts in order to remain in the House. He voted for Dunning's first resolution of April, 1780. In May, 1783, he addressed the House in support of more equitable representation in its membership. He voted for Shelburne's peace terms in 1783. M.P. for Totnes, 1768–88.

Jenyns, Soame. 1704–87

Son of Sir Roger Jenyns (of Bottisham Hall, near Cambridge, Cambridgeshire). Cambridge from 1722. He was a friend of the Yorke family of the Hardwicke peerage, supported the Pelhams, and was a member of the Board of Trade and Plantations, 1755–80. He deserted Newcastle in the crucial divisions of December, 1762, and thereafter supported Bute and in general each successive ministry. He indulged in casual versification and in literary denunciations of the moral degeneration of society. In 1757 he published *The Nature and Origin of*

Evil and in 1776 *Internal Evidence of the Christian Religion,* which went to a 10th edition in 1798. His collected works were published in 1790. M.P. for Cambridgeshire, 1741–54; Dunwich, 1754–58; Cambridge Borough, 1758–80.

Jersey, 4th Earl. See George Bussey Villiers

Jervis, John. 1735–1823

2d son of Swynfed Jervis (of Meaford, near Stone, Staffordshire; from 1747 solicitor to the admiralty); in 1797 created Earl of St. Vincent of Meaford. In 1783 he married his cousin Martha, daughter of Sir Thomas Parker (member of the Treasury Board, 1742–72). He entered the navy as an able seaman ca. 1750 and became lieutenant in 1755 and captain in 1760. In 1778 he commanded a ship under Keppel off Ushant and later testified at the court-martial in support of Keppel's conduct. He was made Knight of the Bath in 1782, rear admiral in 1787, and vice admiral in 1793. In 1797 he defeated the Spanish off Cape St. Vincent and was created baronet. He was admiral from 1795 and admiral of the fleet from 1821. He voted for Shelburne's peace terms in 1783. "As a rule he voted with the Whigs, but seldom spoke except on naval matters" (*DNB*). Two portraits by Beechey, two by Hoppner, and one by Romney. M.P. for Launceston, 1783–84; Great Yarmouth, 1784–90; Chipping Wycombe, 1790–94.

Jervoise, Jervoise Clarke. ca.1733–1808

Of Idsworth Park, near Havant, Hampshire; only son of Samuel Clarke (of West Bromwich, Staffordshire); in 1771 he added the surname Jervoise under the will of his grandfather Thomas Jervoise, and was reputed to have secured an income of nearly £20,000 a year. Cambridge from 1751. In the House of Commons he voted steadily against the North ministry, did not vote on Shelburne's peace terms, voted for Pitt's proposals for the reform of Parliament, and voted for Fox's India Bill in 1783. He opposed the Pitt ministry from 1784, but only one speech by him is reported in the House. M.P. for Yarmouth (Isle of Wight), 1768–69 and 1774–79; Southampton Borough, 1779–90; Yarmouth, 1791–1808.

Jocelyn, Robert. 1731–97

Of Newport, near Limerick, County Tipperary; in 1756 he succeeded his father, Robert Jocelyn, as 2d Viscount Jocelyn and Baron Newport (both Irish); in 1771 created Earl of Roden (Irish). In 1752 he married a daughter of James Hamilton (1st Earl of Clanbrassil, Irish). He was a member of the Irish Parliament, 1743–56; auditor general of the Irish exchequer, 1750–97; and in an unostentatious way one of the most influential men in Irish politics of his time.

Johnes, Thomas. ca.1721–80

Of Croft Castle, near Leominster, Herefordshire; oldest son of Thomas Johnes (of Llanfair, near Lampeter, Cardiganshire). He was enrolled at Inner Temple from 1738, and became receiver general of customs a few years later, serving until his death. He was lord lieutenant of Cardiganshire, 1779–80. He twice won a seat in the House of Commons, which he then passed on, for longer tenure, to his son Thomas Johnes (1748–1816) (*q.v.*). During those 2 brief terms in Parliament he supported the North ministry (as did his son), voting against the Dunning resolution of April 6, 1780. M.P. for Cardigan Borough, 1774; Radnorshire, 1777–80.

Johnes, Thomas. 1748–1816

Of Hafod, near Devil's Bridge, Cardiganshire; oldest son of Thomas Johnes (1721–80) (*q.v.*). Eton from 1760, Edinburgh University (*DNB* says Oxford), followed by the grand tour, 1768–69. Serving with his father in the House of Commons, he too supported the North ministry and voted against the first Dunning resolution of April 6, 1780, receiving at about that time a secret-service pension of £500. In 1781 he became auditor of revenue in Wales and held that post until his death. He voted against Shelburne's peace terms and supported Fox and the coalition in 1783, but there is no record that before 1790 he ever addressed the House. He was a fellow of the Royal Society from 1800 and (again like his father) lord lieutenant of Cardiganshire, 1800–16. He published pamphlets on the improvement of agriculture, especially in Wales, and it was said that in Cardiganshire he planted over 2 million trees in 5 years. He published several significant works, of which the most notable was his translation of Froissart's *Tales*. M.P. for Cardigan boroughs, 1775–80; Radnorshire, 1780–96; Cardiganshire, 1796–1816.

Johnson, Guy. ca.1740–88

Of Guy Hall, Tryon County, New York. He was born of a good Irish family in Ireland, but soon went to America, where he joined his uncle William Johnson (leading British citizen and Indian agent in upstate New York), whom he succeeded as British superintendent of the Iroquois tribes. He served and directed the Indians against the French in Canada, 1757–60. He remained loyal to the crown in 1775 and led British and Indian troops against the colonists in that area, 1776–82, but without notable success. His large inherited estates from Albany westward were confiscated by the Continental Congress, and after the war he repaired to England, where he died. He was respected even by the colonists who were his enemies, though some never forgave him for encouraging the Indians to attack relatively defenseless colonial settlements in the back country.

Johnson, James. 1705–74

Son of James Johnson (clerk and rector of Melford, near Sudbury, Suffolk). Westminster, to Oxford in 1724; B.A., 1728; M.A., 1731; D.D., 1742. He was a master at Westminster school, 1733–48; chaplain to the king, 1748–52; canon of St. Paul's, 1748–53; bishop of Gloucester, 1752–59; and bishop of Worcester, 1759–74. In the House of Lords he opposed the cider tax (a popular opposition) in 1763 but otherwise did not evince disagreement with the temporal powers. He died from a fall from his mount while coursing at Bath, leaving a large private estate.

Johnson, Samuel. 1709–84

For his biography, see standard sources. He published *The Vanity of Human Wishes* in 1749, his *Dictionary* in 1755, *Rasselas* in 1759, and *A Journey to the Western Isles* in 1775. He published his long-delayed edition of Shakespeare in 1765. The first 4 volumes of his *Lives of the Poets* were published in 1779, and the remaining 6 volumes in 1781. In politics he was an ardent and unreconstructed Tory who supported the North ministry (with decreasing enthusiasm) primarily because he believed government by the Whig opposition would be much worse. At North's request he wrote a pamphlet defending North's Falkland Island settlement, 1771–72, for which he was paid, but he resented the ministry's editing of the work, and he never felt adequately rewarded for it. Portrait by Reynolds.

Johnson, William. 1715–74

Born in Ireland; oldest son of Christopher Johnson (of Warrentoun, near Newry, County Down); nephew of Admiral Sir Peter Warren. His uncle owned a large acreage on the Mohawk River in upstate New York, and in 1738 he went to America to develop and manage it. He got along well with the Indians and the Dutch patroons and acquired so much land that his position and holdings were almost feudal in comparison with those of other settlers and of the Indian tribes. In 1744 he was made British colonel of the 6 Iroquois nations, whose confidence he won, and for many years he acted as intermediary between the Indians and the settlers. He organized and commanded the Crown Point expedition against the French in 1755, and was officially superintendent of the 6 nations from 1756 until his death. He was second-in-command at Niagara in 1759 and led the Indians under Amherst in Canada in 1760. In 1768 he concluded a treaty of amity with the Indians at Fort Stanwix. His memoirs and correspondence are "absolutely essential to a proper understanding of . . . America" (*DNB*).

Johnston, Peter. 1749–1837

Of Carnsalloch, near Dumfries, Dumfriesshire; oldest son of Alexander Johnston (of Carnsalloch). Eton, 1762–66; Cambridge, 1766–69; Lincoln's Inn from 1769; barrister in 1775. He was sponsored in politics by Henry Dundas, whom he followed in his votes, supporting the North ministry in early 1782. He voted against Fox's India Bill in 1783 and followed Dundas into support of Pitt in 1784. He was bankruptcy commissioner, 1784–1831. M.P. for Kirkcudbright Stewartry, 1770–81 and 1782–86.

Johnstone, George. ca.1730–87

4th son of Sir James Johnstone (of Westerhall, near Langholm, Dumfriesshire; M.P.; 3d baronet); related to the Scottish Lords of Elibank and to the Earls of Bath. He went to sea at 15 and became lieutenant in 1755 and captain in 1762. In 1748 he distinguished himself for personal bravery in the attack on Port Louis, but in 1759 a court-martial found him guilty of manslaughter in a duel and of insubordination. He was merely severely reprimanded, however, because of his previous "gallant behaviour." He successfully commanded a ship in 1762 and rose to the rank of commodore. In 1763 he was appointed governor of West Florida, where his administration became more notorious than applauded, though he was thereafter, to his own satisfaction, usually called "Governor Johnstone." In Florida he did not get on with the European settlers (who were few), with the Indians (who were not belligerent until goaded), or with the members of his own staff. His officers sent protests to General Gage in New York and Boston about his mistreatment of themselves and others, which Gage, obviously sympathetic, properly sent on to London. He was shortly afterward recalled to England, where he gained election to the House of Commons and vented his bluster, bravado, and belligerence upon his fellow members. Physically no coward, he was reported to have fought many duels, the best known being the one with Lord George Germain in 1770. In politics he opposed the North ministry but was emphatically opposed to recognizing American independence. At the last minute he was named a member of North's peace commission under Carlisle, replacing Richard Jackson (*q.v.*), who had resigned. His attempts to bribe members of the Continental Congress compelled his fellow commissioners to disavow his actions, report them to the ministry, and make public apology to the Americans. By a resolution of Congress he was forced to withdraw from the commission, and returned to England with diminished standing but undiminished effrontery. In 1779 he was temporarily removed from Parliament by being given the command of a small squadron off Portugal, but his naval activities then and in 1781 did neither him nor his nation great credit. In his votes he was somewhat unpredictably guided by his emotions. In January, 1770, he voted against expulsion of Wilkes from the House; in October, 1775, he voted against approval of the address from the throne; in 1783 he voted against Shelburne's peace terms. In 1783 he was a director of the East India Company. He died without having paid any part of a judgment of £5,000 damages awarded against him in the courts and by the House of Lords. M.P. for Cockermouth, 1768–74; Appleby, 1774–80; Lostwithiel, 1780–84; Ilchester, 1786–87.

Johnstone, John. 1734–95

Of Denovan, on River Carron, and Alva, in Ochil Hills, Stirlingshire; 5th son of Sir James Johnstone (of Westerhall, near Langholm, Dumfriesshire; M.P.; 3d baronet); brother of George Johnstone (*q.v.*). He went to Bengal ca. 1750, and was captured in 1756 but soon released. He served under Clive at Plassey and later under Eyre Coote, but in 1765 he resigned under criticism for corruption and returned to England with a fortune reported to be £300,000. Though shrewd and unscrupulous in business, he refused an unexpected bequest of £100,000. In the House of Commons he was consistently pro-American and opposed the North ministry and sometimes his brother. He voted for the Dunning resolution of April 6, 1780. M.P. for Dysart and Kirkaldy burghs, 1774–80.

Johnstone-Pulteney, William. See William Pulteney (Johnstone)

Joliffe, John. ca.1697–1771

Of Petersfield, Hampshire; 3d son of Benjamin Joliffe (of Cofton Hall, near Bromsgrove, Worcestershire). Westminster, to Oxford in 1712; Middle Temple from 1714; Inner Temple from 1720. He was commissioner for wine licenses, 1720–41; receiver general of the Duchy of Lancaster, 1738–51; and a member of the Board of Trade and Plantations in 1771. He was listed as Tory in 1761, and supported Bute and Grenville, voting against repeal of the Stamp Act in 1766. M.P. for Petersfield, 1741–54 and 1761–68.

Joliffe, Thomas Samuel. ca.1746–1824

Of Trotton Place, near Midhurst, Sussex; 2d son of John Joliffe (*q.v.*); brother of William Joliffe (*q.v.*). Winchester, followed by the grand tour. His family "owned" the 2 seats for Petersfield, Hampshire, one of which he filled after his father and in association with his brother. He voted with the North ministry during its final 2 years, voting against Rous's no-confidence motion of March 15, 1782. In 1783 he voted against Shelburne's peace terms, with the coalition, and for Fox's India Bill. He opposed the Pitt ministry throughout 1784. There is no indication that he ever addressed the House of Commons. He was sheriff of Somerset, 1792–93. M.P. for Petersfield, 1780–87.

Joliffe, William. 1745–1802

Oldest son of John Joliffe (*q.v.*); older brother of Thomas Samuel Joliffe (*q.v.*). Winchester, to Oxford in 1764. His family "owned" the 2 seats for Petersfield, and while one was being filled by his father and brother, he filled the other for a longer term. In general, like his brother, he supported the North ministry, though in February, 1775, he opposed North's Massachusetts acts as likely "to make resistance justifiable." But in February, 1776, he told the House of Commons it was now "impossible to retreat" in America, and that therefore "troops must be had." On March 8, 1780, he seconded a motion by Germain questioning the need for auditors and tellers of the Exchequer appointed by Parliament, saying that since they would serve no useful purpose they would be an unnecessary expense. In March, 1780, he spoke opposing Burke's bill to abolish the Board of Trade and Plantations, of which he himself had been a member, 1772–79. He voted against Shelburne's peace terms in 1783, and was a member of the Admiralty Board during the 1783 coalition. M.P. for Petersfield, 1768–1802.

Jones, Henry. ca.1714–92

Son of William Jones (merchant of London). He became a merchant and cloth buyer. During his 4 years in Parliament he supported the North ministry to its end. He did not vote on Shelburne's peace terms or on Fox's India Bill in 1783, and in March, 1784, was listed as a supporter of Pitt. There is no evidence that he ever addressed the House, and he did not seek re-election. M.P. for Devizes, 1780–84.

Jones, Robert. d. 1774

Of Lombard Street, London, and Babraham, near Gog Magog Hills, Cambridgeshire. He became the Earl of Sandwich's man of business and was a director of the East India Company, 1754–58 and 1765–69. In 1762 he moved with Sandwich from support of Newcastle to support of Bute and voted with Sandwich against repeal of the Stamp Act in 1766 and against Chatham's land tax in 1767. He supported the North ministry until his death in 1774, but there is no evidence that he ever addressed the House. M.P. for Huntingdon Borough, 1754–74.

Jones, Skelton. See **Arnoldus Skelton** (formerly **Jones**). ca.1750–93

Jones, William. 1746–94

Born in Westminster, youngest son of William Jones (1675–1749; mathematician; fellow of the Royal Society; friend of Newton and

Halley); knighted in 1783. Harrow from 1753; and at Oxford from 1764; B.A., 1768; fellow from 1776; M.A., 1773. In 1783 he married Anna Maria, oldest daughter of Jonathan Shipley (1714–88; bishop of St. Asaph). He acquired a reputation as a scholar with his translations from French, Latin, and Persian; and from 1773 he was a member of Samuel Johnson's club and an intimate friend of Burke and Gibbon. He became barrister of Middle Temple in 1774 and commissioner for bankrupts from 1776. On the strong recommendation of John Dunning he was judge in the High Court of Calcutta, 1783–94. He was fellow of the Royal Society, like his father, from 1772; published a grammar of the Persian language in 1775; published translations from the Arabic in 1783; was a founder of the Bengal Asiatic Society in 1784; and also published translations from Sanskrit and a study of Hindu law.

Kames, Lord. See **Henry Home**

Keck, Anthony. 1708–67

Of Great Tew, Oxfordshire; son of John Tracy (of Stanway, near Winchcombe, Gloucestershire). In 1736 he married Susan, daughter of James Hamilton (1658–1712; 4th Duke of Hamilton). In 1729 he succeeded through his mother to the Keck estates and adopted that surname. He was a protégé and supporter of the Duke of Marlborough. In 1760, Newcastle gave him a secret-service fund pension of £700 "till he could be otherwise provided for by a court appointment," and that pension (without appointment) continued until 1765. He voted successively with its providers, the Newcastle, Bute, and Grenville ministries, but did not vote on the issue of general warrants in 1774. He died of apoplexy while watching the races at Epsom Downs. M.P. for Woodstock, 1753–67.

Keck, Anthony James. ca.1741–82

Of Stoughton Grange, near Leicester, Leicestershire; oldest son of Anthony Keck (*q.v.*); great-nephew of Sir George Beaumont (4th baronet; M.P.); grandson of James Hamilton (1658–1712; 4th Duke of Hamilton). Eton, 1753–58; Cambridge from 1758; and Lincoln's Inn from 1757. In 1765 he married Elizabeth, daughter of Peter Legh (or Lee) (1706–92) (*q.v.*). In the House of Commons he voted against repeal of the Stamp Act in 1766, for Savile's *Nullum Tempus* Bill in 1768, and against the expulsion of Wilkes in January, 1770. Until 1774 he appears to have been in general opposition to the North ministry, but after 1774 there are no records of any votes or speeches by him in the House of Commons, and John Robinson called him a "bad attender." M.P. for Leicester Borough, 1765–68; Newton, 1768–80.

Keene, Benjamin. 1753–1837

Of Westoe Lodge, Cambridge; oldest son of Edmund Keene (*q.v.*); nephew of Sir Benjamin Keene (ca.1697–1757; M.P.; diplomat). Eton, 1762–70; Cambridge from 1770; Gray's Inn from 1767. The records show only 2 votes cast by him in the House of Commons: one in opposition to the North ministry and the other for Shelburne's peace terms in 1783; and they show no address to the House. M.P. for Cambridge Borough, 1776–84.

Keene, Edmund. 1714–81

3d son of Charles Keene (mercer of King's Lynn, Norfolk); brother of Sir Benjamin Keene (ca.1697–1757; M.P.; diplomat). Charterhouse, to Cambridge in 1730; B.A., 1734; M.A., 1737; fellow, 1736–48; master of Peterhouse College, 1748–54. In 1753 he married Mary, daughter of Lancelot Andrews, with a large fortune. He preached at Whitehall from 1738 and was rector of Stanhope, Durham, 1740–71. He was bishop of Chester, 1752–70; and of Ely, 1770–81, having declined George Grenville's offer of the primacy of Ireland as archbishop of Armagh in 1764. In 1752 Walpole called him "Newcastle's tool at Cambridge, which university he has turned half Jacobite by cramming down new ordinances." He had some opportunity for such immoral indulgence in change while master of Peterhouse College, 1748–54, and vice chancellor of the university, 1749–51; but few men, especially vice chancellors, have ever produced permanent changes in the 2 ancient universities. In the House of Lords he apparently restrained that unorthodox endeavor, for there is no indication that he ever voted against the current ministry. He was good-tempered and generous but "much puffed up with his dignities."

Keene, Whitshed. ca.1732–1822

Of Hawthorne Hill, near Windsor, Berkshire; born in Ireland, only son of Captain Gilbert Keene. B.A., Trinity College, Dublin, 1750. Later described as "an Irish officer of no fortune," he became captain in the army in 1756, major in 1762, a colonel with the army in Portugal, and retired from military service in 1768. He married Elizabeth Legge, sister of William Legge (*q.v.*) and half-sister of Lord North, and according to Horace Walpole "screwed himself into being trusted by Lord North" as he "had very little sense but was a great politician." He was secretary to the lord chamberlain, 1772–82; member of the Board of Trade and Plantations, 1774–77; surveyor general of the Board of Works, 1779–82. In 1779 he was paid £2,000 from secret-service funds for an unstated reason. He voted against Shelburne's peace terms in 1783 and served on the Admiralty Board during the coalition. The records show only one occasion on which he addressed the House of Commons, in April, 1780, on the subject of the Board of Works. M.P. for Wareham, 1768–74; Ludgershall, 1774; Montgomery Borough, 1774–1818.

Keith, 1st Baron and 1st Viscount. See George Keith Elphinstone

Keith, George. 1694–1778

In 1712 succeeded his father, William Keith, as 10th Earl Marischal (Scottish); grandson of the 4th Earl of Perth (Scottish). He became captain of dragoons in 1711, but his career was opposed by the Duke of Argyll, and in 1715 he joined the Jacobites. He escaped to the Continent, but he was attainted for high treason and his estates were forfeited. He commanded the Spanish Jacobite forces that landed in Scotland in 1719, and was wounded in their defeat, but once again escaped and lived for years at Valencia. He took no part in the Jacobite uprising of 1745, and in 1746 he moved to Vienna. In 1751, Frederick the Great appointed him his ambassador to Paris and in 1759, to Spain. In 1759 he was given a free pardon by George II, and in 1761 he succeeded to the estates and title of Earl of Kintore; but in 1764 he returned to Prussia on the urgent entreaties of the Prussian king, whose trusted friend he remained until his death. He was a notable figure on the Continent for nearly 50 years, and an intimate friend of Voltaire and Rousseau.

Keith, Robert Murray. 1730–95

Of Murrayshall, Peeblesshire; oldest surviving son of Robert Keith (d. 1774, of Craig, Kincardineshire). He added the surname Murray upon inheriting from his great-uncle Robert Murray in 1743. He was educated in Edinburgh, and served with the army in the Low Countries and in Germany from 1747. He was on the staff of Lord George Sackville (later Germain) at Minden in 1759 and served until 1763. He was minister to Saxony, 1769–71; envoy to Copenhagen, 1771–72; Knight of the Bath, in 1772; and ambassador to Vienna (a post once held by his father), 1772–92. In 1777 he was made major general and in 1781 lieutenant general. He was a privy councillor from 1789. Although a close friend of Henry Seymour Conway, he favored firm military action toward the American colonists and supported the North ministry. He was able, industrious, unimaginative and opinionated, and an excellent linguist. M.P. for Peeblesshire, 1775–80.

Kellie, 6th Earl. See Thomas Alexander Erskine

Kemp (or Kempe), Thomas. ca.1746–1811

Of Lewes, Sussex; oldest son of George Kemp (or Kempe) (of Lewes). He succeeded his father as a wealthy wool stapler and an independent country gentleman. He steadily opposed the North ministry from his accession to the House of Commons in 1780, but there is no indication that he ever addressed the House before 1790. In 1783 he voted in February for Shelburne's peace terms, in May for Pitt's reforms of Parliament, and in November against Fox's India Bill. From 1784 he supported Pitt. M.P. for Lewes, 1780–1802 and 1806–11.

Kempenfelt, Richard. 1718–82

Born in Westminster; son of Magnus Kempenfelt (Swedish military officer who became lieutenant colonel in the British army). He joined the navy and served with Vernon at Portobello in 1739; was made lieutenant in 1741; was captain and then commodore in the East Indies, 1758–59; was at Pondichéry in 1761; and served in the capture of Manila in 1762. He was a member of the court-martial of Palliser in 1779, and was made rear admiral in 1780. He was in command of a squadron that skirmished with the French fleet off Ushant in December, 1781, and died in the sinking of the *Royal George* in 1782. He developed a greatly improved system of signaling that was adopted by the navy and thereby may have been responsible for more victories or fewer defeats than personal brilliance or courage could have assured.

Kemys-Tynte, Charles. See **Charles Kemys Tynte**

Kenmure, 7th Viscount. See **John Gordon**

Kennedy, David. ca.1727–92

Of Newark, near Ayr, Ayrshire; 3d surviving son of Sir John Kennedy (of Culzean; 2d baronet); in 1775 succeeded his brother Thomas Kennedy as 10th Earl of Cassilis (Scottish). He attended Glasgow University from 1742 and was admitted to the Faculty of Advocates of Edinburgh in 1752. He was a supporter of the Earl of Loudon and of James Stuart Mackenzie, and consistently supported the Grafton and North ministries in the House of Commons until 1773, and as a representative Scottish peer, 1776–90. There is no evidence that he ever addressed the lower House. M.P. for Ayrshire, 1768–74.

Kennet, Lord. See **Robert Bruce**

Kenrick, John. ca.1735–99

Of Bletchingley, Surrey; 2d son of Matthew Kenrick (barrister). Harrow, to Cambridge in 1752; Middle Temple from 1753; barrister in 1759; bencher from 1792; reader from 1798. In 1768 he married Sarah Gifford, daughter and heiress of a wealthy brewer. He was commissioner and then receiver general of stamps, 1762–80, and clerk of deliveries for ordnance, 1780–83. He steadily supported the North ministry, voted against Shelburne's peace terms and for Fox's India Bill in 1783, and opposed Pitt in 1784. M.P. for Bletchingley, 1780–90.

Kensington, 1st Baron. See **William Edwardes**

Kenyon, Lloyd. 1732–1802

Of Gredington Hall, near Hanmer, and Whitchurch, Flintshire; 2d son of Lloyd Kenyon (1697–1788; barrister); created baronet in 1784; created Baron Kenyon in 1788. He was articled to a solicitor in Nantwich, Cheshire, was enrolled at Middle Temple from 1750, and became a barrister in 1756. He "devilled" as a law secretary for Thurlow, "whose idle habits required the aid of a laborious helper"; became king's counsel in 1780; and was chief justice of Cheshire, 1780–84. He was attorney general in the Rockingham-Shelburne ministry, 1782–83; master of the rolls and privy councillor, 1784–88; chief justice of the king's bench, 1788–1802; and lord lieutenant of Flintshire from 1797. On entering the House of Commons in 1780, he complained of the delay in determining the contested election as casting imputations on his "moral character" and demanded quicker decisions. In June, 1782, he told the House that the auditors of the imprest enjoyed large emoluments "without any labour." On June 25, 1782, he demanded that the accounts of Richard Rigby as paymaster and of Welbore Ellis as treasurer of the navy be laid before the House and that each of them be called upon to explain how he could justly continue to receive interest from government funds after leaving office. This motion carried probity beyond comfortable bounds and was roundly defeated. In 1783 he voted for Shelburne's peace terms, opposed the coalition, and then supported Pitt. He was a sound lawyer and a cautious but liberal and capable public servant and citizen. Portraits by Romney and Opie. M.P. for Hindon, 1780–84; Tregony, 1784–88.

Keppel, Augustus. 1725–86

Of Elveden Hall, near Thetford, Suffolk; 2d son of William Anne Keppel (1702–54; 2d Earl of Albemarle) by Anne, daughter of Charles Lennox (1672–1723; 1st Duke of Richmond); one of 15 children; brother of George Keppel (*q.v.*), Frederick Keppel (*q.v.*), and William Keppel (*q.v.*); in 1782 created Viscount Keppel. He was schooled at Westminster, 1733–35, and entered the navy at the age of 10. He served primarily in southern and Mediterranean waters until 1740, was present at the capture of Paita in the South Pacific in 1741, and went around the world with Anson in 1744, when he was made captain. He commanded a ship in American waters in 1754 and escorted Braddock and some of his troops to America. He was at Quiberon Bay in 1759, Belleisle in 1761, and at the capture of Havana in 1762 (where his brother George was in command of the land forces) and received nearly £25,000 in prize money. In 1757 he was a member of the court-martial that found Admiral Byng guilty. In 1759 he took Gorée from the French, and in 1760 was made colonel of marines and in 1762 rear admiral. During the Rockingham ministry he was a lord of the admiralty, 1765–66, his family being strongly Whig in tradition.

In 1767 he secured a royal grant of land in maritime Canada, and in 1770 he was made vice admiral. In 1775 he declared that he would not serve against the American colonists, and only after France entered the war did he accept command of the home fleet as admiral. In the controversy with Palliser, which followed their unsatisfactory skirmish with the French fleet off Ushant in late 1778, he was exonerated by court-martial, but declined further duty under the North ministry. He was first lord of the admiralty and privy councillor in the Portland-Rockingham ministry of 1782–83 and again after the fall of the coalition. He was groom of the bedchamber, 1761–65. In politics he was a staunch Whig; he voted against expulsion of Wilkes in 1770; against approval of the address from the throne in October, 1775; and for the Dunning resolution of April 6, 1780. Six portraits by Reynolds. M.P. for Chichester, 1755–61; Windsor, 1761–80; Surrey, 1780–82.

Keppel, Frederick. 1729–77

4th son of William Anne Keppel (1702–54; 2d Earl of Albemarle); one of 15 children; brother of George Keppel (*q.v.*), Augustus Keppel (*q.v.*), and William Keppel (*q.v.*). Westminster from 1743; Oxford from 1747; B.A., 1752; M.A., 1754; D.D., 1762. In 1758 he married Laura, oldest illegitimate daughter of Sir Edward Walpole. He was chaplain to George II and later to George III; canon and dean of Windsor, 1754–62; bishop of Exeter, 1762–77; and registrar of the Order of the Garter, 1765–77. In 1767 in the House of Lords he recorded dissent to the vote approving the regulation of the East India Company as "injurious to private property and alarming to publick credit." In March, 1776, preaching before the king, he urged immediate peace with the colonies.

Keppel, George. 1724–72

Styled Viscount Bury until 1754, when he succeeded his father, William Anne Keppel (1702–54), as 3d Earl of Albemarle; one of 15 children; older brother of Augustus Keppel (*q.v.*), William Keppel (*q.v.*), and Frederick Keppel (*q.v.*). Westminster, 1732–38. In 1738 he became ensign in the Coldstream Guards and was captain in 1745, colonel in 1749, major general in 1756, lieutenant general in 1759, and general in 1772. He was lord of the bedchamber to the Duke of Cumberland and also served as his military aide, 1746–65. In 1760 he was a member of the court-martial that found Lord George Sackville (later Germain) guilty of disobedience of orders at Minden. In 1761 he was privy councillor, governor of Jersey, and political secretary to the Duke of Cumberland. He led the troops in the successful attack on Havana in 1762 and acquired there some £122,000 in prize money. He received the Order of the Bath in 1764 and Order of the Garter in 1765 (*DNB* says 1771). In politics he supported successively the Pelhams; the Duke of Cumberland; Newcastle against Bute in December, 1762; and the Rockingham ministry, 1765–66. In 1767 he was among those who solicited and secured crown grants of land in maritime Canada. In the House of Lords he recorded his dissent to votes approving (1) Bute's peace preliminaries in 1762, (2) regulation of the East India Company in 1767, (3) the measures taken by the House of Commons against Wilkes in 1770, (4) arbitrary adjournment of the House of Lords on January 15, 1770, and (5) the Royal Marriage Bill in 1772. Portrait by Reynolds. M.P. for Chichester, 1746–54.

Keppel, William. 1727–82

4th son of William Anne Keppel (1702–54; 2d Earl of Albemarle); one of 15 children; brother of George Keppel (*q.v.*), Augustus Keppel (*q.v.*), and Frederick Keppel (*q.v.*). He was schooled at Westminster, and entered the army as ensign in 1744. He became major general in 1762 and lieutenant general in 1772, but his military achievements were not spectacular and were overshadowed by those of his brother George. A good Keppel Whig, in the House of Commons he supported Rockingham and his cousin the Duke of Richmond, voting against expulsion of Wilkes in January, 1770, and for the Dunning resolution of April 6, 1780; but he "troubled himself very little with public business," and by 1781 he was seriously ill and almost incapable of speech. M.P. for Chichester, 1767–82.

Ker (or Kerr), John. 1740–1804

"Born in Hanover Square," London, and styled Marquess of Bow-mont until 1755, when he succeeded his father, Robert Ker (or Kerr), as 3d Duke of Roxburgh (Scottish) and Earl Ker (or Kerr) (English). Eton, 1753–54 and 1756–58; grand tour in 1761. He was a member of the Society of the Dilettante from 1765; lord of the bedchamber, 1767–96; Knight of the Thistle from 1768; lord lieutenant of Roxburgh-shire, 1794–1804; privy councillor from 1796; groom of the stole and first lord of the bedchamber, 1796–1804; fellow of the Society of Arts from 1797; and Knight of the Garter in 1801. He opposed repeal of the Stamp Act in 1766 but in general supported each successive ministry. He was a man of many accomplishments, a sportsman and a book collector whose unrivaled collection of Caxton books sold for more than £23,000 in 1812. The Roxburgh Club, made up of fine-book collectors, was formed and named in his honor.

Ker (or Kerr), William Henry. ca.1710–75

Styled Lord Jedburgh until 1735; then styled Earl of Ancram until 1767, when he succeeded his father, William Ker (or Kerr) (ca.1690–1767), as 4th Marquess of Lothian (Scottish). In 1735 he married Caroline, "with £20,000," only daughter of Robert D'Arcy (d. 1751; 3rd Earl of Holderness or Holdernesse), and embarked on a military career as cornet. He was captain in 1739 and in 1745 was aide to the Duke of Cumberland at Fontenoy, where he was severely wounded. He was shortly afterward made colonel, and distinguished himself at Culloden, where he commanded the cavalry and where his only brother, Robert Ker (or Kerr), was killed. He was made major general in 1755, lieutenant general in 1758, and general in 1770. He secured a seat in the House of Commons for a pocket borough through his brother-in-law Robert D'Arcy (*q.v.*), and supported the Duke of Cumberland until the duke's death. He opposed Bute's peace terms in 1762 and in 1763 "sold" his seat to Henry Fox, who "gave" it to the Dundas family for a political return. He was a Scottish representative peer, 1768–74, and was made Knight of the Thistle in 1768. M.P. for Richmond (Yorkshire), 1747–63.

Ker (or Kerr), William John. 1737–1815

Styled Lord Jedburgh until 1767; then styled Lord Ancram until 1775, when he succeeded his father, William Henry Ker (or Kerr) (*q.v.*), as 5th Marquess of Lothian (Scottish). Unlike most members of his family, he apparently almost invariably added the second *r* to his surname. Eton, 1747–53. He entered his father's regiment with a commission in 1754 and became major general in 1777, lieutenant general in 1782, and general in 1796. He was made Knight of the Thistle in 1776. He was a representative Scottish peer, 1778–90, but demonstrated no great political interest or ability. In 1761, Henry Fox called

511

him "a vain insignificant puppy," but others later praised his character and his military skill. He voted against Fox's India Bill in 1783 and against Pitt's Regency Bill in 1788.

Kildare, 20th Earl and 1st Marquess. See James Fitzgerald

Kilmaine, 1st Baron. See James Charles O'Hara

Kilmarnock, 5th Earl. See James Hay

Kilmaurs, Lord. See **William Cuningham** (or **Cunninghame**)

Kincardine, 9th Earl. See **Charles Bruce**

King, Edward. 1726–97

Of Rockingham, near Boyle, County Roscommon; 2d son of Henry King (3d baronet; Irish); in 1755 succeeded his brother as 5th baronet; in 1764 created Baron Kingston (Irish); in 1766 created Viscount Kingsborough (Irish); in 1768 created Earl of Kingston (Irish). He was a member of the Irish Parliament, 1749–64, and of the Irish Privy Council from 1794. He was grand master of Irish Freemasons, 1761–63 and 1764–70.

King, Richard. 1730–1806

Born at Gosport, near Portsmouth, Hampshire; son of Curtis King (master in the navy); knighted in 1782; created baronet in 1792. His naval career, begun in 1738, included service in the Mediterranean and the West and East Indies from 1745 almost continuously until 1782. He was lieutenant in 1746, was present at the capture of Calcutta in 1757, and was off Madras in 1782. He was made rear admiral in 1787, was in command at the Newfoundland station in 1792, and was made vice admiral in 1793 and admiral in 1795. M.P. for Rochester, 1793–1802.

King, Thomas. 1712–79

Son of Peter King (1669–1734; 1st Baron King); in 1767 succeeded his brother William King (1711–67) as 5th Baron King of Ockham, Surrey. In 1734 he married Wilhelmina, daughter of John Troye (a judge of Brabant with a large fortune). He was sometime partner in a Dutch merchant business and in politics was a vigorous dissenter to the measures of the North ministry. His recorded dissents to majority votes in the House of Lords included opposition to (1) regulation of dividends of the East India Company in 1768; (2) unseating Wilkes in 1770; (3) North's Falkland Islands settlement in 1771; (4) the licensing of a playhouse in Liverpool, which he said was "likely to corrupt public morals"; (5) the East India Company Regulating Bill in 1773; (6) refusal of the peers to accept petitions from the colonies in 1775; (7) the Massachusetts Regulating Bill in 1774; (8) the address from the throne on American policy in 1775; (9) continuance of the Quebec Governing Act in 1775; (10) the hiring of mercenaries without consent of Parliament in 1776; (11) the address from the throne in October, 1776; and (12) refusal to ask the king to dismiss Sandwich in 1779.

Kingsale (or Kinsale), 20th Baron. See John De Courcy

Kingsborough, 1st Viscount. See Edward King

Kingsley, William. ca.1698–1769

Son of William Kingsley (of Maidstone, Kent). He was cornet of dragoons in 1721, and advanced through the Scots Guards to colonel in 1751, having served at Dettingen and Fontenoy, and against the pretender in Scotland in 1745–46. He was active in the raid on Rochefort in 1757 and distinguished himself at Minden in 1759. He became major general in 1758 and lieutenant general in 1760, after which year he was not involved in any major military operations. He was independent, outspoken, and more popular with his men than with the politicians. Portrait by Reynolds.

Kingsmill, Robert Brice. See Robert Brice (later Kingsmill)

Kingston, Duchess. See Elizabeth Chudleigh

Kingston, 1st Baron and 1st Earl. See Edward King

Kingston, 2d Duke. See Evelyn Pierrepont

Kinnoul, 9th Earl. See Thomas Hay. 1710–87

Kinross, Lord. See James Brydges

Kintore, Earl. See George Keith

Kirkman, William John. 1741–80

Of College Hill, London; son of Joseph Kirkman (silk merchant of Coventry and London). He entered his father's business and was an alderman of London, 1768–80. He was elected to the House of Commons in 1780 as a representative of the popular radicals and surviving Wilkites, but died before he took his seat. M.P. for London, September 19, 1780.

Knatchbull, Wyndham. 1737–63

Of Mersham Hatch, near Ashford, Kent; in 1749 succeeded his father, Sir Wyndham Knatchbull, as 6th baronet. Oxford from 1754; grand tour, 1757–60. He was a grandnephew of Lady Hardwicke and supported the Yorke family in politics. In December, 1762, he voted with Newcastle but on the following day reversed his vote on the same issue. M.P. for Kent, 1760–63.

Knight, Henry. 1728–62

Of Barrells Park, near Henley-in-Arden, Warwickshire; only son of Robert Knight (*q.v.*), but predeceased his father. In 1750 he married Frances, daughter of Thomas Heath (of Stanstead, Essex). There is no indication that during the brief interval between his election to Parliament and his sudden death he ever spoke or voted in the House of Commons. M.P. for Great Grimsby, 1761–62.

Knight, Richard Payne. 1750–1824

Of Downton Castle, near Ludlow, Herefordshire; oldest son of Rev. Thomas Knight (1697–1764; of Wormsley Grange, Herefordshire). He inherited wealth from the Shropshire ironworks of his grandfather Richard Knight (1659–1745). Poor health interfered with his formal schooling, but he visited Italy in 1767 and again in 1777 and began a collection of coins and bronzes of some importance, which he bequeathed to the British Museum. He was a minor poet, vice president of the Society of Antiquaries, the author of a diary that was later translated and published by Goethe, and a writer on ancient art, of which he was a recognized authority. In the House of Commons he regularly opposed the North ministry during its last 2 years. In 1783 he voted both for Shelburne's peace terms in February and for Fox's India Bill in November. In 1784 he opposed Pitt. Portrait by Reynolds. M.P. for Leominster, 1780–84; Ludlow, 1784–1806.

Knight, Robert. 1702–72

Of Barrells Park, near Henley-in-Arden, Warwickshire; son of Robert Knight (South Sea Company cashier who fled to France when the company collapsed and became a banker in Paris); in 1745 created Baron Luxborough (Irish); in 1763 created Earl of Catherlough (Irish). He was enrolled at Inner Temple from 1719. In 1727 he married Henrietta, daughter of Henry St. John (1st Viscount St. John). He was recorder of Grimsby from 1761. In the House of Commons he supported the administration until he received his first Irish peerage, after which he appears to have been increasingly in opposition to Newcastle. From 1761 he supported Bute and then Grenville, securing his Irish earldom from Grenville and voting with him against repeal of the Stamp Act in 1766. He supported the North ministry, 1770–72. M.P. for Great Grimsby, 1734–47; Castle Rising, 1747–54; Great Grimsby, 1762–68; Milbourne Port, 1770–72.

Knight, Thomas. 1735–94

Of Godmersham, near Ashford, Kent; son of Thomas May Brodnax (M.P.; in 1737 assumed the surname Knight upon inheriting Chawton, in Hampshire; known as a Tory). Eton, 1753–54; Oxford from 1754; grand tour. He became a country gentleman, and was listed as Tory by Rockingham in 1766. He attended the House of Commons irregularly, and there is no record that he ever addressed it. His recorded votes are very few, but he voted against the North ministry on the Wilkes issues in 1775 and for Dunning's resolution of April 6, 1780. M.P. for New Romney, 1761–68; Kent, 1774–80.

Knightley, Lucy. 1742–91

Of Fawsley, near Daventry, Northamptonshire; oldest son of Valentine Knightly (1718–54; M.P.). Rugby from 1748; Eton, 1755–59; Oxford from 1760. In 1764 he married Catherine, 3d daughter of Sir James Dashwood (*q.v.*), and like his father-in-law was called Tory or its later common equivalent, "country gentleman." He was sheriff of Northamptonshire, 1770–71. According to John Robinson's notes, he always wished "to support government," but his voting record was that of an independent. He voted against the North ministry on Dunning's resolution of April 6, 1780; for Shelburne's peace terms in 1783; and against Fox's India Bill. There is no evidence that he ever addressed the House of Commons. M.P. for Northampton Borough, 1763–68; Northamptonshire, 1773–84.

Knollys, Charles. 1704–77

Of Windsor, Berkshire; reputedly the son of Charles Knollys (titular 4th Earl of Banbury). He served under the Empress of Russia as president of the admiralty, 1765–70.

Knollys, Francis. 1722–72

Of Thame, Oxfordshire; only son of Richard Knollys; created baronet in 1754. Oxford from 1739; M.A., 1744. In 1756 he married Mary, daughter of Sir Robert Cater (sheriff of London). He was sheriff of Oxfordshire, 1757–58, and sat in the House of Commons as an avowed independent. In Bute's 1761 list he was first classified "Tory" and then as "Old Whig," which Bute later altered in his own hand to "Old Walpolian." There is no record of any speech or vote by him in the House. M.P. for Reading, 1761–68.

Knox, William. 1732–1810

Born in Ireland, he accompanied Henry Ellis, the new governor of Georgia, to America in 1757. He bought land in Georgia and the Carolinas and was provost marshal of Georgia, 1757–61. He returned to England and became agent for Georgia and East Florida, but was dismissed by Rockingham in 1765 for writing and publishing pamphlets defending the Stamp Act and for opposing any concessions to the colonists. He was undersecretary of state for the colonies under Germain from 1775 and encouraged Germain in his inflexibility toward the American rebels and in his conviction that they could easily be defeated. He may have been partly responsible for the confusions in strategy that led to Burgoyne's surrender at Saratoga in October, 1777. To the last he remained intransigent in his opposition to reconciliation with the Americans and recognition of their independence. In 1783, during the coalition, he advised North on the future government of colonies in terms of the old mercantile system, which North rejected and incurred Knox's permanent rancor. After 1783 he was not *persona grata* to any ministry and retired disconsolately to Wales. His many published memoranda and unpublished papers from 1764 shed some light on the inner workings of the North administration.

Kynaston, Edward. 1709–72

Of Bryngwyn, near Llanfyllin, Montgomeryshire, and Hardwick Grange, near Shrewsbury, Shropshire; son of John Kynaston (of Hordley, near Ellesmere, Shropshire; M.P.); of Tory extraction. Eton from 1725, Cambridge and Lincoln's Inn from 1726. He married Victoria, daughter of Sir Charles Lloyd (3d baronet). In 1761 he was listed as a Tory country gentleman. Until 1761 he was largely in opposition, but he then supported Bute, and later Grenville, voting with the government on the Wilkes issues and the cider tax, 1763–64. He voted against repeal of the Stamp Act in 1766 and against Chatham's land tax in 1767. He appears to have supported North through 1772, including the Royal Marriage Bill. Though he attended the House of Commons with admirable regularity, he appears never to have addressed it. M.P. for Bishop's Castle, 1734–41; Montgomeryshire, 1747–72.

L

Ladbroke, Robert. ca.1713–73

Of Idlicote, near Shipston, Warwickshire, descended from a Warwickshire family; nephew of Sir Henry Marshall (lord mayor of London, 1744–45). He became a distiller and banker in partnership with his son-in-law Sir Walter Rawlinson (*q.v.*). He was alderman of London from 1741; sheriff of London and knighted, 1743–44; lord mayor in 1747. He was a vehement Presbyterian—an unusual affiliation for a man considered, and listed by Newcastle, a Tory. He voted against Bute's peace preliminaries in 1762 and against Grenville on Wilkes and general warrants, 1763–64. He supported Rockingham, 1765–66, and voted against expulsion of Wilkes in January, 1770. M.P. for London, 1754–73.

Ladbroke, Robert. ca.1740–1814

Only son of Robert Ladbroke (ca.1713–73) (*q.v.*). He became a banking partner of his father and his brother-in-law Sir Walter Rawlinson (*q.v.*). In the House of Commons he opposed the North ministry from his election in 1780. He voted for Shelburne's peace terms, for Pitt's proposals for the reform of Parliament, and for Fox's India Bill in 1783. He opposed Pitt from 1784, but made only one recorded speech in the House of Commons before 1790. M.P. for Warwick Borough, 1780–90; Okehampton, 1791–96; Winchelsea, 1802–1806; Malmesbury, 1806–1807.

Laforey, John. 1729–96

Of Antigua and Stokedamerel, near Devonport, Devon; 2d son of Lieutenant Colonel John Laforey (d. 1753; of Huguenot descent). He became a lieutenant in the navy in 1748 and commander in 1755. He distinguished himself off Louisburg, 1756–58, and in the St. Lawrence in 1759. He was with Rodney at Martinique in 1762 and off Ushant with Keppel in 1778. He was in command in West Indian waters in 1779, when he was made baronet. He was in charge at Plymouth, 1783–87; was made rear admiral in 1789; and was in command at the Leeward Islands station, 1789–93 and in 1795. He became vice admiral in 1793 and admiral just before his death at sea.

Lamb, Matthew. 1705–68

Of Brockett Hall, near Hatfield, Hertfordshire, and Melbourne Hall, near Derby, Derbyshire; 2d son of Matthew Lamb (attorney of Southwell, near Newark, Nottinghamshire); younger brother of Robert Lamb (or Lambe) (*q.v.*); created baronet in 1755, having inherited a fortune from his uncle Peniston Lamb in 1734. Lincoln's Inn from 1726, barrister in 1733, bencher from 1754. In 1740 he married Charlotte, daughter of Sir Thomas Coke, who inherited Melbourne Hall in 1751. He was solicitor to the post office, 1738–68; counsel to the Board of Trade and Plantations, 1746–68; and king's counsel from 1754. He supported Bute from 1761 and thereafter each current ministry, but the records show only one speech, in 1759, in the House of Commons. He left property estimated at £500,000. M.P. for Stockbridge, 1741–47; Peterborough, 1747–68.

Lamb, Peniston. 1745–1828

Of Brockett Hall, near Hatfield, Hertfordshire, and Melbourne Hall, near Derby, Derbyshire; only son of Matthew Lamb (*q.v.*), whom he succeeded as 2d baronet in 1768; in 1770 created Baron Melbourne (Irish); in 1781 created Viscount Melbourne (Irish); in 1815 created

Baron Melbourne (English). Eton, 1755–62; Lincoln's Inn from 1769. In 1769 he married Elizabeth, daughter of Sir Ralph Milbanke (*q.v.*), and became "an eminent land conveyancer, reputed worth £100,000." He supported the Grafton and North ministries, voting against Dunning's resolution of April 6, 1780, and later against attacks on the North administration. He followed North into support of the coalition in 1783, voting against Shelburne's peace terms and for Fox's India Bill. Later he opposed Pitt. He was gentleman of the bedchamber to the Prince of Wales, 1783–96, and lord of the bedchamber, 1812–28. "An easy going man of but little ability who never spoke in the House of Commons," he had other talents and was known as "a confirmed womanizer." M.P. for Ludgershall, 1768–84; Malmesbury, 1784–90; Newport (Isle of Wight), 1790–93.

Lamb (or Lambe), Robert. ca.1703–69

Of Brockett Hall, near Hatfield, Hertfordshire; oldest son of Matthew Lamb (attorney of Southwell, near Newark, Nottinghamshire); older brother of Matthew Lamb (*q.v.*); uncle of Peniston Lamb (*q.v.*). He was dean of Peterborough, 1744–64, and bishop of Peterborough, 1764–69.

Lambart, Richard. ca.1698–74

Son of Hon. Henry Lambart (3d son of Charles Lambart [1649–1702; 3d Earl of Craven, Irish]); in 1772 succeeded his first cousin Ford Lambart (1718–72; grand master of Irish Freemasons) as 6th Earl of Cavan. He was major general in 1772 and lieutenant general in 1774.

Lambton, Henry. 1697–1761

Of Lambton Hall, on River Wear, Durham County; oldest son of Ralph Lambton (of Barnes, Durham); brother of John Lambton (*q.v.*). Oxford from 1715, Lincoln's Inn from 1719. He was reputedly a Whig. M.P. for Durham City, 1734–61.

Lambton, John. 1710–94

Of Lambton Hall, on River Wear, Durham County; 5th son of Ralph Lambton (of Barnes, Durham); brother of Henry Lambton (*q.v.*). He was schooled at Westminster. In 1763 he married Susan, daughter of Thomas Lyon (1704–53; 8th Earl of Strathmore, Scottish). He

519

entered the Coldstream Guards as ensign in 1732 and became lieutenant in 1739, captain in 1740, colonel in 1758, major general in 1761,
lieutenant general in 1770, and general in 1782. In the House of Commons he regularly opposed the North ministry on most major issues.
He voted against unseating Wilkes in January, 1770; for an extension
of the Grenville Disputed Elections Act in 1774; and for Dunning's
resolution of April 6, 1780. He voted for Shelburne's peace terms in
1783 but was largely in opposition to the Pitt ministry, 1784–87. M.P.
for Durham City, 1762–87.

Lane, George Fox. ca.1697–1773

Of Bramham Park, near Tadcaster, Yorkshire; oldest surviving son of
Henry Fox (d. 1719). In 1731 he married Harriet, daughter and heiress
of Robert Benson (1st Baron Bingley). He added the surname Lane
in 1751 upon succeeding to estates of his maternal uncle James Lane
(2d Viscount Lanesborough). In 1762, in view of his father-in-law,
he was created Baron Bingley of Yorkshire. He was always considered
a Tory and voted largely in opposition, 1734–61. He was the father of
Robert Fox-Lane (q.v.). M.P. for Hindon, 1734–41; York City,
1742–61.

Langham, James. 1736–95

Of Cottesbrooke, near Brixworth, Northamptonshire; oldest son of
William Langham (of Rance, Northamptonshire); in 1766 succeeded
his uncle Sir John Langham (ca.1698–1766) as 7th baronet. Oxford
from 1753. He was a captain in the army in 1759, major in 1763, and
lieutenant colonel in 1772; he retired in 1780. He was sheriff of
Northamptonshire, 1767–68. From the year he entered Parliament he
supported Pitt. M.P. for Northamptonshire, 1784–90.

Langlois, Benjamin. ca.1727–1802

4th son of Peter Langlois (Huguenot refugee and Leghorn merchant).
Oxford from 1745. He was secretary of embassy in Vienna, 1763–71;
clerk of ordnance, 1773–78; storekeeper, 1778–80; secretary to Stormont
when Stormont was secretary of state, 1779–82; and a member of the
Board of Trade and Plantations, 1780–82. His career in the House of
Commons was largely due to the sponsorship of Edward Eliot (q.v.),
who provided him with a seat under his control. As a career placeman

he supported the North ministry, which supported him, though sometimes both complained. He was variously pronounced "a diplomatic, old-fashioned coxcombe," "a good and benevolent man," and "fatigueingly ceremonious." Virtue and benevolence often travel in dull company. M.P. for St. Germans, 1768–80.

Langlois, Peter. 1722–88

He was colonel of the regiment that bore his name, commander in Anterior Austria, governor of Antwerp, commander at Trieste, and finally general.

Langrishe, Hercules. 1731–1811

Of Knocktopher, near Thomastown, County Kilkenny; son of Robert Langrishe (d. 1770; sheriff of County Kilkenny); created baronet in 1777. Trinity College, Dublin; B.A., 1753. He was a member of the Irish Parliament, 1761–1800; commissioner of barracks, 1766–74; supervisor of accounts, 1767–75; commissioner of revenue, 1774–1801; commissioner of excise, 1780–1801; and Irish privy councillor from 1777. He supported relief for Roman Catholics and union between Ireland and England but opposed reform of representation in the Irish Parliament. Some of his speeches were published.

Lansdowne, 1st Marquess. See **William Fitzmaurice Petty**

Laroche, James. 1734–1804

Of Over, near Bristol; 3d son of John Laroche (ca.1700–52; M.P.); created baronet in 1776. He was sheriff of Bristol, 1764–65. A Bristol merchant who inherited wealth and increased it, he was master of the Company of Merchant Venturers, 1782–83. In the House of Commons he usually voted with the North administration, opposing the Dunning resolution of April 6, 1780. He addressed the House 3 times, according to existing records, all on minor issues. In 1778 he became bankrupt, and was defeated when he stood again for re-election in 1790. M.P. for Bodmin, 1768–80.

Lascelles, Daniel. 1714–84

Of Goldsborough Hall, near Knaresborough, Yorkshire; 2d son of Henry Lascelles (of Harewood and Stank Hall, near Leeds; formerly of the West Indies; M.P.); brother of Edwin Lascelles (*q.v.*); first cousin of Edward Lascelles (*q.v.*). He inherited extensive plantations in the West Indies. He was enrolled at Inner Temple from 1731, and was almost certainly later connected with the East India Company. In politics he voted with his brother Edwin, and with him signed the Yorkshire petition against the Grafton ministry in September, 1769. In January, 1770, he voted against unseating Wilkes, and in April, 1780, he voted for Dunning's first resolution. He opposed the American measures of the North ministry in its latter years. M.P. for Northallerton, 1752–80.

Lascelles, Edward. 1740–1820

Of Stapleton Park, near Pontrefact, Yorkshire; oldest son of Edward Lascelles (of Barbados); first cousin of Edwin Lascelles (*q.v.*) and Daniel Lascelles (*q.v.*); in 1795 succeeded his cousin Edwin as 2d Baron Harewood; in 1812 created Earl of Harewood. He entered the horse guards in 1756, became captain in 1759, and retired in 1761. In politics he voted with Edwin Lascelles until 1795, against unseating Wilkes in January, 1770, and in general against the North ministry until 1774. M.P. for Northallerton, 1761–74 and 1790–96.

Lascelles, Edwin. 1713–95

Of Harewood House, near Leeds, Yorkshire; oldest son of Henry Lascelles (of Harewood and Stank Hall, near Leeds; formerly of the West Indies; M.P.); brother of Daniel Lascelles (*q.v.*); first cousin of Edward Lascelles (*q.v.*); created Baron Harewood in 1790. He was born in Barbados and with his brother Daniel inherited large sugar plantations there. The family was also connected with the East India Company, of which Henry Lascelles was a director. Cambridge from 1732, Inner Temple from 1731. In 1770 he married (2) Jane, granddaughter of the 8th Duke of Somerset. He was elected to the House of Commons as a Whig and voted with Newcastle and Rockingham. In 1769 he signed the Yorkshire petition against the Grafton ministry. In January, 1770, he voted against expulsion of Wilkes, and in April, 1780, he voted for Dunning's first resolution. But on some other measures he voted with the North ministry, and he opposed Rous's no-confidence motion on March 15, 1782. He voted for Shelburne's peace terms and did not vote on Fox's India Bill in 1783. Thereafter he supported Pitt. M.P. for Scarborough, 1744–54; Northallerton, 1754–61; Yorkshire, 1761–80; Northallerton, 1780–90.

Lauderdale, 1st Baron and 7th and 8th Earls. See James Maitland. 1718–89
and James Maitland. 1759–1839

Laurie, Robert. ca.1738–1804

Of Maxwelton, Dumfriesshire; only son of Sir Robert Laurie (M.P.),
whom he succeeded in 1779 as 5th baronet. In 1763 he married Elizabeth, daughter of James Ruthven (*q.v.*) and niece of John Stuart
(1713–92) (*q.v.*), but divorced her in 1774. He was captain in 1762,
colonel in 1782, lieutenant general in 1798, general in 1803, and knight
marshal of Scotland, 1785–1804. In politics he was supported by, and
supported, his friend the Duke of Queensberry, but was doubtless also
influenced by the Earl of Bute. He was often absent from the House of
Commons and was usually silent when present. He supported in
general the current ministry, voting against the Dunning resolution
of April 6, 1780, and thereafter for the North ministry in every recorded division until its fall in March, 1782. He voted for Shelburne's
peace terms in 1783 and from 1784 supported Pitt. "His inclination is
to be with government," wrote John Robinson in 1784. M.P. for Dumfriesshire, 1774–1804.

Lavington, 1st Baron. See Ralph Payne

Law, Edmund. 1703–87

Born in Cartmel, near Ulverston, Lancashire; son of Edmund Law
(curate and schoolmaster of Lancashire). Cambridge; B.A., 1723;
M.A., 1727; fellow. In 1731 he published *Essay on the Origin of Evil.*
He became rector of Greystoke, Cumberland, in 1737 and archdeacon
of Carlisle in 1743. In 1745 he published *The State of the World with
Regard to the Theory of Religion.* He was master of Peterhouse College, Cambridge, 1756–68; librarian of Cambridge University from
1760; and professor of moral philosophy at Cambridge from 1764. He
was archdeacon of Staffordshire from 1763, prebendary of Lincoln
from 1764, and prebendary of Durham from 1767. On the recommendation of Grafton he was bishop of Carlisle, 1769–87. In 1774 he published a pamphlet supporting religious toleration, which was severely
attacked. He became an ardent disciple of John Locke, whose life and
works he published in 4 volumes in 1777. He sponsored and aided
William Paley (1743–1805), appointing him successively to 4 good
church livings, a prebend at Carlisle, and an archdeaconry. In 1778 he

recorded his dissent in the House of Lords to the address from the throne outlining the ministry's policy toward the colonies. He was "a man of great softness of manners," mild voice, and disposition, but ardent and courageous in his religious convictions. Three portraits by Romney.

Lawley, Robert. 1736–93

Of Canwell Priory, near Tamworth, Staffordshire; in 1779 succeeded his father, Sir Robert Lawley (sheriff of Staffordshire, 1743–44), as 5th baronet. Westminster from 1748, Cambridge from 1753. In 1764 he married Jane, only sister of Beilby Thompson (*q.v.*). He was a country gentleman of an Old Whig family; he professed independence and largely opposed the North ministry from 1780. He voted for Shelburne's peace terms and against Fox's India Bill in 1783. There is evidence that he twice addressed the House of Commons, both times on Warwickshire interests. M.P. for Warwickshire, 1780–93.

Lawrence, William. ca.1723–98

Of Kirkby Fleetham, near Bedale, Yorkshire; 2d son of Thomas Lawrence (navy captain). In 1759 he married Anna Sophia, daughter of William Aislabie (*q.v.*). In the House of Commons he voted against Bute's peace preliminaries in 1762 and voted largely in opposition to the Bute and Grenville ministries, 1762–65. He supported the Rockingham ministry, 1765–66; became an admirer of Charles Fox; and opposed the American measures of the North ministry, 1775–80. He voted for Dunning's resolution of April 6, 1780, and against Shelburne's peace terms in February, 1783. He supported Fox against Pitt from 1783, but there is no evidence, at least before 1790, that he ever addressed the House. M.P. for Ripon, 1761–68, 1775–80, and 1781–98.

Lawson, Wilfred. ca.1707–62

Of Isel Hall, near Cockermouth, and Brayton, Cumberland; in 1752 succeeded his father, Sir Alured Lawson, as 8th baronet. He was sheriff of Cumberland, 1756–57, and became agent for Charles Wyndham (1710–63) (*q.v.*). He was also supported for election to the House of Commons by James Lowther (1736–1802) (*q.v.*); apparently to fill a seat only temporarily. He died without leaving any record of having spoken or voted in the House. M.P. for Cumberland, 1761–62.

Lechmere-Charlton, Nicholas. 1733–1807

Son of Edmund Lechmere (of Hanley Castle, on River Severn, Worcestershire; M.P.); he added the surname Charlton in 1784 upon inheriting the estate of his mother's brother Francis Charlton (*q.v.*). Cambridge from 1751. In the House of Commons he showed traces of his derivation from an Old Tory family. He voted in the interest of Robert Clive and largely in support of the North ministry, but his term was very brief and he did not stand for re-election. M.P. for Worcester City, March–September, 1774.

Le Despencer, 11th Baron. See Francis Dashwood

Lee, Charles. 1731–82

Born at Dernhall, Cheshire; son of Major General Charles Lee, of an old Cheshire County family. He attended school at Bury St. Edmunds and then in Switzerland, and at the age of 14 entered his father's regiment with the rank of ensign. He served in armies on the Continent and then went to America, where he was present at the capture of Fort Duquesne, was wounded at Ticonderoga in 1758, and was with Amherst at the capture of Montreal in 1759. He was in London in 1761 and then became an obvious soldier of fortune. He served on the staff of the Portuguese army under Burgoyne in 1762 and with the Polish army as major general in 1764. He was with the Polish embassy at Constantinople in 1766. In 1773 he went to New York in search of fortune, presumably through military employment, and became an ardent and perhaps sincere supporter of the cause of the colonists against Britain. Because of his military experience and his arrogant confidence, as well as his charm, he greatly impressed the Continental Congress and even Washington, and was made major general in the Continental Army in 1775. In 1776 he was second-in-command under Washington, gave expert service in the Boston area, and then prepared the defenses of New York City in the late spring and summer of 1776. In December, 1776, after Howe had captured New York, Lee was taken prisoner while alone in a public house in northern New Jersey (for reasons that appear obscure and may have been highly personal). While a prisoner of war in New York, he was treated as an honored guest by Howe, Clinton, and the British staff, and was perhaps then privately won over to the British side; he almost certainly then commissioned himself to negotiate personally an end to the war. After being exchanged in early 1778, he was again in high command under Washington until his disobedience of Washington's orders at Monmouth (where but for Lee's unauthorized withdrawal of his troops at a crucial time a very serious defeat might have been inflicted on Clinton's army). He was brought before a court-martial and found guilty of improper conduct toward his commander-in-chief. He was dismissed from further military service and, despite his repeated efforts to gain reinstatement, discredited and rejected. He retired to primitive and almost solitary living in western Virginia and died, almost friendless, almost impoverished, and almost alone, in a tavern in Philadelphia.

Lee, George Henry. 1718–72

Styled Viscount Quarendon until 1743, when he succeeded his father, George Henry Lee (1690–1743), as 3d Earl of Lichfield. Westminster, to Oxford; M.A., 1737; D.C.L., 1743; D.C.L. again, 1762. In 1745 he married Diana, daughter of Sir Thomas Frankland (ca.1683–1747; M.P.). Considered a Tory, and lord of the bedchamber, 1760–62, he supported Bute against Newcastle in 1762, became privy councillor, and was captain of gentlemen pensioners, 1762–72. He was high steward of Oxford University, 1760–62; chancellor of Oxford, 1762–72. He founded a professorship of clinical medicine at Oxford. He was a fellow of the Society of Arts from 1767. He was fourth in direct descent from Charles I, and his wife was fourth in direct descent from Oliver Cromwell. "A red-faced old gentleman, shaking with palsy and drink" was a contemporary description that may not have been without prejudice. M.P. for Oxfordshire, 1740–43.

Lee, John. 1733–93

Of Staindrop, near Bishop Auckland, Durham County; his parentage is now obscure, but he was descended from a family long established in Leeds; he was the youngest of 10 children, whose father died when he was 3 years old. His mother, though a Protestant dissenter, was a friend of Archbishop Secker. He became a barrister of Lincoln's Inn in 1756 and a bencher in 1780. He was recorder of Doncaster from 1768, counsel for Admiral Keppel at his court-martial in 1779, king's counsel and attorney general for the Duchy of Lancaster, solicitor general in

1782, and attorney general in the coalition of 1783. He was a sturdy north-country supporter of Rockingham, to whom, he told the House of Commons in 1782, "he owed his seat, and was proud to have had such a patron." In July, 1782, he attacked Shelburne's competence to maintain a ministry, and in February, 1783, he spoke and voted against Shelburne's peace terms as "infamous and disgraceful." He supported the coalition, and while solicitor general told the House that he was under many professional obligations to Thurlow. From 1784 he supported Fox against the Pitt ministry. He amassed a large fortune, but not by corruption, though he was probably known as "Honest Jack Lee" more for his frankness than for any transparent honesty. Portrait by Reynolds. M.P. for Clitheroe, 1782–90; Higham Ferrers, 1790–93.

Lee, Robert. 1706–76

Of Charlbury, Oxfordshire; 13th son of Edward Lee (1st Earl of Lichfield) by Lady Charlotte Fitzroy (illegitimate descendant of Charles I); in 1772 succeeded his nephew George Henry Lee (*q.v.*) as 4th Earl of Lichfield. In 1745 he married Catherine, daughter of Sir John Stonehouse (of Radley, Berkshire; 3d baronet; M.P.). In 1761 he was listed by Newcastle as Tory. There is no record of any speech or vote by him in the House of Commons, and few clues to his role in the proceedings of the House of Lords. M.P. for Oxfordshire, 1754–68.

Leeds, 5th Duke. See **Francis Godolphin Osborne**

Le Fleming, Michael. 1748–1806

Of Rydal, Westmorland; in 1757 succeeded his father, William Fleming (d. 1756), as 4th baronet; he restored the original particle Le to his surname, in deference, he said, to his father's "veneration for antiquity." Eton, 1760–65. In 1782 he married Diana, daughter of Thomas Howard (1721–83) (*q.v.*). He opposed the North ministry on most major issues, voting against approval of the address from the throne in October, 1775, and voting for the Dunning resolution of April 6, 1780, but he did not vote in any of the 5 crucial divisions recorded in February and March, 1782. He voted for Shelburne's peace terms in February, 1783; against Fox's India Bill in November, 1783; and then with Pitt until 1788. Before 1790 he made only one recorded address to the House of Commons, in 1785, urging the repression of hawkers. M.P. for Westmorland, 1774–1806.

Legge, Henry Bilson. 1708–64

Of Mapledurham, Oxfordshire, near Reading; 4th son of William Legge (1672–1750; 1st Earl of Dartmouth); grandson of Heneage Finch (1st Earl of Aylesford); uncle of William Legge (*q.v.*). Oxford from 1726; D.C.L., 1733. In 1750 he married Baroness Mary Stawell (*q.v.*), daughter of Edward Stawell (ca.1685–1755; 4th Baron Stawell); in 1754 he added the name Bilson upon inheriting from Leonard Bilson. He was a secretary in the treasury and a secretary to the chancellor of the exchequer, 1736–42; surveyor general, 1742–45; member of the Admiralty Board, 1745–46; member of the Treasury Board, 1746–49; special envoy to the king of Prussia in 1748; treasurer of the navy, 1749–54; and chancellor of the exchequer, 1754–55, 1756–57, and 1757–61. Having been a placeman and supporter of the Pelhams, he was courted by the Leicester House party, but opposed it in the Hampshire elections and remained faithful to Newcastle. After he had voted against Bute's peace preliminaries in late 1762, he was dismissed from the exchequer, partly because, it was said, he was greatly disliked by the new king, by Henry Fox, and by the Duke of Bedford. He died within 2 years of that disaster to his career. In 1768 his widow married Wills Hill (*q.v.*). He was ambitious, shrewd in politics, and fairly able in finance, but with a limited range and a dogmatic manner. Though he did not control any constituencies in his own right, he strongly influenced John Buller (1721–86) (*q.v.*), who "managed" East and West Looe. "Nothing ever came amiss to him that might raise him on the ruins of either friends or enemies," was the somewhat unjust comment of Horace Walpole. "He had more masters than any man in England, and never left one with a character." Portrait by Hoare. M.P. for East Looe, 1740–41; Orford, 1741–59; Hampshire, 1759–64.

Legge, William. 1731–1801

Of Patshull House, near Wolverhampton, Staffordshire, and (through the North-Guilford connection) Wroxton, near Banbury, Oxfordshire; the only son of George Legge (d. 1732; Viscount Lewisham); styled Viscount Lewisham from 1732; in 1750 he succeeded his grandfather William Legge (1672–1750) as 2d Earl of Dartmouth. His mother married (2) Francis North (*q.v.*), and he was thus a half stepbrother of Lord North and was his friend from boyhood through-

out his life, though they were not always in political agreement. He
was a nephew of Henry Bilson Legge (*q.v.*) and nephew by marriage
of Sir Walter Bagot (1702–68; M.P.; leading Tory). Westminster, to
Oxford (with North) in 1749; M.A., 1751; D.C.L., 1756; grand tour
with North, 1752–54; fellow of the Society of Arts from 1754. His
family tradition had been Tory, but his own sympathies were liberal,
and by 1765 he was an adherent of the Rockingham Whigs. Personal
loyalty more than political conviction led him to yield to North's pleas
and to join and remain with the North ministry, 1773–82, though he
was often unhappy about the measures of that ministry. He was privy
councillor from 1765; president of the Board of Trade and Plantations,
July 20, 1765–August 16, 1766, in the Rockingham ministry, and again
in the North ministry as part of his function as secretary of state for
the colonies, August 14, 1772–November 10, 1775. He was not a
politician and had no wish to be, but he gave a decade of public service
from a strong sense of *noblesse oblige*. Benjamin Franklin said of him
that he was "a truly good man and wishes sincerely a good understanding with the colonies." When he found his position as secretary of
state for the colonies hopeless in 1775, he withdrew from it into the
less controversial inactivities of lord privy seal, a position he held until
the resignation of the North ministry, March 27, 1782. He rejoined
Lord North in the coalition ministry as lord steward in 1783, and from
1785, at North's instigation, was high steward of Oxford University.
He was a supporter of religion in general and John Wesley in particular, and a generous silent patron of the poet William Cowper. He
was devoted to agriculture, his large family, the improvement of his
estates, and Lord North. In the House of Lords he recorded dissents
to the cider tax in 1763 and to the regulation of East India Company
dividends and management, 1767–68. Dartmouth College in New
Hampshire was named in his honor.

Legge, William George. 1755–1810

Of Patshull House, Wolverhampton, Staffordshire; styled Viscount
Lewisham until 1801, when he succeeded his father, William Legge
(*q.v.*), as 3d Earl of Dartmouth. Harrow, 1770–71; Oxford, 1771–75;
grand tour, 1775–78. In 1782 he married Frances, 2d daughter of Heneage Finch (*q.v.*) and granddaughter of Algernon Seymour (1684–
1750; Duke of Somerset). He was lord of the bedchamber to the

Prince of Wales, 1782–83; warden of the stannaries, 1783–98; president of the Board of Control of India, 1801–1802; privy councillor from 1801; received the Order of the Garter in 1805. With his father he supported the North ministry in every crucial vote until its fall in March, 1782, and then supported North in the coalition ministry, voting against Shelburne's peace terms in February, 1783. After the fall of the coalition he supported Pitt. M.P. for Plymouth, 1778–80; Staffordshire, 1780–84.

Legh (or Lee), Peter. 1706–92

Of Lyme Hall, near Bollington, Cheshire, and Bank Hall, near Preston, Lancashire; 2d but oldest surviving son of Thomas Legh (of Lancaster; M.P.); descended from an old Cheshire family, the Barons of Stoneleigh, who controlled a seat in Parliament for Newton. Westminster, 1721–27; Cambridge from 1727. In 1761 he was listed as Tory, but he supported Newcastle and opposed Bute and then the Grenville ministry, 1762–65, including a vote against general warrants in 1764. Thereafter, though he did not vote against repeal of the Stamp Act in 1766, he usually voted in opposition to the Grafton and then the North ministries until he left Parliament. M.P. for Newton, 1743–74.

Legh (or Lee), Peter. 1723–1804

Of Norbury Booths, near Knutsford, Cheshire; only son of Thomas Pennington Legh (of Cheshire); nephew of Sir Willoughby Aston (1714–72; 5th baronet; M.P.); descended from a family traditionally Tory. He was probably a merchant and government contractor. He supported Newcastle until 1765 but opposed repeal of the Stamp Act in 1766 and Chatham's land tax in 1767, and in general opposed the Grafton ministry thereafter. He voted with the North ministry on most issues, 1770–74, including a vote against continuation of the Grenville Disputed Elections Act in 1774. M.P. for Ilchester, 1765–74.

Legh (or Lee), Thomas Peter. ca.1755–97

Oldest son of Rev. Ashburnham Legh (of Golborne Park, Lancashire); grandson of Sir Holland Egerton; from the same family as Peter Legh (1706–92; M.P.), which Robinson said in 1784 "owned" Newton Borough. He seldom attended the House of Commons and left no record of his votes there, 1780–84. After 1784 he apparently opposed the Pitt ministry. M.P. for Newton, 1780–97.

Leicester, 1st Earls. See **George Townshend.** 1755–1811 and **Thomas William Coke**

Leicester, Peter. 1732–70

Of Tabley, near Knutsford, Cheshire; in 1742 succeeded his father, Sir John Byrne, as 4th baronet; he took the surname Leicester in 1744 upon inheriting estates through his mother. He was enrolled at Oxford in 1750. In 1755 he married Catherine, daughter of Sir William Fleming (d. 1757; M.P.). He was almost immediately unseated on petition. M.P. for Preston, 1767–68.

Leigh, Richard. 1727–72

Of Hawley, near Dartford, Kent; 2d son of Francis Leigh (of Sutton, Kent). Oxford from 1744, Middle Temple from 1750, barrister in 1753. He was serjeant-at-law in 1765, counsel for Wilkes against Halifax in 1769, and king's serjeant from 1771. He was elected to the House of Commons in 1770 with the approval of the ministry, and was thereafter considered a supporter of North, but there is a record of only one vote or speech by him. His health was poor, and he died in 1772. M.P. for East Looe, 1770–72.

Leighton, Charlton. ca.1747–84

Of Loton Park, near Shrewsbury, and Wattlesborough, Shropshire; in 1780 succeeded his father, Sir Charles Leighton, as 4th baronet. He was enrolled at Cambridge in 1763. He was classed by Robinson as a country gentleman, but he voted steadily against the North ministry, including the five crucial divisions reported in February and March, 1782. He voted for Shelburne's peace terms in February, 1783; for Pitt's proposals for the reform of representation in Parliament in May, 1783; and against Fox's India Bill in November, 1783. In 1784 he supported Pitt. He was inclined to vote with his friend Francis Godolphin Osborne (*q.v.*). M.P. for Shrewsbury, 1774–75 and 1780–84.

Leinster, 1st and 2d Viscounts and 1st and 2d Dukes. See **James Fitzgerald** and **William Robert Fitzgerald**

Leith, Alexander Charles George. 1741–80

Of Burgh St. Peter, near Beccles, Norfolk; son of Sir Alexander Leith (killed while commanding artillery at Havana in 1762). He married

(1) Margaret, widowed daughter of Thomas Hay, and (2) in 1775 a daughter of Sir John Cope (d. 1760; M.P.). He was created baronet in 1775. In 1764 he was an army lieutenant; in 1768 he went to India with the East India Company, but was back in England before 1774. He was made lieutenant colonel in 1779. He was brought into the House of Commons with the acquiescence of the North ministry in 1774, but he turned violently to opposition after Burgoyne's surrender at Saratoga in late 1777 and the resultant inquiry in 1778. In January, 1778, he seconded Charles Fox's motion for the papers bearing on Burgoyne's expedition. In 1779 he raised a regiment bearing his name and died while leading it against the Spanish in Jamaica. M.P. for Tregony, 1774–80.

Leland, Thomas. 1722–1785

He entered Trinity College, Dublin, in 1737; B.A., 1737; fellow from 1746. In 1754 he published a Latin translation of the *Philippics* of Demosthenes, followed by the publication of an English translation. In 1758 he published *The History of Philip, King of Macedon*, which impressed the scholarly world. In 1766 he presented to the Trinity College, Dublin, library a rare Irish manuscript chronicle. He was vicar of St. Anne's in Dublin from 1773 and received an honorary D.D. In 1773 he published *The History of Ireland from the Invasion of Henry II*.

Lemon, William. 1748–1824

Of Carclew, near Penryn, Cornwall; oldest son of William Lemon; brother of John Lemon (1754–1814; M.P.); created baronet in 1774. He was enrolled at Oxford from 1765. He inherited a fortune from his grandfather's copper mines in Cornwall. He married a sister of Sir Francis Buller (*q.v.*), thereby establishing a family connection with Henry Bathurst. He was knighted by the North ministry in 1774 and voted with it until late 1777. On November 3, 1775, he told the House of Commons that he approved the ministry's measures toward the American colonies but opposed sending foreign troops to garrison Gibraltar. After 1777 he turned against the ministry and in 1780 voted for Dunning's resolution of April 6. In 1782 he voted against the North ministry in all 5 of the recorded crucial divisions of February and March. He then supported Shelburne and voted for his peace terms in February, 1783, and after 1783 supported Pitt. M.P. for Penryn, 1770–74; Cornwall, 1774–1824.

Lempster (corruption of **Leominster**), **Lord.** See **George Fermor**

Lennox, Charles. 1735–1806

Styled Earl of March until 1750, when he succeeded his father, Charles Lennox (1701–50), as his 3d but 1st surviving son, as 3d Duke of Richmond (2d creation), and 8th Duke of Lennox (Scottish). His family connections included the houses of Cadogan, Fox, Ker, Bathurst, Fitzroy, Campbell, Bruce, and Stewart. He was schooled at Westminster from 1746 and graduated from Leyden University in 1753. In 1757 he married Mary, 3d daughter of Charles Bruce (3d Earl of Ailesbury) and granddaughter of John Campbell (4th Duke of Argyll). He was ensign in the foot guards in 1751, captain in 1753, lieutenant colonel in 1756, and colonel in 1758. He was at the Cherbourg raid in 1758 and distinguished himself at Minden in 1759, where he was aide to Prince Ferdinand and was sent back to England with the news of the victory and of Lord George Sackville's (Germain's) refusal to obey the prince's repeated order to charge with the cavalry. He became major general in 1761, lieutenant general in 1770, and general in 1782. He was later field marshal. He was vice president of the Society of Arts in 1754, fellow of the Royal Society from 1755, and Knight of the Garter from 1782. He was lord of the bedchamber from 1760; lord lieutenant of Sussex, 1763–1806; ambassador to Paris, 1765–66; privy councillor from 1765; secretary of state, southern department, May 23–August 21, 1766; and master general of ordnance, 1782–83. A vigorous, vehement, and independent liberal who toward the end of his career became more conservative, he strongly and invariably opposed the North ministry and its measures toward the colonies. He favored an annually elected Parliament, toleration of Protestant dissenters and Roman Catholics, and universal suffrage. He was handsome, charming in manners except when emotionally aroused, idealistic, downright, and difficult. He was intolerant of guile but capable of astuteness, critical of caution but himself occasionally prudent. He opposed Bute and Grenville, served under Rockingham, 1765–66, and thereafter in general was a Rockingham Whig, though he often preferred to play a lone hand. George III professed to hate him because of his "radicalism" and "factious oppo-

533

sition," which by the king's peculiar doctrines would in a lesser man have seemed close to traitorism, especially after April 7, 1778, when he moved in the House of Lords that the king be asked "to put an end to a system . . . by which . . . wicked men had prevailed in his Court and Administration." In later discussions of new ministries, the king refused to accept any ministry of which he would be a member. After Rockingham's death, he moved slowly, and never unreservedly, into support of the younger Pitt. In the House of Lords he recorded dissents from majority votes (1) approving regulation of the East India Company (as "very injurious to private property and alarming to public credit") in 1767, (2) approving regulation of the dividends of the East India Company in 1768, (3) approving adjournment of the House of Lords on January 15, 1770 (as "uncommon, unreasonable, and neglect of duty"), (4) approving the action of the House of Commons in expelling Wilkes in 1770, (5) rejecting Chatham's motion to reverse the action of the House of Commons expelling Wilkes in 1770, (6) clearing the gallery of the House of Lords (as limiting inquiry and tending "to hide from the public eye the . . . criminal neglect of the ministry") in 1770, (7) approving North's Falkland Islands settlement in 1771, (8) approving the Royal Marriage Bill in 1772, (9) restraining the appointive powers of the East India Company (as "unduly enlarging the powers of the Crown") in 1773, (10) limiting the privileges of the East India Company in 1773, (11) regulating the affairs of the East India Company in 1773, (12) in general supporting the ministry measures affecting the colonies; (13) approving the ministry's colonial policy (which he called "careless futility") in 1775, (14) supporting the address from the throne on American policy in February, 1775, (15) approving the New England Restraint of Trade Bill in 1775, (16) approving the Non-Intercourse Bill for the colonies in 1775, (17) approving the hiring of mercenaries to fight the colonists in 1776, (18) approving the address from the throne in 1776, (19) allowing the continuance of the American war in 1777, (20) approving the address from the throne in 1778, (21) approving the continuance of the American war in 1778, (22) rejecting the motion to ask the king to effect "a total change of System" in 1779, (23) rejecting a motion to ask the king to dismiss Sandwich in 1779, (24) rejecting a motion to examine into public expenditures in 1779, (25) rejecting a motion to protest the dismissal of Pembroke and

Carmarthen from their lord lieutenancies in 1780, (26) approving a declaration of war against the United Provinces in 1781, and (27) accepting the "ruinous prosecution of the unjust war" in 1781. Portraits by Reynolds, Gainsborough, Romney, and Battoni.

Lennox, George Henry. 1737–1805

Of West Stoke House, near Chichester, Sussex; 4th but 2d surviving son of Charles Lennox (1701–50; 2d Duke of Richmond); brother of Charles Lennox (*q.v.*); grandson of William Sloan (1672–1726; 1st Baron Cadogan). He was schooled at Westminster from 1749. In 1758 he married Louisa, daughter of William Henry Ker (or Kerr) (ca.1690–1775; Earl of Ancram and, after 1767, 4th Marquess of Lothian, both Scottish). He was ensign in 1754 and saw military service as aide to the Duke of Cumberland in Germany and France. He was lieutenant colonel in 1758, colonel in 1762, and brigadier general in Portugal in 1763. He was secretary of the legation in Paris, 1765–66, and minister in 1766; major general in 1772; lieutenant general in 1777; constable of the Tower of London, 1783–85; privy councillor from 1784; general and governor of Plymouth in 1793. When in attendance in the House of Commons, he voted steadily in opposition to the North ministry, 1774–82, including a vote for the Dunning resolution of April 6, 1780. In 1783 he did not vote on Shelburne's peace terms, voted for Pitt's proposals for the reform of Parliament, and voted against Fox's India Bill. In 1784 he supported Pitt. M.P. for Chichester, 1761–67; Sussex, 1767–90.

Leslie, David. 1722–1802

Styled Lord Balgonie from 1729; in 1754 he succeeded his father, Alexander Leslie (ca.1699–1754), as 8th Earl of Leven (Scottish). He attended the University of Edinburgh and then the University of Groningen, 1740–42. He entered the army as ensign in 1742 and became captain in 1744. He was grand master of Scottish Freemasons, 1759–61; deputy governor of the Bank of Scotland; lord of Scottish police, 1773–82; and high commissioner of the Church of Scotland, 1783–1801.

Leslie, John. ca.1698–1767

Styled Lord Leslie until 1722, when he succeeded his father, John Leslie

(1679–1722), as 10th Earl of Rothes (Scottish). He entered the army in 1715 as captain of dragoons, was lieutenant colonel in 1720, and was major general in 1743 at Dettingen. He was at Rocourt in 1746, and in command of British troops in Ireland, 1760–74. He was Knight of the Thistle from 1753 and a Scottish representative peer in several Parliaments from 1723 to 1767.

Lethieullier, Benjamin. 1729–97

Of Beckenham, Kent; Belmont, near London; and Middleton, near Andover, Hampshire; oldest surviving son of Christopher Lethieullier (director of the Bank of England); grandson of Edward Lascelles (wealthy Barbados planter). He married a daughter of Sir Matthew Fetherstonehaugh (*q.v.*). With his brother he conducted a prosperous merchant business, especially in trade with Turkey and the Near East. In politics he was, according to John Robinson, "a very independent gentleman," but he inclined to support the current administration only when his friend General Henry Seymour Conway was favorable to it. He voted against unseating Wilkes in January, 1770, against the North ministry on Wilkes issues and on extension of the Grenville Election Act in 1774, for economic reforms in 1778, and for the Dunning resolution of April 6, 1780. He voted for Conway's resolution of February 27, 1782, on promptly ending the war in America, but on two later issues he voted with the North ministry. He voted for Shelburne's peace terms, and did not vote on Fox's India Bill in 1783. There is no evidence that during nearly 30 years in the House of Commons he once addressed its members, at least before 1790. M.P. for Andover, 1768–97.

Leven, Earl. See David Leslie

Leveson-Gower, George Granville. 1758–1833

Styled Viscount Trentham until 1803, when he succeeded his father, Granville Leveson-Gower (*q.v.*), as 3d Earl Gower and 2d Marquess of Stafford; in 1833 created 1st Duke of Sutherland. He was a nephew of the 2d Duke of Bridgwater and in 1803 inherited estates from him; he was also a nephew of the 4th Duke of Bedford. Westminster, 1768–74; at Oxford from 1775. In 1785 he married Elizabeth, daughter of the 18th Earl of Sutherland (Scottish), who was Countess of Sutherland in her own right; through her he came into possession of the greater part of the county of Sutherland. He was elected to fill the family seat in the House of Commons in 1779 and supported the North ministry, of which his father had been a member but had withdrawn, until February 20, 1782. He did not vote on Shelburne's peace terms or on Fox's India Bill in 1783. He supported Pitt's Regency Bill in 1788, became a privy councillor in 1790, and was ambassador to Paris until 1792. There is no evidence that he addressed the House of Commons before 1799, when he was summoned by writ to the House of Lords. He built 450 miles of roads and 134 bridges in Sutherlandshire. M.P. for Newcastle-under-Lyme, 1779–84; Staffordshire, 1787–99.

Leveson-Gower, Granville. 1721–1803

Styled Viscount Trentham from 1746; in 1754 he succeeded his father, John Leveson-Gower, as 2d Earl Gower; in 1786 created Marquess of Stafford. He was a grandson of Evelyn Pierrepont (ca.1665–1726; 1st Duke of Kingston), and his sister married John Russell (1710–71) (*q.v.*), 4th Duke of Bedford, of whose political clique he became a leading member. He was also linked to Thurlow by two still stronger ties: political self-interest and "habits of convivial and social intimacy" (Wraxall). Westminster from 1731; Oxford from 1740. He married (1) in 1746 Elizabeth, daughter and heiress of Nicholas Fazakerley (*q.v.*), (2) in 1748 Louisa, daughter of Scroop Egerton (1st Duke of Bridgwater), and (3) in 1768 Susanna, daughter of Alexander Stewart (ca.1694–1773; 6th Earl of Galloway, Scottish). While in the House of Commons, 1744–54, he made connections with the Leicester House group but continued to support Newcastle until late 1762, when he shifted his support to Bute and then became a member of Bedford's inner circle. He opposed repeal of the Stamp Act in 1766 and recorded dissents in the House of Lords to its majority votes approving the regulation of dividends and of administration of the East India Company. After the death of Bedford in 1771 he became the nominal leader of Bedford's "Bloomsbury Gang," which formed the ministry with North at its head but with plans to dominate his operations. When it was found that North would not be dominated solely by the Bedfordites, he was one of those who on occasion attempted to undermine and oust North. In 1779 he resigned from the North ministry, professing to disagree with North over measures toward Ireland but perhaps also fearing to fall with the ministry, or planning to help it fall in order to replace it. In February, 1783, he condemned Shelburne's peace terms because "we were entitled to better ones." From 1784 he supported and held office in the Pitt minis- He was a member of the Admiralty Board, 1749–51; a privy councillor from 1751; master of the king's horse, 1757–60; lord privy seal, 1755–57; lord lieutenant of Staffordshire, 1755–1800; keeper of the great wardrobe, 1760–63; lord president of the council, 1767–79; and lord privy seal, 1784–94. He received the Order of the Garter in 1771 and was made fellow of the Society of Arts in 1784. M.P. for Bishop's Castle, 1744–47; Westminster, 1747–54; Lichfield, 1754.

Leveson-Gower, John. 1740–92

Of Stittenham, near Malton, Yorkshire; 6th son of John Leveson-Gower (d. 1754, 1st Earl Gower); younger half brother of Granville Leveson-Gower (*q.v.*). Through his brother's marriage he was related to John Russell (1710–71) (*q.v.*). In 1773 he married Frances, daughter of Admiral Edward Boscawen (1711–61). His navy career included a captaincy in 1760 and service in the Mediterranean, the West Indies, and in Newfoundland waters, 1760–77. He was with Keppel off Ushant in 1778 and (at variance with his brother Granville) took Keppel's part in the controversy with Palliser, resigning his ship in protest at Keppel's court-martial. He served on the Admiralty Board, 1783–90; supported Pitt after 1783; and became rear admiral in 1787. M.P. for Appleby, 1784–90; Newcastle-under-Lyme, 1790–92.

Lewes, Watkyn. 1740–1821

Of King's Road, London; 2d son of Rev. Watkyn Lewes (of Penybenglog, near Capel Curig, Carnarvonshire). He was schooled at Shrewsbury, and at Cambridge from 1759; Middle Temple from 1760, barrister in 1766. He married "a substantial fortune." He was alderman of London, 1772–96; and lord mayor of London, 1780–81; and knighted in 1773. He was a leader in the Society for Support of the Bill of Rights, 1769–70, and remained a Wilkite. Defeated in election to Parliament in 1774, he won a seat in 1780 and voted for reform of Parliament and against the North ministry, including 4 of the crucial divisions reported in February and March, 1782. He was especially critical of London's inadequate representation in the House of Commons. In February, 1783, he voted for Shelburne's peace terms, and in May, 1783, he spoke supporting Pitt's reform measures but regretting that they did not go further. He voted against Fox's India Bill in November, 1783, and thereafter supported Pitt. He addressed the House fairly frequently. M.P. for London, 1781–96.

Lewis, Edward.

Of Downton, Radnorshire. His dates of birth and death and his parentage are now obscure. In 1761 he was listed as Tory. In 1767 he was one of those receiving royal grants of land in maritime Canada. From 1774, when North pronounced him an "honest, worthy man" and "a good and steady friend," he held government contracts and supported the North ministry, as he had previously supported every administration since 1761. He voted against the Dunning resolution of April 6, 1780, and voted with the North ministry in all 5 recorded crucial divisions in February and March, 1782. He voted against Shelburne's peace terms and for Fox's India Bill in 1783 and in 1784 opposed Pitt. In 1782 he was forced by the new Crewe Act to resign his government contracts in order to retain his seat in the House of Commons. M.P. for New Radnor boroughs, 1761–90.

Lewis, John. 1738–97

Of Harpton Court, near Radnor; oldest son of Henry Lewis (of Bedford Row, London). He enrolled at Lincoln's Inn in 1755 and became barrister in 1764. He married (2) Ann, daughter of Sir Thomas Frankland (1718–84) (q.v.). In 1763 he became receiver of royal revenues for 3 western counties. He was recorder of Radnor in 1764, 1768, and 1792; bailiff of Radnor in 1766, 1786, and 1791; and sheriff of Radnorshire, 1792–93. His only recorded vote in the House of Commons was against the expulsion of Wilkes in January, 1770, and his only recorded speeches there were 3 in condemnation of the attitude of the ungrateful colonies in 1769 and 1775, expressing a strong wish for their "chastisement." M.P. for New Radnor boroughs, 1768–69, 1774–75, and 1780–81. Unseated in 1781.

Lewis, Thomas. 1690–1777

Of Harpton Court, near Radnor; oldest son of Colonel Thomas Lewis and perhaps an uncle of John Lewis (q.v.). Oxford from 1709. In 1743 he married Ann, daughter of Sir Nathan Wright (3d baronet). He held many local offices in Radnorshire and was known as the "Old Burgess." He was regular in attendance in the House of Commons and voted with the current ministry. M.P. for New Radnor, 1715–61.

Lewisham, Viscounts. See **William Legge** and **William George Legge**

Lichfield, 3d Earl. See **George Henry Lee**

Liddell, Anne. ca.1738–1804

Daughter of Henry Liddell (*q.v.*). In 1756 she married Augustus Henry Fitzroy (*q.v.*). In 1765 he separated from her and in March, 1769, he divorced her for adultery with John Fitzpatrick (*q.v.*), by whom she had a son and whom she married in 1769. It is not to be held against her virtue that she aroused amorous desires in young James Boswell when he first met her in 1762, for that achievement required no skill and no intention, and in her case his desires were unfulfilled. She was attractive and highly intelligent, and in her later life she became a favorite correspondent of Horace Walpole.

Liddell, Henry. 1708–84

Of Ravensworth Castle, near Gateshead, County Durham; oldest son of Thomas Liddell (d. 1715); in 1723 succeeded his grandfather Sir Henry Liddell as 4th baronet; in 1747 created Baron Ravensworth of Durham. Cambridge from 1725. In 1735 he married Anne, daughter of Sir Peter Delmé (lord mayor of London, 1723–24). He was called by Horace Walpole "one of the hottest Whigs in England," and supported Pelham and then Newcastle through 1762. He spoke supporting the Regency Bill in 1765 and opposed the continuance of the Quebec Governing Act in 1775. In 1782, Shelburne wrote to the king that he was one of "the most independent people" in Parliament, but others called him "a warm and honest Whig." He was the father of Anne Liddell (*q.v.*). M.P. for Morpeth, 1734–47.

Lifford, 1st Baron and 1st Viscount. See **James Hewitt**

Ligonier, Edward. ca.1740–82

Son of Colonel Francis Ligonier (d. 1746; son of Seigneur de Monteuquet of Languedoc); in 1770 succeeded his uncle John Louis Ligonier (*q.v.*) as 2d Viscount Ligonier (Irish); in 1776 created Earl Ligonier (Irish). He married (1) in 1766 Penelope, oldest daughter of George

Pitt (*q.v.*), whom he divorced in 1771, and (2) in 1773 Mary, 2d daughter of Robert Henley (ca.1708–72) (*q.v.*). He entered the British army as cornet of horse in 1752 and became captain and aide to Prince Ferdinand at Minden in 1759, where he was one of those who carried orders from the prince to Lord George Sackville (later Germain), which Sackville failed to obey. In the resultant court-martial of Sackville in 1760 he was therefore a chief witness unfavorable to Sackville. He was aide to the king in 1763; secretary of embassy at Madrid, 1763–65; major general in 1775; lieutenant general in 1777; and Knight of the Bath in 1781. In politics he was called a Tory, but he took no significant part in the affairs of court or Parliament.

Ligonier, John Louis. 1680–1770

Of Cobham Place, near Epsom, Surrey; 2d son of Louis de Ligonier (Huguenot; Seigneur de Monteuquet of Languedoc); in 1757 created Viscount Ligonier (Irish); in 1763 created Baron Ligonier (English); in 1766 created Earl Ligonier (English). He came from France to Ireland in 1697 at the age of 16 and became a British citizen in 1701. He promptly enlisted in the British army and fought at Blenheim in 1704, Ramillies in 1706, Audenaarde in 1708, and Malplaquet in 1709. He was governor of Fort St. Philip in Minorca in 1712, adjutant general of the expedition on Vigo in 1718, and governor of Kinsale in County Cork, 1739–40. He was made brigadier general in 1735, major general in 1739, and lieutenant general in 1743. He commanded the British foot at Dettingen in 1743 and at Fontenoy in 1745. He was in command of all British troops in the Netherlands, 1746–47, and was made general in 1746. He was governor of Jersey in 1750, governor of Plymouth in 1752, and commander in chief of all troops in Britain, with a seat in the cabinet, from 1757. He was master general of ordnance, 1759–63; field marshal in 1766. He was a favorite of George II, who had him made a privy councillor, and was intensely admired by nearly all the men he commanded, from general to private. He supported the Pelhams, but in 1762 he opposed Newcastle's wish to continue a subsidy of £2 million to Prussia and thereafter supported Bute. He was a fellow of the Royal Society and a governor of the French Hospital in London. Portrait by Reynolds. M.P. for Bath, 1748–63.

Lilford, 1st Baron. See **Thomas Powys**

Limerick, Viscount. See **James Hamilton.** 1730–98

Lincoln, Earls. See **Henry Fiennes Pelham Clinton.** 1720–94 **Henry Fiennes Pelham Clinton.** 1750–78 **Thomas Pelham Clinton.** 1752–95 and **John Pelham Clinton.** 1755–81

Lind, George. ca.1700–63

2d son of George Lind (of Gorgie, near Edinburgh; merchant). He succeeded his father as an Edinburgh merchant and was lord provost of Edinburgh, 1760–62, and conservator of Scottish privileges in the Netherlands, 1762–63. He was elected to the House of Commons "in the interest" of his friend the Duke of Argyll, but soon resigned his seat to accept a sinecure from Bute, whom he supported politically. M.P. for Edinburgh City, 1761–62.

Lindsay, Alexander. 1752–1825

In 1768 succeeded his father, James Lindsay, as 6th Earl of Balcarres (Scottish). He studied at Gottingen, 1768–70. In 1780 he married his cousin Elizabeth, daughter of Charles Dalrymple. In 1767, before he enrolled at Gottingen, he had entered the army; he became captain in 1771 and major in 1775. He served in America under Burgoyne and was made prisoner of war at the surrender at Saratoga in October, 1777. He was exchanged in 1779, and became colonel in 1782, major general in 1793, lieutenant general in 1798, and general in 1803. He served as a representative Scottish peer, 1784–1825, and was governor of Jersey in 1793 and of Jamaica from 1795.

Lindsay, John. 1737–88

Younger son of Sir Alexander Lindsay (of Evelick, near Pole Hill, Perth; 3d baronet) and grandson of David Murray (Lord Scone and 5th Viscount Stormont). In 1768 he married Mary, daughter of Sir William Milner (M.P.; 1st baronet). He was a navy lieutenant in 1756, commanded a fire ship at Rochefort in 1757, was at Louisburg in 1758, and served at Quebec in 1759. In 1764 he was knighted for gallantry in action at Havana in 1762. In 1764 he traveled extensively in the southern colonies of America with his friend and fellow officer Sir Adam Gordon. He was commodore in East Indian waters, 1769–71, and served notably at Madras. He was with Keppel in the action against the French off Ushant in 1778, supported Keppel in the latter's court-martial in 1779, and resigned his commission in protest at the ministry's treatment of Keppel. After the fall of the North ministry he was placed in command of naval forces in the Mediterranean. He was Knight of the Bath from 1770, a member of the Admiralty Board in 1783, and rear admiral from 1787. "He made no figure in the House if indeed he ever attended" (Haden-Guest). M.P. for Aberdeen burghs, 1767–68.

Linwood, Nicholas. d. 1773

Of Itchel Manor, near Farnham, Hampshire. Of family origins now obscure but certainly not impoverished, he became a partner in the Portuguese wine business and had social as well as political friendships with Henry Fox, John Calcraft, and Richard Rigby, a ubiquitous trio. He was a director of the East India Company, 1749–51 and 1752–54; of the South Sea Company, 1758–64; and of the Sun Fire Assurance Company, 1760–73. He was also part owner of merchant-venture ships and commissioner for the sale of French ships taken as prizes, 1756–61. Desiring government contracts, he usually voted with the current administration, but there is no available evidence that he ever addressed the House of Commons. M.P. for Stockbridge, 1761–68; Aldeburgh, 1768–73.

Lippincott, Henry. 1737–80

Of Stoke Bishop, near Bristol, and Littleton-upon-Severn, near Thornbury, Gloucestershire; only son of Henry Lippincott (of Culmstock and Sidbury, Devon); created baronet in 1778. He became a tobacco merchant in Bristol and was a member of the Bristol Common Council, 1768–80; sheriff of Bristol, 1768–71; sheriff of Gloucester, 1776–77. He was prominent in the Society of Merchant Venturers. He was elected to the House of Commons with the help of the North ministry, which he supported before his death in the same year. M.P. for Bristol, 1780.

Lisburne, 4th Viscount and 1st Earl. See Wilmot Vaughan

Lisle, Warren. ca.1695–1788

Of Upway, near Dorchester, Dorset; son of Warren Lisle (searcher of customs at Poole). He was himself searcher of customs at Weymouth, 1721–73, and became known as the "Terror of Smugglers." Somehow through that supposedly unprofitable occupation he acquired a fortune. His membership in the House of Commons, at the age of 85, was too brief to provide explanations or leave a record of any votes. M.P. for Weymouth and Melcombe Regis, 1780.

Lister, Nathaniel. 1725–93

Of Armitage Park, near Lichfield, Staffordshire; 2d son of Thomas Lister (M.P.); brother of Thomas Lister (1723–61; of Gisburne Park, near Clitheroe, Yorkshire; M.P.); grandson of Sir Ralph Assheton (2d baronet). Westminster from 1736; Oxford from 1744. He was classified as Tory by Bute in 1761, by Rockingham in 1766, and by Newcastle in 1767. He was said to be holding his seat in the House of Commons only during the minority of his nephew Thomas Lister (q.v.), and there is no record that he ever addressed the House or opposed the current ministry after 1768. In 1784 John Robinson referred to Clitheroe as "Mr. Lister's borough." M.P. for Clitheroe, 1761–73.

Lister, Thomas. 1752–1826

Of Gisburne Park, near Clitheroe, Yorkshire; only son of Thomas Lister (1723–61; of Gisburne Park; M.P.); nephew of Nathaniel Lister (q.v.); in 1797 created Baron Ribbesdale. Westminster from ca. 1764; Oxford from 1769. He came from a Tory tradition and ardently supported the war against the colonies until 1780. In 1776 he fitted out a frigate and gave it to the government, and in 1779 he raised at his own expense a regiment known as "Lister's Light Dragoons." But in 1780 he moved into the opposition and supported Rockingham, voting against the North ministry for the Dunning resolution of April 6, 1780, and voting against North in 4 of the crucial recorded divisions in February and March, 1782. He voted against Shelburne's peace terms and for Fox's India Bill in 1783, supporting the coalition. He was in opposition to Pitt in 1784. He was colonel of yeoman cavalry, 1790–1826, and sheriff of Yorkshire, 1794–95. M.P. for Clitheroe, 1773–90.

Littleton, Edward. ca.1725–1812

Of Pillaton Hall, near Penkridge, Staffordshire; and nearby Teddesley Park, Staffordshire; oldest son of Fisher Littleton; in 1742 succeeded his uncle Sir Edward Littleton (of Pillaton Hall; 3d baronet) as 4th

baronet. He was enrolled at Cambridge from 1744. In 1745 he raised
a company and captained it against the Jacobites. He was sheriff of
Staffordshire, 1762–63. In 1784 he was elected to the House of Commons as a supporter of Pitt and did support him, though his only 2
recorded speeches before 1790 were against the tax on bricks in 1784.
M.P. for Staffordshire, 1784–1812.

Liverpool, 1st Earl. See Charles Jenkinson

Livingstone, Adam. ca.1723–95

Of Ardkinglass Castle, Argyllshire, and Bantaskine, near Falkirk,
Stirlingshire; 2d surviving son of Sir James Livingstone (2d baronet).
He followed a military career, 1742–66, as captain in 1751, major in
1758 serving in Canada under Wolfe, and colonel in 1762. He retired
in 1766. He was brought into the House of Commons by the 5th Duke
of Argyll (Scottish), and became "an obscure and silent government
supporter" of the North ministry, voting against the Dunning resolution of April 6, 1780. He was lord treasurer's remembrancer in the
Scottish exchequer in 1785. Samuel Johnson, after hearing him talk,
called him "a mighty misty man." M.P. for Argyllshire, 1772–80.

Lloyd, Charles. 1735–73

Son of Philip Lloyd (of Greenwich; clerk in the Treasury and in
1761 paymaster of gentlemen pensioners). Westminster from 1749;
Oxford from 1754; B.A., 1758; M.A., 1761. He was private secretary
to George Grenville when Grenville was first minister in 1763, receiver of revenues of Gibraltar in 1764 but removed from that office by
Rockingham in 1765, and deputy teller of the exchequer in 1767. He
published many political pamphlets in support of Grenville, and was
a fellow of the Society of Antiquaries from 1763.

Lloyd, Herbert. ca.1719–69

Of Peterwell, Cardiganshire; 4th son of Walter Lloyd (d. 1747; of
Voelallt and Peterwell; M.P.); created baronet in 1763. Oxford from
1738, Inner Temple from 1739, barrister from 1742. In 1761 he was
listed as Tory and supported Bute; he voted against the Grenville
ministry on Wilkes and general warrants, 1763–64, but against repeal
of the Stamp Act in 1766. There is no record that he ever addressed the
House of Commons. He was locally regarded as a petty tyrant and an

unstable character, and had large gambling losses. M.P. for Cardigan boroughs, 1761–68.

Lloyd, Maurice. d. 1796

Of Pall Mall, London. His career before 1780 is now unknown, but in 1784 he married the wealthy widow of George Prowse (of Yeoville, Somerset). In 1782 he gained election to the House of Commons. Soon after he took his seat, he was charged by Luttrell with having engaged in electoral corruption with the support of the North ministry. North stated to the House that he had never been his agent or that of the ministry, and the charges were dismissed by the House. He did not vote on Shelburne's peace terms but voted for Fox's India Bill in 1783. According to the records he addressed the House but once, and then on the subject of the Bank of England. M.P. for Gatton, 1782–87.

Lloyd, Richard Savage. ca.1730–1810

Of Hintlesham Hall, near Hadleigh, Suffolk; oldest son of Richard Lloyd (ca.1696–1761; of Hintlesham Hall; M.P.). Eton, 1742–48; Cambridge from 1748; Middle Temple from 1749. His election to the House of Commons was sponsored by Newcastle, whom he presumably supported, but there is no record of any vote or speech by him in the House. M.P. for Totnes, 1759–68.

Lockhart, Thomas. 1738–75

Of Craighouse, Edinburgh; oldest son of Alexander Lockhart (dean of the Edinburgh Faculty of Advocates). Edinburgh and St. Andrews universities, 1752–55; at Cambridge from 1755; Inner Temple from 1758; and Leyden University from 1759. He became counselor at law. His election to Parliament was sponsored by the North ministry, which he in turn supported. He addressed the House of Commons in support of the Royal Marriage Bill in 1772 and later made several speeches on legal matters. M.P. for Elgin burghs, 1771–74.

Lockhart-Ross, John. See John Lockhart Ross

Lockyer, Joseph Tolson. 1729–65

Of Mapperton, near Beaminster, Dorset; oldest son of Thomas Lockyer (1699–1785; M.P.). He was probably at Eton, 1742–45; certainly at Lincoln's Inn and Leyden from 1747. He married the daughter of a

Leyden merchant. He was a protégé of Newcastle and Egmont, but died "in a lingering consumption" at the age of 35, leaving no record of ever having addressed the House of Commons or cast a vote in it. M.P. for Ilchester, 1756–65.

Londonderry, 1st Baron, 1st Earl, and 1st Marquess. See **Robert Stewart**

Long, James Tylney. 1736–94

Of Draycot Cerne, near Chippenham, Wiltshire; in 1767 succeeded his father, Sir James Long (1705–67; M.P.) as 7th baronet. In 1784, upon inheriting from his uncle John Child (1712–84, M.P.; and 2d Earl Tylney, Irish), he added the surname Tylney. Westminster from 1749, Oxford from 1756. He married (1) in 1775 Harriet, daughter of Jacob Bouverie (1694–1761; M.P.; and 1st Viscount Folkstone) and sister of William Bouverie (1725–76, 1st Earl of Radnor), and (2) in 1785 Catherine, daughter of Other Lewis Windsor (4th Earl of Plymouth). He was classed as Tory by Bute in 1761, by Rockingham in 1765, and by Newcastle in 1766. He voted against Bute's peace preliminaries in 1762, and with the opposition to the Grafton ministry in 1768, when he voted for Sir George Savile's *Nullum Tempus* Bill. He generally supported the North ministry when present in the House of Commons, voting against extension of the Grenville Election Act in 1774 and against Dunning's resolution of April 6, 1780, and voting with the North ministry in 4 of the 5 recorded crucial votes in February and March, 1782. He voted against Shelburne's peace terms and did not vote on Fox's India Bill in 1783. He later supported Pitt. M.P. for Marlborough, 1762–80; Devizes, 1780–88; Wiltshire, 1788–94.

Lonsdale, 4th Viscount and 1st Earls. See **James Lowther.** 1736–1802   and **William Lowther.** 1757–1844

Lorne, Marquess. See **John Campbell.** 1723–1806

Lothian, 4th and 5th Marquesses. See **William Henry Ker (or Kerr)**   and **William John Ker (or Kerr)**

Loudon, 4th and 5th Earls. See **John Campbell.** 1705–82   and **James Mure Campbell**

Loughborough, 1st Baron. See **Alexander Wedderburn**

547

Lovedon (formerly Townshend), Edward. ca.1751–1822

Of Buscot Park, near Faringdon, Berkshire; son of Thomas Townshend (of Cirencester); upon inheriting from a maternal uncle he took the surname Lovedon in 1772. Winchester, 1762–65; Oxford from 1767. "A substantial yeoman" and an accomplished classical scholar, he was sheriff of Berkshire, 1781–82, and of Brecon, 1799–1800. At Buscot he built one of the finest houses in England. He opposed the coalition but did not vote on Fox's India Bill in 1783. In 1784 he professed political independence but thereafter usually voted with Pitt. M.P. for Abingdon, 1783–96; Shaftesbury, 1802–12.

Lovell, 1st and 2d Barons. See John Perceval and John James Perceval

Lovett, Verney. 1705–71

3d son of Colonel John Lovett (of Liscombe House, near Leighton Buzzard, Buckinghamshire); grandson of John Verney (1st Viscount Fermanagh, Irish); from an old Buckinghamshire family settled in Ireland. Rugby from 1713; Trinity College, Dublin, 1723–24. At Trinity he became involved in a serious scrape and perhaps left the country, since for the next 7 years there are no records of his activities. In 1732 he entered the army as ensign. He served in Flanders and then in India until 1756. He was captain in 1743, major in 1754, and retired in 1756. He was brought into the House of Commons by his cousin Lord Verney, and there supported Bute. In 1765 he was made steward of East Hendred and withdrew from Parliament. His seat was then filled by Edmund Burke. M.P. for Wendover, 1761–65.

Lowndes, Charles. ca.1700–83

Of Chesham, near Berkhamstead, Buckinghamshire; 3d son of William Lowndes (M.P.; secretary to the treasury). He was chief clerk of the treasury, 1755–62; keeper of treasury papers, 1762–65; and secretary to the treasury, 1765–67. In 1768 Newcastle supported his election to the House of Commons, where he voted with the opposition on Wilkes issues during his brief tenure. M.P. for Bramber, 1768–69.

Lowndes, Richard. ca.1707–75

Of Winslow Park, near Winslow, Buckinghamshire; oldest son of Robert Lowndes. Eton, to Oxford in 1724. He was sheriff of Buckinghamshire, 1739–40. In the 1754 elections he was a declared Tory and in 1761 was listed as Tory. He supported Bute and then Grenville, 1763–65, voting against repeal of the Stamp Act in 1766 and against Chatham's land tax in 1767. Though he voted for the extension of the Grenville Election Act in 1774, he generally voted with the North ministry. The records show one address to the House of Commons. M.P. for Buckinghamshire, 1741–74.

Lowry-Corry, Armar. 1740–1802

Of Castlecoole, near Enniskillen, County Fermanagh; son of Galbraith Lowry (1706–69; of Ahenis, County Tyrone; member of the Irish Parliament; in 1764 added the name Corry upon inheriting); in 1781 created Baron Belmore (Irish); in 1789 created Viscount Belmore (Irish); in 1797 created Earl Belmore (Irish). He was a member of the Irish Parliament, 1769–81. He married (1) in 1771 a daughter of Somerset Hamilton (1st Earl of Carrick, Irish), and (2) the oldest daughter of John Hobart (2d Earl of Buckinghamshire), a marriage dissolved by act of Parliament in 1793.

Lowth, Robert. 1710–87

2d son of Rev. William Lowth; born at Winchester and schooled there from 1722; to Oxford; B.A., 1733; M.A., 1737; D.D., 1753. He was vicar of Overton, near Basingstoke, in Hampshire from 1735, fellow and professor of poetry at Oxford, 1741–52. In 1749 he was tutor to the sons of the Duke of Devonshire and ciceroned them on a tour to the Continent. Bishop Hoadly appointed him archdeacon of Winchester in 1750 and prebendary of Durham in 1753, when he was also made rector of Woodbury. In 1758 he published his lectures on Hebrew poetry and his *Life of William of Wyckeham*. He was made a fellow of the Royal Society in 1765. He was bishop of St. Davids in 1766 and bishop of Oxford, 1766–77. He was dean of the Chapel Royal, privy councillor, and bishop of London from 1777 to his death. In 1783 he declined appointment as archbishop of Canterbury on grounds of failing health. In 1778 he published his *New Translation of Isaiah with Notes*. He supported John Wesley, who greatly admired him, and sponsored the career of Samuel Horsley. He was strongly criticized by Bishop Warburton, with whom he exchanged uninhibited name calling in a pamphlet controversy. Though less learned than Warburton, he used his learning with greater skill and grace and was perhaps the most cultivated prelate of his day. In 1777 he offered in the House of Lords a bill to prevent abuses in the giving of bonds of resignation. He was greatly interested in extending the influence of the church in the colonies.

Lowther, James. 1736–1802

Of Lowther, near Penrith, and Maulds Meaburn, near Appleby, in Westmorland; 2d but 1st surviving son of Robert Lowther (d. 1745; governor of Barbados, 1711–20), whose large estates in Barbados he inherited. In 1751 he succeeded to the estates and baronetcy of his great-uncle Henry Lowther as 5th baronet; in 1756 he inherited some £2 million from his 3d cousin Sir James Lowther (of Whitehaven; 4th baronet). In 1750 he had succeeded his elderly relation as 4th Viscount Lonsdale (Scottish), and in 1784 he was created Baron Lowther and Earl of Lonsdale (English); in 1797 created Viscount Lowther. His extensive inherited collieries at Whitehaven brought him a large income. Cambridge from 1752. In 1761 he married Mary, oldest daughter of John Stuart (3d Earl of Bute), from whom he acquired a further interest in coal mines, and was reckoned the most wealthy commoner in Britain. He became a powerful political boss and a borough patron "unrivalled in the art of electioneering": at one time he was believed to control 6 to 9 seats in the House of Commons from the Westmorland-Northumberland area. He conducted a famous law suit in which he challenged the Duke of Portland's title to large estates in the north and which he ultimately won. After 1774 he often opposed the North ministry. He voted against approving the address from the throne in October, 1775, and for the Dunning resolution of April 6, 1780. He later moved to end the American war immediately, a motion which was one of the steps leading to the ultimate fall of the North ministry. But in the 5 crucial recorded divisions of February and March, 1782, no votes by him are recorded. He voted for Shelburne's peace terms and against Fox's India Bill in 1783; after entering the House of Lords in 1784 he joined the New Tory party of Pitt, whom he supported until the Regency Bill of 1788. He was lord lieutenant of Westmorland, 1758–1802, and of Cumberland, 1759–1802. He was generally considered "unamiable in public and private" and was widely known in North Britain as "Jimmy Grasp All." M.P. for

Cumberland, 1757–61; Westmorland, 1761–62; Cumberland, 1762–68; Cockermouth, 1769–74; Cumberland, 1774–84.

Lowther, James. 1753–1837

Of Aikton, near Wigton, Cumberland; 2d son of Rev. Henry Lowther (of Aikton). He married Mary Forsythe, believed to be an illegitimate daughter of Sir William Codrington (M.P.; 2d baronet). He was equerry to the Duke of Gloucester, 1782–90, and followed the politics of his patron and probable relative James Lowther (1736–1802) (*q.v.*). In the House of Commons he opposed the North ministry, voting for Dunning's resolution of April 6, 1780, and against the ministry in 4 crucial recorded divisions in February and March, 1782. He voted for Shelburne's peace terms and against Fox's India Bill in 1783 and supported Pitt until his Regency Bill in 1788. There is no indication that before 1790 he ever addressed the House of Commons. M.P. for Westmorland, 1775–1812; Appleby, 1812–18.

Lowther, John. 1759–1844

Of Swillington House, near Leeds, Yorkshire; 2d son of William Lowther (1707–88) (*q.v.*); created baronet in 1824. Westminster, 1771–73; Cambridge from 1776. In 1790 he married Elizabeth, daughter of John Fane (1728–74) (*q.v.*). In the House of Commons he voted with James Lowther (1736–1802) (*q.v.*), and against the North ministry in the 5 crucial recorded divisions in February and March, 1782. He voted for Shelburne's peace terms and against Fox's India Bill in 1783. M.P. for Cockermouth, 1780–86; Carlisle, 1786; Haslemere, 1786–90; Cumberland, 1796–1831.

Lowther, Marcus. d. 1784

Of Kilrue, County Meath; 2d son of Georges Lowther (member of the Irish Parliament). In 1743 he married Katherine Crofton, heiress, and in 1745 added the surname Crofton; created baronet in 1758. He was a member of the Irish Parliament, 1753–76.

Lowther, Robert. 1741–77

2d surviving son of Robert Lowther (d. 1745; governor of Barbados, 1711–20); brother of James Lowther (1736–1802) (*q.v.*). Cambridge from 1753, followed by the grand tour. In politics he broke with his brother over the Wilkes issues in 1763, resigned his seat in the House of Commons, and never re-entered politics. M.P. for Westmorland, 1759–61 and 1763.

Lowther, William. 1707–88

Of Swillington House, near Leeds, Yorkshire; only son of Christopher Lowther (of Little Preston, Yorkshire); created baronet in 1764 upon succeeding to the estate of his cousin Sir William Lowther. Cambridge; B.A., 1730; M.A., 1734. He took orders and became rector of Swillington and vicar of Walton, Yorkshire, in 1742. He was prebendary of York from 1754. He was the father of William Lowther (*q.v.*) and of John Lowther (*q.v.*).

Lowther, William. 1757–1844

Of Uffington, near Stamford, Lincolnshire; oldest son of William Lowther (1707–88) (*q.v.*); older brother of John Lowther (*q.v.*); in 1788 succeeded his father as 2d baronet; in 1802 succeeded by special patent his cousin James Lowther (ca.1736–1802) (*q.v.*) as Baron and Viscount Lowther; in 1807 created Earl of Lonsdale (new creation). Westminster from 1771, Cambridge from 1776. In 1781 he married Augusta, daughter of John Fane (9th Earl of Westmorland). In Parliament he voted largely with his cousin James Lowther against the North ministry, including the 5 crucial recorded divisions in February and March, 1782. He voted for Shelburne's peace terms in 1783. He was a patron of young William Wordsworth, and received the Order of the Garter in 1807. M.P. for Carlisle, 1780–84; Cumberland, 1784–90; Rutland, 1796–1802.

Lucan, 1st Baron and 1st Earl. See Charles Bingham

Lucas, Thomas. d. 1784

Of Lee, Kent. His parentage is now obscure. He was a London merchant, a director of the South Sea Company from 1763, a director of the Union Fire Office from 1767, and president of Guy's Hospital. He was supported for election to the House of Commons by Rockingham, and voted against the North ministry in every recorded crucial division in February and March, 1782. He supported Rockingham until his death in 1782. He then voted for Shelburne's peace terms but did not vote on Fox's India Bill in 1783. He opposed Pitt with Fox in early 1784 and, as a "Fox's martyr," failed of reelection in 1784. There is no evidence that he ever addressed the House. M.P. for Grampound, 1780–84.

Ludlow, 1st Viscount. See Henry Arthur Herbert. ca.1703–72

Ludlow, Peter. 1730–1803

Of Ardsallagh, near Navan, County Meath, and Great Stoughton, near Kimbolton, Huntingdonshire; only surviving son of Peter Ludlow (d. 1750; of Ardsallagh). In 1753 he married Frances, oldest daughter of Thomas Lumley-Saunderson (3d Earl of Scarborough); in 1755 created Baron Ludlow (Irish); in 1760 created Earl Ludlow (Irish). A Whig by family tradition, he voted against the expulsion of Wilkes in January, 1770, against approval of the address from the throne in October, 1775, and for Dunning's resolution of April 6, 1780. He consistently supported the Rockingham Whigs, and in February and March, 1782, voted against the North ministry in 4 of the 5 crucial divisions then recorded. He voted for Shelburne's peace terms and for Fox's India Bill in 1783 and largely opposed Pitt from 1784. He was appointed comptroller of the household and privy councillor by the Rockingham ministry in 1782, but left office with the Rockingham Whigs in 1784. M.P. for Huntingdonshire, 1768–96.

Lumley-Saunderson, George Augusta. 1753–1807

Of Glentworth, near Gainsborough, Lincolnshire, and Sandbeck Park, near Tickhill, Yorkshire; known as Viscount Lumley until 1782, when he succeeded his father, Richard Lumley-Saunderson (*q.v.*), as 5th Earl of Scarborough; nephew of George Savile (*q.v.*). Eton, 1764–70; Cambridge from 1771. Considered a Whig, he opposed the North ministry and voted for the Dunning resolution of April 6, 1780. In November, 1783, he moved the address of thanks to the throne. M.P. for Lincoln City, 1774–80.

Lumley-Saunderson, Richard. ca.1725–82

Styled Viscount Lumley until 1752, when he succeeded his father, Thomas Lumley-Saunderson (ca.1691–1752), as 4th Earl of Scarborough. Eton from 1745, Cambridge from 1748. In 1752 he married Barbara, sister of George Savile (*q.v.*). He was cofferer of the household in 1756 and 1765–66; privy councillor in 1765, but resigned with

Portland in November, 1766; deputy earl marshal, 1765–77; and joint vice treasurer of Ireland in 1782. A staunch Rockingham Whig, he was one of the steadiest dissenters from the measures of the North ministry. His recorded dissents from majority votes in the House of Lords included opposition to (1) restrictions on parliamentary privilege in the Wilkes case in 1763, (2) regulation of East India Company dividends and management, 1767–68, (3) the measures of the House of Commons against Wilkes in 1770, (4) adjournment of the House of Lords on January 15, 1770, (5) the expulsion of Wilkes from the House of Commons in 1770, (6) North's Falkland Islands settlement in 1771, (7) the ministry's measures toward the colonists in 1775, (8) continuance of the Quebec Governing Act in 1775, (9) the address from the throne in October, 1775, (10) the address from the throne on American policy in 1776, (11) the ministry's American measures in 1778, (12) rejection of the motion to ask the king to effect a complete change of "System" in 1779, (13) rejection of the motion to ask the king to dismiss Sandwich in 1779, (14) suspension of the rights of sailors in 1779, (15) rejection of the motion to examine into public expenditures in 1780, and (16) rejection of the bill to exclude holders of government contracts from membership in Parliament.

Lushington, Stephen. 1744–1807

Of Southill Park, near Biggleswade, Bedfordshire; 3d son of Rev. Henry Lushington (d. 1779; vicar of Eastbourne, Sussex); created baronet in 1791. He was a director of the East India Company, 1782–86 and intermittently thereafter until 1805, and its chairman in 1790, 1795, and 1799. He was connected with Charles Fox and the Duke of Portland, and supported them in the House of Commons, which he occasionally addressed on East India affairs. M.P. for Heydon, 1783–84; Helston, 1790–96; St. Michael, 1796–1802; Penryn, 1802–1806; Plympton Erle, 1806–1807.

Luther, John. ca.1739–86

Of Myles, near Ongar, Essex; only son of Richard Luther (of Ongar). Middle Temple from 1755, Cambridge from 1756. He entered the House of Commons with the support of Newcastle and opposed Grenville but did not vote on general warrants in 1764. He was in steady opposition to the Grafton and North ministries, voting against expulsion of Wilkes in January, 1770; against approval of the address from the throne in October, 1775; for the Dunning resolution in April, 1780; and against the North ministry in all 5 of the crucial divisions recorded in February and March, 1782. There is no record that he ever addressed the House. M.P. for Essex, 1763–84.

Luttrell, Francis Fownes. 1756–1823

5th son of Henry Fownes Luttrell (*q.v.*); brother of John Fownes Luttrell (*q.v.*). Eton, 1770–72; Oxford from 1773; Middle Temple from 1770; barrister in 1782. He occupied one of the "family-owned" seats for Minehead and supported the North ministry to its end. In 1781 he opposed Lowther's motion to end the American war immediately. Although he voted for Conway's second motion of February 27, 1782, to end the war, he opposed Cavendish's motion of March 8, 1782, to remove the ministry and voted against Sir John Rous's no-confidence motion on March 15, 1782. He voted for Shelburne's peace terms in February, 1783, and then withdrew from Parliament to accept sinecure offices, "selling" his seat for Minehead for £3,000 in 1784. He was commissioner of taxes, 1784–93; commissioner of customs, 1813–19; and chairman of the Board of Customs, 1813–19. M.P. for Minehead, 1780–83.

Luttrell, Henry Fownes. ca.1720–80

Of Dunster Castle, near Watchet, Somerset; son of John Fownes (of Nethway, near Dartmouth, Devon). He adopted the surname Luttrell in 1747 upon marrying his cousin Margaret, daughter of Alexander Luttrell (M.P.), whose family was said to "own" the 2 Parliament seats for Minehead. Oxford from 1741. In 1769, a year after his election to the House of Commons, he signed the Cornwall petition against the Grafton ministry's measures in the Wilkes case, although in the 1774 election his cousin Henry Lawes Luttrell (*q.v.*) would be the North ministry's candidate against Wilkes. In general he supported the North ministry, but his recorded votes were few, and there is no record that he ever addressed the House of Commons. He was the father of John Fownes Luttrell (*q.v.*) and of Francis Fownes Luttrell (*q.v.*). M.P. for Minehead, 1768–74.

Luttrell, Henry Lawes. 1737–1821

In 1787 succeeded his father, Simon Luttrell (*q.v.*), as 2d Earl of

Carhampton (Irish); brother of Anne Luttrell Horton, who secretly married (2) the young Duke of Cumberland and was a cause of the king's insistence on the passage of the Royal Marriage Bill in 1772. Westminster from 1751, Cambridge from 1755. In 1757 he entered the army as ensign; he was captain in 1759; major in 1762; colonel in 1777; major general in 1782; lieutenant general in 1793; master general of ordnance, 1797–1800; and general in 1798. He served in Portugal as deputy adjutant general in 1762, and was in charge of ordnance in Ireland as adjutant general, 1770–74. In 1796 he was in command of British troops in Ireland. Elected to the House of Commons for Bossiney in 1768, he was persuaded by the Grafton ministry to be its candidate against Wilkes in the 1769 by-election for Middlesex. After a riotous election he was reported to have polled 296 votes against 1,143 for Wilkes, but after debate the House of Commons ruled Wilkes ineligible and declared Luttrell elected. Although in 1772 he opposed the Royal Marriage Bill (which was in a way an insult to his sister), he supported the North ministry in general but was abroad during the crucial votes in February and March, 1782. He supported the coalition in 1783 and adhered to North after its fall but spent much of his time in Ireland, where he was a member of the Irish House of Commons from 1783 and an Irish peer from 1787. Having in earlier years strongly opposed Irish union, he later became its supporter. After 1790 he sought the favor of Pitt. *DNB* called him "a man of wit and daring." M.P. for Bossiney, 1768–69; Middlesex, 1769–74; Bossiney, 1774–84; Plympton Erle, 1790–94; Ludgershall, 1817–21.

Luttrell, James. ca.1751–88

4th son of Simon Luttrell (*q.v.*); brother of Henry Lawes Luttrell (*q.v.*); brother of Ann Luttrell Horton, who secretly married (2) the young Duke of Cumberland and was a cause of the king's insistence on the passage of the Royal Marriage Bill in 1772. He became a lieutenant in the navy in 1770, a captain in 1781, and saw active service in 1782. After taking his seat in the House of Commons in 1775, he became an increasingly strong opponent of the North ministry. In the discussion of North's peace proposals on March 12, 1778, he satirically moved that "the Commissioners for Peace should be authorized to promise the removal of any Ministers to whom the Americans could object." In February, 1780, he urged not only that the proposed vote of thanks be extended to Admiral Rodney for his recent victory but that Rodney be given adequate support for his operations. In March, 1780, he seconded the motion of Lord George Gordon to take up certain anti-Catholic petitions immediately, and 10 days later he opposed North's motion to appoint commissioners from outside Parliament to examine and report on the government's financial accounts. In April, 1780, he voted for the Dunning resolution deploring the excessive influence of the crown. In May, 1780, he spoke opposing the Qualification Bill. He did not vote in any of the 5 crucial divisions recorded in February and March, 1782. From 1784 he supported Pitt. He was surveyor general of ordnance, 1784–88. M.P. for Stockbridge, 1775–84; Dover, 1784–88.

Luttrell, John Fownes. 1752–1816

2d son of Henry Fownes Luttrell (*q.v.*); older brother of Francis Fownes Luttrell (*q.v.*). Eton from 1765, Oxford from 1770. He was an independent country gentleman whose family controlled the elections to both parliamentary seats for Minehead. From 1774 he generally supported the North ministry, though he became increasingly critical of it, or uncertain of its capacity and judgment. In 1780 he sometimes voted in opposition, but he supported North against the Dunning resolution of April 6, 1780. He did not vote in any of the crucial divisions recorded in February and March, 1782. In December, 1782, he spoke at length on Shelburne's army estimates, saying that the security of the nation depended on its maintaining naval power, a statement hardly original to his audience. On March 11, 1783, he defended the past measures of the North ministry as having been at that time in accord with the expressed will of Parliament and the nation. In 1783 he voted for Shelburne's peace terms but did not vote on Fox's India Bill. He opposed Pitt's 1783 proposals for reform of Parliament and said that the power of the crown was not excessive but, if anything, not great enough. After 1783 he was often absent, but was considered a supporter of Pitt. M.P. for Minehead, 1774–1806 and 1807–16.

Luttrell (later Olmius) John. ca.1742–1829

Of Kimpton Lodge, near Andover, Hampshire: 3d son of Simon Luttrell (*q.v.*); brother of Henry Lawes Luttrell (*q.v.*), whom he succeeded in 1821 as 3d Earl of Carhampton. He was also a brother of James Luttrell (*q.v.*), Temple Simon Luttrell (*q.v.*), and Anne Luttrell Horton, who secretly married (2) the young Duke of Cumberland and was a cause of the king's insistence on the passage of the Royal Marriage Bill in 1772. He married (1) in 1766 Elizabeth, daughter of John Olmius (1st Baron Waltham, Irish) and took the added surname Olmius. He entered the navy and as captain led a squadron in the West Indies, 1762–69. He became commissioner of excise in 1784. Like his father he sometimes voted in opposition to the North ministry. In 1775 he spoke "from personal knowledge of the Americans" to condemn North's measures, and that year he also voted for Wilkes' motion to reverse the judgment of the Middlesex election. But, like his father, he supported the North ministry in early 1782 when he voted against Lowther's motion to end the American war immediately, and he voted with the North ministry in 3 other crucial divisions recorded in February and March, 1782. He defended Sandwich, spoke against Conway's later motion to end the war, and did not vote on Rous's no-confidence motion of March 15, 1782. In 1783 he told the House that Shelburne's peace terms were "ignominious" and voted against them, spoke against Pitt's motion to reform the representation in Parliament, and spoke for Fox's India Bill; but in 1784 he asked and received appointment from Pitt as commissioner of excise and held that post until 1826. M.P. for Stockbridge, 1774–75 and 1780–85.

Luttrell, Simon. ca.1713–87

Of Four Oaks, near Sutton Coldfield, Warwickshire; 2d son of Major General Henry Luttrell (of Luttrellstown, County Dublin); in 1768 created Baron Irnham (Irish); in 1781 created Viscount Carhampton (Irish); in 1785 created Earl of Carhampton (Irish). In 1765 his oldest daughter, Anne, married Christopher Horton. After Horton's death Anne secretly married the young Duke of Cumberland, an event which, when the king learned of it in 1771, was a major cause of his insistence on the passage of the Royal Marriage Bill in 1772. He was an admirer of Bute and supported him until 1765, when he opposed the Rockingham ministry and voted with Grenville against repeal of the Stamp Act in 1766. He supported the Chatham-Grafton ministry, 1767–70; voted against North's Royal Marriage Bill in 1772; and after

1775 was a not very dependable supporter of the North ministry. M.P. for St. Michael, 1755–61; Wigan, 1761–68; Weobley, 1768–74; Stockbridge, 1774–80.

Luttrell, Temple Simon. ca.1740–1803

Of Eaglehurst, near Southampton; 2d son of Simon Luttrell (*q.v.*); brother of Henry Lawes Luttrell (*q.v.*), James Luttrell (*q.v.*), John Luttrell (later Olmius) (*q.v.*), and Anne Luttrell Horton (later Duchess of Cumberland). Westminster from 1751. In the House of Commons he was a violent and often abusive critic of the North ministry in its later years, voting against approval of the address from the throne in October, 1775, and for the Dunning resolution of April 6, 1780, when he also spoke attacking North for electoral corruption and inadvertently revealed his own. In May, 1780, he spoke opposing the exclusion of auditors from the gallery of the House, and later he attacked Sandwich for incompetence and corruption. In 1793 he was arrested at Boulogne, taken prisoner to Paris and imprisoned there for 2 years. He died in Paris. M.P. for Milborne Port, 1775–80.

Luxborough, 1st Baron. See **Robert Knight**

Lygon, William. 1747–1816

Of Madresfield Court, near Great Malvern, and Powyck Court, near Worcester, Worcestershire; only son of Richard Pyndar (of Madresfield Court; changed his surname to Lygon upon inheriting); in 1806 created Baron Beauchamp; in 1815 created Earl Beauchamp. Oxford from 1754. He did not attend Parliament regularly, but he often opposed the North ministry and voted against it in 2 of the crucial divisions shortly before its fall. He did not vote on Shelburne's peace terms in 1783 but voted for Pitt's measures to reform Parliament that year. He did not vote on Fox's India Bill. After 1783 he supported Pitt and asked him for a peerage. There is no evidence that before 1790 he ever addressed the House. M.P. for Worcestershire, 1775–1806.

Lymington, 1st Viscount. See **John Wallop**

Lynch, William. ca.1731–85

Of Wingham, near Canterbury, Kent; oldest son of John Lynch (dean of Canterbury, 1734–60). Cambridge from 1748, at Inner Temple from

1749. He married Mary, daughter of Edward Coke (1719–53; M.P.). He was envoy to Sardinia, 1768–79; Knight of the Bath from 1771; and privy councillor from 1773. His election to the House of Commons in 1762 was sponsored by Thomas Thynne (*q.v.*). There he supported Weymouth and the North ministry until he vacated his seat in 1780 upon receiving a pension. M.P. for Weobley, 1762–68; Canterbury, 1768–74; Weobley, 1774–80.

Lyon (later Bowes-Lyon), John. 1737–76

Styled Lord Glamis until 1753, when he succeeded his father, Thomas Lyon (1704–53; M.P.), as 7th Earl of Strathmore (Scottish). Cambridge from 1755; M.A., 1757. In 1767 he married Mary Bowes, daughter and heiress of George Bowes (a very wealthy commoner of Durham) and added the surname Bowes. He traveled in Spain and Portugal, and was a Scottish representative peer, 1767–76. In politics he appears, though with little evidence, to have supported the court. He died at sea en route to Lisbon.

Lyon, Thomas. 1741–96

Of Hallgreen Castle, near Bervie, Kincardineshire, and Pitpointy, Forfarshire; 3d son of Thomas Lyon (M.P.; 6th Earl of Strathmore, Scottish); brother of John Lyon (later Bowes-Lyon) (*q.v.*). Cambridge from 1758. He was supported by Bute for election to the House of Commons, where he consistently supported the North ministry but was, according to Namier, "an obscure member." He vacated his seat in 1778. M.P. for Aberdeen burghs, 1768–78.

Lyster (or Lister), Richard. 1691–1766

Of Rowton Castle, near Shrewsbury, Shropshire; oldest son of Thomas Lyster. Oxford from 1708, Inner Temple from the same year. He was listed as a firm Tory, and was feudal, it appears, in manners, hospitality, and opinions. He was assiduous in his attendance of Parliament, though there is no record that he ever spoke or voted there. By report, however, he voted with the Bute and then with the Grenville ministries. M.P. for Shrewsbury, 1722–23 and 1727–34; Shropshire, 1740–66.

Lyttelton, Charles. 1714–68

Of Hagley Hall, near Stourbridge, Worcestershire; 3d son of Sir Thomas Lyttelton (4th baronet; Eton schoolmaster; and friend of the elder Pitt); grandson of Sir Charles Lyttelton (1629–1716; 2d baronet; M.P.; governor of Jamaica); younger brother of George Lyttelton (*q.v.*); first cousin of George Grenville. Eton, to Oxford in 1732; D.C.L., 1745; Middle Temple from 1731; barrister in 1738; ordained in 1742. He was a fellow of the Society of Arts from 1746; chaplain to George II from 1747; dean of Exeter, 1748–62; and bishop of Carlisle, 1762–68. He was president of the Society of Antiquaries in 1765. He published works on philosophy and archaeology and contributed to *Philosophical Transactions* in 1748 and 1750, and to Volumes I and III of *Archaeologica*.

Lyttelton, George. 1709–73

Of Hagley Hall, near Stourbridge, Worcestershire; in 1751 succeeded his father, Sir Thomas Lyttelton (4th baronet; Eton schoolmaster; friend of the elder Pitt) as 5th baronet; in 1756 created Baron Lyttelton; brother of Charles Lyttelton (*q.v.*), Richard Lyttelton (*q.v.*), William Henry Lyttelton (*q.v.*); first cousin of George Grenville. Eton from 1725, Oxford from 1726, grand tour, 1728–31. He was secretary to the Prince of Wales, 1732–44; member of the Treasury Board, 1744–54; privy councillor from 1754; and cofferer of the king's household, 1754–55. He supported Bute against Newcastle in 1762 and supported the Grenville ministry, 1763–65. In 1765 he declined a post in the Rockingham cabinet, but was briefly chancellor of the exchequer. With Pitt and the Grenvilles he comprised the "Cobhamite" political faction. In 1766 he voted against repeal of the Stamp Act. He was a friend of Alexander Pope and a patron of literature, and in 1747 he published his own poems. Among other works, he published his *Dialogues of the Dead*, 1760, and his *History of the Reign of Henry II*, 1767–71. Thurlow said that his talents were considerable and his industry greater, but Chatham wrote that "there was never so much fine sense and extravagance of Passion jumbled together in any one man." Horace Walpole commented that "when he had been forced to quit virtue [he] took up religion . . . when he had gone to the greatest lengths to promote his earthly interest." Portraits by Reynolds and Benjamin West. M.P. for Okehampton, 1735–56.

Lyttelton, Richard. 1718–70

Of Little Ealing, Middlesex; 5th son of Thomas Lyttelton (4th baronet; Eton schoolmaster; friend of the elder Pitt); brother of George Lyttelton (*q.v.*), William Henry Lyttelton (*q.v.*), and Charles Lyttelton (*q.v.*). He was educated at Besançon, 1737–38. In 1745 he married Rachel, daughter of Wriothesley Russell (2d Duke of Bedford) and wealthy widow of Scroop Egerton (1st Duke of Bridgwater). He was an ensign in the foot guards in 1737, captain of marines in 1741, colonel in 1747, major general in 1757 and lieutenant general in 1759. He was master of the Jewel Office, 1756–62; governor of Minorca, 1762–66; and governor of Guernsey, 1766–70. He was badly crippled by gout from 1757 and could not continue an active life. In politics he supported the Pelhams. M.P. for Brackley, 1747–54; Poole, 1754–61.

Lyttelton, Thomas. 1744–79

Of Hagley Hall, near Stourbridge, Worcestershire; only son of George Lyttelton (*q.v.*), whom he succeeded as 6th baronet in 1773. Eton, 1758–61; Oxford from 1761; grand tour, 1763–65. In 1772 he married Apphia, widow of Joseph Peach (the "very rich and very worthy" former governor of Calcutta), who brought him a fortune. He soon eloped to Paris with a barmaid, but the fortune remained his. He was privy councillor from 1775 and chief justice in Eyre north of Trent, 1775–79. He was a strong supporter of punitive measures against the colonies and of the North ministry until April, 1779, when the revelations of the Howe inquiry may have been the cause of his support of the petition to remove the Earl of Sandwich from his post as head of the Admiralty. He was "a notorious profligate" (*DNB*), "afflicting his father, shocking mankind, and disgracing himself, with great abilities, generally very ill-applied. . . . To banish reflection he flew to company whom he despised and ridiculed" (Horace Walpole). M.P. for Bewdley, 1768–69.

Lyttelton, William Henry. 1724–1808

Of Hagley Hall, near Stourbridge, Worcestershire; 6th son of Sir Thomas Lyttelton (4th baronet; Eton schoolmaster; friend of the elder Pitt); brother of Charles Lyttelton (*q.v.*), George Lyttelton (*q.v.*), and Richard Lyttelton (*q.v.*); in 1779 succeeded his nephew Thomas Lyttelton (*q.v.*) as 7th baronet; in 1776 created Baron Westcote (Irish); in 1794 created Baron Lyttelton of Frankley (English). Eton from ca. 1740; Oxford from 1742; D.C.L., 1781; Middle Temple from 1743; barrister in 1748. He was governor of South Carolina, 1755–62; governor of Jamaica, 1762–66; and envoy to Lisbon, 1766–71. He was a member of the Treasury Board, 1777–82. He sat in the House of Commons as a Whig, 1748–55, but came to be considered a Tory, 1774–80. He supported the North ministry, and in October, 1775, seconded the address of thanks for the speech from the throne and expatiated upon the need to strengthen the hands of government against the American rebels: he proposed sending a few regiments to the southern colonies to bring about a slave uprising that would beneficially "let the blood of their masters." In 1781 he told the House of Commons that he considered the war against the Americans a "holy war." He supported the coalition in 1783 but went over to Pitt early in 1784. He published a study of the Jamaica constitution, and also published minor verse. M.P for Bewdley, 1748–55 and 1774–90.

Macartney, George. 1737–1806

He was born in Ireland, the only son of George Macartney (of Lissanoure Castle, near Ballymoney, County Antrim); in 1776 created Baron Macartney (Irish); in 1792 created Viscount Macartney (Irish); in 1794 created Earl Macartney (Irish); in 1796 created Baron Macartney of Parkhurst, Surrey (English). Trinity College, Dublin, from 1750; M.A., 1759. He made the grand tour, returning to enroll in 1753 in Lincoln's Inn, where he became a friend of Edmund Burke. In 1768 he married Jane, daughter of John Stuart (3d Earl of Bute). He became friendly with George Augustus Selwyn (*q.v.*) and with Henry Fox (*q.v.*). He was knighted and made envoy to Russia in 1764, and in 1767 was named ambassador to Russia but did not take up the mission. He was made Knight of the White Eagle of Poland in 1766. He was a member of the Irish Parliament, 1768–76, and of the Irish Privy Council from 1769, while chief secretary to the lord lieutenant of Ireland. He was made Knight of the Bath in 1772, was constable of Toome Castle in 1774, and was governor of the Caribbean Islands, 1775–79, where he was forced to surrender Grenada to the French in 1779. In 1780 he went to Ireland on a special mission for

Lord North. He was governor of Madras, 1781–85, but declined to accept the governor-generalship in 1785. In 1792 he was made privy councillor and a fellow of the Royal Society, as well as an Irish Viscount. He was ambassador to China, 1792–94. In 1795 he went to Verona on a secret mission. He was governor of Cape of Good Hope, 1796–98, and a trustee of the British Museum, 1801–1806. He also made another trip to Russia in the attempt to arrange a treaty. He wrote accounts of his diplomatic experiences in Russia and China and of his political experiences in Ireland, which were published in the memoir of his life by Barrows. As a civil servant he was competent, dependable, and expediently prone to support the current ministry. Wraxall said he was "of a harsh, severe and unaccommodating temper" but "possessed an enlarged understanding, great knowledge of men, and very sound judgement." His ability was seldom questioned, and his honesty almost never. M.P. for Cockermouth, 1768–69; Ayr burghs, 1774–76; Berealston, 1780–81.

Macaulay (neé Sawbridge), Catherine. 1731–91

Daughter of John Sawbridge (d. 1762; of Kent and London) and sister of John Sawbridge (*q.v.*). She married (1) in 1760 George Macaulay (d. 1766; Scottish physician) and (2) in 1778 William Graham (then aged 21, younger brother of a reputed quack doctor). She became the intellectual mentor and apologist of the London radicals of her time and "a great republican." In 1763 she published the first volume of her history of England from the time of James I. On occasion she visited Paris, where she was received with honors. In 1784 she went to America and while there spent 10 days at Mount Vernon in 1785. She provided the London popular movement with philosophical rationalizations to justify its emotional extravagances and popular excesses. Portrait by Gainsborough.

Macbean, Forbes. 1725–1800

His family origins are now obscure. He attended the Royal Military Academy at Woolwich in 1743 and became an artillery expert. He was lieutenant in 1755, captain in 1759, colonel in 1782, major general in 1793, and lieutenant general in 1798. His career included Fontenoy in 1745; Carlisle in 1745; Flanders, 1746–48; Minden in 1759; Warburg in 1760; Fritzlar in 1761; Portugal, 1762–69; and Canada, 1769–73 and

1778–80. He was inspector general of Portuguese artillery, 1765–69, and was in charge of artillery in Canada during his 2 periods there. He became a fellow of the Royal Society in 1786. He left valuable notes and memoranda on the history and management of artillery.

Macbride, John. ca.1740–1800

Son of Robert Macbride (of Ballymoney, County Antrim; Presbyterian minister). After some years in the merchant marine he entered the navy in 1755. He was lieutenant in 1758, captain in 1765, rear admiral in 1793, and vice admiral in 1794. He was with Keppel off Ushant in 1778 and supported Keppel at his court-martial in 1779. He was prominent at the naval battle off Cape St. Vincent in 1780, and was made admiral in 1799. The Earl of Sandwich thought him "very bold, but with little understanding; busy, violent, troublesome." In the House of Commons from 1784, he voted with Pitt on the reform of Parliament but opposed him on other issues. M.P. for Plympton Erle, 1784–90.

Macclesfield, 3d and 4th Earls. See Thomas Parker and George Parker

Macdonald, Archibald. 1747–1826

Of East Sheen, near Mortlake, Surrey, and Armadale Castle, Skye. He was born at Armadale Castle, the 3d son of Sir Alexander Macdonald (of Sleat, Skye; 7th baronet); grandson of Alexander Montgomerie (ca.1660–1729; 9th Earl of Eglintoun, Scottish); created baronet in 1813. Westminster, 1760–64; Oxford from 1764; B.A., 1768; M.A., 1772; Lincoln's Inn from 1765; barrister in 1770. In 1777 he married Louisa, daughter of Granville Leveson-Gower (*q.v.*), who helped him secure a seat in the House of Commons that year. He was king's counsel from 1778 and justice of Carmarthenshire, 1780–84. Although in 1779 he bitterly attacked North in speeches on North's personal inefficiency, he supported the North ministry on American issues; voted against the Dunning resolution of April 6, 1780, and with North in the 5 recorded crucial divisions in February and March, 1782, including the motion to censure the ministry. He voted for Shelburne's peace terms and against Fox's India Bill in 1783, violently attacked the coalition, and from 1784 supported Pitt. He was solicitor general, 1784–88; knighted in 1788; attorney general, 1788–93; privy councillor from 1793; and lord chief baron of the exchequer, 1793–1813. He was considered one of the most accomplished scholars of his time. Portrait by Romney. M.P. for Hindon, 1777–80; Newcastle-under-Lyme, 1780–93.

Macdonald, James. 1741–1766

Of Sleat, Skye, probably the 2d son of Sir Alexander Macdonald (of Sleat; 7th baronet) and older brother of Archibald Macdonald (*q.v.*). He studied at Oxford, and gained such a reputation for erudition that he was later called "the Marcellus of the North." In 1762, James Boswell liked and envied him, thinking him "a remarkable young man of good points and great application." Horace Walpole called him "a particular friend of Lord Beauchamp . . . rather too wise for his age and too fond of showing it," a fondness with which Walpole should have been familiar. He died young and left no mark on history.

Macdowell, William. ca.1720–84

Of Castle Semple, near Lochwinnoch, Renfrewshire, and nearby Garthland, Wigtownshire; oldest son of Colonel William Macdowell (of St. Kitts and Castle Semple; West Indies planter and merchant). He inherited a considerable commercial empire. Glasgow University from 1735. In politics he was a consistent though silent supporter of the North ministry, notably regular in his attendance at the House of Commons. He did not seek re-election. M.P. for Renfrewshire, 1768–74.

Mackay, Alexander. 1717–89

Of Strathtongue, Kyle of Tongue, Sutherland; 4th son of George Mackay (3d Earl of Reay, Scottish); brother of George Mackay (*q.v.*). He was ensign in the 25th Foot in 1737, captain in 1745, colonel in 1762, major general in 1770, and lieutenant general in 1777. He was governor of Tynemouth Castle, 1771–89; commissioner for forfeited estates in 1781; and governor of Stirling Castle and in command of the forces in Scotland, 1788–89. In the House of Commons he supported the Bute and Grenville ministries, 1762–65, and then, as a close friend of Richard Rigby (*q.v.*), allied with the Bedford junto and supported the North ministry until 1773. But he was extremely sympathetic with the colonists, and before he left the House in 1773, he had become critical of the ministry's attitudes toward them. M.P. for Sutherland, 1761–68; Tain burghs, 1768–73.

Mackay, George. ca.1715–82

Of Skibo Castle, near Dornoch, Sutherlandshire; 3d son of George Mackay (3d Earl of Reay, Scottish); brother of Alexander Mackay (*q.v.*). He inherited Skibo from his uncle Patrick Dowall. Aberdeen University; M.A., 1730; Scots advocate in 1737. In 1766 he married Anne, granddaughter of the attainted 3d Lord Duffus (Scottish). In 1745 he captained one of Loudon's independent companies and in 1746 commanded the regiment. In Parliament he steadily supported the current ministry. M.P. for Sutherlandshire, 1747–60.

Mackellar, Patrick. 1717–78

Descended from an old established Scottish family. He was a clerk in ordnance at Woolwich, 1735–39; an ordnance engineer in Minorca, 1739–54; engineer extraordinary in 1743; and ordinary in 1751. He served under Braddock in America in 1754, and was severely wounded. He was chief engineer of British forts in the colonies in 1756, and was taken prisoner by the French in 1756 and confined in Quebec and Montreal. Exchanged in 1757, he served as captain and engineer at the capture of Louisburg in 1758 and at the capture of Quebec by Wolfe in 1759. He was chief engineer at Halifax in 1760 and was with the expedition against Martinique, 1761–62. He was a lieutenant colonel in the attack on Havana in 1762. He returned to the ordnance service at Minorca, 1763–68, and was in charge of military engineering there at the time of his death.

Mackenzie, Henry. 1745–1831

Born in Edinburgh; son of Joshua Mackenzie (eminent Edinburgh physician). He studied at Edinburgh University. In 1776 he married Penuel, daughter of Sir Ludovic Grant (of Grant on the Spey). He was articled to an Edinburgh attorney, and in 1765 went to London for further legal study. He returned to Edinburgh to become an attorney for the crown but soon began to write books and plays. In 1771 he published, anonymously, *The Man of Feeling*, which was an immediate literary success. He wrote other novels and several plays, one of which was successfully produced in Edinburgh in 1773. He then gave most of his time to writing literary essays and dramatic criticism, and was among the first to proclaim the merits of Robert Burns and Walter Scott. He became an intimate of Hume, of Robertson, and later of Scott, and a notable figure in Edinburgh literary and social life. In politics he was a firm Tory. Portrait by Raeburn.

Mackenzie (later Stuart-Mackenzie), James Stuart. ca.1718–80

Of Rosehaugh, near Fortrose, Ross-shire and Belmont Castle, Angus-shire; 2d son of James Stuart (2d Earl of Bute, Scottish); brother of John Stuart (1713–92; 3d Earl of Bute) (*q.v.*); in 1732 added the surname Mackenzie upon inheriting the estate of his great-grandfather Mackenzie. Eton, 1728–32. He made the grand tour and then attended Leyden University in 1737. In 1749 he married his cousin Elizabeth, 4th daughter of John Campbell (2d Duke of Argyll, Scottish). He was envoy to Turin, 1758–61, and joined his brother in London and became privy councillor under the new king in 1761. He was lord privy seal for Scotland, 1763–64, and a close adviser of his brother Bute. In 1764, George Grenville dismissed him from court office and from court and excluded him from all patronage, as part of the effort to eliminate all Bute influence upon king, court, and government. He continued in the House of Commons, where he supported the Grafton and North ministries, voting against the Dunning resolution of April 6, 1780, and with North in the several crucial divisions of early 1782. M.P. for Argyllshire, 1742–47; Buteshire, 1747–54; Ayr burghs, 1754–61; Ross-shire, 1761–84.

Mackenzie, John. 1727–89

Styled Lord Macleod; oldest son of George Mackenzie (3d Earl of Cromartie, Scottish; attainted in 1746). He joined his father in the Jacobite army in 1745, was taken prisoner, and in 1746 pleaded guilty to high treason. In 1748 he was pardoned on condition that he yield up all his property and title claims. In 1750 he entered the Swedish army as captain and fought through the Seven Years' War as a volunteer. He was decorated and created Count Cromarty by the king of Sweden. In 1777 he returned to Britain and with the help of his cousin Henry Dundas secured permission to raise a highland regiment and become its colonel. In 1779 he took his new regiment to India and commanded its first battalion against Hyder Ali in 1780. He returned to England and was elected to the House of Commons in 1780. He was made a British major general in 1782. Though elected with the support of Henry Dundas, and called by his opponents a mere catspaw of

Dundas, he was absent (reportedly again abroad) and did not vote in any of the crucial divisions during the last 2 months of the North ministry in early 1782. By act of Parliament in 1784 his family estates were returned to him upon payment of £19,000. M.P. for Ross-shire, 1780–84.

Mackenzie, Kenneth. 1744–81

Of Seaforth; only son of Kenneth Mackenzie (1717–61; M.P.); in 1766 created Viscount Fortrose (Irish). But for his grandfather's Jacobite attainder of 1716 he would have succeeded as Earl of Seaforth (Irish) in 1761, but in 1771 he was given that earldom in the Irish establishment. In 1765 he married Caroline, oldest daughter of William Stanhope (1719–79) (*q.v.*) and granddaughter of Charles Fitzroy (1683–1757; 2d Duke of Grafton). In 1771 he raised a regiment called the Seaforth Highlanders, which he commanded as lieutenant colonel. In 1779 he was overwhelmed by debts, and in 1781, perhaps in part to escape from them, he sailed with his regiment for India and died at sea. He was a man of fashion in a circle that was extravagant and profligate. He took little interest in political affairs and had little concern for the problems of Scotland. His attendance of the House of Commons was brief and irregular. Apparently he never addressed the House. On Wilkes issues, at least, he is reported to have voted with the Grafton and North ministries. M.P. for Bute and Cromartie, 1768–74.

Mackenzie, Thomas Frederick. ca.1753–83

Oldest son of Major William Mackenzie; cousin and heir male of Kenneth Mackenzie (*q.v.*), whom he would have succeeded as Earl of Seaforth (Scottish) in 1781 but for the attainder of 1716 attached to that title. In 1774 he assumed the added surname Humbertson. He was cornet of dragoons in 1771, captain in 1777, major in 1778, and lieutenant colonel in 1780. He served at St. Omer against the French in 1779 and on the expedition to the Cape of Good Hope in 1781. He then went to India and saw action against Hyder Ali in 1782. In 1783 he was captured by the Marattas, and died of his wounds at the age of about 29, "an officer of the most exalted promise."

Mackreth, Robert. 1726–1819

Of Ewhurst, near Kingsclere, Hampshire. He was first known as a waiter and billiard marker at White's Club in London. He was enterprising and acquired a vintner's business, which went well, and in 1761 he became proprietor of White's, as well as bookmaker and moneylender to its members, to some of whom he was an intimate friend. On the nomination of Horatio Walpole (1717–97) (*q.v.*), who was said to owe him large sums, and apparently with the lighthearted support of many of the club's influential members, he was elected to the House of Commons and re-elected several times. He generally supported the current ministry. Although he voted against the North ministry in voting for the Dunning resolution of April 6, 1780, he voted with that ministry in all 5 of the recorded crucial divisions in February and March, 1782. He voted for Shelburne's peace terms in 1783. Although he was convicted of assault in 1786 and again in 1792, he was steadily re-elected to Parliament and in 1795 was knighted for his "services to Parliament." His career, according to Namier, "caused amusement more than indignation." M.P. for Castle Rising, 1774–84; Ashburton, 1784–1802.

Mackworth, Herbert. 1737–91

Of Gnoll Castle, near Neath, Glamorganshire; only son of Herbert Mackworth (1687–1765; M.P.); created baronet in 1776. Westminster from 1748, Oxford from 1753, Lincoln's Inn from 1754, barrister in 1759. He became colonel of Gloucestershire militia and a fellow of the Royal Society. He was listed as Tory in 1761 but did not gain election until 1766. Then he appears to have supported the Grafton ministry until the Wilkes issue again arose. In January, 1770, he voted against expelling Wilkes; in February, 1775, he spoke against further "futile" taxation of the colonies; in 1776 he told the House of Commons that he was an independent country gentleman who still hoped for reconciliation with the colonies. In 1779 he voted with the opposition to the North ministry in the Keppel-Palliser controversy, and in April, 1780, he voted for Dunning's first resolution. But whether from absence or other reasons he did not vote in any of the 5 crucial divisions recorded in February and March, 1782. He did vote for Shelburne's peace terms in 1783. M.P. for Cardiff boroughs, 1766–90.

Mackworth-Praed, Humphrey. 1719–1803

Of Trevethoe, near St. Ives, Cornwall; oldest son of William Mackworth (M.P.); added the surname Praed upon inheriting the Praed estates through his wife. Inner Temple from 1739, Cambridge from 1741. He became a banker speculating in mining shares. In 1761 and 1766 he was listed as Tory, but he supported Newcastle through December, 1762, when he voted against Bute's peace preliminaries. He voted with the Grafton ministry for Chatham's land tax in 1767 and generally supported Grafton and North until 1773, when he voted with the opposition on the Middlesex election issues and in 1774 voted to continue the Grenville Disputed Elections Act. M.P. for St. Ives, 1761–68; Cornwall, 1772–74.

Mackworth-Praed, William. 1747–1833

Of Trevethoe, near St. Ives, Cornwall, and Tyringham, Buckinghamshire; oldest son of Humphrey Mackworth-Praed (*q.v.*). Eton from 1757, Oxford from 1767. He emulated his father in becoming a banker, first in Cornwall and, after 1801, in London. He also married the daughter of a London banker. In the House of Commons, which he entered when his father left it, he steadily supported the North ministry. He did not vote on Shelburne's peace terms and voted against Fox's India Bill in 1783. He supported Pitt from 1784. M.P. for St. Ives, 1774–75 and 1780–1806; Banbury, 1806–1808.

Maclean, Allan. ca.1725–84

He was born at Torloisk, near Tobermory, Isle of Mull; son of the Maclean of Torloisk. He entered the Scots brigade in the Dutch service ca. 1746 and was taken prisoner at Bergen-op-Zoom in 1747 but soon paroled. He left the Dutch service and in 1757 was captain in the 77th Highland Foot in America. He was present at the capture of Fort Duquesne in 1758 and served under Amherst against the French in Canada in 1759. In 1775 he helped raise a company of highlanders, and in November, 1775, he joined Carleton at Quebec, just in time to help prevent its capture by General Montgomery and Benedict Arnold. He commanded a fort in Penobscot Bay, Maine, in 1779, and was made colonel in 1780. "A brave and active officer."

Macleane, Lauchlin. ca.1728–78

Of Holles Street, London; oldest son of Rev. John Macleane (vicar of Billy, on River Bush, County Antrim). Trinity College, Dublin, from

1746; took his medical degree from Edinburgh University in 1755. He was in America as a physician, 1756–59, and then became governor of St. Martin's in the West Indies in 1766. Returning to England, he was undersecretary of state to Shelburne, 1766–68. He was one of the few Scots who championed the cause of the American colonists, but during his brief membership in the House of Commons he supported the North ministry, 1770–71. He returned to the colonies as collector of customs in Philadelphia in 1772, went to India as comptroller of army accounts in Bengal in late 1772, and served as commissary general of musters in 1773. A personal friend of Edmund Burke and John Wilkes, in India he became an ardent and trusted satellite of Warren Hastings. He was drowned en route home from India. Utterly unscrupulous despite his intelligence and bravery, he abandoned his wife ca. 1768 and openly cohabited elsewhere, leaving large debts and several illegitimate children for whom he made no adequate provision. M.P. for Arundel, 1768–71.

Macleod, Alexander. ca.1715–90

Of the Isle of Harris and of Theobalds Park, near Cheshunt, Hertfordshire; 2d son of Donald Macleod (of Bernara, Outer Hebrides). He joined the naval service of the East India Company and in 1756 commanded the *Marlborough* in the expedition under Clive and Admiral Watson to recapture Calcutta. He returned to England ca. 1771 with "a noble fortune," settled in the country "in ease and splendour," and kept "a truly hospitable house." He was elected to the House of Commons with the support of the North ministry and a reported contribution of £4,000 but was promptly unseated on petition and did not attempt further election. According to the *English Chronicle*, he was a rough seaman with "the sullen pride of wealth and independence." M.P. for Honiton, 1780–81.

Macleod, John. 1727–89

Oldest son of George Macleod (ca.1703–66; 3d Earl of Cromartie, Scottish; title forfeited as a Jacobite). He was sentenced to death as a Jacobite rebel but was pardoned in 1748 and went to Sweden and earned an excellent reputation as an officer in the Swedish army. He returned to England ca. 1775 and in 1777 raised a regiment of Highland light infantry, which he took to the West Indies. He was in command of field forces at Madras in 1780, but in 1784 the estates of his family, which had been forfeited in the 1745 Jacobite uprising, were restored to him, and he returned to England to claim them. In 1786, at the age of 59, he married Margery, oldest daughter of James Forbes (16th Lord Forbes, Scottish).

Macleod, Lord. See John Mackenzie

Macpherson, James. 1736–96

Of Belville and Ruthven, near Kingussie, Inverness, and of Putney Heath, London; son of Andrew Macpherson ("penurious farmer" of Kingussie, Inverness-shire). King's College, Aberdeen, from 1753; University of Edinburgh. While studying for the Scottish ministry, he maintained himself by odd jobs of teaching, tutoring, and literary hack work, which brought him to the attention and patronage of the Earl of Bute. While still a university student he created the fictional poet Ossian, and in 1762 he published *Fingal*, followed by *Temora* in 1763. Both were widely read and widely accepted at their face value, though Samuel Johnson and a few others promptly challenged their authenticity as products of a poet named Ossian. He nevertheless managed to secure the post of secretary to Governor Johnson of West Florida in 1764. He returned to England in 1766 and in 1775 published his history of Great Britain. The North ministry occasionally employed him to write pamphlets in defense of its measures, and he won election to Parliament in 1780. Though he apparently never addressed the House of Commons, he supported the North ministry in every crucial vote until its fall in late March, 1782. He voted against Shelburne's peace terms and supported the coalition until the controversy over Fox's India Bill, on which he did not vote. From 1784 he supported Pitt. He was a large, handsome man, morose, skeptical, and licentious. With British irony, perhaps unconscious, he is buried in Westminster Abbey. Portrait by Reynolds. M.P. for Camelford, 1780–96.

Macpherson, John. 1745–1821

Of Brompton, Middlesex. He was born at Sleat in Skye, the younger son of John Macpherson (1710–65; Presbyterian minister at Sleat); created baronet in 1786. He attended King's College, Aberdeen, and Edinburgh University. In 1767 he went to Madras with the East India

Company. From 1773 he was paymaster of the troops at Madras, but in 1777 he was dismissed by the company, returned to England, well-to-do, and immediately became a member of Parliament. He supported the North ministry, and in 1781 North appointed him a member of the Supreme Court of Calcutta, where he was also briefly governor in 1785, while Hastings was in England. On his second return to England he was one of the wealthiest of the Company's agents and was pompously active in support of Hastings. Lord North's daughter Anne said of him: "His words come from him like drops of laudanum out of a phial, and have the same effect." M.P. for Cricklade, 1779–82; Horsham, 1796–1802.

Madan, Martin. 1726–90

Older son of Colonel Martin Madan (of Hertingfordbury, Hertford-shire; M.P.); cousin of the poet Cowper. Westminster, to Oxford in 1742; B.A., 1746; barrister in 1748. In 1751 he married Jane, daughter of Sir Bernard Hale (*q.v.*). He led a gay life until he heard John Wesley preach a sermon, which made him an ardent Methodist and led to his ordination. He was chaplain of the Lock Hospital, 1750–80, and also an itinerant preacher and a close supporter and protégé of Lady Huntingdon. He corresponded with John Wesley and wrote and published religious tracts. In 1780 he published *Thelyphthora*, which advocated polygamy and was attacked by his cousin Cowper and aroused wide indignation.

Mahon, Lord. See **Philip Stanhope.** 1714–86   and **Charles Stanhope.** 1753–1816

Maitland, James. 1718–89

Styled Viscount Maitland until 1744, when he succeeded his father, Charles Maitland, as 7th Earl of Lauderdale (Scottish). He married Mary, 14-year-old daughter of Sir Thomas Lombe (silk manufacturer and alderman of London; later sheriff), and with her a fortune of £60,000. He was in military service, 1740–65, serving as lieutenant colonel from 1745. He was a representative Scottish peer, 1747–61 and 1782–84; commissioner of Scottish Police, 1766–82; and rector of Glasgow University, 1780–81. In the House of Lords he spoke on May 10, 1782, in support of the motion of the Marquess of Graham favoring a militia in Scotland. On February 11, 1783, he moved that the peers confer some "Signal Mark of Honour upon Sir George Eliott" (*q.v.*), who had so magnificently defended Gibraltar against a long and bitter Spanish attack. In November, 1783, he supported Fox's India Bill, despite the king's message of disapproval.

Maitland, James. 1759–1839

Styled Viscount Maitland until 1789, when he succeeded his father, James Maitland (*q.v.*), as 8th Earl of Lauderdale (Scottish); in 1806 created Baron Lauderdale of Berwick (English). He studied at Edinburgh University, at Paris in 1774, at Oxford in 1775, at Glasgow University in 1777, and at Lincoln's Inn in 1777, becoming barrister, and in 1780 a member of the Faculty of Advocates in Edinburgh. In the House of Commons he was active in debate and a zealous supporter of Charles Fox. He voted against the North ministry in every crucial division recorded in February and March, 1782. He voted against Shelburne's peace terms in 1783 and supported the coalition. He was a Scottish representative peer, 1790–96; L.L.D., Glasgow University, 1804; privy councillor from 1806; joint commissioner to France in 1806; keeper of the great seal of Scotland, 1806–1807; and Knight of the Thistle from 1821. M.P. for Newport (Cornwall), 1780–84; Malmesbury, 1784–89.

Maitland, John. 1732–79

10th son of Charles Maitland (6th Earl of Lauderdale, Scottish); grandson of James Maitland (4th Earl of Findlater, Scottish); younger brother of James Maitland (1718–89) (*q.v.*); uncle of James Maitland (1759–1839) (*q.v.*). He was captain of marines in 1757, major in 1775, and lieutenant colonel of foot in 1778. He distinguished himself in military operations in America, 1777–79, and died in service at Savannah. He was clerk of the pipe in exchequer from 1769. When in attendance at the House of Commons he voted with the North ministry, but there is no evidence that he ever addressed the House. M.P. for Haddington burghs, 1774–79.

Major, John. 1698–1781

Of Worlingworth Hall, near Framlingham, Suffolk; only surviving son of John Major (of Bridlington Hall, Yorkshire; died at sea in 1709); created baronet in 1765. He first took to sea, but then became a prosperous ironmaster and a director of the South Sea Company. He was an elder brother of Trinity House, 1741–81; sheriff of Suffolk, 1755–56. In Parliament he at first supported Newcastle, but was "won over" by Henry Fox and Sandwich to support Bute and his peace terms in 1762. In 1765 he supported the Rockingham ministry. M.P. for Scarborough, 1761–68.

Malden, Viscount. See **William Anne Holles Capel** and **George Capel-Coningsby**

Malmesbury, 1st Baron and **1st Earl.** See **James Harris.** 1746–1820

Malone, Edmund. 1741–1812

Born in Dublin, 2d son of Edmund Malone (1704–74; attorney of Dublin); nephew of Anthony Malone (ca.1700–76; Irish political leader). He attended Trinity College, Dublin, and was called to the Irish bar in 1767. In 1774 he went to London, where he was soon frequenting the society of Boswell, Johnson, Reynolds, Burke, and Horace Walpole. By 1777 he was permanently settled as a leading London bookseller and publisher. One of his first notable publications was his collected edition of the poems and plays of Goldsmith, published in 1780. His other publications included a critique of Reynolds' paintings with a memoir of Reynolds, 1798; a denial of the authenticity of Chatterton's poems in 1782; and an edition of Shakespeare, 1785–92, setting forth a canon and chronology, much of which is still widely accepted. Portrait by Reynolds.

Malpas, Viscount. See **George Cholmondeley.** 1724–64

Malton, Earl. See **Charles Watson-Wentworth**

Manchester, 7th Earl and **4th Duke.** See **George Montagu.** 1737–88

Mandeville, Viscount. See **George Montagu.** 1737–88

Mann, Horace. 1701–86

2d son of Robert Mann (d. 1752; of Linton Place, Kent; London merchant); created baronet in 1755. Eton, to Cambridge ca.1718. He was assistant to the envoy to Florence and then himself envoy, 1740–86. He was long an intimate correspondent of Horace Walpole from the time of their meeting in Florence in 1740. He was made Knight of the Bath in 1768. Portrait by Astley. M.P. for Sandwich, 1790–96.

Mann, Horatio. 1744–1814

Of Linton Place, near Maidstone, Kent; only surviving son of Galfridus Mann (of Kent; army clothier); nephew and heir of Horace Mann (*q.v.*), whom he succeeded as 2d baronet in 1786. Cambridge from 1760; M.A., 1763. In 1765 he married Lucy, daughter of Baptist Noel (4th Earl of Gainsborough). He inherited some £100,000 from his father, and was knighted in 1772. In the House of Commons he supported the North ministry until 1780, when he voted for Dunning's first resolution in April, and after the surrender at Yorktown opposed the ministry's American policies. In February and March, 1782, he voted against it in all 5 of the crucial recorded divisions. In May, 1782, he spoke opposing Sawbridge's motion to shorten the duration of Parliaments, "even though it was approved by his constituents." He voted against Shelburne's peace terms in February, 1783. M.P. for Maidstone, 1774–84; Sandwich, 1790–1807.

Manners, Charles. 1754–87

Oldest surviving son of John Manners (1721–70) (*q.v.*), whom he succeeded in 1770 as Marquess of Granby; in 1779 succeeded his grandfather John Manners (1696–1779) (*q.v.*) as 4th Duke of Rutland. Eton, 1762–71; Cambridge from 1771; M.A., 1774. In 1775 he married Mary Isabella, daughter of Charles Somerset (4th Duke of Beaufort). He was lord lieutenant of Leicestershire, 1779–87, Knight of the Garter from 1782; privy councillor from 1783; lord steward and privy seal, 1783–84; and lord lieutenant of Ireland, 1784–87. In the House of Commons, though considered a Tory, he strongly disapproved the measures of the North ministry toward the American colonists, and in 1775 he voted against approval of the address from the throne outlining those measures. In 1777 he moved for immediate peace with the colonies. In the House of Lords he recorded dissents to (1) rejection of the motion to examine into public expenditures in 1780, (2) rejection of the protest to the king at the dismissal of Carmarthen and Pembroke from their lord lieutenancies, (3) acceptance of Germain as a peer, and (4) rejection of the motion to curb abuses and mismanagement in public office. From 1784 he was a supporter of

Pitt, but died in his 33d year. He was, according to Barrington, "amiable and extravagant," with no particular talent except for conviviality and heavy drinking. M.P. for Cambridge University, 1774–79.

Manners, George. ca.1746–72

Of Cheveley Park, near Newmarket, Cambridgeshire; illegitimate son of John Manners (1721–70) (*q.v.*). He was cornet of horse guards in 1761 and captain in 1762. He served on his father's staff in campaigns on the Continent but gave up his commission soon thereafter. In the House of Commons he voted with his father. He first supported and then opposed the expulsion of Wilkes, 1769–70, but there is no record that he cast any vote after the death of his father in 1770 or that he ever addressed the House. M.P. for Scarborough, 1768–72.

Manners, John. 1696–1779

Styled Marquess of Granby from 1701; in 1721 he succeeded his father, John Manners (1676–1721; M.P.), as 3d Duke of Rutland. He was descended from one of the great families of the Glorious Revolution, and was nephew of the 2d Duke of Bedford. He was probably at Eton 1706–1707 or longer. He was lord lieutenant of Leicestershire, 1721–79; lord of the bedchamber, 1721–27; Knight of the Garter from 1722; privy councillor from 1727; and chancellor of the Duchy of Lancaster from 1727, resigning in 1736 after a difference of opinion with the king. In 1745 he raised a regiment against the Jacobites. He was lord justice of the realm in 1755; lord steward of the household, 1755–61; groom of the stole in 1761; and master of the horse, 1761–66. He was believed to control at least 4 votes in the House of Commons. He supported the Pelhams and planned to resign as master of the horse when Newcastle was dismissed, but yielded to heavy pressure from the new king and thereafter took few strongly partisan positions, though in 1770 he supported Chatham's motion to revise the action of the House of Commons regarding Wilkes. Horace Walpole called him "an ornament to the peerage of England" and "a gentleman of great worth and goodness." M.P. for Rutland, 1720–21.

Manners, John. 1721–70

Styled Marquess of Granby until 1770, predeceasing his father, John Manners (1696–1779) (*q.v.*), whom he would have succeeded. Eton from 1732, at Cambridge from 1738, grand tour, 1740–42. In 1750 he married Frances, daughter of Charles Seymour (6th Duke of Somerset), "one of the great heiresses." He became a distinguished and highly popular soldier, with character, courage, and integrity. He served in Flanders and in Germany from 1747, having been a colonel in his father's regiment (raised against the Jacobites) from 1745. He was made major general in 1755, and was in command of the British horse at Minden, where despite the counter-orders of Lord George Sackville (later Germain) he led the cavalry in a crucial charge. He replaced Sackville as commander of British forces with Prince Ferdinand, and was made lieutenant general in 1759. He again distinguished himself at Warburg in 1760. He was privy councillor from 1760; master general of ordnance, 1763–70; and commander in chief of armed forces in Britain, 1766–70. He was lord lieutenant of Derbyshire, 1764–66. He was awarded an L.L.D. from Cambridge in 1769. His popularity is indicated by the perhaps unequaled number of public houses in England which still bear his title and display his coat of arms. In politics his qualities were less outstanding than they were in war: he followed the Whig principles of his father and of the Seymour clan into which he married, but he was not an outstanding politician. Portrait by Reynolds. M.P. for Grantham, 1741–54; Cambridgeshire, 1754–70.

Manners, John. 1730–92

Of Grantham Grange, Lincolnshire; oldest illegitimate son of William Manners (2d son of John Manners; M.P.; 2d Duke of Rutland). Westminster, 1741–47. In 1765 he married Louisa, daughter of Lionel Tollemache (4th Earl of Dysart, Scottish). He became a large-scale dealer in annuities and "died worth near half a million." He was housekeeper at Whitehall, 1756–92. In the House of Commons he voted almost invariably in support of the current administration, though he did vote against repeal of the Stamp Act in 1766 and, after first voting for the expulsion of Wilkes in 1769, voted against it in 1770. He then opposed the North ministry until 1774, when he did not seek re-election. There is no record of any speech by him in the House. M.P. for Newark, 1754–74.

Manners, Robert. ca.1717–82

Of Bloxholme, near Sleaford, Lincolnshire; 8th son of John Manners

(1676–1721) (*q.v.*). He was ensign in the foot guards in 1735, captain in 1742, colonel in 1747, major general in 1757, lieutenant general in 1759, and general in 1771. He was lieutenant governor of Hull, 1749–82. In the House of Commons he supported each successive administration except that of Rockingham, 1765–66, when he voted against repeal of the Stamp Act. There is no record that he cast a vote in any of the 5 crucial divisions recorded in February and March, 1782, at the end of the North ministry, or that he ever addressed the House during his 35 years of membership. M.P. for Kingston-upon-Hull, 1747–82.

Manners, Robert. 1758–1823

Of Bloxholme, near Sleaford, Lincolnshire; oldest son of Robert Manners (ca.1717–82) (*q.v.*). Caen Military School, followed by the grand tour. He was cornet in the horse in 1778, captain in 1779, colonel in 1794, major general in 1796, lieutenant general in 1803, and general in 1813. He was equerry to the king, 1784–1808. In politics he supported, and was advanced by, the Pitt ministry. M.P. for Great Bedwin, 1784–90; Cambridgeshire, 1791–1820.

Manners, Robert. 1758–82

2d son of John Manners (1721–70) (*q.v.*). Eton, 1763–71, and then immediately embarked on a naval career. He served under Rodney, Hood, and Keppel, off Ushant in 1778, off Cape St. Vincent in 1779, off Cape Henry in 1782, and off Dominica in 1782, where, at the age of 25, he was fatally wounded. He cared much for the navy and little for politics. According to report, he never took his seat in the House of Commons: he was certainly at sea during all the crucial divisions before the fall of the North ministry in March, 1782. M.P. for Cambridgeshire, 1780–82.

Mansfield, 1st Baron and **1st and 2d Earls.** See **William Murray** and **David Murray**

Mansfield, James. 1734–1821

Son of John James Manfield (attorney of Ringwood, near Christchurch, Hampshire); knighted in 1804. Eton, 1745–50; Cambridge (where he added an *s* to his surname) from 1750; fellow from 1754; Middle Temple from 1755; barrister in 1758; bencher from 1772; and treasurer in 1785. He was legal adviser to Wilkes in 1768 and later to the Duchess of Kingston; king's counsel from 1772; solicitor general, 1780–82 and November–December, 1783; and chief justice of the Court of Common Pleas, 1804–14. He steadily supported the North ministry throughout the crucial divisions which preceded its fall in March, 1782. On May 10, 1782, he spoke opposing Shelburne's motion to arm the people; in February, 1783, he told the House that the king and ministry had legal power to give the colonies their independence; in November, 1783, he spoke in defense of the East India Company. He was a man of energy first, ability second, and grace third. M.P. for Cambridge University, 1779–84.

Manvers, 1st Earl. See **Charles Pierrepont Medows (or Meadows)**

March, 3d Earl. See **William Douglas.** 1724–1810   and **Charles Lennox**

Marchmont, 3d Earl. See **Hugh Hume-Campbell**

Marischal, 10th Earl. See **George Keith**

Markham, William. 1719–1807

Oldest son of Major William Markham; born at Kinsale, County Cork, where his father eked out half pay by maintaining a school. Westminster from 1733; Oxford from 1738; B.A., 1742; M.A., 1745; B.C.L. and D.C.L., 1752. He was considered a fine scholar. According to Jeremy Bentham, "he married a Dutch woman who brought him a considerable fortune." He was headmaster of Westminster, 1753–67; dean of Christ Church, Oxford, 1767–71; preceptor to Prince George and Prince Frederick, 1771–76; bishop of Chester, 1771–77; and archbishop of York, 1777–1807. He was privy councillor from 1777. He was at one time an intimate friend of Edmund Burke, though Chatham once denounced him for preaching "pernicious doctrine." In June, 1780, he was attacked by the Gordon mob, thrown on his face, and had his lace torn away. He actively defended Warren Hastings in the House of Lords. 2 portraits by Reynolds, 1 by Romney, and 1 by Hoppner.

Marlborough, 4th Duke. See **George Spencer**

Marriott, James. ca.1730–1803

Of Twinstead Hall, near Sudbury, Essex; son of Benjamin Marriott (attorney in Hatton Gardens, London). Cambridge from 1746; fellow, 1756–64; master of Trinity Hall, Cambridge, 1764–1803; vice chancellor of Cambridge, 1767–68. He was protégé, agent, pamphleteer, and supporter of the Duke of Newcastle, 1757–62, and in 1762 published *Political Considerations*, urging reconciliation and an alliance between Newcastle and Bute. He was king's advocate, 1764–68; was knighted in 1768; and was judge of the Admiralty Court, 1778–99. In 1799 he was given a pension of £2,000 a year. In the House of Commons he voted regularly with each successive ministry and importuned each for political favors. He supported the North administration and insisted that the American colonists were wrong in asserting that they were not represented in Parliament, since they were specified in their charters to be part of the manor of Greenwich and were therefore represented by the members for Kent. He voted with the North ministry in 4 of the crucial divisions recorded in February and March, 1782. He voted for Shelburne's peace terms and for Fox's India Bill in 1783. He published poems, as well as several legal and political works. M.P. for Sudbury, 1781–84 and 1796–1802.

Marsh, Samuel. ca.1736–95

Of Battersea, Surrey, and Uxbridge, Middlesex; son of William Marsh ("factor"); nephew of Samuel Fludyer (*q.v.*). He joined his uncle's merchant-banking business and in the House of Commons supported the Fludyer interests. After 1779 he was generally in opposition to the North ministry, and in 1780, his last year in Parliament, he voted for the Dunning resolution of April 6. M.P. for Chippenham, 1774–80.

Marsham, Charles. 1744–1811

In 1793 succeeded his father, Robert Marsham (*q.v.*), as 3d Baron Romney; in 1801 created Viscount Marsham and Earl of Romney. Eton, 1753–63; Oxford from 1763; L.L.D. from Cambridge, 1769; fellow of the Royal Society from 1776. In 1776 he married Frances, daughter of Charles Wyndham (1710–63) (*q.v.*). He was a country gentleman whom Wraxall considered "to the last degree coarse and inelegant, yet wanted not ability, and attracted deservedly general consideration in his parliamentary capacity." He voted independently but usually in opposition to both the North and the Pitt ministries. In January, 1770, he voted against the expulsion of Wilkes. In October,

1775, he voted against approval of the address from the throne and proposed a bill of indemnity regarding the hiring of foreign troops to fight in America. In February, 1780, he proposed that the vote of thanks to Rodney should be accompanied by some financial provision. He voted for the Dunning resolution of April 6, 1780, and against North on all 5 crucial divisions recorded in February and March, 1782. He voted for Shelburne's peace terms and Pitt's reforms of Parliament and against Fox's India Bill in 1783. He was vice president of the Society of Arts, a member of the Board of Agriculture in 1793, and president of the Marine Society in 1793. Wraxall called him a man "of good intentions and plain sense, without ornament or decoration of any kind." M.P. for Maidstone, 1768–74; Kent, 1774–90.

Marsham, Robert. 1712–93

Of Romney, Kent; in 1724 succeeded, as 2d but oldest surviving son, his father, Robert Marsham (1685–1724; M.P.), as 2d Baron Romney. Eton from 1728; Oxford from 1731; D.C.L., 1733; fellow of the Royal Society from 1757. He was president of the Society of Arts, 1761–93; fellow of the Society of Antiquaries from 1762; president of the Marine Society from its founding in 1756 until 1793, and "indefatigable" colonel of the West Kent militia from 1759. In 1775 he spoke and wrote in support of Chatham's plan to conciliate the colonies. The *Gentleman's Magazine* pronounced him "highly respected and beloved." Portrait by Reynolds.

Martin, David. 1736–97

The son of the parish schoolmaster of Anstruther, Fifeshire. He studied painting under Allan Ramsay and accompanied him to Rome for further study. He then returned to London, where he acquired a reputation for his portraits and engravings, and was appointed principal painter for Scotland to the Prince of Wales, and later limner for the prince. He painted portraits of many notables, including Bute, Mansfield, and Benjamin Franklin. His fine engravings included portraits of Hume and Rousseau. He also painted a self-portrait.

Martin, James. 1738–1810

Of Overbury, Worcestershire; 3d son of John Martin (1692–1767; M.P.); brother of Joseph Martin (*q.v.*). He became both a successful banker and a country gentleman, "whose incorruptible integrity compensated for the mediocrity of his talents," according to Wraxall. He was scrupulously independent in his votes but on some issues was an enthusiastic extremist about humanitarian reforms and was consequently in strong opposition to the North ministry. In supporting Dunning's resolution of April 6, 1780, he told the House of Commons that the current excessive influence of the crown was derived from the corruption of the ministry, which had brought the nation nothing but disgrace. In February and March, 1782, he voted against the North ministry on all 5 of the recorded crucial divisions. In May, 1782, he supported Shelburne's bill to arm the people; in June, 1782, he supported Pitt's proposals for the reform of Parliament; in July, 1782, he opposed a proposed pension for Isaac Barré (*q.v.*), who was going blind. He voted for Shelburne's peace terms in February, 1783. In March, 1783, he protested as improper the presence of peers in the gallery of the House of Commons during debates. In May, 1783, he supported Sawbridge's motion for shorter Parliaments; in June, 1783, he supported the right of all citizens to petition the crown; in July, 1783, he opposed the possession and award of sinecures by the Exchequer, and in November, 1783, he repeatedly villified the coalition and Fox's India Bill. On that occasion his name lent itself to a witty riposte by North. M.P. for Tewkesbury, 1776–1807.

Martin, Joseph. 1726–76

Of Eastwick and Bookham, near Leatherhead, Surrey; 2d son of John Martin (1692–1767; M.P.); brother of James Martin (*q.v.*). In 1746 he joined the family banking business and in 1760 became its head. Like his brother, he was an ardent advocate of reform and a steady if not always consistent opponent of the North ministry. He was a leader of Rockingham's supporters among the businessmen of London. He was an alderman of London, and was elected sheriff in 1770 but declined that and other municipal offices. In 1769 he moved in support of Wilkes's claims, and he helped draft the London petition critical of the ministry regarding Wilkes. In January, 1770, he voted against unseating Wilkes and in October, 1775, voted against approval of the address from the throne. M.P. for Gatton, 1768–74; Tewkesbury, 1774–76.

Martin, Richard. 1754–1834

Of Ballinahinch Castle, County Galway; oldest son of Robert Martin

(d. 1794; of Dangan House, County Galway). He studied at Harrow and Cambridge and became an Irish barrister in 1781. He was an extensive landowner in Galway and made his principal home there. He supported Catholic emancipation in Ireland, and was said to have declined a peerage. He was a member of the Irish Parliament for the greater part of the period 1776–1827, and high sheriff of Galway in 1782. He was ardent in humanitarian causes, was a founder of the Society for the Prevention of Cruelty to Animals, and was known as "Humanity Martin," though he was always ready for an honorable duel. "His memory is still revered in Galway" (*DNB*).

Martin, Samuel. 1714–88

Of Antigua and Westminster; oldest son of Samuel Martin (of Antigua; speaker of the Antigua assembly, 1753–63). He was born in Antigua and inherited property there, but was educated at Westminster and Cambridge from 1729, and remained in England. He was enrolled at Inner Temple from 1729 and was barrister in 1736, and bencher from 1747. He was the agent for various local governments in the British West Indies, 1742–50, secretary to the chancellor of the exchequer, 1754–55; and secretary in the treasury in 1756, but resigned that post in 1757. He attached himself to the Pelhams and to Henry Bilson Legge, but also sought the favor of the Leicester House group, and secretly supplied Bute with information from Newcastle's private treasury papers while joint secretary to the treasury, 1758–63. In 1763 he called Wilkes a "cowardly scoundrel" to his face after Wilkes had attacked him in the *North Briton*. In the duel which followed he slightly wounded Wilkes in the second exchange. He became treasurer to the Princess Dowager of Wales and supported the proposal to include her among the regents in the 1765 Regency Bill. In 1771 Burke named him to the House of Commons as an example of those exerting a malign secret influence on the government. In 1772 he was granted a pension of £1,200 for life. He was said to be "an obsessional worker." M.P. for Camelford, 1747–68; Hastings, 1768–74.

Martyn, John. 1699–1768

Son of Thomas Martyn (d. 1743; merchant to Hamburg). He was born in London and was dedicated to and trained for a business career, but abandoned it for scientific studies. In 1728, while practicing as a physician in Chelsea, he published *Historia Planatorium Rariorum*. His reputation made, he repaired to Cambridge to study science, and in 1732, within 2 years, became professor of botany there, remaining until 1762. In 1741 he published his translation of Vergil's *Georgics*, and somewhat later the *Eclogues*. He founded a botanical society in London and served as its secretary. He also initiated the *Grub Street Journal*, a weekly satiric review.

Masham, Samuel. 1712–76

In 1758 succeeded his father, Samuel Masham (ca.1680–1758), as 2d Baron Masham. He married (1) in 1736 Henrietta, the niece ("worth £20,000") of Thomas Foley (1712–66; 1st Baron Foley of the 1st creation). He was lord of the bedchamber to George II, and groom of the bedchamber to the Prince of Wales, 1758–61. After the prince became George III in 1761, he served as lord of the bedchamber, 1762–76, and remembrancer of the exchequer, with an annual pension of £1,000. Jonathan Swift professed to detest him. M.P. for Droitwich, 1747.

Mason, William. ca.1724–97

Son of William Mason (d. 1753; vicar of Hull, Yorkshire). Cambridge from 1743; B.A., 1745; M.A., 1749. With encouragement and help from his friend Thomas Gray he was a fellow at Cambridge from 1749. He was also a friend of Horace Walpole, with whom he corresponded frequently over many years. In 1748 he published *Isis*, a polemic against Jacobitism in Oxford. In 1752 he published his quasi-classical play *Elfrida*, which was republished in London in 1772 and again in 1779. In 1754 he became chaplain to Robert d'Arcy (*q.v.*) and was rector of Aston in Yorkshire, 1754–97. He was chaplain to the king, 1757–62; prebendary of York, 1756–62; and canon of York from 1762. Meanwhile, in 1759 he had published his play *Caractalus*, which was briefly produced at Covent Garden Theatre in 1772 and 1776. In 1774 he published *Life and Letters of Thomas Gray*. He was active in the early stages of the Wyvill Yorkshire Association movement in 1780 and later approved Pitt's measures for the reform of Parliament. He opposed, though not as a member of Parliament, Fox's India Bill in 1783, and in that year offended his friend Horace Walpole by his political opinions. He composed poetry and church music. He was Gray's literary executor.

Mason-Villiers, George. See **George Villiers**

Massey, Eyre. 1719–1804

5th son of Colonel Hugh Massey (of Duntryleague, County Limerick); in 1800 created Baron Clarina (Irish). He enlisted in the army in 1739 and served in the West Indies from 1739 and in Scotland, 1745–46, and was made captain in 1747. He married Catherine, sister of Robert Clement (1st Earl of Leitrim, Irish). In 1757 he went to America with the rank of major. He became lieutenant colonel in 1758, and in 1759 he commanded the expedition to Niagara and gained possession of the upper valley of the Ohio River. He commanded the grenadiers at Montreal in 1760. He served at Martinique in 1761; at Havana in 1762; in New York and Quebec, 1763–69; in Halifax, 1776–80; and in Cork, 1794–96. He was made general, marshal of the army in Ireland, and governor of Limerick. He was severely wounded in a number of battles.

Masterman, William. ca.1722–86

Of Trinity House, near Lostwithiel, Cornwall; only son of Thomas Masterman (tanner and small landowner of Little Ayton, near Stokesley, Yorkshire). He became an attorney in London in 1745 and head of a merchant firm in 1750. He was deputy clerk and then clerk of the council and register of the Duchy of Lancaster from 1758, mayor of Lostwithiel in 1764, and town clerk of Bossiney in 1781. In the House of Commons he supported the North ministry from 1780, voting in February and March, 1782, against motions of Conway to end the American war immediately, and against motions by Fox and by Sir John Rous. He voted for Shelburne's peace terms in February, 1783, and for Fox's India Bill in November, 1783. In early 1784 he supported Pitt, but failed of re-election. M.P. for Bodmin, 1780–84.

Masterton, James. 1715–77

Of Newton, Stirlingshire; oldest surviving son of John Masterton (of Edinburgh; merchant). He was a lieutenant in the army in 1742, was captain in 1745, served as aide to the Duke of Cumberland in 1761, was deputy adjutant general in Ireland in 1762, and was barrack master for Scotland in 1769. He was believed by some to have used his army position to assist his friend Lawrence Dundas make a fortune in government supply contracts. He was elected to Parliament in 1768 with the support of Dundas, whom he in turn supported. He voted with the Grafton and North ministries until he left Parliament in 1774, leaving no record of ever having addressed the House. M.P. for Inverkeithing and Stirling burghs, 1768–74.

Mauchline, Lord. See **John Campbell.** 1705–82

Maudit, Israel. 1708–87

A son of Isaac Maudit (d. 1718; refugee French Protestant minister of Bermondsey, London). He went to school at Taunton and then traveled and studied on the Continent and preached at The Hague for a brief period. He and his brother Jasper became woolen merchants and drapers of London and were by inclination as well as inheritance ardent and politically minded dissenters. Jasper became a fellow of the Royal Society in 1751, a dissenting preacher, and a leader of the Royal Society for the Propagation of the Gospel,—"a bachelor, possessed of an ample fortune" (*DNB*). Israel, meanwhile, preached in various dissenting centers and in 1760 published *Considerations on the Present German War*, which was, according to Horace Walpole, widely read and influential and established his reputation as a political journalist. In 1763 Jasper was appointed agent in England for the Massachusetts Bay Colony, and Israel took over most of the work of that agency, largely replacing his brother. He wrote further political pamphlets, some of which were believed to have been commissioned and paid for either by the North ministry or by Lord George Germain in his personal capacity. He supported Governor Hutchinson as a witness in the inquiry into the exchange of letters revealed by Franklin, and later attacked by pamphlet the military conduct of General Howe and (to a lesser degree) the naval conduct of the general's brother Admiral Lord Howe in the American war. In March, 1778, he declared that he was in favor of immediate recognition of American independence, and after 1778 no longer supported the North ministry. He was usually well informed, and he had some public influence.

Mauger, Joshua. 1725–88

Of Warborne, near Lymington, Hampshire; son of José Mauger; born in Jersey. He became master of a ship and then settled as a brewer and distiller in Halifax, Nova Scotia, where per capita demand for his product was naturally high and where he "made a fortune." In 1751, after a brief trip to and from London, he was agent victualer for the navy at Halifax. In 1752 he was accused of smuggling, but the government overlooked the charge, and he became an even more prominent leader in Nova Scotia affairs, and especially in the management of its finances. He was agent for the Nova Scotia Assembly, 1762–68, living from 1765 in Soho, London. In 1768 he won election to Parliament with the support of Rockingham, but was unseated for offering bribes. The following year he was returned unopposed. He voted steadily in opposition to the North ministry and, according to the records, addressed the House twice, on minor issues. He was a director of the French Hospital, 1769–88, and continued his business and political interests in Nova Scotia until his death. M.P. for Poole, 1768–69 and 1769–80.

Maule, William Ramsay. 1700–82

Of Kellie, near Arbroath, Forfarshire; son of Henry Maule (of Kellie; a Jacobite brother of Lord Panmure, Irish); he was commonly called Lord Maule from 1729; in 1743 he was officially given the reinstated Irish titles of Viscount Maule and Earl of Panmure. He attended the universities at Leyden and Paris, 1718–19. He entered the army as ensign in 1727 and served with distinction at Dettingen in 1743; at Fontenoy in 1745; in the Scottish Highlands, 1745–46; in Flanders in 1747; and at Gibraltar in 1748. He was captain in 1737, colonel in 1754, major general in 1755, lieutenant general in 1758, and general in 1770. In 1760 he was a member of the court-martial of Lord George Sackville (later Germain). In politics, "throughout his career he was of the Court party" (*Peerage*). He supported the Old Whigs until 1760, then Bute and Bedford, and then on most issues Grafton and North. He voted against the Dunning resolution of April 6, 1780. There is no evidence that he ever addressed the House of Commons. He was tall, handsome, generous, and popular. M.P. for Forfarshire, 1735–82.

Mawbey, Joseph. 1730–98

Of Botleys, near Chertsey, Surrey; 2d surviving son of John Mawbey (of Ravenstone Hall, near Ashby-de-la-Zouch, Leicestershire); created baronet in 1765. At the age of 17 he became a partner in his uncle's

589

large vinegar distillery. In 1775 he inherited the business and became "an eminent malt distiller and pig dealer," as well as a prosperous merchant of Vauxhall. His business was said to have brought "more than £600,000 per annum to the government in duties." He was sheriff of Surrey, 1757–58, and bought the estate of Botleys there in 1763. In Parliament he supported Newcastle through 1762, voting against Bute's peace preliminaries. He became an active leader in organizing petitions protesting the ministry's measures against Wilkes and in founding the Society of Supporters of the Bill of Rights, 1768–70. He voted against unseating Wilkes in January, 1770, against approval of the address from the throne in October, 1775, and for the Dunning resolution of April 6, 1780, but voted with the North ministry in all 5 of the crucial divisions reported in February and March, 1782. In 1783 he told the House of Commons that "every representative was bound to obey his constituents," and in June he therefore supported the bill to control the expenses of election. In November, 1783, he opposed the receipt tax "on principle," and opposed Fox's India Bill for more tangible reasons, telling the House that he detested the coalition. After 1784 he appears to have been less active in business, and less opinionated in politics. M.P. for Southwark, 1761–74; Surrey, 1775–90.

Mawson, Matthias. 1683–1770

Son of a prosperous brewer of Chiswick, Middlesex. St. Paul's School in London; Cambridge from 1701; fellow, 1707; M.A., 1708; B.D., 1716; and D.D., 1725. He was master of Corpus Christi College, Cambridge, 1724–44, and vice chancellor of Cambridge, 1730–32. He is said to have refused the bishopric of Gloucester in 1734, but he was bishop of Llandaff, 1739–40; bishop of Chichester, 1740–54; and bishop of Ely, 1754–70. In the House of Lords he recorded dissent to approval of the cider tax in 1763 but in all other measures seemed content with the majority decisions of the lords temporal. By inheritance and income he possessed great wealth and left a large part of it to Cambridge colleges.

Maxwell, Robert. ca.1721–79

Of Farnham, near Cavan, in County Cavan; in 1759 succeeded his father, John Maxwell (of Farnham), as 2d Baron Farnham (Irish); in 1760 created Viscount Farnham (Irish); in 1763 created Earl of Farnham (Irish). He married (1) in 1759 Henrietta, widow of William Howard (3d Earl of Stafford), and (2) in 1771 Sarah, with £40,000, sister of Lord Sydney of Leix (Irish). He was a member of the Irish Parliament, 1743–59; member of the Irish Privy Council from 1760; and sheriff of County Cavan in 1757. In 1754 he paid £3,000 for his nomination to a seat for Taunton, but received £3,675 from secret-service funds toward the expenses of a riotous campaign. He supported Newcastle, then Bute, and then Grenville. He became a close friend of Richard Rigby and was therefore something of a Bedford adherent. There is no evidence that he ever addressed the House of Commons. M.P. for Taunton, 1754–68.

Maynard, William. 1721–72

Of Waltons, near Saffron Walden, Essex; in 1738 succeeded his father, Sir Henry Maynard, as 4th baronet. Winchester from 1731, Oxford from 1739, grand tour in 1744. In 1751 he married Charlotte, daughter of Sir Cecil Bishop (or Bisshopp) (*q.v.*). He was considered Tory, but in 1761 he acceded to Newcastle's wish that in standing for re-election he campaign as a Whig in order to "divide the Tory interest there." He supported Newcastle, then Bute from 1762, then Grenville, 1763–65, and Chatham in 1766. No vote or speech by him after 1768 is recorded. He was recorder of Saffron Walden. M.P. for Essex, 1759–72.

Mayne, Robert. 1724–82

Of Jermyn Street, London; 5th son of 21 children of William Mayne (of Powis Logie, Clackmannanshire); brother of William Mayne (*q.v.*). He became a banker in Jermyn Street. From 1776 he held, with Anthony Bacon, important government contracts to victual British troops in America and the West Indies. He voted regularly in support of the North ministry, including votes in all 5 of the recorded crucial divisions in February and March, 1782. There is no evidence that he ever addressed the House of Commons. In 1782 his firm went into bankruptcy, and he committed suicide. M.P. for Gatton, 1774–82.

Mayne, William. 1722–94

Of Gatton, near Reigate, Surrey; Carrick Mayne in County Dublin; and Marston Mortein, near Ampthill, Bedfordshire. He was the 4th son of 21 children of William Mayne (of Powis Logie, Clackmannanshire); created baronet in 1763; created Baron Newhaven (Irish) in 1776; brother of Robert Mayne (*q.v.*). In 1758 he married Frances, sister of John Allen (of Stillorgan; 3d Viscount Allen, Irish), who brought him considerable property. Until 1757 he was engaged in the merchant house of his family in Lisbon, but he then became a partner with his brother Robert in a London merchant-banking house, for which they secured a large government contract to victual British troops in the colonies and West Indies. He was a member of the Irish Parliament, 1761–76, and an Irish privy councillor in 1766. Although reputed a Tory, he became a friend of the elder Pitt, but in 1761 he offered Bute his support in return for future political favors. In 1769 he petitioned, with others, for a crown grant of 100,000 acres in maritime Canada. In the House of Commons from 1774 he supported the North ministry, though he became openly critical of some of its measures. In the House he criticized the boast of Edmund Burke to the House that he was in direct communication with Benjamin Franklin during the war with America, and he voted against Dunning's first resolution in April, 1780. But he opposed North's wish to include non-members of the House in the commission to report on the accounts of the administration. In April, 1782, he spoke in support of Fox's proposed measures for Ireland. He voted against Shelburne's peace terms and from 1784 supported Pitt, but he appears to have addressed the House very seldom after 1782. M.P. for Canterbury, 1774–80; Gatton, 1780–90.

Mayo, 1st Viscount and 1st Earl. See John Bourke

Mayor, John. ca.1735–1817

Of Lacy Court, near Abingdon, Berkshire; son of John Mayor (brass founder of Little Moorfields, London). He became a London banker with influential connections in and about Abingdon and also owned valuable property in Essex. He was sheriff of Berkshire, 1774–75, and became "strongly attached to Lord North" and voted with him "invariably," according to the *English Chronicle*. He opposed the Dunning resolution of April 6, 1780, and hinted for favors from the ministry in return for his steady support. He voted with North on all major issues through March 15, 1782, and North saw to it that in 1782 he was given a pension of £1,000. "A very worthy, honest, upright man," recorded the *English Chronicle*. M.P. for Abingdon, 1774–82.

Meade, John. 1744–1800

In 1745 succeeded his father, Sir Richard Meade, as 4th baronet; created Viscount Clanwilliam (Irish) in 1766; created Earl of Clanwilliam (Irish) in 1776. Dublin University; B.A., 1762. He was a member of the Irish Parliament, 1764–66.

Medley, George. 1720–96

4th son of Thomas Medley (of Buxted Park, near Uckfield, Sussex); grandson of Sir Samuel Dashwood (M.P.; lord mayor of London, 1702). He married (1) in 1757 Elizabeth, daughter of Sir Thomas Palmer (ca.1702–65; M.P.; 4th baronet), and (2) in 1762 Jane, daughter of Sir Timothy Waldo. He became a merchant in Portuguese wine and "amassed a vast property." In the 1768 election he stood in opposition to the Rockingham-Newcastle interests, and after 1770 he supported in general the North ministry until he temporarily left Parliament in 1780, though he voted in favor of extending Grenville's Disputed Elections Act in 1774. He opposed Dunning's resolution of April 6, 1780, and on April 28 told the House of Commons that the House had no right to attack the royal prerogatives. He voted with Pitt after his re-election in 1784. M.P. for Seaford, 1768–80; East Grinstead, 1784–90.

Medlycott (or Medleycott), Thomas. 1697–1763

Of Ven House, near Milbourne Port, Somerset; oldest son of James Medlycott (or Medleycott) (M.P.). Middle Temple from 1720. He was commissioner of hawkers and pedlars in 1742 and commissioner of taxes, 1742–44. He supported Pelham and then Newcastle, who in 1761 provided him with a pension of £600 a year. M.P. for Milbourne Port, 1734–42 and 1747–63.

Medlycott (or Medleycott), Thomas Hutchings. See **Thomas Hutchings**

Medows (or Meadows), Charles Pierrepont. 1737–1816

Of Holme Pierrepont Hall, on River Trent, Nottinghamshire; 2d son of Philip Medows (or Meadows); nephew of Evelyn Pierrepont (*q.v.*); in 1788 assumed the added surname Pierrepont upon inheriting estates from his uncle; in 1796 created Baron Pierrepont and Viscount

Newark; in 1806 created Earl Manvers. He was a lieutenant in the navy in 1755 and captain in 1759. Though elected to Parliament with the support of the Duke of Portland, he voted as an independent country gentleman. He voted for the Dunning resolution of April 6, 1780, and thereafter steadily opposed the North ministry in every crucial division, including the 5 recorded divisions in February and March, 1782. He voted against relief for Roman Catholics but did not vote on Shelburne's peace terms or on Fox's India Bill in 1783. From 1784 he usually supported Charles Fox against Pitt. M.P. for Nottinghamshire, 1778–96.

Medows (or Meadows), William. 1738–1813

3d son of Philip Medows (or Meadows) (deputy ranger of Windsor Park); grandson of the 1st Duke of Kingston; grandson of Sir Philip Medows (or Meadows) (d. 1757; comptroller of army accounts); cousin of Charles Pierrepont Medows (or Meadows) (*q.v.*). He was ensign in 1756; served in Germany, 1760–64; served in America, 1776–78; and was a "gallant defender" of St. Lucia against the French in 1778. He was made colonel in 1780, and in 1781 was in command of reinforcements sent to the Cape of Good Hope. He then went to India, and was governor of Bombay in 1788 and governor of Madras in 1791. He was active in the wars in India until 1793, when he was made lieutenant general. He was governor of the Isle of Wight in 1798, and briefly, after Cornwallis, in command of troops in Ireland in 1801.

Melbourne, 1st Baron and 1st Viscount. See Peniston Lamb

Mellish, Charles. ca.1737–96

Of Blyth, near Worksop, Nottinghamshire; oldest son of William Mellish (*q.v.*). Lincoln's Inn from 1761, and barrister in 1766. He was recorder of Newark, 1770–77 and 1779–94; commissioner of stamps, 1793–96. His father supported the Pelhams, but in October, 1775, he told the House of Commons that he supported the North ministry in all its chief policies. He voted against the Dunning resolution of April 6, 1780, and supported the North ministry in every crucial vote recorded in 1782 until its fall in late March. He voted against Shelburne's peace terms, followed North into the coalition, and voted for Fox's India Bill in November, 1783. He continued to support North in

1784 and failed of re-election. M.P. for Pontrefact, 1774–80; Aldborough, 1780–84.

Mellish, Joseph. ca.1716–90

Of Bush Hill Park, near Edmonton, Middlesex; 3d son of Joseph Mellish (of Blyth, near Worksop, Nottinghamshire); brother of William Mellish (*q.v.*); uncle of Charles Mellish (*q.v.*). He married a daughter of William Gore (lord mayor of London). He was descended from a family long established as London merchants, and became a member of the Russia Company. He also had trade interests in Portugal. He was consulted by Newcastle in matters of public finance, and supported Newcastle, voting in December, 1762, against Bute's peace preliminaries. He remained faithful to Newcastle, but evidently never addressed the House of Commons. He opposed the North ministry: his only recorded vote with that ministry was for the motion to prorogue in 1780. M.P. for Great Grimsby, 1761–80.

Mellish, William. ca.1710–91

Of Blyth, near Worksop, Nottinghamshire; son of Joseph Mellish (of Blyth); older brother of Joseph Mellish (*q.v.*); father of Charles Mellish (*q.v.*). Eton, to Cambridge in 1725; fellow, 1729–35; Lincoln's Inn from 1725; Inner Temple from 1733. He was commissioner of excise, 1757–60; and receiver general of customs, 1760–63 and 1765–85. Like other members of his family, he appears to have supported the Pelhams. M.P. for Retford, 1741–51.

Melville, 1st Viscount. See Henry Dundas

Melville, Leslie Alexander. 1731–94

3d son of Alexander Melville (ca.1699–1754; 7th Earl of Leven and later 4th Earl of Melville, both Scottish). He entered the foot guards in 1753, and became lieutenant colonel in 1766. He served in America in 1774, served in England as colonel and aide to the king in 1775, and served again in America from 1776 as brigadier general under Howe, who praised his gallantry in the field. He was major general under Cornwallis in the Carolinas and in command at Charleston in 1781. Soon afterward ill health forced him to leave military service.

Melville, Robert. 1723–1809

Son of Andrew Melville (minister of Monimail, near Cupar, Fifeshire). He attended Glasgow and Edinburgh universities. In 1744 he began a military career as ensign. He served in Flanders, 1745–48 and 1751–56, and was captain from 1751 and major from 1756. He was present at the capture of Guadeloupe, and was appointed its governor in 1760. He also served as governor of the ceded Leeward Islands: of Grenada, 1763–71; of St. Vincent, 1767–71; and of Tobago, 1767–71. He served under Lord Rollo at the capture of Dominica. He was sent to France to ask for indulgences for the British at Tobago, and on his final return to England devoted himself partly to research into the Roman occupation of Britain. He also published a new theory of Hannibal's route over the Alps to Italy, and invented a naval gun which was in use for nearly a century. He was an L.L.D. of Edinburgh University, fellow of the Society of Arts, and fellow of the Royal Society. He was made general in 1798.

Mendip, 1st Baron. See Welbore Ellis

Mercer, James. 1734–1804

Oldest son of Thomas Mercer (of Aldie Castle, Kinross-shire; Jacobite exile). He was schooled in Paris, and then acquired an M.A. degree from Marischal College, Aberdeen, in 1754. He enlisted in 1756 and served at Cherbourg and Minden and in Ireland from 1770. In 1772 he sold his commission but in 1777 volunteered and became major in the Gordon fencibles. In 1797 he published a volume of lyric poems, which were highly praised in the *Edinburgh Review*, and were republished in 1804 and again in 1806.

Meredith, William. ca.1725–90

Of Henbury Hall near Macclesfield, Cheshire, and Pierrepont, near Farnham, Surrey; oldest son of Amos Meredith (of Newbury, Gloucestershire); in 1752 succeeded his grandfather Sir William Meredith (1665–1752) as 3d baronet. Westminster from 1738; Oxford from 1743; D.C.L., 1749. He was called "A Tory under George II and a liberal Whig under George III," but he insisted that it was not he but the parties which had changed their principles. He was elected to Parliament as an avowed Tory in 1754, and was listed by Newcastle as Tory in 1761. Horace Walpole pronounced him "a convert from Jacobitism, inflexibly serious, and of no clear head . . . an honest man."

In 1765 he supported the Rockingham Whig ministry, and was a member of the Admiralty Board, 1765–66. In 1766–67 he made an analysis of the voting blocs in the House of Commons. He supported the Whig opposition on the Wilkes and Middlesex election issues in 1770 but rescued North from a Wilkes mob outside Westminster Hall. In March, 1774, he left the Whig opposition to the extent of serving as comptroller of the king's household, 1774–77, and became a privy councillor in 1774, thus losing some credit with the opposition. But he was independent of the ministry and of the court in his repeated motions, beginning in 1773, to secure relief for dissenters from subscription to the 39 articles in order to secure admission to the universities or to public service. In 1775 he approved North's Declaratory Act and other measures aimed at coercing the Massachusetts colonists, but in 1777 he resigned his court post and in 1778 voted for repeal of the Declaratory Act. In June, 1779, he moved that the king be directed to bring an immediate end to the American war, and in April, 1780, he voted for Dunning's first resolution. From 1773 he was "hot in the pursuit of Clive" and seconded Burgoyne's resolution condemning Clive's conduct in India. After 1780 he was in general a supporter of Rockingham and Fox. His pamphlets reveal his liberalism and his independence. M.P. for Wigan, 1754–61; Liverpool, 1761–80.

Metham, George. 1713–93

Of North Cave, near Hull, Yorkshire; only son of Hugh Montgomery; added the surname Metham in 1756, upon inheriting from his mother's brother Philip Metham. Cambridge from 1734, Inner Temple from 1734, then studied in Paris. He was clerk of the wardrobe, 1766–82. He was elected to the House of Commons as a supporter of Newcastle, and opposed Bute's peace preliminaries in 1762 and the Grenville ministry, 1763–65. Upon securing his court appointment under the Rockingham ministry, he withdrew from the House and did not stand for re-election. M.P. for Kingston-on-Hull, 1757–66.

Methuen, Paul. 1723–95

Of Corsham Court, near Chippenham, Wiltshire; oldest son of Thomas Methuen (of Bradford-on-Avon, Somerset). Oxford from 1741. In 1749 he married Christian, daughter of Sir George Cobb (of Adderbury, Oxfordshire; 3d baronet). In 1757 he succeeded to the estate of Sir Paul Methuen (ca.1672–1757; M.P.) and an income of £16,000 a year. He supported the Earl of Warwick and the Grenville ministry, 1763–65, when Newcastle listed him as Tory. He voted against repeal of the Stamp Act in 1766 and opposed Rockingham. After 1766 he appears to have attended the House of Commons very irregularly but when present to have voted mostly with Grafton and North. In 1781 he resigned his seat in favor of his son Paul Cobb Methuen (*q.v.*). M.P. for Westbury, 1747–48; Warwick Borough, 1762–74; Great Bedwin, 1774–81.

Methuen, Paul Cobb. 1752–1816

Of Corsham Court, near Chippenham, Wiltshire; oldest son of Paul Methuen (*q.v.*). Oxford from 1769. He was a country gentleman with a large inherited income, and was regarded as politically "very independent." Like his father he attended the House of Commons "but little," and he left few recorded votes and no recorded speeches. He apparently supported the North ministry through 1781, but he was absent from 4 of the 5 crucial divisions recorded in February and March, 1782. He voted against Rous's no-confidence motion of March 15, 1782, however. He was sheriff of Wiltshire, 1780–81, and did not stand for re-election to Parliament in 1784. M.P. for Great Bedwin, 1781–84.

Mexborough, 1st Earl. See John Savile. 1719–78

Meynell, Hugo. 1735–1808

Of Bradley, near Ashbourne, Derbyshire; son of Littleton Pointz Meynell (M.P.; a successful gambler). He was sheriff of Derbyshire, 1758–59, and master of the royal staghounds, 1770–76. In politics he followed the lead of his friend the Duke of Grafton. He voted against Bute's peace preliminaries in December, 1762. He supported Newcastle and the Rockingham ministry, 1765–66; Chatham and Grafton, 1767–70; and then the North ministry until Grafton resigned from it, when he followed Grafton into opposition. He voted against approving the address from the throne in October, 1775, and for the Dunning resolution of April 6, 1780. He was a gambling and racing man, the founder of the Quorn Hunt, and was considered the finest foxhunter in England. M.P. for Lichfield, 1762–68; Lymington, 1769–74; Stafford Borough, 1774–80.

Meyrick, Owen. ca.1705–70

Of Bodorgan, near Holyhead, Anglesey; son of Owen Meyrick (of Bodorgan; M.P.). Westminster, 1721–24; Cambridge from 1724. In 1745 he married Hester, daughter of John Putland of London. During his 8 years in the House of Commons no vote or speech appears in the surviving records. He did not vote against Bute's peace terms in 1762, did not vote against repeal of the Stamp Act in 1766, and did not vote against Chatham's land tax in 1767. M.P. for Anglesey, 1761–70.

Michel, David Robert. ca.1736–1805

Of Dewlish, near Dorchester, Dorset; son of John Michel (of Kingston Russell, near Dorchester). Oxford from 1753. In the House of Commons for 4 years from 1780, he supported the North ministry in every recorded crucial division during its final months and voted against Shelburne's peace terms in 1783. He left no record of any speech in the House of Commons, and did not seek re-election. M.P. for Lyme Regis, 1780–84.

Michell, John. 1710–66

Of Boston, Lincolnshire; 2d son of Simon Michell (M.P.). Charterhouse; Cambridge, 1727–30; Lincoln's Inn from 1727. He became a wine merchant in Boston; was mayor of Boston, 1744, 1755; recorder of Boston, 1759. In 1754 he was an avowed Tory, and in 1761 he was listed as Tory by Bute. There is no indication that he ever addressed the House of Commons. M.P. for Boston, 1741–54 and 1761–66.

Middlesex, Lord. See **Charles Sackville**

Middleton, Charles. 1726–1813

Of Teston and Barham Court, near Maidstone, Kent; 2d son of Robert Middleton (collector of customs at Linlithgow, Scotland); created baronet in 1781; created Baron Barham in 1805. He entered the navy in 1741 and became lieutenant in 1745 and captain in 1758. He gave distinguished service in the West Indies from 1761. He was comptroller of the navy, 1778–90; rear admiral from 1787; vice admiral in 1793; and admiral in 1795. He was a highly competent and influential member of the Admiralty Board from 1794; first lord of the admiralty, 1805–1806; privy councillor from 1805; and elder brother of Trinity

House, 1781–1813. He was an important figure in the development of the navy and in its historiography. In politics he was considered a Tory, and warmly supported Sandwich while he was in office. M.P. for Rochester, 1784–90.

Middleton, 4th Baron. See **Thomas Willoughby**

Middleton, William. 1738–95

Of Belsay Castle, near Morpeth, Northumberland; in 1768 succeeded his father, Sir John Lambert Middleton (1705–68; merchant), as 5th baronet. He was cornet of horse in 1756 and lieutenant in the horse guards in 1759 at Minden, where he lost a leg. He was made captain in 1762; in 1774 he retired from active military service and won election to the House of Commons as an independent, at great expense, against a candidate supported by the Duke of Northumberland. "He did not attend much," but when present he opposed the North ministry's continuation of the American war after 1778. He voted for Dunning's first resolution in April, 1780, and against the North ministry in all 5 of the crucial divisions recorded in February and March, 1782. He voted for Shelburne's peace terms in 1783 and from 1784 opposed the Pitt ministry. M.P. for Northumberland, 1774–95.

Midleton, 3d and **4th Viscounts.** See **George Brodrick.** 1730–65 and **George Brodrick.** 1754–1836

Milbanke, Mark. ca.1725–1805

3d son of Sir Ralph Milbanke (ca.1688–1748; of Halnaby Hall, near Darlington, Yorkshire; 4th baronet; sometime sheriff of Yorkshire); younger brother of Ralph Milbanke (*q.v.*). He was descended from an old Northumberland family of standing. He entered the navy as a student at Portsmouth in 1737 and became lieutenant in 1744. He commanded the *Serpent* in 1746, was commissioner to Morocco in 1759, was rear admiral and a member of the court-martial for Keppel in 1779, and was vice admiral in 1780. He was port admiral for Plymouth, 1783–86; in command of the Newfoundland station, 1790–92; admiral in 1793; and in command at Portsmouth, 1799–1803.

Milbanke, Ralph. 1722–98

Of Halnaby Hall, near Darlington, Yorkshire; in 1748 succeeded his father, Sir Ralph Milbanke (ca.1688–1748; of Halnaby Hall, 4th baronet; sometime sheriff of Yorkshire), as 5th baronet; brother of Mark Milbanke (*q.v.*). Westminster from 1733. In 1748 he married Elizabeth, daughter of John Hedworth (1683–1747; M.P.). He was sheriff of Yorkshire, 1753–54. Connected with Robert D'Arcy (*q.v.*), he supported each administration, 1761–68, in apparent silence in the House, and did not seek re-election in 1768. M.P. for Scarborough, 1754–61; Richmond, 1761–68.

Milford, 1st Baron. See **Richard Philipps** (or **Phillips**)

Mill, Richard. 1717–70

Of Montisford and Newton Berry, Hampshire; in 1760 succeeded his father, Sir Richard Mill (1690–1760), as 6th baronet. He was descended from "an old Whig family, possessed of a very noble property." Oxford from 1735; M.A., 1738. He was classed by Newcastle as "country gentleman, doubtful," and no vote or speech by him in the House of Commons is recorded. M.P. for Southampton, 1765–68.

Millar, Andrew. 1707–68

Born in Scotland. By 1729 he had become a leading bookseller in the Strand, London. He soon took up book publishing as well. He shared in the financing and the printing of Samuel Johnson's dictionary and published Thomson's *Seasons*, Fielding's *Tom Jones*, and the histories of Hume and Robertson. In 1767 he resigned his business to Thomas Cadell the elder and retired to Kew Green.

Miller, John.

Printer of the *London Evening Post*. In 1771 he was summoned before the bar of the House of Commons to answer for having printed a full report of debates in the House, against its standing order.

Miller, Thomas. 1717–89

Of Glenlee, near New Galloway, Kirkcudbright, and Barskimming, near Mauchline, Ayrshire; son of William Miller (writer to the signet in Edinburgh); created baronet in 1788. Glasgow University from 1730, Edinburgh University from 1738. He was collector of excise for Scotland, 1755–59; solicitor general for Scotland, 1759–60;

lord advocate for Scotland, 1760–66; lord justice of Scotland, with the title of Lord Glenlee, 1766–87; and lord president of the Scottish Court of Sessions, 1787–89. He was also rector of Glasgow University, 1762–64. In the House of Commons he supported George Grenville from 1762 but avoided involvement and debate on the issues of Wilkes and general warrants, 1763–64. In 1766 he voted against repeal of the Stamp Act and then left Parliament for his legal appointment. M.P. for Dumfries burghs, 1761–66.

Miller, Thomas. ca.1731–1816

Of Lavant, near Chichester, Sussex; in 1772 succeeded his father, John Miller (of Lavant), as 5th baronet. Cambridge from 1753. In Parliament he steadily opposed the North ministry from 1774, voting against approval of the address from the throne in October, 1775, and for the Dunning resolution of April 6, 1780. Apparently he never addressed the House of Commons. M.P. for Lewes, 1774–80; Portsmouth, 1806–16.

Miller, William. 1755–1846

Of Glenlee, near New Galloway, Kirkcudbright, and Barskimming, near Mauchline, Ayrshire; in 1789 succeeded his father, Sir Thomas Miller (1717–89) (*q.v.*), as 2d baronet. He attended Edinburgh University and became Scots advocate in 1777. In the House of Commons he followed the politics of his father and the interests of the Duke of Queensberry, contesting a seat against Sir Lawrence Dundas and supporting the North ministry during his year in the House. In his only recorded speech there he defended the ministry's appointment of Palliser to Greenwich Hospital. He was chief clerk of the judiciary in Scotland from 1783 and, as Lord Glenlee, like his father, lord of sessions in Scotland, 1795–1840. M.P. for Edinburgh Burgh, 1780–81.

Milles, Richard. ca.1735–1820

Of Nackington, near Canterbury, Kent; oldest son of Christopher Milles (of Nackington). Westminster, 1749–52; Cambridge from 1753; Lincoln's Inn from 1753. In 1765 he married Elizabeth, daughter of Rev. Thomas Tanner (prebendary of Canterbury). When elected to the House of Commons in 1761, he was listed as a Tory country gentleman of large estate. He supported Newcastle, 1761–62, and opposed the Grenville ministry, 1763–65. Belying his reputation as a Tory, he then supported the Rockingham ministry, 1765–66, and opposed the Grafton-Chatham ministry, 1767–70. He voted against unseating Wilkes in January, 1770, and voted for Dunning's first resolution of April, 1780. The records show only 2 addresses to the House of Commons. M.P. for Canterbury, 1761–80.

Milner, William. ca.1725–74

Of Nun Appleton Hall, near Cawood, Yorkshire; in 1745 succeeded his father, William Milner (ca.1696–1745; M.P.), as 2d baronet. In 1747 he married a granddaughter of John Mordaunt (1627–75; 1st Viscount Mordaunt). In 1745 he subscribed £100 to the defense of Yorkshire against the Jacobites. He was sheriff of Yorkshire, 1747–48, and receiver general of excise at £2,500 a year from 1748.

Milsington, Viscount. See Charles Colyear

Milton, 1st and 2d Barons. See Joseph Damer and **John Damer. 1744–76**

Milton, Lord. See Andrew Fletcher

Milton, Viscount. See William Wentworth Fitzwilliam

Minchin, Humphrey. ca.1728–96

Of Soberton, near Bishop's Waltham, Hampshire; oldest son of Paul Minchin (of Billinakill, County Queens, Ireland). Trinity College, Dublin, from 1742. In the House of Commons from 1778, he voted for the Dunning resolution of April 6, 1780. In his only recorded speech in the House, on March 25, 1781, he discussed at length the mismanagement of the navy and moved an inquiry into government expenditures at the dockyards—a motion defeated, 147–45, in a half-empty House. In February and March, 1782, he voted against the North ministry in all 5 of the crucial divisions of which voting records are available. In June, 1782, after North's fall and the installation of the Rockingham-Shelburne ministry, he spoke opposing Lord Mahon's bill for preventing bribery at elections, as "disenfranchising" many voters, who, he said, could not travel to the polls unless their expenses were paid. In February, 1783, he voted against Shelburne's peace terms; in March, 1783, he urged a more open presentation of government accounts; in

May, 1783, he opposed the Custom House Reform Bill; in June, 1783, he voted against Pitt's bill to reform representation in Parliament, and in December, 1783, he voted for Fox's India Bill. He supported the coalition on every major issue. He was clerk of ordnance in 1783. M.P. for Okehampton, 1778–90; Bossiney, 1790–96.

Minto, 1st Earl. See **Gilbert Elliot.** 1751–1814

Mitchell, Andrew. 1708–71

Of Westshore, Shetland, and Thainstone, near Kintore, Aberdeenshire; only son of Rev. William John Mitchell (king's chaplain), whom he succeeded in 1739 as 2d baronet; grandson of Sir Hugh Cunningham (lord provost of Edinburgh). He attended Edinburgh University and then Leyden and Paris universities, and traveled in Italy, 1729–34. He was enrolled at Inner Temple from 1734 and became barrister in 1738. He was undersecretary of state for Scotland, 1742–46; commercial commissioner to Brussels, 1752–55; envoy to Frederick of Prussia, 1756–65 and 1765–71; and Knight of the Bath in 1765. He became a firm friend of Newcastle and supported Newcastle and then Rockingham in the House of Commons, voting to repeal the Stamp Act in 1766. He died in Berlin during his mission there. M.P. for Aberdeenshire, 1747–54; Elgin burghs, 1755–71.

Mitford, William. 1744–1827

Of Beaulieu, near Exbury, Hampshire; in 1761 succeeded his father, John Mitford (barrister), as 5th baronet; brother of John Freeman Mitford (1748–1830; a judge in Wales from 1789; M.P.; later solicitor general; 1st Baron Redesdale in 1802); cousin of the 1st Duke of Northumberland. Cheam School, to Oxford in 1761, Middle Temple from 1763. He was colonel of the South Hampshire militia, a Greek scholar, and a friend of Gibbon. He published his *History of Greece*, 1784–1810, a literary and historical landmark and almost a classic. He also published miscellaneous works. In the House of Commons he sat in the interest of the Duke of Northumberland. M.P. for Newport (Cornwall), 1785–90; Berealston, 1796–1806; New Romney, 1812–18.

Moira, 2d Earl. See **Francis Rawdon-Hastings**

Molesworth, John. 1729–75

Of Pencarrow, near Bude Haven, Cornwall; in 1766 succeeded his father, John Molesworth (1705–66; M.P.), as 5th baronet; father of Sir William Molesworth (1758–98, M.P.). Oxford from 1749. He became a colonel in the Cornwall militia and a member of the House of Commons for Cornwall. He signed the 1769 Cornwall petition against the Grafton ministry for its measures in the Wilkes case and was generally in opposition to the North ministry. He voted against approving the address from the throne in October, 1775. M.P. for Cornwall, 1765–75.

Molyneux, Charles Richard William. 1748–95

Of Croxteth Hall, near Prescot, Lancashire; only son of Hon. Thomas Joseph Molyneux (of Croxteth Hall); in 1759 succeeded his uncle William Molyneux as 8th Viscount Molyneux (Irish); in 1771 created Earl of Sefton (Irish). He was educated at St. Omer and Oxford. In 1768 he married Isabella, daughter of William Stanhope (1719–79) (*q.v.*). He was born a Roman Catholic, but in 1769 conformed to the Church of England. He was attached to the Duke of Grafton in politics and supported the North ministry, as Grafton did, through 1774, when he left the House of Commons with no record of ever having addressed it. M.P. for Lancashire, 1771–74.

Molyneux, Crisp. 1730–92

Of Thundersley Hall, near Rayleigh, Essex, and Garboldisham Hall, near Thetford, Norfolk; son of Charles Molyneux (of St. Kitts). He was born in St. Kitts. Cambridge from 1748, Inner Temple from 1749. He returned to the West Indies but in 1754 was back in London with an "ample" fortune. He was high sheriff of Norfolk, 1767–68, and was elected to the House of Commons in 1771. In that year he supported Wilkes, and did so again in 1774; all his recorded votes were against the North ministry. He voted against approving the address from the throne in October, 1775, for Dunning's first resolution in April, 1780, and against the North ministry in 3 crucial divisions recorded in February and March, 1782. After 1784 he sometimes supported Pitt, but his attendance became increasingly irregular. He returned to St. Kitts and died there. M.P. for Castle Rising, 1771–74; Lynn, 1774–90.

Molyneux, Francis. ca.1736–1812

Of Wellow, near Tuxford, Nottinghamshire; in 1781 succeeded his father, Sir William Molyneux, as 7th baronet. He was gentleman usher of the black rod from 1765. He was knighted in 1765. In 1793 he was made D.C.L. of Oxford.

Molyneux, Thomas More. ca.1724–76

Of Loseley Park, near Guildford, Surrey; son of Sir More Molyneux. Oxford from 1742. He entered the army as ensign in 1747, was lieutenant in 1751, and captain in 1753. He served in Germany during the Seven Years' War, and was made colonel in 1761. He entered the House of Commons as a country gentleman, supported Bute and then Grenville, and voted against repeal of the Stamp Act in 1766. He supported the North ministry in general until his death, but there is no evidence that he ever addressed the House. M.P. for Haslemere, 1759–76.

Monboddo, Lord. See James Burnet (or Burnett)

Monckton, Edward. 1744–1832

Of Somerford Hall, near Wolverhampton, Staffordshire; 5th surviving son of John Monckton (ca.1695–1751; 1st Viscount Galway, Irish); grandson of John Manners (2d Duke of Rutland); younger half brother of William Monckton-Arundell (*q.v.*) and Robert Monckton (*q.v.*); uncle of Henry William Monckton-Arundell (*q.v.*) and Robert Monckton-Arundell (*q.v.*). In 1776 he married Sophia, an illegitimate daughter of George Pigot (*q.v.*). He joined the East India Company and was in Madras, 1762–78. He returned to England, and in the House of Commons he voted steadily against the North ministry from 1780 and supported Charles Fox. He voted against Shelburne's peace terms in February, 1783, for Fox's India Bill in November, 1783, and regularly against Pitt from 1784. There is no evidence that before 1790 he ever addressed the House. M.P. for Stafford Borough, 1780–1812.

Monckton, Robert. 1726–82

2d surviving son of John Monckton (1st Viscount Galway, Irish); grandson of John Manners (2d Duke of Rutland); brother of William Monckton-Arundell (*q.v.*) and Edward Monckton (*q.v.*); uncle of Henry William Monckton-Arundell (*q.v.*) and Robert Monckton-Arundell (*q.v.*). Westminster from 1737. He entered the army as ensign in 1741. He served in Flanders from 1742 and was captain in 1744, major in 1747, lieutenant colonel in 1751, colonel in 1757, major general in 1761, lieutenant general in 1770. He was sent to Nova Scotia in 1752, was governor of Annapolis and lieutenant governor of Nova Scotia, 1755–61, and was second-in-command under Wolfe at Quebec, where he was wounded in 1759. He was governor of New York in 1761, commanded at Martinique in 1762, and returned to England in 1763. There he served as governor of Berwick-on-Tweed, 1765–68. He was again on foreign service with Rodney in the West Indies in 1770. He was governor of Portsmouth, 1778–82. Meanwhile his nonmilitary life had been not uneventful. He had speculated heavily in stock of the East India Company with Macleane, 1767–68, and had lost heavily. To redeem his finances, the company had offered him command of its forces in India in 1773, but he had declined to interrupt his regular army career. In politics he voted, apparently without speechmaking, with the current ministry. He voted against the Dunning resolution of April 6, 1780, but was ill and absent from the House of Commons during the votes crucial to the North ministry, during February and March, 1782. In politics he was, according to John Watts, "impartial and independent," and according to Namier, he was "the best type of English officer . . . just and moderate in his American dealings." M.P. for Pontrefact, 1751–54 and 1774; Portsmouth, 1778–82.

Monckton-Arundell, Henry William. 1749–74

In 1772 succeeded his father, William Monckton-Arundell (*q.v.*), as 3d Viscount Galway (Irish); nephew of Robert Monckton (*q.v.*); brother of Robert Monckton-Arundell (*q.v.*), who succeeded him as 4th Viscount Galway in 1774. Eton, 1760–66. He entered the House of Commons in 1772 but died in 1774 at the age of 24. There is no evidence that he ever addressed the House, and his only recorded vote was against continuation of the Grenville Disputed Elections Act in 1774. M.P. for Pontrefact, 1772–74.

Monckton-Arundell, Robert. 1752–1810

Younger son of William Monckton-Arundell (*q.v.*); in 1774 succeeded his brother Henry William Monckton-Arundell (*q.v.*) as 4th Viscount Galway; nephew of Edward Monckton (*q.v.*) and Robert Monckton (*q.v.*). He was regarded as Tory, and voted with the North ministry from 1780 until its fall in March, 1782. He supported Shelburne and Fox in their proposals for reform of Parliament in 1782, opposed the coalition, voted against Fox's India Bill in 1783, and supported Pitt from 1784 until 1788, when he opposed Pitt's Regency Bill. He was comptroller of the king's household, 1784–87; privy councillor from 1784; and Knight of the Bath from 1786. Wraxall said that he was generally drunk when he addressed the House of Commons, and Eden reported from The Hague in 1792 that while in Holland he was continually drunk and that "his understanding (such as it was) is quite gone." M.P. for Pontrefact, 1780–83; York City, 1783–90; Pontrefact, 1796–1802.

Monckton-Arundell, William. 1725–72

In 1751 succeeded his father, John Monckton, as 2d Viscount Galway (Irish); brother of Robert Monckton (*q.v.*) and Edward Monckton (*q.v.*); father of Henry William Monckton-Arundell (*q.v.*) and Robert Monckton-Arundell (*q.v.*); added the surname Arundell (which was maintained by his sons) upon inheriting from an aunt, Lady Frances Arundell, in 1769. Westminster, 1737–47; Cambridge. He was receiver general of crown rents for Yorkshire and County Durham in 1748 and was master of the royal staghounds, 1765–70. In Parliament he supported Pelham and then Newcastle until 1762. He voted against the Grenville ministry on general warrants in 1764 and with the Grafton-Chatham ministry on the land tax in 1767. He voted for a Wilkes petition in 1769 and usually against the North ministry until his death. There is no evidence that he ever formally addressed the House of Commons. M.P. for Pontrefact, 1747–48; Thirsk, 1749–54; Pontrefact, 1754–72.

Moncrieff, James. 1744–93

Son of James Moncrieff (of Sauchop, Fifeshire). He entered the Royal Military Academy at Woolwich in 1759 and served as a military engineer at Havana and elsewhere in the West Indies. He was ensign in 1762, lieutenant in 1770, and captain in 1776. He distinguished himself at Savannah in 1779 and Charleston in 1780, when he was made lieutenant colonel. He was quartermaster general to the allies in the Netherlands, and chief engineer at Valenciennes in 1793. He was fatally wounded at Dunkirk, and buried at Ostend. He never married.

Moneagle, 1st Baron. See **John Browne**

Money, John. ca.1752–1817

Of parentage now obscure, he apparently entered the army at the age of 10 in 1762 and became cornet of horse shortly thereafter, captain in 1770, colonel in 1795, major general in 1798, lieutenant general in 1805, and general in 1814. (Since he is also reported in *DNB* and elsewhere to have begun his military career with the Norfolk militia, his birth date of 1752 is to be questioned.) He was with Burgoyne in 1777, and was made prisoner of war at Saratoga. Later exchanged, he fought with the Dutch against the Austrians in 1792. One of the first British aeronauts, he made 2 balloon ascents in 1785 and in 1803 published *A Treatise on the Use of Balloons*. He also wrote and published *A History of the Campaign of 1792*.

Monson, George. 1730–76

3d son of John Monson (1693–1748; 1st Baron Monson); grandson of Lewis Watson (1st Earl of Rockingham). Westminster School from 1738; grand tour, 1747–49. In 1757 he married Anne, daughter of Henry Vane (d. 1758; 1st Earl of Darlington). He entered the army as ensign of foot guards in 1750 and was captain in 1752, major in 1757, colonel in 1761, brigadier general in 1763. He was groom of the bedchamber to the Prince of Wales, 1756–60, and to the king, 1760–63. He served in India from 1758, and distinguished himself at Pondichéry in 1760 and at Manila in 1762. He returned to England in 1764 and was aide to the king in 1769. In 1773 he accepted an appointment, sponsored by North, as a member of the new Supreme Council of Bengal. There he joined in the bitter campaign against Warren Hastings. In the House of Commons, when present, he supported Newcastle and Rockingham. Though not a member of Parliament during the North ministry, he appears to have been in general support of it. M.P. for Lincoln City, 1754–68.

Montagu, Lord. See **John Hussey-Montagu**

Montagu, Charles Greville. 1741–84

2d son of Robert Montagu (3d Duke of Manchester); younger brother of George Montagu (1737–88) (*q.v.*). Oxford from 1759. He was made major general, and governor of South Carolina, 1765–73. On his return to England he was made Knight of the Bath. In 1780 and 1782 he raised troops for the American and French wars. He was given land rights in Nova Scotia, and in 1783 he went there with members of his provincial troops to establish a new colony, but died there the following year. In the House of Commons for 3 years, he voted against Grenville and general warrants in 1764 and then supported Rockingham. M.P. for Huntingdonshire, 1762–65.

Montagu, Edward. 1692–1775

Of Sandleford, near Newbury, Berkshire, and Allerthorpe, near Pocklington, Yorkshire; oldest son of Hon. Charles Montagu (d. 1759; M.P.); grandson of Edward Montagu (1625–1672; 1st Earl of Sandwich); cousin of Edward Wortley Montagu (*q.v.*). Eton from 1706, Cambridge from 1710, Lincoln's Inn from 1710. In 1742 he married Elizabeth, daughter of Matthew Robinson, who became in her own right a distinguished social, literary, and epistolary figure. He inherited rich coal mines from a cousin. In the House of Commons, which he attended only irregularly, he was considered a Tory, and was so listed by Bute in 1761. In 1767 he voted to reduce the land tax (i.e., against the Grafton-Chatham ministry) and in 1768 declined to stand for re-election. He was a good mathematician and agricultural scientist. M.P. for Huntingdon Borough, 1734–68.

Montagu, Edward (Hussey). See John Edward Hussey-Montagu

Montagu, Edward Wortley. 1713–76

Of Borehamwoods, near St. Albans, Hertfordshire; only son of Edward Wortley Montagu (1678–1761; M.P.) and Lady Mary Wortley Montagu (1689–1762; neé Pierrepont). He attended Westminster School intermittently, but ran away from it several times; he then traveled extensively in Italy, Egypt, and the Near East and studied briefly at Leyden in 1741. He married Sally, "an industrious washerwoman." He indulged in a brief military career, which ended in his resignation as captain-lieutenant in 1748, after having served as secretary to the Congress of Aix-la-Chapelle. In 1764 he eloped with the wife of a Danish consul on the Continent and concurrently became a Roman Catholic. Later, "smitten by a beautiful Arabian," he embraced her and Mohammedanism together. During these amatory and religious ubiquities he was also engaged lightly in politics and a little more seriously in historiography. In politics he was originally sponsored by his cousin the Earl of Sandwich, and after 1761 was considered a member of the Bedford junto, but he had little interest or influence in political affairs. In 1758 he revealed his only creative intellectual interest, publishing *Reflections on the Rise and Fall of Ancient Republics*, a work whose merits appear to have been transitory. He died in Padua. M.P. for Huntingdonshire, 1747–54; Bossiney, 1754–68.

Montagu, Elizabeth (neé Robinson). 1720–1800

Born at York, the older daughter of Matthew Robinson (1694–1778; of West Layton, near Richmond, Yorkshire; rich and well connected); sister of Matthew Robinson (1713–1800; 2d Baron Rokeby). In 1742 she married Edward Montagu (1692–1775) (*q.v.*). By 1750 she had made their London house a center of conversational cultivation and fashionable intellectual pretensions, and was becoming known as "the Madame du Deffand of London"—a reputation which by no means displeased her. She was not without talent, though in some London circles her status as an intellectual was perhaps enhanced by her inheritance of large estates from her husband in 1775 and by her enthusiastic hospitality at the handsome Sandleford Priory near Newbury, which she built in 1781. In 1791 she entertained the king and queen in her own town house in Portman Square. In 1769 she published an attack on Voltaire, and she contributed to Lyttelton's *Dialogues of the Dead*. Four volumes of her excellent letters were published, 1809–13. Portrait by Reynolds.

Montagu, Frederick. 1733–1800

Of Popplewick, Nottinghamshire; only surviving son of Charles Montagu (d. 1759; of Popplewick; M.P.); nephew of George Montagu Dunk (*q.v.*) and through him a cousin of Francis North (*q.v.*) and of his son Frederick North (*q.v.*). He was also on intimate family terms with William Legge (*q.v.*) and exchanged many delightful letters with Mary Delany (neé Granville) (*q.v.*). Eton, 1742–48; Cambridge from 1751; Lincoln's Inn from 1751; barrister in 1757; bencher from 1782. On friendly terms with Newcastle, he became a loyal Rockingham New Whig "of distinguished probity," as Wraxall rightly put it. He opposed the North ministry and the American war with polite firmness; voted against the expulsion of Wilkes in January, 1770; voted against approving the address from the throne in November, 1774, and again in October, 1775; and voted for the Dunning resolution of April 6, 1780. He helped George Grenville frame his Disputed Elections Act, which was renewed in 1774. In 1780, despite the difference in party and measures, he was Lord North's first choice to succeed Sir Fletcher Norton as speaker in the House of Commons, partly because North liked and trusted him personally, partly because most other men did, and partly because the choice might mollify the increasingly dangerous opposition. Montagu, despite much urging, declined to be a candidate for the speakership, and Cornwall was chosen. He did, however, act for North in the endeavors to form a coalition cabinet in the last years of the North ministry, but he also voted against North in all 5 of the crucial divisions recorded in February and March, 1782. He was a member of the Treasury Board with Rockingham in 1782; opposed Shelburne's ministry and voted against his peace terms in February, 1783; supported the coalition and served on its Treasury Board; and opposed Pitt in 1784. He helped prepare the articles of impeachment advanced against Warren Hastings in 1787. He was privy councillor in 1790 but retired that year from public life. He was a fellow of the Royal Society from 1792. M.P. for Northampton Borough, 1759–68; Higham Ferrers, 1768–90.

Montagu, George. 1712–90

Born George Brudenell, in 1732 he succeeded his father, George Brudenell, as 4th Earl of Cardigan; on the death of his father-in-law in 1749 he added the surname and arms of Montagu and in 1766 became Duke of Montagu of a new creation, derived from his marriage in 1730 to Mary, 3d daughter of John Montagu (ca.1688–1749; 2d Duke of Montagu). Cambridge, 1731–32. He was Knight of the Garter in 1762, governor of the Prince of Wales and master of the king's horse in 1776. He was governor of Windsor Castle, privy councillor, lord lieutenant of Huntingdonshire, and president of the London Hospital and of the Society of Arts. He took very little part in politics, almost invariably supported the court, and usually supported the North ministry.

Montagu, George. See **George Montagu Dunk**

Montagu, George. 1737–88

Styled Viscount Mandeville from 1739; in 1762 succeeded his father, Robert Montagu (ca.1710–62; M.P.), as 4th Duke and 7th Earl of Manchester; brother of Charles Greville Montagu (*q.v.*). Eton, 1747–50; Oxford, 1750–54; D.C.L., 1763; grand tour, 1754–56. In 1762 he married Elizabeth, oldest daughter of Sir James Dashwood (*q.v.*). His connections included the houses of Halifax, Marlborough, Sussex, Suffolk, Leeds, Torrington, Greville, Grenville, and Temple. He entered the army as ensign in 1757, was colonel of militia in 1759 and 1779, and was lord lieutenant of Huntingdonshire, 1762–88. Before entering the peerage he was a member of the House of Commons for Huntingdonshire, 1761–62. He was collector of subsidies for the port of London and a lord of the bedchamber, 1762–70, but resigned his court appointments in 1770 in protest at the dismissal of Charles Pratt (Lord Camden) and became "one of the Lords of the Opposition" to the North ministry, 1770–82, though he made "no great figure in politics," according to the *Peerage* of 1775. He usually supported the Rockingham party and "sided with the colonies." He signed dissenting protests to majority votes in the House of Lords for (1) adjourning the House on January 15, 1770, which he denounced as "uncommon, unreasonable, and neglect of duty," (2) approving measures of the House of Commons against Wilkes in 1770, (3) approving the expulsion of Wilkes in 1770, (4) excluding visitors from the gallery of the House of Lords, which he protested as "limiting free inquiry" and attempting "to hide from the public eye the . . . criminal neglect of the ministry," in 1770, (5) approving North's Falkland Islands settlement in 1771, (6) approving the Massachusetts Justice Bill in 1774, (7) approving the New England Restraint of Trade Bill in 1775, (8) approving the colonial Non-Intercourse Bill in 1775, (9) approving the address from the throne in October, 1775, (10) continuing the Quebec Governing Act in 1775, (11) approving the employment of mercenaries without formal advance consent of Parliament in 1776, (12) continuing the ministry's policy toward the colonies in October, 1776, (13) continuing the war in America in 1778, (14) rejecting a motion to ask the king to dismiss Sandwich in 1778, (15) rejecting a motion to ask the king to effect "a total change of System" in 1779, (16) suspending the rights of sailors in 1779, (17) rejecting a motion to examine into public expenditures in 1780, (18) rejecting a protest against the king's dismissal of Pembroke and Carmarthen from their lord lieutenancies, as "a violation of the Bill of Rights," and (19) rejecting a bill to exclude holders of government contracts from membership in Parliament in 1781. In 1775 he supported Chatham's motion to conciliate the colonies; in 1776 he supported Richmond's motion to make immediate peace with the colonies; in March, 1778, he moved to advise the king that he would be supported only if he removed his incompetent advisers. His liberalism did not extend to easing restrictions on Protestant or Catholic dissenters in 1778, and he opposed the Catholic Relief Bill. After the fall of the North ministry he was privy councillor and lord chamberlain, 1782–83, and ambassador to Paris to make peace in 1783. He supported the coalition and opposed Pitt's commercial treaties in 1786. He was grand master of English Freemasons, 1777–82. He was dignified, affable, and consistent, but Wraxall thought that "neither his abilities nor his fortune corresponded with his figure, which was distinguished." M.P. for Huntingdonshire, 1761–62.

Montagu, James. 1752–94

3d son of John Montagu (1719–95) (*q.v.*); brother of Admiral George Montagu (1750–1829) and of Edward Montagu (1755–99). He was a lieutenant in the navy in 1771 and a commander in 1773. He served at the capture of Rhode Island and was in American and West Indian waters and in the Channel until 1782. He was killed in an engagement with the French off Ushant in 1794, and appears to have taken no part in politics.

Montagu, John. 1718–92

Oldest son of Edward Richard Montagu (d. 1722; Viscount Hinchingbroke); styled Viscount Hinchingbroke from 1722; in 1729 he succeeded hs grandfather Edward Montagu (1670–1729) as 4th Earl of Sandwich. Eton, 1728–32; Cambridge from 1735; grand tour, 1737–39. In 1740 he married Dorothy Fane (sister of 1st Earl of Stanhope). He became a fellow of the Royal Society in 1740, colonel in 1745, major general in 1755, lieutenant general in 1759, and general in 1772. He served on the Admiralty Board, 1744–48, as a plenipotentiary for peace at Breda in 1746, and at Aix-la-Chapelle in 1748. He was first lord of the admiralty, 1748–51 and April 23–September 10, 1763. He was secretary of state, northern department, September 10, 1763–July 12, 1765. He was also joint vice treasurer of Ireland, 1755–63. In the House of Lords he recorded dissent from the vote approving repeal of the Stamp Act in 1766 and from the decision in the Douglas-Hamilton case, "because it is proved that the appellant is not the son of Lady Jane Douglas," in 1769. His attack on his former crony John Wilkes in 1768 led to his permanent acquisition of the sobriquet "Jemmy Twitcher," from the character in *The Beggar's Opera*. He was postmaster general in 1768; again secretary of state, northern department, 1770–71; and again first lord of the admiralty, January 12, 1771–March 30, 1782. Both a "gastronomic atrocity" and the Sandwich Islands were named for him. He was involved and influential in the affairs of the East India Company, but there is no evidence that in them he worked adversely to the ends sought by Lord North. He was intensely loyal to the king, and, although sometimes openly critical of North, he supported him, and was supported by him, throughout the long ministry and during the coalition of 1783. Criticisms (only partly justified) of his management of naval affairs nearly led to a vote of censure in both houses of Parliament and made him a crucial figure in the party struggles of 1779–82. He defended himself with dignity and was personally and socially popular even among many of his most bitter political critics. Boswell thought him in 1762 "a jolly, hearty, lively man." Horace Walpole, a bitter political opponent, nevertheless did him rough justice in his summation: "His industry to carry any point he had in view was so remarkable, that for a long time the world mistook his abilities; but as his manner was awkward and unpolished, so his talents were but slight, when it was necessary to exert them in any higher light than in art and intrigue . . . his passion for maritime affairs, his activity, industry and flowing complaisance, endeared him to the profession, re-established the marine, and effaced a great part of his unpopularity. No man in the Administration was so much a master of business, so quick and so shrewd, and no man had so many public enemies who had so few private; for though void of principles, he was void of rancour, and bore with equal good humour the freedom with which his friends attacked him, and the satire of his opponents." Portraits by Gainsborough and Zoffany.

615

Montagu, John. 1719–95

Of Fareham, Hampshire; son of James Montagu (d. 1747; of Lackham House, near Chippenham, Wiltshire); cousin of John Montagu (1718–92) (*q.v.*). He attended Portsmouth Naval Academy from 1733. He was lieutenant in 1741, rear admiral in 1770. He was in command in American waters, 1771–74; governor, naval commander at Newfoundland and vice admiral in 1776; admiral in 1782; and in command at Portsmouth, 1783–86. In the House of Commons he voted with the court. M.P. for Huntingdon Borough, 1748–54.

Montagu, John. 1743–1814

Styled Viscount Hinchingbroke until 1792, when he succeeded his father, John Montagu (1718–92) (*q.v.*), as 5th Earl of Sandwich. Eton, 1753–58. He married (1) in 1766 Elizabeth, daughter of George Montagu (2d Earl of Halifax), and (2) in 1772 Mary, daughter of Harry Powlett (*q.v.*). He was cornet of horse in 1759, captain in 1761, and retired from military service in 1767. He was vice chamberlain to the king and privy councillor, 1771–82; master of the royal buckhounds, 1783–1806; and joint paymaster general, 1807–14. While in the House of Commons, 1765–92, he supported his father, voting with the North ministry, 1770–82, and against the Dunning resolution of April 6, 1780. He voted against Shelburne's peace terms, supported the coalition, and voted for Fox's India Bill in 1783, but after 1784 he often voted with Pitt. He was not an influential figure and in his later years was deeply in debt. If he lacked his father's pleasant vices, he also lacked his father's durable virtues. M.P. for Brackley, 1765–68; Huntingdonshire, 1768–92.

Montagu (Hussey), John. See **John Hussey-Montagu**

Montagu, William Augustus. 1752–76

2d surviving son of John Montagu (1718–92) (*q.v.*); brother of John Montagu (1743–1814) (*q.v.*). Eton from 1759, Cambridge from 1768; Lincoln's Inn from 1768. In his 2 years in the House of Commons he made no recorded vote or speech, but he was surely a supporter of his father and of the North ministry. He was a favorite of his father, to whom his death at Lisbon at the age of 23 was a hard blow. M.P. for Huntingdon Borough, 1774–76.

Montagu (Dunk), George. See **George Montagu Dunk**

Montagu of Boughton, 1st Baron. See **John Montagu Brudenell**

Montgomerie, Alexander. 1723–69

4th but oldest surviving son of Alexander Montgomerie (ca.1660–1729; 9th Earl of Eglintoun, Scottish); older brother of Archibald Montgomerie (*q.v.*); in 1729 succeeded his father as 10th Earl of Eglintoun. He was schooled in Scotland, at Westminster from 1738, and at Paris from 1742. He was sheriff of Renfrewshire in 1748; grand master of Scottish Freemasons, 1750–51; governor of Dumbarton Castle, 1759–61; lord of the bedchamber, 1760–67; and a Scottish representative peer, 1761–69. He was strongly opposed to increases in the public debt and in 1754 published a tract on that subject. He dissented from repeal of the Stamp Act in 1766 and opposed regulation of the dividends and administration of the East India Company, 1767–68. He supported Bute and conservative and Scottish interests but took little active part in national politics. He was able but indolent, a sportsman, a friend of the Duke of York, a prominent member of the Catch Club, and something of a charming rake. Henry Fox (Lord Holland) called him, in what must have been a moment of frustration in some political deal, "a worthless and silly wretch," but the Duchess of Hamilton corroborated to the extent of saying that Eglintoun was always "whistling to himself for want of thought." Boswell, who met him when both were young men, and who received kindness and generosity from him, said of him that he "loved wit more than wine, and men of genius more than sycophants." In 1769 he was shot and killed, probably accidentally, by Mungo Campbell, an excise officer.

Montgomerie, Archibald. 1726–96

Of Minnoch, near Newton Stewart, Ayrshire; 2d surviving son of Alexander Montgomerie (ca.1660–1729; 9th Earl of Eglintoun, Scottish); younger brother of Alexander Montgomerie (*q.v.*), whom he succeeded in 1769 as 11th Earl of Eglintoun. Eton, 1738–41; briefly at Winchester. He then studied in London, 1742–43, and at Geneva, 1743–44. He married (1) in 1772 Jean, oldest daughter of George Lindsay (21st Earl of Crawford and Lindsay, Scottish), and (2) the daughter of Sir William Twisden. He was cornet in the Scots Greys in

1743, captain in 1744, and lieutenant colonel in 1757, when he raised a regiment of highlanders, which he then commanded in America. He was at Fort Duquesne in 1758 and again in the colonies in 1769. He was governor of Dumbarton Castle, 1764–82; equerry to the queen, 1761–69; deputy ranger of Hyde and St. James's Parks, 1766–68; and governor of Edinburgh Castle, 1782–96. He was major general in 1772, lieutenant general in 1777, and general in 1793. In 1788 he divorced his 2d wife for adultery with the Duke of Hamilton. As a member of the House of Commons, 1761–68, and then as a representative Scottish peer, 1776–96, he supported Bute and then Grenville, voting against repeal of the Stamp Act in 1766. He opposed the North ministry but supported the coalition. He was an able, genial, hot-tempered, and hard-drinking man. M.P. for Ayrshire, 1761–68.

Montgomerie (or Montgomery), Hugh. 1739–1819

Of Skelmorlie, near Largs, and Coilsfield Hall, near Tarbolton, Ayrshire; oldest son of Alexander Montgomerie (of Coilsfield); in 1783 succeeded to the estates of his mother's family; in 1796 succeeded his cousin Archibald Montgomerie (*q.v.*) as 12th Earl of Eglintoun, (Scottish); in 1806 created Baron Ardrossan (English). He entered the army as ensign in 1756 and served in the war in America; he was captain in 1772 and colonel in 1782. In the 1790's he raised 2 regiments and commanded one of them. He was a member of the House of Commons almost continuously, 1780–96; a Scottish representative peer, 1798–1806; lord lieutenant of Ayrshire, 1796–1819; and governor of Edinburgh Castle, 1794–96. In the House of Commons he was silent, and few votes or partisan affiliations are indicated. He supported Pitt, 1784–85, but opposed Pitt's Regency Bill in 1788. He rebuilt Eglintoun Castle in 1798 and greatly improved the family estates. He was known as "munificent, patriotic, enterprising." He was made Knight of the Thistle in 1812. M.P. for Ayrshire, 1780–81, 1784–89, and 1796.

Montgomery, James William. 1721–1803

Of The Whin and Stanhope, near Broughton, Peeblesshire; 2d son of William Montgomery (of Peebles; advocate); created baronet in 1801. He studied at Edinburgh University and became Scots advocate in 1743. He was deputy sheriff of Peeblesshire, 1748–60, and joint solicitor general for Scotland, with Francis Gordon, 1760–64. After Gordon was promoted to the bench, Montgomery was solicitor general, 1764–66. He was lord advocate for Scotland, 1766–75, and chief baron of the Scottish exchequer, 1775–1801. In 1767 he secured a crown grant of land in maritime Canada. He was a regular supporter of the current ministry and confined his speeches in the House of Commons largely to Scottish concerns. Boswell spoke favorably of him in his journal in 1774. M.P. for Dumfries burghs, 1766–68; Peeblesshire, 1768–75.

Montgomery, 7th and 8th Earls. See **Henry Herbert.** 1734–94 and **George Augustus Herbert**

Monthermer, Marquess. See **John Montagu Brudenell**

Montresor, James Gabriel. 1702–76

Born at Fort William, Inverness-shire; son of James Gabriel Le Mon Trésor (naturalized French officer; lieutenant governor of Fort William). He was ensign in the British army in 1732, lieutenant in 1737, and military engineer extraordinary in 1742. He was at Port Mahon, 1743–47; chief engineer at Gibraltar, 1747–54; and chief engineer with Braddock in America, 1754–59. He built roads over the Alleghenies in 1755, surveyed Lake Champlain in 1756, and in 1759 designed and constructed Fort George. He superintended the building of new powder magazines at Purfleet, 1763–65, and was chief engineer at Chatham in 1769.

Montrose, 3d Duke. See **James Graham (or Grahame)**

Moore, Charles. 1730–1822

In 1758 succeeded his father, Edward Moore, as 6th Earl of Drogheda (Irish); in 1791 created Marquess of Drogheda (Irish); in 1801 created Baron Moore (English); grandson of 1st Earl of Bessborough (Irish). In 1766 he married Anne, daughter of Francis Seymour Conway (*q.v.*) and granddaughter of the 2d Duke of Grafton. He was cornet of horse in 1744, captain in 1750, lieutenant colonel in 1755, colonel in 1762, major general in 1770, lieutenant general in 1777, general in 1793, and field marshal in 1821. He was a member of the Irish Parliament, 1756–58; governor of County Meath in 1759; secretary to the lord lieutenant of Ireland, 1763–65; lord justice of Ireland in 1766; master general of ordnance for Ireland, 1770–97; joint postmaster general for Ireland, 1797–1806; and constable of Maryborough Castle. As a member of the English House of Commons he was seldom in attendance, and no votes are recorded from him, 1776–79; but he was considered a supporter of the North ministry. He was a Knight of St. Patrick from 1783. "A very eccentric character, passionately fond of play, and subject to great pecuniary embarrassments," according to Raikes's diary. M.P. for Horsham, 1776–80.

Moore, Henry. 1713–69

Born in Vere, Jamaica, the son of Samuel Henry Moore (Jamaica planter); created baronet in 1762. Eton, to Leyden in 1731. He received military training in the militia. He returned to Jamaica and was a member of the council there from 1752 and was its secretary in 1753. As lieutenant governor of Jamaica, 1755–62, and sometimes acting governor, he did his best to allay quarrels between the two houses of the legislature. He was governor of New York Province, 1765–69, and to ease dangerous dissensions suspended enforcement of the Stamp Act. He also tried to settle boundary arguments with Massachusetts. He died in New York.

Moore, John. 1718–79

Of Hersant, Buckinghamshire; 3d son of Rev. Henry Moore (rector of Malpas, near Chester, Cheshire); created baronet in 1766. He entered the navy in 1729 and was lieutenant in 1738 and commander in 1743. In 1747 he distinguished himself in the action with L'Étendière. He commanded at the Leeward Islands station in 1756 and at Martinique and Guadeloupe in 1759. He was made rear admiral in 1762 and put in command of the Downs. He was made Knight of the Bath in 1772 and admiral in 1778.

Moore, John. 1730–1805

Son of Thomas Moore (of Gloucester). Oxford, 1745–51; B.A., 1748; M.A., 1751; took orders; B.D. and D.D., 1763. He tutored the sons of the 2d Duke of Marlborough and was prebendary of Durham in 1761; canon of Christ Church, Oxford, in 1763; dean of Canterbury, 1771–75; bishop of Bangor, 1775–83; and archbishop of Canterbury, 1783–1805. He was "an amiable and worthy prelate, a competent administrator, and a promotor of the Sunday School movement and of missionary enterprise," but he "dispensed his patronage with somewhat more than due regard to the interests of his own family" (*DNB*). In the House of Lords he supported the current ministry. Portrait by Romney.

Morant, Edward. 1730–91

Of Brockenhurst, near Lymington, Hampshire; oldest surviving son of John Morant (Jamaica planter); cousin of Henry Dawkins and Richard Pennant (like himself, former residents of Jamaica; owners of large plantations there; members of the 1761–68 House of Commons in London). Oxford from 1747. He was a member of the Jamaica Assembly, 1752–56, and of the Jamaica Council, 1756–59. Returning again to England, he secured, through the good offices of William Beckford (who also had a fortune derived from the West Indies), a seat in the House of Commons for Hindon. He voted as an independent, and was irregular in attendance, 1761–68. He was again elected in 1774 through the influence of the Duke of Bolton, in the expectation that he would support the North ministry, but he acted in opposition on the Wilkes election issues of 1775 and voted against the North ministry in all 5 of the crucial divisions recorded in February and March, 1782. He supported Shelburne and voted for his peace terms, 1782–83, but also voted for Fox's India Bill in November, 1783. In 1784 he opposed Pitt. M.P. for Hindon, 1761–68; Lymington, 1774–80; Yarmouth (Isle of Wight), 1780–87.

Moray, 8th and **9th Earls.** See **James Stuart.** 1708–67 and **Francis Stuart**

Mordaunt, Charles. ca.1698–1778

Of Walton D'Eiville, near Kineton, Warwickshire, and Massingham Parva, near King's Lynn, Norfolk; in 1721 succeeded his father, Sir John Mordaunt (ca.1650–1721, M.P.), as 6th baronet. Oxford from 1714; Lincoln's Inn from 1718; D.C.L., 1759. In 1730 he married (2) Sophia, daughter of Sir John Wodehouse (4th baronet). He was an avowed Tory in the 1754 elections and was generally in opposition, 1734–61. In December, 1762, he was regarded as a parliamentary leader of the Tories, and supported Bute and then Grenville, voting against repeal of the Stamp Act in 1766. On some issues he supported the Grafton and North ministries, but he apparently never addressed the House of Commons. He did not stand for re-election in 1774. M.P. for Warwickshire, 1734–74.

Mordaunt, Charles. 1708–79

Son of Colonel John Mordaunt (died of smallpox in 1710); styled Viscount Mordaunt from 1710; in 1735 succeeded his grandfather Charles Mordaunt (1658–1735) as 4th Earl of Peterborough. Westminster from 1719, Oxford from 1727. Before 1735 he married Mary, daughter of Thomas Cox (Quaker wholesale grocer of London). He was an Old Whig and supported the Pelhams until 1760 but was thereafter politically inactive. "A whimsical character . . . easy and convivial . . . perhaps uxorious to excess."

Mordaunt, John. 1697–1780

Of Freefolk, near Whitchurch, Hampshire; oldest son of Henry Mordaunt; nephew of Charles Mordaunt (1658–1735; 3d Earl of Peterborough); uncle of Charles Mordaunt (1708–79) (*q.v.*). He entered the army in 1721 and was captain in 1724, colonel in 1741, brigadier general in 1745, major general in 1747, lieutenant general in 1754, and general in 1770. He was Knight of the Bath in 1749; governor of Sheerness, 1752–78; and governor of Berwick Castle, 1778–80. He served in Scotland, 1745–46, and in the Low Countries from 1747. In 1757 he commanded the unsuccessful raid on Rochefort for which he was censured by a military court of inquiry, which included Lord George Sackville (later Germain) (who was himself later more seriously censured), but was afterward fully acquitted by a court-martial. Though he was from an ancient family that was still reputed Tory, in the House of Commons he usually supported the court, though he opposed the Rockingham ministry, speaking and voting against repeal of the Stamp Act in 1766. He declined to stand for re-election in 1768. M.P. for Pontrefact, 1730–34; Whitchurch, 1735–41; Cockermouth, 1741–68.

Mordaunt, Lord. See Alexander Gordon

Morden, 1st Baron. See Charles Yorke

More, Hannah. 1745–1833

Of Stapleton, near Bristol; 4th daughter of Jacob More (Tory schoolmaster of Stapleton). In 1773 she published a pastoral drama entitled *The Search after Happiness,* which (especially since it was written by a young woman) attracted attention, and in Bristol circles she developed a reputation as a literary figure and bluestocking. In 1774 she went to London and was sponsored by Elizabeth Montagu. She developed friendships with Mary Delany, Garrick, Samuel Johnson, Burke, and Reynolds, and was accepted and made much of in cultivated, if not fashionable, society. She published several plays and wrote and published a number of tracts on manners and morals "for the humble." In 1777 her tragedy *Percy* was produced by Garrick. She retired to Somerset about 1789 and there devoted most of her time and remarkable energies to working for the welfare of the miners and their families, for whom she established advanced schools in and near the Mendip Hills. Portrait by Opie.

Morgan (born Gould), Charles. 1726–1806

Of Ealing, Middlesex; oldest son of King Gould (deputy judge advocate general); assumed the surname Morgan upon inheriting through his wife in 1792, and in that year was created baronet. Westminster from 1735; Oxford from 1743; M.A., 1750; D.C.L., 1773; Lincoln's Inn from 1743; barrister in 1750. He was king's counsel from 1754; deputy judge advocate general, ca.1754–69; judge advocate general, 1769–1806; chancellor of Salisbury Cathedral from 1772; knighted in 1779. He supported the North ministry from 1778 and voted with it in all the crucial divisions of February and March, 1782, except that he voted for Conway's second motion February 27, 1782, to end the American war. He voted for Shelburne's peace terms and also for Fox's India Bill in 1783, and became privy councillor in 1802. M.P. for Brecon Borough, 1778–87; Brecknockshire, 1787–1806.

Morgan, Charles. 1736–87

Of Tredegar, Monmouthshire; 2d son of Thomas Morgan (1702–69) (*q.v.*); brother of Thomas Morgan (1727–71) (*q.v.*) and John Morgan (1732–92) (*q.v.*); connected with the Cavendish family. He was lieutenant in the foot guards but did not pursue a military career. "Independent, desirous of peace, a friend of the constitution," he supported Newcastle and then Rockingham, 1763–69. In 1769 he went over to Grafton and then to North. But he remained independent, and in April, 1780, he voted against North in voting for Dunning's first resolution and opposed the North ministry in all the 5 crucial divisions in February and March, 1782. His only recorded address in the House of Commons was made in 1780, when he presented a petition from Brecon urging reform. M.P. for Brecon Borough, 1763–69; Brecknockshire, 1769–87.

Morgan, John. 1710–67

Of Kinnersley, Herefordshire; in 1716 succeeded his father, Sir Thomas Morgan (M.P.), as 4th baronet. Westminster from 1721, Oxford from 1726. He became a director of the South Sea Company. Listed in 1761 as Tory, he supported Bute in 1762, voted against Grenville in 1764, and did not vote with Grenville against repeal of the Stamp Act in 1766. He did vote against the Grafton ministry in voting against Chatham's land tax in 1767, his last year in Parliament. M.P. for Hereford Borough, 1734–41; Herefordshire, 1755–67.

Morgan, John. 1732–92

Of Tredegar, Monmouthshire; 3d son of Thomas Morgan (1702–69) (*q.v.*); brother of Charles Morgan (1736–87) (*q.v.*) and Thomas Morgan (1727–71) (*q.v.*). Politically he was professedly "unconnected," but he often voted in opposition to the North ministry. He voted for the Dunning resolution of April 6, 1780, and for Conway's first motion in February, 1782, to end the American war immediately, but after that vote he supported North in 3 crucial divisions recorded in February and March, 1782. He voted for Shelburne's peace terms in 1783. The records show that the only occasion upon which he addressed the House of Commons was on a local issue. M.P. for Brecon Borough, 1769–71; Monmouthshire, 1771–92.

Morgan (or Morgann), Maurice. 1726–1802

His family origins are obscure. He was a clerk in the office of the secretary of state and became private secretary to Shelburne in 1766. He served in Quebec, 1768–70; was an undersecretary of state in 1782; and was secretary of the peace commission of 1782–83. He also wrote and published essays and was a commentator on Falstaff and other Shakespearean characters.

Morgan, Thomas. 1702–69

Of Tredegar, Monmouthshire, and Ruperra Castle, near Caerphilly, Glamorganshire; 2d son of John Morgan (M.P.). He was lord lieutenant of Monmouthshire and Breconshire, 1731–69; judge advocate general, 1741–68. He supported Robert Walpole, then Pelham, then Newcastle, and opposed George Grenville on general warrants in 1764. In 1765 Rockingham counted on him as "a friend." He voted against Chatham's land tax in 1767. M.P. for Brecon Borough, 1723–34; Monmouthshire, 1734–47; Breconshire, 1747–69.

Morgan, Thomas. 1727–71

Of Tredegar, Monmouthshire; oldest son of Thomas Morgan (1702–69) (*q.v.*); brother of John Morgan (1732–92) (*q.v.*) and Charles Morgan (1736–87) (*q.v.*). In politics he followed the lead of his father, supporting Newcastle and opposing Grenville and then supporting Rockingham. In 1769 he voted with the Grafton ministry to seat Luttrell in place of Wilkes. He was lord lieutenant of Breconshire and Monmouthshire, 1770–71. There is no evidence that he ever addressed the House of Commons. M.P. for Brecon Borough, 1754–63; Monmouthshire, 1763–71.

Morgan, William. 1725–63

Of Tredegar, Monmouthshire; oldest son of Sir William Morgan (M.P.); grandson of William Cavendish (2d Duke of Devonshire); nephew of Thomas Morgan (1702–69) (*q.v.*); cousin of Thomas Morgan (1727–71) (*q.v.*), John Morgan (1732–92) (*q.v.*), and Charles Morgan (1736–87) (*q.v.*). Westminster from 1738, Oxford from 1743. In his votes he followed the politics of his cousin William Cavendish (1720–64) (*q.v.*) but seldom addressed the House of Commons. M.P. for Monmouthshire, 1747–63.

Morice, Humphry. 1723–85

Of Werrington, near Launceston, Devon; oldest son of Humphry Morice (London merchant; M.P.); in 1750 succeeded his cousin Sir William Morice as 4th baronet. Of a Tory family, he was never known to vote against the current ministry, though he often did not vote at all. He was clerk comptroller of the green cloth, 1757–61; comptroller of the household, 1762–63; privy councillor from 1763; warden of the stanneries, 1763–83; high steward and lord warden of the Duchy of Cornwall from 1774; and recorder of Launceston, 1771–82. He did not stand for re-election in 1780. He died at Naples. M.P. for Launceston, 1750–80.

Morris, Roger. 1727–94

3d son of Roger Morris (of Netherby, near Knaresborough, Yorkshire). He was in the army in France under Ligonier, and was captain in 1745. He went to America as aide to Braddock in 1755 and was wounded at Fort Duquesne. In 1758 he married Mary Phillipse, 2d daughter of Frederick Phillipse (2d Lord of the Phillipse Manor in New York Province) with the intention of settling in America, but was unsympathetic with the demands of the colonists. He was at the siege of Louisburg as major in 1758, and was wounded again while with Wolfe at Quebec in 1759. He was an aide to Amherst and then to Gage, with the rank of lieutenant colonel in 1764. He returned to England in 1776.

Morris, Staats Long. 1728–1800

Of New York and (later) Huntly Lodge, Strath Bogie, Aberdeenshire; 2d son of Lewis Morris (judge and leading citizen of New York); half brother of Gouverneur Morris (of New York). Yale, 1743–46. He was captain of the New York Provincial Infantry in 1751. He went to England and in 1756 married Catherine, widow of Cosmo George Gordon (*q.v.*). He was elected to the House of Commons in 1774. He supported the North ministry in its American measures. He voted against the Dunning resolution of April 6, 1780, and voted with the North ministry on 3 crucial divisions recorded in February and March, 1782. He voted for Shelburne's peace terms but supported the coalition in 1783. After the 1784 elections he supported Pitt. He became a major general in the British army in 1777, lieutenant general in 1782, and general in 1786, but did not see action in America. M.P. for Elgin burghs, 1774–84.

Morse, Robert. 1743–1818

2d son of Thomas Morse (rector of Langall, near Taunton, Somerset). He entered Woolwich Military Academy in 1756 and was ensign in 1757. In 1758 he took part in raids on the French coast. In 1759 he served in the West Indies and in 1761 was at the attack on Belleisle. He was on active duty in Germany, 1762–63. In 1763 he was made captain and engineer extraordinary. He commanded in the West Indies and was chief military engineer in America under Carleton in 1782. He commanded the engineers at Gibraltar in 1791, and was made major general in 1793, lieutenant general in 1799, inspector general of fortifications in 1802, and general in 1808.

Morshead, John. 1747–1813

Of Trenant Park, near Liskeard, and Levethan, Cornwall; oldest son of William Morshead (d. 1784; sheriff of Cornwall in 1753); created baronet in 1784. Oxford from 1766. In 1778 he married Elizabeth, daughter of Sir Thomas Frederick (3d baronet, a director of the South Sea Company). He was a personal friend of the Earl of Sandwich, and therefore supported the North ministry in the House of Commons from 1780, voting with it in every crucial recorded division in February and March, 1782. He voted against Shelburne's peace terms in February, 1783, and then supported the coalition. Though he had inherited considerable property in Cornwall, he was in financial straits in 1780, but kept his seat in the House of Commons. He was surveyor general to the Prince of Wales in 1796 and warden of the stanneries, 1798–1800. M.P. for Callington, 1780–84; Bodmin, 1784–1802.

Mortimer, Hans Winthrop. 1734–1807

Of Caldwell Hall, near Burton, Derbyshire; only son of Cromwell Mortimer (physician; secretary of the Royal Society). Lincoln's Inn from 1755, barrister in 1761. Considered an independent in the House of Commons, from 1775 he voted chiefly in opposition to the North ministry. He voted for the Dunning resolution of April 6, 1780, but voted against Lowther's motion of December, 1781, to end the American war immediately. He voted against Shelburne's peace terms in February, 1783, and for Fox's India Bill in November, 1783. After the 1784 elections he generally supported Pitt. There is no evidence that he ever addressed the House of Commons. M.P. for Shaftesbury, 1775–80 and 1781–90.

Morton, 14th and **15th Earls.** See **James Douglas** and **Sholto Charles Douglas**

Morton, John. ca.1715–80

Of Tackley, near Woodstock, Oxfordshire; oldest son of John Morton (of Tackley). Oxford from 1730, Inner Temple from 1732, barrister in 1740, bencher from 1758, reader from 1765, treasurer in 1766. He affiliated with Leicester House, and in 1761 was listed as Tory. Newcastle called him "a very low, inconsiderable man." He was recorder of Woodstock from 1743; chief justice of Chester, 1762–80; attorney general to the queen, 1770–80; and deputy high steward of Oxford University, 1770–80. In 1763 North consulted him regarding the legality of Wilkes's position, and he supported North on the Wilkes issues from 1763. He opposed repeal of the Stamp Act in 1766, opposed Chatham's land tax in 1767, and supported the North ministry on the Wilkes and American issues, 1770–80. M.P. for Abingdon, 1747–70; New Romney, 1770–74; Wigan, 1775–80.

Moss, Charles. 1711–1802

Son of William Moss (country gentleman of Postwick, near Norwich, Norfolk); nephew of Robert Moss (1666–1729; dean of Ely from 1713). Cambridge from 1727; B.A., 1731; M.A., 1735; fellow from 1735. He received preferments from Bishop Sherlock of Salisbury and was prebendary of Salisbury Cathedral in 1738; archdeacon of Colchester in 1749; bishop of St. David's, 1766–74; and bishop of Bath and Wells, 1774–1802. He was reputed a Tory, was a fellow of the Royal Society and, according to *DNB*, was "a good average prelate."

Mostyn, John. 1709–79

2d son of Sir Roger Mostyn (1675–1739; M.P.); grandson of Daniel Finch (7th Earl of Winchilsea). Westminster from 1722, Oxford from 1728. He entered the foot guards as ensign in 1733 and was captain in 1736, major general in 1757, lieutenant general in 1759, and general in 1772. He was groom of the bedchamber, 1746–79; governor of Minorca and in military command there, 1758–68; acting commanding officer of British forces on the Continent, 1759–60; and governor of Chelsea Hospital from 1768. He secured his seat in the House of Commons "in the interest" of Rockingham, and was a regular supporter of the Whig ministries until 1766, when he voted against repeal of the Stamp Act. He never otherwise voted against Rockingham, as far as the records show. M.P. for Malton, 1741–68.

Mostyn, Roger. 1734–96

Of Mostyn, near Holywell, Flintshire, and Leighton, near Crewe, Cheshire; in 1758 succeeded his father, Sir Thomas Mostyn, as 5th baronet; nephew of John Mostyn (*q.v.*). Westminster, 1745–51; Oxford from 1751. He was lord lieutenant of Flintshire, 1761–96. In the House of Commons he supported Newcastle, 1758–62; sometimes voted against the Grenville ministry, 1763–65; supported the Rockingham ministry, 1765–66; and left no clear voting record during the Grafton ministry, 1766–70. He opposed the North ministry, especially from 1780, when he voted for Dunning's resolution of April 6, and in February and March, 1782, he voted against the North ministry in 4 of the 5 crucial divisions. He voted for Shelburne's peace terms and then supported the coalition in 1783. He opposed the Pitt ministry in early 1784. M.P. for Flintshire, 1758–96.

Mostyn-Owen, William. See **William Mostyn Owen**

Mountcastle, Baron. See **James Hamilton.** 1712–89

Mount Charles, 1st Baron. See **Henry Conyngham**

Mount Edgcumbe, 1st Viscount and 1st Earl. See **George Edgcumbe**

Mount Florence, 2d Baron. See **William Willoughby Cole**

Mountmorris, 1st Earl. See **Arthur Annesley**

Mountstuart, Viscount. See **John Stuart.** 1744–1814

Moutray, John. d. 1785

He was a naval lieutenant in 1749 and a commander in 1759. In 1780 he convoyed a valuable merchant fleet for the East Indies, nearly all of which were captured or destroyed by a French-Spanish fleet off Spain. He was tried and censured by a court-martial. He became resident commissioner at Antigua in 1783, but was recalled in 1785.

Moysey, Abel. 1743–1831

Of Hinton Charterhouse, near Bath, Somerset; only son of Abel Moysey (distinguished physician of Bath). Westminster from 1756, Oxford from 1760, Lincoln's Inn from 1758, barrister in 1767, bencher from 1802, treasurer in 1810. In 1774 he married Charlotte, daughter of Richard Warwick Bamfylde (or Bampfyld) (*q.v.*). He secured a seat in the House of Commons through strong mercantile support in Bath and with the help of the North ministry, which gave him appointments in 1771 and 1777. He was a personal follower of North, but in 1775 he supported Sawbridge's motion to shorten the duration of Parliaments, in 1776 opposed the employment of foreign mercenaries without the formal consent of Parliament, and also opposed the ministry's militia bill "as an unnecessary extension of the prerogative." He voted against Shelburne's peace terms and for Fox's India Bill in 1783 and in general opposed the Pitt ministry, 1784–90. He was commissioner for bankruptcy, 1771–74; justice of the Brecon circuit, 1777–1819; deputy remembrancer in exchequer, 1795–1813; and mayor of Bath in 1792 and 1810. M.P. for Bath, 1774–90.

Mulgrave, 1st and **2d Barons.** See **Constantine Phipps** and **Constantine John Phipps**

Muncaster, 1st Baron. See **John Pennington.** ca.1737–1813

Munro, Hector. 1726–1805

Of Novar, near Dingwall, Ross-shire; oldest son of Hugh Munro (of Sutherland; merchant). He was ensign in 1747, captain in 1756, colonel in 1777, major general in 1782, lieutenant general in 1793, and general in 1798. His military career was largely in India. He suppressed a mutiny at Patna in 1764, captured Pondichéry in 1778 and Nagapatam in 1781, but was not successful against Hyder Ali in 1780. He was at odds with Warren Hastings from 1778. When present in the House of Commons, he generally supported the North ministry. In the crucial divisions of February and March, 1782, he voted for Fox's motion to censure Sandwich and for Conway's first motion to end the war immediately, but after that he supported North in 3 divisions. M.P. for Inverness burghs, 1768–1802.

Murphy, Arthur. 1727–1805

Son of Richard Murphy (merchant of Dublin; lost at sea in 1729). In 1735 he moved with his widowed mother to London. He was schooled at St. Omer, 1738–44. In April, 1749, he was clerk to a merchant in Cork, but moved back to London, where he clerked in a London

banking house until 1751. He then joined with others in publishing
Gray's Inn Journal. In 1754 he took up another new vocation: he tried
acting on the stage and became one of the most noted and popular
comedians of his time. In 1803 he received a crown pension of £200
a year. He was a favorite in high society, a guest at the country houses
of peers, and a friend of Garrick and Sheridan. Two portraits by
Nathaniel Dance Holland.

Murray, Alexander. 1736–95

Of Murrayfields, Edinburgh, and Henderland, on Megget Water,
Peeblesshire; oldest son of Archibald Murray (of Murrayfields;
advocate); grandson of Lord William Hay. He attended Edinburgh
University and became Scots advocate in 1758. In 1773 he married
Katherine, daughter of Sir Alexander Lindsay. He was deputy
sheriff for Peeblesshire, 1761–75, and solicitor general for Scotland,
1775–83. In 1783 he became lord of sessions in the Court of Judiciary
for Scotland, with the legal title of Lord Henderland. He was clerk of
the pipe in the Scottish exchequer, 1786–95. In the House of Commons
he supported the North ministry when present, but he was often absent. For example, owing to illness, he did not vote in 4 of the 5
crucial recorded divisions of February and March, 1782, but he rose
from his bed to vote with North against Rous's no-confidence motion
on March 15, 1782. In one of his few speeches in the House, in 1781, he
opposed the petitions of grievance as unconstitutional. M.P. for
Peeblesshire, 1780–83.

Murray, David. 1727–96

4th son of David Murray (5th Viscount Stormont and Lord Scone,
Scottish); in 1748 succeeded his brother as 7th Viscount Stormont;
in 1793 succeeded his uncle William Murray (*q.v.*) as 2d Earl of
Mansfield (English). Westminster, to Oxford in 1744; B.A., 1748;
D.C.L., 1793. He was attaché at the British embassy in Paris in 1751;
envoy to Saxony, 1756–59; envoy to Warsaw in 1761; envoy to Vienna,
1763–72; envoy to Paris, 1772–78. He was privy councillor from 1763;
secretary of state, southern department, 1779–82; and lord president of
the council in 1783 and 1794–96. He narrowly escaped with his life
when he and his uncle's London home were attacked by Gordon
rioters in June, 1780. He supported the North ministry, of which he

was a member from 1778, and then the coalition. Later he supported Pitt. He was a Scottish representative peer, 1754–93, and chancellor of Marischal College, Aberdeen, from 1793. In manner he was formal, in character good, in perception weak, in judgment dubious.

Murray, James. 1690–1764

In 1724 succeeded his father, John Murray, as 2d Duke of Atholl (Scottish), his elder brother William Murray (known as Marquess of Tullibardine) having been attainted as a Jacobite traitor after the 1715 uprising. He was captain of foot guards in 1712 and lieutenant colonel in 1714. He was a representative Scottish peer, 1733–37; lord privy seal for Scotland, 1733–63; and Knight of the Thistle from 1734. In 1745–46 he served with the Duke of Cumberland against the Jacobites. He was lord justice general of Scotland, 1763–64. M.P. for Perthshire, 1715–24.

Murray, James. ca.1719–94

7th son of Alexander Murray (1677–1736; 4th Lord Elibank, Scottish); brother of Patrick Murray (*q.v.*). He entered the army ca. 1728 and served in the West Indies from 1738. He was captain of grenadier guards at L'Orient in 1748, major in 1749, and purchased a lieutenant colonelcy in 1751. He commanded a regiment at Rochefort in 1757 and in 1758 won the praise of Wolfe for his conduct while commanding a brigade at Louisburg, where he was made brigadier general. He served as governor of Quebec, 1760–66, and defended it against the French, but was recalled to England and charged with showing partiality to the French Canadians. He was exonerated by the House of Lords and, having been made a major general in 1762, was made lieutenant general in 1772. He was governor of Minorca, 1774–81. There he was obliged to surrender Fort St. Philip, after 7 months of stubborn resistance, to a siege by much stronger French and Spanish forces. He was made general in 1783. "A good and able soldier," he had met every kind of difficult situation well, from quelling a mutiny at Quebec in 1763 to raising at his own expense a battalion of high-landers when troops were needed in 1779. In 1767 he was one of those granted a large tract of land in maritime Canada.

Murray, James. 1727–99

Of Broughton, Wigtownshire, and Cally, near Gatehouse of Fleet,

Kirkcudbright; only son of Alexander Murray (M.P.); grandson of James Stewart (5th Earl of Galloway, Scottish). Glasgow University, 1741–45; grand tour in 1752. In 1752 he married his cousin Catherine, daughter of Alexander Stewart (6th Earl of Galloway). He became a close friend of Rockingham and voted with his party in the House of Commons, voting against Bute's peace preliminaries in December, 1762, and against the expulsion of Wilkes in January, 1770. Having inherited estates of considerable value in Scotland, he was appointed receiver of land tax for Scotland by the coalition in 1783. M.P. for Wigtownshire, 1762–68; Kirkcudbright Stewartry, 1768–74.

Murray, James. 1734–94

Of Strowan, near Blair Atholl, Perthshire; 2d son of Lord George Murray (officer in the Jacobite army in 1715 and 1745); grandson of John Murray (1659–1724; 1st Duke of Atholl). Eton; Utrecht, 1749–51; Besançon, 1754–55. He was a captain in the army in 1757, colonel in 1777, major general in 1782, and lieutenant general in 1793. He was wounded at Ticonderoga in 1758 and again at Martinique in 1762. In 1779 he raised a battalion of Scots to defend against the French. In the House of Commons he supported the North ministry, 1773–82, voting against the Dunning resolution of April 6, 1780, and with North in all 5 recorded crucial divisions in February and March, 1782. He voted for Shelburne's peace terms in 1783 and after 1784 supported Pitt. M.P. for Perthshire, 1773–94.

Murray, John. 1711–87

Of Pitnacree, near Aberfeldy, Perthshire, and Banner Cross, near Sheffield, Yorkshire; 13th child of John Murray (1659–1724; 1st Duke of Atholl). He studied at Leyden in 1728. He was lieutenant in the guards in 1733; aide to the king in 1743; colonel of the Black Watch, 1745–87; major general in 1755; lieutenant general in 1758; and general, 1770. He served in Flanders, 1743–47. Though politics was an extremely secondary interest to this professional soldier, he was a member of the House of Commons for more than 25 years and supported Robert Walpole, then Pelham, and finally Newcastle. M.P. for Perthshire, 1734–61.

Murray, John. 1729–74

Of Strowan, near Blair Atholl, Perthshire; oldest son of Lord George

Murray (ca.1700–60; officer in the Jacobite armies in 1715 and 1745); grandson of John Murray (1659–1724; 1st Duke of Atholl); older brother of James Murray (1734–94) (*q.v.*); in 1764 succeeded his uncle James Murray (ca.1690–1764) (*q.v.*) as 3d Duke of Atholl (Scottish). Eton, 1742–45; Gottingen, 1751–53. In 1753 he married his cousin Charlotte, daughter of James Murray (2d Duke of Atholl). Though his father's title was attainted, his own was confirmed by the House of Lords in 1764. He was captain of a regiment raised by Sir James Lowther, and was a Scottish representative peer, 1766–74. Considered a Tory, he supported Bute, then Grenville, then North. He was considered virtuous, courageous, and benevolent. He was made Knight of the Thistle in 1767, and was grand master of Scottish Freemasons, 1773–74. He drowned himself "in a fit of delirium" in the River Tay at the age of 44. M.P. for Perth, 1761–64.

Murray, John. 1732–1809

In 1756 succeeded his father, William Murray, as 4th Earl of Dunmore (Scottish). He entered the army as ensign in 1750. He married Charlotte, daughter of Alexander Stewart (ca.1699–1773; 6th Earl of Galloway, Scottish). He was governor of New York Province and of Virginia, 1769–76. In 1775 he nearly provoked the colonists to immediate armed action by removing gunpowder belonging to the colonists to a British man-of-war, and was forced to withdraw to a warship during the riots that followed. He returned to England in 1776, where he supported the Bedford bloc and hence, less dependably, the North ministry. He was a Scottish representative peer, 1761–68, and 1776–96, and governor of the Bahamas, 1787–94. In 1767 in the House of Lords he recorded dissent from the vote to continue the war in Germany, and in 1769 he recorded dissent from the decision in the Douglas-Hamilton case "because it is proved that the appellant is not the son of Lady Jane Douglas."

Murray, John. 1755–1830

In 1774 succeeded his father, John Murray (1729–74) (*q.v.*), as 4th Duke of Atholl (Scottish); in 1786 created Baron Murray and Earl Strange (both English titles). He married (1) in 1774 Jane, oldest daughter of Charles Cathcart (1721–76; 9th Baron Cathcart, Scottish), and (2) in 1794 Margery, oldest and widowed daughter of James

Forbes (16th Lord Forbes, Scottish). He raised a regiment of high-landers in 1777. He was grand master of Scottish Freemasons, 1778–80; a Scottish representative peer, 1780–86; fellow of the Royal Society from 1780; governor of the Isle of Man from 1783; lord lieutenant of Perthshire, 1794–1830; privy councillor from 1797; and Knight of the Thistle from 1800. During the Napoleonic Wars he raised a large number of volunteers and militia. In 1805 he secured on petition one-quarter of the customs revenue of the Isle of Man, which he later sold for £409,000. Deeply interested in afforestation, he planted trees on a large scale on his estates in Scotland.

Murray, Patrick. 1703–78

In 1736 succeeded his father, Alexander Murray (1677–1736), as 5th Earl of Elibank (Scottish); brother of James Murray (1719–94) (*q.v.*); succeeded his younger brother Alexander Murray as titular Earl of Westminster. In 1735 he married Maria, widow of William North (Lord North and Grey; cousin of Frederick, Lord North). He was Scots advocate in 1723, but in that year joined the army, became lieutenant colonel of marines in 1739, and distinguished himself at Cartagena in 1740. In his later life in London he associated with writers and intellectuals and wrote and published pamphlets and books on the currency in 1758, on entails in 1765, on Scottish history in 1773, and on the peerage of Scotland in 1774. Samuel Johnson told Boswell that he had a very high opinion of him.

Murray, William. 1705–93

Of Perthshire and of Kenwood, Hampstead, Middlesex; 4th son of David Murray (5th Viscount Stormont, Scottish); brother of David Murray (6th Viscount Stormont); uncle of David Murray (*q.v.*); in 1756 created Baron Mansfield (English); in 1792 created Earl Mansfield (English). Westminster, 1718–23; Oxford from 1723; B.A., 1727; M.A., 1730; Lincoln's Inn from 1724; barrister in 1730. In 1738 he married Elizabeth, daughter of Daniel Finch (1647–1730; M.P.; and 7th Earl of Winchilsea). He was king's counsel from 1742; solicitor general, 1742–54; L.L.D. from Glasgow in 1754; attorney general, 1754–56. Though in 1756 Newcastle offered him a large pension to remain in the House of Commons as his spokesman, he removed himself from Parliament and was chief justice of the king's bench, as well as privy councillor and king's serjeant-at-law, 1756–88. He was ex officio chancellor of the exchequer, April–June and September–October, 1757. He was speaker of the House of Lords in 1760 and 1770–71. As a peer he was nominally a Whig, but his extreme caution made him above all a conservative, and he supported the court on most major issues during his incumbency in office. In 1768 he reversed the outlawry of Wilkes on a technicality and substituted a sentence of fine and imprisonment. In 1770 he declared in effect that in libel cases the only function of the jury was to rule on the facts of publication and sale and that the determination of whether a libel had taken place lay wholly with the judge. That decision was denounced by Camden and attacked by Whigs in opposition. He insisted that the American colonies must recognize the complete sovereignty of Parliament, and urged as much coercion as necessary to that end. In 1780 his house was sacked and burned by the Gordon rioters. As an advocate he was almost unrivaled; as a judge he was considered by conservatives an oracle; but on controversial issues he was notoriously timid. Horace Walpole wrote that "all men reverenced his abilities, feared his art . . . and derided his pusillanimity." George III wrote to Bute: "He is but half a man . . . and cries out against everything but moderation." He derived "a princely income" from his legal practice. Macaulay called him "the father of modern Toryism"; Foss in his *Judges of England* pronounced him "the founder of commercial jurisprudence." M.P. for Boroughbridge, 1742–56.

Musgrave, George. ca.1740–1824

Of Kepyer, on River Wear, County Durham; 2d son of George Musgrave (storekeeper of ordnance at Chatham). He was descended from an old north country Tory family. Westminster from 1752, Oxford from 1758, Lincoln's Inn from 1761. In the House of Commons he voted with the Rockingham Whigs, including his vote against expulsion of Wilkes in January, 1770. He made 7 reported speeches in the House of Commons. M.P. for Carlisle, 1768–74.

Musgrave, Philip. ca.1713–95

Of Edenhall, near Penrith, Cumberland, and Kempton Park, near Kingston, Middlesex; in 1736 succeeded his father, Sir Christopher Musgrave (1688–1736; M.P.), as 6th baronet. Eton, to Oxford in 1733.

In politics his interests appear to have been entirely local and north country. M.P. for Westmorland, 1741–47.

Musgrave, Samuel. 1732–80

Son of Richard Musgrave (of Washfield, near Tiverton, Devonshire). Oxford from 1749; B.A., 1754; M.A., 1756; traveling fellow, 1754. He was a fellow of the Royal Society from 1760, M.D. of Leyden in 1763, and M.D. of Oxford in 1775. He became a classical scholar, a physician, a political polemist, and in some things an extremist. In 1763 he wrote and published pamphlets charging that the ministry had sold Britain's interests and honor to the enemy in the peace just made; in the 1770's his condemnations of the North ministry were so extravagant that he was several times threatened with libel suits. He also published books on medicine and annotated editions of the plays of Sophocles and Euripides. As a scholar of Greek and a writer on medical subjects he had few peers in his time.

Musgrave, William. 1735–1800

Of Hayton Castle, Cumberland; younger son of Sir Richard Musgrave (ca.1701–66; 4th baronet); in 1755 succeeded his brother Sir Richard Musgrave (1724–55) as 6th baronet. Middle Temple from 1753, barrister in 1758, bencher from 1789, treasurer in 1795. In 1759 he married Isabella, dowager Countess of Carlisle. He was commissioner of customs from 1763 and commissioner of accounts from 1785. He was a fellow of the Royal Society from 1774 and its vice president in 1780; fellow of the Society of Arts from 1788 and its vice president in 1786. He was a trustee of the British Museum from 1783.

Myddelton, Richard. 1726–95

Of Chirk Castle, near Wrexham, Denbighshire; only son of John Myddelton (M.P.). Eton, 1739–43; and at Oxford from 1744. In 1761 he married (1) Elizabeth, daughter of John Rushout (ca.1684–1775) (q.v.). He was lord lieutenant of Denbighshire, 1748–95. In the House of Commons he supported Pelham and then Newcastle through 1762. He opposed the Bute and Grenville ministries, 1763–65; supported Rockingham and then Grafton; but voted against the ministry over Wilkes in 1769 and thereafter. He sometimes supported Rockingham against the North ministry, 1770–82, though in 1780 John Robinson classed him as a friend of the ministry. He "stayed away" during most of the crucial divisions in February and March, 1782, but voted for Conway's motion of February 27 to end the American war immediately. There is no evidence that he ever addressed the House of Commons. M.P. for Denbigh boroughs, 1747–88.

Naas, 1st Baron. See **John Bourke**

Nagle, Edmund. 1757–1830

Son of Edmund Nagle (d. 1762); cousin of Edmund Burke. He entered the navy at the age of 13 in 1770 and was lieutenant in 1777, commander in 1782, and knighted in 1794. In 1798 he married "a lady of ample fortune," the widow of John Lucie of London. He served in North American waters, 1777–82. In 1782 he was captured by the French. He was later exchanged, and became a great favorite of the Prince of Wales, since he was a man of high spirit, endless good nature, and Irish charm. That sponsorship and those qualities may account for a series of promotions not due to impressive achievements. He was rear admiral in 1805 and vice admiral in 1810, governor of Newfoundland in 1813, Knight Commander of the Bath in 1815, and admiral in 1819.

Napier, Francis. 1733–79

3d son of Francis Napier (5th Lord Napier, Scottish). He was lieutenant of marines in 1755, captain in 1757, major in 1772, and lieutenant colonel in 1779.

Napier, Francis. 1758–1823

Born at Ipswich; in 1775 succeeded his father, William Napier, as 7th Baron Napier (Scottish; adjutant general of the forces in Scotland). He entered the army as ensign in 1774, became lieutenant in 1776, and was taken prisoner at Burgoyne's surrender at Saratoga in October, 1777. Released on parole, he returned to England in 1779, became captain in 1784, became major in 1785, and retired from active military service in 1789. He was grand master of Scottish Freemasons and lord lieutenant of Selkirkshire, 1797–1823; high commissioner for the Church of Scotland, 1802–16; and president of the Scottish Society for the Propagation of Christian Knowledge from 1805. He was a Scottish representative peer, 1796–1815. He compiled a genealogical account of the Napier family.

Napier, George. 1751–1804

Born in Edinburgh, the oldest son of Francis Scott (later Napier; 5th Baron Napier of Merchiston). He was educated under the tutorship of David Hume, and entered the army as ensign in 1767, becoming lieutenant in 1771. He served in America, and was made captain in 1778. He then withdrew from active military service, marrying (2) Sarah, 4th daughter of the 2d Duke of Richmond, divorced in 1776 from her first husband, Sir Charles Thomas Burnham (M.P.). He re-entered the army in 1782 and was superintendent of the Woolwich laboratory ca. 1788, and quartermaster general under the Earl of Moira in 1793. During the Irish rebellion of 1798 he strongly fortified his own house. In 1788 he published a monograph on the composition of gunpowder.

Napier, Gerard. 1739–65

Of Middlemarsh Hall, near Cerne Abbas, and Critchell More, near Cranborne, Dorset; in 1759 succeeded his father, Sir William Gerard Napier (ca.1696–1759), as 6th baronet. Eton, 1755–57; Oxford from 1758. In 1762 he married Elizabeth, daughter of Sir John Oglander (of the Isle of Wight; 4th baronet). He was a Scot whose family had long lived in England and had acquired wealth. He was supported for election to the House of Commons by Lord Ilchester and the Duke of Newcastle. He was listed as Tory by Bute in 1761, and then was regarded as a supporter of first Bute and then Grenville. There is no record that he ever voted with the minority or ever addressed the House. M.P. for Bridport, 1761–65.

Napier, 7th Baron. See **Francis Napier.** 1758–1823

Nares, George. 1716–86

Of Reading, Berkshire; 2d son of George Nares (of Albury, Oxfordshire; steward to the Earl of Abingdon); brother of James Nares (*q.v.*); father of Edward Nares (1762–1841; regius professor of modern history at Oxford). Oxford University; D.C.L., 1773; Inner Temple from 1738; barrister in 1741. In 1751 he married Mary, daughter of Sir John Strange. He was king's serjeant-at-arms from 1759, and was supported for election to the House of Commons by the Duke of Marlborough. In 1771 he was knighted and appointed a justice of the Court of Common Pleas, thus vacating his seat in the House. M.P. for Oxford City, 1768–71.

Nares, James. 1715–83

Born at Stanwell, near Staines, Middlesex; oldest son of George Nares (of Albury near Thame, Oxfordshire; steward to the Earls of Abingdon); brother of George Nares (*q.v.*). He was a chorister in the Chapel Royal, then assistant organist at Windsor, then organist at York Cathedral from 1734 (the date given in *DNB* but to be questioned because he would have been only 19). In 1756 or 1757 he returned to the Chapel Royal as organist and composer to the king. He was made a doctor of music by Cambridge University, and remained at the Chapel Royal until 1780. He composed harpsichord etudes, 6 organ fugues, a chromatic ode, 20 anthems and many catches and glees. He also wrote 2 treatises on vocal music.

Nassau, Richard Savage. 1723–80

2d son of Frederick Nassau Zuylestein (1682–1738; 3d Earl of Rochford); brother of William Henry Nassau Zuylestein (*q.v.*). Westminster, 1734–39. In 1751 he married (1) Anne Spencer, widow of James Hamilton (1703–43; 5th Duke of Hamilton, Scottish). He was groom of the bedchamber from 1760 and was clerk of the Board of the Green Cloth, 1771–80. He regularly supported the North ministry, but made no reported speeches before the House of Commons. He opposed the Dunning resolution of April 6, 1780. M.P. for Colchester, 1747–54; Malden, 1774–80.

Nedham, William. ca.1741–1806

Of Howbery Park, at Wallingford, Oxfordshire, and Newry, Carlingford, County Down; 3d son of Robert Nedham (M.P.); nephew of William Pitt (1708–78) (*q.v.*). His family had long been established in Jamaica, though he himself never lived there. Eton, 1756–61; Cambridge from 1762; Inner Temple from 1758. He was sheriff of Oxford-shire, 1774–75, and a member of the Irish Parliament, 1767–76. In the English House of Commons he consistently opposed the North ministry, voting against approval of the address from the throne in October, 1775, for Dunning's first resolution in April, 1780, and against the North ministry in all 5 crucial divisions reported in February and March, 1782. In 1783 he voted against Shelburne's peace terms and supported the coalition but did not vote on Fox's India Bill. No votes are recorded after 1784, and he seldom addressed the House. M.P. for Winchelsea, 1774–80; Pontrefact, 1780–84; Winchelsea, 1784–90.

Nesbitt, Arnold. ca.1722–79

Of West Wickham, Kent, and Icklesham, near Winchelsea, Sussex; son of Thomas Nesbitt (of Lismore, County Cavan). In 1758 he married Susanna, sister of Henry Thrale (*q.v.*). A London merchant who was apparently at one time in America, he owned a large sugar plantation in Jamaica. In 1766, in partnership with Adam Drummond, he held a contract to victual British troops in America, at what were said by some to be exorbitant rates. In 1767 he received a royal grant of land in maritime Canada. In the House of Commons he supported Newcastle, opposed Grenville, and in general supported the Rockingham, Grafton, and North ministries. There is no evidence that he ever addressed the House during his membership of some 24 years. He left at least 2 illegitimate sons. M.P. for St. Michael, 1753–54; Winchelsea, 1754–61; Cricklade, 1761–68; Winchelsea, 1770–74; Cricklade, 1774–79.

Nesbitt, John. ca.1745–1817

Of Keston Park, near Bromley, Kent; 2d son of Cosby Nesbitt (Irish M.P.). He inherited a fortune, though one heavily encumbered with debt, from his uncle Arnold Nesbitt (*q.v.*), and established himself as a banker in Dublin. In 1780 he was elected to the English Parliament, and in the same year received a pension from Lord North. In 1782, having become a protégé of the Prince of Wales and a familiar of Charles Fox, he abandoned his previous support of North and voted with the opposition in the crucial divisions on Conway's motion of February 27 to end the American war immediately and on Rous's no-confidence motion of March 15, 1782. In 1784 he was compelled by the new Clerke Act to give up his government contracts in order to retain his seat in the House of Commons. He voted against Shelburne's peace terms but did not vote on Fox's India Bill in 1783. From 1784 he supported Pitt, but there is no evidence that he addressed the House before 1790. He was commissioner for hackney coaches, 1814–17. M.P. for Winchelsea, 1780–90; Gatton, 1790–96; Bodmin, 1796–1802.

Neville, George. 1727–85

Godson of George II; in 1744 succeeded his father, William Neville, as 17th Baron Abergavenny; in 1784 created Earl of Abergavenny. Oxford from 1745. In 1753 he married Henrietta, sister of Thomas Pelham (1728–1805) (*q.v.*) and widow of Richard Temple (ca.1669–1749; 1st Viscount Cobham). He was lord lieutenant of Sussex, 1757–61. From 1762 he was in steady opposition to the ministry in power (except the Rockingham ministry, 1765–66) until the fall of the North ministry in March, 1782. In politics perhaps, as well as in activities in which he was presumably more successful, Walpole may have been right in saying that "His Lordship's heart is more inflammable than tender." In recorded dissents from majority votes in the House of Lords he opposed (1) the cider tax in 1763, (2) restriction on parliamentary privilege in the Wilkes case in 1763, (3) regulation of the management and dividends of the East India Company, 1767–68, (4) the actions of the House of Commons regarding Wilkes in 1770, (5) North's Falkland Islands settlement in 1771, (6) the Royal Marriage Act in 1772, (7) the Massachusetts Regulating Bill in 1774, (8) the New England Restraining Bill in 1775, (9) the rejection of petitions from the colonies in 1775, (10) the policies enunciated in the addresses from the throne in February and October, 1775, (11) the Non-Intercourse Act in 1775, (12) the hiring of mercenaries without formal consent of Parliament in 1776, (13) the policies in the address from the throne in October, 1776, (14) the continuation of the war in America in 1778, (15) rejection of the motion to ask the king to effect "a total change of System" in 1779, (16) suspension of the rights of sailors in 1779, (17) rejection of the motion to examine into public expenditures in 1780, and (18) the king's dismissal of Pembroke and Carmarthen in 1780.

Neville, Richard Aldworth. See **Richard Aldworth-Neville Aldworth (later Griffin)**

Newark, 1st Viscount. See **Charles Pierrepont Medows (or Meadows)**

Newborough, 1st Baron. See **Thomas Wynn**

Newcastle, 1st and **2d Dukes.** See **Thomas Pelham-Holles** and **Henry Fiennes Clinton.** 1720–94

Newdigate, Roger. 1719–1806

Of Arbury Hall, near Nuneaton, Warwickshire, and Harefield, near Uxbridge, Middlesex; 7th son of Sir Richard Newdigate (1668–1727, 3d baronet); in 1734 succeeded his brother Sir Edward Newdigate as 5th baronet. Westminster from 1727; Oxford from 1736; M.A., 1738; D.C.L., 1749; grand tour, 1738–40. In 1743 he married (1) Sophia, daughter of Edward Conyers (ca.1693–1742; M.P.). He inherited large land holdings in Middlesex and Warwickshire. Throughout his career he was considered a high Tory and was listed as Tory by Newcastle in 1761. He was a strong supporter of the priorities and privileges of the Church of England and in general resisted change. He took his Parliament duties very seriously, kept daily notes of events in the House of Commons, and voted as an independent conservative. He often opposed Newcastle, Chatham, Rockingham, and Grafton but in general supported the North ministry, especially against Wilkes and reform. He was an active promoter of the development of inland canals and an eager traveler and antiquarian. He endowed an annual prize for poetry and gave his collection of ancient marble sculptures to Oxford University, which he represented in Parliament for nearly 30 years. M.P. for Middlesex, 1742–47; Oxford University, 1751–80.

Newhaven, 1st Baron. See **William Mayne**

Newnham, George Lewis. ca.1734–1800

Of Newtimber Place, near Brighton, Sussex; oldest son of Nathaniel Newnham (ca.1699–1778; of Swithen's Lane, London; M.P.). Eton 1745–48; Cambridge from 1751; Lincoln's Inn from 1749; barrister in 1757; bencher and king's counsel from 1772. He voted in steady opposition to the North ministry, including a vote for the Dunning resolution of April 6, 1780, but there is no evidence that he ever addressed the House of Commons, and he did not seek re-election in 1780. M.P. for Arundel, 1774–80.

Newnham, Nathaniel. 1742–1809

Of Newtimber Place, near Brighton, Sussex, and Inner Temple, London; 4th son of Nathaniel Newnham (ca.1699–1778, of Swithen's Lane, London; M.P.); brother of George Lewis Newnham (*q.v.*). He was a director of the East India Company intermittently, 1738–59, and was an alderman of London from 1774; sheriff of London, 1775–76; and lord mayor of London, 1782–83. Though not a follower of Wilkes, he "was always ranked among the political doubtfuls," according to Namier, and opposed the North ministry, especially its measures toward the colonies. He was a supporter of popular reform. In November, 1780, he made his first recorded address in the House of Commons, opposing the address from the throne because it gave countenance to ministers who neglected the nation's commerce and imposed unjust taxes to pay for an unjust war. He voted against the North ministry in all recorded crucial divisions in February and March, 1782. He then supported the Rockingham ministry, voted against Shelburne's peace terms, and voted for Fox's India Bill in 1783. In a speech in June, 1783, he supported the London petition against the receipt tax, which he called burdensome and oppressive. After 1784 he usually opposed Pitt but supported Pitt's measures for reform. M.P. for London, 1780–90; Ludgershall, 1793–96.

Newport, 2d Baron. See Robert Jocelyn

Newton, Michael Archer. ca.1727–1803

Of Barr's Court, Gloucestershire, and Culverthorpe, near Kesteven, Lincolnshire; 2d son of William Archer (ca.1680–1739; M.P.); took the surname Newton after inheriting through his mother in 1743. He was from an old Tory family, and in 1767 Newcastle still classified him as Tory. He left no record of any speech or vote in the House of Commons and did not stand for re-election. M.P. for Beverley, 1761–68.

Newton, Thomas. 1704–82

Born at Lichfield, Staffordshire, the son of John Newton (of Lichfield; brandy and cider merchant). Westminster from 1717; Cambridge from 1723; B.A., 1727; fellow from 1729; M.A., 1730; D.D., 1745. He was rector of St. Mary-le-Bow in London, 1744–68, and rector of St. George's, Hanover Square from 1747. In 1749 he published his edition of Milton's *Paradise Lost*, which went to an 8th edition in 1775. He was Boyle lecturer in 1754; chaplain to George II, 1755–60; prebendary of Westminster, 1757–61; precentor of York, 1759–61; president of Sion College and dean of St. Paul's from 1760; and bishop of Bristol ("worth only £300 a year"), 1761–82. He claimed to have been offered, and to have declined, the primacy of Ireland in 1764. In the House of Lords he recorded dissent to repeal of the Stamp Act in 1766 and supported the American measures of the North ministry throughout the war. Just before his death in 1782 he published his autobiography and collected works. Portrait by Reynolds.

Nicholls, John. ca.1746–1832

Of Ockley, near Dorking, Surrey, and Goring on Thames, Oxfordshire; son of Frank Nicholls (physician to George II). Oxford from 1761, Lincoln's Inn from 1761, barrister in 1767. He married a granddaughter of Edmund Gibson (bishop of London). He supported the coalition during his first year in the House of Commons and voted that year for Fox's India Bill. From 1784 he opposed the Pitt ministry. He spent his later years in France and in 1820 published his *Recollections and Reflections*. M.P. for Bletchingley, 1783–87; Tregony, 1796–1802.

Nisbett, William Arnold Hamilton (later Hamilton-Nisbett). 1747–1822

Of Dirleton and Belhaven, near Dunbar, Haddingtonshire; oldest son of William Nisbett (of Dirleton). By the acquisitions of inheritance and marriage he was reputed one of the wealthiest lairds in Scotland. Eton, 1756–65. In 1777 he married Mary, daughter of Robert Manners (ca.1717–82) (*q.v.*). He was cornet of dragoons in 1767 and adjutant in 1769 and retired from the army in 1774. In the House of Commons from 1777, he supported the North ministry, though there is no evidence that he ever addressed the House. In 1797 he took the added surname Hamilton upon inheriting through his mother. M.P. for Haddingtonshire, 1777–80; East Grinstead, 1790–96; Newport (Isle of Wight), 1796–1800.

Noel, Edward. 1715–74

Of Kirkby Mallory, near Market Bosworth, Leicestershire; in 1723 succeeded his father, Sir Clobery Noel (ca.1695–1723; M.P.), as 6th baronet. Eton from 1725; at Oxford from 1733; M.A., 1736; D.C.L.,

1744; in 1745 succeeded, through his cousin Martha Wentworth, as 9th Baron Wentworth; in 1762 créated Viscount Wentworth on the recommendation of Bute. He was "in effect a Tory" and generally voted with the court but in 1766 opposed repeal of the Stamp Act.

Noel, Thomas. ca.1705–88

Of Exton Park, near Oakham, Rutland; 2d son of John Noel, of a family frequently represented in Parliament from 1550. In 1756 he married Elizabeth Chapman, widow of Baptist Noel (4th Earl of Gainsborough). While a Tory by inclination and tradition, he appears to have supported, though very independently, Newcastle and then Rockingham. He voted against Bute's peace preliminaries in December, 1762. During the North ministry he attended the House of Commons but seldom, and when present usually opposed it, though he cast no vote in the 5 crucial recorded divisions in February and March, 1782. He did not disclose his political thinking by political speaking. As Robinson wrote to Pitt in 1784, "His ideas are not known, but he does not attend much." In Parliament, as at home in Rutland, "he hunted with his own hounds until his death" at 82. M.P. for Rutland, 1728–41 and 1753–88.

Noel, Thomas. 1745–1815

In 1774 succeeded his father, Edward Noel (*q.v.*), as 2d Viscount Wentworth. Eton, 1757–63; Oxford from 1763; M.A., 1766; D.C.L., 1773. In 1788 he married Mary, widow of Edward Ligonier (1740–82) (*q.v.*) and daughter of Robert Henley (ca.1708–72) (*q.v.*). He was elected to the House of Commons in 1774, but succeeded to the peerage before he could cast a vote in the lower House. He was lord of the bedchamber, 1790–1815; and lieutenant colonel of the West Leicestershire volunteers from 1798. The lack of recorded dissents in the records of the House of Lords indicates that he supported the North ministry. M.P. for Leicestershire, 1774.

Nollekens, Joseph. 1737–1823

Born in London; 2d son of Joseph Francis Nollekens (1702–48; native of Antwerp; Roman Catholic; lived in Soho, London and gained some repute as a painter). He practiced at sculpture as well as at painting from the age of 13. In 1760 he went to Rome for further study; there both Garrick and Sterne sat for busts. While in Rome he acted as agent for the collection of antiques or works of art for several English and other collectors, and later speculated profitably on the stock exchange. When he returned to London in 1770, his reputation as an artist was already established, and his financial position was better than when he had first reached Rome. He very soon married Mary, daughter of Saunders Welch (a friend of Samuel Johnson), and became a member of the Royal Academy, where he exhibited annually, 1771–86. As London's most fashionable portrait sculptor of his time, his works included busts of George III, Pitt, Charles Fox, and the Prince of Wales. In his last years he was partly paralyzed and increasingly senile. Reputedly niggardly, he left a large fortune, some of it to charities.

Norfolk, 11th Duke. See **Charles Howard.** 1746–1815

Norreys, Baron. See **Willoughby Montagu Bertie**

Norris, John. 1740–74

Of Hemsted, near Cranbrook, Kent; oldest son of John Norris (M.P.), who with his family had represented Rye for at least 3 generations. Cambridge from 1757. He was captain of Deal Castle, 1766–74. In the House of Commons he steadily supported Newcastle, voting against Bute's peace preliminaries in 1762 and opposing Grenville on Wilkes issues in 1763 and general warrants in 1764. After 1770 he fell badly into debt and "retired" to the Continent during his last 4 years as a member of Parliament. Just before he left, he voted against unseating Wilkes in January, 1770, and was said to have seen much of Wilkes on the Continent. There is no record that he ever addressed the House, on which he had little or no influence. M.P. for Rye, 1762–74.

North, Brownlow. 1741–1820

2d son of Francis North (*q.v.*); half brother of Frederick North (*q.v.*), who notably forwarded his career and is said to have commented on this nepotism that "though Brownlow was probably too young to be a bishop, when Brownlow was older he might not have a brother who was first minister." He was also a half stepbrother of William Legge (*q.v.*). Eton, to Oxford in 1760; B.A., 1762; M.A., 1766; D.C.L., 1770; fellow of All Souls from 1763. In 1771 he married Henrietta Maria, daughter and co-heiress of John Bannister, a West Indies merchant. He was canon of Christ Church, Oxford, from 1768, dean of Canterbury in 1770 (the year Lord North became first minister); bishop of Lichfield and Coventry, 1771–74; bishop of Worcester, 1774–81; bishop of Winchester, 1781–1820. He organized clerical charities, restored old clerical buildings, and voiced old clerical saws. But he was as generous to literary aspirants as he was in providing church livings and patronage to members of his family. In the House of Lords he devotedly supported the North ministry and the coalition, even to opposing any easing of the restrictions on dissenters or Roman Catholics. He spent his latter years almost entirely on the Continent, though retaining his bishopric (one of the most lucrative in the hierarchy). He published a collection of his sermons. Two portraits, in his episcopal robes, by Henry Howard. Portrait also by Nathaniel Dance Holland.

North, Dudley Long. 1749–1829

Of Hurts Hall, near Saxmundham, Suffolk; 2d son of Charles Long (of Hurts Hall); great-grandson of Sir Dudley North (1641–91); in 1789 adopted the surname North upon inheriting from a distant cousin. Cambridge from 1766; M.A., 1774; Lincoln's Inn from 1769. In 1802 he married Sophia, daughter of Charles Anderson (later Pelham) (*q.v.*). He was elected to the House of Commons with the support of Rockingham in 1780, and became a staunch supporter of Charles Fox and a friend of Lord Richard Cavendish. In all the 5 crucial recorded divisions of February and March, 1782, he voted against the North ministry. He was a manager of the impeachment proceedings of Warren Hastings, and was said to have had an acute and witty mind. M.P. for St. Germans, 1780–84; Great Grimsby, 1784–90; Banbury, 1790–93; Great Grimsby, 1793–96; Banbury, 1796–1806 and 1808–12; Richmond, 1812–18; Haddington burghs, 1818–20; Newton (Isle of Wight), 1820–21.

North, Francis. 1704–90

Of Wroxton, near Banbury, Oxfordshire, and Waldershare, near Canterbury, Kent; in 1729 succeeded his father, Francis North, as 3d Baron Guilford; in 1734 succeeded his kinsman William North (of Kirtling, Cambridgeshire) as 7th Baron North; in 1752 created Earl of Guilford. Eton from 1718, Oxford from 1721; there is no record that he took a degree. He married (1) in 1728 Lucy, daughter of

George Montagu (2d Earl of Halifax), (2) in 1736 Elizabeth, daughter of Sir Arthur Kaye and widow of George Legge (Viscount Lewisham), and (3) in 1751 Catherine, 2d daughter of Sir Robert Furnese and widow of Lewis Watson (2d Earl of Rockingham). He was the father of Frederick North (*q.v.*) and of Brownlow North (*q.v.*). From a family traditionally Tory, he professed to be, and was regarded as, a leading Whig of Oxfordshire, and controlled the elections for Banbury. He was lord of the bedchamber to Frederick, Prince of Wales, at £600 a year, 1730–51, and treasurer to Queen Charlotte, 1773–90. He was governor of the two older sons of Prince Frederick, 1750–51, but replaced in that post because, it was believed, he was not a sufficiently dependable and enthusiastic promulgator of Whig doctrine. The king sometimes consulted him, most notably in 1783, about how to make Lord North do what the king wanted him to do. Horace Walpole, who never quite made up his mind whether his personal liking for Lord North outweighed his political dislike of North's measures, pronounced Francis North to have been "an able, worthy man, of no great genius," but with a passion, which he very considerably gratified, for advancing the material interests of his family. M.P. for Banbury, 1727–29.

North, Frederick. 1732–92

Of Wroxton, near Banbury, Oxfordshire; Dillington, near Ilminster, Somerset; Bushey Park, Richmond, near London; and Lower Grosvenor Street, London. Styled Lord North from 1752; in 1790 he succeeded his father, Francis North (*q.v.*), as 2d Earl of Guilford; half stepbrother of William Legge (*q.v.*); half brother of Brownlow North (*q.v.*). He was connected with the families of Montagu, Burgoyne, Furnese, Pelham, and Watson-Wentworth. Eton, 1742–48; Oxford, 1749–52; grand tour with William Legge, 1752–54. In 1756 he married Anne, daughter of George Speke (of White Lackington, Somerset) and presumed heiress of the wealthy William Pynsent (ca.1681–1765; of Burton Pynsent, Somerset). For his career, see standard works. Elected to the House of Commons with the support of Newcastle, Halifax, and Henry Bilson Legge (a stepuncle) (*q.v.*). In 1754 he supported the Newcastle party. He was a clerk in the treasury, 1759–65; was joint paymaster to the forces, 1766–67; and (after declining to displace Charles Townshend in 1767) succeeded

649

Townshend upon the latter's death a few months later and retained that post until March, 1782. He was 1st lord of the treasury, February 10, 1770–March 27, 1782, though he frequently begged (sometimes with absolute sincerity) to be relieved of that post. In alliance with Charles Fox from December, 1782, he opposed Shelburne's peace terms, and after Shelburne's defeat on that issue he formed a coalition government with Fox in April, 1783, to the bitter distress of the king. After the connived defeat of Fox's India Bill in the House of Lords on December 20, 1783, he was immediately and ungraciously dismissed by the king. He was in steady opposition to the Pitt ministry in the House of Commons, 1784–90, and (though seldom able to attend and for the last few years completely blind) in the House of Lords, 1790–92. He was chancellor of Oxford University, 1773–92; lord lieutenant of Somerset, 1774–92; lord warden of the Cinque Ports, 1778–92; and elder brother of Trinity House. M.P. for Banbury, 1754–90.

North, George Augustus. 1757–1802

Of Wroxton, near Banbury, Oxfordshire, and Lower Grosvenor Street, London; as oldest son succeeded his father, Frederick North (*q.v.*), as 3d Earl of Guilford in 1792. Eton, 1766–74; Oxford, 1774–77. He married (1) in 1785 Maria, 3d daughter of George Hobart (*q.v.*), and (2) in 1796 Susan, daughter of Thomas Coutts (*q.v.*). He was colonel of a regiment of Cinque Ports volunteers in 1778 but saw no active military service. He was secretary to his father in the Exchequer in 1782; comptroller of the queen's household, 1781–84; and under-secretary of state to his father in the coalition ministry, April–December, 1783. He was named one of the proposed commissioners for India in Fox's defeated bill in 1783. He played a part in bringing his father and Charles Fox together to form a coalition and voted against Shelburne's peace terms in 1783. He was one of the managers of the impeachment proceedings against Warren Hastings in 1787, and was authoritatively said to have declined an offer from Pitt to become governor general of India in 1792. He rarely addressed the House of Commons, but in the House of Lords after his father's death in 1792, he was more vocal. He was frank, conciliatory, and sometimes witty but extremely lazy, with little strength of character and only moderate ability. M.P. for Harwich, 1778–84; Wootton Bassett, 1784–90; Petersfield, 1790; Banbury, 1790–92.

Northampton, 8th Earl. See **Spencer Compton**

Northesk, 6th Earl. See **George Carnegie**

Northey, William. ca.1722–70

Of Compton Bassett, near Calne, and Ivy House, near Chippenham, both in Wiltshire; oldest son of William Northey (ca.1686–1738; M.P.). Cambridge; Middle Temple from 1739. He married (1) in 1742 Harriet, daughter of Robert Vyner (or Viner) (*q.v.*), and (2) Anne, daughter of Edward Hopkins (M.P.; secretary of state in Ireland). He was groom of the bedchamber, 1760–70; member of the Board of Trade and Plantations in 1770. He was considered a Tory and was so listed in 1761. He supported Newcastle and then Grenville but did not vote in 1766 against repeal of the Stamp Act, and he gave general support to the Grafton ministry, 1767–70. M.P. for Calne, 1747–61; Maidstone, 1761–68; Great Bedwin, 1768–70.

Northington, 1st and 2d Earls. See **Robert Henley.** ca.1708–72 and **Robert Henley.** 1747–86

Northumberland, 1st and 2d Dukes. See **Hugh Percy.** 1715–86 and **Hugh Percy.** 1742–1817

Northwick, 1st Baron. See **John Rushout.** 1738–1800

Norton, Chapple. 1746–1818

3d son of Fletcher Norton (1716–89) (*q.v.*); brother of William Norton (*q.v.*), Fletcher Norton (1744–1820) (*q.v.*), and Edward Norton (*q.v.*). He became captain in the 19th Foot in 1763. He distinguished himself in the American war and was made colonel in 1780, major general in 1787, lieutenant general in 1797, and general in 1798. Though tending toward political independence, he voted with his family, which was allied to Sir James Lowther (1736–1802) (*q.v.*), and generally supported Pitt. He seldom addressed the House of Commons. M.P. for Guildford, 1784–90, 1796–1806, and 1807–12.

Norton, Edward. 1750–86

4th son of Fletcher Norton (1716–89) (*q.v.*); brother of Chapple Norton (*q.v.*), William Norton (*q.v.*), and Fletcher Norton (1744–1820) (*q.v.*). Oxford from 1766, Middle Temple from 1772, barrister in

1775. He sat in the House of Commons "in the interest of" James Lowther (1736–1802) (*q.v.*). In the 5 crucial divisions recorded in early 1782, he voted against the North ministry. He voted for Shelburne's peace terms in 1783, opposed the coalition and Fox's India Bill, and supported Pitt from 1784. There is no record that he ever addressed the House. M.P. for Haslemere, 1780–84; Carlisle, 1784–86.

Norton, Fletcher. 1716–89

Of Grantley, Yorkshire, and Wonersh, near Guildford, Surrey; son of Thomas Norton (of Grantley; d. 1719); knighted in 1762; created Baron Grantley on April 9, 1782, immediately after the fall of the North ministry, with which he had broken in 1780. Cambridge and Middle Temple from 1734, barrister in 1739, bencher from 1754. He was king's counsel from 1754; king's attorney and serjeant for the Duchy of Lancaster, 1758–63; solicitor general, 1763–65; member of the Admiralty Board in 1766; privy councillor from 1769; and chief justice in Eyre south of Trent, 1769–89. He entered Parliament as a Whig but later was often called Tory. He took office under Bute and Grenville and in 1768 and 1769 defended Mansfield's ruling in the Wilkes outlawry case. On the motion of North and the second of Richard Rigby, he was elected speaker of the House of Commons in 1770, succeeding Sir John Cust. He was re-elected speaker in 1774, and until nearly 1780 supported the North ministry as a King's Friend. But he developed increasing doubts about the wisdom of the ministry's measures in the American war and ceased to be a King's Friend (indeed he incurred the king's hot anger) when he made remarks in the House of the "more than ample" grants made to the court by Parliament. In 1780 he was also critical of North for considering Alexander Wedderburn for appointment as chief justice, a post he wanted for himself. He also supported Burke's Establishment Bill. Consequently, to his intense displeasure, after the 1780 elections the North ministry replaced him as speaker with Charles Cornwall (or Cornewall). He voted for Dunning's resolution of April 6, 1780, and with the opposition in 3 of the crucial divisions reported in February and March, 1782, including Sir John Rous's no-confidence motion of March 15, 1782. On the formation of the coalition in 1783 he went over to Pitt. Shrewd, able, and experienced, he was not high-principled and was sometimes arrogant; his opponents called him "Sir Bullface Double-face." "As bold as blunt . . . yet his abilities were so good, and his knowledge was so great, that no man had more extensive practice in Westminster Hall," wrote Horace Walpole. He was D.C.L. of Oxford in 1762, fellow of the Royal Society in 1776, and fellow of the Society of Arts in 1779. M.P. for Appleby, 1756–61; Wigan, 1761–68; Guildford, 1768–82.

Norton, Fletcher. 1744–1820

2d son of Fletcher Norton (1716–89) (*q.v.*); brother of William Norton (*q.v.*), Chapple Norton (*q.v.*), and Edward Norton (*q.v.*). Harrow; Eton, 1756–62; Oxford from 1762; Middle Temple from 1765; barrister in 1769; bencher from 1795; treasurer in 1808. In the House of Commons he supported the interests of his family and of Sir James Lowther (1736–1802) (*q.v.*), and presumably supported the North ministry until he withdrew from Parliament in 1775, but there is no record of any vote or speech by him. He was a baron of the Scottish exchequer, 1776–1820. M.P. for Appleby, 1773–74; Carlisle, 1774–75.

Norton, William. 1742–1822

In 1789 succeeded his father, Fletcher Norton (1716–89) (*q.v.*), as 2d Baron Grantley; brother of Chapple Norton (*q.v.*), Edward Norton (*q.v.*), and Fletcher Norton (1744–1820) (*q.v.*). Harrow and Cambridge; Middle Temple from 1755. In politics he followed the lead of his father and the interests of Sir James Lowther (1736–1802) (*q.v.*). He was also politically allied to Lord Stair and to the Onslow family, and was elected with the added support of Sir Lawrence Dundas. He generally supported the North ministry until 1780 and then went with his father into opposition, voting for the Dunning resolution of April 6, 1780, and generally supporting Pitt. He was often absent in connection with his duties as peripatetic minister to Switzerland, 1765–83. M.P. for Richmond (Yorkshire), 1768–74; Wigtown burghs, 1774–75; Richmond, 1775–80; Guildford, 1782–84; Surrey, 1784–89.

Norwich, 1st Earl. See Alexander Gordon

Nottingham, 3d and 4th Earls. See Daniel Finch and George Finch

Nugent, Christopher. 1698–1775

Of Bath and of Queen Anne Street, London. He was born in Ireland, a Roman Catholic, studied in France, and took his medical degree there. He practiced medicine first in Ireland and then in Bath, where he became a prominent physician. Shortly after 1764, he went to London where his daughter married Edmund Burke, who became greatly attached to him. He was an original member of Samuel Johnson's Literary Club. In 1753 he published the results of his researches into hydrophobia. He was a fellow of the Royal Society from 1765.

Nugent, Edmund. 1731–71

Of Gosfield, near Halstead, Essex; son and heir of Robert Nugent (later Craggs Nugent) (*q.v.*) and with him changed his surname to Craggs Nugent ca. 1737, but predeceased his father. He was captain of the 85th Foot in 1759 and lieutenant colonel in 1762. He was groom of the bedchamber, 1760–71. With his father he defected from support of Newcastle in October, 1762, and thereafter he followed his father in his votes, and supported the Grafton ministry on the Wilkes issues. His excesses were probably the cause of his chronic bad health and early death in his 40th year. M.P. for Liskeard, 1754–59; St. Mawes, 1761–70.

Nugent, George. 1757–1849

Of Waddesdon House, near Little Marlow, Berkshire; illegitimate son of Edmund Nugent (*q.v.*); half brother of Charles Edmund Nugent (ca.1759–1844; admiral of the fleet in 1833); grandson of Robert Nugent (later Craggs Nugent) (*q.v.*). He entered the army in 1773 and was lieutenant in 1777, major in 1782, lieutenant colonel in 1783, major general in 1796, and general in 1813. He saw service in America, 1777–83, and in the Netherlands in 1793. He raised troops in Buckinghamshire to defend against the French. He was in command in Ireland, 1796–1801. In 1797 in Belfast he married Maria, daughter of Courtland Skinner (sometime attorney general of New Jersey). He was lieutenant governor of Jamaica, 1801–1806, and on his return to England was created baronet. He was in India as commander in chief, 1811–13. He was made Grand Commander of the Bath in 1815 and field marshal in 1846. M.P. for Buckinghamshire, 1790–1802; Aylesbury, 1806–12; Buckingham Borough, 1818–32.

Nugent (later Craggs Nugent), Robert. 1702–88

2d son of Michael Nugent (of Carlowstown, County Meath), whom he succeeded in 1739 as 10th baronet (Irish); in 1767 created Baron

Nugent and Viscount Clare (both Irish); in 1776 created Earl Nugent (Irish). He married (1) in 1730 Emilia, 2d daughter of Peter Plunkett (4th Earl of Fingall, Irish); (2) in 1737 Anne, widow of John Knight and daughter of James Craggs (postmaster general, 1715–21), and added not only the surname Craggs but £150,000 to his assets; and (3) Elizabeth, widow of Augustus (4th Earl of Berkeley). He gained election to the House of Commons for St. Mawes, a borough in Cornwall controlled by the family of his third wife. While comptroller of the household of Prince Frederick from 1747, he lent the prince large sums, which were repaid in terms of "places, pensions and peerages" by George III. He was a member of the Treasury Board, 1754–59; privy councillor from 1759; vice treasurer of Ireland, 1759–65 and 1768–82; and 1st lord of trade and plantations, 1766–68. He normally supported the ministry currently in power, abandoning Newcastle when he fell in 1762 and taking with him his reputed control of 4 seats in the House of Commons. He was considered a Whig until 1770, when he began to support the North ministry, and he voted with that ministry, or was paired, in all 5 of the crucial divisions recorded in February and March, 1782. In 1783 he did not vote on Shelburne's peace terms or on Fox's India Bill, but he spoke in favor of the receipt tax. He was on friendly if somewhat patronizing terms with Oliver Goldsmith, and wrote verses, some of which he published. His daughter married George Nugent-Temple Grenville (*q.v.*). "A jovial and voluptuous Irishman who left Popery for the Protestant religion, money, and widows" (Glover). "A thoroughly unprincipled, if amusing, blackguard" (1775 *Peerage*). "An Irish converted Catholic stallion" (Horace Walpole). M.P. for St. Mawes, 1741–54; Bristol, 1754–74; St. Mawes, 1774–84.

Nugent, 1st and 2d Earls. See **Robert Nugent** (later **Craggs Nugent**) and **George Nugent-Temple Grenville**

Nuneham, Viscount. See **George Simon Harcourt**

O'Brien, Murrough. 1726–1808

Of Taplow, near Maidenhead, Buckinghamshire; oldest son of James

O'Brien (3d son of the 3d Earl of Inchiquin, Irish); in 1777 succeeded his uncle William O'Brien as 5th Earl of Inchiquin; in 1800 created Marquess of Thomond (Irish); in 1801 created Baron Thomond (English). He married (1) in 1753 his cousin Mary, daughter of William O'Brien (4th Earl of Inchiquin), and (2) in 1792 Mary, niece of Sir Joshua Reynolds. He was ensign in the foot guards in 1743 and captain in 1747, but retired from the army in 1756. He inherited with his uncle's title an estate worth about £9,000 a year and was a member of the Irish Parliament, 1757–68. In 1769 he signed the Buckinghamshire petition against the Grafton ministry's measures against Wilkes. In the English House of Commons he voted for Pitt's reforms but often opposed him on other issues. M.P. for Richmond, 1784–96; Liskeard, 1797–1800.

Offaly, Lord and 1st and 2d Earls. See James Fitzgerald and William Robert Fitzgerald

Offley, John. ca.1718–84

Of Wichnor, near Lichfield, Staffordshire; oldest son of Crewe Offley (of Wichnor; M.P.). He was a man of fashion with political loyalties to the Pelhams, whom he supported as loyally as they supported him. In 1762 he resigned his post as groom of the bedchamber, as well as a secret-service pension of £400 a year, in protest against the treatment of Newcastle. He opposed the Grenville and supported the Rockingham ministry, 1763–67. In 1768 Newcastle used his influence to help him secure a seat for East Retford, after he had declined an offer of a court appointment from Grafton. He was surveyor of the king's private roads, 1756–57, and groom of the bedchamber, 1757–62. There is no indication that he ever addressed the House of Commons. M.P. for Bedford Borough, 1747–54; Orford, 1754–68; East Retford, 1768–74.

Ogilvy, Charles. ca.1731–88

Of Pall Mall, London; 4th son of James Ogilvy (of Auchiries, Aberdeenshire). Because his brother had served with the Jacobite army in 1745, he thought it expedient to emigrate to South Carolina, where he became a prosperous merchant in Charleston, exporting rice and importing wine. About 1760, still a young man, he returned to Britain

and established his business in London, though retaining a considerable property in Carolina, to which he returned briefly in 1774. He
was elected to Parliament with the support of the North ministry.
During his year of membership he supported the North ministry in
general, but there is no evidence that he took part in the debates on the
colonies, or of what he thought regarding them. M.P. for West Looe,
1774–75.

Ogilvy, James. ca.1714–70

Styled Lord Deskford from 1730; in 1764 he succeeded his father,
James Ogilvy, as 6th Earl of Findlater and Earl of Seafield (both titles
Scottish). He made the grand tour ca. 1740. In 1749 he married Mary,
18th child of John Murray (1st Duke of Atholl, Scottish). He was
commissioner of customs for Scotland, 1754–61; chancellor of King's
College, Aberdeen, 1761–70; and Scottish lord of police from 1765 to
1770, when he committed suicide. He had also been trustee for the
improvement of fisheries and manufactures for Scotland. Walpole
pronounced him "a mighty sensible man (but) mighty grave."

Oglethorpe, James Edward. 1696–1785

Born in London; 3d son of Sir Theophilus Oglethorpe (d. 1702; of
Westbrook, near Godalming, Surrey); in 1727 succeeded his brother
Theophilus Oglethorpe (ca.1682–1727) as 2d baronet. Eton, to Oxford
in 1714; M.A. 1731. He was ensign in the foot guards at the age of 11
and fought as lieutenant under Prince Eugene at the capture of
Belgrade in 1717 when about 21. In the House of Commons from 1722,
he was active in debate, and often "his exceeding shrill voice could be
heard in the lobby," according to his obituary in the *Gentleman's
Magazine* in 1785. In 1729 he became chairman of a committee of the
House to inquire into the state of the prisons in Britain. It was certainly
in part as a result of that experience that he sought more humane ways
of dealing with imprisoned debtors and other victims of the sometimes
barbaric traditional laws for the treatment of criminals. He proposed
to found a colony in Georgia, where such offenders could be given
the opportunity to start new lives. His project had the approval of the
king and court, since his colony would serve as a barrier between the
other British colonies and the Spaniards south of them. He began his
settlement in 1732–34 and commanded the troops that defended it

from the Spanish attacks in 1742, but himself failed in an attack on Spanish St. Augustine in 1740. He was much criticized for his management of the colony because he prohibited the importation of Negro slaves and of rum; he also had difficulties with the Wesley brothers and Whitefield. In 1743 he returned to England and was made brigadier general, and in 1745, when he served against the Jacobites, he became major general, but was accused by Cumberland of being too "soft" with the Jacobites. In the resultant court-martial he was acquitted of the heinous charge of humanity, and though he did not return to further active service, he was made lieutenant general in 1747 and general in 1765. His interest in his colony had scientific aspects: in June, 1734, he escorted a group of Cherokee Indians to England. He was made a fellow of the Royal Society in 1749. Pope mentioned him in his verses, and Samuel Johnson accepted him as a member of his circle. M.P. for Haslemere, 1722–54.

O'Hara, Charles. 1740–1802

Illegitimate son of James O'Hara (*q.v.*); grandson of Charles O'Hara (ca.1640–1724). In 1756 he entered the Coldstream Guards, of which his father was colonel. He was aide to Granby in 1759 and quartermaster general in Portugal in 1762. He commanded the troops in action at Gorée in Senegal in 1766 and in 1781 served under Cornwallis in America in the Carolina campaign, and was wounded at Guilford. He represented Cornwallis, who pleaded illness, in the negotiations for the surrender at Yorktown in 1781. Exchanged, he became major general in 1782 and lieutenant general in 1783. He was again wounded and again captured, this time by the French, at Toulon in 1793, but was exchanged in 1795, and, like his father, was governor of Gibraltar, 1795–1802. He died in Gibraltar, a wealthy man. He was for some years engaged to marry Horace Walpole's young friend Mary Berry, who called him "the most perfect specimen of a soldier and a courtier of the past age" but apparently decided not to marry perfection.

O'Hara, James Charles. 1690–1773

In 1724 succeeded his father, Charles O'Hara (ca.1640–1724), as 2d Baron Tyrawley, having succeeded him as colonel of the Royal Fusiliers in 1713; in 1722 created Baron Kilamine (Irish). In 1724 he married the sister of the 1st Earl of Blessington (Irish). He was a lieutenant in his father's regiment in 1703 at 13 and a captain in 1704 at 14 and served with his father in Spain, 1706–1707. He was wounded at Almanza in 1707 and was severely wounded again while aide to Marlborough at Malplaquet in 1709. He was colonel at Minorca in 1713; aide to George I and then to George II, 1727–43; envoy to Portugal, 1728–41. He was brigadier general in 1735, major general in 1739, lieutenant general in 1743, general in 1761, and field marshal in 1763. He was ambassador to Russia, 1743–45; governor of Minorca, 1747–56; and governor of Gibraltar, 1756–57. In 1757, Lord George Sackville (later Germain) charged him in the House of Commons with waste in strengthening the fortifications of Gibraltar. He demanded to be heard by the House and there defended himself with such wit and force that he won over the House and discredited Sackville. In 1762 he was made privy councillor and returned to Portugal. He was governor of Portsmouth in 1763. Horace Walpole said that he had "a great deal of humour, and occasionally good breeding . . . but imperiously blunt, haughty," and high-spirited.

Oliver, Richard. 1735–84

Of Fenchurch Street, London; son of Rowland Oliver (a judge and planter in Antigua). He was born in Antigua, but became a West Indies merchant in London. He was alderman for Billingsgate, 1770–78, and sheriff of London, 1772–73. He was a leader in forming the Society of Supporters of the Bill of Rights, 1769–71. In 1771 he was called before the House of Commons with Wilkes and Crosby to answer for his conduct in impeding and arresting the messenger of the House in the performance of his duty in the Wilkes case. He was committed to the Tower but soon released, and in the same year, as a member of the House, he voted against declaring printers Wheble and Thompson in contempt of the House. In 1773 he supported Sawbridge's motion for annually elected Parliaments. In 1775 he opposed acceptance of the address from the throne and proposed a vote of censure of the North ministry for its corruption and its American measures, and demanded to know who were the king's harmful "secret advisors." In 1778 he returned to Antigua to look after his estates there and died at sea on the return voyage. He seldom addressed the House, but was effective when he did so. He had quarreled with Wilkes but remained an advocate of reform and "liberty" and an opponent of the North ministry. M.P. for London, 1770–80.

Olmius, Drigue Billiers. 1746–87

Of New Hall, near Boreham, and Chelmsford, Essex; in 1762 succeeded his father, John Olmius (*q.v.*), as 2d Baron Waltham (Irish). In general he supported the current ministry, though he voted against North's Royal Marriage Bill in 1772. After 1784 he opposed Pitt, though in 1785 he voted for Pitt's Reform Bill. His only recorded speech in the House of Commons was a brief seconding of a motion against Wilkes in 1768. M.P. for Weymouth and Melcombe Regis, 1768–74; Malden, 1784–87.

Olmius, John. 1711–62

Of New Hall, near Boreham, and Chelmsford, Essex; only son of John Olmius (a Dutch merchant settled in Braintree, Essex; deputy governor of the Bank of England); in 1762 created Baron Waltham (Irish). He was high sheriff of Essex, 1746–47. In Parliament he was regarded as a staunch Whig; it was from Bute that he secured his Irish peerage. M.P. for Weymouth and Melcombe Regis, 1737–41; Colchester, 1741–42 and 1754–61; Weymouth and Melcombe Regis, 1761–62.

O'Neill, John. 1740–98

Of Shane's Castle, on Lough Neagh, County Antrim; oldest son of Charles O'Neill (of Shane's Castle); in 1793 created Baron O'Neill (Irish); in 1795 created Viscount O'Neill (Irish). Trinity College, Dublin, from 1757, Oxford from 1762. In 1777 he married Henrietta, granddaughter of John Boyle (*q.v.*). He was a member of the Irish Parliament, 1761–93, and an Irish privy councillor from 1780. He supported the Irish nationalists and in 1781 moved approval of the address from the throne and a vote of thanks to the Irish volunteers. He opposed Pitt in 1785 and 1787. A Protestant, toward the end of his career he declared himself in favor of Irish emancipation but died, while governor of County Antrim, while fighting rebels in Antrim.

Ongley, 1st Baron. See Robert Henley-Ongley

Onslow, Arthur. 1691–1768

Of Imber Court, near Thames Ditton, Surrey; oldest son of Foot Onslow (M.P.). Winchester from 1706, Oxford from 1708, Middle

Temple from 1707, barrister in 1713, bencher from 1728. He was
secretary to the chancellor of the exchequer, 1714–15; recorder of
Guildford from 1719; speaker of the House of Commons, 1727–61,
during the entire reign of George II; privy councillor from 1728;
chancellor to the queen, 1729–37; treasurer of the navy, 1734–42; and
trustee of the British Museum. The marriage of his son, George
Onslow (1731–1814) (*q.v.*), to a niece of the Duke of Newcastle further cemented his political affiliations with the Pelhams, and he usually
gave his personal support to the Whig ministry in power, though as
speaker he set a high standard of impartiality and good management
of the House. Upon his retirement the House voted him an annuity
of £3,000 a year for life for him and his son. M.P. for Guildford,
1720–27; Surrey, 1727–61 (41 consecutive years).

Onslow, Edward. 1758–1829

Of Imber Court, near Thames Ditton, Surrey; 2d son of George
Onslow (1731–1814) (*q.v.*). Westminster from 1766, Oxford from
1774, Middle Temple from 1768, barrister from 1778. He was especially
esteemed for his good manners because, it was said, they were in such
contrast to those of other members of his family. Upon election to
Parliament in 1780 he was thought to have an important career before
him in the House. But in 1781 he was accused of homosexual practice
and after first denying it admitted it. He withdrew to France, married,
and lived there as a respected citizen. M.P. for Aldborough, 1780–81.

Onslow, George. 1731–1814

Of Imber Court, near Thames Ditton, Surrey; only son of Arthur
Onslow (*q.v.*) and inherited the £3,000 annual pension voted to his
father by the House; in 1776 created Baron Cranley; in that year succeeded his cousin Richard Onslow (1713–76) (*q.v.*) as 4th Baron
Onslow; created Earl Onslow in 1801. Westminster from 1739, Cambridge from 1749. In 1753 he married Henrietta, daughter of Sir John
Shelley (1692–1771; M.P.; and 4th baronet) and niece of Thomas
Pelham-Holles (1st Duke of Newcastle, new creation). He was outranger of Windsor Great Park, 1754–63; surveyor of the royal gardens
and waters, 1761–63. In December, 1762, he voted against Bute's peace
preliminaries and soon after was dismissed from court office. He continued to support Newcastle and made for his use a list of members of

the House of Commons and their party affiliations. In 1765 he supported the Rockingham ministry. He served on the Treasury Board, 1765–67, and on the Privy Council. Though at first he defended Wilkes, in 1769 he moved that the election of Wilkes be declared invalid, and in 1770 he took legal action against Horne Tooke, though judgment was withheld on technical grounds. He supported the North ministry, and was comptroller of the household, 1777–79; treasurer of the household, 1779–80; lord of the bedchamber, 1780–84; high steward of Guildford and lord lieutenant of Surrey, 1776–1814, and colonel from 1794. In 1767 he was granted 10,000 acres in East Florida at a quitrent of a halfpenny an acre. In 1778 he voted against permitting peers to attend funeral services for Lord Chatham in the House of Commons. In 1783 he voted for Fox's India Bill; in 1788 he supported Pitt's Regency Bill. Horace Walpole, a political opponent, called him "a noisy, indiscreet man" but could not deny that he was sometimes effective. He was once hanged in effigy by a London mob. M.P. for Rye, 1754–61; Surrey, 1761–74.

Onslow, George. 1731–92

Of Ockham, near Guildford, Surrey; oldest son of Lieutenant General Richard Onslow (ca.1697–1760; M.P.); cousin of George Onslow (1731–1814) (*q.v.*). He was ensign in 1748 and captain in the foot guards in 1750, lieutenant colonel in 1759, and retired from service in 1762. He was outranger of Windsor Forest, 1765–92. He supported successively the administrations of Newcastle, Rockingham, Grafton, and North, voting for repeal of the Stamp Act in 1766 and against the expulsion of Wilkes in 1770. But he supported North against Burke's conciliation proposals, against Dunning's resolution of April 6, 1780, and later against "any invasions of the prerogative of the crown." He supported the bill to control gambling in 1782, denied the importance of holding Gibraltar at all costs in 1782, and in February and March, 1782, voted with the North ministry in all 5 of the crucial divisions recorded. He thought well of the 1783 coalition, voted against Shelburne's peace terms, and "reprehended" Pitt for his harsh attack on North in February, 1783. He was small, pompous, opinionated, generous, intelligent, effective. M.P. for Guildford, 1760–84.

Onslow, Middleton. d. 1801

Of Drungewicke Manor, near Loxwood, Sussex; oldest son of Denzil

Onslow (M.P.); 3d cousin of George Onslow (1731–1814) (*q.v.*). He was elected to fill a seat until Thomas Onslow (*q.v.*) came of age. Though he presumably followed the family line in politics, there is no record of any vote or speech in the House of Commons. M.P. for Rye, 1774–75.

Onslow, Richard. 1713–76

In 1740 succeeded his father, Thomas Onslow (1679–1740; M.P.), as 3d Baron Onslow. Eton, 1728–30; Cambridge from 1730; L.L.D., 1749. He was lord lieutenant of Surrey and high steward of Guildford, 1740–76, and Knight of the Bath from 1753. He was related through the Speke family to Lord North. M.P. for Guildford, 1734–40.

Onslow, Richard. 1741–1817

Son of Lieutenant General Richard Onslow (ca.1697–1760; M.P.); brother of George Onslow (1731–92) (*q.v.*); nephew of Arthur Onslow (*q.v.*); cousin of George Onslow (1731–1814) (*q.v.*); created baronet in 1797. He served in the navy as lieutenant from 1758 and commander from 1761. He served under Howe, 1777–78, and was in action against D'Estaing in 1778 and at the relief of Gibraltar, 1781–82. He was made rear admiral in 1793 and vice admiral in 1794 and was made second in command in the North Sea operations in 1796 and at Camperdown. He was made admiral in 1799. In politics he supported Newcastle and then North but was never a member of Parliament. He was made Grand Commander of the Bath in 1815.

Onslow, Thomas. 1754–1827

Of West Clandon, near Guildford, Surrey; oldest son of George Onslow (1731–1814) (*q.v.*), whom he succeeded in 1814 as 2d Earl Onslow; brother of Edward Onslow (*q.v.*); styled Viscount Cranley from 1801 until he succeeded his father as earl. Westminster, 1767–71; Cambridge from 1771. He supported the North ministry, including all 5 crucial divisions recorded in February and March, 1782; supported North in the coalition; voted for Fox's India Bill in November, 1783; and opposed Pitt in 1784. He became colonel of the Surrey militia and in 1793 succeeded his father as outranger of Windsor Park. He made little effort to be influential in politics but was talented, wrote humorous verse, and was regarded as a great wit. "His predominant passion was driving four-in-hand," according to Wraxall. M.P. for Rye, 1775–84; Guildford, 1784–1806.

Opie, John. 1761–1807

Born at St. Agnes near Truro, Cornwall, the son of a Cornish carpenter. He became an itinerant portrait painter and in 1780 made his way to London in company with John Wolcot ("Peter Pindar") (*q.v.*). He was introduced to the court by Mrs. Boscawen, and soon became fashionable as "the Cornish wonder." He received commissions from the royal family and painted many ladies of the court. From 1782 he exhibited at the Royal Academy, of which he became a member in 1787 and was a teaching professor from 1798. He painted 508 portraits, mostly in oil, including those of Charles Fox, Edmund Burke, Samuel Johnson, Robert Southey, and Mrs. Inchbald. His second wife, Amelia Alderson, whom he married in 1798, was something of a novelist and poet and prefixed her memoir of him to his *Lectures in Painting*, published in 1809.

Ord, John. 1729–1814

Of Bingfield, near Corbridge, Northumberland; only son of Robert Ord (*q.v.*). Cambridge from 1746; B.A., 1750; fellow from 1752; Lincoln's Inn from 1747; barrister in 1754. He was attorney general of the Duchy of Lancaster, 1777–1810; master in chancery, 1778–1809; fellow of the Royal Society from 1780; and chairman of several important committees in the House of Commons. He supported the North ministry in every crucial vote to its end in late March, 1782. In 1783 he voted for both Shelburne's peace terms and Fox's India Bill. In 1784 he opposed Pitt. M.P. for Midhurst, 1774–80; Hastings, 1780–84; Wendover, 1784–90.

Ord, Robert. 1700–78

Of Newbiggin, near Carlisle, Northumberland, and Petersham, Surrey; 9th son of John Ord (of Newcastle-on-Tyne; solicitor). Lincoln's Inn from 1718, barrister in 1724. He was secretary to the chancellor of the exchequer, 1742–43; deputy cofferer, 1743–44; chief baron of the exchequer of Scotland, 1755–75. He appears to have supported Pelham and Newcastle. With an ample fortune, he built "an elegant house and lived in it magnificently in Scotland," according to Boswell. M.P. for St. Michael, 1734–41; Morpeth, 1741–55.

Orde, John. 1751–1824

Son of John Orde (of East Orde and Morpeth, Durham County); younger brother of Thomas Orde (later Orde-Powlett) (*q.v.*); created baronet in 1790. He entered the navy in 1766 and was lieutenant in 1774. He saw service in American and West Indies waters during and after the American war, with Byron, Howe, Collier, and Arbuthnot. He commanded the *Zebra* in the Delaware River estuary in 1778 and was with Clinton at the capture of Charleston in 1780. He was governor of Dominica in 1783, rear admiral in 1795, and vice admiral in 1799. He commanded a squadron off Finisterre, 1804–1805, and was made admiral in 1805. M.P. for Yarmouth (Isle of Wight), 1807–12.

Orde (later Orde-Powlett), Thomas. 1746–1807

Of Hackwood Park, near Basingstoke, Hampshire; son of John Orde (of East Orde and Morpeth, Durham County); older brother of John Orde (*q.v.*); in 1797 created Baron Bolton of Bolton Castle, Yorkshire. Eton, 1755–65; Cambridge from 1765; fellow, 1768–78; M.A., 1773; Lincoln's Inn from 1769; barrister in 1765. In 1778 he married Jean, illegitimate daughter of Charles Powlett (ca.1718–65; M.P.; 5th Duke of Bolton); assumed the surname Orde-Powlett, and inherited large estates in 1765. Considered a Tory, he was auditor of the Duchy of Cornwall, 1772–74; receiver general of taxes, 1774–1807; and secretary to the treasury in the Shelburne ministry in 1782. He supported the North ministry from the time he entered the House of Commons in late 1780, voting with it in every recorded crucial division in February and March, 1782. In 1781 he drew up for that ministry the report of the secret committee on East India affairs. In 1783 he voted for Shelburne's peace terms and against Fox's India Bill. In 1784 he became a staunch adherent of Pitt. He was secretary to the lord lieutenant of Ireland and member of the Irish Privy Council, 1784–87, and member of the Irish Parliament, 1784–90. He was English privy councillor from 1785; member of the Board of Trade, 1786–1807; governor of the Isle of Wight, 1791–1807; and lord lieutenant of Hampshire, 1800–1807. He was a close friend of George Romney (*q.v.*), the portrait painter. M.P. for Aylesbury, 1780–84; Harwich, 1784–96.

Orford, 3d and 4th Earls; 1st and 2d Earls of a new creation. See **Horatio Walpole (Horace).** 1717–97   **George Walpole.** 1730–91   **Horatio Walpole.** 1723–1809   and **Horatio Walpole.** 1752–1822.

Orme, Robert. 1728–1801

Born at Anjengo, Travancore, India, 2d son of Alexander Orme (surgeon for the East India Company). He was sent to England at the age of 2 and was schooled at Harrow. He was back in Calcutta in 1742 and entered the service of the company in 1743 at the age of 14. In 1748 he was a writer with the company. He returned with Clive to England in 1753, but was again in India as a member of the Madras Council, 1754–58, and commissary general for India, 1757–58. In 1759 he was captured by the French on shipboard en route to England, but was later released. In England from late 1760, he wrote his *History of the Military Transactions of the British Nation in Indostan from 1745,* the 1st volume of which was published in 1763, the 2d and 3d volumes in 1778. The original of that work is preserved at the India Office. He broke with Clive and from 1769 was historiographer for the company, living in England, and in 1782 published his *Historical Fragments of the Mogul Empire, the Morattoes, and English Concerns in Indostan from 1659.* He became a friend of Samuel Johnson. Portrait by Nollekens.

Orwell, 1st Baron and 1st Viscount. See Francis Vernon

Osbaldeston, Fountayne Wentworth. 1696–1770

4th son of Sir Richard Osbaldeston (of Hunmanby, near Scarborough, Yorkshire; M.P.); brother of William Osbaldeston (*q.v.*). Cambridge from 1712, barrister of Lincoln's Inn in 1725. In 1766 he succeeded his brother William in Parliament without a contest and there supported Newcastle and Rockingham. Only 1 vote by him (against the Grafton ministry on the Middlesex election issue) is recorded after 1768, and there is no evidence that he ever addressed the House of Commons. M.P. for Scarborough, 1766–70.

Osbaldeston, Richard. 1690–1764

2d son of Richard Osbaldeston (of Havercroft, West Riding, Yorkshire, and Osbaldeston, near Blackburn, Lancashire; baronet). Cambridge from 1707, B.A., 1711; M.A., 1714; fellow from 1714; D.D., 1726. With the aid of the Duke of Portland he secured and held the rich living of Hinderwell, Yorkshire, 1715–62. He was royal chaplain to George II from 1727 and later tutor of the future George III. He was dean of

York Cathedral, 1728–47; bishop of Carlisle, 1747–62; and bishop of London, 1762–64, when he prohibited the introduction of statuary into St. Paul's. "A Whig in politics, and liberal in his church views, rich, indolent and [as bishop of Carlisle] chiefly non-resident, leaving his diocese to be administered by his vigorous Chancellor" (*DNB*).

Osbaldeston, William. 1688–1766

Of Hunmanby, near Scarborough, Yorkshire; oldest son of Richard Osbaldeston (of Hunmanby; M.P.); brother of Fontayne Wentworth Osbaldeston (*q.v.*). Cambridge from 1706. He was a Whig country gentleman of the old school, a steady supporter of Sir Robert Walpole and then of the Pelhams, but not an office seeker. He did not follow Newcastle into opposition in 1763 but did support Rockingham, 1765–66, and did not vote in 1766 against repeal of the Stamp Act. There is no evidence that he addressed the House of Commons after 1754. M.P. for Scarborough, 1736–47 and 1754–66.

Osborn (or Osborne), George. 1742–1818

Of Chicksands Priory, near Ampthill, Bedfordshire; in 1753 succeeded his father, Sir Danvers Osborn (or Osborne) (1715–53; M.P.), as 4th baronet; nephew of George Montagu (1st Earl of Halifax); distantly connected to Lord North. Westminster from 1750, Cambridge from 1759. In 1778 he married (2) Heneage, daughter of Daniel Finch (7th Earl of Winchilsea). He was captain in 1759, major in 1762, colonel in 1777, major general in 1779, lieutenant general in 1787, and general in 1797. He was groom of the bedchamber, 1770–1812, and was elected to Parliament "in the interest of" George Edgcumbe (*q.v.*). He supported the North ministry to its end, voting against the Dunning resolution of April 6, 1780, and with North on all 5 crucial divisions recorded in February and March, 1782. He made 7 speeches on minor issues, voted against Shelburne's peace terms and for Fox's India Bill in 1783, and was not re-elected in 1784. M.P. for Northampton, 1768–69; Bossiney, 1769–74; Penryn, 1774–80; Horsham, 1780–84.

Osborne, Francis Godolphin. 1751–99

Styled Marquess of Carmarthen from 1761; in 1789 he succeeded his father, Thomas Osborne (*q.v.*), as 5th Duke of Leeds. His family was connected with the Beauforts, Berties, Harleys, Herberts,

Herveys, and Walpoles. Westminster, 1764–67; Oxford from 1767; M.A., 1769; D.C.L., 1773. In 1773 he married (1) Amelia, daughter of Robert D'Arcy (*q.v.*), but in 1778 she eloped with John Byron (later father of the poet). He was a fellow of the Royal Society from 1773, and in 1776 was summoned to the House of Lords as Baron Osborne. He was lord of the bedchamber, 1776–77; chamberlain to the queen, 1777–80; privy councillor from 1777; and lord lieutenant of East Riding, 1777–80. In 1780 he told the king privately that he could no longer support the measures of the ministry and offered to resign his court appointment. Like Pembroke, who had done the same thing at almost the same time, he found himself suddenly and unexpectedly removed from his lord lieutenancy. He reported that dismissal, and its background, to the House of Lords, calling the North ministry "pusillanimous, incapable and corrupt." He was supported by opposition peers, but their motion of protest to the king was defeated. He recorded protests in the House of Lords to (1) rejection of a bill to exclude holders of government contracts from membership in Parliament in 1780, (2) passage of a bill to raise government funds by annuities and lotteries in 1781, (3) rejection of a bill to protest the admission to the House as a peer of Lord George Germain as Viscount Sackville in 1782, and (4) rejection of a bill to prevent abuses in public life in 1783. Under the Rockingham ministry of 1782 he was reinstated as lord lieutenant of East Riding, 1782–99. He was ambassador to Paris in 1783; secretary of state, 1784–91; governor of the Scilly Isles, 1785–99; governor of the Levant Company, 1792–99; and Knight of the Garter in 1790. He supported Pitt, 1784–91. According to Wraxall he was "highly accomplished . . . with pleasing manners and very elegant deportment," but Walpole thought him "of very moderate parts, and less principles." M.P. for Eye, 1774; Helston, 1774–75.

Osborne, Thomas. 1713–89

Styled Earl of Danby until 1729 and Marquess of Carmarthen until 1731, when he succeeded his father, Peregrine Hyde Osborne (1691–1731), as 4th Duke of Leeds. Westminster, to Oxford in 1731; D.C.L., 1733. In 1740 he married Mary, daughter of Francis Godolphin (2d Earl Godolphin) and granddaughter of John Churchill (1st Duke of Marlborough). He was a fellow of the Royal Society from 1739; lord of the bedchamber from 1748; chief justice in Eyre south of Trent,

1748–56; Knight of the Garter from 1749; cofferer of the household, 1756–61; privy councillor from 1757; and chief justice in Eyre north of Trent, 1761–64. He was in general a supporter of the North ministry until his son Francis Osborne (Lord Carmarthen) broke with it in 1780. He opposed the coalition and Fox's India Bill in 1783. He was benevolent without ostentation, affable to his inferiors without being patronizing, and "strictly regular in the discharge of his debts" (1775 *Peerage*).

Ossory, Upper, 1st Baron and 2d Earl. See John Fitzpatrick

Ossulton, Lords. See Charles Bennet. 1716–67 and **Charles Bennet. 1743–1822**

Oswald, James. 1715–69

Of Dunnikier, near Colinsburgh, Fifeshire; oldest son of Captain James Oswald (merchant of Fife; provost of Kirkaldy; M.P.). He studied at Edinburgh University, Lincoln's Inn, and Leyden from 1733. He was Scots advocate in 1738 and made the grand tour. In 1747 he married Elizabeth, daughter of Joseph Townshend (London brewer; M.P.). He was commander in the navy in 1745 and Scottish commissioner for the navy, 1745–47; a member of the Board of Trade and Plantations, 1751–59; a member of the Treasury Board, 1759–63; a member of the Privy Council from 1763; and joint vice treasurer of Ireland, 1763–68. He supported Pelham and then, less dependably, Newcastle; he was active in opposition to repeal of the Stamp Act in 1766. A friend of Halifax and of Adam Smith, he was something of a financial expert, and was consulted by Halifax on state finances and later by Shelburne on American affairs. Horace Walpole thought him one of the 30 best speakers in the House of Commons, but he spoke infrequently and not inspiringly. He was certainly one of the abler members of Parliament. M.P. for Dysart burghs, 1741–47; Fifeshire, 1747–54; Dysart burghs, 1754–68.

Oswald, James Townshend. 1748–1814

Of Dunnikier, near Colinsburgh, Fifeshire; only son of James Oswald (*q.v.*). Edinburgh University, 1764–66; Oxford from 1766; traveled in France in 1767. He was secretary for the Leeward Islands in 1772 and auditor general of the Scottish exchequer from 1779. He supported

Grafton and then North, though in 1774 he voted against North in voting to continue the Grenville Disputed Elections Act. M.P. for Dysart burghs, 1768–74; Fifeshire, 1776–79.

Oswald, Richard. 1705–84

2d son of Rev. James George Oswald (minister of Dunnett, near Thurso, Caithness). In 1750 he married Mary, only daughter and heiress of Alexander Ramsay (of Jamaica), who brought him valuable estates in America and the West Indies and enabled him to buy the estate of Auchincruive in Ayrshire. He became a London merchant, acquired a government contract to supply British troops on the Continent, and was commissary general to the army of Prince Eugene during the Seven Years' War. He was a friend of Adam Smith, who recommended him to Shelburne, who used him as his agent in peace negotiations with Franklin in Paris in 1782, and as a chief negotiator of the peace treaty with the United States, 1782–83.

Oughton, James Adolphus Dickenson. 1720–80

Illegitimate son of Sir Adolphus Oughton (ca.1685–1736; of Tachbrooke Mallory, near Warwick, Warwickshire; M.P.; brigadier general). He was a lieutenant in the army in 1741 and captain in 1742. He saw service at Culloden in 1746 and in Flanders, 1747–48. He was long lieutenant governor of Antigua, and in command of the forces in North Britain, 1768–80. He was major general in 1761, lieutenant general in 1770, and Knight of the Bath from ca. 1770. Through friendship with James Boswell, who called him one of the "most universal scholars" he ever knew, he became a favored acquaintance of Samuel Johnson. He appears to have taken no active part in politics.

Ourry, Paul Henry. 1719–83

Of Plympton Erle, Devon; 2d son of Louis Ourry (naturalized Huguenot). In 1747 he married Charity, daughter of George Treby (ca.1684–1742; M.P.; secretary at war). He was lieutenant in the navy in 1742, captain in 1757, and resident commissioner of Plymouth dockyard, 1775–83. In the House of Commons he appears to have supported each ministry currently in office; there is no record of his ever having addressed the House. M.P. for Plympton Erle, 1763–75.

Owen, Hugh. See Hugh Oliver Barlow

Owen, Hugh. ca.1730–86

Of Orielton, near Pembroke, Pembrokeshire; in 1781 succeeded his father, William Owen (*q.v.*), as 5th baronet. Cambridge from 1749. In the House of Commons he voted largely in opposition to the North ministry, 1770–74; thereafter he attended irregularly and voted with the ministry until 1780, when he voted for the Dunning resolution of April 6, 1780. In the 5 crucial divisions recorded in February and March, 1782, he cast no reported votes. In 1783 he voted against Shelburne's peace terms and for Fox's India Bill. In 1784 he opposed Pitt, against whom, according to John Robinson (who had become a supporter and political analyst for Pitt), he "has some grievances, indeed some fair ones." He was lord lieutenant of Pembrokeshire, 1778–86. M.P. for Pembrokeshire, 1770–86.

Owen, William. ca.1697–1781

Of Orielton, near Pembroke, Pembrokeshire, and Bodowen, Anglesey; in 1753 succeeded his father, Sir Arthur Owen, as 4th baronet. Oxford from 1713. He was lord lieutenant of Pembrokeshire under the aegis of Newcastle, 1761–78, and was succeeded in that office by his son Hugh Owen (ca.1730–86) (*q.v.*). During his 52 years in the House of Commons he left no record of a single speech and apparently attended only infrequently. His interest was chiefly in local affairs and local patronage. Though he was opposed in his 1761 election by a candidate supported by Newcastle, he steadily supported Newcastle from that time and after Newcastle held his lord lieutenancy by supporting nearly every current ministry. M.P. for Pembroke boroughs, 1722–47; Pembrokeshire, 1747–61; Pembroke boroughs, 1761–74.

Owen, William Mostyn. ca.1742–95

Of Woodhouse, near Rednal, Shropshire, and Bryngwyn, near Llanfyllin, Montgomeryshire; oldest son of William Mostyn (of Bryngwyn). He added the surname Owen upon inheriting the estate of John Lloyd Owen, a distant cousin. Oxford from 1761, Middle Temple from 1759. His candidacy for the House of Commons was supported by the Herbert family of the Powis peerage. He supported the North ministry from 1774 until about the time of Burgoyne's surrender, when he opposed it primarily on the issue of the American war, and voted against it in 4 of 5 of the crucial issues recorded in

671

February and March, 1782. He did not vote on Shelburne's peace terms but voted for Fox's India Bill in 1783 and opposed Pitt in 1784. There is no evidence that he ever addressed the House of Commons. M.P. for Montgomeryshire, 1774–95.

Oxford, 4th Earl. See **Edward Harley**

Page, Francis. ca.1728–1803

Of Middle Aston, near Deddington, Oxfordshire; oldest son of Richard Bourne (of Ombersley, near Droitwich, Worcestershire); in 1741 took the surname Page upon inheriting from his maternal uncle Sir Francis Page. Oxford from 1743. He was sheriff of Oxfordshire, 1752–53. He was a conservative country gentleman, emotionally devoted to the prerogatives of king, church, and university. He opposed on occasion the Grafton ministry and the North ministry, 1770–74, but supported North in his church and American measures. He opposed Dunning's first resolution in April, 1780, and in February and March, 1782, he voted with North in all 5 crucial recorded divisions. He voted against Shelburne's peace terms but did not vote on Fox's India Bill in 1783, and opposed Pitt from 1784. Before 1775 he addressed the House at least 11 times in defense of the privileges and priorities of the Established Church, but there is no record of any speech thereafter. M.P. for Oxford University, 1768–1801.

Page, John. 1697–1779

Of Watergate House, near Havant, and Chichester, Sussex; son of Edward Page (of Chichester). He married (1) Catherine, daughter of Robert Knight (cashier of the South Sea Company who fled to France after that bubble burst) and sister of Robert Knight (*q.v.*). He was a director of the East India Company, 1730–33; deputy paymaster general, 1755–57; and searcher of customs at Chester and Liverpool, 1761–79. His family had long been active and influential in Chichester Whig politics, and though he became a London businessman, he maintained the status of a Whig country gentleman. He supported

Newcastle, who consulted him on financial matters and especially on awards of pensions and sinecures. He voted against Bute's peace preliminaries in 1762 and against Grenville on general warrants and the Wilkes issues, 1763–64. In 1768 he retired in ill health. M.P. for Great Grimsby, 1727–34; Chichester, 1741–68.

Paget, 10th Baron. See Henry Bayly

Paine, Thomas. 1737–1809

Born at Thetford, Norfolk, the son of Joseph Paine (Quaker farmer and staymaker of Thetford). From the age of 13 he worked in his father's shop; at 19 he joined a privateer but soon returned home. In 1758 he moved to Dover; he then set up as a staymaker at Sandwich in 1759 but failed and in 1760 moved again, this time to Margate. In 1761 he returned to Thetford as an excise officer. In 1772, however, he was dismissed for leading a movement for higher pay. In 1774 he separated from his wife and went to America, arriving in November, 1774, with a letter of introduction from Benjamin Franklin to Franklin's son-in-law in Philadelphia. He became connected with a Philadelphia bookseller and also won the help of Dr. Benjamin Rush. During the height of the controversy between the colonies and the London government he wrote and published *Common Sense*, 1776, and then *Additions to Common Sense*. He served as aide to General Nathaniel Greene and as a secretary to the committee on public affairs of the Continental Congress in 1777. In 1781 he went to France with President Laurens of the Congress. He returned to Boston and in 1787 went to Europe. He published *The Rights of Man*, 1791–92, and *The Age of Reason* in 1794, supporting the French Revolution. He returned to America in 1802, where he opposed Washington in politics. He died in New York. Portrait by Romney.

Palk (or Palke), Robert. 1717–98

Of Haldon House, near Exeter, Devon; 2d son of Walter Palk (or Palke) (of Ashburton, near Totnes, Devon); created baronet in 1782. Oxford from 1736. He took orders and was a chaplain in the navy from 1747. In 1749 he went to India as chaplain to the Company and was a member of the Madras Council, 1753–55, and governor of Madras, 1763–67. In 1766 he concluded a treaty with the Nizam of Hyderabad

which was widely criticized as weak and unsatisfactory. In 1767 he
returned to England and secured a seat in the House of Commons. He
first associated with Calcraft, Shelburne, and Dunning, but nevertheless supported the North ministry on several issues, 1772–78. In
1778 he went into steady opposition, voting against the North ministry
in 4 out of 5 crucial divisions recorded in February and March, 1782.
He voted for Shelburne's peace terms in February, 1783, opposed the
coalition and Fox's India Bill, and from 1784 supported Pitt. There is
no record that he ever addressed the House. M.P. for Ashburton,
1767–68; Wareham, 1768–74; Ashburton, 1774–87.

Palliser, Hugh. 1723–96

Of Deptford, Kent, and the Vache, near Chalfont St. Giles, Buckinghamshire; only son of army Captain Hugh Palliser (of North Deigh-
ton, near Wetherby, Yorkshire); created baronet in 1773. He entered
the navy in 1735 under the command of his uncle Nicholas Robinson
and became lieutenant in 1741 and captain in 1746. He was severely
wounded in action in the Mediterranean in 1744, and was made commander in 1746. He was governor and officer in command at Newfoundland, 1764–69; comptroller of the navy, 1770–75; rear admiral
and lieutenant general of marines in 1775; vice admiral in 1778; and
a member of the Admiralty Board, where he was a protégé and a
supporter of Sandwich, 1775–79. From the beginning of hostilities in
1775 he expressed grave doubts about the ability of the British land
forces to subdue the Americans. In 1778 he was put in command of a
squadron under Keppel, and after the unsatisfactory engagement with
the French off Ushant he became involved in charges and counter-
charges regarding his own conduct and that of Keppel in that affair.
He was supported by Sandwich and the North ministry; Keppel, by
the opposition Whigs. At his own instigation, to have opportunity to
answer the charges made against him, Keppel was brought before a
court-martial in early 1779 in a case that aroused national interest,
strong partisan emotions, and harmful dissensions among officers in
the navy. Keppel was completely exonerated of misconduct by the
court-martial. In a subsequent court-martial Palliser was exonerated
in less downright terms. He then resigned his offices in navy and court
and had no further combat service. He was partly compensated for his
losses in honor and income when the North ministry appointed him

674

governor of Greenwich Hospital, 1780–96, but the opposition attacked that action in Parliament and blew it up as a cause for the ministry's resignation or dismissal. He was, however, made admiral under Pitt's ministry in 1787 and became governor of Scarborough Castle. In 1767 he was one of those naval officers who applied for and received large grants of crown land in maritime Canada. Although he took comparatively little part in partisan politics, he supported the North ministry in the House of Commons in all 5 of the crucial divisions recorded in February and March, 1782. He voted for Fox's India Bill in 1783. M.P. for Scarborough, 1774–79; Huntingdon Borough, 1780–84.

Palmer, John. 1735–1817

Of Carlton Park, near Market Harborough, Northamptonshire, and Carlton Curlieu, near Market Harborough, Leicestershire; in 1765 succeeded his father, Thomas Palmer (*q.v.*), as 5th baronet. Cambridge from 1752. In 1768 he married Charlotte, daughter of Sir Henry Gough (1708–74; M.P.). In general he supported the Rockingham ministry, 1765–66, though he was classed as Tory in 1767. He was largely in opposition, 1767–74, voting against Chatham's land tax in 1767, against the ministry in voting for Sir George Savile's *Nullum Tempus* Bill in 1768, and against the expulsion of Wilkes in 1770. After 1770 he supported the measures of the North ministry toward the American colonists, but his name seldom appears in the division lists. He voted with the opposition for reforms and voted for the first Dunning resolution of April, 1780. There is no evidence that he ever addressed the House of Commons. M.P. for Leicestershire, 1765–80.

Palmer, Peregrine. ca.1703–62

Of Fairfield, near Bridgwater, Somerset; 2d son of Nathaniel Palmer (M.P.); grandson of Sir William Wyndham (ca.1687–1740; M.P.; 2d baronet). Oxford from 1719, fellow of All Souls from 1727. In 1761 he was listed as Tory, and he appears to have been largely in opposition throughout his years in the House of Commons. Namier branded his service as "totally undistinguished"—words Oxford men rarely apply to fellows of All Souls. M.P. for Oxford University, 1745–62.

Palmer, Thomas. ca.1702–65

Of East Carlton, Northamptonshire, and Carlton Curlieu (both near

Market Harborough), Leicestershire; 2d but 1st surviving son of Robert Palmer (of Medbourne, near Market Harborough, Leicestershire); in 1732 succeeded his uncle Sir Jeffery Palmer (1655–1732; M.P.) as 4th baronet. Cambridge from 1718. He was sheriff of Northamptonshire, 1740–41. Listed in 1761 as Tory, he voted against the Grenville ministry on the Wilkes issues and on general warrants, 1763–64. There is no record of any speech by him in the House of Commons. He was the father of John Palmer (*q.v.*). M.P. for Leicestershire, 1754–65.

Palmerston, 2d Viscount. See Henry Temple

Panmure, 1st Earl. See William Ramsay Maule

Pardoe, John. ca.1757–96

Of Leyton, near Stratford, Essex; only son of John Pardoe (director of the East India Company). Lincoln's Inn from 1774, Cambridge from 1775. His father paid the Treasury £4,000 for his seat in the House of Commons in 1780. There he supported Sandwich and the North administration, with which he voted in 4 of the 5 crucial divisions reported in February and March, 1782. In 1783 he voted against Shelburne's peace terms and did not vote on Fox's India Bill. There is no record that, at least before 1790, he ever addressed the House. M.P. for Camelford, 1780–84; Plympton Erle, 1784–90; West Looe, 1790–96.

Parker, Armsted (or Armstead). ca.1699–1777

Of Burghberry Manor, near Peterborough, Northamptonshire; only son of Charles Parker (M.P.). In 1761 he was listed as Tory, and was called by Sandwich "very independent." Before 1760 he was largely in opposition. He supported Bute and then Grenville. He opposed Rockingham and repeal of the Stamp Act in 1766. There is no record of any speech by him in the House of Commons. M.P. for Peterborough, 1734–41, 1742–47, and 1761–68.

Parker, George. 1755–1842

Styled Viscount Parker until 1795, when he succeeded his father, Thomas Parker (*q.v.*), as 4th Earl of Macclesfield; cousin of George Lane Parker (*q.v.*). Eton, to Oxford in 1773. He was elected to the House of Commons "in the interest of" the Duke of Marlborough, and supported the North ministry to its end in late March, 1782, opposing the Dunning resolution of April 6, 1780, and voting with North in all 5 of the crucial divisions recorded in February and March, 1782. He supported the Shelburne ministry and voted for Shelburne's peace terms, but did not vote on Fox's India Bill in 1783. He was lord of the bedchamber to the Prince of Wales, 1780–89, and with him supported Charles Fox against Pitt. He was comptroller of the household, 1791–97; privy councillor from 1791; again lord of the bedchamber, 1797–1804; captain of the yeomen of the guard, 1804–30; and lord lieutenant of Oxfordshire, 1817–42. M.P. for Woodstock, 1774–84; Minehead, 1790–95.

Parker, George Lane. 1724–91

Of Woodbury, near Caxton, Cambridgeshire; 2d son of George Parker (1697–1764; M.P.; 2d Earl of Macclesfield); younger brother of Thomas Parker (*q.v.*); uncle of George Parker (*q.v.*). Oxford from 1741. He was lieutenant and then captain of foot guards in 1749, colonel in 1762, major general in 1770, and lieutenant general in 1777. He consistently supported the North ministry but did not attend the House regularly and addressed it seldom if at all. M.P. for Yarmouth (Isle of Wight), 1769–74; Tregony, 1774–80.

Parker, Hyde. 1714–83

Born at Tredington, on River Stour, Worcestershire; younger son of Hyde Parker (rector of Tredington; well connected); in 1782 succeeded his brother Harry Parker as baronet. He served for several years in the merchant marine and then joined the navy in 1738. In 1745 he was a lieutenant with the East India squadron. In 1748 he was captain of the *Lively*, which he brought back to England in 1749. In 1755, commanding the *Squirrel*, he went to Morocco to negotiate a treaty to redeem captured and enslaved Europeans. In 1757 he commanded a ship off France under Howe. In 1760 he was again in the East Indies and took part in the reduction of Pondichéry in 1761 and the attack on Manila in 1762. In 1764 he returned to England and saw no further important active service until 1776. In 1778 he served as rear admiral with 6 ships of the line under Byron in American waters and in 1779 was in action off Grenada. While in command of the Leeward Islands station in 1779, he captured several French ships. He

677

served under Rodney in April, 1780, when, lacking clear orders, he unwittingly rendered Rodney's action against the French less effective. In 1781, as vice admiral, he fought the Dutch off Dogger Bank. Bitterly critical of the lack of support for Sandwich in 1781–82, he insisted on resigning. In 1782, as baronet, he accepted a command in East Indian waters, but was lost at sea somewhere between Río de Janeiro and India in early 1783. Portrait by Romney.

Parker, Hyde. 1739–1807

2d son of Hyde Parker (1714–83) (*q.v.*). He followed his father into the navy and was a captain in 1763. He served under Admiral Howe in American waters during the American Revolution and led ships in a raid up the Hudson River to Tarrytown and again to Fort Washington on the Hudson in late 1776, while General Howe occupied New York. In 1778 he commanded the *Phoenix* (44 guns) under Howe against D'Estaing off Rhode Island. In 1779 he convoyed troops to Savannah and was knighted. He was shipwrecked in West Indies waters in October, 1780, but was rescued. When the American war ended, he experienced a decade of inaction, but was made rear admiral in 1793, vice admiral in 1794, and later admiral. In 1801 he was in command in the action off Copenhagen, where he was believed to have shown irresolution and was replaced by Nelson. Portraits by Reynolds and Romney.

Parker, John. ca.1735–88

Of Boringdon, Devon; oldest surviving son of John Parker (of North Molton, near Barnstaple, Devon); grandson of John Poulet (or Powlett) (ca.1688–1743; 1st Earl Poulet); in 1784 created Baron Boringdon. Oxford from 1753. In 1769 he married (2) Theresa, daughter of Thomas Robinson (1695–1770) (*q.v.*). He secured his seat in the House of Commons in 1761 with the support of Bute and "in the interest of" William Irby (*q.v.*), who controlled it. He was primarily a country gentleman, was listed as Tory in 1761, and supported Bute and then Grenville, 1761–65. He was in general opposition to the Grafton and North ministries, 1767–82. In 1769 he signed the Devonshire-Cornwall petition against the ministry over the Wilkes case. He voted for the Dunning resolution of April 6, 1780, and against the North ministry in all 5 of the crucial divisions recorded in February and March, 1782. He voted for Shelburne's peace terms in February, 1783, but did not vote on Fox's India Bill in November, 1783. From 1784 he supported Pitt in the House of Lords. His only recorded speech in the lower House was in 1763, on a minor issue. M.P. for Bodmin, 1761–62; Devonshire, 1762–84.

Parker, John. ca.1755–97

Only son of Edward Parker (of Browsholme, near Clitheroe, Yorkshire). Eton from 1766, Cambridge, 1771–74. In 1778 he married Beatrix, daughter of Thomas Lister (1723–61; M.P.) and sister of Thomas Lister (*q.v.*). In his 2 years in the House of Commons he voted against the North ministry, including his votes in all 5 of the crucial divisions recorded in February and March, 1782. There is no record that he ever addressed the House. M.P. for Clitheroe, 1780–82.

Parker, Peter. 1721–1811

Of Bassingbourne, Cambridgeshire; 3d son of Admiral Christopher Parker; created baronet in 1783. He entered the navy at a very early age and was captain in 1747. In 1759 he commanded the *Woolwich* (44 guns) and then the *Norfolk* (74 guns). He commanded the *Buckingham* (70 guns) in the action at Belleisle in 1761. He was knighted in 1772. In 1776 he commanded a squadron from Cork, with Sir Henry Clinton in charge of land forces, in the unsuccessful attempt to take Charleston. He supported General Howe's capture of New York later in 1776 and remained in New York waters and about Rhode Island until 1777, when he was made rear admiral. He was in command of the Jamaica station, 1780–82. He was vice admiral in 1787 and admiral of the fleet in 1799, but was seldom considered a very brilliant or very forceful naval leader. His attendance of the House of Commons was limited by his overseas service, but in general he supported Pitt. He was an early patron of young Horatio Nelson. M.P. for Seaford, 1784–86; Maldon, 1787–90.

Parker, Thomas. 1723–95

Styled Lord Parker from 1732; in 1764 he succeeded his father, George Parker (ca.1697–1764; M.P.), as 3d Earl of Macclesfield; older brother of George Lane Parker (*q.v.*). Oxford from 1740; M.A., 1743; D.C.L., 1773. In 1749 he married his cousin Mary, oldest daughter of Sir

William Heathcote (1693–1757; M.P.; 1st baronet). He was a fellow of the Royal Society from 1747. He was one of the Whig protagonists in the bitterly contested Oxfordshire elections of 1754. He supported the Pelhams until 1761, when Bute helped him to re-election and secured him a pension, after which he supported Bute and then Grenville. He rarely addressed the House of Commons. He was rear admiral in 1762 and a member of the Admiralty Board from 1766. M.P. for Newcastle-under-Lyme, 1747–54; Oxfordshire, 1755–61; Rochester, 1761–64.

Parnell, John. ca.1720–82

Of Rathleague, County Queens; the son of John Parnell (judge; member of the Irish Parliament); created baronet (Irish) in 1766. In 1745 he married Anne, sister of Bernard Ward (1st Viscount Bangor). He was a barrister in Dublin from 1744, sheriff of County Queens in 1753, and a member of the Irish House of Commons, 1761–82. He was the father of John Parnell (ca.1744–1801) (*q.v.*).

Parnell, John. ca.1744–1801

Of Rathleague, County Queens; in 1782 succeeded his father, John Parnell (ca.1720–82) (*q.v.*), as 2d baronet (Irish). Eton, Harrow, and Trinity College, Dublin; Lincoln's Inn from 1766; bencher from 1786. He was a member of the Irish Parliament, 1761–68, 1776–83, and 1783–1801, and a leader of the Irish nationalist movement. He was chancellor of the Irish exchequer, 1785–89; British privy councillor from 1786. In 1792 he helped dissuade Pitt and Dundas from taking certain Irish measures unacceptable to the Irish nationalists. He was commissioner of customs and excise for Ireland from 1780. He opposed Flood's reform bill in 1783 and in 1799 opposed union of Ireland with England. In 1801 he became representative of County Queens to the English House of Commons under the new dispensation.

Parry, John. ca.1724–97

2d son of Love Parry (of Wernfawr, Carnarvonshire). Cambridge and Lincoln's Inn from 1742, barrister in 1748, bencher from 1772, treasurer in 1785. He was constable of Conway Castle, 1769–97; attorney general for North Wales, 1769–97. In the House of Commons he voted against the North ministry from 1780, including all 5 crucial divisions recorded in February and March, 1782. He voted for Shelburne's peace terms and against Fox's India Bill in 1783 and supported Pitt from January, 1784. M.P. for Carnarvonshire, 1780–90.

Pasley, Thomas. 1734–1808

5th son of James Pasley (of Craig, Dumfriesshire); connected with the family of Gilbert Elliot (1722–77) (*q.v.*); created baronet in 1794. He entered the navy in 1751, was with Hawke in the raid on Rochefort in 1759, and saw much active service in American and West Indies waters, 1774–84. He served in the Mediterranean and in the Channel, 1788–94; lost a leg in action; and was given a baronetcy and a pension of £1,000 a year. He was vice admiral in 1795 and admiral in 1801. Portrait by Beechey.

Paterson, John. ca.1705–89

Of Epping, Essex; son of Lieutenant Colonel Alexander Paterson. In 1761 he married "an heiress with £30,000." He was successively clerk, warden, and master of the Barber Surgeons' Company, 1745–76; a member of the London Common Council; and alderman, 1759–61. He was chairman of the ways and means committee of the House of Commons, 1765–68, and clerk to the Land Tax Commission, 1772–89. He supported Bute, then Grenville, then Chatham and Grafton. He sat "in the interest of" George Selwyn. M.P. for Ludgershall, 1761–68.

Paterson, John. ca.1730–82

Of Eccles, Berwickshire; only son of John Paterson (of Eccles); in 1759 succeeded his grandfather as 3d baronet. In 1755 he married Anne, daughter of Hugh Hume-Campbell (*q.v.*). He posed as a conservative country gentleman but was a heavy gambler and a dissolute character. He supported the North ministry from 1779, voting against the Dunning resolution of April 6, 1780. There is no evidence that he ever spoke in a House debate. M.P. for Berwickshire, 1779–80.

Paulet (or Powlett), George. 1722–1800

Of Amport, Hampshire; only surviving son of Norton Paulet (of Amport; M.P.); 3d cousin of Harry Paulet (or Powlett) (*q.v.*), through whose influence he secured a seat in the House of Commons and whose policies he followed, supporting Chatham and Grafton, 1766–70, and the North ministry, 1772–74, though he voted against expulsion of Wilkes in January, 1770. He was groom porter, 1767–82, and in 1794 succeeded Harry Paulet as 12th Marquess of Winchester. M.P. for Winchester, 1765–74.

Paulet (or Powlett), Harry. 1720–94

2d son of Harry Paulet (later 4th Duke of Bolton); in 1765 succeeded his brother Charles Paulet as 6th Duke of Bolton and 11th Marquess of Winchester. Winchester, 1728–29; Portsmouth Naval Academy from 1733. In 1765 he married (2) Katherine, sister of James Lowther (1736–1802) (*q.v.*). He was a navy lieutenant in 1739; was captain in 1740; served in the West Indies, 1746–50; and was rear admiral in 1756, vice admiral in 1759, and admiral in 1770. He was privy councillor from 1766; governor of the Isle of Wight, 1766–70; and lord lieutenant of Hampshire, 1782–93. He supported Newcastle and in 1762 supported Bute but voted against the cider tax and the Grenville ministry on Wilkes in 1763. He supported Rockingham, 1765–66; Grafton, 1767–70; and the North ministry until late 1777, when he strongly opposed continuing the American war and attacked Sandwich for mismanagement of the navy. He supported Keppel against Palliser in 1779. He spoke occasionally when in the House of Commons and perhaps somewhat less when in the House of Lords, mostly on naval matters. In 1772 his oldest daughter married John Montagu (1744–1814) (*q.v.*). In 1787 his youngest daughter married her cousin William Henry Vane (1766–1842; later 1st Duke of Cleveland). An illegitimate daughter married Thomas Orde (later Orde-Powlett) (*q.v.*). Horace Walpole called him "a silly, brutal, proud man." M.P. for Christchurch, 1751–54; Lymington, 1755–61; Winchester, 1761–65.

Payne, Ralph. 1739–1807

Oldest son of Ralph Payne (chief justice of St. Kitts) and almost certainly related to Edward Payne (prominent venture merchant shipowner) and to John Willett Payne (1752–1803; M.P.); in 1795 created Baron Lavington (Irish). He was educated at Christ's Hospital School from 1752, followed by the grand tour. In 1767 he married Frances, daughter of General Baron Kolbel of Austria. He inherited wealth and continued a prosperous West Indies family business. He became a friend of Charles Fox, was first elected to Parliament "in the interest of" Chatham and Grafton in 1768, and in general supported Grafton and then the North ministry, though he was extremely irregular in attendance. He was Knight of the Bath from 1771; governor of the Leeward Islands, 1771–76 and 1799–1807; clerk of the Board of the Green Cloth, 1777–82; fellow of the Royal Society from 1779; and fellow of the Society of Arts from 1781. He was a privy councillor from 1799. He approved Mansfield's decisions in the Wilkes and libel cases; supported the North ministry in all 5 crucial divisions recorded in February and March, 1782; supported the coalition; and as a "Fox's martyr," failed of re-election in 1784. He continued to support Fox and North and oppose Pitt until 1795, when he was given an Irish peerage. Wraxall pronounced him good-natured, pleasing, and well bred. He died in the West Indies. M.P. for Shaftesbury, 1768–71; Camelford, 1776–80; Plympton Erle, 1780–84; Fowey, 1790–91; New Woodstock, 1795–99.

Peach, Samuel. 1725–90

Of Minchinhampton, Gloucestershire; son of John Peach (of Chalford, Gloucestershire). He was a silk merchant in London, a partner in a London bank, and a director of the East India Company, 1773–74, 1776–79, and 1781. He went bankrupt in 1781. He was too briefly a member of the House of Commons to have left any record there. M.P. for Cricklade, 1775–76.

Peach-Hungerford, John. 1719–1809

Of Dingley Hall, near Market Harborough, Northamptonshire; oldest son of John Hungerford (of Coombe Bassett, Wiltshire); added the surname Peach upon inheriting from his stepfather Thomas Peach in 1770. An independent country gentleman, he opposed the North ministry on the Wilkes issues in 1775 and on the American war from 1778; supported the ministry on the contractors' bill in 1779; and voted for the Dunning resolution of April 6, 1780, but against Lowther's motion to end the American war immediately in 1781. He voted with the North ministry in the crucial divisions throughout February, 1782, but voted for Cavendish's motion to remove the ministry, and for Sir John Rous's no-confidence motion on March 8 and 15, 1782. In 1783 he voted for Shelburne's peace terms and did not vote on Fox's India Bill. Thereafter he usually supported Pitt. M.P. for Leicestershire, 1775–90.

Peachey, James. 1723–1808

Of West Dean, Sussex; 2d son of Sir John Peachey (ca.1680–1744; M.P.; 2d baronet); in 1765 succeeded his brother Sir John Peachey (ca.1720–65; M.P.) as 4th baronet; in 1794 created Baron Selsey of Sussex. Westminster, 1730–37; Oxford from 1739. In 1747 he married Georgiana, daughter of Henry Francis Scott (1st Earl Deloraine, Scottish). He was groom of the bedchamber to the Prince of Wales and then the king, 1751–91, and master of the robes, 1791–1808. From an old Tory family, he supported the ministries of Newcastle, Bute, Grenville, Rockingham, and Grafton. M.P. for Leominster, 1747–54; Seaford, 1755–68.

Peachey, John. 1749–1816

Of West Dean, Sussex; in 1808 succeeded his father, James Peachey (*q.v.*), as 5th baronet and 2d Baron Selsey. Eton, 1758–61. In the House of Commons he supported the North ministry from 1776, voting against the Dunning resolution of April 6, 1780, and against Fox's motion to censure Sandwich on February 20, 1782. He voted for Conway's motions of February 22 and 27 to make immediate peace with the United States, but voted against Cavendish's and Rous's motions of March 8 and 15, 1782. He voted for Shelburne's peace terms and did not vote on Fox's India Bill. He later supported Pitt. M.P. for St. Germans, 1776–80; New Shoreham, 1780–90.

Pearce, Zachariah. 1690–1774

Son of Thomas John Pearce (d. 1752; wealthy London distiller). Westminster from 1704; Cambridge from 1710; fellow, 1716–20. In 1722 he married Mary, daughter of Benjamin Adams (another wealthy distiller of London). He was chaplain to Lord Chancellor Thomas Parker (1666–1732; 1st Earl of Macclesfield), who aided him to rapid preferment. Through Parker he secured the rectorship of St. Barnabas in 1720. In 1724 he was named by Parker to the vicarage of St. Martins-in-the-Fields with £500 a year, and dedicated to Parker his translation of Longinus' *On the Sublime*. (In 1724, Parker was indicted for misuse of funds, and resigned.) He was also aided by friendship with William Pulteney (1684–1764; Earl of Bath), who secured the aid of the queen in offering him preferments. He became dean of Windsor in 1739, and was shortly afterward proposed by Pulteney for a bishopric. In 1747 he was offered the See of Bangor in addition to the deanery of Westminster. He at first declined but later accepted, and was consecrated in 1748. He visited his diocese annually until 1753, but then his health failed and he exchanged Bangor for Rochester. In 1761 he declined Pulteney's offer to secure him the bishopric of London. In the House of Lords he usually voted with the crown. A good scholar, he published many tracts and sermons, as well as an edition of Cicero.

Pearson, Richard. 1731–1806

Born at Lanton Hall, near Appleby, Westmorland, perhaps the son of General Sir Richard Pearson (d. 1781). He entered the navy in 1745 and served in the Mediterranean until 1749. He was involved in several of the naval actions in East Indies waters, 1758–59. He is chiefly noted for having been in command of the *Serapis* when it was defeated and captured by John Paul Jones in 1779, soon after which he was knighted, "for his brave resistance to a superior force." When Jones heard of that event, he commented: "Should I have the good fortune to fall in with him again, I'll make a lord of him." He was lieutenant governor of Greenwich Hospital, 1800–1806.

Pechell, Samuel. (?–?)

An East Indies merchant, a friend of Warren Hastings, and one of his spokesmen in England, who did his best to reconcile North with Hastings' later operations and with Hastings' withdrawal of his proffered resignation. (Some of that interesting correspondence is in the Additional Manuscripts collection of the British Museum.)

Peebles, Viscount. See **William Douglas.** 1724–1810

Peirse, Henry. ca.1754–1824

Of Bedale, near Northallerton, Yorkshire; only son of Henry Peirse (of Bedale; M.P.); of an old Yorkshire family. Eton, 1764–70; Cambridge from 1771. In 1777 he married Charlotte, daughter of John Monson (3d Baron Monson). An independent Whig country gentleman, he voted against approval of the address from the throne in October, 1775, and for Dunning's resolution of April 6, 1780. In 15 divisions, 1775–82, he voted against the North administration each time. He did not vote on Shelburne's peace terms but voted against Fox's India Bill and from 1784 supported Pitt's reform proposals.

There is no evidence that before 1790 he addressed the House of Commons. M.P. for Northallerton, 1774–1824.

Pelham, Charles Anderson. See Charles Anderson (later Pelham)

Pelham, Henry. 1759–97

2d son of Thomas Pelham (*q.v.*). Westminster from 1770, Caen military academy, 1775–76. Ensign of foot guards in 1775, captain in 1778, lieutenant colonel in 1791, and retired in 1792. In the House of Commons from 1780, he supported the North ministry in all the crucial divisions of February and March, 1782, except that he voted for Conway's motion of February 27 to make immediate peace with the Americans. He voted for Shelburne's peace terms and also for Fox's India Bill in 1783. From 1784 he opposed the Pitt ministry. There is no record that he addressed the House of Commons before 1790. M.P. for Lewes, 1780–96.

Pelham, Thomas. 1728–1805

Of Stanmer, near Lewes, Sussex; oldest son of Thomas Pelham (one-time merchant of Constantinople; M.P.); in 1768 succeeded his cousin Thomas Pelham-Holles (1693–1768) (*q.v.*) as 6th baronet and 2d Baron Pelham; in 1801 created Earl of Chichester. Westminster, 1740–45; Cambridge from 1745; grand tour, 1746–50. His political career was sponsored by his Pelham cousins, whom he supported in return. He was a member of the Board of Trade and Plantations, 1754–61; a member of the Admiralty Board, 1761–62; comptroller of the household, 1765–74; privy councillor from 1765; chief justice in Eyre north of Trent, 1774–75; and keeper of the great wardrobe, 1775–82. In 1762 he voted against Bute's peace preliminaries, but he did not resign office with Newcastle, and was subsequently dismissed from the Admiralty Board by Henry Fox and Bute. He supported the Rockingham and then the North ministry in the House of Lords, and in 1783 was appointed surveyor general of ordnance by the coalition ministry. He voted for Fox's India Bill in 1783 and opposed Pitt until the French Revolution. M.P. for Rye, 1749–54; Sussex, 1754–68.

Pelham, Thomas. 1756–1826

Of Stanmer, near Lewes, Sussex; oldest son of Thomas Pelham (1728–1805) (*q.v.*); brother of Henry Pelham (*q.v.*); in 1805 succeeded his father as 2d Earl of Chichester. Westminster, 1766–73; Cambridge, 1773–76; grand tour, 1775–78. In 1801 he married Mary Henrietta, daughter of Francis Godolphin Osborne (*q.v.*). He was chief secretary to Lord Northington and Lord Camden when each served as lord lieutenant of Ireland, 1783–84 and 1795–98; privy councillor from 1795; member of the Board of Control for India in 1801; home secretary, 1801–1803; chancellor of the Duchy of Lancaster, 1803–1804; and postmaster general, 1807–26. Though his father supported the North ministry, he considered North "a most abominable minister" and voted with the opposition on reform measures in 1781 and against continuing the American war, 1781–82. Under family pressure, however, he supported the North ministry in the motions of March 8 and 15, 1782, by Cavendish and Rous. He voted for Shelburne's peace terms in 1783 and, though dubious of the coalition, took service under Northington in Ireland. He generally opposed the Pitt ministry. M.P. for Sussex, 1780–1801.

Pelham-Holles, Thomas. 1693–1768

Oldest son of Sir Thomas Pelham (1650–1712; M.P.; 1st Baron Pelham); took the name Holles in 1711 upon inheriting estates of his maternal uncle John Holles (1662–1711; M.P.; 1st Duke of Newcastle from 1694); in 1712 succeeded his father as 5th baronet and 2d Baron Pelham; in 1714, in connection with an inheritance from John Holles, created Earl of Clare of Suffolk; in 1715 created 1st Duke of Newcastle-upon-Tyne (a new creation but in continuation of the old); a brother of Henry Pelham (ca.1695–1754; M.P.; first minister). For a complete account of his career, see standard sources. Westminster, to Cambridge in 1709; L.L.D., 1728; chancellor of Cambridge University in 1748. He married his cousin Henrietta, sister of Francis Godolphin (*q.v.*) and granddaughter of the Duke of Marlborough. He was Knight of the Garter from 1718 and served in high political office almost continuously, 1724–63, becoming first minister in 1754, upon the death of his brother. He resigned that office in 1756, but was again first minister in a coalition with the elder Pitt and retained that post after the accession of George III. He resigned in a conflict with Bute and the court on May 25, 1762. He was lord privy seal in Rockingham's ministry, August 25, 1765–July 30, 1766. He was the greatest political party organizer and dispenser of patronage of his time, and perhaps the poorest statesman. "A master of political corruption, he was not himself corrupt" (*DNB*), and was said to have died £300,000 the poorer for having spent his career in politics. Horace Walpole, who was seldom a kindly critic of men of affairs, said that "he never conferred a favour till it was wrested from him" and had "no pride, but infinite self-love . . . he loved business immoderately, yet was always doing it, never did it."

Pembroke, 10th and 11th Earls. See Henry Herbert. 1734–94   and **George Augustus Herbert**

Penn, John. 1729–95

Born in London, the oldest son of Richard Penn (d. 1771); grandson of William Penn (1644–1718; founder of Pennsylvania). In 1766 he married Ann, daughter of William Allen (chief justice of Philadelphia). He was lieutenant governor and chief proprietor of Pennsylvania, 1763–71 and 1773–76. He died at Philadelphia, ending the last administrative link of the Penn family with the government of the new state. Portrait by another Pennsylvanian, Benjamin West.

Penn, Richard. 1736–1811

Of Laleham, Middlesex; 2d son of Richard Penn (d. 1771); grandson of William Penn (1644–1718; founder of Pennsylvania); younger brother of John Penn (*q.v.*). Eton from 1748, Cambridge and Inner Temple from 1752. About 1775 he married Mary, daughter of William Masters (of Philadelphia). He substituted for his brother as deputy lieutenant governor of Pennsylvania, 1771–73. In 1775 he and his brother presented to king and Parliament the "Olive Branch" petition from the citizens of Pennsylvania, especially its Quakers, expressing their ardent desire to avoid forceful resistance to Britain and urging that the British government make concessions to the colonies that would bring conciliation. After 1783 he supported Pitt. M.P. for Appleby, 1784–90; Haslemere, 1790–91; Lancaster Borough, 1796–1802; Haslemere, 1802–1806.

Pennant, Richard. 1737–1808

Of Penrhyn Hall, Carnarvonshire, and Winnington, Cheshire; son of Richard Pennant (merchant of Liverpool); probably a nephew of Sir Samuel Pennant (West Indies merchant and shipowner; lord mayor of London in 1750); grandson of Edward Pennant (chief justice of Jamaica); in 1783 created Baron Penryn (or Penrhyn) (Irish). He was related to Edward Morant and Henry Dawkins, both wealthy West Indies merchants in London, and was himself the absentee owner of a large plantation in Jamaica. He owed his seat in the House of Commons to the support of William Beckford (*q.v.*). Cambridge from 1754. In the House of Commons he voted regularly with the opposition after 1768, voting against expulsion of Wilkes in 1770 and for the Dunning resolution of April 6, 1780. He supported Charles Fox in 1782 and the coalition in 1783, and opposed Pitt, 1784–90. M.P. for Petersfield, 1761–67; Liverpool, 1767–80 and 1784–90.

Pennington, John. ca.1710–68

Of Pennington, Lancashire, and Muncaster, Cumberland; in 1744 succeeded his father, Joseph Pennington (1677–1744; M.P.), as 3d baronet. He came from an old Cumberland family politically allied with James Lowther (1736–1802) (*q.v.*). He was comptroller of excise, 1734–38; colonel of Cumberland militia from 1745; lord lieutenant of Westmorland, 1756–58. He supported Bute and then Grenville, 1761–65, and voted against repeal of the Stamp Act in 1766. He is not known to have addressed the House of Commons. M.P. for Cumberland, 1745–68.

Pennington, John. ca.1737–1813

Of Muncaster, Cumberland; in 1768 succeeded his father, John Pennington (ca.1710–68) (*q.v.*), as 4th baronet; in 1783 created Baron Muncaster (Irish). Winchester from 1754. He entered the army as ensign in 1756 and was captain in 1762, major in 1765, lieutenant colonel in 1773, and retired in 1775. Entering the House of Commons in 1781, he opposed the North ministry and voted against it in the 3 final crucial divisions in February and March, 1782. He supported the Rockingham and Shelburne ministries, 1782–83, voting for Shelburne's peace terms and against Fox's India Bill. He later supported Pitt's ministry. He made 6 unimportant speeches in the House, 1782–89. M.P. for Milbourne Port, 1781–96; Colchester, 1796–1802; Westmorland, 1806–13.

Pennyman, James. 1736–1808

Of Ormesby, Yorkshire; only son of Ralph Pennyman ("with a thumping landed property" at Beverley, according to Rockingham); in 1770 succeeded his uncle Sir Warton Pennyman (ca.1701–70) as 6th baronet. Westminster from 1749, Oxford from 1756. In 1762 he married (1) Elizabeth, daughter of Sir Henry Grey (of Howick, Northumberland; 1st baronet). A Rockingham Whig, he opposed the North ministry, voting against approval of the address from the throne in October, 1775, for the Dunning resolution of April 6, 1780, and for all 5 crucial opposition motions recorded in February and March, 1782. He supported the Rockingham ministry in 1782, voted for Shelburne's peace terms and against Fox's India Bill in 1783, and then supported Pitt. M.P. for Scarborough, 1770–74; Beverley, 1774–96.

Penruddock (or Penruddocke), Charles. 1743–88

Of Compton Chamberlayne, Wiltshire; only son of Charles Penruddock (or Penruddocke); of an old Wiltshire family. Oxford from 1761. He supported the Wiltshire petition of 1769 against the Grafton ministry, and in the House of Commons voted steadily against the North ministry from 1770 until its fall, including opposition votes in all 5 of the recorded crucial divisions of February and March, 1782. He voted for Shelburne's peace terms in February, 1783, then supported the coalition, and voted for Fox's India Bill in November, 1783. He afterward continued in opposition to Pitt. In 1784 Robinson listed him as a "moderate" country gentleman. M.P. for Wiltshire, 1770–88.

Penryn (or Penrhyn), 1st Baron. See Richard Pennant

Penton, Henry. 1736–1812

Of Eastgate House, near Winchester, Hampshire; son of Henry Penton (ca.1705–62, M.P.). Winchester, to Cambridge and Lincoln's Inn in 1753, barrister in 1762, grand tour. He was letter carrier to the king, 1761–1812, and a member of the Admiralty Board, 1774–82. He supported Bute; opposed the Grenville ministry on Wilkes issues, 1763–64; supported the Rockingham ministry, 1765–66; and supported the Grafton and North ministries, voting with North in all 5 of the crucial divisions reported in February and March, 1782. He seldom addressed the House of Commons, but in 1781 strongly defended the ministry's expenditure on the dockyards and the efficiency of Sandwich. He voted against Shelburne's peace terms, followed North into the coalition in 1783, and afterward opposed the Pitt ministry. M.P. for Winchester, 1761–96.

Pepys, William Weller. 1741–1825

Oldest son of William Pepys (1698–1743; of London; banker); created baronet in 1801. In 1777 he married a daughter of William Dowdeswell (*q.v.*). He was on friendly terms with Elizabeth Montagu (neé Robinson) (*q.v.*) and for a time with Samuel Johnson, but quarreled with Johnson over the life of Lord Lyttelton. He was master in chancery, 1775–1807.

Perceval, Charles George. 1756–1840

3d son of John Perceval (*q.v.*); half brother of John James Perceval (*q.v.*); in 1784 succeeded through his mother as 2d Baron Arden (Irish); in 1802 created Baron Arden of Warwickshire (English). Harrow, 1771–74; Cambridge from 1774; Lincoln's Inn from 1777. He was a lord of the admiralty, 1783–1801; registrar of the Admiralty Court, 1790–1840; also master of the mint, 1801–1802. In the House of Commons he steadily supported the North ministry from 1780. He spoke against Burke's bill to regulate the civil list because, he said, it would "reduce the Sovereign to humiliating dependency." In March, 1781, he opposed Crewe's bill to bar revenue officers from voting. In 1783 he voted against Shelburne's peace terms and against Fox's India Bill, and thereafter supported the Pitt ministry, serving on the India Board, 1801–1803. M.P. for Launceston, 1780–90; Warwick Borough, 1790–96; Totnes, 1796–1802.

Perceval, John. 1711–70

Styled Viscount Perceval from 1733; in 1748 he succeeded his father, John Perceval (1683–1748), as 2d Earl of Egmont (Irish); in 1762 created Baron Lovell and Holland of Enmore (English). In 1737 he married (1) Catherine, daughter of James Cecil (5th Earl of Salisbury). He was a member of the Irish Parliament, 1731–48; lord of the bedchamber to the Prince of Wales, 1748–51; joint postmaster general, 1762–63; privy councillor from 1765; member of the Admiralty

Board and first lord of the admiralty, 1763–66; he resigned from the Admiralty Board more in opposition to Pitt than in loyalty to Rockingham. He headed the group that successfully applied to the crown for large grants of land on St. John's Island in maritime Canada. In the House of Commons he opposed Robert Walpole and later joined the Leicester House group. In 1761 he supported Newcastle but in 1762 voted with Bute and took office under him, retaining office under Grenville and Rockingham. He was a fellow of the Society of Arts from 1736 and of the Royal Society from 1764. He published political pamphlets. "Strong and manly . . . his greatest talent was indefatigable application" (Horace Walpole). M.P. for Westminster, 1741–47; Weobley, 1747–54; Bridgwater, 1754–62.

Perceval, John James. 1738–1822

Styled Viscount Perceval from 1748; in 1770 succeeded his father, John Perceval (*q.v.*), as 3d Earl of Egmont (Irish) and 2d Baron Lovell (English). Eton, 1753–54; Cambridge from 1756. In 1765 he married Isabella, granddaughter of Charles Paulet (or Powlett) (2d Duke of Bolton). He was captain of foot guards in 1760 and served in Germany as lieutenant colonel under Prince Ferdinand. He was lord lieutenant of Somerset, 1773–74. In the 1760's he was rated Tory; he supported Bute and then Grenville, and was later a "doubtful" occasional supporter of the Rockingham and the Chatham-Grafton ministries. There is no evidence that he ever addressed the House of Commons, and in the House of Lords from 1770 he almost invariably supported the court. He opposed Pitt's Regency Bill in 1788. M.P. for Bridgwater, 1762–69.

Percy, Algernon. 1750–1830

2d son of Hugh (Smithson) Percy (*q.v.*); grandson of Algernon Seymour (1684–1750; 7th Duke of Somerset); brother of Hugh Percy (*q.v.*); in 1790 created Earl of Beverley. Eton, 1756–63; grand tour in 1767. In the House of Commons he supported the North ministry from 1774, but according to existing records addressed that House but once. After 1780 he seldom attended Parliament because of poor health, and was "abroad" during all the crucial divisions as recorded in early 1782. After 1784 he supported the Pitt ministry. "A mild and amiable man." M.P. for Northumberland, 1774–86.

Percy, Elizabeth Seymour. 1716–76

Daughter of Algernon Seymour (1684–1750; 7th Duke of Somerset). In 1740 she married Hugh (Smithson) Percy (*q.v.*), who adopted the surname Percy. In 1750 she succeeded her father as Baroness Percy. She was heiress to the Percy estates, and in 1756 was created Duchess of Northumberland of the third creation, in her own right, while her husband was in the same year created Earl of Northumberland and in 1766 Duke of Northumberland of a new creation. She was a famous hostess at Northumberland House in London, as well as lady of the bedchamber to the queen. Thomas Percy (*q.v.*) dedicated *Reliques of Ancient Poetry* to her; Goldsmith wrote a ballad to amuse her; Boswell ingratiated himself with her in pursuit of a commission for himself in the Life Guards. Horace Walpole described her, certainly ungallantly and perhaps ungenerously, as "mischievous under the appearance of frankness, generous and friendly without delicacy or sentiment, and a fond wife without curbing her Lord's amours, or her own."

Percy, Hugh. 1742–1817

Styled Lord Warkworth, 1750–66; Lord Percy, 1766–86; in 1776 succeeded his mother, Elizabeth Seymour Percy (*q.v.*), as Baron Percy; in 1786 succeeded his father, Hugh (Smithson) Percy (*q.v.*), as 2d Duke of Northumberland. Eton, 1753–58; Cambridge from 1760. He married (1) in 1764 Anne, 3d daughter of John Stuart (1713–92) (*q.v.*), but divorced her for the usual reason in 1779, and (2) in 1779 Frances, sister of Peter Burrell (1754–1820) (*q.v.*). He entered the army as ensign; he was captain in 1759 and served under Prince Ferdinand at Minden. In 1775 he was in America under Gage and commanded the forces sent to relieve the troops at Concord and lead their retreat to Boston on April 20, 1775. He commanded with distinction 4 brigades at the Battle of Brooklyn on Long Island on August 27, 1776, and was left in command of New York City when Howe attacked Washington in Westchester County in October, 1776. He commanded a column of Hessians against Fort Washington on the Hudson in November, 1776. Because he disagreed openly with General Howe, he successfully demanded to be recalled to England in 1777. He was major general in 1775, lieutenant general in 1777. He supported Grenville, 1762–65, and voted against repeal of the Stamp

Act in 1766. He supported the Grafton administration and voted against the expulsion of Wilkes in January, 1770. He opposed the North ministry, 1770–72, but later supported it on the issue of forcible coercion of the American colonists, whose military ability he openly derided. "His temper in politics was impracticable and he was in perpetual opposition," according to *DNB*; but despite that verdict, his major votes were often in support of government. M.P. for Westminster, 1763–76.

Percy (Smithson), Hugh. 1715–86

Son of Langdale Smithson (of Stanwick, Yorkshire); in 1733 succeeded his grandfather Hugh Smithson as 4th baronet. In 1740 he married Elizabeth, only daughter of Algernon Seymour (1684–1750; 7th Duke of Somerset and Earl of Northumberland) (see Elizabeth Seymour Percy). He adopted the surname Percy, since his wife was heiress to the Percy estates, and in 1756 he succeeded her father as Earl of Northumberland, while she became Baroness Percy in her own right. In 1766 he was created Duke of Northumberland (new creation). Oxford from 1730. He was a fellow of the Society of Arts and of the Royal Society from 1736. He was high sheriff of Yorkshire in 1738; lord of the bedchamber, 1753–63; lord lieutenant of Northumberland, 1753–86, vice admiral of Northumberland in 1755; Knight of the Garter from 1756; and a trustee of the British Museum, 1753–86. He also bore the title vice admiral of North America from 1764. In 1760 he urged Newcastle not to resign, but in 1761 he attached himself to Bute, in 1762 supported Bute against Newcastle, and was rewarded with the additional appointment of lord chamberlain to the queen, 1762–68. Upon Bute's fall he supported Grenville and was lord lieutenant of Ireland, September 22, 1763–May 15, 1764. In 1764 he said that he would support "whatever ministry the King appointed," and 2 years later was made Duke of Northumberland. As lord lieutenant of Middlesex, 1762–86, he opposed Wilkes, but on one occasion in 1768 was forced by a mob to drink Wilkes' health. In the House of Lords he supported the crown and the North ministry, though he recorded his dissent from its vote supporting the expulsion of Wilkes from the House of Commons. He was considered by North for several ministry posts, including that of lord president of the council in 1779. In 1780 he was roughly handled once again by a mob of Gordon rioters while serving as master of the king's horse, 1778–80. He is said to have increased the annual income of the Percy family from £8,000 to £50,000, at the same time restoring Alnwick Castle, Stanwick in Yorkshire, Sion House, and Northumberland House in London. In Northumberland alone he planted "above 12,000 trees" annually for some years. The Smithsonian Institution in Washington was established from a bequest by his illegitimate son, James Smithson (James Lewis [or Louis] Macie) (1765–1829). He was "one of the most accomplished noblemen of the present age," according to the *Peerage* of 1775. M.P. for Middlesex, 1740–50.

Percy, Thomas. 1729–1811

Son and grandson of grocers of Bridgnorth, Shropshire. Oxford from 1746; B.A., 1750; M.A., 1753; D.D. from Cambridge, 1770. He was rector of Easton-Maudit, Northamptonshire, 1753–82; bishop of Dromore, Ireland, 1782–1811. In 1765 he published his 3-volume *Reliques of Ancient Poetry* (dedicated to his presumed but distant relative the Duchess of Northumberland), for which Dodsley the printer paid him 100 guineas. The work was immediately recognized as a major contribution to English literature, and the 4th edition (edited by his nephew Thomas Percy) was published in 1794. In 1770 he published *Northern Antiquities*, and later published other works of antiquarian interest. Portrait by Reynolds.

Perryn, Richard. 1723–1803

Of Twickenham, London; son of Benjamin Perryn (of Flintshire; merchant). Oxford from 1741, Lincoln's Inn from 1740, Middle Temple from 1746, barrister in 1747. He was knighted and made circuit judge in 1776, and was later a baron of the exchequer. He retired in 1799. Portrait by Gainsborough.

Pery, Edmund Sexton. 1719–1806

Oldest son of Rev. Stackpole Pery (of Stackpole Court, County Clare); in 1785 created Viscount Pery (Irish). He was called to the Irish bar in 1745 and was a member of the Irish House of Commons, 1751–85, serving as its speaker, 1771–85, and was made an Irish peer upon his retirement. "A man of great abilities—a cursed jobber—hates English government and tries by all means to raise the consequence of Irishmen." That far from impartial comment was made in 1775 by Sir John Blaquiere, secretary of Lord Lieutenant Harcourt, who was unable to cope with Pery and other Irishmen who sought political equality.

Peterborough, 4th Earl. See **Charles Mordaunt.** 1708–79

Petersham, Lord. See **William Stanhope.** 1719–79 and **Charles Stanhope.** 1753–1829

Petty, William Fitzmaurice. 1737–1805

Of Bowood, Wiltshire; styled Viscount Fitzmaurice from 1753; in 1761 succeeded his father, John Fitzmaurice Petty (ca.1706–61; M.P.), as 2d Earl of Shelburne (Irish) and 2d Baron Wycombe (English); in 1784 created Marquess of Lansdowne (English). Westminster, to Oxford in 1755. He married (1) in 1765 Sophia, daughter of John Carteret (*q.v.*) and aunt of the 3d Earl of Bute, and (2) in 1779 Louisa, daughter of John Fitzpatrick (1719–58; 1st Earl of Upper Ossory, Irish). He was an army lieutenant at Rochefort in 1757, at Minden in 1759, and colonel at Kempen in 1760. He was major general in 1765, lieutenant general in 1772 and general in 1783, but he was not primarily a military man. He declined office under Bute and declined the presidency of the Board of Trade and plantations under Grenville in 1763. He became the political lieutenant of the elder Pitt, and was secretary of state, southern department, August 2, 1766–October 21, 1777. Talk of dismissing him led to his resignation and accelerated that of Chatham from the Grafton ministry. He strongly opposed the North ministry and especially its colonial measures, though like Chatham he opposed granting independence to the Americans. He was secretary of state, home and colonial, in the Rockingham ministry, March–July, 1782, and after Rockingham's death was first lord of the treasury and first minister, July, 1782–April, 1783. The terms of his peace treaty and the coalition against them of Fox and North brought about his fall. He was a patron of the arts, and his political service to his nation was greater than has generally been recognized. Horace Walpole, who disliked him, contributed to the unjust reputation which tradition has given him. In the House of Lords he recorded dissents to (1) adjournment of the House on January 15, 1770, as "uncommon, unreasonable, and neglect of duty," (2) acceptance of the House of Commons action unseating Wilkes in January, 1770, (3) rejection of Chatham's bill to reseat Wilkes in 1770, (4) the closing of the gallery of the House of Lords to visitors, as limiting proper inquiry and tending "to hide from the public eye the . . . criminal neglect of the ministry" in 1770, (5) North's Falkland Islands settlement in 1771, (6) the ministry's measures toward the colonies in 1774, (7) the address from the throne in February, 1775, (8) the New England Restraint of Trade Bill in 1775, (9) continuance of the ministry's American war policy in 1778, (10) rejection of the motion to ask the king to dismiss Sandwich in 1779, (11) suspension of the rights of sailors in 1779, (12) refusal to examine into public expenditures in 1779, (13) refusal to exclude holders of government contracts from membership in Parliament in 1780, (14) the declaration of war against the United Provinces in 1781, and (15) the dismissal of Pembroke and Carmarthen from their lord lieutenancies. M.P. for Chipping Wycombe, 1760–61.

Peyton (Dashwood), Henry. 1736–89

Of Doddington, Cambridgeshire; oldest son of George Dashwood; took the surname Peyton in 1771 upon inheriting from his mother's brother; created baronet in 1776. He was called "a moderate Tory"; he voted for Shelburne's peace terms and did not vote on Fox's India Bill in 1783. He supported Pitt's reform measures after 1784, but there is no record that he ever addressed the House of Commons. M.P. for Cambridgeshire, 1782–89.

Phelips (or Phelipps), Edmund. 1725–97

Of Montacute, Somerset; oldest son of Edward Phelips (or Phelipps) (M.P.); from an old and wealthy political family of Somerset. Westminster from 1737, Oxford from 1741. He voted with the North ministry, 1774–79; in 1780 he voted mostly in opposition. His interests were primarily local, and there is no evidence that he ever addressed the House of Commons or influenced it in other ways on any major measure. M.P. for Somersetshire, 1774–80.

Philips (or Philipps), George. ca.1743–84

Of Coedgain, Carmarthenshire; son of John Philips (or Philipps) (of Coedgain). Westminster, to Cambridge in 1761. He was sheriff of

Carmarthenshire, 1767–68, and mayor of Carmarthen, 1773–74. A west-country gentleman who was considered a supporter of the North ministry, he voted and attended irregularly, but voted with North in the final crucial divisions of March 8 and March 15, 1782, on the motions of Cavendish and Sir John Rous. He voted for Shelburne's peace terms in 1783. M.P. for Carmarthen Borough, 1780–84.

Philipps, Griffith. ca.1715–81

Of Cwmgwili, Carmarthenshire; oldest surviving son of Grismond Philipps (of Cwmgwili). Lincoln's Inn from 1741, barrister in 1744. He was a leader of the Whigs in Carmarthen, and in the House of Commons he supported Pelham and Newcastle. He did not seek re-election in 1761, but upon re-entering the House in 1768 he regularly supported the Grafton and then the North ministry, even voting against the continuance of Grenville's Disputed Elections Act in 1774. He is not known to have addressed the House. M.P. for Carmarthen, 1751–61 and 1768–74.

Philipps (or Phillipps), John. ca.1701–64

Of Picton castle, Pembrokeshire; 2d son of Sir John Philipps (or Phillipps) (4th baronet); in 1743 succeeded his brother as 6th baronet. Oxford from 1720. His only political appointment before 1761 was to the Board of Trade and Plantations, 1744–45, and he apparently took no important part in national politics until after his 60th year. He was a Tory and a distant cousin of Horace Walpole, who does not seem to have cherished the relationship. Newcastle listed him as a Tory in 1760 and privately called him "a broken Jacobite," but supported him against William Beckford (whom Newcastle called "a wild West Indian") for a seat in the House of Commons in 1761. There he supported Newcastle in turn, though not for long. A "busy, restless man," he turned to Bute in 1762, who made him a privy councillor in 1763. Grenville, whom he professed to support in 1763, complained in disillusion that "he pretended to answer for the Tories but could not." M.P. for Carmarthen Borough, 1741–47; Petersfield, 1754–61; Pembrokeshire, 1761–64.

Philipps (or Phillipps), Richard. 1743–1823

Of Picton Castle, Pembrokeshire; in 1764 succeeded his father, John

Philipps (or Phillipps) (*q.v.*), as 7th baronet; in 1776 created Baron Milford (Irish). Oxford from 1761. He served as *Custos Rotulorum* of Haverford West, 1764–70. Like his father he was listed as Tory in 1761, and in his own case again in 1765 by Newcastle and Rockingham, but he voted as an independent gentleman. He opposed Chatham's land tax and the Grafton ministry in 1767. From 1770 he generally supported the North ministry until he went into opposition in 1779. After 1784 he professed himself a Pitt supporter. He seldom addressed the House of Commons. He was lord lieutenant of Pembrokeshire, 1781–1823. M.P. for Pembrokeshire, 1765–70; Plympton Erle, 1774–79; Haverford West, 1784–86; Pembrokeshire, 1786–1812.

Phillips, Charles. ca.1720–74

Of Camelford, Cornwall; son of John Phillips (attorney of Camelford). He was recorder of Camelford, 1761–74. He supported the Grafton ministry and the North ministry until 1774, but there is no indication that his interest went beyond local affairs and favors, or that he ever addressed the House of Commons. M.P. for Camelford, 1768–74.

Phillipps, William. ca.1731–81

His parentage is obscure, and he was apparently of humble origin. His military career began in 1745 as ensign, when he was about 14 years old. In 1746 he was a cadet in the royal artillery, and in 1756 he was in command of a company of miners raised for the defense of Minorca. He commanded the British artillery at Minden with distinction, and did so again at Warburg in 1766, becoming colonel in 1772. He became a friend as well as companion in arms of General Sir Henry Clinton, and through Clinton a friend of the 2d Duke of Newcastle. Serving as major general with Burgoyne in 1777, his strategic placement of his artillery resulted in the almost bloodless capture of Ticonderoga. He was made prisoner of war at Burgoyne's surrender at Saratoga in October, 1777, and was not exchanged from his internment at Cambridge, Massachusetts until late 1779. He then joined Clinton in New York and in early 1781 led a small expedition into Tidewater Virginia; he became ill and died near Richmond on May 13, 1781. In general he supported the North ministry when not absent on duty, but with increasing reservations and regret at fighting his "brother" Americans, as he called them in a letter to Clinton in 1779. He was a brave, loyal, honorable, and modest expert in artillery warfare. M.P. for Boroughbridge, 1775–80.

Phillipson, Richard Burton. ca.1724–92

Of Ipswich; son of William Burton (of Herringswell, Suffolk); added the name Phillipson upon inheriting in 1766. Eton from 1732, Cambridge from 1742, Middle Temple from 1741. He was a close friend of Lord Charles Cornwallis, whose family controlled the seat for Eye to which he was elected in 1762. He was cornet of horse in 1744, captain in 1751, and major in 1759. In 1777–78 he was colonel of the First Royal Dragoons and aide to the king. In October, 1777, Burgoyne sent to him from America a copy of his dispatch to Germain reporting his surrender at Saratoga—a copy which Burgoyne doubtless hoped would find its way to the king's eye before Phillipson forwarded it, as requested, to Burgoyne's nephew the Earl of Derby—as a protection against misrepresentation by Germain. He supported the North ministry in all 5 of the crucial divisions recorded in February and March, 1782, voted for Shelburne's peace terms and against Fox's India Bill in 1783, and in 1784 adhered to Pitt. He was a supporter of Newcastle, 1762–65; of Rockingham, 1765–67; and of Grafton, 1767–69. He was major general from 1779 and lieutenant general from 1787. In his later years he grew "very deaf and very stout." M.P. for Eye, 1762–68 and 1770–92.

Phipps, Charles. 1753–86

Of Mulgrave, Yorkshire; 2d son of Constantine Phipps (*q.v.*); brother of Constantine John Phipps (*q.v.*). He was a naval lieutenant in 1771 and captain in 1776. When not absent on navy duty, he supported, though silently, the North ministry from his entrance to the House of Commons in 1779. In all 5 of the crucial divisions recorded in February and March, 1782, he voted with the North ministry. He did not vote on Shelburne's peace terms or on the coalition issues in 1783, and early in 1784 he displayed an allegiance to the Pitt ministry. M.P. for Scarborough, 1779–84; Minehead, 1784–86.

Phipps, Constantine. 1722–75

Of Mulgrave, Yorkshire; son of William Phipps (d. 1730; innkeeper);

grandson of James Annesley (3d Earl of Anglesey); in 1767 created Baron Mulgrave (Irish). Middle Temple from 1739. In 1743 he married Lepell, oldest daughter of John Hervey (son and heir of John Hervey, 1st Earl of Bristol). He died at the age of 53 at Spa in Germany, having left little mark on history or his contemporaries.

Phipps, Constantine John. 1744–92

Of Mulgrave, Yorkshire; in 1775 succeeded his father, Constantine Phipps (q.v.), as 2d Baron Mulgrave (Irish); brother of Charles Phipps (q.v.). He was called "Ursa Major" to distinguish him from his less robust and less distinguished brother. Eton, 1755–58. He entered the navy in 1760 and was lieutenant in 1762 and captain in 1765. In 1773, serving under his uncle John Hervey, he commanded a ship in a voyage of discovery to the Arctic and a search for a northwest passage. He was a member of the Admiralty Board, 1777–82; with Keppel off Ushant in 1778; privy councillor from 1784; member of the Board of Trade, 1784–86; member of the Board of Control, 1784–91; and joint paymaster, 1784–91. He was a personal friend and political supporter of Sandwich, and he supported the North ministry in every crucial vote of which there is a record in February and March, 1782. He was especially opposed to Burke's proposed reforms of Parliament. He spoke and voted against Shelburne's peace terms in 1783, opposed the reform bills of May, 1783, and opposed the printing of the report of the secret committee on India in 1783. He was a fellow of the Royal Society from 1771 and a fellow of the Society of Arts from 1776. He owned the best nautical library in England. M.P. for Lincoln City, 1768–74; Huntingdon Borough, 1776–84; Newark-on-Trent, 1784–90.

Phipps, James Farrell. 1745–86

Of Peterborough, Northamptonshire. He was born in St. Kitts, oldest son of Constantine Phipps (of St. Kitts). Oxford from 1761, Middle Temple from 1763. "A gentleman of small fortune," according to the *English Chronicle*, he strongly opposed the North ministry from his entrance into Parliament in 1780, and voted against it in all 5 of the recorded crucial divisions in February and March, 1782. He then voted for Shelburne's peace terms and for Pitt's 1783 proposals for the reform of Parliament but against Fox's India Bill. He supported Pitt in early 1784, but was thereafter silent and perhaps inactive. M.P. for Peterborough, 1780–86.

Pierrepont, Evelyn. 1711–73

Only son of William Pierrepont (d. 1713; M.P.); styled Earl of Kingston, 1713–15; styled Marquess of Dorchester, 1715–26; in 1726 succeeded his grandfather Evelyn Pierrepont (ca.1665–1726) as 2d Duke of Kingston. Eton from 1725, and then tutored in France. In 1769 he married, or went through the semblance of marriage to, Elizabeth Chudleigh, secret wife of Augustus John Hervey (3d Earl of Bristol), from whom she had separated. He was master of the royal staghounds north of Trent in 1738, Knight of the Garter, and lord of the bedchamber from 1741. In 1745 he raised and led as colonel a regiment of light horse which distinguished itself against the Jacobites at Culloden. He became major general in 1755, lieutenant general in 1759, and general in 1772. He was lord lieutenant of Nottinghamshire, and steward of Sherwood Forest, 1763–65. Horace Walpole called him "a very weak man, of the greatest beauty and finest person in England," but the *Peerage* of 1775 pronounced him a man of "manly frankness ... generosity and courage." Upon Pierrepont's death, members of his family challenged the legality of Elizabeth Chudleigh's position as Duchess of Kingston and as heiress of the duke's fortune. In the notorious case which followed, she was found guilty of bigamy by the House of Lords, but as a peeress she escaped serious sentence, retired to France, and died there.

Pierrepont, 1st Baron. See Charles Pierrepont Medows (or Meadows). 1737–1816

Pigot, George. 1719–77

Of Patshull, Staffordshire, and Westminster; oldest son of Richard Pigot (of Westminster); brother of Hugh Pigot (*q.v.*) and Robert Pigot (*q.v.*); brother-in-law of the 3d Duke of Grafton. Created baronet in 1764; created Baron Pigot (Irish) in 1766. From 1737 he was a writer with the East India Company. He was governor of Madras and commanding officer of Fort St. George, 1755–63, defending it against the French, 1758–59. He returned to England ca. 1765 with a fortune and purchased the estate in Patshull in Staffordshire for a reputed £100,000. He was again in India, 1775–77, but was soon at odds with the council there, through his attempts to override it. The council, probably illegally, arrested and imprisoned him, and he died in the company's guard house in 1777. He was regarded as a Tory, and supported the North ministry from 1770 until he went into opposition in 1774. He strongly supported Clive. "A vain, despotic, energetic man." M.P. for Wallingford, 1765–68; Bridgnorth, 1768–77.

Pigot, Hugh. ca.1722–92

Of Wychewood Forest, Oxfordshire; 3d son of Richard Pigot (of Westminster); brother of George Pigot (*q.v.*) and Robert Pigot (*q.v.*); brother-in-law of the 3d Duke of Grafton; father of General Sir Henry Pigot (1750–1840). He entered the navy in 1734 as an able seaman and became lieutenant in 1742, captain in 1746, rear admiral in 1775, and vice admiral in 1775. He was a member of the Admiralty Board, 1782–83, and in 1783 was made admiral of the blue. In 1782 he commanded the fleet in the West Indies, succeeding Rodney. In the House of Commons from 1768, he voted with the Grafton ministry and then with the North ministry until his brother-in-law Grafton left it and went into opposition. In 1778 he supported Keppel against Palliser and the ministry. In 1780 he voted for the Dunning resolution of April 6, and in February and March, 1782, he voted against the North ministry in all 5 of the crucial divisions recorded. He supported Rockingham in 1782 and the coalition in 1783, voting for Fox's India Bill in November. On November 9, 1783, he moved to increase the sea service by 26,000 men, including 4,495 marines. He spoke in the House but seldom, and then chiefly on naval matters. M.P. for Penryn, 1768–74; Bridgnorth, 1778–84.

Pigot, Robert. 1720–96

2d son of Richard Pigot (of Westminster); brother of George Pigot (*q.v.*) and Hugh Pigot (*q.v.*); in 1777 succeeded his brother George as 2d Baron Pigot (Irish). He was ensign in the army in 1741 and fought at Fontenoy; he was captain in 1751, major in 1758, and colonel in 1772. In 1774 he went on duty to America and in 1775 commanded a regiment at Bunker Hill. He was made major general in 1777; was in command of land troops at Newport, Rhode Island, when D'Estaing attacked in August, 1778; and became lieutenant general in 1782. He held the military sinecure of governor of St. Mawes' Castle, 1772–96; and was also warden of the mint. Like his brothers, he supported the ministry of their brother-in-law Grafton, 1766–70, and then supported the North ministry until Grafton left it, though he left the House in 1772. M.P. for Wallingford, 1768–72.

Pilkington, Lionel. 1707–78

Of Stanley, near Wakefield, Yorkshire, and Chench, near Royston, Yorkshire; in 1716 succeeded his father, Sir Lyon Pilkington (1683–1716; of Stanley), as 5th baronet. Westminster from 1721, Oxford from 1725. A Yorkshire country gentleman, his interests were largely in that county, of which he was sheriff, 1740–41. In the House of Commons he usually voted with the current ministry, even voting with the Grenville ministry on general warrants in 1764 and with Grafton on Chatham's land tax in 1767, but there is no indication that he ever addressed the House, and he did not seek re-election in 1768. M.P. for Horsham, 1748–68.

Pitt, George. 1721–1803

Of Strathfieldsaye, Hampshire; oldest son of George Pitt (d. 1745; M.P.); in 1776 created Baron Rivers and added the surname Rivers; in 1802 created Baron Rivers of Sudley Castle, Gloucestershire. Winchester from 1731; Oxford from 1737; M.A., 1739; D.C.L., 1745. In 1754 he was in open opposition to the Whig ministry, and in 1761 Newcastle listed him as Tory. He was colonel of Dorset militia from 1757; groom of the bedchamber, 1760–70; lord lieutenant of Hampshire, 1780–82; lord lieutenant of Dorset, 1793–1803; lord of the bedchamber, 1782–1803. He served in several diplomatic posts, including that of envoy to Turin (which had been offered to and declined by Lord North), where he was said to "have led a life of debauchery." He supported succeeding ministries, reputedly in quest of a peerage, which he finally secured from the North ministry. In 1784 he published *Letters to a Young Nobleman*. Horace Walpole, seldom the kindliest of critics, called him brutal and half-mad. M.P. for Shaftesbury, 1742–47; Dorset, 1747–74.

Pitt, George. 1751–1828

Of Strathfieldsaye, Hampshire; son of George Pitt (1721–1803) (*q.v.*), whom he succeeded as 2d Baron Rivers in 1803. In the House of Commons from 1774, he supported the North ministry in general until it fell in March, 1782, though he voted for the Dunning resolution of April 6, 1780. He voted with the North ministry against the motion of Cavendish on March 8 and against the motion of Sir John Rous on March 15, 1782. In 1783 he voted for Shelburne's peace terms but did not vote on Fox's India Bill. After 1784 he supported Pitt. He was lord of the bedchamber, 1804–19. There is no record that, at least before 1790, he ever addressed the House, and in his later years he lived much on the Continent. "A pleasant and elegant man." M.P. for Dorset, 1774–90.

Pitt, John. ca.1706–87

Of Encombe, Dorset; 2d surviving son of George Pitt (d. 1735; M.P.) and uncle of George Pitt (1721–1803) (*q.v.*). Oxford from 1722. An avowed Tory in 1754, he followed his cousin William Pitt into opposition in 1755, and was dismissed from the Board of Trade and Plantations, on which he had served since 1744. After William Pitt returned to office, he was a member of the Admiralty Board, 1756–57; surveyor of the king's woods, 1756–63 and 1768–86. He opposed the Grenville ministry over Wilkes and general warrants, 1763–64; supported Newcastle and Rockingham, 1765–66; and then supported the Grafton ministry until he left Parliament in 1768. His only recorded address to the House, in 1765, was on the subject of Newfoundland. M.P. for Wareham, 1734–47 and 1748–50; Dorchester, 1751–61; Wareham, 1761–68.

Pitt, John. 1756–1835

Son of William Pitt (1708–78) (*q.v.*), whom he succeeded as 2d Earl of Chatham in 1778; brother of William Pitt (1759–1806) (*q.v.*). In 1783 he married Mary Elizabeth, daughter of Thomas Townshend (1733–1800) (*q.v.*). He entered the army in 1774, but resigned his first military commission in 1776, at the urging or direction of his father, because he would not fight against the Americans. He re-entered the army as lieutenant when France entered the war in 1778 and was captain in 1779. He served at Gibraltar throughout its long siege, 1779–83. He was colonel in 1793; master general of ordnance, 1801–1806; lieutenant general in 1802; and general in 1812. He was first lord of the admiralty, 1788–94; privy councillor from 1789; Knight of the Garter from 1790; lord privy seal, 1794–96; president of the council, 1796–1801; governor of Jersey in 1807; and governor of Gibraltar, 1820–35.

Pitt, Thomas. 1737–93

Of Boconnoc, Cornwall; only surviving son of Thomas Pitt (ca.1705–61; of Boconnoc; M.P.); cousin of William Pitt (1708–78) (*q.v.*); in 1784 created Baron Camelford. Cambridge from 1754; B.A., 1758; M.A., 1759. He married Anne, daughter of Pinckney Wilkinson (*q.v.*) and described as "a commercial heiress." At first a supporter of Newcastle, in 1762 he abandoned Newcastle for Grenville, who appointed him to the Admiralty Board, 1763–65. He opposed the ministry of Grafton and his cousin William Pitt and signed the Devon and Cornwall petitions against the ministry in the Wilkes case, supporting the election of Wilkes in 1768. He became a violent opponent of the North ministry and supported Sir William Meredith's motions to relax the discriminations against dissenters. He voted for Dunning's resolution of April 6, 1780; for the Yorkshire petitioners' reforms; and for motions to make prompt peace with the Americans. In early March, 1782, he voted for Cavendish's motion to dismiss the ministry and for Rous's no-confidence motion. In 1783 he voted for Shelburne's peace terms, hotly condemned the coalition, and declined the speakership of the House of Commons. In 1784 the Pitt ministry made him a peer. From 1762 he lived at Twickenham and shared Horace Walpole's interest in pseudo-Gothic architecture. He was also a friend of Mrs. Mary Delany (*q.v.*), who called him "high minded, well-bred, sensible, a little irresolute, even effeminate in manner." He died in Florence. M.P. for Old Sarum, 1761–68; Okehampton, 1768–74; Old Sarum, 1774–84.

Pitt, William. 1708–78

Of Hayes, Kent, and later of Burton Pynsent, Somerset; 2d son of Robert Pitt (of Baconnoc, Cornwall); in 1766 created Earl of Chatham. Eton, 1719–26, and studied at Utrecht. In 1754 he married Hester, only daughter of Richard Grenville (1678–1728; M.P.), and sister of Richard Temple Grenville (*q.v.*). For his career see standard reference works. M.P. for Old Sarum, 1735–47; Seaford, 1747–54; Aldborough, 1754–56; Buckingham Borough, December, 1756; Okehampton, 1756–57; Bath, 1757–66.

Pitt, William. 1759–1806

2d son of William Pitt (1708–78) (*q.v.*). Cambridge from 1773; M.A., 1776; Lincoln's Inn from 1778; barrister in 1780. For his career see standard reference works. He opposed the North ministry, declined Rockingham's offer of a cabinet post in 1782, but joined Shelburne as privy councillor and chancellor of the exchequer in July, 1782. He voted for Shelburne's peace terms and opposed the coalition in 1783, but declined the king's repeated invitations to form a ministry to forestall the coalition. Later he connived with the king, Thurlow, and Temple to bring about the sudden fall of the coalition and was ready to replace it with a ministry under his own leadership, at the age of 25, just before Christmas, 1783. By ignoring the attacks of the majority in the House of Commons and the usual traditions of procedure, he managed to remain in office, and then roundly won the general election he arranged in the spring of 1784. Portrait by Hoppner. M.P. for Appleby, 1781–84; Cambridge University, 1784–1806.

Pitt, William Morton. 1754–1836

Of Kingston, near Dorchester, Dorset; oldest son of John Pitt (1706–87) (*q.v.*). Oxford from 1772, Lincoln's Inn from 1774. He entered the House of Commons as "a North independent" (an amusing fantasy) but voted consistently against the North ministry, including all 5 crucial votes recorded for February and March, 1782. He voted for Shelburne's peace terms and did not vote on Fox's India Bill in 1783. From 1784 he generally supported the Pitt ministry, but there is no evidence that before 1790 he ever addressed the House. He was an ardent philanthropist in behalf of the poor and in the promotion of Sunday schools. M.P. for Poole, 1780–90; Dorset, 1790–1826.

Playfair, John. 1748–1819

Oldest son of James Playfair (parish minister at Liff Benvie, near Dundee, Forfarshire). From the age of 14 he was schooled at St. Andrews, from which he graduated in 1765 at the age of 17. He succeeded his father as minister at Benvie, 1773–82, but continued his scientific study, and in 1785 was called to Edinburgh University as professor of mathematics. In 1805 he became professor of natural philosophy, and in 1795 he published *Elements of Geometry*, which went through many editions. He was a fellow of the Royal Society from 1807.

Pleydell-Bouverie. See Bouverie.

Plumb, Samuel. d. 1784

Brother-in-law of Henry Thrale (*q.v.*), and through Thrale a friend of Samuel Johnson. He strongly supported the ministry against Wilkes and the popular party.

Plumer, William. 1736–1822

Of Blakesware and Gilston Park, Hertfordshire; only surviving son of William Plumer (1687–1767; M.P.). Cambridge from 1732. In 1760 he married Frances, daughter of Lucius Charles Cary (7th Viscount Falkland, Scottish; M.P.). In 1791 he married (2) Jane, daughter of George Hamilton and granddaughter of James Hamilton (7th Earl of Abercorn, Scottish). He was a man of good character who did not enter politics in quest of personal favors, being "one of the most opulent country gentlemen in the kingdom." He supported Newcastle, then Rockingham, and later Charles Fox, and was constant and dutiful in attendance of Parliament. In 1770 he voted against expulsion of Wilkes; in April, 1780, he voted for Dunning's first resolution against the excessive influence of the crown; and in February and March, 1782, in every crucial division in which the votes of members were listed, he voted against the North ministry. He voted for Shelburne's peace terms in 1783 but later joined Fox in opposition to Pitt's ministry. M.P. for Lewes, 1763–68; Hertfordshire, 1768–1807; Higham Ferrers, 1812–22.

Plumtre (or Plumtree), John. 1710–91

Of Nottingham and Fredville, Kent; oldest son of John Plumtre (or Plumtree) (1679–1751; of Nottingham; M.P.). Cambridge from 1728. In 1750 he married (1) Margaret, daughter of Brook Bridges (*q.v.*). He supported Newcastle and opposed Bute and Grenville, supported the Rockingham ministry, and opposed the North ministry, voting against Bute's peace terms in 1762 and against unseating Wilkes in

January, 1770. There is no record that he made a speech in Parliament. He was commissioner of stamps, 1739–53. M.P. for Penryn, 1758–61; Nottingham Borough, 1761–74.

Plymouth, 5th Earl. See Other Hickman Windsor

Pochin, William. 1731–98

Of Barkby Hall, Leicestershire; oldest son of Thomas Pochin (of Barkby Hall and Loughborough, Leicestershire). Cambridge from 1750. He was high sheriff of Leicestershire, 1756–57. An independent country gentleman but a friend of the Duke of Rutland, he voted against the North ministry from entering the House of Commons in 1780, and in February and March, 1782, he voted against North in every recorded crucial division. In 1783 he voted for Shelburne's peace terms, for Pitt's proposals for the reform of Parliament, and against Fox's India Bill. There is no record that before 1790 he ever addressed the House. M.P. for Leicestershire, 1780–98.

Pocock, George. 1706–92

Of Twickenham, Middlesex; oldest son of Rev. Thomas Pocock (chaplain of Greenwich Hospital and rector of Danbury, Essex). He entered the navy in 1718; held a command at the Leeward Islands, 1747–48; and was captain in 1748, rear admiral in 1755, vice admiral in 1757. He was in command at the East India station, 1758–59, and was admiral and Knight of the Bath in 1762, when he commanded the fleet that captured Havana and received £122,000 as his share of the prize money. Thus fortified against the hazards of matrimony, in 1763 he married Sophia, daughter of George Drake (son of Sir Francis Drake; 3d baronet) and widow of Captain Digby Dent of the navy. Three years later he retired from naval service. In Parliament, when present, he supported the Bute and Grenville ministries and voted against repeal of the Stamp Act in 1766. Thereafter he seldom attended. M.P. for Plymouth, 1760–68.

Pole, Reginald. See Reginald Pole Carew

Polhill, Nathaniel. 1732–82

Of Peckham, Kent, near London, and Howbury Hall, near Bedford, Bedfordshire; oldest son of William Polhill (of Burwash, Sussex).

He became a leading London broker and tobacco merchant and won election to the House of Commons in 1774 as a supporter of Wilkes. He voted regularly against the North ministry: against approval of the address from the throne in October, 1775; for the Dunning resolution of April 6, 1780; and against the ministry in all 5 of the crucial divisions reported in February and March, 1782. He supported Lord George Gordon's anti-Catholic declarations that initiated the riots of June, 1780. M.P. for Southwark, 1774–82.

Pollington, 1st Baron and Viscount. See John Savile

Polwarth, 3d and 6th Barons. See Hugh Hume-Campbell and Hugh (or Hew) Scott

Pomfret, 2d Earl. See George Fermor

Ponsonby, Frederick. 1758–1844

Styled Viscount Duncannon until 1793, when he succeeded his father, William Ponsonby (*q.v.*), as 3d Earl of Bessborough (Irish) and 3d Baron Ponsonby (English). Oxford from 1774, and then made the grand tour. In 1780 he married Henrietta, daughter of John Spencer (*q.v.*). He left no record of his role in the House of Commons during the last 2 years of the North ministry, 1780–82, but in 1783 he voted against Shelburne's peace terms. He was "a man of the most amiable and mild manners . . . an excellent speaker . . . against the union" of Ireland and England. M.P. for Knaresborough, 1780–93.

Ponsonby, John. 1713–87

Descended from an influential Irish family, the 2d son of Brabazon Ponsonby (1697–1758; 2d Viscount Duncannon and 1st Earl of Bessborough, both titles Irish; 1st Baron Ponsonby, English); younger brother of William Ponsonby (*q.v.*). In 1743 he married Elizabeth, daughter of William Cavendish (1698–1755; 3d Duke of Devonshire). He entered the Irish Parliament in 1739 and in 1744 became first commissioner of Irish revenue, a sinecure he held until 1771. In 1745 he raised 4 companies of horse to help put down the Jacobite uprising. He was an Irish privy councillor from 1748 and speaker of the Irish House from 1756. His party competed with that of the lord lieutenant (Viscount Townshend) for control of the Irish Parliament until he resigned the speakership in 1771, and was then dismissed from the revenue board because of his opposition to the lord lieutenant's measures. Thereafter he took a less important part in Irish politics.

Ponsonby, William. 1704–93

In 1758 succeeded his father, Brabazon Ponsonby (1697–1758), as 2d Earl of Bessborough (Irish) and 2d Baron Ponsonby (English). He made the grand tour. In 1739 he married Caroline, oldest daughter of William Cavendish (3d Duke of Devonshire) (in 1743 his younger brother, John Ponsonby, married her younger sister Elizabeth). He was a member of the Irish Parliament, 1725–58; chief secretary to the lord lieutenant of Ireland and member of the Irish Privy Council, 1741–44. He was a member of the Admiralty Board, 1746–56, a member of the Treasury Board, 1756–59; joint postmaster general, 1759–62 and 1765–66; and governor of County Kilkenny from 1758. In 1762 he resigned his court offices in protest against the dismissal of his brother-in-law the Duke of Devonshire and in the House of Lords also dissented from its approval of Bute's peace preliminaries. The Rockingham ministry reappointed him joint postmaster general and also privy councillor in 1765, but he resigned again in 1766 in protest against the dismissal of Lord Edgcumbe. In 1773 he strongly opposed North's support of the proposed measure to tax absentee Irish landlords, and in general he supported the Rockingham opposition to the North ministry. He was a trustee of the British Museum. In the House of Lords he recorded dissents from its majority votes (1) approving the cider tax in 1763, (2) approving restrictions on parliamentary privilege in the Wilkes case in 1763, (3) approving regulation of dividends of the East India Company, 1767–68, (4) approving actions of the House of Commons in the Wilkes case in 1770, (5) clearing the gallery of auditors in 1770, as "limiting inquiry" into the "criminal neglect of the ministry," (6) approving North's Falkland Islands settlement, (7) approving the East India Company Regulating Bill in 1773, (8) approving the Massachusetts Regulating Act in 1774, (9) approving North's measures toward the colonies in 1774, (10) refusing to accept petitions from the colonies in 1775, (11) approving the New England Restraint of Trade Bill in 1775, (12) approving continuance of the Quebec Governing Act in 1775, (13) rejecting a motion to ask the king to end the American war in 1778,

711

(14) rejecting a motion to ask the king to effect "a total change of System" in 1779, (15) rejecting a motion to protest the dismissals of Pembroke and Carmarthen from their lord lieutenancies, as "a violation of the Bill of Rights" in 1780, (16) rejecting a motion to prevent holders of government contracts from membership in Parliament, and (17) rejecting a motion to oppose raising funds for the government by lotteries and annuities. Portrait by Copley. M.P. for Derby Borough, 1742–54; Saltash, 1754–56; Harwich, 1756–58.

Ponsonby, William Brabazon. 1744–1806

Oldest son of John Ponsonby (*q.v.*); in 1806 created Baron Ponsonby. As yet another Ponsonby grandson of William Cavendish (3d Duke of Devonshire), he was a sturdy Whig of the old school in both English and Irish politics and became a dependable adherent of Charles Fox. He was a leader in the Irish Parliament, 1764–1806; joint postmaster general of Ireland, 1784–89. He voted against Flood's reform bill for Ireland in 1783 and against union between England and Ireland in 1799. He was said to have kept "the best hunting establishment in Ireland."

Poole, Francis. ca.1682–1763

Of The Friars, near Lewes, Sussex; oldest surviving son of Sir James Poole (of Stretton Grandison, near Ledbury, Herefordshire), whom he succeeded as 2d baronet ca. 1730. Eton and Oxford. In 1723 he married Frances, daughter of Henry Pelham (M.P.) and thus gained a connection with Newcastle. He was deputy paymaster for Minorca in 1747. Newcastle assisted him to gain and keep his seat in the House of Commons and in 1761 secured him a pension of £300 a year from secret-service funds—later raised to £500 a year in consideration of his son Henry Poole, who was appointed commissioner of excise in 1761. Father and son supported Newcastle through 1762, voting against Bute's peace preliminaries. The son, who succeeded his father as 3d baronet in 1763, became electoral agent for Newcastle at Seaford, but died in 1767. He was succeeded by another son, Francis Poole (4th baronet), who died in 1804. M.P. for Lewes, 1743–63.

Popham, Alexander. ca.1729–1810

Of Taunton, Somerset; oldest son of Rev. Alexander Popham (rector of West Monckton, near Taunton, Somerset). Oxford from 1746; M.A., 1755; Middle Temple from 1746; barrister in 1755; bencher from 1785; reader from 1793; treasurer in 1800. He was recorder of Wells, 1766–67; master in chancery, 1786–92; and auditor of the Duchy of Lancaster in 1802. In the House of Commons he generally opposed the Grafton and North ministries, voting against approval of the address from the throne in October, 1775, and for the Dunning resolution of April 6, 1780. After 1784 he supported Pitt. He was deeply interested in prison reform. M.P. for Taunton, 1768–74, 1775–80, and 1784–96.

Popham, Edward. ca.1712–72

Of Littlecote, near Marlborough, Wiltshire; oldest surviving son of Francis Popham (M.P.); descended from a family often represented in Parliament. Oxford from 1729. He won election to the House of Commons in 1738, where he was regarded as a Tory in 1754. In 1762, however, Newcastle listed him as a "sure friend," and he voted against Bute's peace preliminaries. He supported the Rockingham ministry, 1765–66; supported the Wiltshire petition against the Grafton ministry for its measures toward Wilkes; voted against unseating Wilkes in January, 1770; and continued to oppose the North ministry until his death. There is no record that he ever addressed the House. M.P. for Great Bedwin, 1738–41; Wiltshire, 1741–72.

Porchester, 1st Baron. See Henry Herbert. 1741–1811

Porteus, Beilby. 1731–1808

Born in York, the 18th child of Robert Porteus (Virginia planter who returned to England in 1720). Cambridge from 1748; B.A., 1752; fellow, 1752–55; ordained, 1757; D.D., 1767. He was chaplain to Thomas Secker, archbishop of Canterbury, from 1762; rector of Wittersham, Kent, 1762–65; rector of Rucking, Kent, from 1764; rector of Hunton, Kent, from 1766; rector of Lambert, Surrey, 1767–97; prebendary of Peterborough, 1764–76; chaplain to the king from 1769; bishop of Chester, 1776–87; bishop of London, 1787–1808. He was an early patron of the Church Missionary Society and of the British and Foreign Missionary Society, always an energetic worker, with more of a spirit for reform than most prelates of his time. He was a great ad-

713

mirer of Archbishop Secker and in 1770 published a pamphlet praising Secker and defending him against his critics. In 1778 he petitioned unsuccessfully for reform of the liturgy and of the 39 articles. A leading evangelist, he encouraged Sunday schools, promoted the welfare of Negroes, and helped Wilberforce, in and out of Parliament, in his crusade against the slave trade. He was often denounced as a Methodist and was a friend of Hannah More, but he was not so idealistic that he rejected the plurality of church livings by which he prospered.

Portland, 3d Duke. See William Henry Cavendish-Bentinck

Portmore, 2d Earl. See Charles Colyear

Portsmouth, 1st Earl. See John Wallop

Potter, Christopher. d. 1817

Of Colchester, Essex. His parentage and early history are obscure, but in 1777 he owned a good estate in Cambridgeshire and was "a gentleman of business and very fair character in the City, and a good friend to Government upon all occasions," according to Lord North in 1778. In 1781 he held a government contract to victual troops in the West Indies. Though he voted for Lowther's motion to end the war immediately and was soon thereafter unseated for corrupt election practices, he received another contract and regained his seat within the year, in 1782, and this time voted for Conway's motion to end the war. In 1789 he went to live in Paris, where he encouraged the development of printing on porcelain and on glass, and re-opened the potteries at Chantilly. M.P. for Colchester, 1781, 1782, and 1784.

Potter, Thomas. 1740–1801

Of Ridgmont, near Bedford, Bedfordshire; only son of Thomas Potter (ca.1718–59, M.P.). He was schooled at Eton, 1753–54, and at Cambridge from 1756; Lincoln's Inn from 1767, barrister in 1772. He was a judge on the Welsh circuit, 1778–1801. A friend of John Robinson, he supported the North ministry, voting against the Dunning resolution of April 6, 1780, but left the House of Commons that year, with no further votes and no speech recorded. M.P. for Lostwithiel, 1776–80.

Poulet (or Paulet, Poulett, or Powlett), Anne. 1711–85

4th son of John Poulet (1st Earl Poulet); brother of Vere Poulet (or

Paulet, Poulett, or Powlett) (*q.v.*); grandson of Peregrine Bertie. Oxford from 1729. In the House of Commons from 1769, he supported the Grafton ministry in its final year and then the North ministry. He voted against Dunning's resolution of April 6, 1780, and with North in all of the 5 crucial divisions that were recorded during February and the first half of March, 1782. He then voted for Shelburne's peace terms and for Fox's India Bill in 1783 and opposed the Pitt ministry until his death. M.P. for Bridgwater, 1769–85.

Poulet (or Paulet, Poulett, or Powlett), Vere. 1710–88

Of Poulet Lodge, Twickenham, London; 3d son of John Poulet (ca.1688–1743; 1st Earl Poulet); in 1764 succeeded his brother John Poulet (1708–64) as 3d Earl Poulet. Oxford from 1729, with his brother Anne Poulet (*q.v.*). He was recorder of Bridgwater and was lord lieutenant of Devon, 1771–88. He was a "very affable" old school Whig who took little part in politics outside Devonshire but who usually sided with the court. In the House of Lords, he did not vote on Fox's India Bill after the king's threat in December, 1783. M.P. for Bridgwater, 1741–47.

Powell, Harcourt. 1718–82

Of Brightstone, near Newport, Isle of Wight; son of Thomas Powell; nephew of Simon Harcourt (ca.1661–1727; 1st Viscount Harcourt). He was enrolled at Lincoln's Inn from 1736, but there is no record that he became a barrister. He was an independent country gentleman of Whig traditions and voted against Bute's peace preliminaries in December, 1762, and against the Grenville ministry, 1763–65. He supported the Rockingham ministry, 1765–66, and in general supported Grafton and then North, until he left the House of Commons in 1775, without any record that he ever addressed it. M.P. for Newtown, 1754–75.

Powis, 1st Baron and 1st Earl. See Henry Arthur Herbert. ca.1703–72

Powis, 1st Earl. See Edward Clive

Powlett. See also Paulet, Poulet, and Poulett.

Powlett, Harry. 1720–94

2d son of Harry Powlett (1691–1759; M.P.; 4th Duke of Bolton); in

1765 succeeded his brother Charles Powlett (ca.1718–65; M.P.) as 6th Duke of Bolton. Westminster from 1728, Portsmouth Naval Academy in 1735. In 1765 he married (2) Katherine, younger sister of James Lowther (1736–1802) (*q.v.*). He was in naval service from 1733 and was lieutenant in 1739, captain at Cartagena in 1743, rear admiral in 1756, vice admiral in 1759, and admiral in 1770. He was admiral of Hampshire and Dorset from 1767. During his time in the House of Commons, 1751–65, he supported Pelham and Newcastle and spoke 14 times, largely on naval affairs. He voted against Grenville on the Wilkes issues; on general warrants, 1763–64; and against the cider tax in 1763. In 1765 he supported the Rockingham ministry and made a violent polemic attack on George Grenville in the House. He was privy councillor in 1766 and governor of the Isle of Wight, 1766–70 and 1782–91. He was also lord lieutenant of Hampshire, 1782–94. After Rockingham fell, he supported the Chatham-Grafton ministry, 1767–70, and then the North ministry in the House of Lords, until he broke with it over Keppel in 1778. He recorded dissents in the upper House to (1) arbitrary adjournment of that House on January 15, 1770, (2) North's Falkland Islands settlement in 1771, (3) clearing of the galleries of the House in 1770, (4) approval of the address from the throne in 1778, (5) rejection of the motion to ask the king to dismiss Sandwich in 1779, (6) restriction of the rights of sailors in 1779, (7) refusal of the peers to examine into public expenditures in 1780, and (8) the raising of government revenue by lotteries in 1781. His daughter married the son and heir of Lord Sandwich, whom he had attacked so severely in the House of Lords. He was called "a silly, brutal, proud man" by Horace Walpole and was believed to have been the original of Captain Whiffle in Smollett's *Roderick Random*. M.P. for Christchurch, 1751–54; Lymington, 1755–61; Winchester, 1761–65.

Powlett, Thomas Orde. See **Thomas Orde** (later **Orde-Powlett**)

Pownall, John. 1720–95

Of Wykeham, near Louth, Lincolnshire; oldest son of William Pownall (of Saltfleetby, near Louth, Lincolnshire); brother of Thomas Pownall (*q.v.*). He was a clerk in the office of the Board of Trade and Plantations, 1741–45; solicitor and clerk of reports, 1745–53; an officer of the navy in

Jamaican waters, 1755–68; undersecretary of state for the colonies, 1768–76; commissioner of excise, 1776–85; and commissioner of customs, 1785–88. In those posts, and through the Board of Trade and Plantations, he was influential in forming and implementing policies and measures for the American colonies, especially before 1777. In 1767 he received one of the royal grants of land on St. John Island in maritime Canada. As an officeholder he supported the North ministry, sometimes, however, with private complaints. M.P. for St. Germans, 1775–76.

Pownall, Thomas. 1722–1805

Of Saltfleetby, near Louth, Lincolnshire; 2d son of William Pownall (of Saltfleetby); brother of John Pownall (*q.v.*). Cambridge from 1740. He was sponsored by the 2d Earl of Halifax, and served as his assistant in 1732, when Halifax headed the Board of Trade and Plantations. He was secretary to the governor of New York Province in 1753; lieutenant governor of New Jersey Province, 1755–56; and lieutenant governor of Massachusetts Bay Colony, 1757–59. In 1759 he led an expedition to Penobscot Bay, Maine, against the French. In 1760 he was appointed governor of South Carolina, but soon resigned and returned to England, where he explained and sometimes defended the points of view of the colonists, though he did not concede their right to refuse to accept British taxation or to use force in revolt. In 1761 he was sent to Germany to check on reported frauds and mismanagement by army contractors. In 1762 he headed the control department of the commissariat. In 1764 he published *The Administration of the Colonies*, and in 1770 (having secured a seat in the House of Commons in 1767) he moved to repeal the tax on tea. But in 1775 he supported the North ministry and opposed Burke's conciliation bill, though he continued to advocate concessions to gain peace with the colonists and opposed the use of Indians against them. In 1770 he voted against unseating Wilkes. M.P. for Tregony, 1767–74; Minehead, 1774–80.

Powney, Penyston Portlock. 1744–94

Of Maidenhead, Berkshire; oldest son of Penyston Powney (ca.1699–1757; of Old Windsor; M.P.; an avowed Tory). He inherited extensive estates near Windsor, though he was never a man of great wealth. Oxford from 1761. His election to the House of Commons in 1780 was supported by the North ministry and the king, and he voted with the ministry in every recorded crucial division in February and March, 1782. In 1783 he voted against Shelburne's peace terms and against Fox's India Bill. From 1784 he generally supported the Pitt ministry, though he voted against it in 1786 on the impeachment of Warren Hastings. He was ranger of Windsor Park, 1788–94. M.P. for Windsor, 1780–94.

Powys, Thomas. 1743–1800

Of Lilford Hall, near Oundle, Northamptonshire; oldest son of Thomas Powys (1719–67; of Lilford); in 1797 created Baron Lilford of Northamptonshire. Eton, 1755–59; Cambridge from 1760. He was sheriff of Northamptonshire, 1768–69. A country gentleman with no apparent liking for politics or yearning for office, he avoided party factions, yet opposed the reform of Parliament. He could and occasionally did speak with force and even passion on issues important to him. A member of the House of Commons from 1774, he supported the North ministry in its measures toward the Americans and in its opposition to "innovations" in church, Parliament, or court; but in 1778 he moved to authorize North's peace commission to declare the independence of the former colonies. He became increasingly critical of that ministry's failures; and though in May, 1780, he opposed Conway's motion to end the war with America immediately, he had the previous month voted against the North ministry on the first Dunning resolution. In the 1780 elections North wanted him to be the ministry's candidate to contest a seat for Westminster, but he declined, and was re-elected for Northamptonshire. In the new Parliament of 1780 he supported the economic reforms proposed by Burke and the Rockingham party, and in February, 1781, he "contended warmly" for the right of the House to control public expenditure by the court or ministry, supporting Burke's bill to regulate the civil list. In December, 1781, he seconded Lowther's motion to end the war in America and spoke critically of the ministry, but he supported North in opposition to Mahon's bill to reform the electoral system. In February and March, 1782, however, he voted against the North ministry in all 5 of the crucial divisions recorded. Though he was considered a Rockingham Whig in 1782, he voted for Shelburne's peace terms and denounced the coalition and Fox's India Bill. In 1784 he proposed in the House that North be made a peer to remove him from the House of Commons and thus make more likely an alliance between Pitt and Fox. Later he voted increasingly in opposition to the Pitt ministry. M.P. for Northamptonshire, 1774–97.

Praed, Humphrey Mackworth. See **Humphrey Mackworth-Praed**

Praed, William. 1747–1833

Of Tyringham House, near Newport Pagnell, Buckinghamshire, and Trevethoe, near St. Ives, Cornwall; oldest son of Humphrey Mackworth-Praed (*q.v.*). Eton from 1757, Oxford from 1767. He became a banker, first in Cornwall and after 1801 in London. He steadily supported the North ministry and voted with it in all 5 of the crucial divisions recorded in February and March, 1782. He did not vote on Shelburne's peace terms and voted against Fox's India Bill in 1783. Afterward he supported the Pitt ministry. M.P. for St. Ives, 1774–75 and 1780–1806; Banbury, 1806–1808.

Pratt, Charles. 1714–94

Of Camden Place, near Chislehurst, Kent; 4th son of John Pratt (ca.1658–1734; of Seale, near Sevenoaks, Kent; chief justice of the king's bench, 1717–25); in 1765 created Baron Camden; in 1786 created Earl Camden. Eton, 1725–31, where he established a lifelong friendship with the elder Pitt; Cambridge from 1731; B.A., 1734; fellow from 1734; M.A., 1740; Inner Temple from 1728; barrister in 1738. He was a fellow of the Royal Society from 1742; king's counsel from 1755; attorney general to the Prince of Wales, 1756–57; and recorder of Bath from 1759. He was knighted in 1761, was made a privy councillor in 1762, and was serjeant-at-law and lord justice of the Court of Common Pleas, 1761–66. In 1763 he ruled in the Wilkes case that general warrants were unconstitutional and challenged Mansfield's ruling that in libel cases the powers and duties of juries were limited to determining the facts of publication—an argument in which he eventually triumphed in the passage of Fox's Libel Act in 1792. As a peer he opposed the tax measures proposed for the colonies as taxation without representation and declared the Stamp Act unconstitutional. He was lord chancellor, 1766–70, but was dismissed, largely on the insistence of the king, for open disagreements with other members of the North ministry. Thenceforth he opposed that ministry and the 1783 coalition. He was lord president of the council with Rockingham and Shelburne, March, 1782–April, 1783, and again under Pitt in 1784. In the House of Lords he recorded further dissents against (1) the action of the House of Commons in unseating Wilkes in January, 1770, (2) rejection of Chatham's motion to reseat Wilkes in 1770, (3) the ministry's measures toward the colonies in 1775, (4) the New England Restraint of Trade Bill in 1775, (5) the hiring of mercenaries without approval of Parliament in 1776, (6) rejection of protests against the American war in 1778, (7) rejection of the motion to ask the king to dismiss Sandwich in 1779, (8) rejection of the motion to examine into public expenditures in 1779, (9) the dismissal of Pembroke and Carmarthen from their lord lieutenancies in 1780, and (10) the declaration of war against the United Provinces in 1781. In sympathy with his political conduct, the mayor and Corporation of London commissioned Reynolds to paint his portrait, and his title was given to new towns in several colonies or states in America. Horace Walpole described him as "steady, warm, sullen, stained with no reproach, and a uniform Whig." M.P. for Downton, 1757–62.

Pratt, John Jeffries. 1759–1840

Of Camden Place, near Chislehurst, Kent; styled Viscount Baynham from 1786; in 1794 succeeded his father, Charles Pratt (*q.v.*), as 2d Earl Camden; in 1812 created Earl of Brecknock and Marquess of Camden. Cambridge from 1776. In the House of Commons from 1780, he voted steadily against the North ministry, including all 5 of the critical divisions recorded in February and March, 1782. In 1783 he voted for Shelburne's peace terms and for Pitt's reform of Parliament but against Fox's India Bill and supported Pitt from 1784. He was teller of the exchequer, 1786–1834; a member of the Admiralty Board, 1782–83 and 1783–89; secretary for war and colonies, 1804–1805; lord president of the council, 1805–1806 and 1811–12; and Knight of the Garter. M.P. for Bath, 1780–94.

Pratt, Robert. 1726–75

Of Coscomb, near Winchcomb, Gloucestershire; 2d son of Sir John Pratt (ca.1658–1734; M.P.); half brother of Charles Pratt (*q.v.*). Oxford from 1745, Inner Temple from 1747, barrister in 1751. He was master in chancery, 1767–75. In the House of Commons from 1763, he voted against the main measures of the Grenville ministry and of the Grafton ministry and opposed the North ministry in its early years, but there is no record that he ever addressed the House of Commons. M.P. for Horsham, 1763–74.

Prescott, George. ca.1712–90

Of Theobald's Park, near Cheshunt, Hertfordshire; from an old Cheshire family; his father was an eminent lead merchant. He was schooled on the Continent and then established himself as a banker in Italy. About 1760 he came to England and, according to Horace Walpole, became "a very rich banker" connected with the Leghorn trade. He supported and was politically sponsored by Henry Fox (*q.v.*). He voted against repeal of the Stamp Act and later often voted with Grafton. In general he supported the North ministry in its early years. M.P. for Stockbridge, 1761–68; Milbourne Port, 1772–74.

Prescott, Robert. 1725–1816

Born in Lancashire of a family that had lost its estate by opposing the revolution settlement of 1688. He was captain in the army at Rochefort in 1757, Louisburg in 1758, and Martinique in 1761, when he was made major. He was in several actions against the Americans and became major general in 1781. He reduced Martinique and became lieutenant general in 1793 and governor of Martinique in 1794. He was governor of Canada, 1796–99, and was general in 1798.

Price, Charles. 1708–72

Of Rose Hall, Jamaica; oldest son of Colonel Charles Price (of Rose Hall); created baronet in 1768. He was sent to England to school, and was at Oxford from 1724, followed by the grand tour. He returned to Jamaica in 1730 and was a member of the Jamaica Assembly, 1732–63, and its speaker, 1746–63. He was judge of the Jamaica Supreme Court and major general of its militia. He was known as "the Jamaica patriot." His son Charles Price (1732–88) succeeded him as 2d baronet and as speaker of the Jamaica Assembly, 1763–75.

Price, Chase. ca.1731–77

Of Knighton, on River Teme, Radnorshire; son of John Price (of

Knighton). Westminster from 1745, Oxford from 1749, Inner Temple from 1751, barrister in 1757. He was listed as Tory in 1761. He steadily supported the Grenville ministry. In 1767, perhaps through the good offices of his friend Charles Townshend, he was appointed receiver of fines in customs and thereafter appears to have supported the Grafton ministry. In 1770, however, he voted against unseating Wilkes and continued largely in opposition to the North ministry. Considered an "original," he appears to have addressed the House of Commons twice, on both occasions effectively. M.P. for Leominster, 1759–67; Radnor, 1768–77.

Price, Richard Thelwall. 1720–75

Of Rhiwlas, near Bala, Merionethshire; son of William Price (of Rhiwlas); grandson of Price Devereux (9th Viscount Hereford); added the name Thelwall in 1767 upon inheriting from his cousin Thelwall Price. He became a nonconformist minister and a writer on morals and politics, and in 1756 published *Review of the Principal Questions in Morals*. Though from a family tradition that was strongly Tory, and though he himself was listed as Tory in 1761, he was on occasion sponsored by Shelburne. In the House of Commons he was essentially independent and voted chiefly in opposition. In 1771, no longer in Parliament, he proposed a reduction in the national debt. He was on friendly terms with Benjamin Franklin and wrote pamphlets attacking the harsh measures of the Grenville and North ministries toward the American colonists. There is no record that he ever addressed the House. M.P. for Beaumaris, 1754–68.

Priestley, Joseph. 1733–1804

Born at Fieldhead, near Birstall, West Riding, Yorkshire; oldest son of Joseph Priestley (cloth dresser of Yorkshire). In his youth he was adopted by his aunt, a strong Calvinist, and was locally schooled. He became a Presbyterian minister, but also a student and experimenter in chemistry and electricity and something of a political philosopher as well. In 1756 he published *Early Opinions Concerning Jesus* and in 1767 *Essay on Government*, which influenced Jeremy Bentham. His *History of Electricity* was an important contribution to scientific thought, and his *History of the Corruptions of Christianity*, published in 1782, pleased and fortified the religious liberals while inducing some conservatives to accuse him of atheism. In October, 1774, he accompanied Shelburne to Paris and there met and held discussions with Lavoisier and other French scientists. In politics he opposed the measures of the North ministry toward the Americans, supported Shelburne, and influenced Shelburne's brief ministry, 1782–83. Cuvier called him "the father of modern chemistry . . . who would never acknowledge his daughter." In 1793 his three sons emigrated to America, where he joined them in 1794. He received a warm welcome upon his arrival in New York. He established himself at Northumberland, Pennsylvania, where he lived quietly until his death and where he was buried in the Quaker burial ground. Portraits by Opie, Rembrandt Peale, Gilbert Stuart, and others.

Primrose, Neil. 1729–1814

Styled Lord Dalmeny until 1755, when as 4th but oldest surviving son, he succeeded his father, James Primrose (ca.1691–1755), as 3d Earl of Roseberry (Scottish). As a younger son he had embarked on a mercantile career and did not entirely abandon it. He was a Scottish representative peer, 1768–84, and was created Knight of the Thistle in 1771. He spent much of his later years in travel on the Continent.

Pringle, James. 1726–1809

Of Stichill House, near Kelso, Roxburghshire; in 1779 succeeded his father, Sir Robert Pringle, as 4th baronet. He was a 2d lieutenant in the army in 1744, captain in 1755, and lieutenant colonel in 1762. He was in military service in America during the reactions to the Stamp Act, 1765–66. He retired from the army in 1770. In the House of Commons from 1761 he was "silent and undistinguished," according to Namier. He supported Bute and then Grenville and on his return from America in 1766 opposed repeal of the Stamp Act. In general he supported the current ministry, including the colonial measures of the North administration. He was master of the works in Scotland from 1774. M.P. for Berwickshire, 1761–79.

Pringle, John. 1707–82

Of Pall Mall, London; 4th son of Sir John Pringle (2d baronet); cousin of Gilbert Elliot (*q.v.*); created baronet in 1766. He was educated at St. Andrews, and at Edinburgh from 1727, and studied medicine at Leyden, receiving his M.D. degree there in 1730. He returned to practice in Edinburgh. He was professor of metaphysics and moral philosophy at Edinburgh, 1734–44, but from 1742 was in Flanders as physician and then physician general to the British army. In 1749 he was physician to the Duke of Cumberland, in 1761 physician to the queen's household, and physician to the king in 1774. He was a fellow of the Royal Society from 1745 and its president, 1772–78. From 1768 he also conducted a private medical practice in London and acquired a reputation as a scientist. He improved military medicine and sanitation. He was a friend of Benjamin Franklin and of James Boswell's father, Lord Auchinleck. Portrait by Reynolds.

Pringle, John. ca.1716–92

Of The Haining, Selkirk, and Clifton Hill, near Yetholme, Roxburghshire; 2d son of John Pringle (of The Haining). As a young man he went to Madeira and rapidly made a modest fortune in the wine trade; later he added to that fortune as a merchant in London. He was elected to the House of Commons in 1765, and supported Grenville in voting against repeal of the Stamp Act in 1766, calling Chatham "that charlatan." In general he supported the North ministry, though he was frequently absent from the House, especially in 1779 and 1780. In the votes on crucial motions by Cavendish and Sir John Rous on March 8 and March 15, 1782, he voted with the North ministry. He supported Shelburne's ministry and voted for his peace terms in 1783. Late that year he voted against Fox's India Bill and afterward supported Pitt (son of "that charlatan"). He was known as a generous and kindly man. M.P. for Selkirkshire, 1765–86.

Proby, John. 1720–72

Of Glenart Castle, near Arklow, County Wicklow, and Elton Hall, near Oundle, Huntingdonshire; oldest son of John Proby (ca.1695–1762; M.P.); grandson of John Leveson-Gower (1675–1709; 1st Baron Gower); in 1751 created Baron Carysfort (Irish). Westminster, to Cambridge in 1736; M.A., 1742; Inner Temple from 1740. In 1754 he was known as an active Tory and a friend of Sandwich and was supported by the "Bedford gang." He voted with Bute and Grenville; against the Rockingham ministry, 1765–66; and against the Grafton ministry until he left the House of Commons in 1768. He was grand master of English Freemasons, 1747–54; Irish privy councillor from 1758; Knight of the Bath from 1761; and a member of the Admiralty Board, 1757 and 1762–65. M.P. for Stamford, 1747–54; Huntingdonshire, 1754–68.

Proby, John Joshua. 1751–1828

Of Norman Cross, near Yaxley, Huntingdonshire; in 1772 succeeded his father, Sir John Proby (*q.v.*) as 2d Baron Carysfort (Irish); in 1789 created Earl of Carysfort (Irish); in 1801 created Baron Carysfort (English). Westminster, ca.1764–67; Cambridge from 1767; M.A., 1770; D.C.L., 1810; L.L.D., 1811. He was a fellow of the Royal Society from 1779. He was active in Irish political affairs, Irish privy councillor, and keeper of the rolls in Ireland from 1789. In 1783 he energetically supported a Wyvill Association petition, but his Huntingdonshire constituents were apathetic to reform. From 1784 he supported Pitt, and in 1787 Buckingham wrote of him to Pitt: "He is very warm and zealous, and has a certain degree of talents and application." He was envoy to Berlin, 1800–1802; English privy councillor, commissioner of the Board of Control, and joint postmaster general, 1806–1807. He published poems, essays, and several tragedies. M.P. for East Looe, 1790; Stamford, 1790–1801.

Prowse, Thomas. 1707–67

Of Compton Bishop, near Axbridge, Somerset; only son of John Prowse (M.P.). In 1754 he was an active and avowed Tory (Namier called him "a typical West Country Tory"). He was a friend of Henry Bilson Legge and before 1761 a friendly opponent of the Pelhams. To ingratiate the Tories in 1761, Newcastle sounded him out for election as speaker of the House of Commons, but he declined. He was critical of the ministry's handling of the Wilkes issues in 1763, when Gibbon called him "a very agreeable, sensible man," but after 1763 he was often ill and absent from Parliament. In 1766 Chatham offered him the postmaster generalship, but he declined that office also, and died the following year. M.P. for Somerset, 1740–67.

Pryse, John Pughe. 1739–74

Of Gogerddan, near Aberystwyth, Cardiganshire; only son of Thomas Pryse (1707–67; M.P.; owner of large estates in Wales). Westminster, to Oxford in 1756. When elected to the House of Commons in 1761, he was listed by Newcastle as Tory, and he supported Bute but sometimes voted independently. Newcastle listed him as a "sure friend" in 1764, but Rockingham again listed him as "Tory" in 1767. He voted against Chatham's land tax in 1767 and against Grafton in voting for Sir George Savile's *Nullum Tempus* Bill in 1768. His last recorded votes were with the opposition on Wilkes issues in 1769. M.P. for Cardiganshire, 1761–68; Merionethshire, 1768–74.

Pulteney, Harry. 1686–1767

Brother of William Pulteney (1684–1764; 1st Earl of Bath). He was colonel in 1733, major general in 1743, and general in 1765 but took no active part in politics after 1760. M.P. for Hedon, 1722–34 and 1739–41; Hull, 1744–47.

Pulteney (Johnstone), William. 1729–1805

Of Westerhall, near Langholm, Dumfriesshire; 3d son of Sir James Johnstone (1697–1772; 3d baronet; M.P.); in 1794 succeeded his brother as 5th baronet. In 1760 he married (1) Frances, daughter and heiress of William Pulteney (1684–1764; 1st Earl of Bath) and in 1767 took the surname Pulteney when he succeeded to the landed estates of Lord Bath and to "an immense fortune." He became a friend of Adam Smith and of David Hume, and in the House of Commons appears to have voted with complete independence. In January, 1770, he voted against unseating Wilkes and in October, 1775, against approval of the address from the throne. In 1778–79, nevertheless, he was used by North to conduct secret negotiations, under the name Williams, with Benjamin Franklin in Paris, negotiations which were totally unsuccessful. He voted for Dunning's resolution of April 6, 1780, but on November 6, 1780, in effect defended the North ministry by telling the House of Commons that the American war was just and necessary "to protect our American friends from the tyranny and oppression of Congress." On December 4, 1780, he spoke in support of the North ministry's appointment of Palliser to Greenwich Hospital. He voted with the North ministry in the crucial divisions of February 22 and 27, 1782, but voted against the North ministry in voting for the motion of Cavendish on March 8 and of Sir John

Rous on March 15, 1782. In June, 1783, he opposed the Receipt Tax Bill and the Malt Duties Bill, and in July, 1783, he opposed the Exchequer Regulation Bill, but he also moved that the officers of the Exchequer "shall receive no greater emoluments in time of war than in time of peace." He became a friend and supporter of the younger Pitt. He was buried in Westminster Abbey. "As a politician he was upright and honest . . . in private life frugal . . . supposed to be the noblest commoner in the Kingdom." M.P. for Cromartie and Nairn, 1768–74; Shrewsbury, 1775–1805.

Purling, John. ca.1722–1800

Of Bradford Peverell, near Dorchester, Dorset. He entered the shipping business with the East India Company in 1753, and was so successful that 10 years later he became a director of the company, serving in that office, 1763–67 and 1768–80. He was deputy chairman and then chairman of the company, 1770–72. In the House of Commons from 1770, he was a steady supporter of the North ministry. He opposed the Dunning resolution of April 6, 1780, and voted with North in the crucial divisions of February and March, 1782, including a vote against Rous's no-confidence resolution on March 15, 1782. A friend of Lord Sandwich, he followed Sandwich into support of the coalition in 1783, voting against Shelburne's peace terms. After 1784, however, he supported Pitt. M.P. for New Shoreham, 1770; Lewes, 1770–72; East Looe, 1772–74; Weymouth and Melcombe Regis, 1774–80.

Pye, Henry. 1709–66

Of Faringdon, Berkshire; oldest son of Henry Pye (of Faringdon); nephew of Benjamin Bathurst (*q.v.*); brother of Thomas Pye (*q.v.*). Oxford from 1725. A member of the House of Commons from 1746, he was listed as Tory in 1754 and 1761. There is no record that he ever addressed the House, and his only recorded vote was against general warrants, and consequently against the Grenville ministry, in 1764. M.P. for Berkshire, 1746–66.

Pye, Thomas. 1713–85

2d son of Henry Pye (of Faringdon, Berkshire); brother of Henry Pye (*q.v.*); nephew of Sir Benjamin Bathurst (*q.v.*). He entered the navy in 1727 and became captain in 1741, rear admiral in 1758, vice admiral in 1762, and admiral in 1773, in which year he was also knighted. He had no notable naval achievements, and was thought to be "a man of slender ability, thrust into office by the Bathurst interests" (*DNB*). He was considered a Tory, and supported the North ministry without exception, 1771–74. M.P. for Rochester, 1771–74.

Pynsent, William. ca.1681–1765

Of Erchfont, near Devizes, Wiltshire, and Burton Pynsent, near Langport, Somerset; ca. 1719 succeeded his father, Sir William Pynsent (twice sheriff of Wiltshire), as 2d baronet. He was sheriff of Somerset, 1741–42. He was a wealthy merchant of strong and often unpredictable opinions and, in his later years, of erratic conduct. He had given strong reason to believe that he would bequeath his considerable fortune to his nearest young relation, Lady North. But perhaps because he had been angered by North's support of the cider tax in 1763, or perhaps because he had developed a tremendous admiration for the elder Pitt, whom it was said he never met, he left nothing to the Norths and willed his estate of Burton Pynsent, and £30,000, to Pitt. After litigation the will was declared valid. M.P. for Taunton, 1715–22.

Quarendon, Viscount. See George Henry Lee

Queensberry, 3d, 4th and 5th Dukes. See Charles Douglas. ca.1698–1778
  William Douglas. 1724–1810   and Henry Scott

Radcliffe, John. 1738–83

Of Hitchin Priory, near Stevenage, Hertfordshire; 3d son of John Radcliffe (merchant of Turkey). Eton, 1754–55. In 1768 he married Frances, daughter of Henry Howard (4th Earl of Carlisle). He was elected to Parliament with the support of the Newcastle Whigs, but his attendance was very irregular and he invariably voted against the ministry in office. He opposed approving the address from the throne in October, 1775; voted for the Dunning resolution of April 6, 1780; voted against the North ministry in all 5 of the crucial divisions recorded in February and March, 1782; and voted against Shelburne's peace terms in 1783. No speech by him in the House of Commons is recorded. M.P. for St. Albans, 1768–83.

Radnor, 1st and **2nd Earls.** See **William Pleydell Bouverie** and **Jacob Bouverie (or Pleydell-Bouverie)**

Rainsford, Charles. 1728–1809

2d son of Francis Rainsford. He was cornet of horse in 1744, at Fontenoy as ensign in 1745, lieutenant in 1751, captain of foot guards and then lieutenant colonel in 1761. He was equerry to the Duke of Gloucester, 1766–80; colonel and aide to the king in 1774; governor of Chester Castle, 1776–96; major general in 1777; lieutenant general in command at Minorca in 1782; and governor of Tynemouth Castle, 1796–1809. There is no evidence that he ever took much interest in politics or addressed the House of Commons, but he steadily supported the North ministry. He left 40 volumes of manuscript material now in the British Museum. M.P. for Maldon, 1773–74; Berealston, 1787–88; Newport (Isle of Wight), 1790–96.

Ramsay, Allan. 1713–84

Born in Edinburgh, the oldest son of Allan Ramsay (1686–1758; author of *The Gentle Shepherd*). About 1733 he went to London to study painting and then studied in Italy, 1736–38. Upon his return to Edinburgh in 1741 he rapidly acquired a reputation as a fashionable portrait painter. He was again in Italy, 1755–57, and ca. 1760 settled in London, where he painted royalty, peers, and prominent government figures, employing assistants and giving more and more of his time to politics and classical studies. He was a member of Samuel Johnson's club and from 1767 was painter to the king. Horace Walpole declared his portraits of women to be superior to those of Reynolds; many would disagree. Examples of his work, including a self-portrait, are in the Tate and National galleries. He published 4 pamphlets on political topics, 1769–83.

Ramsay, George. ca.1728–87

2d son of George Ramsay (ca.1700–39; styled Lord Ramsay as the son of the 6th Earl of Dalhousie, Scottish); in 1764 succeeded his brother Lieutenant Colonel Charles Ramsay as 8th Earl of Dalhousie; in 1782 succeeded to the large estates of his maternal uncle William Maule (Earl of Panmure, Irish). He was a Scots advocate from 1757; grand master of Scottish Freemasons, 1767–69; lord of Scottish Police, 1775–82; representative Scottish peer, 1774–87; and high commissioner of the General Assembly of the Church of Scotland, 1777–82. He died at Abbeville, France.

Ramsay-Irvine, Alexander. 1717–1806

Of Balmain, Kincardineshire; only son of Charles Ramsay (merchant of Montrose, Forfarshire); in 1754 succeeded his uncle Sir Alexander Ramsay (provost of Montrose) as 6th baronet. Through a secret and dubious marriage in 1744 he had acquired as a child-wife the heiress of the Irvine estates; he added the surname Irvine and became a "rich and independent" supporter of Bute for 3 years in the House of Commons, though Bute had already been discarded by the king. No vote or speech by him is recorded. M.P. for Kincardineshire, 1765–68.

Ramsden, Frecheville. 1715–1804

Of Longley Hall, near Huddersfield, Yorkshire; 6th son of Sir William Ramsden (of Byam Longley, Yorkshire); younger brother of Thomas Ramsden (*q.v.*). In 1761 he married Isabella, sister of Charles Ingram (*q.v.*). He was present at Fontenoy and Dettingen; was major in the Earl of Effingham's troop in 1751; served in Germany as lieutenant colonel under Prince Ferdinand; was lieutenant governor of Carlisle; and in 1762 was equerry to the king. From that time his career appears to have faded away.

Ramsden, John. 1735–1839

Of Longley Hall, near Huddersfield, Yorkshire; in 1769 succeeded his father, Sir John Ramsden (of Byam Longley, Yorkshire), as 4th baronet. Oxford from 1754. In 1787 he married Louisa Susan, daughter of Charles Ingram (*q.v.*) (in 1761 his sister married Frecheville Ramsden [*q.v.*]). His half sister married Rockingham, through whom he secured his seat in the House of Commons in 1780 and with whom he voted regularly, voting against the North ministry in all 5 of the recorded crucial divisions of February and March, 1782. He voted against Shelburne's peace terms but did not vote on Fox's India Bill in 1783. In 1784 he opposed the Pitt ministry, and was not re-elected. There is no evidence that he ever addressed the House. He was high sheriff of Yorkshire, 1797–98. M.P. for Grampound, 1780–84.

Ramsden, Thomas. 1709–91

5th son of Sir William Ramsden (of Byam Longley and Longley Hall, near Huddersfield, Yorkshire); older brother of Frecheville Ramsden (*q.v.*); grandson of John Lowther and nephew of the 3d Viscount Lonsdale. In 1743 he married Anne, daughter of Sir Philip Medows (or Meadows). He was Latin secretary to the king and collector of state papers, at a combined stipend of £700 a year.

Rashleigh, Jonathan. 1693–1764

Of Menabilly, near Fowey, Cornwall; 2d surviving son of Jonathan Rashleigh (M.P.). In 1728 he married Mary, daughter of Sir William Clayton (d. 1744; M.P.; 1st baronet) and sister of Kenrick Clayton (*q.v.*) and William Clayton (*q.v.*). He was a Cornish country gentleman who owned considerable landed property, and was also a merchant. In the 1754 elections he took the Tory side, and in 1761 was listed as Tory. All his recorded votes in the House of Commons from 1760 were against the current ministry, and he is not known ever to have addressed the House. He was recorder of Fowey, 1714–64. M.P. for Fowey, 1727–64.

Rashleigh, Philip. 1729–1811

Of Menabilly, near Fowey, Cornwall; oldest son of Jonathan Rashleigh (*q.v.*), with whom he represented Fowey in the House of Commons for 75 consecutive years. Oxford from 1749. He developed a great interest in mineralogy which he maintained throughout his life. Like his father he was called a Tory, but he was independent to the point of unpredictability. He spoke but little in the House, but during his later years there was called "Father of the House of Commons" because of his long tenure. He voted against Chatham's land tax in 1767, against unseating Wilkes, and for Grenville's Disputed Elections Act in 1770. He usually opposed the measures of the North ministry, but he supported North against most reform proposals. He did not vote on Dunning's resolution of April 6, 1780. On February 20, 1782, he voted for Fox's motion to censure Sandwich and on February 22 for Conway's first motion to end the American war immediately; but on February 27 he voted against Conway's second motion to end the war. He did not vote on the Cavendish motion to dismiss the ministry on March 8, 1782, or on Rous's no-confidence motion on March 15. He voted against Shelburne's peace terms in 1783 and from 1784 generally supported the Pitt administration. He was a fellow of the Society of Arts, and of the Royal Society from 1788. Portrait by Opie. M.P. for Fowey, 1765–1802.

Ravensworth, 1st Baron. See Henry Liddell

Rawdon-Hastings, Francis. 1754–1826

In 1790 created Baron Rawdon (English); in 1793 succeeded his father as 2d Earl of Moira (English); in 1817 created Marquess of Hastings (English). Harrow, to Oxford in 1771. In 1804 he married a daughter of the 5th Earl of Loudon (Scottish). He served under the Duke of York in Flanders, was wounded at Bunker Hill in 1775, served under Clinton at Monmouth in 1778, and served notably under Cornwallis in the Carolinas, 1780–81. Illness forced him to take ship for England in July, 1781, and he was captured by the French while at sea. He was made general in 1803 and was governor general of Bengal, 1813–22, and in active military service in India until 1820. Wraxall called him "the Timon of the present age, whose chivalrous spirit, impelled by a magnificent temper, has completely exhausted a splendid fortune." Portrait by Reynolds.

Rawlinson, Abram (or Abraham). 1738–1803

Of Ellell Hall, near Lancaster, Lancashire; oldest son of Thomas Hutton Rawlinson (an affluent merchant). He was connected with the Cavendish family. He followed his father into trade and by 1780 was reputedly worth £50,000. In the House of Commons from 1780, he voted against the North ministry. In February and March, 1782, he voted against the ministry in 3 of the 5 crucial divisions recorded, and did not vote in the fourth. In 1783 he voted for Shelburne's peace terms but then supported the coalition. After 1784 he generally opposed the Pitt ministry, but voted with it for parliamentary reform in 1785. M.P. for Lancaster Borough, 1780–90.

Rawlinson, Henry. 1743–86

Of Grassyard Hall, near Caton, Lancashire; oldest son of Abram Rawlinson (of Lancaster); first cousin of Abram (or Abraham) Rawlinson (*q.v.*). He was a merchant with interests in the West Indies. In Parliament from 1780, he supported the North ministry until 1781, when he spoke in the House of Commons denying his subservience to the ministry, and on occasion thereafter opposed it. But in the crucial votes of February and March, 1782, of which records now exist, he voted with the ministry in the last 3. In 1783 he voted for Shelburne's peace terms, but later supported the coalition and (unlike his cousin) voted against Pitt's reform measures. M.P. for Liverpool, 1780–84.

Rawlinson, Thomas. d. 1769

Of London and Stowlangtoft Hall, near Ixworth, Suffolk; cousin of Sir Thomas Rawlinson (1647–1708; lord mayor of London). Apparently in trade in London, he was an alderman from 1746; sheriff of London in 1748; master of the Company of Grocers; lord mayor of London, 1753–54; colonel of militia; and knighted in 1760. His only daughter, Susannah, married George Wombwell (*q.v.*).

Rawlinson, Walter. 1734–1805

Of Stowlangtoft Hall, near Ixworth, Suffolk; only son of Thomas Rawlinson (*q.v.*). Cambridge from 1753, Lincoln's Inn from 1752. He was a London banker in partnership with Robert Ladbroke (1713–73) (*q.v.*) and Robert Ladbroke (1740–1814) (*q.v.*). He was a London alderman, 1773–77. He was elected to the House of Commons in 1774, and supported the North ministry, voting against Dunning's resolution of April 6, 1780. Although in December, 1780, he supported the move for an immediate end to the war in America, in February and March, 1782, he voted with the North ministry in 4 of 5 of the crucial divisions recorded. In 1783 he voted for Shelburne's peace terms but then followed Sandwich into support of the coalition and opposed Pitt. M.P. for Queenborough, 1774–84; Huntingdon Borough, 1784–90.

733

Rebow-Martin, Isaac. 1731–81

Of Wivenhoe Park, near Colchester, Essex; only surviving son of Isaac Lemyng Rebow (of Colchester; of Dutch ancestry; M.P.). Eton, 1745–48; Cambridge from 1749. In 1776 he married his cousin Mary, daughter of Thomas Martin, and added the surname Martin. He was recorder of Colchester, 1763–81. In the House of Commons, where he very seldom spoke and voted almost as seldom, he had little influence. Except in 1764, when he voted against general warrants and Grenville, he generally supported the ministry in office, including the North ministry, 1770–81. M.P. for Colchester, 1755–81.

Reeve, Clara. 1729–1807

Born at Ipswich, the oldest daughter of William Reeve (rector of Freston, Suffolk, and perpetual curate of St. Nicholas, Ipswich; "an old-fashioned Whig"). From 1772 she was an industrious and prolific producer of verse and prose, with a special flair for sentimental novels in romantic settings and popular style, exemplified by *The Old English Baron*, 1777, and rationalized in *The Progress of Romance*, 1785, which were widely read. She led a quiet and retired life, chiefly at Ipswich.

Reid, Thomas. 1710–96

Born at Strachan, near Banchory, Kincardineshire, the son of Lewis Reid (1676–1762; dissenting minister). Aberdeen University, 1722–26. He then studied divinity, and in 1731 was licensed to preach. He was librarian at Aberdeen, 1733–36, and in 1737 secured the nearby living of Newmachar. In 1740 he married his cousin Elizabeth, daughter of George Reid (London physician). In 1748 he published *Essays on Quantity*, and in 1752 became professor of moral philosophy at Aberdeen. In 1764 he published *An Inquiry into the Human Mind*, and in 1785 *On the Intellectual Powers of Man*. He was founder of the "Scottish School" of philosophy, which reacted against the skepticisms of David Hume. Portrait by Raeburn and a medallion by Tassie.

Reynolds, Francis. d.1773

Of Strangeways, near Wigan, Lancashire; oldest son of Thomas Reynolds (of South Mimms, Middlesex; a director of the South Sea

Company, 1715–22). He was provost marshal of Barbados, 1741–61; clerk of the crown for the Duchy of Lancaster, 1741–61; and surveyor of woods for the Duchy of Lancaster, during which time he supported the Pelham and Newcastle interests. After 1761 he appears to have supported the current ministry. He voted with the Grafton ministry on the land tax in 1767 and on the *Nullum Tempus* Bill in 1768. He appears never to have addressed the House of Commons. Presumably in appreciation of his votes (or his silence), he was given a secret-service pension of £600. M.P. for Lancaster Borough, 1745–73.

Reynolds, Joshua. 1723–92

Born at Plympton Erle, near Plymouth, Devonshire, the 7th child of Rev. Samuel Reynolds (1681–1746; fellow of Balliol College, Oxford; master of a grammar school near Plymouth). He began to paint portraits before he had completed his local schooling and by the age of 20 had determined to make painting his career. Before 1749 he went to London for further study and then spent 3 years in Italy as a protégé of Augustus Keppel (*q.v.*). After his return to England about 1760 he rapidly established a reputation as England's pre-eminent portrait painter. In 1764 he organized the Literary Club—primarily, he said, to give Samuel Johnson opportunity to talk. In 1768 he became the first president of the Royal Academy. He was knighted in 1769 and in 1773 was elected lord mayor of Plymouth. He continued to paint until 1789, when his eyes failed him.

Ribbesdale, 1st Baron. See **Thomas Lister**

Rice, George. ca.1724–79

Of Newton Castle, Carmarthenshire; only son of Edmund Rice (of Newton; M.P.). Oxford from 1742. In 1756 he married Cecil, daughter and heiress of William Talbot (Earl Talbot), who succeeded as Baroness Dynevor in her own right in 1782. He entered the House of Commons in 1754, supported Bute and Bedford from 1761, and was a member of the Board of Trade and Plantations (at £1,000 a year), 1761–70. From 1768 he supported the Grafton and North ministries, was a privy councillor in 1770, and was treasurer of the king's chamber, 1770–79. In the House of Commons he spoke strongly against concessions to the Americans, and Burke named him as an example of men with undue influence over the crown and ministry. He was lord lieutenant of Carmarthenshire, 1755–79. M.P. for Carmarthenshire, 1754–79.

Rich, Robert. 1685–1768

Of Roos Hall, near Beccles, Suffolk; 2d son of Sir Robert Rich (1648–99; M.P.); kinsman of the Earls of Warwick; in 1706 succeeded his brother Sir Charles Rich (ca.1680–1706) as 4th baronet. He was page of honor to William III until 1702. He was an ensign in the army in 1700 and colonel in 1709. He was wounded at Schellenberg, at Blenheim, and again at Ramillies. He was made major general in 1735, lieutenant general in 1739, general in 1745, and field marshal in 1757. He was groom of the bedchamber to the king (at £500 a year), 1727–59, and governor of the bedchamber to George II as Prince of Wales and as king. He was governor of Chelsea Hospital (at £500 a year), 1740–68. M.P. for Dunwich, 1715–22; Berealston, 1724–27; St. Ives, 1727–41.

Rich, Robert. 1714–85

Of Roos Hall, near Beccles, Suffolk; in 1768 succeeded his father, Robert Rich (*q.v.*), as 5th baronet. In 1752 he married (1) Mary, sister of Peter Ludlow (*q.v.*). He was a lieutenant in the army in 1739, held a command as lieutenant colonel at Falkirk in 1746, and lost his left hand in action at Culloden in 1746. He defended Minorca in 1754, was made major general in 1758, and fought at Minden in 1759. He was governor of Londonderry and Culmore forts in 1756, and was made lieutenant general in 1760. Though he took little or no part in politics, in 1774 he began a long controversy with General Conway over military affairs in which he ultimately came off second best.

Richmond, Richard. 1729–80

Son of Sylvester Richmond (clerk of Walton-on-the-Hill, near Liverpool, Lancashire). Cambridge from 1746; L.L.D., 1758. He was rector of Walton-on-the-Hill, 1757–80; chaplain to the Duke of Atholl; and bishop of Sodor and Man, 1773–80.

Richmond, 3d Duke. See Charles Lennox

Ridley, Matthew. 1711–78

Of Blagdon, near Morpeth, and Heaton, near Cornhill, Northumberland; 2d son of Richard Ridley. Westminster from 1724, Oxford from 1727, Gray's Inn from 1728, barrister in 1732, bencher from 1749, treasurer in 1765. He usually supported the current ministry, but in January, 1770, he voted against unseating Wilkes. He addressed the House of Commons fairly frequently, mostly on local matters, but was considered to be on the whole a supporter of the North ministry, 1770–74. He was mayor of Newcastle-on-Tyne in 1733, 1745, 1751, and 1759 and governor of the Company of Merchant Adventurers in 1739. M.P. for Newcastle-on-Tyne, 1747–74.

Ridley, Matthew White. 1745–1813

Of Blagdon, near Morpeth, and Heaton, near Cornhill, Northumberland; 2d son of Matthew Ridley (*q.v.*); in 1778 succeeded his maternal uncle Matthew White (1727–78; M.P.) as 2d baronet. Westminster, to Oxford in 1764. A country gentleman, he opposed change and professed political independence, but was cast by his traditions and his temperament into the arms of North, a man rather like him. Walpole commented in 1775 that he was "always with administration," but Walpole was not always right, and Ridley voted against unseating Wilkes, against the Royal Marriage Bill, and for the renewal of Grenville's Disputed Elections Act. In 1780 he voted for Dunning's first resolution deploring the excessive influence of the crown. Although he supported the ministry in opposing Crewe's bill to disenfranchise revenue officers, he opposed North on all 5 of the crucial votes in February and March, 1782. On May 23, 1782, he told the House of Commons that he favored the Election Bribery Bill of the new Rockingham ministry in principle but opposed many of its clauses. After 1784 he generally opposed the Pitt ministry in its early years. He was, like his father, mayor of Newcastle-on-Tyne, 1774, 1782, and 1791. M.P. for Morpeth, 1768–74; Newcastle-on-Tyne, 1774–1812.

Rigby, Richard. ca.1722–88

Only son of Richard Rigby (of Mistley Hall, near Manningtree, Essex; wealthy woolen merchant). Cambridge, Middle Temple from 1738, grand tour. He attached himself to Frederick, Prince of Wales, and with the support of Leicester House won a seat in the House of Commons in 1745. Shortly after the death of the prince in 1751 he became a political lieutenant and friend of the Duke of Bedford and in 1752 saved the Duke

from "a murderous riot at the Lichfield races." He was secretary to
Bedford when Bedford was lord lieutenant of Ireland, 1754–61, and
later became Bedford's political agent, parliamentary floor manager,
well-salaried private secretary, and a member of the inner circle of
the "Bloomsbury gang." He was vice treasurer of Ireland, 1762–65 and
1768, and master of the rolls for Ireland from 1765. As paymaster of
the forces from 1768 he made a fortune and died immensely rich, leaving "near half a million of public money." He took a prominent part
in the opposition to Wilkes and, to the extent that Bedford factional
politics permitted, supported the North ministry, 1770–82, though in
1778, in support of his friends the Howe brothers, he moved for the
parliamentary inquiry into the causes of the surrender of Burgoyne
at Saratoga, which, as the evidence emerged, discredited the ministry's,
and especially Germain's, management of the war. In 1778 he also
objected to a public funeral, or to raising a public fund, in honor of
the first Earl of Chatham, with whose politics he had disagreed. After
1778 he became increasingly doubtful of the ability of the North ministry to continue in office and spoke privately of the need to discard
North in order to save the other ministers. In 1781–82 he insisted that
there was no popular demand, and no need, for the reform of representation in the House of Commons. He opposed Dunning's resolution of April 6, 1780, and supported the North ministry (except for
attacks with Dundas on Germain and Sandwich in late 1781 and early
1782) until its fall, voting with it in all the crucial divisions recorded
in February and March, 1782. In 1783 he voted for Shelburne's peace
terms, and thereafter inclined toward Pitt. In 1784 he was threatened
with impeachment for his personal use of public funds acquired when
paymaster. Though he was called "the brazen bosun of the Bloomsbury crew" and "an unblushing placeman during the worst period
of Parliamentary corruption" (DNB), he did not lack ability, public
spirit, and some private scruples; he did little more than to capitalize
more efficiently than most other politicians upon the ethical laxity of
a political and social system he had not created. Many Whig opponents who self-righteously condemned him, and some later Whig
historians who have done likewise, may secretly have wished that they
could emulate his success. He did not lack cultivation in both the
classics and French vintages, and he dressed in unique and mag-

nificent velvet sobriety. M.P. for Castle Rising, 1745–47; Sudbury, 1747–54; Tavistock, 1754–88.

Rivers, 1st and 2d Barons. See **George Pitt.** 1721–1803   and **George Pitt.** 1751–1828

Riversdale, 1st Baron. See **William Hull**

Roberts, John. 1712–72

Son of Edward Roberts (registrar of Chester). Westminster from 1723, Oxford from 1728. He studied medicine but abandoned it to become a very faithful and greatly trusted secretary to Henry Pelham. In that capacity he dispensed large sums of secret-service money, and was rewarded with several sinecures and backstairs connections at court. He was deputy paymaster for Gibraltar, 1743–61; inspector of customs, 1746–62; and receiver of quit-rents for Virginia, 1748–72. He assisted Newcastle in the general elections of 1754 and in that year received a pension (in the Irish establishment) of £800 a year. He was in charge of secret-service expenditures under Newcastle, 1754–56, and again assisted Newcastle in the 1761 elections. In that year he was appointed to the Board of Trade and Plantations. He resigned that post in 1762 in protest at the dismissal of the Duke of Devonshire but continued to manage the treasury-controlled boroughs of Harwich and Orford. He voted against Bute's peace preliminaries in 1762, with the opposition to Grenville against general warrants, and for Wilkes, 1763–64, but joined the Grenville forces in opposing repeal of the Stamp Act in 1766. In 1767 he voted for Chatham's land tax but thereafter attended only about half the meetings of the Board of Trade and Plantations, to which he had been reappointed in 1765. He appears never to have addressed the House of Commons. In honor of that inspiring career he has a marble monument in Westminster Abbey. M.P. for Harwich, 1761–72.

Roberts, John Christopher. 1739–82

Of Taunton, Somerset. He was army captain in 1755, colonel in 1777, commissary general, and major general (on half pay) in 1781. He was mayor of Taunton in 1774, and that year stood for election to the House of Commons. He was found guilty of making false returns in his own favor in his capacity of mayor, and was unseated. But he was a strong supporter of the North ministry and of the American war, and in 1780 the North ministry contributed £3,000 toward the expenses of his election, which he won. In his first reported speech in the House of Commons in November, 1781, he opposed a vote of thanks to retiring speaker Fletcher Norton, on the grounds that since he had voted against Norton's continuance as speaker he could not consistently now thank him for his services. In that year he was also forced to make apology to Speaker Cornwall for his absence from the House, which he had been ordered to attend. He cast no votes in the 5 crucial divisions reported in February and March, 1782; his seat was reported at that time vacant. Since he died that year, the conclusion seems clear. M.P. for Taunton, 1780–82.

Robertson, James. ca.1720–88

Born in Fifeshire of parentage now unknown. He entered the army as a private, ca. 1735, served at Cartagena, and became ensign in 1740. In 1756 he was in service in the colonies and became major general (provincial class) of American colonial troops. In 1772 he was colonel (English class), and in 1776 he commanded a brigade in Howe's army in the battle on Long Island. He was military governor of New York City in 1779, and in that year he returned to England to give testimony in the Howe inquiry. There he tended to support the conclusions and claims of Germain, but his evidence was outweighed by the contrary conclusions and opinions of the Howe brothers, Burgoyne, Cornwallis, Carleton, and General "Flintlock" Grey. His evidence was consequently challenged and even derided by the opposition, and although he returned to his governorship of New York, 1779–81, and served there as lieutenant general until he returned to England in 1782, he held no important military post thereafter.

Robertson, William. 1721–93

Oldest son of William Robertson (d. 1745; Scotch Presbyterian minister at Dalkeith, near Edinburgh). He was schooled at Dalkeith and then at Edinburgh University. In 1751 he married his cousin Mary, daughter of James Nisbet (1677–1756; minister of Edinburgh). He served both as a minister and as a teacher at Edinburgh University. In 1759 he published his *History of Scotland*, and the reputation gained from that painstaking compilation of facts probably helped him secure appointment as principal of the university. In 1769 he published his *History of the Reign of Charles I*, and in 1777 a history of America. Both were thorough, pedantic, and uninspired. Portrait by Reynolds.

Robinson, Charles. ca.1732–1807

Of Maxton, near Dover, Kent; 7th son of Matthew Robinson (of Edgeley, Yorkshire); brother of Matthew Robinson Morris (1713–1801; M.P.). As a boy he entered the navy, but soon withdrew to embark upon the study of law; Middle Temple from 1749, barrister in 1753. He was recorder of Canterbury from 1763; recorder of Hythe, New Romney, and Sandwich from 1766; and recorder of Dover from 1770. He was bankruptcy commissioner, 1776–92. In Parliament from 1780, he voted steadily against the North ministry, including opposition votes in all 5 of the crucial divisions recorded in February and March, 1782. He voted for Shelburne's peace terms and against Fox's India Bill in 1783. From 1784 he generally supported Pitt and reform. He is known to have addressed the House twice on Pitt's shop tax, but there is no record of other speeches. M.P. for Canterbury, 1780–90.

Robinson, Frederick. 1746–92

Of Newby Hall, near Boroughbridge, Yorkshire; 2d son of Sir Thomas Robinson (1695–1770; of Rokeby, Edgeley, and Newby, Yorkshire; M.P.; 1st Baron Grantham); brother of Thomas Robinson (1738–86) (*q.v.*); cousin of William Aislabie (*q.v.*); allied to Lord Hardwicke. Westminster, to Cambridge in 1763; Lincoln's Inn from 1764; barrister in 1770. In 1785 he married Catherine, daughter of James Harris (1709–80) (*q.v*). He was secretary of the embassy at Madrid, 1772–79. In the House of Commons from 1780, he voted with the North ministry in all 5 of the crucial divisions reported in February and March, 1782. He voted for Shelburne's peace terms and against Fox's India Bill in 1783 and supported Pitt, 1784–87. In 1787 he received a pension of £900 a year for life and vacated his seat. M.P. for Ripon, 1780–87.

Robinson, George. 1730–1815

Of Cranford St. Andrew, near Kettering, Northamptonshire; in 1765 succeeded his father, Sir John Robinson (1702–65; sheriff of Northamptonshire), as 5th baronet, and inherited a considerable estate. Cambridge from 1749; fellow from 1755; M.A., 1756. Like his father, he was sheriff of Northamptonshire, 1766–67. In the House of Commons from 1774, all his recorded votes were against the North ministry, including opposition to approval of the address from the throne in October, 1775, and a vote for Dunning's first resolution in April, 1780. He was said by the *Public Ledger* to be "an honest, independent country gentleman," which, from that source, meant that he was a good opposition Whig. There is no record that he ever addressed the House. M.P. for Northampton Borough, 1774–80.

Robinson, John. 1727–1802

Of Islesworth on Thames, Middlesex, and Sion Hill, at Twickenham, London; oldest son of Charles Robinson (1702–60; merchant of Appleby, Westmorland). He was articled to his uncle Richard Wordsworth (grandfather of the poet William Wordsworth and attorney of Westmorland). Gray's Inn from 1759. In 1759 he married Mary, daughter of Nathaniel Crowe (West Indies merchant). He began his political career as a protégé and aide of James Lowther (1736–1802) (*q.v.*), became a secretary in the treasury in 1770; and was later North's trusted undersecretary, political agent, and confidant, 1770–82. He was "a steady, sober-minded man of business," trusted by the king, who used him to urge and energize North to action, 1778–82. He was a member of the House of Commons from 1764 and supported the North ministry in every recorded vote, including the Dunning resolution of April 6, 1780, which was aimed partly at his own influence over North and the king. His preliminary analysis of the potential vote in the 1780 general election was a major factor in the North ministry's decision to call that election earlier than was traditional. After North's fall, he voted against Shelburne's peace terms in February, 1782, but did not follow North into the coalition. Later he openly supported Pitt. North took that defection bitterly but on his deathbed effected a reconciliation. He was an honorary D.C.L. of Oxford in 1773 and was surveyor of woods and forests, 1786–1802. His daughter married a son of Lord Abergavenny. His letters and papers, and especially his notes on election estimates and deals and his comments on individuals involved in them, are valuable historical material. M.P. for Westmorland, 1764–74; Harwich, 1774–1802.

Robinson, Richard. 1709–94

Of Rokeby, near Richmond, North Riding, Yorkshire; 6th son of William Robinson (1675–1720; of Rokeby); in 1777 created Baron Rokeby of Armagh (Irish). Westminster, to Oxford in 1726; B.A., 1730; M.A., 1733; B.D. and D.D., 1748. He was successively or simultaneously chaplain to Lancelot Blackburne (archbishop of York, 1724–43), rector of Etton in the East Riding from 1738, prebendary of York from 1738, and rector of Hutton, Yorkshire, from 1742. In 1751 he went to Ireland as chaplain to Lionel Sackville (first Duke of Dorset and then lord lieutenant of Ireland). Warmly sponsored by the Duke of Cumberland, he was bishop of Killala, 1752–59; bishop of Leighlin and Ferns, 1759–61; and bishop of Kildare, 1761–65. He succeeded George Stone as archbishop of Armagh, 1765–94. He was also dean of Christ Church, Dublin, from 1761; Irish privy councillor from 1765; vice chancellor of Dublin University, 1765–91; and chief justice for Ireland from 1787. He was a fellow of the Society of Arts from 1776. Horace Walpole called him "a proud but superficial man," but Richard Cumberland (who seldom spared superlatives in laudatory memoirs of great men he but slightly knew) called him "splendid, liberal, lofty . . . benefitted a whole nation by his works." Portrait by Reynolds.

Robinson, Thomas. 1695–1770

Of Edgeley and Newby, West Riding, Yorkshire; 4th son of Sir William Robinson (d. 1736; of Newby; 1st baronet; M.P.), whom he succeeded in 1736 as 2d baronet; in 1761 created Baron Grantham of Lincolnshire. Westminster, to Cambridge in 1712; M.A., 1718; fellow from 1719; Middle Temple from 1723. In 1737 he married Frances, daughter of Thomas Worseley of Yorkshire. He early became a friend of the Duke of Newcastle and supported him through 1762. He was secretary to the embassy at Paris, 1723–30; envoy to Vienna, 1730–48; Knight of the Bath from 1742; plenipotentiary at the peace negotiations at Soissons, 1728–29, and at Aix-la-Chapelle in 1748. He was a member of the Board of Trade and Plantations, 1748–49; master of the wardrobe, 1749–54 and 1755–61; and privy councillor from 1750. He was secretary of state, southern department, leader of the House of Commons for Newcastle, 1754–55; joint postmaster general under Rockingham, 1765–66. He greatly influenced 4 votes in the House of

Commons, as well as several electoral constituencies in Yorkshire and Lincolnshire. As a peer he strongly protested the limitations on parliamentary privilege in the Wilkes case in 1763. Henry Fox called him "a very dull man . . . a very honest and a very good-natured man . . . worse than a bad speaker." To Henry Fox, honesty and dullness probably seemed inseparable. M.P. for Thirsk, 1727–34; Christchurch, 1748–61.

Robinson, Thomas. ca.1703–77

Of Rokeby, near Richmond, North Riding, Yorkshire; oldest son of William Robinson (1675–1720; of Rokeby); brother of Richard Robinson (*q.v.*); created baronet in 1731. Oxford from 1721, Middle Temple from 1722, extensive grand tour. He married (1) in 1728 Elizabeth, oldest daughter of Charles Howard (3d Earl of Carlisle) and widow of Nicholas Lechmere (Baron Lechmere), and (2) at Barbados, ca. 1743, the widow "with £10,000" of Samuel Salmon (wealthy ironmonger). She declined to return with him to England, though presumably her dowry did. He studied architecture in Greece and Italy, and then took a commission in the army, which he soon resigned. He was commissioner for excise, 1735–42; governor of Barbados, 1742–47. Still devoted to architecture, and a fellow of the Royal Society, he spent large sums on building and entertainment, especially at Rokeby, which he rebuilt extensively. In 1769 he was forced to sell Rokeby, which had been in the family for 160 years, to meet his debts. In the House of Commons, 1727–34, he made several long speeches, but they did not alter the general conclusion that he was "a specious, empty man." Samuel Johnson said to him on one occasion: "You talk the language of a savage." M.P. for Morpeth, 1727–34.

Robinson, Thomas. 1738–86

Born in Vienna where his father, Thomas Robinson (1695–1770) (*q.v.*), was envoy; in 1770 succeeded his father as 2d Baron Grantham. Westminster from 1750; Cambridge from 1755; M.A., 1757; grand tour. He supported Newcastle in the general election, and in 1761, for services rendered, he was appointed secretary to the embassy to the Congress of Augsburg at £2,800 a year, although it had been for some time apparent that the congress would never meet. In December, 1762, having won a seat in the House of Commons, he voted

against Bute's peace preliminaries, and was soon afterward dismissed
by Bute with other Newcastle supporters and placemen. In 1766 he
was appointed by Rockingham to the Board of Trade and Plantations
(of which his father had once been a member), and held that post
until 1770. He supported the North ministry and was privy councillor
in 1770; vice chamberlain, 1770–71; ambassador to Madrid, 1771–79;
and first lord of trade, 1780–82. He was secretary of state for foreign
affairs under Shelburne, 1782–83, and supported Shelburne's peace
terms. Upon his dismissal he displayed "an eager rapacity" for a
larger pension and acquired one of £2,000 a year, though he had already secured one from North of £3,000 a year. From 1784 until his
death he supported Pitt. According to Horace Walpole, he "possessed
solid though not eminent parts." Portrait by Romney. M.P. for Christchurch, 1761–70.

Rochford, 4th Earl. See William Henry Nassau Zuylestein

Rockingham, 2d Marquess. See Charles Watson-Wentworth

Rocksavage, 1st Earl. See George James Cholmondeley

Roddam, Robert. 1719–1808

2d son of Edward Roddam (of Roddam Hall, near Alnwick, Northumberland). He entered the navy in 1735 and was lieutenant in 1741,
commander in 1746, captain in 1747, rear admiral in 1758, and admiral
in 1793. He saw service in the North Sea, the West Indies, and American waters, 1735–57. In 1757 he was captured by the French after a
gallant fight, but was soon exchanged. He was in command at the
Nore.

Roden, 1st Earl. See Robert Jocelyn

Rodney, George. 1753–1802

In 1792 succeeded his father, George Brydges Rodney (*q.v.*), as 2d
Baron Rodney. Harrow, 1766–67; grand tour. In 1781 he married Anne,
daughter of Thomas Harley (*q.v.*). He was ensign in the foot guards in
1773 and captain in 1777. He was elected to the House of Commons in
1780, where, though regarded as a Tory, he was "universally esteemed"
and supported the North ministry in every crucial recorded division

from 1780 until its end in late March, 1782. He voted for Shelburne's peace terms and for Fox's India Bill in 1783, but early in 1784 he switched to support Pitt. There is a record of only one address in the House of Commons. M.P. for Northampton Borough, 1780–84.

Rodney, George Brydges. 1719–92

Of Rodney Stoke, near Wells, Somerset, and Great Alresford, near Winchester, Hampshire; 2d son of Henry Rodney (of Walton-on-Thames, Surrey); created baronet in 1764; created Baron Rodney in 1782. Harrow, 1730–32. In 1753 he married a sister of Spencer Compton (*q.v.*). He entered the navy in his 14th year and was lieutenant in 1739, captain in 1743, rear admiral in 1759, vice admiral in 1763, and admiral in 1778. He was present at the actions off Finisterre in 1747 and was in command at the Newfoundland station, 1749–50. While in command of the Leeward Island station, 1761–63, he captured Martinique, St. Lucia, Grenada, and St. Vincent. In 1761 he petitioned, with others, for a grant of the entire island of St. John in maritime Canada, and in 1767 was given a large royal grant there. He was governor of Greenwich Hospital, 1765–70, and in command of the Jamaica station, 1771–74. "A complete slave to women and to play," according to Lecky (who was given to superlatives of dubious accuracy), in 1775 he was so badly in debt that he went to Paris to escape his creditors and did not return to Britain and naval service until called in 1778 and made admiral. During the latter half of the war against the American colonies he held command of West Indies waters, and then of substantially the entire Atlantic area. He defeated the Spanish off Cape St. Vincent, helped to relieve Gibraltar, and was made Knight of the Bath. He resigned his command to Hood but in 1782 rejoined active service and defeated the French under DeGrasse off Dominica. For his later career, see standard sources. In politics he was by tradition and inclination Tory and by ambition opportunist. He supported, even while sometimes almost openly condemning, whatever ministry was currently in office. Frequent active naval service, and the demands of his creditors, prevented his regular attendance when a member of the House of Commons, but he professed to support successively Newcastle, Bute, Grenville, Rockingham, Chatham and Grafton, and North. He was at sea during all the crucial divisions of February and March, 1782, that led to the fall of the North ministry. He was said to have spent some £30,000 to win election for Northampton in 1768. He was perhaps the most enterprising and irascible, able and bombastic, intolerant, intolerable, and successful British naval officer between Drake and Nelson. Portraits by Reynolds and Gainsborough. M.P. for Saltash, 1751–54; Okehampton, 1759–61; Penryn, 1761–68; Northampton Borough, 1768–74; Westminster, 1780–82.

Rodrigues, Joseph Jeshurum. d. 1787

Better known as Joseph Salvador. A wealthy Portuguese Jew, he came to England from Holland soon after 1700, acquired a bloc of East India Company stock, and became the company's first Jewish director. He negotiated loans for the government and was president of the Portuguese Jewish Congregation in London. He was a noted philanthropist. In the credit crisis of 1772–73 he lost all he had owned in Europe but saved his property in America and went there to live, dying in North Carolina.

Roebuck, John. 1718–94

Son of John Roebuck (prosperous Sheffield manufacturer); born at Sheffield and schooled there and in Northampton. He studied medicine at Edinburgh and took his M.D. at Leyden in 1742, but developed special interests in chemistry and in the classics. In 1746 he introduced new methods, at first crude but soon greatly improved, for manufacturing sulfuric acid and with Samuel Garbett started a plant at Preston Pans to produce it. In 1760 he established an ironworks at Carron, near Stirling, and introduced new methods of smelting. He helped James Watt develop his steam engine but later turned over his two-thirds interest in Watt's engine to Matthew Boulton to cancel a debt of £1,200. He was a fellow of the Royal Society and contributed to *Philosophical Transactions*. He was strongly opposed to using military force against the American colonists.

Rogers, Frederick Leman. 1747–97

Of Blackford, near Cornwood, Devonshire, from a Plymouth family long involved in politics; in 1777 succeeded his father, Sir Frederick Rogers, as 5th baronet and recorder of Plymouth. In the House of Commons from 1780, he supported the North ministry until February, 1782, when he voted for Conway's motion for an immediate end to the American war. But on March 8 and 15, 1782, he voted with North against the motions of Cavendish and Rous. He voted against Shelburne's peace terms, did not vote on Fox's India Bill in 1783, and was not re-elected in 1784. M.P. for Plymouth, 1780–84 and 1790–97.

Rogers, John. 1750–1832

Of Penrose, near Helston, Cornwall; only son of Hugh Rogers (of Penrose). Oxford from 1768, Inner Temple from 1771. In 1776 he married Margaret, sister of Francis Basset (1757–1835) (*q.v.*). "A country gentleman and an uncertain voter," according to Namier, he supported the North ministry in all 5 of the crucial divisions recorded in February and March, 1782. He supported Pitt, 1784–86. There is no evidence that he ever addressed the House of Commons. M.P. for West Looe, 1775–80; Penryn, 1780–82; Helston, 1784–86.

Rogers, Thomas. 1735–93

Of The Hill, near Amblecote, Stourbridge, Worcestershire; only surviving son of Thomas Rogers (glassmaker of Amblecote); grandson of Richard Knight (ironmaster of Herefordshire). In 1760 he married the daughter of a merchant in Cheapside who also conducted a warehouse business, and became a partner in those enterprises. With his wife he also embraced the Presbyterian faith. In 1766 he successfully embarked upon a career as banker in Cornhill. He was elected to the House of Commons in 1780 as an opponent of the North ministry, but was almost immediately unseated on petition, and left no recorded speech or vote. M.P. for Coventry, 1780–81.

Rokeby, 1st Baron. See Richard Robinson

Rolle, Denys. ca.1726–97

Of Stevenstone, near Torrington, Devonshire; 4th son of John Rolle (M.P.); brother of John Rolle-Walter (*q.v.*). Oxford from 1742. Considered a Tory, and so listed when elected to Parliament in 1761, he supported Newcastle against Bute in 1762, voting against Bute's peace preliminaries. He voted in steady opposition to Grenville, 1762–64. In May, 1764, he obtained a royal grant of 20,000 acres in East Florida, and his efforts to colonize that tract diverted his interest and attendance in Parliament. In 1764 he embarked for Florida with 14 settlers, but was unsuccessful and returned to England in 1765. He went to Florida again in 1767 and again was unsuccessful. M.P. for Barnstaple, 1761–74.

Rolle, John. 1756–1842

Of Stevenstone, near Torrington, Devonshire; oldest son of Denys Rolle (*q.v.*); in 1796 created Baron Rolle. Winchester from 1764, Cambridge from 1769. In 1822 he married (2) Louisa, daughter of Robert Trefusis (17th Lord Clinton). In the House of Commons from 1780, he professed independence, and his votes were evidently unpredictable: between January and April, 1780, he voted 5 times against the North ministry but in later votes supported it; in the final crucial recorded divisions of February and March, 1782, he voted 4 times against the North ministry and once for it. In May, 1782, after Rockingham's accession, he moved a protest against the recall of Rodney, and in 1783 his violent dislike of Edmund Burke led to bitter exchanges on the floor of the House. He did not align himself with Pitt in 1784 but later became Pitt's strong adherent. He was the "hero" of *The Rolliad*. Portrait by Cruikshank. M.P. for Devonshire, 1780–96.

Rolle-Walter, John. ca.1714–79

Of Stevenstone, near Torrington, and Bicton, near Sidmouth, Devonshire; 2d son of John Rolle (M.P. and 2d baronet); brother of Denys Rolle (*q.v.*); added the surname Walter in 1731 upon inheriting the estates of his uncle Sir Robert Walter. Oxford from 1729. In 1754 he was elected to the House of Commons, where he was considered a Tory and was so listed in 1761. He voted against repeal of the Stamp Act in 1766 and against expulsion of Wilkes in 1770 and was thereafter in constant opposition to the North ministry until his death. There is no record that he ever addressed the House. M.P. for Exeter, 1754–76; Devonshire, 1776–79.

Rolt, Edward. See Edward Bayntun-Rolt

Romney, George. 1734–1802

Born at Dalton-in-Furness, Lancashire; son of "Honest John" Romney (cabinet maker and builder). His talent for drawing was so evi-

749

dent in his childhood that he was apprenticed to an itinerant painter. In 1756 he married Mary Abbott, the admirable daughter of his landlord in Kendal, and established himself as a painter of portraits. In 1762 he went to London, where he soon won prizes from the Society of Arts for his portraits. In 1764 he went to Paris for further study, and in 1773 to Italy, where he remained until 1775. He was patronized by the Duke of Richmond and others as a rival of Sir Joshua Reynolds, who showed Romney marked hostility over the years. He repeatedly painted the portrait of "Lord Nelson's Lady Hamilton."

Romney, 2nd and 3d Barons and 1st Earl. See **Robert Marsham** and **Charles Marsham**

Rose, George. 1744–1818

Of Duke Street, Westminster; 2d son of David Rose (dissenting clergyman of Lethnot, near Brechin, Forfarshire; imprisoned as a Jacobite after the 1745 uprising). He was briefly schooled at Westminster, and entered the navy in 1758. He saw service in the West Indies but resigned from the navy in 1762 to enter political self-service. In 1763 he gained a place in the office of the Exchequer and became joint keeper of records in 1773, and a member of the Tax Board from 1777. He was also a financial assistant and adviser to Lord North and learned from John Robinson how to manage electors and win elections. As a secretary of the treasury under Shelburne in 1782–83 he became a satellite of Thurlow in plans to upset the coalition. He was later associated with the Pitt administration and served on the Board of Trade, as privy councillor from 1802, as joint paymaster, and as treasurer of the navy, 1804–12. He wrote and published essays on finance. He was a trustee of the British Museum from 1804 and was long an elder brother of Trinity House. Portrait by Beechey. M.P. for Launceston, 1784–88; Lymington, 1788–90; Christchurch, 1790–1818.

Rosebery, 3d Earl. See **Neil Primrose**

Rosewarne, Henry. ca.1732–83

Of Truro, Cornwall; son of Walter Rosewarne (of Truro). He probably attended Cambridge from 1749. He became a merchant and mining speculator in Truro and was mayor of Truro in 1774 and recorder in 1782. He was vice warden of the stanneries in 1776. Professing political independence, he supported the North ministry, 1780–82, including all 5 of the crucial divisions recorded in February and March, 1782. He addressed the House of Commons in February, 1781, opposing Burke's reform bill as ill-conceived, and said that by restricting the prerogatives of the crown it would be certain to make government either chaotic or futile. In May, 1782, he seconded John Rolle's motion protesting the recall of Rodney by the Rockingham ministry. In February, 1783, he voted against Shelburne's peace terms, and in March, 1783, he condemned the economy estimates as certain to weaken the armed forces and endanger the safety of the nation. M.P. for Truro, 1780–83.

Ross, Alexander. 1742–1827

5th son of Ross of Auchlossin, near Aboyne, Aberdeenshire. He was ensign in the army in 1760, lieutenant in 1765, and captain in 1775. He saw service in Germany and from 1775 in America, where he was a friend of Cornwallis and his aide. He became major in 1780 and in 1781 acted for Cornwallis, who professed illness, in negotiating the terms of the surrender at Yorktown. He later served in India and in 1793 was colonel and later governor general of Fort George. In 1795 he was major general, under Cornwallis once again, was surveyor general of ordnance in 1795, and was made general in 1812. He was also deputy adjutant general for Scotland. His son Charles Ross edited and in 1859 published the correspondence of Cornwallis, which is still the standard edition.

Ross, Charles. ca.1729–97

Of Morangie, Ross-shire; 2d son of David Ross (of Invercassley, Sutherland). He became ensign in 1747, captain in 1756, colonel in 1777, major general in 1781, and lieutenant general in 1793. He was at Gibraltar, 1773–79, and on his return to England was supported for election to the House of Commons by his friend John Stuart (1744–1814) (q.v.). He often voted against the North ministry, 1780–82, including votes in 3 of the most crucial divisions recorded in February and March, 1782. On March 13, 1783, he spoke at length in the House, reviewing the conduct and management of the war in America, and moved that lists of all officers who had served in America during that war, together with their past records and orders, be laid before the

House. He voted against Shelburne's peace terms, supported the coalition, and voted for Fox's India Bill in 1783. M.P. for Tain and Kirkwall, 1780–84.

Ross, 1st Earl. See Ralph Gore

Ross, George. 1700–86

Of Cromartie, near Inverness; only son of Andrew Ross (of Pitkerrie, Ross-shire). For many years he was confidential clerk to Duncan Forbes (1685–1747; of Culloden, near Inverness; lord president of the Court of Sessions in Scotland). He then operated an army agency business in London, from which he acquired wealth. In 1780 he won election to Parliament, where he supported the North ministry in 2 of the crucial divisions recorded in February and March, 1782, and did not vote in 2 others. He voted against Shelburne's peace terms and for Fox's India Bill in 1783, and after the fall of the coalition in December, 1783, he continued to support Fox. There is no evidence that he ever addressed the House of Commons. M.P. for Cromartie and Nairn, 1780–84; Tain burghs, 1786.

Ross (or Rosse), John. 1719–92

Only son of John Ross (or Rosse) (attorney, of Ross, Herefordshire). Cambridge, 1737–41; M.A., 1744; B.D., 1756; fellow, 1743–70. He was chaplain to the king from 1757. In 1760, Viscount Weymouth, who had been one of his private pupils, gave him the valuable benefice of Frome in Somerset, which he held until his death. He was canon of Durham, 1769–78, and also prebendary of Durham. He was successively prebendary, archdeacon, and bishop of Exeter, 1778–92, and at the same time rector of Sherbrooke in Devonshire. He enthusiastically engaged in theological polemics of the pen, and in 1749 published an edition of Cicero's somewhat less dogmatic letters. He was a fellow of the Royal Society from 1758. "A man of sense, honest and just," extremely hospitable but extremely frugal, tolerant of dissenters but intolerant of Sunday schools, he was a narrator of long anecdotes and a quoter of conversations with the great.

Ross, John Lockhart. 1721–90

Of Balnagowan, near Tain, Ross-shire; 5th son of Sir James Lockhart (of Carstairs, near Lanark, Lanarkshire); in 1778 succeeded his brother George Lockhart as 5th baronet; assumed the surname Ross in 1760 upon succeeding to the Ross estate of Balnagowan. He was in the navy from 1735 and was lieutenant in 1743; captain in operations in the Channel, 1756–57; in the North Sea and at Quiberon Bay, 1758–60; commander in 1765; again in the Channel, the North Sea, and in the Mediterranean, 1779–82, including the relief of Gibraltar, 1780–81, and further service in the Channel in 1782. In the House of Commons (when not absent on duty) from 1761, he successively voted with Bute, Grenville, Grafton, and North until 1774, including a vote in 1766 against repeal of the Stamp Act. He was rear admiral in 1779 and vice admiral in 1787. M.P. for Linlithgow burghs, 1761–68; Lanarkshire, 1768–74.

Rosslyn, 1st and 2d Earls. See **Alexander Wedderburn** and **James St. Clair Erskine**

Rossmore, 1st Baron. See **Robert Cuningham** (or **Cunninghame**)

Rothes, 10th Earl. See **John Leslie**

Rous, George. ca.1744–1802

Of Bedford Square, London; 3d son of Thomas Rous (of Piercefield Park, near Chepstow, Monmouthshire; a director of the East India Company); brother of Thomas Bates Rous (*q.v.*). Eton, to Oxford in 1760; Middle Temple from 1763; Inner Temple from 1764; barrister in 1768; bencher from 1802. In 1776 he won a seat in the House of Commons, and before that year had ended, he had spoken against revising those acts of Parliament objected to by the colonists as a weak and dangerous concession to rebels. Until 1778 he usually voted with the North ministry, but thereafter, partly because of its ill success in America, he voted against it until he left Parliament, without standing for re-election, in 1780. In that final year he was especially vocal in the House. In March, 1780, he described the inefficiencies and corruptions of the East India Company. In April he supported Dunning's resolution and joined in the attack on the "corrupting and unconstitutional" actions of the court and ministry. In May he spoke at length opposing Conway's bill for an immediate end to the war in America, as limiting the proper powers of the executive branch of the government. Later in May he attacked North for "blustering and mere manoeuvering" in his opposition to Burke's Establishment Bill. Despite (or possibly because of) his comments on agents of the East India Company, he served as its counsel, 1781–1803. M.P. for Shaftesbury, 1776–80.

Rous, John. ca.1727–71

Of Henham Hall, near Halesworth, Suffolk; in 1735 succeeded his father, Robert Rous, as 5th baronet. Cambridge from 1744. He was sheriff of Suffolk, 1759–60. In the House of Commons he was regarded as "a typical Tory," according to Namier. His only 4 recorded votes during his 3 years of membership were in opposition. In 1770 he voted against unseating Wilkes and in 1771 against approving North's Falkland Islands settlement. Apparently he never addressed the House. M.P. for Suffolk, 1768–71.

Rous, John. 1750–1827

Of Henham Hall, near Halesworth, and Stradbroke, near Eye, Suffolk; in 1771 succeeded his father John Rous (ca.1727–71) (*q.v.*), as 6th baronet; in 1796 created Baron Rous; in 1821 created Viscount Dunwich and Earl of Stradbroke. Westminster, 1764–67; Oxford from 1768; M.A., 1771. He was captain of Suffolk yeomanry in 1794. In Parliament he voted with the North ministry in 1780, but from December, 1781 (perhaps after news of the surrender of Cornwallis at Yorktown), he served the ministry notice that he could no longer support it. In February and March, 1782, he voted against the ministry in the first 4 crucial divisions recorded and was the author of the final motion of March 15 of no confidence in the North ministry, which, though defeated by 136 to 227, presaged the resignation of the ministry only 5 days later. Horace Walpole commented that, although Rous had been "till this time much devoted to Lord North, and a Tory by principle, as he avowed," his motion had been the shrewdest blow yet dealt against it. He declined to take office with Shelburne in 1782 and voted for Shelburne's peace terms and against Fox's India Bill in 1783. From 1784 he steadily supported Pitt and became a statesman of consequence. M.P. for Suffolk, 1780–96.

Rous, Thomas Bates. ca.1739–99

Of Berners Street, London; son of Thomas Rous (of Piercefield

Park, near Chepstow, Monmouthshire); brother of George Rous
(*q.v.*). "Under the patronage of Lord Clive" he soon acquired a handsome fortune and became a director of the East India Company in
1773. (In January, 1768, he had appeared by invitation before the
House of Lords to explain the affairs of the Company and had made
an impression of fairness and authority.) Later in 1773 he was elected
to the House of Commons, and though almost immediately unseated
on petition, he was again elected in 1774. He steadily opposed the
North administration, voting for the Dunning resolution of April 6,
1780, and against the ministry in all 5 crucial divisions recorded in
February and March, 1782. In 1783 he voted for Shelburne's peace
terms, for Fox's and Pitt's bills to reform Parliament, and for Fox's
India Bill. He was not re-elected in 1784. M.P. for Worcester City,
1773–84.

Rouse-Boughton, Charles William. 1747–1821

Of Rouse Lench, near Alcester, Warwickshire; 2d son of Shuckburgh
Boughton (of Poston Court, Herefordshire); changed his surname
in 1768, upon inheriting the estate of Rouse Lench from his cousin
Thomas Rouse; created baronet in 1791; in 1794 succeeded his older
brother Sir Edward Boughton as 9th baronet. In the House of Commons from 1780, he left no record of any vote for or against the North
ministry until February, 1782, when he seconded the motion of Richard Smith (*q.v.*) for a committee on the petitions against the Bengal
Supreme Court, and on that occasion he reportedly spoke at length
and with weight. The passage of that motion opened the door to a
general reform of legal procedure in India. In 1783 he voted for Shelburne's peace terms, for Pitt's reforms of Parliament, and for Fox's
India Bill. In 1784 he supported Pitt and promptly became secretary
of the Board of Control, a post he held until 1791. He continued to
support Pitt. M.P. for Evesham, 1780–90; Bramber, 1796–99.

Rowley, Joshua. ca.1730–90

Oldest son of William Rowley (*q.v.*); created baronet in 1786. In
1759 he married Sarah, daughter of Bartholomew Burton (deputy
governor of the Bank of England). He was a lieutenant in the navy
under his father in the Mediterranean in 1747. In 1779 he was in command of reinforcements to Admiral Byron in the West Indies and

became rear admiral. He was in command of the Jamaica station, 1782–83, and was made vice admiral in 1787.

Rowley, William. ca.1690–1768

Of Tendring Hall, near Colchester, Essex; son of William Rowley (of Whitehall, London). He entered the navy in 1704 at the age of 14 and was lieutenant in 1708, captain in 1716, rear admiral in 1743, vice admiral in 1744, admiral in 1747, and admiral of the fleet in command of the home fleet in 1762. He was a member of the Admiralty Board, 1751–56 and again in 1757, and was Knight of the Bath from 1753. A friend of Lord Egremont, in the House of Commons he supported (by vote though not by speech) Egremont's measures and usually those of the current ministry. M.P. for Taunton, 1750–54; Portsmouth, 1754–61.

Roxburgh, 3d Duke. See John Ker (or Kerr)

Royston, 1st and 2d Viscounts. See Philip Yorke. 1690–1764 and Philip Yorke. 1720–90

Rumbold, Thomas. 1736–91

Of Woodhall, near Watford, Hertfordshire; 3d son of William Rumbold (of the East India Company); created baronet in 1779. In 1772 he married (2) Joanna, daughter of Edmund Law (bishop of Carlisle). From 1752 he was an agent for the East India Company. In 1757 he was captain and aide to Clive at Plassey. He was a member of the Bengal Council, 1766–69. In 1772 he was made a director of the East India Company, serving in that capacity again, 1775–77, and in 1777 becoming governor of Madras. In 1780 he resigned in ill health and returned to England, where he had been a member of the House of Commons, 1770–75. He promptly gained election in 1780. From 1770 he supported the North ministry. In 1772 he spoke in favor of an inquiry into the affairs of the East India Company. In 1773 he addressed the House in support of Clive. In 1774 he voted against continuance of the Grenville Disputed Elections Act, and (ironically) was that year challenged for having bribed his own way to election, though the charge was dismissed. After 1780 he was vocal in the House chiefly in defense of his own earlier conduct in India. In February and March, 1782, he voted with the North ministry in all 5 of the crucial divisions recorded. In 1783, Henry Dundas accused him of mismanagement and corruption in India, and on June 2, 1783, he made "a most pathetic speech & asked that his trial be accelerated so that his name might be cleared" or else that he be given "a speedy sentence." He was acquitted by Parliament inquiry. M.P. for New Shoreham, 1770–74; Shaftesbury, 1774–75 and 1780–81; Yarmouth (Isle of Wight), 1781–84; Weymouth and Melcombe Regis, 1784–90.

Rumbold, William Richard. 1760–86

Oldest son of Thomas Rumbold (*q.v.*). Harrow, 1771–76. In 1777 he was an ensign in the army and in 1778 went to India with his father. He served there with some distinction as captain in 1780 and fought at Pondichéry. He returned to England with his father in 1780 and won a seat in the House of Commons in 1781. In general he voted with his father for the North ministry, 1781–82. He did not vote on Shelburne's peace terms in 1783 and died in his 26th year. M.P. for Weymouth and Melcombe Regis, 1781–84.

Rumford, Count. See **Benjamin Thompson**

Rushout, John. 1685–1775

Of Northwick Park, near Moreton-in-the-Marsh, Gloucestershire; 4th son of Sir James Rushout (d. 1698); in 1711 succeeded his nephew as 4th baronet. In 1729 he married Anne, daughter of George Compton (4th Earl of Northampton). He entered the horse guards as cornet in 1705 and was lieutenant in 1706, captain in 1710, and retired in 1712. He sat for 55 years in the House of Commons, where he spoke frequently, and upon his retirement at the age of 83 he was called (like several others with comparable records) "Father of the House of Commons." He supported Pelham and Newcastle and opposed Grenville. There is no record of any speech or vote by him during the Grafton ministry. He was high steward of Malmesbury from 1743; a member of the Treasury Board, 1742–43; treasurer of the navy, 1743–44; and privy councillor from 1744. He died at 90 with "his memory, good humour and politeness in their full bloom." M.P. for Malmesbury, 1713–22; Evesham, 1722–68.

Rushout, John. 1738–1800

Of Northwick Park, near Moreton-in-the-Marsh, Gloucestershire; in

1775 succeeded his father, John Rushout (*q.v.*), as 5th baronet; grandson of George Compton (4th Earl of Northampton); in 1797 created Baron Northwick. Eton, 1753–56; Oxford from 1756. In the House of Commons he professed political independence. He opposed Grenville in 1764 and did not vote against repeal of the Stamp Act in 1766. He opposed the Grafton ministry on the Wilkes issues, 1769–70, and the North ministry on Wilkes and on continuing the Grenville Disputed Elections Act in 1774. He voted against approving the address from the throne in October, 1775, and voted for the Dunning resolution of April 6, 1780. Until 1775 he supported the American measures of the North ministry but thereafter opposed them. He voted for Shelburne's peace terms and for Fox's India Bill in 1783 and in general opposed Pitt until after 1788. M.P. for Evesham, 1761–96.

Rushworth, Edward. 1755–1817

Of Freshwater House, near Yarmouth, Isle of Wight; oldest son of Captain John Rushworth of the navy. Winchester, to Oxford in 1770. He began a career in law but abandoned it to enter first the church and then politics. Though no votes by him are recorded, he appears from other reports to have opposed the North ministry from entering the House of Commons in 1780 until he left it in 1781, to return in 1784. He later supported Charles Fox and in 1785 voted against Pitt's proposals for reform of the representation of Parliament. M.P. for Yarmouth (Isle of Wight), 1780–81; Newport (Isle of Wight), 1784–90; Yarmouth, 1790 and 1796–97.

Russell, Francis. 1739–67

Only surviving son of John Russell (1710–71) (*q.v.*); styled Marquess of Tavistock until 1767, when he predeceased his father; grandson of John Leveson-Gower (d. 1754; 1st Earl Gower). Westminster, 1749–57; Cambridge, 1757–59. In 1764 he married Elizabeth, daughter of William Anne Keppel (1702–54; 2d Earl of Albemarle). He was a member of the Irish Parliament, 1759–60. In the English House of Commons, he followed his father in politics, and there is a record of only one speech in that House, which was to move congratulations to the queen on the birth of the Prince of Wales in 1762. His attendance of the House was irregular, and his first interest was in military affairs; he confessed an aversion to politics. He was killed by a fall from his horse in his 28th year. He was widely believed to be in love with Lady Pembroke, wife of the 10th Earl, but his devotion was either platonic or discreet, since he was pronounced "of amiable and unblemished character." M.P. for Bedfordshire, 1761–67.

Russell, Francis. 1765–1802

The son of Francis Russell (*q.v.*); styled Marquess of Tavistock from 1767; in 1771 he succeeded his grandfather John Russell (1710–71) (*q.v.*) as 5th Duke of Bedford. He was schooled at Westminster and Cambridge. He attached himself to Charles Fox and the Prince of Wales. He rebuilt Russell Square and Tavistock Square in London, was a member of the first Board of Agriculture, and was first president of the Smithfield Club. Portrait by Hoppner.

Russell, John. 1710–71

2d son of Wriothesley Russell (1680–1711; 2d Duke of Bedford); in 1732 succeeded his brother Wriothesley Russell (1708–32) as 4th Duke of Bedford. He married (1) in 1731 Diana, daughter of Charles Spencer (1674–1722; 3d Earl of Sunderland) and granddaughter of John Churchill (1650–1722; 1st Duke of Marlborough), and (2) in 1737 Gertrude, oldest daughter of John Leveson-Gower (d. 1754; 1st Earl Gower), a woman with great political interest and force. He became colonel in 1745, major general in 1755, and lieutenant general in 1759. He was a privy councillor from 1744; first lord of the admiralty, 1744–48; lord justice of Great Britain in 1745, 1748, and 1750. He was secretary of state, southern department, 1748–51, and lord lieutenant of Ireland, 1756–57. He was ambassador to Paris to negotiate peace, 1762–63; lord president of the council, 1763–67; lord lieutenant of Bedfordshire, 1745–71; lord lieutenant of Devonshire, 1751–71; warden of New Forest, 1746–71; and master of Trinity House, 1756–60. He was extremely influential in politics, especially from 1760. After his death the party or faction he headed (known as the "Bloomsbury gang" from his residence in Bloomsbury Square) continued to be important far beyond its numbers and its talents, and was thought by many to dictate the measures of the North ministry. He recorded dissents from majority votes in the House of Lords disapproving (1) continuation of the war in Germany in 1762, (2) repeal of the Stamp Act in 1766, and (3) disagreement with the verdict of the peers in the Hamilton-Douglas paternity case. His political opponent Horace Walpole pronounced him "a man of inflexible honesty and good will to his country . . . though immensely obstinate . . . . If he could have thought less well of himself the world would probably have thought better of him." The *Royal Register* praised him as "an honest man in not sacrificing his opinions to gratify his wishes." He was apparently a man with more honor and more honors than wit and was good-natured, passionate, stubborn, and generous. He represented a class with no more political vision than himself, and less virtue. Portraits by Gainsborough and Reynolds.

Russell, John. 1745–1806

Born at Guildford, Surrey; son of John Russell (bookseller of Guildford and 5 times mayor of Guildford). As a boy he studied painting in London with Francis Cotes, R.A. In 1767 he set up his own studio. In 1770 he won a gold medal from the Royal Academy, where he exhibited until 1775. His works in crayon made him famous, and his special treatment of his crayons kept his works in near-perfect condition over many years. He was also deeply interested in the science of astronomy and invented apparatus to aid in its study. Having become an ardent Methodist at the age of 19, he "never ceased from preaching and disputation."

Ruthven, James. d. 1783

A collateral descendant of the Earls of Ruthven (Scottish), he claimed that title through his mother in 1732. Although his claim was never formally accepted or denied, from 1733 to 1774 he voted without being challenged as Lord Ruthven at the special elections of Scottish representative peers, and after 1774 he was accepted by George III as Lord Ruthven. His claim carried more weight (though not in some circles more popularity) because in 1736 he had married (2) a sister of the 3d Earl of Bute.

Rutland, 3d and 4th Dukes. See John Manners. 1679–1779 and Charles Manners

Ryder, Nathaniel. 1735–1803

Of Shiplake, near Reading, Oxfordshire; only son of Dudley Ryder

(1691–1756; M.P.); in 1776 created Baron Harrowby of Lincolnshire. Cambridge from 1753. In 1762 he married Elizabeth, daughter of Richard Terrick (*q.v.*). He supported Pelham and Newcastle in the House of Commons and in 1764 opposed George Grenville on the issue of general warrants. He supported the Rockingham ministry, 1765–66, but did not vote on repeal of the Stamp Act in 1766. Ambitious for a peerage, he supported Grafton and, in general, North, though he spoke seldom and briefly in the House of Commons. Having secured his peerage from the North ministry in 1776, he moved to the House of Lords and there paid his debt by continued support of that administration. He voted for Fox's India Bill in 1783 and afterward supported Pitt. M.P. for Tiverton, 1756–76.

S

Sackville, Charles. 1711–69

Of Knole, near Tunbridge Wells, Kent; styled Lord Middlesex until 1765, when he succeeded his father, Lionel Sackville, as 2d Duke of Dorset; older brother of George Sackville (later Germain) (*q.v.*). Westminster, 1720–28; Oxford from 1728; M.A., 1730; grand tour. In 1744 he married Grace, daughter of Richard Boyle (1682–1764; 2d Viscount Shannon, Irish). In his youth he was an ardent cricketeer and spendthrift and continued the latter characteristic throughout his life. As a young man he broke with his father over his politics and his debts; the former breach was more easily healed than the latter. He attached himself to Leicester House, and (according to circumstantial evidence as well as gossip) his intimacy with Prince Frederick was only exceeded by the intimacy of his wife. He successfully contested a seat in the House of Commons for Sussex, against his father's wishes, and supported principles opposed by the duke. He also continued to deplete the Sackville fortune by his extravagances in London, and especially by his almost singlehanded financing of London opera. Later, through the mediation of Bubb Dodington, he was somewhat reconciled with his father, and lived partly at Knole during his father's final years. Before 1760 he voted with Leicester House, then supported Bute, then Grenville, but later shifted his support to Rockingham. He was as erratic in politics as in his private life, and no more effective. In the House of Lords from 1765, he recorded dissents to its majority votes to regulate the dividends of the East India Company, 1767–68, and to the Royal Marriage Bill in 1772. He was a member of the Treasury Board, 1743–47; master of horse to the Prince of Wales, 1747–51; privy councillor in 1766; and lord lieutenant of Kent, 1766–69. According to Shelburne "a proud, disgusted, melancholy, solitary man," he had little good sense and less stability, his only redeeming features being a love of music and a trivial talent for versification. M.P. for East Grinstead, 1734–41; Sussex, 1742–47; Old Sarum, 1747–54; East Grinstead, 1761–65.

Sackville (later **Germain**), George. 1716–85

3d son of Lionel Sackville (1688–1765; 1st Duke of Dorset); brother of Charles Sackville (1711–69; M.P.; 2d Duke of Dorset) (*q.v.*); in 1770 assumed the surname Germain upon inheriting from his parents' friend Lady Betty (Berkeley) Germain; in 1782 created Viscount Sackville. Westminster, 1723–31; Trinity College, Dublin, from 1731; B.A., 1733; M.A., 1734; Irish barrister, 1734. While his father was lord lieutenant of Ireland, he acted as his father's private secretary and was a member of the Irish Parliament from 1733; ranger of Phoenix Park, Dublin, 1736–85; and clerk of the Irish Privy Council, 1737–85. He entered the army as captain in 1737 and was lieutenant colonel in 1740 and aide to the king in 1743. He was wounded at Fontenoy in 1745, and in the same year was made colonel. In 1746 he was with the Duke of Cumberland (the two sharing a friendship that later ended abruptly) in Scotland, where he relentlessly pursued and punished fleeing Jacobites. He became major general in 1755 and lieutenant general of ordnance in 1757. In that year he was also a member of a court of inquiry into the conduct of John Mordaunt (*q.v.*) at Rochefort and rendered a verdict censoring Mordaunt which was later abrogated by a court-martial. He was second-in-command at the abortive raid on St. Malo in 1758, when his criticisms of Richard Howe's sea management roused Howe's permanent animosity. He then served in Germany as commander of the British contingent of cavalry, under Prince Ferdinand. His drastic criticisms of the prince's financial management of his army and of his military strategy angered the prince. At the Battle of Minden in 1759 his refusal to obey the prince's repeated order to lead his cavalry in a charge prevented what might have been a crushing defeat of the French. He was dismissed from the service and in 1760 declared by a court-martial unfit to serve king and country in any military capacity. He lived in deep disgrace for several years, having been dismissed by George II and Pitt from his court and military offices and from both the English and the Irish Privy Council. He slowly rebuilt his position in politics and through the Rockingham ministry was a vice treasurer of Ireland, 1765–68. In 1762, George III restored him to the Privy Council, and in 1770 he somewhat redeemed himself from the reputation for personal cowardice by fighting a duel with George Johnstone (q.v.). He became influential in Rockingham's party and opposed the North ministry until 1774, when he joined it in favoring a "firm" policy toward the colonies. In December, 1775, North appointed him secretary of state for the colonies, to take the executive lead in implementing that firmness. Objecting to all conciliation, concessions, or peace talks, he successively lost the confidence and acquired the enmity of all 4 of his leading generals, Carleton, Howe, Burgoyne, and Clinton (with Cornwallis only more discreetly reticent in expressing his opinion). The Whig opposition made him the central target of its condemnation of the American war and of the blunders made in the pursuit of that war. After Burgoyne's surrender in late 1777, he was a recognized liability to the North ministry, but he refused to resign voluntarily without a peerage, and the king refused to create the peerage. In February, 1782, he was at last given the promise of a peerage if he would resign, and in his interview with the king he managed to secure a viscountcy instead of the baronage the king had intended. His peerage was the topic of irate debate and strong minority protest in the House of Lords (he was present, and voted for his own admission). After that virtual dismissal from office in 1782, he carried little weight and retired to his country estate of Drayton, Northamptonshire. M.P. for Dover, 1741–61; Hythe, 1761–68; East Grinstead, 1768–82.

Sackville, John Frederick. 1745–99

Only son of John Philip Sackville (2d son of Lionel Sackville; 1st Duke of Dorset); nephew of Charles Sackville (q.v.); nephew of George Sackville (later Germain) (q.v.); grandson of John Leveson-Gower (1st Earl Gower); in 1769 succeeded his uncle Charles Sackville as 3d Duke of Dorset. Westminster from ca. 1754. In 1790 (at the age of 45) he married Arabella, daughter of Sir Charles Cope. He was agreeable but weak, with little ability or enthusiasm except for amorous pursuits. During his year in the House of Commons there is no record that he ever spoke or voted. In the House of Lords from 1769, he supported the North ministry, of which his uncle George Sackville was a member from December, 1775. After 1783 he supported Pitt. He became a member of the privy council and was ambassador to Paris, 1783–89, a post in which many thought him notably incompetent. He was lord lieutenant of Kent, 1769–97; Knight of the Garter from 1788; and lord steward of the household, 1789–99. M.P. for Kent, 1768–69.

St. Albans, 3d and **5th Dukes.** See **George Beauclerk.** 1730–86 and **Aubrey Beauclerk**

St. Aubyn, John. 1726–72

Of Clowance, near Helston, and St. Michael's Mount, near Penzance, Cornwall; in 1744 succeeded his father, Sir John St. Aubyn (1696–1744; M.P.), as 4th baronet. Oxford from 1744; M.A., 1747. He was an overt and active Tory in 1754, and was listed as Tory in 1761. He voted against Grenville and general warrants in 1764, did not vote against repeal of the Stamp Act in 1766, and voted against Grafton on the land tax in 1767. He was in general opposition to the Grafton and North ministries, 1768–72, and voted against unseating Wilkes in January, 1770. M.P. for Launceston, 1747–54 and 1758–59; Cornwall, 1761–72.

St. Clair, James. See **James Sinclair** (sometimes **St. Clair**)

St. Helens, 1st Baron. See **Alleyne Fitzherbert**

St. John, Frederick. 1734–87

In 1748 succeeded his father, John St. John, as 3d Viscount St. John; in 1751 succeeded his uncle Henry St. John (1678–1751; M.P.) as 2d Viscount Bolingbroke; brother of Henry St. John (*q.v.*) and John St. John (*q.v.*). Eton. In 1757 he married Diana, oldest daughter of Charles Spencer (1706–58; 3d Duke of Marlborough), but divorced her in 1768 for adultery with Topham Beauclerk (*q.v.*), whom she married later that month. He was lord of the bedchamber, 1762–65 and 1768–80. He opposed repeal of the Stamp Act in 1766. In general he supported the North ministry, though in 1780 he recorded his dissent to the rejection of a bill to exclude holders of government contracts from membership in Parliament. From 1781 he was mentally incompetent.

St. John, George Richard. 1761–1824

In 1787 succeeded his father, Frederick St. John (*q.v.*), as 3d Viscount Bolingbroke; grandson of Charles Spencer (1706–58; 3d Duke of Marlborough). Harrow from 1774, Oxford from 1777. In 1804 he married (2) Isabella, Baroness Hompesch of Germany. He was a follower of Charles Fox, and from his entrance of the House of Commons at the age of 21 he supported Fox, voting against Shelburne's peace terms and for Fox's India Bill in 1783. After succeeding to the peerage in 1787, he generally lived on the Continent and died at Pisa. M.P. for Cricklade, 1782–84.

St. John, Henry. 1738–1818

Of Rockley, near Marlborough, Wiltshire; 2d son of John St. John (1678–1751; M.P.; 2d Viscount St. John); brother of Frederick St. John (*q.v.*); related by marriage to Lord North. Eton, 1747–53. In 1771 he married Barbara, daughter of Thomas Bladen (ca.1698–1780; M.P.). He was ensign in the army in 1754, major in 1760, colonel in 1776, major general in 1779, lieutenant general in 1787, and general in 1797. He was groom of the bedchamber to the Duke of York, 1763–67; and to the king, 1771–1812. He was a Bedford party man and in the House of Commons opposed the Rockingham ministry, 1765–66; opposed Chatham and Grafton, 1767–70; and generally supported the North ministry, 1770–82, voting against the Dunning resolution of April 6, 1780. He opposed Shelburne's peace terms, supported the coalition, and voted for Fox's India Bill in 1783. M.P. for Wootton Bassett, 1761–84 and 1802.

St. John, Henry Paulet. 1737–84

Of Dogmersfield Hall, near Odiham, Hampshire; in 1780 succeeded his father, Sir Paulet St. John (1694–1780; of Farley, Southampton; M.P.), as 2d baronet. Winchester from 1750, Oxford from 1755. He was knighted in 1760. There is no evidence that he ever addressed the House of Commons, and his only recorded vote was for the Dunning resolution of April 6, 1780. M.P. for Hampshire, 1772–80.

St. John, John. ca.1746–93

3d son of John St. John (1678–1751; M.P.; and 2d Viscount St. John); brother of Henry St. John (*q.v.*). His family was connected with that of Lord North, whom he rescued from the Gordon mob in 1780. Eton, 1756–63; Oxford from 1763; Lincoln's Inn from 1765; Middle Temple from 1767; barrister from 1770. He was surveyor general of the land revenues of the crown, 1775–84. He was a member of the Bedford-Gower-Sandwich political alliance, opposed to any concessions to the American colonists, and supported the North ministry to its end, opposing the Dunning resolution of April 6, 1780. He supported the coalition and Fox's India Bill in 1783. He indulged literary ambitions by writing several prose fancies and plays, including *Mary, Queen of Scots.* M.P. for Newport (Isle of Wight), 1773–74; Eye, 1774–80; Newport, 1780–84.

St. Leger, Anthony. 1731–86

Of Park Hill, near Bantry, County Cork; 4th son of Sir John St. Leger (baron of the Irish exchequer). Eton, 1745–48; Cambridge from 1750. He was a sportsman and a soldier whom Granby encouraged and sponsored in his earlier years. He was lieutenant in 1754, captain in 1756, colonel in 1777, and major general in 1781. In 1777 he led the small and unsuccessful diversionary force from Canada into central New York State and the Mohawk Valley in connection with Burgoyne's campaign. He was again active in that area in 1781. He had political connections with John Calcraft (*q.v.*), and hence with Chatham and Shelburne, and voted in opposition to the North ministry until he left Parliament. There is no indication that he ever addressed the House of Commons. M.P. for Great Grimsby, 1768–74.

St. Vincent, 1st Earl. See **John Jervis**

Salisbury, 6th and 7th Earls and 1st Marquess. See **James Cecil.** 1713–80 and **James Cecil.** 1748–1823

Salt, Samuel. ca.1723–92

Son of Rev. John Salt (vicar of Audley, near Newcastle, Staffordshire). Eton, to Oxford in 1743; Middle Temple in 1741; Inner Temple in 1745; barrister in 1753; bencher of Inner Temple from 1782; reader from 1787; treasurer in 1788. He was a director of the South Sea Company, 1769–75, and its deputy governor, 1775–92. He became legal agent for the Eliot family and a follower of Charles Fox. He voted with the opposition, 1768–82: against unseating Wilkes in 1770; against approving the address from the throne in October, 1775; for the Dunning resolution of April 6, 1780; and against the North ministry in all 5 of the crucial divisions recorded in February and March, 1782. There is no evidence that he ever addressed the House of Commons. The father of Charles Lamb, whom he befriended, was his clerk for nearly 40 years. M.P. for Liskeard, 1768–84; Aldeburgh, 1784–90.

Saltersford, 1st Baron. See James Stopford

Salusbury-Brereton, Owen. See Owen Salusbury Brereton

Salvador, Joseph. See Joseph Jeshurum Rodrigues

Sandilands, James. 1759–1815

In 1765 succeeded his father, Walter Sandilands (*q.v.*), as 9th Lord Torpichen (Scottish). He served as lieutenant with the Royal Scots Fusiliers in America under Burgoyne, and was made prisoner of war at the surrender at Saratoga in October, 1777. Exchanged, he became captain in 1781 and lieutenant colonel in the Coldstream Guards in 1783 and served in Flanders with the Duke of York, 1793–94. He was burgess of Edinburgh in 1784 and a Scottish representative peer, 1790–1802.

Sandilands, Walter. ca.1707–65

2d but 1st surviving son of James Sandilands (7th Earl Torpichen, Scottish, whom he succeeded in 1754 as 8th Lord Torpichen). He was a Scots advocate from 1727 and sheriff depute of Midlothian in 1748. He did much to preserve order in the Edinburgh area during the Jacobite uprising of 1745.

Sandwich, 4th and 5th Earls. See **John Montagu.** 1718–92 and **John Montagu.** 1744–1814

Sandys, Edwin. 1726–97

In 1770 succeeded his father, Samuel Sandys (*q.v.*), as 2d Baron Sandys. Eton from 1742, Oxford from 1743. At Oxford he was considered one of the finest Greek scholars of his time, and he was awarded an honorary D.C.L. in 1756. In 1769 he married Anne Maria, sister of Sir James Colebrooke (*q.v.*). A professional Whig, he supported the Pelhams and served in the Admiralty Board in 1757. He later successively supported the ministries of Rockingham, Grafton, and North, 1765–82, and the coalition of 1783. After 1770 he was in the House of Lords. He was an authority on English history and a constant attender of Parliament. He died "immensely rich," though the source of his wealth is not now clear. M.P. for Droitwich, 1747–54; Bossiney, 1754–61; Westminster, 1762–70.

Sandys, Samuel. 1695–1770

Of Ombersley Court, near Droitwich, Worcestershire; oldest son of Edwin Sandys (M.P.) and grandson of Sir James Rushout (1st baronet); father of Edwin Sandys (*q.v.*); in 1743 created Baron Sandys. Oxford from 1711. He was a member of the Treasury Board, 1741–43; privy councillor from 1742; chancellor of the exchequer, 1742–43; cofferer and treasurer of the chamber, 1743–55; speaker of the House of Lords in 1756; chief justice in Eyre south of Trent, 1755–56, and north of Trent 1759–61; and first lord of trade and plantations, 1761–63. Lord North called him "a very useful diligent senator, a warm steady friend." Horace Walpole wrote: "He never laughed but once, and that was when his best friend broke his thigh." John Owen pronounced him "one of the dullest but most persistent of opponents." M.P. for Worcester City, 1718–43.

Sargent, John. ca.1715–91

Of Downing Street, London, and Halstead Place, near Sevenoaks, Kent; only son of John Sargent (storekeeper of Deptford Navy Yard). He became a merchant and was a director of the Bank of England, 1753–67. In 1763 his sympathy with the American colonists led him to advocate a bounty on hemp grown in the colonies, to encourage its development there in the interests of the colonists, as well as of British trade. He was an original promoter of the Ohio land-development scheme. He became a friend of Benjamin Franklin; upon leaving London in 1766 Franklin gave him charge of his personal affairs there. They renewed their friendship after the war. In 1766 the Assembly of New York Province "voted him the gift of a piece of plate worth £100 sterling" for his friendship and for his support of the repeal of the Stamp Act. He established a gold-medal award at the University of Pennsylvania. He supported Pelham and Newcastle but opposed the Grenville ministry. M.P. for Midhurst, 1754–61; West Looe, 1765–68.

Saunders, Charles. 1713–75

Of Hambledon, near Fareham, Hampshire; son of James Saunders (of Bridgwater, Somerset). His naval career began in 1727: he was a lieutenant in 1734, with Anson in 1739, and captain in 1741. He was on the home station under Hawke in 1745; in command at the Newfoundland station, 1752–55; rear admiral in the Mediterranean in 1756; in command in the St. Lawrence and at Quebec in 1759; and in command in Mediterranean waters in 1760. He was comptroller of the navy in 1755, a member of the Admiralty Board in 1756, and Knight of the Bath in 1761. A trusted supporter of Rockingham, he became first lord of the admiralty on September 16, 1766, but resigned on December 13, 1766, in protest against dismissal of the Rockingham Whigs. With Rodney and others (mostly navy officers) he applied for a crown grant of land on St. John's Island in maritime Canada, and in 1767 secured it. He became lieutenant general of marines in 1770 and admiral in the same year. In the House of Commons, which he could not attend regularly, he occasionally spoke on naval matters, urging further preparedness and in general supporting the current ministry. But in January, 1770, he voted against unseating Wilkes and in October, 1775, against approving the address from the throne. Horace Walpole called him a pattern of bravery, modesty, simplicity, and good nature—an indication that he was at least a good Walpole Whig. Portrait by Reynolds. M.P. for Plymouth, 1750–54; Heydon, 1754–75.

Saunderson, Richard Lumley. See Richard Lumley-Saunderson

Savile, George. 1726–84

In 1743 succeeded his father, Sir George Savile (of Thornhill, near Dewsbury, Yorkshire, and Rufford Abbey, near Mansfield, Nottinghamshire; M.P.), as 8th baronet. He was captain against the Jacobites in the 1745 uprising. In late 1745 he went to Cambridge and became M.A. and then L.L.D. in 1749. He was a Rockingham Whig and, from his election to the House of Commons in 1759, was in steady opposition to Bute, Grenville, Grafton, and North. He was an ardent and persistent advocate of reforms. In 1762 he voted against Bute's peace preliminaries; in 1766 he voted to repeal the Stamp Act; in 1768 he introduced his *Nullum Tempus* Bill; in 1769 he signed the Yorkshire petition against the Grafton ministry in the Wilkes controversy; in 1770 he opposed the unseating of Wilkes; in 1771 he voted against declaring printers Wheble and Thompson in contempt of the House; in 1775 he opposed approval of the October address from the throne; in 1778 he urged an immediate end to the war in America; and in 1780 he voted for Dunning's resolution of April 6, 1780. In the recorded crucial divisions of February and March, 1782, he cast no recorded vote in 3 cases, but he voted for Conway's motion of February 27 to end the American war immediately, and he voted for Rous's no-confidence motion of March 15. From 1782 he continued to support the Rockingham Whig party. He promoted bills for the relief of dissenters from subscription to the 39 articles and for the abolition of the political disabilities maintained against Roman Catholics, and presented the Wyvill Yorkshire petition to the House of Commons. He was a fellow of the Royal Society, long a vice president of the Society of Arts, and a benefactor to the universities. Though Tory Samuel Johnson called him, outrageously, "a little dirty scoundrel," there is no doubt that, as another contemporary said, "his reason was sharp, his soul was candid, having none of the acrimony or vengeance of party." He came close to being "of unimpeachable character, large fortune and still larger mind." Portrait by Richard Wilson. M.P. for Yorkshire, 1759–83.

Savile, John. 1719–78

Only son of Charles Savile (of Methley Hall, Leeds, Yorkshire); in 1753 created Baron Pollington (Irish); in 1766 created Viscount Pollington and Earl of Mexborough (both Irish). Cambridge from 1739. In 1760 he married Sarah, sister of Francis Blake Delaval (*q.v.*) and John Hussey Delaval (or Hussey-Delaval) (*q.v.*). He supported Pelham and then Newcastle; voted against Bute's peace preliminaries in December, 1762; but then generally supported George Grenville's ministry, 1763–65. He supported the Rockingham ministry, 1765–66, sacrificing his political principles and loyalties, if any, to his overt desire for a peerage. He was Knight of the Bath from 1749 and honorary L.L.D. of Cambridge in the same year. M.P. for Heydon, 1747–54; Shoreham, 1761–68.

Sawbridge, John. 1732–95

Of London and Olantigh Towers, near Ashford, Kent; oldest son of John Sawbridge (of Olantigh), from whom he interited considerable estates in Kent and Middlesex. He married (1) in 1763 Mary Diane, daughter and heiress of Sir Orlando Bridgman (ca.1679–1738; of Weston Park, Staffordshire; 4th baronet; M.P.), and (2) in 1766 Anne, daughter and heiress of Sir William Stephenson. Thus doubly fortified against the hazards of radicalism, he became the voluble leader of the popular radical movement in London. He was an alderman of London from 1769; sheriff, 1769–70; and lord mayor, 1775–76. With his sister Catherine Macaulay (neé Sawbridge) (*q.v.*), he was an ardent supporter of Wilkes, a leader in the Society for Defense of the Bill of Rights, and thus naturally a strong opponent of the North ministry. He voted against unseating Wilkes in January, 1770; against approving the address from the throne in October, 1775; for the Dunning resolution of April 6, 1780; and against the North ministry in all 5 of the crucial divisions recorded in February and March, 1782. In 1783 he opposed Shelburne's peace terms, supported Fox, opposed Pitt, and happily continued to urge radical measures upon the House of Commons until his death. Portrait by Benjamin West. M.P. for Hythe, 1768–74; London, 1774–95.

Sawyer, Herbert. ca.1730–98

Of parentage now obscure, he was in naval service from 1747 and was lieutenant in 1756 and captain in 1759. He served off the coast of France and then in West Indies waters, 1778–79, where he distinguished himself at St. Lucia in 1779. He was at the relief of Gibraltar in 1781 and later was in command at the Halifax station. He was admiral in 1795. Horace Walpole pronounced him "an extreme sensible and well-educated man." His oldest son, Sir Herbert Sawyer, became admiral and Commander of the Bath.

Saxton, Charles. 1732–1808

Of Circourt, Berkshire; 4th son of Edward Saxton (merchant of London; mayor of Abingdon); created baronet in 1794. He was in naval service from 1745; was in the West Indies, 1753–60; and was captain in 1762. After the outbreak of the American war he was again in the West Indies in 1780 and was off Chesapeake Bay before and after the Yorktown surrender of Cornwallis in late 1781. He was in command of the Jamaica station, 1782–83, and was commissioner of the navy at Portsmouth in 1789. He retired in 1806 with a pension of £750 a year.

Scarborough, 4th and 5th Earls. See Richard Lumley-Saunderson and George Augusta Lumley-Saunderson

Scarsdale, 1st and 2d Barons. See Nathaniel Curzon. 1727–1804 **and Nathaniel Curzon.** 1751–1837

Scawen, James. 1734–1801

Of Carshalton, near Sutton, in Surrey, and Maidwell, near Market Harborough, Northamptonshire; only son of Thomas Scawen (d. 1774; M.P.; of a Cornish family). He inherited a large family estate in Surrey. He supported Newcastle against Bute and Grenville, 1761–65, and supported the Rockingham ministry, 1765–66. He opposed the Chatham-Grafton and North ministries, 1767–80, voting against unseating Wilkes in January, 1770, voting against approving the address from the throne in October, 1775, and voting for the Dunning resolution of April 6, 1780. M.P. for St. Michael, 1761–74; Surrey, 1774–80.

Schaw, Charles. See Charles Schaw Cathcart

Scone, Lord. See David Murray

Scott, David. 1689–1766

Of Scotstarvet Tower, near Cupar, Fifeshire; only son of David Scot (or Scott) (of Scotstarvet). In 1712 he qualified as Scots advocate. In 1716 he married Lucy, daughter of Sir Robert Gordon (3d baronet; M.P.). In the House of Commons from 1741, he generally opposed the Whig ministries. He supported Bute, 1761–63, and supported Grenville on Wilkes and general warrants, 1763–64, but was recorded as absent at the division on the repeal of the Stamp Act—perhaps owing to illness, since he died the same year. M.P. for Fifeshire, 1741–47; Aberdeen burghs, 1751–66.

Scott, George Lewis. 1708–80

Born in Hanover, the oldest son of George Scott (of Brisco, Scotland; diplomat). He was schooled chiefly at Leyden. He became barrister of Middle Temple in 1736, fellow of the Society of Arts in 1736, and fellow of the Royal Society in 1737. About 1751 he married Sarah, younger daughter of Matthew Robinson (d. 1778; of West Layton, near Richmond, Yorkshire) (see Sarah Scott [neé Robinson]). Though considered to have strong Jacobite leanings, he was sub-preceptor to Prince George (later George III) and commissioner of excise, 1758–80. He was a brilliant mathematician but "very sociable," a friend of the family of James Boswell, and a friend and patron of James Thomson (author of *The Seasons*). He took no active part in politics.

Scott, Henry. 1746–1812

Oldest surviving son of Francis Scott (1721–50; styled Earl of Dalkeith; M.P.); in 1751 succeeded his grandfather Francis Scott (1695–1751) as 3d Duke of Buccleuch (Scottish). Eton from 1757. He made the grand tour with Adam Smith as tutor. In 1767 he married Elizabeth, only daughter of George Montagu (1737–88) (*q.v.*), and through her acquired the vast Montagu estates. In 1794 he succeeded through his mother to the landed estate of her father the Duke of Argyll, though not to that title. In 1810 he succeeded his cousin William Douglas (1724–1810) (*q.v.*) as 5th Duke of Queensberry (Scottish). He was made Knight of the Thistle in 1767 and Knight of the Garter in 1794 (resigning the Thistle in order to accept the new office). He was first president of the Royal Society of Edinburgh; governor of the Royal Bank of Scotland, 1777–1812; and captain general of the Royal Company of Archers, 1778–1812. In 1778 he raised a regiment of fencibles, of which he was colonel in command and which helped quell the anti-Catholic riots in Edinburgh. He was lord lieutenant of Midlothian and Haddingtonshire, 1794–1812, and of Roxburghshire, 1804–12. He was a friend of Sir Walter Scott and a notable patron of literature.

Scott, Hugh (or Hew). 1758–1841

Of Harden Tower, near Hawick, Roxburghshire, and Mertoun, near St. Boswells, Berwickshire; 2d but 1st surviving son of Walter Scott (*q.v.*); nephew of Hew Hume (1708–93; M.P.; 3d Earl of Marchmont, Scottish), through whom he assumed the surname Hepburne in 1820, having inherited from his cousin James Hepburne in 1793. In 1835 he was allowed to claim the title of 6th Baron Polwarth (Scottish). In politics he was a professed independent, and from 1780 he voted with the North ministry, including votes in all 5 of the crucial divisions reported in February and March, 1782. He then voted against the Rockingham ministry in early 1782; against Shelburne's peace terms in February, 1783; but with the coalition and for Fox's India Bill. He seldom spoke in the House of Commons, and in 1784, in his 26th year, he retired from active national politics. M.P. for Berwickshire, 1780–84.

Scott, John. ca.1725–75

Of Balcomie Castle, near Crail, Fifeshire; 2d son of David Scott (*q.v.*). He married (1) in 1770 Mary, daughter of James Hay (15th Earl of Errol, Scottish), but in 1771 divorced her for the usual reason. In 1773 he married (2) Margaret, daughter of Robert Dundas. He was ensign in the army in 1741, captain in 1744, and colonel in 1762. He served in America from 1769 and was made major general in 1770. In politics he supported Newcastle in the House of Commons, 1754–61, and thereafter, though a close friend of Shelburne, each successive ministry until 1775. He was a notorious gambler and was credited with having won in his lifetime a total of £500,000. M.P. for Caithness-shire, 1754–61; Tain burghs, 1761–68; Fifeshire, 1768–75.

Scott, John. 1739–98

Son of Thomas Scott (of Urlings, near Thurles, County Kilkenny). He attended Trinity College, Dublin, from 1756 and then Middle Temple. He was an Irish barrister from 1765 and a member of the Irish Parliament from 1769. He was solicitor general for Ireland, 1774–77, and attorney general for Ireland from 1777. He was trusted by the North administration and personally by North, to whom he wrote several times, 1778–79, warning that, unless the British government very promptly instituted political and economic reforms in Ireland, serious trouble would soon break out there. North did nothing for several months, and when serious riots broke out in Dublin in late 1779, Scott, who had loyally enforced the laws imposed by England, barely escaped from the mob with his life. When North and the English Parliament then began to pass somewhat mollifying legislation for Ireland, North called on Scott to help arouse the acceptance and gratitude of the Irish Parliament. In 1782, however, he was dismissed from office by the Rockingham ministry for denying the right of the British Parliament to bind Ireland by legislation unacceptable to Irish citizens. In 1784 he was nevertheless named chief justice of the king's bench in Ireland. In 1789 he was created Viscount Clonmell (Irish), and in 1793 he was created Earl of Clonmell (English). Some thought him "unscrupulous, passionate and greedy," but he was able and independent, and his letters are those of a man of character.

Scott, Robert. ca.1746–1808

Of Blackheath, Kent; only son of Robert Scott (of Lauder, Berwickshire; Scottish merchant of Madeira wine). Eton from 1757, Cambridge and Lincoln's Inn from 1762, grand tour in 1765. He disapproved of the American war and voted in the House of Commons against acceptance of the speech from the throne in October, 1775. Thereafter he voted steadily against the North ministry until he left the House in 1780, including a vote for the Dunning resolution of April 6, 1780. He left an estate of some £400,000. M.P. for Wootton Bassett, 1774–80.

Scott (née Robinson), Sarah. d. 1795

Younger daughter of Matthew Robinson (d. 1778; of West Layton, near Richmond, Yorkshire); younger sister of Matthew Robinson (1713–1800; 2d Baron Rokeby, Irish) and Elizabeth Montagu (née Robinson) (q.v.). About 1751 she married George Lewis Scott (q.v.), of whom Mary Delany (q.v.) strongly disapproved. They soon parted "through disagreement of tempers." She then lived with Lady Barbara Montagu (sister of George Montagu Dunk) (q.v.) until Lady Barbara died in 1765. She became an industrious but uninspired writer, though in her time she was considered "an excellent historian." From 1750 she published novels, moral tales, and histories, some of which were highly praised.

Scott, Thomas. 1723–1816

Of Shepperton on Thames, Middlesex; son of Thomas Scott ("brick-maker" of Fulham). In 1782 he married the widow of Arnold Nesbitt (*q.v.*) and sister of Henry Thrale (*q.v.*). He opposed the North ministry from the time he entered the House of Commons in 1780 and voted against it in all 5 of the recorded crucial divisions in February and March, 1782. He supported Shelburne's ministry, 1782–83, and voted for Pitt's reforms of Parliament and against Fox's India Bill in 1783. Thereafter he supported Pitt's reform proposals, but on most other occasions he opposed the ministry. M.P. for Bridport, 1780–90.

Scott, Walter. 1724–93

Of Harden Tower, near Hawick, Roxburghshire, and Mertoun, near St. Boswells, Berwickshire; oldest son of Walter Scott (of Harden and Whitefield, Roxburghshire); uncle of Hugh (or Hew) Scott (*q.v.*). Glasgow University from 1743. In 1754 he married Diana, daughter of Hugh Hume (1708–94; 3d Earl of Marchmont, Scottish). He was a member of the House of Commons for some 18 years and from 1761 supported Bute and then Grenville. He was (perhaps consequently) receiver general of customs in Scotland, 1765–93, and trustee for fisheries and manufactures in Scotland, 1769–93. M.P. for Roxburghshire, 1747–65.

Scott, William. 1745–1836

Born at Heworth, near Gateshead, Durham County, the oldest son of William Scott (d. 1776; coal factor to ships at Newcastle-on-Tyne); older brother of John Scott (1751–1838; 1st Baron and Earl of Eldon); in 1821 created Baron Stowell. In 1813 he married (2) Louisa Catherine, youngest daughter of Richard Howe (*q.v.*). Newcastle Grammar School, to Oxford in 1761; B.A., 1764; fellow from 1765; M.A., 1767; B.C.L., 1772; Middle Temple from 1762; barrister in 1780; bencher from 1794; reader from 1799. He was register of the court of faculties in 1783 and advocate general, 1788–98. He was knighted in 1788, when he was made judge of the Consistory Court, a post which he held until 1821 and where he formulated and recorded several important doctrines since recognized in international law. He was fellow of the Society of Arts from 1792 and of the Royal Society from

1793. In 1798 he became a privy councillor and was a member of the Board of Trade, 1798–1836. A good north-country man and border Scot, he had an affinity for clear thinking, port wine, and hard cash. M.P. for Downton, 1790–1801; Oxford University, 1801–21.

Scott, Waring, John. 1747–1819

Of Kinton, near Shrewsbury, Shropshire; oldest son of Jonathan Scott (of Shrewsbury); in 1798 added the surname Waring upon inheriting from his cousin Richard Hill Waring. He was married 3 times. In 1766 he was employed as cadet by the East India Company, in 1767 was an officer in the Bengal army, was regimental adjutant in 1774, and was an aide to Warren Hastings in 1778. In 1781 he returned to England, and in 1784, when he was a candidate for election to the House of Commons, Warren Hastings contributed £4,000 to his election expenses. After his election he supported Pitt. He was sheriff of Cheshire, 1801–1802. He published several essays on political issues. M.P. for West Looe, 1784–90; Stockbridge, 1790–93.

Scrope (or Scroope), Thomas. 1723–92

Of Coleby Hall, Kesteven, Lincolnshire; 5th son of Gervase Scrope (or Scroope) (of Cockerington, near Louth, Lincolnshire). Oxford from 1740; grand tour, 1751–52. For 14 years he tried unsuccessfully to gain election to the House of Commons, and became so eccentric that in 1764 he was declared insane and taken into custody. In 1768 he was released and again sought election. Being then legally of sound mind, he bribed so openly and extensively that he won election, and was allowed to take his seat. He voted against the unseating of Wilkes in 1770. There is no record of any further votes or any speech in the House. M.P. for Lincoln City, 1768–74.

Scudamore, Charles Fitzroy. See Charles Fitzroy-Scudamore

Scudamore, John. 1727–96

Of Kentchurch Court, on River Monnow, Herefordshire; oldest son of Richard Scudamore; descended from a family with great political interest and influence in Herefordshire. Lincoln's Inn from 1746. In the House of Commons from 1764, he voted against Grenville and general warrants in 1764; supported the ministry of Rockingham,

1765–66; and opposed the Grafton and North ministries, 1767–82. He voted against unseating Wilkes in January, 1770; against approving the address from the throne in October, 1775; for Dunning's resolution of April 6, 1780; and against the North ministry in all 5 crucial divisions recorded in February and March, 1782. From 1782 he supported Fox and voted for his India Bill in November, 1783. He stood by Fox and opposed Pitt from 1784. According to the records, he addressed the House of Commons once in 1772 and once in 1780. M.P. for Hereford City, 1764–96.

Seafield, 6th Earl. See **James Ogilvy**

Seaforth, 1st Earl. See **Kenneth Mackenzie**

Sebright, John Saunders. 1725–94

Of Beechwood, near Hemel Hempstead, Hertfordshire, and Bessford Court, Worcestershire; 2d son of Sir Thomas Saunders Sebright (4th baronet); in 1761 succeeded his brother Sir Thomas Saunders Sebright (M.P.) as 6th baronet. Westminster, 1735–41. He entered the army as ensign and was captain in 1744, colonel in 1758, major general in 1761, lieutenant general in 1770, and general in 1782. In the House of Commons from 1763, he supported the Grenville ministry until 1765 and voted against repeal of the Stamp Act in 1766, against Chatham's land tax in 1767, and against Savile's *Nullum Tempus* Bill in 1768. He supported the North ministry until he left Parliament in 1780, opposing Dunning's first resolution of April, 1780. He did not seek re-election. M.P. for Bath, 1763–74 and 1775–80.

Secker, Thomas. 1693–1768

Son of Thomas Secker (a pious dissenter with a small estate at Sibthorpe, near Markham, Nottinghamshire). He attended dissenter schools and then audited lectures in Paris, 1718–19; M.D., Leyden, 1721; B.A., Oxford, 1722. In 1725 he married Caroline, sister of his friend and mentor Bishop Benson. He took orders, obtained the rich living of Houghton-le-Spring in Durham County, and became prebendary of Durham. He was rector of St. James's, Piccadilly, from 1733 and (while retaining his other posts and revenues) bishop of Bristol (for which the stipend was notably low), 1735–37. He was bishop of Oxford, 1737–58, and dean of St. Paul's from 1750. He was archbishop of Canterbury, 1758–68. Though Horace Walpole wrote that he deplored Methodism and "laboured truly for the encouragement of the good cause," he was intimately acquainted with John Wesley and "with every step he took" and did not call on him or other Methodists to leave the Church of England. In 1723 he helped Bishop Joseph Butler (1692–1772) obtain the lucrative living of Stanhope in Durham County. He had "a morbid dread of enthusiasm" and sought to maintain "a decent middle ground" in the church. Against strong public disapproval he "boldly advocated" a scheme for establishing bishoprics in the colonies. A notable Hebrew scholar, he published *Concio ad Clerum* in 1761. He stood very well with Frederick, Prince of Wales, and the prince's mother, the queen, but as archbishop was not greatly esteemed or consulted by either George II or George III. In 1748 he advocated toleration of Scottish episcopal orders even though they were not confirmed by English bishops, and in 1753 and 1754 he supported toleration of the Jews. He was calm and judicial, but in his later years illness reduced his influence in church and court. In 1761 he urged Newcastle to remain in office "as his duty."

Sedley, Charles. ca.1722–78

Of Nuthall, near Nottingham; in 1730 succeeded his father, Sir Charles Sedley, as 2d baronet. Westminster from 1732, Oxford from 1739. He was elected to the House of Commons as a Tory. His only recorded vote during the North ministry was against it on the conduct of the war in America in 1778. There is no evidence that he ever addressed the House. M.P. for Nottingham Borough, 1747–54 and 1774–78.

Sefton, 1st Earl. See Charles Richard William Molyneux

Selkirk, 4th Earl. See Dunbar Hamilton

Selsey, 1st and 2d Barons. See James Peachey and John Peachey

Selwyn, George Augustus. 1719–91

Of Matson House, near Gloucester; 2d but oldest surviving son of Colonel John Selwyn (1688–1751; of Matson; M.P.); closely connected by marriage with the Townshend family. Eton, to Oxford in 1739, but was expelled for preparing the sacrament at a drinking party; Inner Temple from 1737. He became a friend and frequent correspondent of Horace Walpole and the Earl of Carlisle and was a member of White's Club and of the Jockey Club from 1767. He was a wit, a minor literary figure, a would-be politician who did not arrive, and perhaps above all a seeker of sinecures who supported the court in order to secure, maintain, and increase them, and condemned the court privately if it failed to co-operate. He was surveyor of the mint, 1740–91; registrar of the Court of Chancery in Barbados, 1753–91; and surveyor general of crown lands, 1783–91—his duties in those offices being performed by others. When he was refused further "favours" by the North ministry, he became bitter toward North but had no alternative but to support his ministry. He opposed the Dunning resolution of April 6, 1780, and voted with North in all 5 of the recorded crucial divisions of February and March, 1782. His claim for favors rested largely upon his virtual control of the elections of members for Ludgershall. In 1761 he offered Bute control of those two elections; Bute accepted the offer and secured the election of Thomas Whately and John Patterson. North later had the same opportunity and made all he could of it, but Selwyn was not the only man who had to be paid in kind. In the House of Commons he more than once openly burlesqued North's apparent somnolence by pretending to sleep with him "except when taking part in a division" (DNB). Portrait, with the Earl of Carlisle, by Reynolds. M.P. for Ludgershall, 1747–54; Gloucester City, 1754–80; Ludgershall, 1780–91.

Selwyn, William. 1732–1817

Of Boxley, near Maidstone, Kent; 2d son of Henry Selwyn (of Westminster); 1st cousin of George Augustus Selwyn (q.v.) and Thomas Townshend (1733–1800) (q.v.). Westminster from 1740, Cambridge from 1749, Lincoln's Inn from 1749, barrister in 1754, bencher from 1780, treasurer in 1793, and king's counsel from 1780. He usually followed the political line of Carlisle, opposing the coalition ministry and then supporting Pitt. According to the records he addressed the House of Commons but once, and then on legislation to discourage burglaries. M.P. for Whitchurch, 1783–90.

Sergison, Thomas Warden. 1701–66

Of Cuckfield Place, near Hayward's Heath, Sussex; son of Thomas

Warden (of Cuckfield). In 1732, upon inheriting from his maternal great-uncle Charles Sergison (M.P.), he added the name Sergison. In the elections of 1734 and 1741 he unsuccessfully opposed the Pelham interest, but in 1747 he "took the Newcastle living" for Lewes and for 19 years in the House of Commons faithfully repaid his obligation by supporting Pelham and Newcastle. He voted against Bute's peace preliminaries in 1762 and opposed the Grenville ministry. There is no record that he addressed the House after 1760. M.P. for Lewes, 1747–66.

Serle, Ambrose. 1742–1812

Born of a Calvinist father. He entered the navy and became captain in 1755. He was undersecretary of state for the colonies under Dartmouth, 1772–74. He was with the British army in America from 1776 as clerk of reports and served briefly as private secretary to Admiral Howe and then to the Carlisle peace commission in 1778. He returned to England in late 1780, settled in Heckfield, Hampshire, and published an account of his political and military experiences in America, in which he was emotionally extravagant in his condemnation of the morals and military incapacities of the Americans and the general sinfulness of nearly everyone except himself. He was forced to conclude that American military incompetence had not resulted in American disaster simply because the British military forces were only slightly less incompetent. He also published religious books with a melancholy, Calvinistic strain. He was commissioner of transport and of prisoners of war in 1795, 1803, and 1809.

Sewell, Thomas. ca.1712–84

Of Ottershaw, near Chertsey, Surrey; son of Thomas Sewell (of West Ham, Essex). Middle Temple from 1729, barrister in 1734, bencher from 1754, reader from 1762, and treasurer in 1765. He married (1) in 1769 Catherine, daughter of Thomas Heath (M.P.), and (2) in 1773 Elizabeth, daughter of Humphrey Sibthorp (professor at Oxford). In 1760–61 he was supported for re-election by Newcastle, whom he in turn supported until switching his support to George Grenville from 1763, with rewarding results. He was king's counsel from 1764, master of the robes and privy councillor from 1764. He voted for general warrants in 1764. In 1767, Charles Townshend listed him as a supporter of the Chatham-Grafton ministry. He addressed the House of Commons seldom, and is not known to have cast a vote against any current ministry. M.P. for Harwich, 1758–61; Winchelsea, 1761–68.

Seymour, Edward. 1718–92

Styled Lord Seymour from 1750; in 1757 he succeeded his father, Edward Seymour (1695–1757; M.P.), as 9th Duke of Somerset. Westminster from 1730, Oxford from 1736. He was considered a Whig, but his interest did not lie in politics, and he carried less political weight than most men of his rank and other members of his family. He had a mania about smallpox inoculation which kept him from risking attendance at the House of Lords, where infection might lurk in the blood of some vaccinated viscount. Consequently, he was absent from many crucial divisions, and also from meetings of the Privy Council, of which he was a member from 1770. The *Peerage* of 1775 reported: "He interferes very little in the public transactions of his time, living mostly in his country seats, in a private peaceable manner." In 1783 the king gave him a pension of £1,200 a year, though for what service it remains in doubt.

Seymour, Henry. 1729–1807

Of Sherborne, Dorset; he was the oldest son of Francis Seymour (of Sherborne; M.P.); half brother of John Montagu (1718–92; 4th Earl of Sandwich); cousin of Edward Seymour (1695–1757) (*q.v.*). Westminster, 1739–47; Oxford from 1747; grand tour. In 1753 he married (1) Caroline, only daughter of William Cowper (2d Earl Cowper). A country gentleman of Tory inclinations, he entered the House of Commons in 1763, supported the Grenville ministry, and was groom of the bedchamber, 1763–65. Upon Grenville's dismissal he resigned his court post and went into opposition, speaking frequently and voting against repeal of the Stamp Act in 1766. He signed the 1769 petition from Somerset against the Grafton ministry's measures toward Wilkes; and in January, 1770, he voted against unseating Wilkes. In 1772 he accused North of turning against the measure to ease the discriminations against dissenters which he had promised to support, and drew from North a characteristically disarming, amusing, and unsatisfactory reply. He voted against approving the address from the throne in October, 1775, and though allied to the Bedford party, he supported Charles Fox on the issue of the war in America. In 1778 he went to France and settled near Versailles and became a paramour of Madame Du Barry. He did not vote in Parliament from 1778 or permanently return to England until 1792. M.P. for Totnes, 1763–68; Huntingdon Borough, 1768–74; Evesham, 1774–80.

Seymour-Conway. See **Robert Seymour Conway. Henry Seymour Conway. 1719–95   Henry Seymour Conway. 1746–1830   Francis Seymour Conway. 1719–94   and Francis Ingram Seymour Conway. 1743–1822**

Shaftesbury, 4th Earl. See **Anthony Ashley-Cooper**

Shafto (or Shaftoe), Robert. ca.1732–97

Of Whitworth, near Bishop Auckland, Durham County; son of John Shafto (or Shaftoe) (of Whitworth and London; M.P.). Eton and Westminster, 1740–49; Oxford from 1749. Though he was of a Tory family, he voted for Newcastle, 1760–62; voted against the Grenville ministry over Wilkes and general warrants, 1763–64; and received a pension of £200 a year from the Rockingham ministry in 1765. On returning to the House of Commons, he supported the North ministry, voting against Dunning's resolution of April 6, 1780. In February and March, 1782, he voted with the North ministry in all 5 of the recorded crucial divisions. In 1783 he voted for Shelburne's peace terms but then supported the coalition and Fox's India Bill. In 1784 he opposed Pitt. He spoke very seldom in the House, but according to John Robinson he carried considerable influence because he "owned" the 2 seats for Downton. M.P. for Durham County, 1760–68; Downton, 1780–96.

Shafto (or Shaftoe), Robert Jenison. ca.1728–71

Of Wratting Park, near Newmarket, Cambridgeshire; 2d son of Robert Shafto (or Shaftoe) (of Benwell Tower, Northumberland). He was ensign in the army in 1745, lieutenant in 1750, retired in 1755. He supported Newcastle and then Grenville, voting against repeal of the Stamp Act in 1766. On the Wilkes issues he supported the Grafton ministry, but his only recorded address to the House was a brief one said to have been made on a bet in 1762. He was a well-known sportsman and a notorious gambler. He died by a self-inflicted gunshot wound. M.P. for Leominster, 1761–68; Castle Rising, 1768–71.

Shannon, 1st and 2d Earls. See Henry Boyle and Richard Boyle

Sharp, Granville. 1735–1813

9th son of Thomas Sharp (1693–1758; dean of Durham Cathedral); grandson of John Sharp (archbishop of York, 1691–1714). He was apprenticed to a Quaker linen draper in London, and meanwhile taught himself Greek and Latin and advanced his general education and prospects. In 1757 he became a member of the Company of Fishmongers, and in 1764 a clerk in ordinary in ordnance. In 1767 he declined an offer of church orders and a church living and remained in ordnance until 1776. He supported the cause of the American colonists, favored a revision of representation in Parliament but opposed Wyvill's move for triennial elections because he favored annual elections, joined a movement to abolish press gangs, and established the Society for the Conversion of Jews. The first man of ability and energy to espouse the cause of freeing the slaves, in 1787 he helped found the Society for the Abolition of Slavery and became its chairman. His activities in politics, pamphleteering, and legal suits were chiefly directed at those objectives. Portrait by Nathaniel Dance; memorial in Westminster Abbey.

Sharpe, Fane William. ca.1728–71

Of South Lodge, Enfield Chase, Middlesex; oldest son of John Sharpe (ca.1700–56; M.P.; agent for several West Indies islands). Westminster from 1738, Oxford and Lincoln's Inn from 1747. In 1752 he married Mary, daughter of George Newport (prosperous London merchant). A member of the House of Commons from 1756, he supported Newcastle through 1762, voted with Grenville on general warrants in 1764, and voted against repeal of the Stamp Act in 1766. He opposed the Grafton ministry and opposed North's settlement with Spain on the Falkland Islands in 1771. He was "very rich and very shy," and there is no indication that he ever addressed the House. M.P. for Callington, 1756–71.

Shaw-Stewart, John. 1739–1812

Of Greenock, Renfrewshire; in 1796 succeeded his father, Michael Stewart, as 4th baronet; in 1752 added the surname Shaw upon inheriting "great wealth and property" from his great-uncle Sir John

Shaw. In the House of Commons from 1780, he opposed the North ministry's American policies and measures, joined the Portland and Rockingham Whigs, and voted against the ministry in every crucial division recorded after February 20, 1782. He voted against Shelburne's peace terms and supported Fox in the 1783 coalition and afterward, voting against Pitt through 1786. He was "inconspicuous in politics" but led a "roistering social life." M.P. for Renfrewshire, 1780–83 and 1786–96.

Sheffield, 1st Baron and Earl. See **John Baker-Holroyd**

Shelburne, 2d Earl. See **William Fitzmaurice Petty**

Shelley, John. ca.1730–83

Of Mitchelgrove, near Arundel, Sussex; in 1771 succeeded his father, Sir John Shelley (1692–1771), as 5th baronet. He was related to George Montagu Dunk (*q.v.*) and supported him in politics. Westminster from 1745, Cambridge from 1748. He was keeper of records in the Tower of London, 1755–83; clerk of the pipe in exchequer, 1758–83; treasurer of the king's household, 1766–67; and privy councillor during the Rockingham ministry in 1766. In the House of Commons he supported Newcastle against Bute and voted against Bute's peace preliminaries in December, 1762. He was equivocal in partisanship during the Grenville ministry but voted for repeal of the Stamp Act in 1766, and was rewarded with a court appointment. He supported the Grafton and then the North ministry until he ended his career in Parliament. M.P. for East Retford, 1751–68; Newark, 1768–74; New Shoreham, 1774–80.

Sheraton, Thomas. 1751–1806

Born at Stockton-on-Tees, Durham County, the son of Thomas Sheraton, a zealous Baptist. He was largely self-taught and became a cabinet maker of the greatest skill and highest reputation. In 1791 he enhanced his standing and influence by publishing *The Cabinet Maker's Drawing Book*, and in 1803 he published *The Cabinet Dictionary*. Those books and, even more, the many examples of his own style and craftsmanship, set fashions in domestic furniture which almost dominated in his time, and have ever since been held in high esteem.

Sherborne, 1st Baron. See James Dutton

Sheridan, Richard Brinsley. 1751–1816

2d son of Thomas Sheridan (Irish actor; manager of the Theatre Royal in Dublin; teacher of rhetoric and elocution; author of a dictionary published in 1780). Harrow, 1762–68; Middle Temple from 1773. He made his reputation as a playwright in 1775 with the production of *The Rivals* at the Covent Garden Theatre and then began a career in public affairs as well. A member of the House of Commons from 1780 and an intimate of Fox and Burke, he spoke in strong opposition to the policies and measures of the North ministry toward the Americans, and was offered but refused a gift of money by the Continental Congress in appreciation of his speeches justifying the resistance of the colonies. In February and March, 1782, he voted against the ministry in all 5 of the crucial divisions recorded. After North's fall he was undersecretary of state for foreign affairs under Fox in the Rockingham ministry, April–July, 1782, and supported Fox after Rockingham's death. In the coalition ministry he was secretary to the treasury, April–December, 1783. He defended Fox's India Bill in the House of Commons in late 1783 and after Fox's fall remained with Fox in opposition to Pitt. In 1787, when he, through Fox, had become very friendly with the Prince of Wales, he was a manager of the impeachment proceedings against Warren Hastings. He was receiver for the Duchy of Cornwall from 1805, privy councillor from 1806, and treasurer of the navy, 1806–1807. He was an ardent and eloquent supporter of popular reforms and upon his death received a large public funeral. M.P. for Stafford Borough, 1780–1806; Westminster, 1806–1807; Ilchester, 1807–12.

Sherrard, Bennet. 1709–70

Styled Lord Sherrard from 1732; in 1750 succeeded his father, Philip Sherrard (ca.1680–1750; M.P.), as Baron Sherrard (Irish) and 3d Earl of Harborough (English). Eton, ca.1728–29. He married (1) in 1748 Elizabeth, oldest daughter of Ralph Verney (1st Earl Verney, Irish), (2) in 1757 Frances, daughter of William Noel (1695–1762; M.P.), (3) in 1761 Margaret, half sister of Noel Hill (1st Baron Berwick), and (4) in 1767 Elizabeth, oldest daughter of Thomas Cave (*q.v.*). The variety and intensity of his domestic life comprised his major career, and perhaps accounts for the relative unimportance of his public and political activities. His younger brother Philip Sherrard, less complicated in his home life, became a major general in 1762 and as lieutenant general commanded with distinction the guards at the battle at Bruckmuhl, Bavaria.

Shiffner, Henry. 1721–95

Of Pontrilas, on River Dore, Herefordshire; born in St. Petersburg, the oldest son of Matthew Shiffner (an affluent merchant to Russia related to the Grenville family). He was sent to England at the age of 3 and at 7 was "put to a public school." Before 1742 he joined his father's business and made several trips to Russia. In 1754 the firm became insolvent, but in 1761 he was elected to the House of Commons with the support of Bute and Grenville, whom he in turn supported, receiving in 1763 a secret-service pension of £500 a year. Though he voted against the cider tax proposed by Grenville, he supported Grenville on all other major issues and spoke and voted against repeal of the Stamp Act in 1766. In 1767 he opposed the land tax of the Chatham-Grafton ministry. In 1768 he did not stand for re-election but retired to the life of "a rather self-conscious country gentleman" who urged firm action against the intransigent American colonists. M.P. for Minehead, 1761–68.

Shipbrook, 1st Earl. See **Francis Vernon**

Shipley, Jonathan. 1714–88

Son of Jonathan Shipley (d. 1749; of Leeds; stationer of London). Schooled at Reading, to Oxford in 1731; M.A., 1738; took orders; D.D., 1748. In 1743 he became rector of Silchester and Sherborne St. John, Hampshire. About 1743 he married Anna Maria, niece of Charles Mordaunt (3d Earl of Peterborough). In 1745 he was chaplain general to the Duke of Cumberland's troops in the Fontenoy campaign, and in 1748 he was canon of Christ Church, Oxford. In 1760 he returned to Hampshire as rector of Chilbolton, and was also dean of Westminster. In 1769 he became bishop of Llandaff, and later in that year became bishop of St. Asaph, a bishopric he held until his death. He was, with Bishop Hinchcliffe, the most vehement of the clerical peers in opposition to the North ministry's measures toward the colonies. He recorded dissents to majority votes in the House of Lords on (1) the raising of government funds by annuities and lotteries, which he called "improvident, corrupt and partial," in 1781, (2) the address from the throne, with its continuing colonial policy, which he called "short-sighted," in 1778, (3) the rejection by the peers of a motion to examine into public expenditures in 1779, and (4) rejection by the peers of a motion to exclude holders of government contracts from membership in Parliament, in 1780. Portrait by Reynolds.

Shirley, Robert. 1723–87

Son of Laurence Shirley (1720–60; 4th Earl of Ferrers); in 1778 succeeded his brother Washington Shirley (*q.v.*) as 6th Earl Ferrers of Chartley, Staffordshire. He supported Grafton, 1767–70, and the North ministry until 1775, when Grafton resigned and Shirley also resigned his court office. He then voted largely with the Rockingham Whigs and signed many dissents to majority votes in the House of Lords. He supported the motion to ask the king to dismiss Sandwich in 1779, the motion to ask the king to effect "a total change of System" in 1779, the motion to examine into public expenditures in 1780, and the motion to exclude holders of government contracts from membership in Parliament in 1780. He opposed a declaration of war against the United Provinces in 1781 and supported the bill to prevent abuses in public life in 1783. In the same year he opposed the coalition, and from 1784 he supported Pitt.

Shirley, Washington. 1722–78

Son of Laurence Shirley; in 1760 succeeded his brother Laurence Shirley (1720–60; hanged for the murder of his land steward) as 5th Earl Ferrers; older brother of Robert Shirley (*q.v.*). He entered the navy ca. 1738 and was captain in 1746, rear admiral in 1775, vice admiral in 1776. He was a fellow of the Royal Society from 1761 and grand master of English Freemasons, 1762–64. In 1763 the king restored to him the estates forfeited by his brother Laurence. In the House of Lords he recorded dissents against (1) the cider tax in 1763 and (2) repeal of the Stamp Act in 1766. He supported Chatham's bill to alter the action of the House of Commons in unseating Wilkes in 1770 and Chatham's bill to conciliate the colonies in 1775. Nominally a Grenville Whig, he supported the North ministry when Grenville or Suffolk did so.

Shirley, William. 1694–1771

Born at Preston, near Worthing, Sussex, the son of William Shirley (mercer of London). He attended Old Merchant Taylors' School, and Cambridge from 1710 and became a barrister of Middle Temple. In 1731 he went to Boston and was governor of Massachusetts Bay Colony, 1741–56. In 1755 he directed the colonial troops at the capture of Louisburg; in 1758–59, after Braddock's defeat and death, he organized and led a partly successful but disappointing expedition against the French and Indians at Oswego and Niagara, with the rank of lieutenant general. He was then summoned to London to answer criticisms of his management of that expedition, and was ably supported in his defense before Parliament by a young American of Scottish descent named William Alexander, who had been his aide and commissary supplier in the campaign, who would shortly lay claim to the Scottish earldom of Stirling and become known by that title, and who would then become a general under Washington in the American Continental army. Shirley was finally exonerated by Parliament and was compensated by appointment as governor of the Bahamas, where he served 1759–67. He then returned to Massachusetts as a private citizen and at Roxbury built a handsome mansion with bricks brought from England at great expense. He died at Roxbury.

Shrewsbury, 14th Earl. See George Talbot

Shuckburgh-Evelyn, George Augustus William. 1751–1804

Of Shuckburgh Park, near Southam, Warwickshire; oldest son of Lieutenant Colonel Richard Shuckburgh (of a Warwickshire family frequently represented in Parliament); in 1773 succeeded his uncle Sir Charles Shuckburgh (1722–73; sheriff of Warwickshire) as 6th baronet; in 1793 added the surname Evelyn from his wife's family. Rugby from 1760; Oxford from 1768; B.A., 1772; grand tour. He was a fellow of the Society of Arts from 1777 and of the Royal Society from 1774. According to John Robinson, he was politically "much connected with Mr. Fox," and in February and March, 1782, he voted against the North ministry in all 5 crucial divisions recorded. He did not vote on Shelburne's peace terms, and, though he admired Fox, he did not like his alliance with North and did not support the coalition, voting against Fox's India Bill. A distinguished mathematician and gentleman scientist, he published papers on his scientific investigations and built an observatory. M.P. for Warwickshire, 1780–1804.

Shuldham, Molyneux. ca.1717–98

2d son of Rev. Lemuel Shuldham (of Dublin); in 1776 created Baron Shuldham (Irish). In 1732 he began a naval career and was lieutenant in 1739, served at Cartagena in 1741, and was captain in 1746. In 1756 he was captured by the French off Martinique but was soon exchanged and was present at the reduction of Guadeloupe in 1759. He was governor and in sea command of the Newfoundland station, 1772–74 (though others questioned his competence) and was then appointed by Sandwich in command in American waters. He was recalled against Sandwich's wish in 1776, and Sandwich insisted he be given a peerage (albeit an Irish one) and put him in command of the Plymouth dockyards, where he served, 1777–82. He broke with Sandwich in late 1778, however, when he "was warm in Keppel's praises" in the Keppel-Palliser controversy after Ushant. He continued to support the North ministry, voting against Dunning's first resolution in April, 1780, and voting with the ministry in all 5 of the crucial divisions recorded in February and March, 1782. He did not vote on Shelburne's peace terms in February, 1783, or on Fox's India Bill in November, 1783, but he otherwise supported the coalition. He failed of re-election in 1784. He was made admiral in 1787. M.P. for Fowey, 1774–84.

Shuttleworth, James. 1714–73

Of Gawthorpe Hall, near Burnley, Lancashire, and Forcett Park, Yorkshire; oldest surviving son of Richard Shuttleworth (of Gawthorpe). He was schooled at Westminster. He secured a seat in the House of Commons in 1741. In the 1754 elections he was an avowed and demonstrated Tory, and in 1761, when sheriff of Yorkshire, he was listed as Tory. His only recorded votes in the House of Commons after 1760 were against the Grenville ministry on the Wilkes issues in 1763 but with Grenville against repeal of the Stamp Act in 1766. There is no indication that he ever addressed the House, and he did not seek re-election in 1768. M.P. for Preston, 1741–54; Lancashire, 1761–68.

Sibthorpe, Coningsby. 1706–79

Of Canwick, Kesteven, Lincolnshire; 2d son of John Sibthorpe (M.P.). Westminster from 1718, Oxford, 1724–28. He was sheriff of Lincolnshire, 1733–34. Listed as Tory in 1761 and 1766, he supported Bute and his peace preliminaries in December, 1762, voted with Grenville against repeal of the Stamp Act in 1766, and voted against Grafton and Chatham's land tax in 1767. M.P. for Lincoln City, 1734–41, 1747–54, and 1761–68.

Sibthorpe, Humphrey Waldo (later **Waldo-Sibthorpe**). 1744–1815

Of Canwick, Kesteven, Lincolnshire; oldest surviving son of Humphrey Sibthorpe (botanist; professor at Oxford); nephew of Coningsby Sibthorpe (*q.v.*); in 1804 added the surname Waldo upon inheriting through his mother from Peter Waldo. Harrow from 1755, Westminster from 1756, Oxford from 1758, Lincoln's Inn from 1760, barrister in 1766. He professed political independence but voted regularly with the North ministry, including votes with North in all 5 of the crucial divisions recorded in February and March, 1782. He did not vote on Shelburne's peace terms or on Fox's India Bill in 1783. He addressed the House of Commons only one time, at least before 1790, in 1780. M.P. for Boston, 1774–84; Lincoln City, 1800–1806.

Simpson, Edward. ca.1701–64

Of Acton, near Paddington, Middlesex; son of Francis Simpson (of Fishlake, near Thorne, Yorkshire). Cambridge from 1718; Lincoln's Inn from 1719; barrister in 1726; fellow at Cambridge, 1724–35; master of Trinity Hall, Cambridge, 1735–64; vice chancellor of the university, 1740–41. He was advocate of doctors' commons in 1736; chancellor of the Diocese of Bath and Wells in 1738; chancellor of the Diocese of London, 1749–59; judge of the Consistory Court in London, 1747–58; judge of the Cinque Ports and dean of the arches, 1758–64. He was knighted in 1761. In politics he supported Newcastle and voted against the Grenville ministry on Wilkes issues in 1763. In 1764 he spoke and voted against general warrants and the Grenville ministry. M.P. for Dover, 1759–64.

Sinclair (or St. Clair), James. ca.1688–1762

Of Balblair, near Bonar Bridge, Sutherlandshire, and Sinclair, near Dysart, Fifeshire; 2d son of Henry Sinclair (10th Lord Sinclair, Scottish). Since his older brother was attainted in 1716 for supporting the Jacobite rising, he succeeded his father to the family estates in 1716; he resigned them to his brother when his brother was pardoned in 1726, and succeeded to them again on the death of his brother in 1750. He was colonel of a Scottish regiment from 1737, major general in 1741, lieutenant general and in command of British troops in Flanders in 1745, and led an expedition against Port L'Orient in 1746. He was ambassador to Vienna and to Turin in 1761 and was governor of Cork in 1762. Politically he was a protégé and supporter of the Duke of Argyll, and in 1762 he supported Bute. Pitt called him the officer best qualified to succeed Ligonier in 1760. "A patriarchal figure of great wealth derived from his collieries." M.P. for Dysart burghs, 1722–34; Sutherlandshire, 1736–47; Dysart burghs, 1747–54; Fifeshire, 1754–62.

Sinclair, John. 1754–1835

Of Ulbster, near Wick, and Thurso Castle, Caithness; oldest surviving son of George Sinclair (of Ulbster); nephew of William Sutherland (7th Earl of Sutherland, Scottish); created baronet in 1786. Edinburgh University, 1765–67 and 1768–70; Glasgow University, 1773–74; Lincoln's Inn from 1774; barrister in 1782. In the House of Commons from 1780, he professed independence. He spoke in support of North's declaration of war on the United Provinces in January, 1781, but later in that year spoke against North and in favor of prompt peace with the Americans. He supported Sandwich against the attacks in January, 1782, and voted with the North ministry in all 5 of the crucial divisions reported in February and March, 1782. He voted for Shelburne's peace terms and paired on Fox's India Bill in 1783. He usually supported Pitt, 1784–88. In 1784 he published *A History of the Public Revenues* and later occasionally published pamphlets critical of Pitt's measures. He was president of the Scottish Board of Agriculture, 1793–98 and 1806–14; cashier of excise in Scotland, 1811–35; and privy councillor from 1810. M.P. for Caithness-shire, 1780–84; Lostwithiel, 1784–90; Caithness-shire, 1790–96; Petersfield, 1797–1802; Caithness-shire, 1807–11.

Skelton (formerly Jones), Arnoldus. ca.1750–93

Of Branthwaite, near Brigham, Cumberland; son of James Jones (captain of foot guards); brother-in-law of Charles Cornwallis (*q.v.*), who in 1768 married his sister Jemima. He took the surname Skelton in 1772 upon inheriting from his father's friend Lieutenant General William Skelton. He was ensign in 1772, captain in 1776, and retired in 1779. In the House of Commons from 1780, he supported the North ministry in all 5 of the crucial divisions reported in February and March, 1782, but there is no evidence that he ever addressed the House. He left Parliament in 1782, possibly with a pension from the North ministry. M.P. for Eye, 1780–82.

Skene, Robert. 1719–87

Of Hallyards, near Lochgelly, Fifeshire; oldest son of David Skene (of Hallyards); cousin of Adam Smith (*q.v.*). He was ensign in 1743, lieutenant in 1745, captain in 1756, adjutant general in 1763, colonel in 1772, major general in 1777, and lieutenant general in 1782. He was master of baggage and inspector of roads in the Scottish highlands, 1767–80. He supported the North ministry from entering the House of Commons in 1779, and in February and March, 1782, voted with North in all 5 of the crucial divisions recorded. He supported the coalition and Fox's India Bill in 1783 and opposed Pitt, 1784–87. M.P. for Fifeshire, 1779–87.

Skinner, William. 1700–80

Of Croom's Hill, Greenwich; son of Thomas Skinner (merchant of St. Christopher, West Indies). He was educated by his uncle as an engineer, and served in the ordnance office in the Tower of London in 1719 and at the Gun Wharf in Devonport in 1720. He was at Minorca in 1722, at Gibraltar in 1724, and was mentioned in dispatches during the siege of Gibraltar in 1727. He was appointed engineer extraordinary in 1729, and was then chief engineer at Gibraltar. In 1746 he went to Scotland to construct defense posts, and in 1755 went to Ireland to report on the state of its defenses. From 1757 he was, by royal patent, chief engineer of Great Britain. In 1758, at the instance of Germain, he exchanged variant opinions before Parliament with Tyrawley on the fortifications of Gibraltar, on which he was adviser in 1759, 1769, and 1770. In that verbal duel with the rugged old Irish soldier he came off second best. He was made major general in 1761 and lieutenant general in 1770, and he supervised old and new fortifications in Scotland, Milford Haven, Portsmouth, and Plymouth.

Skipwith, Thomas George. 1736–90

Of Newbold Pacey Hall, near Warwick; in 1778 succeeded his father, Sir Francis Skipwith (ca.1705–78), as 4th baronet. Rugby from 1743, Cambridge from 1754. In 1785 he married Selina, daughter of George Shirley and granddaughter of Robert Shirley (1st Earl Ferrers). Considered a Tory in 1761 elections, in 1769 he won a seat as a supporter of the Rockingham Whigs and consistently opposed the Grafton and then the North ministries. He voted against unseating Wilkes in January, 1770, for Dunning's resolution of April 6, 1780, and against the North ministry in all 5 of the crucial divisions recorded in February and March, 1782. He voted for Shelburne's peace terms, did not vote on Fox's India Bill in 1783, and was not returned in 1784. M.P. for Warwickshire, 1769–80; Steyning, 1780–84.

Skryne (or Skrine), William. ca.1722–83

Of Arlington Street, London; son of William Skryne (physician of Bath). Oxford from 1738. He became a close friend of Lord Orford and Lord Barrington, and was elected to the House of Commons in 1771 in Orford's "interest." Though he apparently never addressed the House, he regularly supported the North ministry until 1780. He killed himself in a tavern after losing at cards at Brooks Club. M.P. for Callington, 1771–80.

Skynner, John. 1724–1805

Of Great Milton, Oxfordshire; son of John Skynner (of Great Milton). Westminster from 1735, Oxford from 1742, Lincoln's Inn from 1739, barrister in 1748, bencher from 1771. He was attorney general of the Duchy of Lancaster, 1770–77; judge on the Chester circuit, 1772–77; king's counsel from 1771; chief baron of the exchequer, 1777–87; recorder of Woodstock, 1771–80; recorder of Oxford, 1776–97; and privy councillor from 1787. He was knighted in 1777. Though critical of details in North's Massachusetts Governing Act, he supported the North ministry until he withdrew from the House in 1777, and he spoke frequently in defense of the prerogatives of the established church. M.P. for New Woodstock, 1771–77.

Slingsby, Henry. ca.1693–1763

Of Scriven and Red House, near Knaresborough, Yorkshire; in 1726 succeeded his father, Sir Thomas Slingsby, as 5th baronet. Oxford from 1710. In 1729 he married Mary, daughter of John Aislabie (M.P.; chancellor of the exchequer, 1718–21) and sister of William Aislabie (*q.v.*). In the 1754 elections he was an overt Tory, having since 1714 voted regularly with the opposition to the long Whig hegemony, but one of his last votes was against Bute's peace preliminaries in December, 1762. M.P. for Knaresborough, 1714–15 and 1722–63.

Sloane-Stanley, Hans. 1739–1827

Of South Stoneham, near Southampton, Hampshire; oldest surviving son of William Sloane (of South Stoneham); added the surname Stanley after inheriting the estate of Hans Stanley in 1780. Inner Temple from 1755, Cambridge from 1757. He was deputy cofferer of the household, 1770–82, and a member of the Board of Trade and Plantations, 1780–82. He voted steadily in support of the North ministry in every crucial division to its end in late March, 1782; he had received his appointments from it and was also following the example of his benefactor, Hans Stanley. He voted against Shelburne's peace terms, supported the coalition, and voted for Fox's India Bill in 1783. In 1788 he opposed Pitt's Regency Bill. M.P. for Newport (Isle of Wight), 1768–80; Southampton Borough, 1780–84; Christchurch, 1788–96; Lostwithiel, 1796–1806.

Sloper, William Charles. born ca.1730

Of Twyford, near Winchester, Hampshire; oldest son of William Sloper (1709–89; of West Woodhay, near Hungerford, Berkshire; M.P.). In 1774 he married Amelia, daughter of Jonathan Shipley (*q.v.*). He was ensign in the army in 1753, captain in 1758. As aide to Prince Ferdinand at the Battle of Minden in 1759, he was one of those who conveyed to Lord George Sackville (later Germain) the orders to charge with the cavalry, orders which Sackville did not obey, and in 1760 he was a chief witness at the court-martial of Sackville (who he insinuated was in a frightened trauma). He was immediately promoted by George II, and retired as lieutenant general in 1773. In the House of Commons from 1780, he voted against the North ministry in all 5 of the crucial divisions recorded in February and March, 1782. He voted against Shelburne's peace terms, against Fox's India Bill in 1783, and for Pitt's proposals for reform of representation in Parliament in 1784, but he did not regularly thereafter support Pitt. He was a friend of the family of Lord Spencer and gave it electoral support. M.P. for St. Albans, 1780–90.

Small, John. 1726–96

Born at Strath Ardle, near Atholl, Perthshire, and served in the Scottish brigade in the Dutch service as ensign in 1747. He was lieutenant in 1756. He served under John Campbell (4th Earl of Loudon); under Amherst in Canada, 1757–59; and was at Martinique as captain in 1772. In 1775 he recruited the Scots in Nova Scotia, led a battalion of engineers against the Americans, and was present at Bunker Hill. He was lieutenant governor of Guernsey from 1793 and major general in 1794.

Smart, Christopher. 1722–71

Born at Shipbourne, near Tunbridge, Kent; son of Peter Smart (1687–1771; of an old north-country family; estate agent in Kent). He was schooled at Maidstone, Kent, at Cambridge (with financial help from the Duchess of Cleveland, who was impressed by his talents) from 1739; B.A., 1742; fellow from 1745; M.A., 1747. In 1750 he published an imitation of Horace under a pen name, and ca. 1754 he left Cambridge for a literary life in London. At about that time he published the *Hilliad*, a satire in epic form, and in 1756 a prose translation of Horace. Meanwhile he was living in poverty, unable to support his wife and children, who went to Ireland to live with relatives. Sometime before 1763 his mind, always on the edge of imbalance, failed him, and he was committed to a mental asylum. It may have been while there that he wrote *A Song to David*, published 1763–1765, 1819, and 1895. His later poems were less impressive and less widely read. He was released from the asylum, but soon confined again for unpaid debts, and died in his 49th year. Portrait, perhaps by Reynolds.

Smith, Abel. 1717–88

3d son of Abel Smith (of East Stoke, near Newark, Nottingham; banker). In 1756 he became head of the family bank and expanded it rapidly. He became associated with the 2d Duke of Manchester and with his help won a seat in the House of Commons in 1774. There he supported the North ministry (from which he received government war contracts from 1776) and voted with North in all 5 of the crucial divisions recorded in February and March, 1782. In 1784 he was compelled by the Clerke Act of 1782 to give up his contracts with the Treasury in order to retain his seat in Parliament. In 1783 he voted against Fox's India Bill and until 1788 supported Pitt. He made only one recorded speech in the House. M.P. for Aldborough, 1774–78; St. Ives, 1780–84; St. Germans, 1784–88.

Smith, Abel. 1748–79

Of Welford, Northamptonshire; 2d son of Abel Smith (*q.v.*). He died only 3 months after election to the House of Commons, and his only recorded vote during that time was against the North ministry with regard to the Carlisle peace commission to America, when he apparently voted in opposition to his father. M.P. for Nottingham Borough, October, 1778–January, 1779.

Smith, Adam. 1723–90

The only and posthumous son of Adam Smith (writer to the Signet and comptroller of customs at Kirkaldy, Fifeshire). University of Glasgow, 1737–38; Oxford from 1740. He spent 6 years at Oxford, returning to Scotland in 1746. He became professor of logic at Glasgow in 1751 and was professor of moral philosophy, 1752–64. He was a friend of David Hume. For his career see standard sources. In 1759 he published his *Theory of the Moral Sentiments*, which was applauded in the limited circles interested in the abstractions of ethics and which led to a visit to London in 1761. He traveled extensively on the Continent, 1763–66, as tutor to the young Duke of Buccleuch (Scottish). He then returned to Kirkaldy and worked for 10 years on *The Wealth of Nations*, which was published in 1776 and immediately made him a notable figure in intellectual circles. The book influenced economic thinking in Britain, America, and western Europe more profoundly than any other economic monograph for at least half a century. Both North and the younger Pitt echoed some of its conclusions and aphorisms, and in 1778 North appointed him commissioner of customs for Scotland, at £600 a year. He moved to Edinburgh, but he was also rector of Glasgow University in 1787.

Smith, Edward. ca.1705–62

Of Edmondthorpe, near Melton Mowbray, Leicestershire; oldest son of Rev. Roger Smith (of Husbands Bosworth, near Market Harborough, Leicestershire). Rugby from 1714, Cambridge from 1722. Throughout his career he was considered a Tory; he was overtly active on the Tory side in the 1754 elections, and was listed as Tory by Newcastle in 1761. There is no record of any speech or vote by him during his last 8 years in the House of Commons. M.P. for Leicestershire, 1734–62.

Smith (or Smyth), Jarrit. ca.1692–1783

Of Long Ashton, near Bristol, Somerset; only son of John Smith (of Bristol); created baronet in 1763. A Bristol attorney made affluent by marrying a fortune, he founded a Tory club in Bristol and was listed as Tory in 1761. He opposed Newcastle and Henry Fox from 1756, supported Bute and his peace preliminaries in 1762, and supported Grenville and general warrants in the Wilkes issues, 1763–64. "To please his constituents" he did not vote against repeal of the Stamp Act in 1766. In 1767 he voted against the Grafton ministry on Chatham's land tax and in 1768 voted for Savile's *Nullum Tempus* Bill. He did not stand for re-election in 1768. M.P. for Bristol, 1756–68.

Smith, John. ca.1727–75

Of Coombe Hay, near Bath, Somerset; oldest son of Robert Smith (of Foxcote, near Bath, and Stony Littleton, near Radstock, Somerset). Oxford from 1744. In 1757 he married Anne, daughter of Thomas Charles Tracy (5th Viscount Tracy, Irish). A west-country gentleman, he usually voted in opposition to the Grafton and North ministries. He voted against Chatham's land tax in 1767 and again against the Grafton ministry on the Wilkes issues in 1769, signing the Bath petition against the ministry. In October, 1775, very shortly before his death, he voted against approval of the address from the throne. M.P. for Bath, 1766–75.

Smith, John. d. 1797

Of Drapers' Hall, London; son of John Smith (of London). In 1773 he became clerk to the Company of Drapers and was solicitor for the East India Company, 1775–97. He was elected to Parliament "in the interest" of Edward Dering (or Deering) (*q.v.*) as a placeholder, and served only a few months until replaced by Michael Atkinson (1738–

95; M.P.). There is no evidence that he ever spoke or voted in the House of Commons. M.P. for New Romney, 1784.

Smith, John. 1754–1837

Born at Brighton, Sussex. He entered Woolwich Military Academy in 1768 and became lieutenant in 1771. He went to Canada on military service in 1773, was twice wounded, and then was captured at Fort St. John in 1775. He was exchanged in January, 1777, and served successively under Generals Percy, Howe, Clinton, and Cornwallis in America, 1777–81. He was present at the Brandywine, at Germantown, and at Monmouth, and was made a prisoner of war at the surrender of Cornwallis at Yorktown in October, 1781. He was soon put on parole and then exchanged. He was made captain in 1782 and major in 1784. He commanded the infantry at St. Vincent and at Trinidad, 1795–97, and served on the expedition against the Dutch in 1799. He was made major general in 1810 and lieutenant general in 1819. He was knighted in 1831, and just before his death he was made full general.

Smith, John Mansel. 1759–?

Of Chilton Ffoliat (or Ffolliat), near Hungerford, Wiltshire; only son of Richard Smith (*q.v.*). Harrow, to Cambridge in 1776. In 1780 his father purchased for him a seat in the House of Commons from Lord Verney. With his father he voted against the North ministry, including all 5 crucial divisions recorded in February and March, 1782. He spoke in behalf of Conway's motion to end the American war immediately, but in 1783 spoke and voted against Shelburne's peace terms. He supported Charles Fox and the coalition in 1783, voting for Fox's India Bill in November, 1783. He was not re-elected in 1784. M.P. for Wendover, 1780–84.

Smith, Joseph. 1682–1770

From the age of 18 he appears to have been settled in Venice, presumably first as clerk to a merchant firm and then as a merchant in his own right. In 1740 he was appointed resident consul in Venice, a post he held until 1760. He came known as "the merchant of Venice" and was admired for his skill and devotion in collecting rare paintings and coins, which he later sold to George III for £10,000. In 1729, in the flush of middle age, he produced an exact reproduction of the 1527 edition of *The Decameron*, which is now in the British Museum.

Smith, Joseph. ca.1732–90

He was ensign under Clive in the Carnatic in 1752 and captain in 1754. He fought at Madura in 1755 and commanded the garrison at Trichinopoly in 1757. He was at the reduction of Karikal in 1760, when he was made major. He led troops against Hyder Ali, 1766–68, and in 1773, as major general, captured Tanjore. "He served in India with an unblemished reputation"—a fact which in itself made him historically distinguished; "his fortune was not enlarged by rapine," according to his obituary in the *Gentleman's Magazine*.

Smith, Richard. 1734–1803

Of Chilton Ffoliat (or Ffolliat), near Hungerford, Wiltshire; son of John Smith (of London). He was ensign in the Bengal army in 1752, lieutenant in 1753, captain in 1756, colonel in 1764, and brigadier general in 1768. In 1770 he retired from military service and returned to England "with a fortune." He was eager to secure a seat in the House of Commons and set about it immediately: his attempts at the open purchase of a seat for New Shoreham in 1770 violated the traditional discretions of corruption and caused a minor scandal. In 1774 he won the election, but his victory was declared void, and he was prosecuted for bribery, fined 1,000 marks, and sentenced to 6 months' imprisonment. In 1776, again at large, he again gained election for Hindon, and was again unseated by the House in 1777. In 1780, his standing having been enhanced by service that year as sheriff of Berkshire, he "bought" by more accepted methods (a private deal with the "owner," Lord Verney) the 2 seats for Wendover and installed himself in one of them and his son in the other. That gentlemanly deal with Lord Verney was not found improper by the members of the House, and he immediately began a vigorous opposition to the North ministry. In February and March, 1782, he voted against North in all 5 of the crucial recorded divisions. He became chairman of the select committee to study and report on the situation in India and the East India Company. His report was repeatedly attacked by George Johnstone as partial to the company, and for a year the kettle was defending itself against the pot. To lessen public criticism of his position, he sold all his shares in the East India Company and refused to disclose to interested members of the House the nature of his later committee reports before they had been formally presented in Parliament. In 1783 he opposed a suspension by the House of its earlier order recalling Sir Elijah Impey for accepting a position in violation of an act of Parliament. In February, 1783, he voted against Shelburne's peace terms. On March 13, 1783, he urged the government to take immediate action to save the East India Company from bankruptcy and its affairs in India from chaos. In June, 1783, he supported the motion to provide funds to give the Prince of Wales a separate establishment, arguing that the heir to the throne should be enabled to live with a dignity comparable to that displayed by some wealthy peers. In November, 1783, he spoke in strong support of Fox's India Bill. In 1784, deeply in debt from gambling, he sold the estate at Chilton Ffoliat, which he had bought in 1770, and fled to the Continent to escape his creditors. He had considerable ability and obviously great energy, though he was thought to be haughty and insolent. He returned to sit again in Parliament from 1790. M.P. for Hindon, 1774–75 and 1776–77; Wendover, 1780–84; Wareham, 1790–96.

Smith, Robert. 1752–1838

Of Bulcot, near Bingham, Nottinghamshire; 3d son of Abel Smith (1717–88) (*q.v.*); brother of Abel Smith (1748–79) (*q.v.*); brother of Samuel Smith (1754–1834) (*q.v.*); in 1796 created Baron Carrington (Irish); in 1797 created Baron Carrington of Upton, Nottinghamshire. He became a founding partner of the banking house of Smith and Payne and a man of excellent financial reputation. In the House of Commons from 1779, he opposed the North ministry in every crucial division during February and March, 1782, and in February, 1783, voted for Shelburne's peace terms. On April 25, 1783, he complained that his bank had not been given participation in the new government loan and claimed that the ministry could have secured the loan on better terms had it not played favorites among the bankers. He voted against Fox's India Bill and from 1784 supported Pitt, whose personal friend he had become. His support was ultimately rewarded with an Irish, and then an English, peerage. He was treasurer of the Levant Company from 1790; president of the Board of Agriculture, 1800–1803; captain of Deal Castle, 1802–38; and president of the London Institution, 1812–27. He was a fellow of the Royal Academy and an honorary D.C.L. M.P. for Nottingham Borough, 1779–97.

Smith, Samuel. 1754–1834

Of Wilford, near Nottingham; 4th son of Abel Smith (1717–88) (*q.v.*); brother of Robert Smith (*q.v.*), and Abel Smith (1748–79) (*q.v.*). He became a partner in the family bank and succeeded his father in the seat for St. Germans in the House of Commons, where he sat continuously, 1788–1832, and in general supported the Pitt ministries. M.P. for St. Germans, 1788–90; Leicester Borough, 1790–1818; Midhurst, 1818–20; Wendover, 1820–32.

Smith, Samuel. 1755–93

Of Cherington Park, near Stroud, Gloucestershire, and Putney, Surrey; oldest son of Samuel William Smith of London; related to Richard Smith (*q.v.*). He became a tea merchant and was a director of the East India Company, 1783–86. He entered the House of Commons in 1780 and supported the North ministry to its fall, voting with it in all 5 of the crucial divisions recorded during February and March, 1782. He voted against Shelburne's peace terms and spoke vigorously against Fox's India Bill in 1783, supporting Lawrence Sulivan's criticisms of it and protesting that Fox had made deliberate misrepresentations and that the House had not allowed the directors of the company a fair hearing. He later opposed Pitt. M.P. for Ilchester, 1780–84; Worcester City, 1784–90; Ludgershall, 1791–93.

Smith, Thomas Assheton. See **Thomas Assheton-Smith**

Smithson, Hugh Percy and **Hugh.** See **Hugh Percy.** 1715–86 and **Hugh Percy.** 1742–1817

Smith-Stanley, James. See **James Stanley** (later **Smith-Stanley**)

Smith-Stanley, Thomas. ca.1753–79

2d son of James Stanley (later Smith-Stanley) (*q.v.*); brother of Edward Stanley (*q.v.*); grandson of Edward Stanley (11th Earl of Derby). Eton, 1764–70; Cambridge from 1771. He entered the military service as cornet of horse in 1775 and became captain of dragoons in 1776 and major in 1777. He was briefly a member of the House of

Commons and died on active military service in Jamaica. M.P. for Lancashire, 1776–79.

Smollett, Tobias George. 1721–71

Born in Cardross on Clyde, Dumbartonshire; son of Archibald Smollett (of Leven Bank, Cardross; a cultivated but weak and petulant Scot); grandson of Sir James Smollett (sometime provost of Dumbarton). Glasgow University from 1736. In 1739, aged 17, he went to London with a play in his pocket with which he hoped to make his fortune. Finding no takers, he became a surgeon's assistant and was a surgeon with the West Indies squadron, 1741–43. On his return he established himself in near penury in Downing Street. He published *Roderick Random* in 1748, *Peregrine Pickle* in 1751, and *Humphrey Clinker* in 1771; though never wealthy, he was from that time far from penurious. In 1757 he began publishing, in parts, his *History of England*. In 1759 or 1760 (authorities differ) he was briefly imprisoned for libel, and was again imprisoned in 1769, after which he left England permanently and died near Leghorn, Italy. He was a literary caricaturist of great and ruthless power, with profound moral ardor but only occasionally equally deep human sympathy.

Smyth, John. 1748–1811

Of Heath Hall, near Pontrefact, Yorkshire; only son of John Smyth (of Heath Hall). Westminster until 1776, Cambridge. In 1778 he married Georgiana, daughter of Augustus Henry Fitzroy (*q.v.*). He was a Yorkshire country gentleman who was brought into national politics primarily through his support of Wyvill's Yorkshire Association and its petitions. From his election to the House of Commons in 1783, he supported the Pitt ministry. He was a member of the Admiralty Board, 1791–94; a member of the Treasury Board, 1794–1802; privy councillor from 1802; master of the mint, 1802–1804; member of the Board of Trade, 1783–1807. M.P. for Pontrefact, 1783–1807.

Smyth, Robert. 1744–1802

Of Berechurch Hall, near Colchester, Essex; oldest son of Rev. Robert Smyth (vicar of Woolavington, Sussex); in 1765 succeeded his cousin Sir Trafford Smyth (ca.1720–65; of Upton, near London) as 5th baronet. Westminster, to Cambridge in 1762. He became a banker in

Paris and then returned to London to acquire a country estate and on that foundation secure membership in Parliament. He achieved both aims in 1774. Though Horace Walpole said that in the House of Commons he "generally voted with the court," he voted with the opposition on the Wilkes issues in 1775, after 1779 generally opposed the North ministry, and in February and March, 1782, voted against it on all 5 recorded crucial motions. He was a strong supporter of the reform of Parliament and headed the Essex Association of the Wyvill movement in 1780. He did not vote on Shelburne's peace terms and voted against Fox's India Bill in 1783. In 1784 he supported Pitt and received £2,000 from secret-service funds. M.P. for Cardigan boroughs, 1774–75; Colchester, 1780–90.

Smythe, Philip. 1715–87

In 1724 succeeded his father, Endymion Smythe, as 4th Viscount Strangford (Irish). In 1733, on recommendation of Archbishop Boulter, he was granted a pension of £200 a year to support his studies at Trinity College, Dublin. There he became B.A. in 1736 and L.L.D. in 1751. He took orders in 1742, became rector of a living in County Cork, and was prebendary of Cork Cathedral, 1743–52. He was dean of Derry, 1752–69, and archdeacon of Derry, 1769–74. In 1784 the Irish House of Lords disqualified him from sitting in that or any future Irish Parliament for having tried to obtain a bribe of £200 for his vote in that House.

Smythe, Sydney Stafford. 1705–78

Born in London, the son of Henry Smythe (of Old Bounds, Bidborough, near Tunbridge Wells, Kent); knighted in 1750. Westminster, to Cambridge in 1721; B.A., 1724; Inner Temple from 1724; barrister in 1728; bencher from 1747. He was steward of the king's palace at Westminster from 1740; king's counsel from 1747; puisne baron of the exchequer, 1750–77; commissioner of the great seal, 1756–57, and in January, 1771 (with Henry Bathurst and Sir Richard Aston after the sudden death of Charles Yorke). In 1777 he was made privy councillor and given a pension of £2,400 a year. He was a supporter and placeholder of the North ministry; there is no record that during his 3 years in the House of Commons he ever addressed the House. M.P. for East Grinstead, 1747–50.

Solway, 1st Earl. See **Charles Douglas.** ca.1698–1778

Somerset, Henry. 1744–1803

In 1756 succeeded his father, Charles Noel Somerset (1709–56; M.P.), as 5th Duke of Beaufort. Oxford from 1760; D.C.L., 1763. In 1766 he married Elizabeth, daughter of Admiral Edward Boscawen (1711–61) and sister of George Evelyn Boscawen (3d Viscount Falmouth). He was grand master of English Freemasons, 1767–72; master of horse to the queen, 1768–70; lord lieutenant of Monmouthshire, 1771–1803; lord lieutenant of Brecknockshire, 1787–1803; lord lieutenant of Leicestershire, 1787–99. He was made Knight of the Garter in 1786, and secured the barony of Botetourt in 1803. In politics he was considered a Tory; in general he supported the North ministry.

Somerset, 9th Duke. See **Edward Seymour**

Somerville, James. 1698–1765

Of Drum, near Edinburgh; in 1709 succeeded his father, James Somerville (1674–1709), as 12th Lord Somerville (Scottish), and was confirmed in that title in 1723. He married (1) in 1724 Anne, widow of Edward Rolt (d. 1722; of Sacombe, Hertfordshire) and sister-in-law of Edward Baynton-Rolt (*q.v.*), and (2) in 1736 Frances, "a woman of Wealth," widow of Peter Curgenoun (an East Indies merchant). He was a representative Scottish peer, 1741–47, and lord of the Scottish police, 1744–65—a strong supporter of the Hanoverian cause in 1745. Sir James Bland Burgess said that he was "warm and hasty, beyond measure crazy after matrimonial alliances," which he achieved with only moderate success.

Somerville, James. 1727–96

Of Drum, near Edinburgh; in 1765 succeeded his father, James Somerville (1698–1765) (*q.v.*), as 13th Lord Somerville (Scottish). He studied at Westminster, 1742–43, and at Caen, 1744–45. He was cornet in the horse guards in 1743, lieutenant in 1744, aide to Sir John Cope at Preston Pans in 1745, and aide to General Hawley at Falkirk and Culloden in 1746. He was captain in 1751 and major general in 1761. He served under Granby in Germany, 1760–63, and then retired from the military. He was a Scottish representative peer, 1793–96.

Sommers (or Somers), 1st Baron and 1st Earl. See **Charles Cocks** and **John Sommers Cocks**

Sondes, 1st and 2d Barons. See **Lewis Thomas Watson.** 1728–95 and **Lewis Thomas Watson.** 1754–1806

Southampton, 1st Baron. See **Charles Fitzroy**

Southwell, Edward. 1738–77

Of Henbury, near Bristol, Gloucestershire; only son of Edward Southwell (of King's Weston, near Bristol, Gloucestershire); nephew of Thomas Watson-Wentworth (3d Earl of Rockingham); in 1776 succeeded as 20th Baron DeClifford. Westminster from 1748, Cambridge from 1754. In 1761 he was listed as a Tory, but he supported Newcastle against Bute in 1762, voted against Grenville and general warrants in 1764, voted against Chatham's land tax in 1767, voted against unseating Wilkes in 1770, voted against the North ministry and for extension of Grenville's Disputed Elections Act in 1774, and voted against the North ministry on Wilkes issues in 1775. As a peer he continued to oppose the North ministry and strengthened his connection with the Rockingham Whigs. There is no evidence that he ever addressed the House of Commons. M.P. for Bridgwater, 1761–63; Gloucestershire, 1763–76.

Southwell, Thomas George. 1721–80

In 1766 succeeded his father, Thomas Southwell (1698–1766), as 3d Baron Southwell (Irish); in 1776 created Viscount Southwell (Irish). Lincoln's Inn from 1736, Oxford from 1739. He was a member of the Irish Parliament, 1747–66; constable of Limerick Castle, 1749–80; grand master of Irish Freemasons, 1753–57; and governor of County Limerick, 1769–80.

Sparrow, Robert. 1741–1822

Of Worlingham, near Beccles, Suffolk; oldest son of Robert Sparrow (of Worlingham). Cambridge and Middle Temple from 1759. In 1771 he married (1) Mary, sister of Robert Bernard (*q.v.*). He opposed the Bedford party and voted against the North ministry on Wilkes issues in 1775. There is no evidence that he addressed the

House of Commons in his single year in the House. He was sheriff of Suffolk, 1777–78. M.P. for Bedford Borough, 1774–75.

Spence, Joseph. 1699–1768

Born at Kingsclere, near Basingstoke, Hampshire, the son of Joseph Spence (rector of Winnall, near Winchester, Hampshire). Eton; Winchester from 1715; and Oxford from 1717; B.A., 1724; M.A., 1727. He took orders in 1724 and became a fellow at Oxford. He was professor of poetry at Oxford, 1728–38; Regius professor of history from 1742; and special tutor to the Earl of Lincoln in 1739. In 1747 he published *Polymetis*, a treatise on classical mythology. He was a friend of Alexander Pope and took notes on Pope's conversations. Samuel Johnson praised his candor and his judgment but thought his mind not powerful and his learning not great. Johnson nevertheless made use of his literary anecdotes in his *Lives*. The anecdotes were published on their own account in 1820. *DNB* recorded him as "amiable and high-principled."

Spencer, Charles. 1740–1820

Of Wheatfield, near Thame, Oxfordshire; 2d son of Charles Spencer (5th Earl of Sunderland and 3d Duke of Marlborough); known as Lord Charles Spencer. Eton, 1747–54; Oxford, 1756–59; studied in Holland, 1759–60. In 1762 he married Mary, daughter of Vere Beauclerk (1st Baron Vere). He became a member of the Bedford junto, supported Bute's ministry, and made his first speech in the House of Commons when he seconded the motion to approve the address from the throne in 1762. He voted against Grenville and general warrants in 1764 and against repeal of the Stamp Act in 1766. In 1774 he voted, against the North ministry, for extension of Grenville's Disputed Elections Act. He was a member of the Admiralty Board from 1768, but resigned from it in 1778, saying that he would no longer serve with the Earl of Sandwich as first lord. The king thereupon wrote to North that Lord Charles Spencer "ought to be promised an Employment of £1,500 a year" (June 11, 1778). He opposed the Dunning resolution of April 6, 1780, and voted with the North ministry in all 5 of the crucial divisions recorded in February and March, 1782. He took office under Rockingham as "a moderate Whig" in 1782, as vice treasurer of Ireland. He voted for Shelburne's peace terms in February, 1783, but remained in office and voted for Fox's India Bill in 1783. On January 16, 1784, he moved that the House declare the Pitt ministry contrary to constitutional principles "and injurious to the interests of His Majesty and the people" and won his motion by 21 votes. He supported Fox against Pitt, 1784–90. He was verdurer of Wychewood Forest, outranger of Windsor Forest, and surveyor of the king's gardens and waters, 1762–63; comptroller of the king's household, 1763–65; joint postmaster general, 1801–1806; and master of the mint from 1806. M.P. for Oxfordshire, 1761–90 and 1796–1801.

Spencer, George. 1739–1817

Styled Marquess of Blandford until 1758, when he succeeded his father, Charles Spencer (1706–58), as 4th Duke of Marlborough; older brother of Charles Spencer (*q.v.*). Eton. In 1762 he married Caroline, daughter of John Russell (1710–71) (*q.v.*). He was ensign in the army in 1755 and captain of the 20th Foot in 1756, but left the army in 1758. He was ranger of Wychewood Forest, 1758–62; lord lieutenant of Oxfordshire, 1760–1817; lord chamberlain, 1762–63; privy councillor from 1762; lord privy seal, 1763–65; D.C.L. of Oxford and Knight of the Garter in 1771; master of Trinity House, 1768–70; and fellow of the Royal Society from 1786. He opposed repeal of the Stamp Act with Grenville in 1766 but thereafter took little part in court and London politics, though he was long a leader of the Whigs in Oxfordshire. Curiously, in 1762 Bute listed him as Tory. In 1783 he supported Fox's India Bill but later became an adherent of Pitt. He was "ceremonious, humane and hospitable," adjectives which suggest that his contemporaries preferred to avoid describing his intellectual powers.

Spencer, George John. 1758–1834

Of Althorpe Park, near Northampton, and Brington, Northamptonshire; styled Viscount Althorpe from 1765; in 1783 he succeeded his father, John Spencer (*q.v.*), as 2d Earl Spencer of Althorpe; brother-in-law of the 5th Duke of Devonshire, and also connected with the Marquess of Rockingham. Harrow, 1770–75; Cambridge from 1776; M.A., 1778; D.C.L. of Oxford, 1794. He made the grand tour, 1778–80. In 1781 he married Lavinia, daughter of Charles Bingham (*q.v.*). He became a fellow of the Royal Society in 1780. Of a Whig family, he was prominent in the final attacks on the North ministry, 1781–82, and then served on the Treasury Board with Rockingham in 1782 but resigned with Fox after Rockingham's death. He voted against Shelburne's peace terms and supported the coalition in 1783 but went over to Pitt with Portland in 1784. He was privy councillor and ambassador to Vienna in 1794; first lord of the admiralty, 1794–1801; home secretary, 1806–1807. He was high steward of St. Albans, 1783–1807; mayor of St. Albans in 1790; colonel of yeomanry in 1794; Knight of the Garter in 1799. A trustee of the British Museum for 40 years, he was a notable book collector, and his collection of prints was said to be the finest in Europe in his time. M.P. for Northampton Borough, 1780–82; Surrey, 1782–83.

Spencer, John. 1734–83

Of Althorp Park, near Northampton, and Brington, Northamptonshire and Wimbleton Park, Surrey; oldest son of John Spencer (1708–46; of Althorp); grandson of Charles Spencer (1674–1722; 3d Earl of Sunderland and 5th Baron Spencer); nephew of Charles Spencer (1706–58; 3d Duke of Marlborough); in 1761 created Viscount Spencer; in 1765 created Earl Spencer. Grand tour ca. 1754. In 1762 he went with Newcastle into opposition, and on the urging of Newcastle was made a peer by the Rockingham ministry in 1765. He was opposed to Bute's peace preliminaries in 1762 and the cider tax in 1763. He supported the Marlborough interests first and the Chatham ministry second, 1766–70. In the House of Lords he generally voted against the North ministry in major divisions, recording dissent against the Quebec Governing Act in 1775 and against approval of the address from the throne in October, 1775; he supported Chatham's bill to conciliate the colonies in 1775. In 1779 he protested the refusal of the House of Lords to ask the king to dismiss Sandwich from the Admiralty. He was high steward of St. Albans, 1772–83. In 1774 his daughter Georgiana (1757–1806) married William Cavendish (5th Duke of Devonshire) and became a leading figure in Whig political society, and at fashionable gaming tables. M.P. for Warwick Borough, 1756–61.

Spencer, Robert. 1747–1831

3d son of Charles Spencer (1706–58; 3d Duke of Marlborough); brother of George Spencer (*q.v.*) and Charles Spencer (*q.v.*). Oxford, 1762–65; grand tour, 1766–68. He entered the House of Commons in

1768 as a supporter of the Marlborough interests and a Bedford Whig, but he attended irregularly and made only 2 reported speeches in the House. He supported the North ministry through 1780, opposing Dunning's resolutions in April, 1780, and served on the Board of Trade and Plantations, 1770–81. But he had become a close friend of Charles Fox, and in January, 1781, he joined the opposition. In February and March, 1782, he voted against the North ministry in all 5 of the crucial recorded divisions. He then joined the Rockingham ministry as joint vice treasurer of Ireland and a member of the Privy Council; he followed Fox into opposition to Shelburne upon the death of Rockingham in July, 1782; voted against Shelburne's peace terms and for Fox's India Bill in 1783; and in 1784 won re-election as a Foxite. He was at one time so nearly bankrupt that he dealt faro at Brooks Club for £5 an hour. He was surveyor general of woods and forests, 1806–1807. M.P. for Woodstock, 1768–71; Oxford City, 1771–90; Wareham, 1790–99; Tavistock, 1802–1807 and 1817–18; Woodstock, 1818–20.

Spencer-Stanhope, Walter. 1749–1822

Only surviving son of Walter Stanhope (of Cannon Hall, near Barnsley, and Horsforth Hall, near Leeds, Yorkshire; merchant of Leeds); added the surname Spencer upon inheriting from his uncle John Spencer in 1775. Oxford, 1766–69; grand tour, 1769–70. He was elected to Parliament with the support of Sir James Lowther (later 1st Earl of Lonsdale) in 1775, and voted steadily against the North ministry, addressing the House of Commons at least 35 times between 1775 and 1780. He voted against approving the address from the throne in October, 1775; condemned North's peace terms in 1778 as so watered down that they were futile; and voted for Dunning's resolution of April, 1780. He supported the Yorkshire petitions and told the House that they were widely supported by public opinion. In February and March, 1782, he voted against the North ministry in all 5 crucial recorded divisions. In February, 1783, he voted for Shelburne's peace terms, opposed the coalition and Fox's India Bill in November, 1783, and from 1784 supported Pitt's reform proposals. M.P. for Carlisle, 1775–80; Haslemere, 1780–84; Kingston-on-Hull, 1784–90; Cockermouth, 1800–1802; Carlisle, 1802–12.

Spicer, William. ca.1735–88

Of Weare Park, near Exeter, Devonshire; oldest son of Edward Spicer (of Exeter). He began his career as a glovemaker; was sheriff of Devonshire, 1764–65; and was elected as a stopgap to the House of Commons. During his few months in the House he left no record of any speech, vote, or impression. M.P. for Exeter, 1767–68.

Spode, Josiah. 1754–1827

Son of Josiah Spode (1733–97; potter of Stoke-on-Trent). He adopted his father's trade. At 19 he married a Miss Barker, the daughter of a pottery manufacturer, and, with Wedgwood, became the leading china manufacturer of his time. He improved the quality of English bone paste and opened a large warehouse in London to market his manufactures. He developed the willow pattern and in 1808 became pottery maker to the king. He built himself a fine mansion at Penkoll, Staffordshire, and left a large fortune.

Spry, Richard. 1715–75

2d son of George Spry (1684–1730; of Place House, Cornwall). He entered the navy in 1733. Serving against Spain, 1744–45, he was captured, but was soon exchanged; he served under Boscawen against the French at Pondichéry and was at Louisburg in 1758. In 1767 he joined with Rodney, Saunders, and others in a petition to the crown for grants of land on the island of St. John in maritime Canada, and in time he secured a grant there. He became rear admiral in 1770, commanded a squadron in the Channel in 1772, and was knighted in 1773.

Squire, Samuel. 1713–66

Son of Thomas Squire (1687–1761; apothecary of Warminster, near Trowbridge, Wiltshire). In 1730 he secured a fellowship to Cambridge; B.A., 1734; M.A., 1737. He curried favor with Newcastle and Chesterfield and in 1760 obtained a deanery at Bristol. In 1761 he became bishop of St. Davids and held that post until his death. While at Cambridge he fostered the study of Anglo-Saxon (an act of sadism which may account for his unpopularity there). He was a fellow of the Royal Society from 1746 and of the Society of Arts from 1747 and published historical essays. He was considered servile to the powers and to miss no opportunity to advance himself.

Stafford, 1st and 2d Marquesses. See **Granville Leveson-Gower** and **George Granville Leveson-Gower**

Stair, 4th, 5th and 6th Earls. See **William Dalrymple-Crichton.** **John Dalrymple.** 1720–89 and **John Dalrymple.** 1749–1821

Stamford, 4th and 5th Earls. See **Harry Grey** and **George Harry Grey**

Standert, Frederick. ca.1705–85

Of Greenwich, Kent. Merchant Taylors' School, 1717–19. In 1735 he married Mary, daughter of Sir Harcourt Master (alderman of London). Until at least 1780 he conducted a merchant business in St. Martin's Lane. He was elected to the House of Commons "in the interest" of his son-in-law Robert Clayton (*q.v.*) and with him voted regularly in opposition to the North ministry, opposing the unseating of Wilkes in 1770, opposing declaring printers Wheble and Thompson in contempt in 1771, and opposing approval of the address from the throne in October, 1775. There is no record that he ever addressed the House. M.P. for Bletchingley, 1769–80.

Standish, Frank. ca.1746–1812

Of Duxbury, near Chorley, Lancashire; oldest son of Thomas Standish; in 1756 succeeded his grandfather Sir Thomas Standish (sheriff of Lancashire, 1711–12) as 3d baronet. Westminster, to Oxford in 1763. He was sheriff of Lancashire, 1782–83. He was elected to the House of Commons in 1768 in opposition to Lord Strange, but was unseated on petition the same year, and left no mark there. M.P. for Preston, 1768.

Stanhope, Charles. 1753–1816

Styled Lord Mahon from 1763; in 1786 succeeded his father, Philip Stanhope (1714–86), as 3d Earl of Stanhope; nephew of Thomas Hamilton (7th Earl of Haddington, Scottish). Eton, 1761–63; studied science in Geneva, 1764–74. He served as major of dragoons in the

Swiss army, 1771–73. He married (1) in 1774 Hester, oldest daughter of William Pitt (1st Earl of Chatham), and (2) in 1781 Louisa, daughter of Henry Grenville (1717–84; M.P.). He became a fellow of the Royal Society in 1772. In 1774 he stood unsuccessfully for Parliament as a Wilkite candidate for Westminster, but with Shelburne's support he gained a seat in 1780. He opposed the North ministry and continuation of the war in America and in 1781 urged an immediate end to both. In February and March, 1782, he voted against the North ministry in every major recorded division. He advocated reform of Parliament and was active in the petition movement in Kent and Buckinghamshire. In February, 1783, he voted for Shelburne's peace terms, opposed the coalition, and he ardently supported Pitt's reform measures in 1783 and again in 1785. He supported Pitt's Regency Bill in 1788 but broke with Pitt over the French Revolution and in 1794 moved to recognize the French Republic. A voluble and vehement speaker, he addressed the House of Commons more than 90 times in less than 6 years, usually at length. He had scientific talent and in 1777 invented 2 calculating machines, a microscopic lens, and in 1805 a process of stereotype which until very recently was used by Oxford University Press. He experimented in printing and electrotyping and in musical tones and also advocated a rapid development of England's canals. Regarded in his day as a slightly mad radical, he was certainly an eccentric; he disinherited all his children on principle. He was tall, lank, bald, pale, and impetuous in thought and action but also learned, eloquent, artistic, scientific, musical, and something of a genius. M.P. for Chipping Wycombe, 1780–86.

Stanhope, Charles. 1753–1829

Styled Viscount Petersham from 1757; in 1779 succeeded his father, William Stanhope (1719–79) (*q.v.*), as 3d Earl of Harrington. He was a cousin of the Duke of Grafton. Eton, 1767–69. In 1769 he entered the army as ensign and was captain in 1773, lieutenant colonel in 1777, colonel in 1782, major general in 1793, lieutenant general in 1798, and general in 1803. He served in Canada in 1776, was aide to Burgoyne and was made prisoner of war at Saratoga in October, 1777. Exchanged, he raised and commanded the 85th Foot in Jamaica, 1779–82, and was aide to the king, 1782–83. He was in command of British troops in Ireland, 1805–12, and was governor of Windsor

Castle, 1812–29. His election to the House of Commons in 1774 was sponsored by the Bedford clique. Though considered a Whig, he does not appear in the opposition lists in any important division, 1774–79 (partly, at least, owing to his military service and captivity overseas). In 1779 he voted with the North ministry against the motion to censure the Earl of Sandwich. As a Bedford adherent he presumably supported North when not on active military service; his office-holding and promotions ended for a time when the North ministry fell in March, 1782, and did not begin again for a decade. In the House of Lords from 1779, he voted for Fox's India Bill in 1783 and for Pitt's Regency Bill in 1788. He was made a member of the Privy Council in 1798, and was ambassador to Vienna and Berlin, 1805–1806. He was a fellow of the Society of Arts from 1787. His domestic life was praised in contrast with that of his father, and he is said to have been greatly beloved by his officers and men. M.P. for Thetford, 1774; Westminster, 1776–79.

Stanhope, Henry Fitzroy. 1754–1828

2d son of William Stanhope (1719–79) (*q.v.*); brother of Charles Stanhope (1753–1829) (*q.v.*). Eton, 1767–70. He entered the army as cornet in 1772. He was captain in 1776, commanded troops in Tobago in 1781, was secretary to the master general of ordnance in 1782, was colonel in 1794, and retired in 1794. During his 2 years in the House of Commons he voted against the North ministry in all 5 of the crucial divisions recorded in February and March, 1782. He supported Fox against Shelburne in 1782 and voted against Shelburne's peace terms and for Fox's India Bill in 1783. M.P. for Bramber, 1782–84.

Stanhope, Lovell. 1720–83

Of Winchester, Hampshire; 4th son of Rev. Michael Stanhope (canon of St. Paul's and Windsor; cousin of the 4th Earl of Chesterfield). Lincoln's Inn from 1743, barrister in 1747. He was law clerk to the secretaries of state, 1747–74; agent for Jamaica, 1757–63; gentleman usher to the queen from 1761; and undersecretary of state, 1764–65. From 1770 he supported the North ministry, and in 1771 he received a pension of £564 a year; in 1774 an annual further £100 from secret-service funds was added. He was clerk comptroller of the

Green Cloth, 1780–82, during which time he opposed the Dunning resolution of April 6, 1780, and voted with the North ministry in all 5 of the crucial divisions recorded in February and March, 1782. There is no evidence that he ever addressed the House of Commons. M.P. for Winchester, 1774–83.

Stanhope, Philip. 1714–86

Styled Viscount Mahon from 1718; in 1721 succeeded his father, James Stanhope (1673–1721), as 2d Earl Stanhope. He was educated at Utrecht and Geneva, and in 1735 became a fellow of the Royal Society at age 21. A cousin and great admirer of the elder Pitt, in the House of Lords he was a steady opponent of the policies and measures of the North ministry until 1778, after which time he either relaxed in discouragement or gave up opposition because of poor health. He recorded dissents against (1) the address from the throne in November, 1774, (2) the "careless facility" of the ministry's attitude toward colonial problems in 1774, (3) the New England Restraining Act in 1775, (5) the colonial policy in the address from the throne in October, 1775, and (6) the continuance of the ministry's American policy and measures in December, 1778. George Macartney called him "a queer little man ... a furious patriot."

Stanhope, Philip. 1732–68

Born in Holland, the illegitimate son of Philip Dormer Stanhope (1699–1773; 4th Earl of Chesterfield). Westminster, 1743–46; grand tour, 1746–51. He married, secretly and against his father's wishes, Eugenia Peters, illegitimate daughter of "one Domville of Ireland" (Namier). He served in minor diplomatic posts on the Continent until his early death in 1768, in his 36th year. He was resident at Hamburg, 1757–63; envoy to the Imperial Diet in 1763; and envoy to Saxony, 1764–68. He secured a seat in the House of Commons in 1754, through the heavy pressure placed upon Pelham and Newcastle by his father, but his first speech in the House of Commons, on November 13, 1755, was by general agreement "very bad"; indeed, he broke down completely. His election in 1761 cost his father £2,000, and in 1765 he "sold" his seat, having left no mark upon the House except the memory of his initial elocutionary disaster. M.P. for Liskeard, 1754–61; St. Germans, 1761–65.

Stanhope, Philip Dormer. 1699–1773

In 1726 succeeded his father, Philip Stanhope, as 4th Earl of Chesterfield. Cambridge from 1712. He was elected to the House of Commons when under 21 years of age. He was captain of the yeomen of
the guard when 19, 1723–25; and was privy councillor at the age of 33
in 1727. He was lord steward, 1730–33; Knight of the Garter in 1730;
and ambassador to The Hague, 1728–32, at the age of 34. He opposed
the ministry of Robert Walpole and in 1733 offended George II by
marrying the Countess of Walsingham, "with £50,000 and £3,000
a year," the illegitimate daughter of George I. His previously extremely rapid advancement at court thereupon ceased for a decade.
He was secretary of state, northern department, 1746–48. In the 1760's,
though his own active political career was waning, he became a strong
opponent of coercion and punitive legislation against the American
colonists. He urged the creation of a third secretary of state for the
colonies and felt that if greater sympathy with colonial problems and
emotions was not shown by government the colonies would soon be
lost to Britain. He was a notable man of fashion, a skilled courtier, and
the author of the famous letters to his illegitimate son. He was an
excellent Latin scholar and a master of the French language, French
manners, and French morals. He had keen perceptions and great
political insight but lacked loftiness of mind and character, as well as
the forcefulness that sometimes supports disinterested principle.
C. R. L. Fletcher concluded that "he set a bad example for his age";
it would be more fair to say that he was an aristocratic mirror of the
weaknesses of his age as well as of its strengths. He was professionally
expedient, and Horace Walpole commented that "his speeches were
fine, but as much labored as his extempore sayings." Portrait by Hoare.
M.P. for St. Germans, 1715–22; Lostwithiel, 1722–23.

Stanhope, Walter Spencer. See Walter Spencer-Stanhope

Stanhope, William. 1702–72

Of Eythrope, near Aylesbury, Buckinghamshire; 2d son of Philip
Stanhope (3d Earl of Chesterfield); younger brother of Philip Dormer Stanhope (q.v.); grandson of George Savile (1633–95; 1st Marquess of Halifax). He inherited large estates from the Dormer family
and an income of £8,000 a year, and in 1725 was made Knight of the

Bath. His third marriage, to the daughter of Sir Ambrose Crowley (M.P.; alderman of London; wealthy Durham ironmaster) added to his wealth. He was a founder of Whites club and spent much time there. He frequently visited Italy and in 1758 brought to England an extensive collection of paintings he had purchased there. He was little interested in politics and when present in the House of Commons usually voted with his brother. He voted against Grenville on the Wilkes issues in 1763 and against general warrants in 1764. In 1765 he again went to the Continent and took no further recorded part in Parliament. He died at Dijon. M.P. for Lostwithiel, 1727; Buckinghamshire, 1727–41 and 1747–68.

Stanhope, William. 1719–79

Styled Viscount Petersham from 1742; in 1756 succeeded his father, William Temple Stanhope (ca.1683–1756; M.P.; general), as 2d Earl of Harrington. Probably at Eton from 1732. In 1756 he married Caroline, oldest daughter of Charles Fitzroy (2d Duke of Grafton). He was ensign in the 10th Foot in 1738, colonel at Fontenoy in 1745, major general in 1755, lieutenant general in 1758, and general in 1770. He did nothing of great distinction in military affairs and even less in politics, and was known from his peculiar gait as "Peter Shambler." He appears to have supported, without unduly exerting himself, the successive Whig ministries under George II. The *Royal Register* for 1778 called him "a nobleman who sacrifices all appearance of decency and good morals, neglecting every domestic duty, every public concern, for the lowest amusements of the lowest brothels." Others considered him, sometimes with a note that seemed envious, as "of quite exceptional immorality." M.P. for Aylesbury, 1741–47; Bury St. Edmunds, 1747–56.

Stanley, Edward. 1752–1834

Oldest son of James Stanley (later Smith-Stanley) (*q.v.*); in 1776 succeeded his grandfather as 12th Earl of Derby; brother of Thomas Smith Stanley (*q.v.*). Eton from 1764, Cambridge from 1771. He married (1) Elizabeth, daughter of James Hamilton (6th Duke of Hamilton, Scottish), and (2) in 1797 Elizabeth Farren, actress and his mistress. He was a strong supporter of firm measures toward the colonies and in 1775 voted against North's conciliatory proposals. A nephew of General John Burgoyne and under his influence, he defended Burgoyne's conduct of the Saratoga campaign and by exhibiting about London in late 1777 a copy of Burgoyne's dispatch (which Burgoyne had sent to him for that purpose) to Germain reporting on Saratoga, defending his own conduct and criticizing the inflexible orders Germain had sent to him, helped open the door to a later parliamentary inquiry. In 1778 he went with Burgoyne into steady opposition and thereafter supported Charles Fox. In the House of Lords he registered dissents against (1) continuance of the North ministry's American war policy in 1778, (2) failure of the peers to ask the king to effect "a total change of System" in 1779, (3) refusal of the peers to examine into public expenditure, 1779–80, and (4) admittance of Germain as a peer in 1782. Field sports were his greatest devotion and excellence in them his greatest talent. M.P. for Lancashire, 1774–76.

Stanley, Hans. 1721–80

Of Paultons Park, near Romsey, New Forest, and Ventnor, Isle of Wight, the only son of George Stanley (of Paultons Park; committed suicide in 1734). He was educated chiefly in Switzerland. In 1743 he began in politics as a supporter of Pelham and Newcastle but was soon praising Pitt and seeking favors from him. In 1759 he asked Newcastle to make him a lord of the treasury, but he was solaced instead by membership on the Admiralty Board, 1759–65. He supported Bute in 1762 in hopes of being appointed secretary at war, but was again disappointed and went angrily off to Paris as chargé d'affaires for Bedford in his peace negotiations. He became privy councillor in 1762 and in 1763 hopefully promised Grenville his support. He was governor of the Isle of Wight, 1764–66 and 1770–80; and was cofferer of the king's household, 1766–74 and 1776–80. As a placeman he supported the North ministry but had little influence in politics. He was a trustee of the Sloane bequest. His sisters married Welbore Ellis and Christopher D'Oyley. He killed himself at Althorpe in 1780. M.P. for St. Albans, 1743–47; Southampton Borough, 1754–80.

Stanley (later Smith-Stanley), James. 1717–71

Oldest son of Edward Stanley (1689–1776; 11th Earl of Derby) but pre-deceased him; styled Lord Strange. In 1747 assumed the added surname Smith after his marriage to Lucy, daughter of Hugh Smith (of Weald Hall, Essex). He was a schoolboy friend of General John Burgoyne, who eloped with his sister Charlotte. Westminster from 1729; Leyden in 1735; grand tour, 1736–37. He was lord lieutenant of Lancashire, 1757–71; privy councillor from 1762; and chancellor of the Duchy of Lancaster, 1762–71. He was considered a Tory, and supported Bute and then Grenville, 1762–66. He spoke and voted against repeal of the Stamp Act in 1766, supported the Grafton ministry on Chatham's land tax and on the *Nullum Tempus* Bill and strongly opposed Wilkes, 1767–71. He supported the North ministry until his death. "A busy young Lord, very disinterested, often quick, as often injudicious" (Horace Walpole). M.P. for Lancashire, 1741–71.

Stanley, Thomas. 1749–1816

Of Cross Hill, near Lancaster, Lancashire; oldest son of Rev. Thomas Stanley. Manchester Grammar School, 1758–66; Cambridge from 1767. From his election to Parliament in 1780 he consistently opposed the North ministry and voted against it in all 5 of the crucial divisions recorded in February and March, 1782. He voted against Shelburne's peace terms and for Fox's India Bill in 1783. In early 1784 he tried to bring Pitt and Fox together and, failing, continued to support Fox. Between 1780 and 1785 he spoke frequently and at length in the House of Commons. M.P. for Lancashire, 1780–1812.

Stanley, Thomas Smith. ca.1753–79

2d son of James Stanley (later Smith-Stanley) (*q.v.*); brother of Edward Stanley (*q.v.*). Eton, 1764–70; Cambridge from 1771. He entered the army as cornet in 1775 and became captain in 1776 and major in 1777. He went with his regiment to Jamaica in 1779 and soon died there. In his brief time in the House of Commons he followed his brother's politics. M.P. for Lancashire, 1776–79.

Stanmer, 2d Baron. See **Thomas Pelham.** 1728–1805

Stanwix, John. ca.1693–1766

Of Carlisle, Cumberland; son of Rev. John Roos (rector of Widmerpool, near Kinoulton, Nottinghamshire); changed his name to Stanwix in 1725 upon inheriting from his uncle, Thomas Stanwix (M.P.). He entered the army as ensign at age 16 in 1706 and was captain in 1722, colonel in 1756, major general in 1759, and lieutenant general in 1761. He was governor of Carlisle Castle, 1752–66, and was deputy lieutenant governor of the Isle of Wight, 1763–66. In 1756 he volunteered for service in America and commanded the Royal American Regiment against the French and Indians, building Fort Stanwix in 1757. In politics he followed the line of his political sponsor Sir James Lowther (later 1st Earl of Lonsdale), and supported the Grenville ministry but did not vote against repeal of the Stamp Act in 1766. He was lost at sea in the Irish Channel in 1766. M.P. for Carlisle, 1741–42 and 1746–61; Appleby, 1761–66.

Stapylton (or Stapelton), Thomas. 1727–81

Of Rotherfield, Greys Court, near Henley, Oxfordshire; 2d but oldest surviving son of Sir William Stapylton (ca.1698–1740; M.P.), whom he succeeded in 1740 as 5th baronet. Eton from 1742; Oxford from 1744; D.C.L., 1754. In 1765 he married Mary, daughter of Henry Fane and niece of the 8th Earl of Westmorland. He was listed by Bute as Tory in 1761. He supported Bute and then Grenville, 1761–65. He opposed the Rockingham ministry, 1765–66, but did not vote against repeal of the Stamp Act in 1766. There is no record of any later vote or speech in the House of Commons. M.P. for Oxford City, 1759–68.

Starkie, Edmund. ca.1693–1773

Of Preston and Huntroyd Hall, near Burnley, Lancashire; 2d son of Nicholas Starkie (attorney general of the County Palatine of Lancaster). Inner Temple from 1710, barrister in 1718, bencher from 1746, reader from 1755, treasurer in 1758. He was recorder of Preston, 1767–71. He was reputed a Jacobite and was certainly a Tory to the extent that that term was significant in 1760. He opposed Newcastle through 1762 and supported Grenville from 1763, but there is no record of any speech or vote by him. M.P. for Preston, 1754–68.

Staunton, George Leonard. 1737–1801

Son of Colonel George Staunton (1700–1780; of Cargin, near Roscommon, Ireland, County Galway). He studied in France from 1753 and took a medical degree from Montpelier in 1758, returning to

London in 1759. He practiced medicine in the West Indies, 1761–70, and was attorney general there. He was active in the defense of Grenada, 1772–79; was secretary to Macartney at Madras in 1782; and in 1784 negotiated a treaty with Tippoo Sultan. He was again secretary to Macartney during his embassy to China in 1792. Having been in the employ of the East India Company during much of his career, he was pensioned by the company and was created an Irish baronet in 1785. He received the D.C.L. degree from Oxford in 1790, and was buried in Westminster Abbey.

Staunton, Thomas. ca.1706–84

Of Stockgrove, near Leighton Buzzard, Bedfordshire, and Holbrook Hall, Suffolk; the only son of John Staunton (of County Galway). Trinity College, Dublin, from 1723, and Inner Temple from 1727. He was called to the Irish bar in 1729, and became a barrister of Lincoln's Inn in 1740. He married (1) Jane, 3d daughter of Gilbert Vane (2d Baron Barnard) and sister of Henry Vane (1st Earl of Darlington). He was a member of the Irish Parliament, 1727–61. In British politics he was very independent and was considered a Tory. He supported Newcastle in 1762, voting against Bute's peace preliminaries in December, 1762. He supported the Grafton ministry from 1767 and the North ministry until 1778, when he voted against it on American issues and voted for the Dunning resolution of April 6, 1780. In February and March, 1782, he voted against the North ministry in all 5 of the crucial recorded divisions. In February, 1783, he voted against Shelburne's peace terms, and in November, 1783, did not vote on Fox's India Bill. In 1784 he opposed Pitt, and was not re-elected. M.P. for Ipswich, 1757–84.

Stavordale, Lord. See Henry Thomas Fox-Strangways

Stawell, Mary. 1726–80

Daughter of Edward Stawell (ca.1685–1755; 4th Baron Stawell). She married (1) in 1750 Henry Bilson Legge (*q.v.*); in 1760 created Baroness Stawell in her own right; in 1768 married (2) Wills Hill (*q.v.*). She was a forceful personality, and her connection with the Halifax Whigs through her first marriage later strongly influenced the political conduct of her second husband.

Steele, Thomas. 1753–1823

Of Westhampnett, near Chichester, Sussex; oldest son of Thomas Steele (recorder of Chichester). Westminster, to Cambridge in 1771; Middle Temple from 1772. In November, 1780, almost immediately after his election to the House of Commons, he addressed it in support of a vote of thanks to retired Speaker Fletcher Norton. He opposed the North ministry, and in February and March, 1782, voted against it in all 5 of the crucial recorded divisions. He supported Shelburne in 1782 and voted for his peace terms in February, 1783. He opposed the coalition and supported Pitt from 1784. He was secretary to the master of ordnance, 1782–83, and supported his chief in the debate on the ordnance estimates in March, 1783. He was joint secretary to the Treasury Board, 1783–91; privy councillor from 1791; joint paymaster general, 1791–1804; and a member of the Board of Control, 1791–93. M.P. for Chichester, 1780–1807.

Steevens, George. 1736–1800

Born at Poplar, London, the only child of George Steevens (d. 1768; affluent captain in the East India Company fleet and director of the company). Eton; Cambridge, 1753–56; Middle Temple. While still a student he began to collect a library of Elizabethan literature, which later proved very valuable. In 1766 he published reprints of Shakespeare quartos and in 1773, with the editorial help of Samuel Johnson, published a complete edition of Shakespeare's works. In 1793 he produced another edition of Shakespeare, edited entirely by himself. He was the first man to introduce the text of most of the quartos to the general public; to point out their importance in textual criticism, and to establish a canon and order of composition of Shakespeare's plays—a canon which for nearly 2 centuries has been the standard from which all emendations have been challenged departures. He also helped expose the Chatterton forgeries. Portraits by Zoffany and George Dance.

Stephens, Philip. 1723–1809

Of Fulham, near Putney, Middlesex, and Horsford, near Norwich, Norfolk; 3d son of Rev. Nathaniel Stephens (rector of Alphamstone, near Halstead, Essex); created baronet with a special pension in 1795. He was secretary in the victualing office before 1759, when he was made second secretary to the Admiralty Board. He soon became its first secretary and served it continuously, 1759–95, and was a member of the board, 1795–1806. He supported each successive ministry while it was in office, opposing the Dunning resolution of April 6, 1780, and voting with the North ministry in all 5 of the recorded crucial divisions of February and March, 1782. He voted for Shelburne's peace terms in 1783. In 1806 he was granted a further pension of £1,500 a year. There is no record that, at least between 1759 and 1790, he ever addressed the House of Commons, but he was regular in his attendance. M.P. for Liskeard, 1759–68; Sandwich, 1768–1806.

Stephenson (or Stevenson), John. ca.1709–94

Of Brentford, near Ealing, Middlesex. His origins were probably in Cumberland, but his parentage is now obscure; it was apparently not humble, for he was a landowner there, and presumably inherited. He also seems to have been a cousin, or possibly a nephew, of Sir William Stephenson (lord mayor of London in 1764). In 1763 he was "a very considerable Spanish and Portugal merchant," and was a director of the East India Company, 1765–68. He was on friendly terms with the Earl of Sandwich, who through Charles Courtenay assisted him to win election to Parliament in 1761. In late 1762 he left Newcastle for Bute and then supported the Grenville ministry. He opposed the Rockingham ministry, 1765–66, voting against repeal of the Stamp Act in 1766. He appears to have been in general support of the Grafton ministry and after 1770 supported the North ministry throughout its entire course, opposing the Dunning resolutions in April, 1780, and voting with the ministry in all the recorded crucial divisions in February and March, 1782. During those years his support of the administration may not have been wholly unrelated to his extensive dealings in government loans. The Clerke Act of 1782 compelled him in 1784 to give up his war contract with the Treasury in order to keep his seat in the House of Commons. In February, 1783, he voted against Shelburne's peace terms; he then supported the coalition and voted for Fox's India Bill in November, 1783, but in January, 1784, moved over to the support of Pitt. In his 39 years in the House of Commons he is reported to have addressed it twice. M.P. for St. Michael, 1754–55 and 1761–80; Tregony, 1780–84; Plympton Erle, 1784–90; Tregony, 1790–94.

Stepney, John. 1743–1811

Of Prendegast, near Haverfordwest, Pembrokeshire, and Llanelly, near Swansea, Carmarthenshire; in 1772 succeeded his father, Sir Thomas Stepney, as 8th baronet. Oxford from 1760. He became a protégé and supporter of the Duke of Beaufort. He was envoy to Dresden, 1776–82, and to Berlin, 1782–84. When able to attend the House of Commons he appears to have voted steadily in support of the North ministry, from whom his blessings flowed. He did vote against the unseating of Wilkes in January, 1770, but he voted against Dunning's 3 resolutions in April, 1780, and with the ministry in every crucial division in 1782 until North's fall in late March. M.P. for Monmouth Borough, 1767–70 and 1774–88.

Sterne, Lawrence. 1713–68

Born at Clonmell, County Tipperary, the son of Roger Sterne (lieutenant in the army); spent much of his boyhood at various army posts in Ireland and England. He was educated chiefly at Halifax, and then at Cambridge from 1732; B.A., 1736; ordained, 1738; M.A., 1740. In 1741 he married Elizabeth Lumley. He was canon of St. Ives, Huntingdonshire, in 1737, and vicar of Sutton-in-the-Forest, Yorkshire, 1738–68. He secured additional (plural) livings at Stillington in 1741 and at Coxwold in 1760. He was prebendary of York Cathedral, 1741–68, and chaplain to the 4th Earl of Aboyne (Irish). He traveled on the Continent, 1762–67, after having published *Tristram Shandy*, 1759–67, which established him as a leading literary figure. He published *A Sentimental Journey* in 1768 and *Sermons of Mr. Yorick*, intermittently, 1760–1769. Though criticized by Samuel Johnson, Richardson, and Horace Walpole for having, while a man of the cloth, written "immoral passages," he became an established figure accepted in high London society in his last years but died very shortly after his reputation was made. He had rare talents for literary high comedy, but did not try to create characters that came alive. Portraits by Reynolds and Gainsborough.

Stevens, Richard. (?–?)

Of Winscott, near Torrington, Devon. His origins are obscure. He became agent to Lady Orford for her estates in Devon and Cornwall and through the Walpole interest gained a seat in the House of Commons. There he voted against the Grenville ministry on general warrants in 1764; supported the Rockingham ministry, 1765–66; voted against Chatham's land tax and the Grafton ministry in 1767; and retired in poor health in 1768. There is no record of any important speech by him in the House. M.P. for Callington, 1761–68.

Steward, Gabriel. 1731–92

Of Nottington, near Weymouth, Dorset; oldest son of Gabriel Steward. He served in India with the India Company, ca.1763–78, and after his return to England gained a seat in the House of Commons. He supported the North ministry from 1778, and in 1779 was appointed paymaster to the marines, a post he held until his death. After receiving that sinecure he evidently never cast a vote against the North ministry. He voted against Dunning's resolution of April 6, 1780, and with the ministry in all the recorded crucial divisions of February and March, 1782. He voted for Shelburne's peace terms in 1783 and from 1784 supported Pitt. His only known speech in the House of Commons was in July, 1784, in support of Pitt's India Bill. M.P. for Weymouth and Melcombe Regis, 1778–86 and 1788–90.

Stewart, Alexander. ca.1739–94

Of Afton, near Tarbolton, Ayrshire; 2d son of John Stewart (of Castle Stewart; M.P.). He was lieutenant in the army in 1756, captain in 1761, brigadier general in America in 1781, and major general in 1790. He served in Germany during the Seven Years' War. In 1781 he was wounded at Eutaw Springs, North Carolina, where he succeeded Rawdon-Hastings in command under Cornwallis. He served in Jamaica in 1782 and 1783. He was politically independent of his family; he opposed Pitt on the Regency Bill in 1788 and lost his chance of preferment. M.P. for Kirkcudbright Stewartry, 1786–94.

Stewart, Archibald James Edward. 1748–1827

Oldest son of Colonel John Stewart (of Grandtully on Tay, Perthshire) and of Lady Jane Douglas (1698–1753), daughter of the 2d Marquess of Douglas. Rugby and Westminster. He married (1) in 1771 the only daughter of William Graham (2d Duke of Montrose), and (2) a sister of Henry Scott (*q.v.*). On the death of his uncle the 3d Duke of Douglas, his guardians advanced his claim to the Douglas estates, and after long litigation and much counterclaiming he won a famous case in the House of Lords. He then paid off large debts owing by his parents and continued the rebuilding of Douglas Castle. In 1790 he was elected to Parliament but in the same year was created Baron Douglas of Douglas of the English peerage, and took his seat in the House of Lords.

Stewart, John. ca.1723–81

Of Mitcham, near Wimbledon, Surrey, and London; son of Archibald Stewart (wine merchant; M.P.; tried and acquitted as a Jacobite supporter in 1747). Before 1759 he was a partner in his father's business and was connected with the East India Company. In 1764 he was an aide and supporter of Clive and in 1766 an assistant of Sir George Colebrooke. He wrote and published articles on East India Company affairs from 1773 and in his 3 years in Parliament supported Colebrooke's interests, though there is no record that he ever addressed the House of Commons. In 1775 he was in financial straits, and he took no further active part in politics. M.P. for Arundel, 1771–74.

Stewart, John. 1736–1806

Styled Lord Garlies from 1746; in 1773, as 4th but oldest surviving son, succeeded his father, Alexander Stewart (ca.1694–1773), as 7th Earl of Galloway (Scottish); in 1796 created Baron Stewart of Garlies (English). Glasgow University. He married (1) in 1762 Charlotte, daughter of Francis Greville (1st Earl Brooke of Warwick), and (2) in 1764 Anne, daughter of Sir James Dashwood (*q.v.*). At the beginning of his political career he was considered a Tory, but he was an ambitious opportunist in search of advancement and was often thought insincere as well as arrogant. Elected to the House of Commons in 1761, he supported Bute, and then Grenville but broke with Grenville when refused patronage (at the age of 28). He was gentleman of the Scottish police, 1768–73, and lord of Scottish police, 1774–82. In 1766 he voted against repeal of the Stamp Act. He supported the North ministry, 1770–80, first in the House of Commons until 1773, and then in the House of Lords as a representative Scottish peer. He served on the Board of Trade and Plantations, 1768–74; was made Knight of the Thistle in 1775; and was lord of the bedchamber, 1784–1806. He opposed the coalition in 1783 and in 1784 supported Pitt. In

1788 he asked for a lucrative sinecure with the plea that he needed it to support his 14 children, and was lord lieutenant of Wigtownshire, 1794–1806. He was much devoted to agricultural pursuits and "was long remarkable for his attendance at the opera," according to the *Gentleman's Magazine*. M.P. for Morpeth, 1761–68; Ludgershall, 1768–73.

Stewart, John Shaw. See **John Shaw-Stewart**

Stewart, Keith. ca.1735–95

Of Glasserton, near Whithorn, Wigtownshire; 8th child and 2d surviving son of Alexander Stewart (6th Earl of Galloway, Scottish); brother of John Stewart (1736–1806) (*q.v.*). In 1782 he married Georgina Isabella, daughter of Simha D'Aguilar (naturalized Portuguese Jew). He entered the navy ca. 1753 and was lieutenant in 1759, captain in 1762, rear admiral in 1790, and vice admiral in 1794. He served in the West Indies and the Mediterranean until 1768. He was in command of the *Berwick*, of 74 guns, with Keppel in his engagement with the French fleet off Ushant in 1778. In 1781 he was commodore under Parker against the Dutch at Dogger Bank. In 1782 he commanded the *Cambridge* under Howe at Gibraltar. In 1762, having been elected to the House of Commons for Wigtown burghs, he yielded to an agreement between Bute and Rockingham and vacated his seat in favor of their compromise candidate, John Hamilton. Elected again in 1768, he supported the Grafton and then the North ministries, though his only recorded vote was in favor of increasing the pay of half-pay navy captains, as moved, after petition, by Admiral Howe in 1773. In general he followed the politics of his brother-in-law Earl Gower and his friend Sandwich, and he voted with the North ministry in all 5 of the crucial divisions recorded in February and March, 1782. In February, 1783, he spoke in support of Shelburne's peace terms as being the best that could be secured: "we had no right to expect better." He spoke against the coalition and voted against Fox's India Bill in 1783 and afterward steadily supported Pitt. He was receiver of land tax in Scotland, 1784–95, though his first interest had by then become the care of his estates and the management of his coal and iron mines. He was "a generous and loyal friend." M.P. for Wigtown burghs, February–March, 1762; Wigtownshire, 1768–84.

Stewart, Robert. 1739–1821

Oldest son of Alexander Stewart (of Ballylarn Castle, County Donegal, and Mountstewart, on Lough Strangford, County Down); in 1789 created Baron Londonderry (Irish); in 1795 created Viscount Castlereagh (Irish); in 1796 created Earl of Londonderry (Irish); in 1816 created Marquess of Londonderry (Irish). He was a member of the Irish Parliament, 1769–83, and of the Irish Privy Council from 1782. He was lord lieutenant of County Down, 1801–21, and of County Londonderry, 1803–21. He married (1) in 1766 Sarah Frances, 2d daughter of Francis Seymour Conway (1st Marquess of Hertford), and (2) in 1775 Frances, oldest daughter of Charles Pratt (1st Earl of Camden). He was a Tory who favored removing the restrictions on Irish Roman Catholics and served as Irish representative peer under the new dispensation, 1801–21. *DNB* pronounced him to be "a sagacious though never a prominent public man."

Stewart, William. 1737–97

Of Castle Stewart, Wigtownshire; oldest son of John Stewart (of Castle Stewart; M.P.); brother of Alexander Stewart (*q.v.*). Glasgow University from 1749. In 1771 he married Euphemia, daughter of Kenneth Mackenzie (Lord Fortrose, Scottish). He was lieutenant of foot in 1756 and captain in 1757, but retired from the army in 1769. His family, large landowners but saddled with debt, were connected with the Duke of Argyll, who assisted his career and his election to Parliament in 1770. There he opposed the North ministry on navy captains' pay in 1773 but thereafter supported it on every recorded vote. His finances were so desperate that he did not stand for re-election in 1780, and in 1783 he was obliged to sell his estates. M.P. for Wigtown burghs, 1770–74; Kirkcudbright Stewartry, 1774–80.

Stewart-Moore, Andrew Thomas. 1725–1809

Only son of Robert Stewart (1700–42; 8th Baron Castle Stewart). He was sheriff of County Tyrone in 1755; In 1774 claimed and was granted the title of Baron Castle Stewart (Irish); in 1793 was created Viscount Castlestewart (Irish); in 1800 created Earl of Castlestewart (Irish). Presumably he added the surname Moore upon inheriting.

Stirling, Thomas. 1733–1808

Of Struwan, near Blair Atholl, and Ardoch, near Crieff, Perthshire;

2d son of Henry Stirling (1688–1753; 3d baronet); in 1799 succeeded his brother William Stirling as 5th baronet. He served in the Scots brigade in Holland, 1747–57 and was captain in 1757. He served in Canada and in Martinique in 1759 and at Havana in 1762 and was major in 1770 and lieutenant colonel in 1771. He commanded the 42d Highlanders against the Americans, 1776–80, when he was severely wounded. There is no evidence that he ever encountered his distant cousin William Alexander ("Lord Stirling"; aide and personal friend of Washington) though he must have known of him. He was made general in 1801.

Stockdale, Percival. 1736–1811

Only child of Thomas Stockdale (vicar of Branxton, near Coldstream, Northumberland). He was schooled at Berwick-on-Tweed and was a student at Aberdeen in 1754. In 1756 he was lieutenant of Welsh Fusiliers and was with Byng at Minorca. He left military service in October, 1756, and became (often concurrently) journalist, poet, playwright, literary hack, rector of the established church, and sycophant to the near-great. Having somewhere taken orders, he became in 1780 rector of Hinxworth in Hertfordshire and after 1783 held several minor livings. He thought himself badly treated when London booksellers selected Samuel Johnson instead of himself to write *Lives of the Poets*. His only importance lies in the occasional light thrown upon history by his memoirs, which are however vitiated by highly adulatory and often untrustworthy accounts of important men whom he knew less intimately than he implied, or by his wallowings in what *DNB* called his "unbounded egotism."

Stone, Andrew. 1703–73

Oldest son of Andrew Stone (goldsmith and banker of Lombard Street, London). Westminster, 1715–22; Oxford, 1722–26; M.A., 1728. He was private secretary to Newcastle, 1732–34; undersecretary of state, 1734–49 and 1750–51; keeper of the state paper office, 1742–73; secretary to the government of Barbados, 1742–73; and joint secretary to the lords justice from 1744. He was a member of the Board of Trade and Plantations, 1749–61; registrar of chancery in Jamaica, 1753–73; sub-governor to the Prince of Wales, 1751–56; secretary to the Prince of Wales, 1756–60; and treasurer to Queen Charlotte, 1761–73. Though he was accused of having once toasted the pretender, he retained the confidence of the king and was a trusted adviser to Newcastle, 1754–61. In 1761 he told Newcastle that he could not remain in office with honor. He did not follow Newcastle into opposition in 1762 but continued to support the court and hold his offices. M.P. for Hastings, 1741–61.

Stone, George. ca.1708–64

Younger son of Andrew Stone (goldsmith and banker of Lombard Street); brother of Andrew Stone (*q.v.*). Westminster; B.A., Oxford, 1729; M.A., 1732; D.D., 1740. He was bishop of Ferns and Leighlin, 1740–43; bishop of Kildare, 1743–45; bishop of Derry, 1745–47; and archbishop of Armagh and primate of Ireland, 1747–64. He was an Irish privy councillor and lord justice from 1747. He supported the British interests in Ireland with an enthusiasm second only to his support of his own. He was active, influential and sometimes unscrupulous in Irish politics and far from popular with Irish nationalists. He effected an alliance with Lord George Sackville (later Germain), then chief secretary to his father, the 1st Duke of Dorset (lord lieutenant of Ireland, 1749–54). Their mutual aim was to drive or bribe through the Irish Parliament certain measures so disliked by the Irish public that Stone was obliged to hide from resentful Irish mobs and was reproved by the English court, while Dorset and his son were soon recalled to London. Stone was greedy for power, and his interests were more secular than spiritual. Horace Walpole called him "generous and charitable, and of a soul above revenge" but also said that his death was "a sacrifice to drunkenness."

Stonehewer, Richard. ca.1728–1809

Son of Richard Stonehewer (1727–69; rector of Houghton-le-Spring, near Durham, Durham County). Cambridge from 1745; B.A., 1750; fellow from 1751; M.A., 1753. He was tutor and private secretary to Augustus Henry Fitzroy (*q.v.*) and undersecretary of state, northern department, 1765–66, southern department, 1766. He held no office during the Grafton administration, despite (or perhaps because of) his former connection with the duke. In general he supported the North ministry from 1770 and was permanent auditor for excise, 1772–89. He avoided partisan politics as much as possible after 1770.

He was a friend of Thomas Gray and helped to secure him appointment to a Cambridge professorship. Through William Mason he inherited Gray's library and papers.

Stopford, James. 1731–1810

Oldest son of Edward Stopford (1732–70; lieutenant general); in 1770 he succeeded, by court ruling, his uncle James Stopford (1721–58; of Courtown, County Wexford; M.P. of Ireland) as 2d Earl of Courtown (Irish); in 1796 created Baron Saltersford of Cheshire (English). Trinity College, Dublin, from 1749. In 1762 he married Mary Powys, niece of George Brudenell (1712–90; M.P.; 4th Earl of Cardigan). He was a member of the Irish Parliament, 1761–68, and of the Irish Privy Council from 1775. In the English House of Commons he voted largely with the North ministry from 1780. He voted for Shelburne's peace terms but did not vote on Fox's India Bill in 1783. From 1784 he supported Pitt, and was called a Tory. He was lord of the bedchamber to the Prince of Wales, 1780–84, and privy councillor and treasurer of the king's household, 1784–93. M.P. for Great Bedwin, 1774; Marlborough, 1780–93.

Storer, Anthony Morris. 1746–99

Of Golden Square, London; oldest son of Thomas Storer (of Jamaica and Westminster). Eton, 1754–64; Cambridge from 1764; Middle Temple from 1762. In his youth he developed friendships with the young Earl of Carlisle and with George Selwyn and later corresponded frequently with both. In the 1770's he became a domestic favorite of Lady North and her daughters and long pestered North for an appointment to the Board of Trade and Plantations, a post for which he had few claims or qualifications except his self-confidence, and which he ultimately and ungratefully received from North in 1781. In 1778 he accompanied Carlisle as his aide in the peace mission to America and in 1782 claimed to have been an intermediary between North and Fox in effecting the coalition. He voted against Shelburne's peace terms; supported the coalition, and secured from it appointment as secretary to the embassy at Paris in 1783, and then as minister to Paris. He held that post for 6 days before the coalition was dismissed. He later broke with Carlisle. He was socially ingratiating, prosperous, and intelligent and was an excellent musician, dancer, and skater—a member of the Dilettante Society from 1790 and a fellow of the Society of Arts from 1777. He willed his excellent collection of prints and books to Eton. He appears to have addressed the House of Commons but once in his decade of membership—in 1775, when he praised the administration of Lord North. M.P. for Carlisle, 1774–80; Morpeth, 1780–84.

Stormont, 7th Viscount. See **David Murray**

Stowell, 1st Baron. See **William Scott**

Strabane, Viscount. See **James Hamilton.** 1712–89

Strachey, Henry. 1737–1810

Oldest son of Sir Henry Strachey (of Sutton Court, near Bristol, Somerset); created baronet in 1801. Westminster from 1750. He served as a clerk in the War Office, ca.1760–64. In 1764 he went to India as private secretary to Robert Clive. He returned to England in 1774 and became secretary to the Howe brothers' peace commission to the colonies. In 1778 he emerged from that unsuccessful undertaking with a pension of £587 a year for life. He was storekeeper of ordnance, 1780–82; a secretary to the Treasury Board in 1782; a joint undersecretary of state for home affairs, 1782–83; clerk of deliveries for ordnance in 1783; and master of the household, 1794–1810. He had the political support of Clive and of the Howe brothers and was a close friend of Christopher D'Oyley, secretary to Germain until 1779. As a placeholder he supported the North ministry, opposing the Dunning resolutions of April, 1780, and voting with the ministry in all 5 of the crucial divisions recorded in February and March, 1782. He seldom addressed the House of Commons, and then usually in support of Clive or of the Howes. He voted for Shelburne's peace terms in 1783 and opposed the Pitt ministry from 1784. M.P. for Pontrefact, 1768–74; Bishop's Castle, 1774–78; Saltash, 1778–80; Bishop's Castle, 1780–82; East Grinstead, 1802–07.

Stradbroke, 1st Earl. See **John Rous.** 1750–1827

Strahan, William. 1715–85

Of London, the only son of William George Strahan (writer to the signet and clerk of the customs at Leith, near Edinburgh). He was apprenticed to an Edinburgh printer and then became a partner in London of John Millar, printer and publisher. Later he entered into partnership with Thomas Cadell the elder, printing and publishing bookseller. He published Johnson's *Dictionary*, Blackstone's *Commentaries on the Laws of England*, Gibbon's *Decline and Fall of the Roman Empire*, Adam Smith's *The Wealth of Nations*, and the works of David Hume. He also served briefly as printer to the king. He was successively critical of the political measures of Bute, Grenville, Rockingham, Chatham, and Grafton. He was favorable to North in 1770 and supported him through 1783; he voted against Dunning's resolutions in April, 1780, and with the ministry in all 5 of the recorded crucial divisions of February and March, 1782; he encouraged the coalition between Fox and North and voted against Shelburne's peace terms. M.P. for Malmesbury, 1774–80; Wootton Bassett, 1780–84.

Strange, Lord and **1st Earl.** See **James Stanley** (later **Smith-Stanley**). 1717–71 and **John Murray.** 1755–1830

Strange, Robert. 1721–92

Born at Kirkwall, Orkney, the oldest son of David Strang (or Strange) (of Kirkwall). He was apprenticed to an engraver and then to a lawyer in Edinburgh, but in 1745 he joined the Jacobite army and fought at Preston Pans, Falkirk, and Culloden. He escaped to Rouen, married, and settled in Paris; but in 1753 he returned to London and was pardoned. There he made a reputation as a master engraver of the Italian baroque painters. He traveled and worked in Italy, 1760–65. In 1775 he published a pamphlet attacking the narrow views of the Royal Academy. He was knighted in 1787. He stands in the top rank for his engravings of works by Vandyck, Titian, and Raphael, together with his portraits of the royal family. Portraits by Greuze, Romney, and Raeburn.

Strangford, 4th Viscount. See **Philip Smythe**

Stratford, Edward Augustus. ca.1734–1801

Of Baltinglass, County Wicklow, near Athy, and Great Glemham, near Saxmundham, Suffolk; oldest son of John Stratford (1st Baron Baltinglass from 1763; 1st Earl of Aldborough from 1777, both titles

Irish); in 1777 succeeded his father as 2d Baron Baltinglass and 2d Earl Aldborough. He was a member of the Irish Parliament, 1759–68 and 1775–77. He was elected to the English House of Commons for Taunton in 1774, but was unseated on petition in early 1775—he would, it was thought, have supported Shelburne and opposed North. M.P. for Taunton, 1774–75.

Strathallan, Viscounts. See Drummond

Strathmore, 7th Earl. See John Lyon (later Bowes-Lyon)

Strathnaver, Lord. See William Sutherland

Stratton, George. ca.1734–1800

Of Great Tew, near Chipping Norton, Oxfordshire; oldest son of John Stratton (counsel to and member of the Council of Madras). He became a writer in the East India Company in 1750, and a member of the Governor's Council in India in 1768. In 1776 he opposed Pigot and became acting governor after Pigot's arrest by the council. He returned to England with a considerable fortune in 1778, and was promptly elected to the House of Commons with the support of the Earl of Sandwich. In March, 1779, he spoke defending his actions in India, and insisting that the company administration there was not corrupt. He supported Sandwich and the North ministry, opposed the Dunning resolution of April 6, 1780, and voted with the ministry against all 5 crucial divisions recorded for February and March, 1782. He voted against Shelburne's peace terms and did not vote on Fox's India Bill in 1783. He did not return to Parliament in 1784. M.P. for Callington, 1778–84.

Strode, William. 1738–1809

Oldest son of William Strode (ca.1712–55; M.P.). Oxford from 1755. He was elected to the House of Commons in 1768 "in the interest" of Sir Thomas Worsley (1711–78; M.P.), but there is no evidence that he ever spoke or voted in the House, and he soon withdrew. M.P. for Yarmouth (Isle of Wight), 1768–69.

Strutt, Jedediah, 1726–97

Born at Perth Normanton, Derbyshire, 2d son of William Strutt (of

Blackwell, Derbyshire). He was educated to become a farmer, but after a trial at farming apprenticed himself to Robert Massey, a wheelwright at Findern, near Derby. He soon revealed remarkable mechanical aptitude and before 1758 had invented a ribbing machine that helped revolutionize textile manufacture. He was then put in touch with Richard Arkwright, with whom he took over a cotton mill at Nottingham. In 1780 he owned several mills at Belper, Derbyshire, and Milford, Staffordshire, where he developed further improvements in clothmaking machinery.

Strutt, John. ca.1727–1816

Of Terling Place, near Chelmsford, Essex; only son of Joseph Strutt (prosperous miller in Essex). He became a progressive farmer, a considerable landowner, an independent country gentleman with Tory ideas, a steady supporter of the North ministry, and a local philanthropist "of large fortune and consummate integrity." He was the only member of the House of Commons to oppose openly a vote of thanks to Keppel for his services in 1779. He voted against Dunning's resolutions in April, 1780, and with the North ministry in all the crucial divisions in February and March, 1782. He opposed the Rockingham ministry in 1782 and voted against Shelburne's peace terms in 1783. Initially a hesitant supporter of the coalition, he turned against it and from early 1784 supported Pitt. M.P. for Malden, 1774–90.

Stuart, Andrew. 1725–1801

Of Craigthorn, Lanarkshire; 2d son of Archibald Stuart (of Lanarkshire). He became tutor to the children of the 6th Duke of Hamilton (Scottish) and in 1759 a writer to the signet. He was king's remembrancer for Scotland, 1770–71, and joint keeper of the signet for Scotland, 1777–79. In 1770 he was legal counsel in the Hamilton-Douglas lawsuit and was challenged to a duel by Thurlow, the opposing counsel. He slightly wounded Thurlow, but there is no indication that he even slightly punctured Thurlow's overbearing self-confidence. In 1773 he published a pamphlet attacking Lord Mansfield's decision in that case. He was active for the East India Company from 1774 but also maintained a very cordial relationship with Lord North and in general supported the North ministry until 1782, voting with it in all 5 of the recorded crucial divisions of February and March, 1782. He served on the Board of Trade and Plantations, 1779–82, and from 1781 was also clerk of the register for Scotland. He voted for Shelburne's peace terms in 1783 but then supported the coalition, though he did not vote on Fox's India Bill. From 1784 he frequently opposed the Pitt ministry. In 1790, presumably after the mature consideration of one aged 65, he overcame Scottish caution sufficiently to enter into marriage with Margaret, daughter of Sir William Stirling of Perth (4th baronet). M.P. for Lanarkshire, 1774–84; Weymouth and Melcombe Regis, 1790–1801.

Stuart, Charles. 1753–1801

4th son of John Stuart (1713–92; 3d Earl of Bute, Scottish); grandson of Lady Mary Wortley Montagu; brother of Frederick Stuart (*q.v.*), brother of James Archibald Stuart (later Wortley-Mackenzie [*q.v.*]), and brother of John Stuart (1744–1814) (*q.v.*). In 1778 he married Louisa, daughter of Lord Vere Bertie (ca.1712—68; M.P.). He was ensign in the army in 1768, lieutenant in 1770, captain in 1773, major in 1775, colonel in 1782, major general in 1793, and lieutenant general in 1798. He arrived in America the day after the battle of Bunker Hill and was at the capture of New York in late 1776. He was nearly killed at the battle of the Brandywine in 1777. In 1778 he returned to England, and in the House of Commons, to which he had gained election soon after he left for America in 1776, he condemned Sandwich's management of naval operations. In January, 1779, he was very critical of Germain as well, but in most other matters he supported the North ministry in preference to the policies of the opposition. He went to America again in July, 1779, and became a confidant of Clinton, who was, in frustration, threatening to resign. Once more back in England, he again supported the North ministry until its fall, voting against the motions of Cavendish and Rous in early March, 1782. He then supported Fox until after 1783 but was often absent on the Continent until 1788. He captured Minorca from the Spaniards in 1798 and was governor of Minorca, 1799–1801. He was Knight of the Bath from 1799 and deputy ranger of Richmond Park. He was able, ambitious, conceited, critical, and difficult. M.P. for Bossiney, 1776–90; Ayr boroughs, 1790–94; Poole, 1796–1801.

Stuart, Francis. 1737–1810

Styled Lord Doune until 1767, when he succeeded his father, James Stuart (*q.v.*), as 9th Earl of Moray (Scottish); in 1796 created Baron Stuart (English). In 1763 he married Jean, daughter of Lord Gray. He was a representative Scottish peer, 1784–96, and thereafter a member of the English peerage. He was lord lieutenant of Morayshire, 1794–1810.

Stuart, Frederick. 1751–1802

3d son of John Stuart (1713–92) (*q.v.*); brother of John Stuart (1744–1814) (*q.v.*), James Archibald Stuart (later Wortley-Mackenzie) (*q.v.*), and Charles Stuart (*q.v.*). Winchester, to Oxford in 1768; he ran away from Oxford to Paris in his 17th year and was with difficulty brought back to England. In 1769 his family sent him to India, but he managed to make his way home in 1772. Sent again to India, he was befriended by Warren Hastings and remained in India until 1775, when he again returned to England and gained a seat in the House of Commons. There he defended Hastings and in general supported the North ministry. In 1776 he told the House that it must use sterner measures against the Americans, who, he said, had no money to buy support from any foreign power. He opposed Dunning's resolution of April 6, 1780. In 1782 he was so heavily in debt that he decamped to Paris, and thereafter he took no significant part in British affairs. M.P. for Ayr burghs, 1776–80; Buteshire, 1796–1802.

Stuart, James. 1708–67

Styled Lord Doune from 1735; in 1739 succeeded his father, Francis Stuart (ca.1673–1739), as 8th Earl of Moray (Scottish). He married (1) in 1734 Grace, widow of John Gordon (3d Earl of Aboyne, Scottish), and (2) in 1740 Margaret, daughter of David Wemyss (Earl of Wemyss, Scottish). He was Knight of the Thistle from 1741; grand master of Scottish Freemasons, 1744–45; and a Scottish representative peer, 1741–67.

Stuart, James. ca.1702–62

Of Kerrimoran, Buteshire; 3d son of Sir Robert Stuart (M.P.; 1st baronet); grandson of Sir Robert Hamilton; distant cousin of the Earls of Bute. He was ensign in 1720, captain in 1736, major in 1758, and lieutenant colonel in 1761. He was little known to many of his contemporaries, and is included here because they and their successors have often confused him with other James Stuarts, as in obituary notices in the *London Magazine* and the *Gentleman's Magazine* in 1762. M.P. for Buteshire, 1761–62.

Stuart (later Wortley-Mackenzie), James Archibald. 1747–1818

Of Admaleish, Buteshire; 2d son of John Stuart (1713–92) (*q.v.*); brother of John Stuart (1744–1814), *q.v.*), Charles Stuart (*q.v.*), and Frederick Stuart (*q.v.*); added his mother's name Wortley upon inheriting much of the vast Wortley fortune in 1794; in 1800 added the further name Mackenzie upon acquiring the estate of his uncle James Stuart Mackenzie. Edinburgh University, 1766–67, studied in France, 1767–68. He was ringleader in a student riot at Edinburgh University in 1767. That year he also married secretly, was ordered home, and was then sent with a governor to France. In 1780 he served briefly with his regiment in the West Indies but fell ill and was invalided home. In the House of Commons from 1768, he consistently supported the North ministry throughout its career, voting with North in every recorded crucial division in February and March, 1782. He voted against Shelburne's peace terms in February, 1783, and then supported the coalition. From 1784 he opposed Pitt's ministry; but in the meantime he had become a heavy drinker and gambler, and his influence, never great, had declined. After 1784 he led a more sober life, but his "numerous infidelities" encouraged his wife to indulge similar "gallantries." M.P. for Ayr burghs, 1768–74; Buteshire, 1774–80; Plympton Erle, 1780–84; Buteshire, 1784–90; Bossiney, 1797–1802; Buteshire, 1806–1807.

Stuart, John. 1713–92

Born at Edinburgh, the grandson of Archibald Campbell (d. 1703; 1st Duke of Argyll, Scottish); in 1723 succeeded his father, James Stuart, as 3d Earl of Bute. Schooled at Eton. In 1736 he married Mary, only daughter of Edward and Lady Mary Wortley Montagu, from whom she inherited great wealth (in 1761 she was created Baroness Mountstuart of Wortley, English, in her own right). He was commissioner of police for Scotland from 1737; Knight of the Thistle from 1738; and a representative Scottish peer, 1737–41 and 1760–80. He was lord of the bedchamber to Frederick, Prince of Wales, until the prince's death in 1751, and became the mentor and friend of his son, next Prince of Wales and later George III. Admired, feared, maligned, and toadied to as the new king's favorite and potential first minister, he was groom of the stole; ranger of Richmond Park, 1761–92; Knight of the Garter from 1762; and secretary of state, northern department, March 25, 1761–May 29, 1762, when he became first lord of the treasury, a post he held until April 16, 1763. Always unpopular with the London citizenry and the anti-Scots, his fall was as rapid and complete as his rise. He resigned as first minister when his peace preliminaries with France were severely criticized and when he felt, justifiably, that he was not receiving loyal support from many other members of his ministry. George Grenville, his successor as first minister, and others in the new administration then forced him not only to retire from London and from politics but to sever all personal communication with the king—for they continued to fear his influence. It was charged that he continued to communicate with George III, but his later influence was slight. In the House of Lords he voted against the Stamp Act in 1765. He was chancellor of Marischal College, Aberdeen, from 1761; first president of the Society of Scottish Antiquaries in 1780; and a trustee of the British Museum, 1765–92. In his later years he traveled much, often incognito, on the Continent. Portrait by Reynolds.

Stuart, John. 1744–1814

Styled Lord Mountstuart from his mother's English peerage until 1776, when, through his marriage (1) to Jane, daughter of Viscount Windsor (of the family of the Earls of Pembroke), he became Baron Cardiff (English); in 1792 succeeded his father, John Stuart (1713–92) (*q.v.*), as 4th Earl of Bute (Scottish); in 1796 created Earl of Windsor (English) and 1st Marquess of Bute (Scottish). He attended Harrow from 1757 and then Winchester. During their respective grand tours, 1761–65, he and James Boswell met and traveled together in Italy, though the two exuberant young egotists did not always get on easily. In 1800 he married (2) Frances, daughter of Thomas Coutts (*q.v.*). He was lord lieutenant of Glamorganshire, 1772–93 and 1794–1814, and lord lieutenant of Buteshire, 1794–1814. He served briefly in the American war, where he was impatiently critical of his superiors because he was not more rapidly advanced. He was a privy councillor, 1779–83, and auditor of the impress, 1781–82; when the latter office was discontinued in 1782, he was given a pension of £7,000 a year for life. He was envoy to Turin, 1779–83, and ambassador to Spain in 1783 and 1795–96. He supported the Grafton and North ministries and (in the House of Lords) the coalition of 1783. He was a trustee of the British Museum, 1800–14. He was handsome, conventional, indolent, and sometimes arrogant, but with a good mind and good intentions. M.P. for Bossiney, 1766–76.

Stuart, Simeon. ca.1721–79

Of Hartley Maudit, near Alton, Hampshire; in 1761 succeeded his father, Sir Simeon Stuart (M.P.), as 3d baronet; a cousin of the Earls of Bute; descended from a family that had lived and intermarried in England since the 15th century and had more than once represented Hampshire constituencies. Westminster, 1734–37. He was elected to the House of Commons in 1761 with the support of Lord Carnarvon, who largely controlled the seat for Hampshire. Regarded as Tory, in 1761 he offered the ministry his support in return for "any part of Administration," and in the same year was made chamberlain of the exchequer (where he served until 1769), and in 1764 was made chamberlain of the tally court—both posts in which an incompetent man could do little harm and an able man could do little good. In return he supported Bute and then Grenville, voting against repeal of the Stamp Act in 1766. Later he supported the Grafton and North ministries. A fox-hunting gentleman "of great merit," he appears to have addressed the House of Commons but once, in 1774, on how to pack hops. He was declared bankrupt in 1775. M.P. for Hampshire, 1761–79.

Stuart-Mackenzie, James. ca.1719–1800

Of Rosehaugh, near Fortrose, Ross-shire, and Belmont, Angusshire; 2d son of James Stuart (2d Earl of Bute); grandson of Archibald Campbell (d. 1703; 1st Duke of Argyll); brother of John Stuart (1713–92) (q.v.). Eton, 1728–32. He then made the grand tour and studied at Leyden University in 1737. In 1749 he married his cousin Elizabeth, daughter of John Campbell (1674–1743, 2d Duke of Argyll), and under the entailed estate of his great-grandfather Sir George Mackenzie he added the surname Mackenzie. He was envoy to Turin, 1758–61; privy councillor from 1761; and lord privy seal for Scotland, 1763–65 and 1766–1800. He supported and was sponsored by his brother the Earl of Bute, to whom he made himself invaluable in the management of Scottish affairs and patronage. Friction with Grenville in 1763, and fear that he would perpetuate Bute's influence over the king, led Grenville and his ministers to force Stuart-Mackenzie to leave court and administration after "an affecting scene with the King" in May, 1765, when Newcastle and Rockingham refused to take office if he was continued. In 1766 he voted in the House of Commons against repeal of the Stamp Act. In 1766 he was reinstated as Scottish lord privy seal, and became a close adviser to Grafton. He was retained by North and supported his ministry until 1780, but was apparently not ambitious for further office. M.P. for Argyllshire, 1742–47; Buteshire, 1747–54; Ayr burghs, 1754–61; Ross-shire, 1761–80.

Stubbs, George. 1724–1806

Son of John Stubbs (of Liverpool; currier). Determined to become a painter, he studied anatomy, first at Liverpool and then at London. In 1754 he went to Italy to study art. In 1756 he returned to London with a considerable reputation as a landscape painter. He came to be considered the pre-eminent English painter of landscapes of his time and was particularly noted for his paintings of horses against English-countryside backgrounds. He long exhibited at the Royal Academy, and was called upon by such men as the Duke of Richmond and Earl Grosvenor to paint their favorite mounts or Newmarket winners. In 1766 he published *The Anatomy of the Horse*. Self-portrait, on a white horse.

Sturt, Humphrey. ca.1724–86

Of Crichel More, near Wimborne, Dorset; only son of Humphrey Sturt (of Horton, near Cranborne, Dorset). Oxford from 1741. Wealthy and independent, in 1761 and 1767 he was listed as Tory. In the House of Commons from 1754, his voting record seems to have been erratic, and there is no record that in 30 years he ever addressed the House. Before 1761 he was chiefly in opposition, and in 1764 he voted against the Grenville ministry on general warrants. He did not vote with Grenville against repeal of the Stamp Act in 1766; he voted for Chatham's land tax in 1767 but with the opposition on the Wilkes issues in 1769 and 1770. He voted against North's Falklands Islands settlement in 1771 and against the ministry on the Middlesex election issues. From 1774 he steadily opposed the North administration, voting for the Dunning resolution of April 6, 1780, and with the opposition in 4 out of 5 of the crucial votes recorded in February and March, 1782. He opposed Shelburne's peace terms and supported Fox through 1783. M.P. for Dorset, 1754–84.

Succoth, Lord. See **Ilay Campbell**

Suckling, Maurice. 1726–78

Oldest surviving son of Maurice Suckling (prebendary of Westminster Abbey); uncle of Lord Nelson. In 1764 he married his cousin Mary, daughter of Horatio Walpole (1st Baron Walpole). He became a navy lieutenant in 1745 and captain in 1755 and fought a spirited action against the French in 1757. He was comptroller of the navy, 1775–78. He was elected to the House of Commons, probably with the support of the Admiralty Board and the administration, and supported the North ministry, but there is no record that he ever spoke or voted in the House. M.P. for Portsmouth, 1776–78.

Suffield, 1st Baron. See **Harbord Harbord** (formerly **Morton**)

Suffolk, 12th and 14th Earls. See **Henry Howard** and **Thomas Howard.** 1721–83

Sulivan, Lawrence. ca.1713–86

Of Ponsbourne Park, near Hatfield, Hertfordshire; born in Ireland; of a family well known in County Cork. His early years are obscure. He was in India as aide to the governor of Bengal in 1740 and was a member of the Bombay Council in 1751. In 1753 he returned to England with a moderate fortune and was thereafter intermittently a director of the East India Company, 1755–86, serving for 3 years as its deputy chairman and as its chairman, 1758–59, 1760–62, and 1781–82. He was a friend and political follower of Shelburne, and in company politics a violent enemy of Clive. In 1769 he left Shelburne and supported Grafton, and supported the North ministry until 1773. He then complained of North's measures against the East India Company and conduct toward himself, and gave his support to the Rockingham opposition. In 1780 he rejoined North and supported Warren Hastings. In 1783 he opposed Fox's India Bill and in 1784 supported Pitt. M.P. for Taunton, 1762–68; Ashburton, 1768–74.

Sunbury, Viscount. See George Montagu Dunk

Sundridge, 1st Baron. See John Campbell. 1723–1806

Surrey, Earl. See Charles Howard. 1746–1815

Sussex, 3d (and 17th) Earl. See Henry Yelverton.

Sutherland, Earl. See William Sutherland

Sutherland, 1st Duke. See George Granville Leveson-Gower

Sutherland, William. 1735–66

Styled Lord Strathnaver until 1750, when he succeeded his father, William Sutherland (1708–50, M.P.), as 18th Earl of Sutherland (Scottish). Winchester, 1745–46; Harrow, 1747–50; Enfield, 1750–52; and Göttingen, 1752–55. He was ensign of foot, in his 11th year, in 1747, captain in 1755, lieutenant colonel in 1759, and colonel and aide to the king, 1763–66. Portrait by Ramsey.

Suttie, George. 1715–83

Of Balgone, near North Berwick, Haddingtonshire; oldest son of Sir James Suttie, whom he succeeded in 1736 as 3d baronet; cousin of John Dalrymple (1749–1821) (*q.v.*), who assisted his career. He was lieutenant in 1737, major in 1747, and lieutenant colonel in 1751 and resigned from the army in 1752. Elected to the House of Commons in 1768, he usually supported the Grafton and then the North ministries, including the war with the colonies. He spoke frequently and was influential in the House. In 1777 he vacated his seat in accordance with a pre-election agreement with William Hamilton Nisbet. M.P. for Haddingtonshire, 1768–77.

Sutton (or Manners-Sutton), George. 1723–83

Of Kelham Hall, near Newark, Nottinghamshire; 3d son of John

Manners (1696–1779) (*q.v.*); brother of John Manners (1721–70) (*q.v.*) and Robert Manners (or Manners-Sutton) (ca.1722–62; M.P.); added the surname Sutton in 1762 upon succeeding his brother Robert to the Lexinton estates. Eton, 1739–40. He entered the House of Commons in 1754. In 1761 Bute listed him as a supporter of Newcastle, and he appears not to have voted for Bute's peace preliminaries in 1762. He voted against repeal of the Stamp Act in 1766 but did not vote on Chatham's land tax in 1767. From 1768 his attendance of the House of Commons was infrequent, and he voted both ways on the Wilkes-Middlesex issues, 1769–70, but voted against unseating Wilkes in January, 1770. By 1774 he was classed as in opposition to the North ministry. He was chairman of the Wyvill Association committee in Nottinghamshire in 1780 and voted with the Rockingham opposition, 1781–82, including votes against the North ministry in all 5 of the crucial divisions recorded in February and March, 1782. M.P. for Grantham, 1754–80; Newark, 1780–83.

Sutton, James. ca.1733–1801

Son of Prince Sutton (clothing merchant of New Park, Devizes, Wiltshire). He continued his father's business. He was elected to Parliament in 1765, and supported the Rockingham ministry, 1765–66. He opposed the Grafton ministry on the Wilkes issues, 1767–70. He was generally in opposition to the North ministry until 1776, after which time he supported it until he left the House of Commons, voting against the Dunning resolution of April 6, 1780. There is no record that he ever addressed the House, and he did not seek re-election in 1780. He was sheriff of Wiltshire, 1785–86. M.P. for Devizes, 1765–80.

Sutton (or Manners-Sutton), John Manners. 1752–1826

Of Kelham Hall, near Newark, Nottinghamshire; 2d son of George Sutton (or Manners-Sutton) (*q.v.*); first cousin of William Montagu (1768–1843; 5th Duke of Manchester). In 1778 he married his cousin Anne, illegitimate daughter of John Manners (1721–70; Marquess of Granby). He was page of honour to George III, 1765–76. He was ensign in the army in 1768, lieutenant in 1773, captain in 1775, lieutenant colonel in 1780, and retired in 1791. In 1783 he replaced his father as member of the House of Commons for Newark and voted for Shelburne's peace terms and for reform of Parliament but against Fox's India Bill. He supported the Pitt ministry from 1784, but there is no evidence that, at least before 1790, he ever addressed the House. M.P. for Newark, 1783–96; Ilchester, 1804–1806.

Sutton, Richard. 1733–1802

Of Norwood Park, near Southwell, Nottinghamshire; 2d surviving son of Sir Robert Sutton (d. 1747; M.P.; minister to The Hague, Paris, and Constantinople); created baronet in 1772; closely related to Lord North. Westminster from 1744; Cambridge from 1749; M.A., 1752; Middle Temple from 1754; barrister of Inner Temple in 1759. He married (1) in 1765 Susanna, sister of Philip Champion Crespigney (or de Crespigney) (*q.v.*); made 2 later marriages. He was undersecretary of state, 1766–72; counsel to the Ordnance Board in 1768; commissioner of the privy seal in 1768. In 1769 he received an annual pension of £500 for life. He was recorder of St. Albans from 1763. In the House of Commons he frequently though not always opposed the North ministry, but Horace Walpole commented that he was "too necessary to be dismissed" from his court offices. He spoke frequently in House debates and voted against unseating Wilkes in January, 1770. In 1772 he spoke 17 times in favor of amendments to North's Royal Marriage Bill, but he supported North's policies and measures toward America. He opposed Dunning's resolution of April 6, 1780. He served on the Admiralty Board, 1780–82. He voted with North in all 5 crucial divisions recorded during the last 10 weeks of North's ministry in 1782. He voted against Shelburne's peace terms and supported the coalition in 1783, and afterward continued in opposition to Pitt. M.P. for St. Albans, 1768–80; Sandwich, 1780–84; Boroughbridge, 1784–96.

Sutton (or Manners-Sutton), Robert. 1722–62

Of Kelham Hall, near Newark, Nottinghamshire; 2d son of John Manners (1696–1769) (*q.v.*); brother of John Manners (1721–70) (*q.v.*) and George Sutton (or Manners-Sutton) (*q.v.*) and like the latter added the surname Sutton upon inheriting estates through his mother in 1734. He was captain in 1745 and lieutenant colonel in 1746.

He served in Flanders, 1747–48, and became colonel in 1760. He was lord of the bedchamber to the Prince of Wales, 1749–51, and master of foxhounds, 1754–62. He died in his 39th year without having played a significant role in national affairs. M.P. for Nottinghamshire, 1747–62.

Swymmer, Anthony Langley. ca.1724–60

Of Longwood House, near Winchester, Hampshire; oldest son of Anthony Swymmer (planter of Jamaica); cousin of Hans Stanley (*q.v.*) and Rose Fuller (*q.v.*). Winchester, to Cambridge in 1741. In 1748 he married Arabella, daughter of John Astley (*q.v.*). He inherited plantations in Jamaica but established himself near Winchester. Classed as Tory, he voted with Hans Stanley and in general supported the Pelhams. M.P. for Southampton Borough, 1747–60.

Sydney, 1st Baron and 1st Viscount. See Thomas Townshend. 1733–1800

Sydney, 1st Baron (Irish). See Dudley Alexander Sydney Cosby

Sykes, Francis. 1732–1804

Of Basildon Park, near Reading, Berkshire; 4th son of Francis Sykes (of Thornhill, near Dewsbury, Yorkshire; "yeoman"); created baronet in 1781. He went to India for the Company in 1749 and served there under Clive, accumulating wealth by dubious methods in private trade. In 1770 he returned to England and married (2) a daughter of William Monckton-Arundell (*q.v.*). With Clive's support he gained a seat in the House of Commons in 1771 and followed Clive into support of the North ministry. In 1773 he addressed the House (his only recorded speech before 1790), defending Clive's conduct in India and his own. In 1775 he was fined £11,000 and unseated for open bribery in the election at Shaftesbury (where such matters were normally arranged more discreetly), but he regained the seat in the 1780 election. He voted with the North ministry in every recorded critical division during its last 10 weeks in early 1782. He opposed Shelburne's peace terms and Fox's India Bill in 1783 and thereafter (except as regarded the attacks on his close friend Warren Hastings) supported the Pitt ministry. He was high steward of Wallingford. M.P. for Shaftesbury, 1771–75 and 1780–84; Wallingford, 1784–1804.

Symons (or Symmons), John. 1701–64

Of Llanstinan, near Fishguard, Pembrokeshire; 4th son of John Symons (or Symmons) (of Llanstinan). A Welsh country gentleman, he was listed as Tory in 1761 and generally so considered throughout his career in the House of Commons. He followed the lead of that unregenerate Tory Sir John Philipps and voted in steady, dogged opposition to the Pelham and Newcastle Whigs, asking no quarter and receiving none, but holding the respect of his associates. There is no record that he ever addressed the House. M.P. for Cardigan Borough, 1746–61.

Symons (or Symonds), John. 1708–63

Of Mynde Park, The Meend, near Hereford, Herefordshire; only son of Richard Symons (or Symonds), successful London merchant. Middle Temple from 1724, Oxford from 1728. In 1735 he married Anne, daughter of James Colebrooke (London banker) and sister of James Colebrooke (*q.v.*) and George Colebrooke (*q.v.*). He was classed as Tory, and supported Bute. He opposed the cider tax in 1763, and his only recorded speech was against it. M.P. for Hereford Borough, 1754–63.

Symons-Peers (or Symonds-Peers), Richard. ca.1744–96

Of Mynde Park, The Meend, near Hereford, Herefordshire; only son of Richard Peers (alderman of London); added the surname Symons (or Symonds) in 1763 upon inheriting Mynde Park from his maternal uncle John Symons (or Symonds) (*q.v.*), and acquiring a fortune; created baronet in 1774. In Parliament from 1768, in 1769 he voted against the Grafton ministry on the Wilkes issues but in 1774 supported the North ministry in opposing renewal of Grenville's Disputed Elections Act. In 1780 he opposed Dunning's resolution on excessive influence, and in 1782 he voted with North in all 5 of the crucial divisions of the final 10 weeks before the fall of the ministry in late March. He voted against Shelburne's peace terms in 1783, but he expressed the fear that the coalition was neither "natural nor noble," and in March, 1783, declared that he would "watch them narrowly" before he "gave them any support." He voted against Fox's India Bill and supported Pitt from January, 1784. M.P. for Hereford Borough, 1768–84.

T

Talbot, George. 1719–87

Oldest son of George Talbot (d. 1753); in 1743 succeeded his uncle Gilbert Talbot (1673–1743) as 14th Earl of Shrewsbury and Waterford (Irish). In 1743 he married a daughter of the 7th Baron Dormer.

Talbot, 3d Baron and **1st Earl.** See **John Chetwynd-Talbot**

Talbot, William. 1710–82

2d son of Charles Talbot (1st Baron Talbot, Irish), whom he succeeded in 1737 as 2d Baron Talbot; in 1761 created Earl Talbot (Irish); in 1780 created Baron Dinevor (English). Eton and Oxford. He became lord steward of the king's household. He was a correspondent and friend of Francis North (1st Earl of Guilford), father of Lord North. M.P. for Glamorganshire, 1734–37.

Tankerville, 3d and **4th Earls.** See **Charles Bennet.** 1716–67 and **Charles Bennet.** 1743–1822

Tarleton, Banastre. 1754–1833

Born in Liverpool, the 3d son of John Tarleton (1719–73; merchant of Liverpool). Oxford and the Inns of Court. He entered the army as cornet in 1775 and went to America with Cornwallis in 1776. He took part in the unsuccessful attempt to take Charleston in 1776, in Howe's capture of New York in late 1776, in the battles of Brandywine and Germantown in 1777, and in the Battle of Monmouth during Clinton's retreat from Philadelphia in 1778. As brigade major of cavalry, he shared in the capture of Charleston by Clinton and in the subsequent operations under Cornwallis in the Carolinas, 1780–81. He was in command at the Battle of Cowpens, in which he displayed great personal courage but questionable military judgment. He was made prisoner of war at Cornwallis' surrender at Yorktown in October, 1781, but was soon returned to England on parole. He was major general in 1794, served in Portugal in 1798, became lieutenant general in 1801, served in Ireland in 1803, was made full general in 1812, and was made Knight of the Bath in 1820. In 1787 he published an account of the campaigns of 1780–81 in America. He was unquestionably a brave, gallant, and competent officer, and the charges of unnecessary brutality lodged against him by the colonists in the Carolinas were perhaps exaggerated or, owing to his parlous situation there, were perhaps militarily justified. Portraits by Reynolds and Gainsborough. M.P. for Liverpool, 1790–1806 and 1807–12.

Tassie, James. 1735–99

The 4th child of William Tassie (of Pollokshaws, near Glasgow; tanner). He began his career as a stonemason but in his spare time studied painting. In 1763 he went to Dublin as an assistant to a physician but developed skill in gem engraving and helped invent a white enamel compound of great usefulness in the production of medallion portraits and the reproduction of precious stones. In 1766 he went to London, where he received many commissions, including orders from the Empress of Russia, and exhibited at the Royal Academy, 1769–91. He executed many medallion portraits of notable contemporaries and in 1775 and 1791 published catalogues of his works. Portrait by Paxton.

Tavistock, Marquesses. See Francis Russell. 1739–67 and **Francis Russell.** 1765–1802

Taylor, Clement. d. 1804

Of Tovil House, near Maidstone, Kent; 2d son of Clement Taylor (of Wrotham, Kent; paper manufacturer), from whom he inherited prosperous paper mills. He was independent in politics, but in the House of Commons he voted regularly against the North ministry from 1780, and in his one reported speech in the House, in early 1782, he condemned the ministry's mismanagement of naval affairs. He voted against North in all 5 of the crucial divisions recorded in February and March, 1782. He voted for Shelburne's peace terms and for Fox's India Bill in 1783 and opposed Pitt until he left Parliament. He retired to Ireland and died there. M.P. for Maidstone, 1780–96.

Taylor, Peter. 1714–77

Of Burcott, near Wells, Somerset, and Purbrooke Park, near Portsmouth, Hampshire; 2d son of Robert Taylor (of Wells; grocer). He was orphaned at the age of 13, and from that time earned his own living. In 1755 he was a silversmith in the Strand in London, and soon struck up friendships with Henry Fox and John Calcraft (*q.v.*), among the most "practical" politicians of their time. He was deputy paymaster of British troops in Germany, 1757–63, and was suspected of appropriating for his own use some of the funds that passed (or did not pass) through his hands. In 1763 he returned to England with a good income and a bad reputation and settled down to enjoy the former and gild the latter. He built "an elegant mansion" at Burcott and engaged in a "ferocious" election contest at Wells, in which he was said to have campaigned exuberantly and drunkenly. After his election he broke with Henry Fox and was unseated on petition by the House of Commons. He stood again for Wells, but after large expenditures was defeated. In 1774, however, he won election at Portsmouth with the support of the North ministry. It was a mutually unsatisfactory bargain, for there is no record that he ever addressed the House in behalf of the North ministry, and he received no further "favours." His attendance was irregular, and he died less than 3 years later. M.P. for Wells, 1765–66; Portsmouth, 1774–77.

Taylor, Robert. 1714–88

A highly successful architect who built many country houses and London landmarks, as well as buildings for Lincoln's Inn in 1756 and additions to the Bank of England. He sculptured several monuments for Westminster Abbey, 1743–46. He left most of his considerable estate to finance the teaching of modern languages at Oxford. He was knighted, and was sheriff of London, 1782–83.

Taylor, Robert Paris. ca.1741–92

Of Burcott, near Wells, Somerset, and Grately Lodge, near Andover, Hampshire; oldest son of Peter Taylor (*q.v.*). He served as deputy paymaster under his father in Germany, 1759–63, and was sheriff of Somerset, 1765–66. In 1765 he aided in his father's notoriously corrupt campaign. In 1768 he himself gained a seat in the House of Commons. He voted against the ministry on the Wilkes issues. The record shows only one occasion upon which he addressed that House, and then on a point of order. Demonstrating the power of heredity, he was imprisoned in Fleet Street in 1780 for sharp dealings with his debtors. He was believed to have become insane at some time before his death in prison 12 years later. M.P. for Berwick-on-Tweed, 1768–74.

Taylour, Thomas. 1724–95

Of Headfort House, near Kells, County Meath. He was born in Dublin, and in 1757 succeeded his father, Sir Thomas Taylour, as 3d baronet (Irish); in 1760 created Baron Headfort (Irish); in 1762 created Viscount Headfort (Irish); in 1766 created Earl of Bective (Irish). Trinity College, Dublin, from 1741; B.A., 1745. In 1754 he married Elizabeth, oldest daughter of Hercules Langford Rawley and Countess Langford in her own right. He was a member of the Irish Parliament, 1747–60, and was sheriff of County Meath in 1756. From 1783 he was a Knight of St. Patrick, and from 1785 an Irish privy councillor.

Tempest, John. 1710–76

Of Sherburn, near Durham, and Wynyard, near Stockton, Durham County; oldest son of John Tempest (of Durham; M.P.). Cambridge from 1728. In 1738 he married Frances, daughter of Richard Shuttleworth (1683–1749; M.P.). He came from an old Tory family of Durham and was listed as Tory in 1761. He became mayor of Hertlepool, and from 1742 a member of the House of Commons, where he voted mainly against the Whig ministries. In 1761, however, he supported Newcastle, and in 1764 he voted against Grenville on general warrants. He did not vote against repeal of the Stamp Act in 1766 but did not support the Rockingham ministry. He voted for Chatham's land tax. No speech by him in the House is recorded. M.P. for Durham City, 1742–68.

Tempest, John. ca.1741–94

Of Wynyard, near Stockton, Durham County; oldest son of John Tempest (1710–76) (*q.v.*); inherited a very large landed estate. Westminster from 1750, Cambridge from 1758. In 1767 he married Anne, daughter of Joseph Townsend (M.P.). He voted regularly in opposition to the North ministry, including a vote for the Dunning resolution of April 6, 1780. He voted for Shelburne's peace terms and against Fox's India Bill in 1783 and in 1784 tried to bring about a union of parties. Thereafter he opposed the Pitt ministry. M.P. for Durham City, 1768–94.

Temple, 1st and 2d Earls. See Richard Grenville. 1711–79 and George Nugent-Temple Grenville. 1753–1813

Temple, Henry. 1739–1802

Of East Sheen, near Mortlake, Surrey, and Broadlands, near Romsey, Hampshire; only son of Henry Temple; in 1757 succeeded his grandfather Henry Temple (ca.1673–1757; M.P.) as 2d Viscount Palmerston (Irish). Cambridge from 1757; M.A., 1759. He was a member of the Irish House of Lords from 1761, and in 1762 he won a seat in the English House of Commons with the help of Newcastle and Henry Bilson Legge. He supported Bute's peace terms in 1762. He traveled abroad, 1763–64, and returned to oppose Grenville on general warrants in his maiden speech. He became friendly with the Rockingham party leaders and served on the Board of Trade and Plantations, 1765–66. He regularly supported the current ministry, 1766–82. He was a member of the Admiralty Board, 1766–77; was a vice treasurer of Ireland, 1775–77; and served on the Treasury Board, 1777–82. He opposed the Dunning resolution of April 6, 1780, opposed Shelburne's peace terms, supported the coalition and Fox's India Bill in 1783, and opposed the Pitt ministry from 1784. He was fond of travel and social life; wrote light verse and travel diaries; and in 1784 was a member of Dr. Johnson's Literary Club. Sheridan's wife called him "a good natured stuttering Viscount." M.P. for East Looe, 1762–68; Southampton Borough, 1768–74; Hastings, 1774–84; Boroughbridge, 1784–90; Newport (Isle of Wight), 1790–96; Winchester, 1796–1802.

Temple, John. ca.1735–1800

Son of Sir William Temple (of Stowe, near Buckingham; 6th baronet); in 1786 succeeded his older brother Richard Temple (*q.v.*) as 8th baronet; related to the Grenville family. In 1760 he was appointed surveyor general of the customs in North America. In 1767 he was one of the original 5 members of the new Board of Customs for America, commissioned with the unpopular task of collecting colonial duties more effectively. He increased the complications of that assignment by marrying the daughter of James Bowdoin (ardent patriot and governor of Massachusetts, 1785–87). In 1770 he was removed from his appointment and returned to England. In 1772 he became surveyor general of customs in England, and in 1785 he was named consul general to the United States.

Temple, Richard. 1731–86

Of Nash House, Kempsey, near Worcester; in 1761 succeeded his father, Sir William Temple (of Stowe, near Buckingham), as 7th baronet. He was commissioner of the navy from 1761 and was comptroller of excise, 1763–86.

Templeton, 1st Baron. See **Clotworthy Upton**

Terrick, Richard. 1710–77

Oldest son of Samuel Terrick (rector of Weldrake and prebendary of York). Cambridge from 1726; B.A., 1729; M.A., 1733; fellow, 1731–38; D.D., 1747. He was preacher at the Rolls Chapel, 1736–57; chaplain to the speaker of the House of Commons, 1741–42; canon of Windsor, 1742–49; vicar of Twickenham, 1749–64; and canon of St. Paul's, 1749–57. With the help of the Duke of Devonshire he became chaplain to George II, and he was also bishop of Peterborough, 1757–64, and privy councillor and bishop of London, 1764–77. He left the Duke of Devonshire after Devonshire's resignation and supported Bute and then Grenville, 1762–65. Horace Walpole said that he had no assets save "a sonorous delivery and an assiduity of back stairs address" and that "ambition, creeping upstairs by little intrigues, formed his whole character."

Thanet, 8th Earl. See **Sackville Tufton**

Thistlethwaite, Robert. 1755–1802

Of Southwick Park, near Fareham, Hampshire; oldest son of Rev. Robert Thistlewaite (of Broughton, Hampshire). Oxford from 1772. In 1780 he was supported for election to the House of Commons by the Duke of Chandos. He voted consistently against the North ministry, including his votes in all 5 of the critical divisions reported in February and March, 1782. He voted for Shelburne's peace terms and against Fox's India Bill in 1783. He opposed Pitt, 1784–87, but thereafter usually supported him. M.P. for Southampton Borough, 1780–90.

Thomas, Edmund. 1712–67

Of Wenvoe Castle, near Cardiff, Glamorganshire; in 1723 succeeded his father, Sir Edmund Thomas, as 3d baronet. Westminster from 1725, Middle Temple from 1728, Oxford from 1730. In 1740 he married Abigail, daughter of Sir Thomas Webster (of Battle Abbey, Sussex). He attached himself to the court of the Princess of Wales as groom of the bedchamber to her young son, 1742–51; as clerk of the household, 1756–57; and as clerk treasurer to the Princess Dowager of Wales, 1756–61. He followed the political lead of Leicester House; in 1761 he pledged to support Bute in hopes of a place and was a member of the Board of Trade and Plantations, 1761–63. He was surveyor of the king's woods and forests, 1763–67. There is no record of any speech or vote by him in the House of Commons after 1763. M.P. for Chippenham, 1741–54; Glamorganshire, 1761–67.

Thomas, John. 1691–1766

He was said to have been the son of a drayman at St. Nicholas' brewery and of a washerwoman of All Hallows, London, but though his origins may have been somewhat lowly, that story seems unlikely. Merchant Taylors' School in London, to Cambridge; M.A., 1717; D.D., 1728. Because of his good knowledge of the German language he was a favorite of George II. He was bishop of St. Asaph, 1743–44; bishop of Lincoln, 1744–61; and bishop of Salisbury, 1761–66.

Thomas, John. 1696–1781

Son of Stremer Thomas (of Westminster; colonel of the guards). Charterhouse, to Oxford in 1713; B.A., 1716; M.A., 1719; fellow of All Souls' from 1720; B.D., 1727; D.D., 1731. He was prebendary of St. Paul's from 1731; canon of St. Paul's, 1742–48; chaplain to the king from 1742; preceptor to the Prince of Wales (later George III), from 1752; bishop of Peterborough, 1747–57; bishop of Salisbury, 1757–61; and bishop of Winchester, 1761–81. In the House of Lords he recorded his dissent to the vote of the peers approving the cider tax in 1763. He was "a useful bishop as well as a good preacher" (*DNB*). Portrait by Benjamin Wilson.

Thomas, John. 1712–93

Born at Carlisle, the oldest son of John Thomas (d. 1747; vicar of Brampton, near Carlisle, Cumberland). Oxford from 1730; B.C.L.

and D.C.L. in 1742; ordained in 1737. He became private tutor to the son of Sir William Clayton, and later married the son's sister. He was rector of Bletchingley from 1738, dean of Peterborough from 1740, chaplain to the king in 1749, and later to King George III. He was made dean of Westminster Cathedral and a member of the Order of the Bath in 1768, and was bishop of Rochester, 1774–93. He published at least one volume of sermons. Portrait by Reynolds.

Thomlinson, John. 1731–67

Of East Barnet, north of London, Hertfordshire; only son of Major John Thomlinson ("one of the best planters in Antigua," and a London merchant holding victualing contracts). Cambridge from 1750, Lincoln's Inn from 1752. He married (1) in 1757 Elizabeth, sister of Arthur Young (*q.v.*), and (2) in 1759 Mary, daughter of Thomas Warden Sergison (*q.v.*). In his youth he was extremely extravagant, but he sobered after joining his father's merchant company and also became a partner of Barlow Trecothick (*q.v.*). In 1761 he was returned for Steyning with the help of Newcastle and his second father-in-law, Thomas Sergison. In Parliament he supported Newcastle, voting against Bute's peace preliminaries in late 1762, and reflected in his politics his family's commercial contracts with America. He died in his 36th year, 4 days after his father's death. M.P. for Steyning, 1761–67.

Thomond, 1st Marquess, 1st Baron and **1st Earl.** See **Murrough O'Brien** and **Percy Wyndham-O'Brien**

Thompson, Beilby. 1742–99

Of Escrick, near York; oldest son of Beilby Thompson (of Escrick). Cambridge, 1759–64. He secured a seat in the House of Commons in 1768, when he was reported to have an income of £8,000 a year. He supported the Rockingham Whigs but seldom attended the House longer than "a fortnight every year" and had little political influence. He voted against unseating Wilkes in 1770 and voted for Dunning's resolution of April 6, 1780. He voted against the North ministry in 3 of the most critical divisions of February, 1782 and paired against North in the votes on motions of Cavendish and Rous in March. In 1783 he solicited Shelburne for a peerage and voted for Shelburne's peace terms, and on Shelburne's fall he supported the coalition with the same hope. That ministry also failed to make him a peer, and Pitt, though he created many more peers than his predecessors, proved equally unrewarding. He was mayor of Heydon in 1777. M.P. for Heydon, 1768–80; Thirsk, 1780–84; Heydon, 1790–96.

Thompson, Benjamin. 1753–1814

Born at North Woburn, Massachusetts, the son of Benjamin Thompson (d. 1754; a fairly prosperous and well-respected citizen of Massachusetts Colony). He attended Harvard in 1769 but did not take a degree. He became a schoolmaster in Massachusetts and New Hampshire and was a major in a colonial regiment. An able, ambitious, and assertive youth, in 1775 he attempted to ingratiate himself both with the rebellious colonists and with Governor Wentworth and the British and loyalist elements of Yankee society. Suspecting this maneuver, the patriots took him into custody for lukewarmness to the revolutionary cause, and he was thus forced to choose sides and declare himself. He elected loyalty to the crown, and, assisted by General Howe, who armed him with letters to English politicians, he took ship for England in 1776. There he quickly ingratiated himself with Lord George Germain, and even more intimately, it was rumored, with Germain's wife and daughters, who did indeed give many evidences of their friendship with him. Germain made him a secretary to the Board of Trade and Plantations, over which he himself presided, and later took him into his office of secretary of state for the colonies. He was charged by other officials with having indulged in corruptions in those offices to his personal financial profit. He denied the charge, and was warmly supported by Germain. But criticism of his conduct in office continued so strong that in early 1781 Germain expediently facilitated his return to America as lieutenant colonel of dragoons. He conducted himself well in several minor engagements in the southern states and meanwhile wrote letters of great intimacy, and professing great devotion, to Germain. At the end of the war in America he returned to England. His talent for scientific investigation had been convincingly demonstrated during his earlier years there, and he had been elected fellow of the Royal Society in 1779. He soon went to the Continent in search of further fortune, took service with the elector of Bavaria, and became a trusted and prosperous favorite of the elector, who created him Count Rumford. He made occasional brief visits to England and increasingly devoted himself to scientific research, in which he achieved an excellent reputation. He published important scientific papers, especially on thermodynamics. In 1799 he helped found the Royal Institution in London. He left to Harvard a bequest which still bears his title.

Thornhagh, John. See **John Thornhagh Hewett**

Thornton, Henry. 1760–1815

Of Clapham, Surrey; 3d son of John Thornton (1720–90; an ardent financial supporter of the evangelicals). In 1778 he was apprenticed to a London merchant, and in 1784 became a partner in his father's London banking firm. He also became a governor of the Bank of England, an authority on public finance, and a large subscriber to government loans. In the House of Commons he supported Shelburne in 1782 and voted for removing discriminations against Roman Catholics. He did not, however, vote on Shelburne's peace terms in 1783, and he opposed the receipt tax as badly drawn and easily evaded. He voted against Fox's India Bill and from 1784 supported Pitt. He was active in the Bible Society and in the Church Missionary Society, and was the first treasurer of the latter society. He gave very large sums to charity. In 1802 he published his papers on public credit. M.P. for Southwark, 1782–1815.

Thorold, John. 1734–1815

Of Syston Park, near Grantham, Lincolnshire; in 1775 succeeded his father, Sir John Thorold (1703–75; sheriff of Lincolnshire), as 9th baronet. Oxford from 1752. He also became sheriff of Lincolnshire. As a member of the House of Commons from 1779, he opposed the war in America and voted steadily in opposition to the North ministry, voting for the Dunning resolution of April 6, 1780, and voting against North in all 5 of the critical divisions reported in February and March, 1782. In 1782–83 he seemed to incline toward Fox against Shelburne; he did not vote on Shelburne's peace terms and voted for Fox's India Bill. After 1783 he usually opposed the measures of the Pitt ministry. He occasionally addressed the House, not eloquently but sensibly. M.P. for Lincolnshire, 1779–96.

Thoroton, Thomas. ca.1723–84

Of Screveton Hall, near Bingham, Nottinghamshire; oldest son of Robert Thoroton; grandson of Sir Richard Levett (lord mayor of London). Westminster from 1736, Cambridge from 1742, Lincoln's Inn from 1745. In 1751 he married Rosita Drake, an illegitimate daughter of John Manners (1696–1779) (*q.v.*), and also gained a connection with the Duke of Newcastle. Although his father was reputed a Tory, he himself was, according to Granby, "an extreme good Whig." He served both Rutland and Newcastle as a political agent. In the House of Commons he voted against repeal of the Stamp Act in 1766; voted against unseating Wilkes in January, 1770; followed Granby into opposition to the North ministry; and voted for the Dunning resolution of April 6, 1780. In June, 1780, he played the hero by rescuing several men attacked by the Gordon mobs. He was secretary of the Ordnance Board, 1763–70, and in 1782 was agent for the Leicestershire militia. His daughter married Charles Manners-Sutton (archbishop of Canterbury, 1805–28); her son was speaker of the House of Commons, 1817–35. M.P. for Boroughbridge, 1757–61; Newark, 1761–68; Bramber, 1769–82.

Thrale, Henry. ca.1729–81

Of Streatham Place and Southwark, London; only son of Ralph Thrale (brewer of Southwark; M.P.), whose business he inherited. Oxford from 1744, followed by the grand tour. In 1763 he married Hester Lynch (niece of Lynch Salusbury Cotton) (*q.v.*). He developed close connections with the Grenville family and made several attempts to secure a seat in Parliament. In 1765 he succeeded, with the acceptance of Newcastle, and supported the Rockingham ministry, 1765–66. He voted for Chatham's land tax in 1767 and after 1770 generally supported the North ministry, especially on issues involving Wilkes and popular reform. His only recorded votes in opposition to the North ministry were his vote for an increase in the pay of half-pay navy officers in 1773 and his vote to extend the Grenville Disputed Elections Act in 1774. He and his wife were close friends of Samuel Johnson, and he once suggested to North that he find a seat in the House of Commons for Johnson—a suggestion upon which North did not act. Johnson called Thrale (ironically, in view of his urban career and trade) "a plain independent English squire." His brewery

produced at least 4,000 barrels a year, and after his death it sold for
£135,000. M.P. for Southwark, 1765–80.

Thurlow, Edward. 1731–1806

Oldest son of Rev. Thomas Thurlow (rector of Knapton, near North
Walsham, Norfolk); brother of Thomas Thurlow (*q.v.*); in 1778
created Baron Thurlow, and in 1792 created Baron Thurlow (with a
special remainder). As a boy he was incorrigible; he was sent to a
small school for difficult boys and later to King's School, Canterbury.
Although his defiance of control continued, apparently his potential
ability caused a Cambridge college to overlook his past conduct and
admit him in 1748. He was expelled in 1751 for insolence and misconduct. In 1752 he enrolled at Middle Temple, and in his London lodg-
ings he became a friend of the poet Cowper, despite their utter
dissimilarity in manners and temperament. He at length became a
champion of the social and legal order he had earlier defied. He was
barrister in 1754, bencher from 1762, and treasurer of Middle Temple
in 1792. In 1762 he became king's counsel and allied himself with the
Bedford party. He became chief secretary to Viscount Weymouth
upon Weymouth's appointment as lord lieutenant of Ireland, but
because of a change in ministry neither he nor Weymouth went to
Ireland. In 1770 he became solicitor general in North's new ministry
and was attorney general, 1771–78. His quick wits, readiness to distort
facts to suit his end, ponderous eloquence, and overbearing self-confidence probably saved Lord George Germain from a vote of censure
for the mismanagement of the 1777 campaigns that ended in the surrender of Burgoyne at Saratoga. Partly for that service to the ministry he was made privy councillor and lord chancellor on June 2,
1778, a post he held until the coalition took office on April 9, 1783.
Though a member of North's cabinet and in several political crises
North's effective supporter, he was often openly and bitterly critical
of North. In 1781 and 1782 the king, who was impressed by his forcefulness and decision as compared to North, personally enlisted his
services to try to form a coalition ministry, but, as North had previously learned, no coalition ministry could be formed as long as the
king insisted on terms which none of the opposition leaders would
accept. He was lord chancellor again in the Pitt ministry, 1785–92, and
teller of the exchequer, 1786–1806. He presided at the trial of Warren

Hastings in 1788 and on another occasion defended the property rights of slaveholders in their slaves. His legal self-confidence was greater than his legal knowledge, and both were greater than his legal ethics, but he asserted his opinions with such impressive beetle-browed assurance that his legal opinions were seldom openly defied. Charles Fox once said that "no man could be as wise as Thurlow looks," and Lecky later concluded with justice that Thurlow's "complete freedom from every vestige of deference, modesty or hesitation all added to the impression of overbearing and exuberant strength." He won his way, certainly with North, and often with king and cabinet, as much by bullying as by ability. M.P. for Tamworth, 1765–78.

Thurlow, Thomas. 1737–91

2d son of Rev. Thomas Thurlow (rector of Knapton, near North Walsham, Norfolk); younger brother of Edward Thurlow (*q.v.*) to whose influence he largely owed his advancement in the church. Oxford, 1754–59; B.A., 1758; fellow, 1759; M.A., 1761; B.D., 1769; D.D., 1772. He was rector of Stanhope, in Durham County, in 1771; dean of Rochester in 1775; bishop of Lincoln, 1779–87; dean of St. Paul's 1782–87; and bishop of Durham, 1787–91. In 1780 he was attacked by Gordon rioters and escaped from them by fleeing in disguise across the housetops of London. Though *DNB* pronounced him "a zealous patron of literary merit," he was certainly not a stimulating spiritual or intellectual force and was therefore an acceptable if not distinguished prelate.

Thynne, Henry Frederick. 1735–1826

Of Kempsford, near Fairford, Gloucestershire, and Hawnes, Bedfordshire; 2d son of Thomas Thynne (1710–51; 2d Viscount Weymouth); younger brother of Thomas Thynne (*q.v.*); in 1776 added the surname Carteret after inheriting in 1763 from his maternal uncle John Carteret (*q.v.*); in 1784 created Baron Carteret. Cambridge from 1752. In 1810, at the age of 75, he married Eleanor Smart, "who had been his mistress for 43 years." He was clerk comptroller of the Board of the Green Cloth, 1762–65; master of the household, 1768–70; privy councillor and joint postmaster general, 1770–89. In politics he followed the lead of his brother, supporting Bute and then Grenville, opposing repeal of the Stamp Act in 1766, and then supporting Grafton and North to the extent that membership in the Bedford junto and observance of his brother's "interests" permitted. M.P. for Staffordshire, 1757–61; Weobley, 1761–70.

Thynne, Thomas. 1734–96

Of Longleat, near Warminster, Wiltshire; oldest son of Thomas Thynne (1710–51; 2d Viscount Weymouth); brother of Henry Frederick Thynne (*q.v.*); in 1751 succeeded his father as 3d Viscount Weymouth; in 1789 created Marquess of Bath. He was briefly at Cambridge University and then traveled on the Continent and perfected his talent for aristocratic dissipation. In 1759 he married Elizabeth Cavendish-Bentinck, older daughter of the 2d Duke of Portland, who proceeded to present him with 10 daughters, "all beautiful and good," according to Mary Delany (*q.v.*). Despite his connection with the Duke of Portland, who was a political ally of Rockingham, he became an important member of the Duke of Bedford's "Bloomsbury gang." In the early 1760's his debts made it expedient for him to plan a retirement to the Continent. Just in time, his friends and family made financial contributions, and on May 15, 1764, a helpful ministry, partly to rehabilitate him, appointed him lord lieutenant of Ireland. Before he went to Ireland (having served in that post *in absentia* from June to August), the Grenville ministry fell, and he was replaced by an appointee of the Rockingham ministry. In the House of Lords he opposed repeal of the Stamp Act in 1766 and recorded his dissent to the Grafton ministry's proposals to regulate the dividends and management of the East India Company, 1767–68. He was, however, secretary of state, northern department, January 20, 1768–October 21, 1768, and of the southern department from late October to December 19, 1770, when he withdrew in resentment at North's overruling policy toward Spain over the Falkland Islands affair, which was not as belligerent as his own. He rejoined the North ministry as secretary of state, southern department, on November 10, 1775, and on the death of Suffolk added, nominally, the duties of the northern department to his portfolio until November 24, 1779, when he again resigned from the North ministry, this time in a break with North which many thought to be part of a Bedford scheme to upset North and bring the Bedford group into undisputed control of the ministry.

861

From that point his political influence waned. The king had liked him
personally and had sometimes maneuvered for his advancement, but
North had never liked or greatly trusted him. He was a pleasing and
sometimes brilliant private conversationalist, but, according to Horace
Walpole, "there was nothing in Weymouth's character that recommended his morality." Certainly his talents, though not wholly lacking, were not of the substantial and mature sort that justified his being
given posts of such high responsibility. His abilities were better illus-
trated by an entry in the betting book at Whites Club dated April 13,
1769: "Ld. Ashburnham bets Lord Weymouth twenty guineas that
Sr. Peniston Lamb has a child born alive by Lady Lamb before Sir
Watkin Williams has by Lady Harriot Williams." Portrait by Lawrence.

Titchfield, Marquess: See William Henry Cavendish-Bentinck

Tollemache, Lionel. 1734–99

Styled Lord Huntingtower until 1770, when, as 3d but oldest surviving son, he succeeded his father, Lionel Tollemache, as 5th Earl of
Dysart (Scottish). In 1760 he married (1) Charlotte, "with £10,000,"
illegitimate daughter of Sir Edward Walpole. He supported the North
ministry, the coalition, and North after the coalition.

Tollemache, Wilbraham. 1739–1821

Of Calveley Hall, Cheshire; 2d son of Lionel Tollemache (4th Earl
of Dysart, Scottish); grandson of John Carteret (1st Earl of Granville); younger brother of Lionel Tollemache (*q.v.*), whom he succeeded in 1799 as 6th Earl of Dysart. He was captain in 1761, major
in 1771, and retired from military service in 1772. In the House of
Commons from 1771, he voted regularly against the North ministry.
He was chairman of the Wyvill Association for Cheshire, 1779–80;
voted for Dunning's resolution of April 6, 1780; and voted against
the North ministry in all 5 of the critical divisions recorded in February and March, 1782. He voted for Shelburne's peace terms but
supported the coalition in 1783, and was not re-elected in 1784. M.P.
for Northampton Borough, 1771–80; Liskeard, 1780–84.

Tonson, Richard. d. 1772

Of Water Oakley, near Windsor, Berkshire; 2d son of Jacob Tonson;

brother-in-law of William Baker (*q.v.*). He became a partner with his brother in the notable bookselling and publishing firm but "took little part in the concerns of the business." He was also part owner of several merchant-venture ships. In the House of Commons he seems to have supported in general the Pelham and Newcastle ministries, then the Grafton ministry, and briefly the North ministry, but few votes and no speech by him are recorded. He was popular, hospitable, and benevolent. M.P. for Wallingford, 1747–54; Windsor, 1768–72.

Tooke, John Horne. 1736–1812

Son of John Horne (poulterer of Leicester Square, London); in 1782 assumed the surname Tooke upon inheriting from his friend and admirer William Tooke. Westminster from 1744; Eton (where he lost the sight of one eye in a schoolboy fight) from 1746; Cambridge from 1756; B.A., 1758. He enrolled at Inner Temple in 1756, but his father wished him to take orders and bought him the curacy at New Brentford, which he held, 1760–63. "Being unsuited to clerical duties," he gave up the ministry life in 1765 and traveled on the Continent as a tutor. In 1765 he published a pamphlet defending Wilkes, in language certainly not clerical. From that point he developed an enthusiasm for popular reform and for the causes of Wilkes, whom from 1768 he volubly, violently, and effectively supported. He also helped organize the Society for Support of the Bill of Rights. But in 1771 he quarreled with Wilkes and later seceded from the Wilkites and formed the Constitutional Society to pursue popular objectives independently. In 1774 he was reproved by the House of Commons for a violent verbal attack on Speaker Fletcher Norton. In 1778 he was fined and briefly imprisoned for making a public attempt to raise funds to support the American revolutionaries and was also refused admission to the bar. By inheriting from his father about this time, he was able to give famous (or notorious) suppers in London, at which politics and reform were loudly discussed. He continued to pose belligerently in political controversy in the role of an old-fashioned radical and to write and publish political and philological pamphlets. He was tried for high treason in 1794 and won acquittal. He finally gained election to the House of Commons in 1801, but Parliament almost immediately passed an act declaring clergymen ineligible to sit in that House. M.P. for Old Sarum, 1801–1802.

Torpichen, 8th and 9th Lords. See **Walter Sandilands** and **James Sandilands**

Torrington, 4th Viscount. See **George Byng.** 1740–1812

Touchet, Samuel. ca.1705–73

Of Epping, Essex; son of Thomas Touchet (prominent dissenter and Manchester's "most considerable merchant and manufacturer of linen and cotton goods"). By 1750 he had established himself in London as a leading Lancashire merchant with a large American trade. Later he also owned merchant-venture ships, traded in slaves, held government contracts, and subscribed to government loans. He was a director of the Sun Assurance Company, 1756–64. From 1757 he exchanged favors and profits with Henry Fox; later he supported Bute. In 1763 he successfully fought off impending bankruptcy and regained great prosperity. He became a friend of Charles Townshend but tended to support the ministry currently in office. In November, 1762, he was reputed to have been the first to receive the news that peace preliminaries had been signed in Paris. In 1766 he was among those (most of the others being navy officers) who successfully applied for grants of land on St. John's Island in maritime Canada. He later secured iron-mine prospects near Lake Superior. In 1773 he hanged himself. M.P. for Shaftesbury, 1761–68.

Townsend, Chauncy. 1708–70

Of Austin Friars, London; only son of Jonathan Townsend (d. 1710; brewer of London). By 1744 he was a prosperous London linen merchant and until his death continuously held contracts to provision British forces and settlements in Nova Scotia. By 1750 he had acquired mines in Wales and gained a seat in the House of Commons. There he supported the Pelhams, then Bute, and then Grenville, voting against repeal of the Stamp Act in 1766. He supported the Chatham-Grafton ministry, but there is no evidence that he ever addressed the House of Commons. In 1767 he was one of those who secured large grants of land on St. John's Island in maritime Canada. M.P. for Westbury, 1748–68; Wigtown burghs, 1768–70.

Townsend, Isaac. 1685–1765

Of Thorpe, near Chertsey, Surrey; nephew of Sir Isaac Townsend (captain in the navy and resident commissioner at Portsmouth). He entered the navy ca. 1699 and became captain in 1720, rear admiral in 1744, vice admiral in 1746, and admiral in 1747. He was at Cartagena in 1741. While governor of Greenwich Hospital in 1756, he had custody of Admiral Byng. In Parliament from 1744, he supported Pelham and then Newcastle. He voted for Bute's peace preliminaries in December, 1762, did not vote on general warrants in 1764, but supported Rockingham in 1765. There is no evidence that he ever addressed the House of Commons. M.P. for Portsmouth, 1744–54; Rochester, 1757–65.

Townsend, James. 1737–87

Of Bruce Castle, Tottenham, Middlesex; oldest surviving son of Chauncy Townsend (*q.v.*). He was at Oxford from 1756. In 1763 he married Rosa Peregrina, illegitimate but wealthy daughter of Henry Hare (3d Baron Coleraine, Irish). He did not follow his father's political line of expedient support of the current ministry, but became a "veteran radical." He supported Shelburne in the early 1760's and with Shelburne's help secured a seat in the House of Commons in 1767. He immediately became an ardent defender of Wilkes and the popular causes. He was alderman of London from 1769; sheriff of London, 1769–70; lord mayor of London, 1772–73. In 1769 he was a founder of the Society for the Support of Civil Rights and at that time was also speculating, with Shelburne and MacLeane, in shares of the East India Company. In 1770 he voted against unseating Wilkes and contributed to a fund to pay Wilkes's debts and meet his living expenses. In 1771 he refused to pay his land tax in Middlesex on the ground that Middlesex was not constitutionally represented in Parliament since Wilkes had been arbitrarily replaced by Luttrell. Later he broke with Wilkes and supported John Horne Tooke. He strenuously opposed the North ministry on almost every issue and occasionally denounced it in the House of Commons in extreme terms. He was a leader of Shelburne's supporters in London and active in the Wyvill Association movement to reform Parliament, 1778–82. He voted for Shelburne's peace terms and spoke against Fox's India Bill in 1783. After 1784 he supported Pitt's reform measures but usually opposed his ministry on other issues. In 1787, just before his death, he strenuously defended Warren Hastings in the House. M.P. for West Looe, 1767–74; Calne, 1782–87.

Townshend, Charles. 1725–67

Of Adderbury, near Banbury, Oxfordshire, and Grosvenor Square, London; 2d son of Charles Townshend (1700–64; M.P.; 3d Viscount Townshend). Cambridge, 1742–45; Lincoln's Inn from 1742; Leyden University (with Wilkes and Dowdeswell), 1745–46; barrister in 1747. In 1755 he married Caroline, daughter of John Campbell (1678–1743; 2d Duke of Argyll, Scottish) and widow of the Earl of Dalkeith (Scottish). He was a member of the Board of Trade and Plantations, 1749–54; a member of the Admiralty Board, 1754–55; privy councillor from 1757; and secretary at war, 1761–62. He voted against Bute's peace preliminaries in December, 1762, and resigned, but was brought back into the Grenville administration to serve as president of the Board of Trade, March 1, 1763–September 9, 1765. In 1764, however, he opposed Grenville when he spoke brilliantly against general warrants. He was paymaster under Rockingham, 1765–66, and was chancellor of the exchequer in the Grafton-Chatham ministry from 1766 until his sudden death in 1767, when he was succeeded by Lord North. In his last year he was at odds with Chatham over East India policies and further angered Chatham by suddenly and casually promising the House of Commons that he would take immediate steps to secure greater revenue from the colonies. He tightened the enforcement of colonial customs and excise payments in ways that increased American resentment and helped lead to the revolution. At the time of his death Chatham had already demanded that Grafton dismiss him. "His phenomenon of genius was, perniciously to himself and uselessly to his country, lavished in unexampled profusion of parts in wanton buffoonery, only to excite transient and barren applause," wrote Horace Walpole. "His fame illustrates the willingness of his colleagues to let bombast and wit atone for instability in character." M.P. for Great Yarmouth, 1747–56; Saltash, 1756–61; Harwich, 1761–67.

Townshend, Charles. 1728–1810

Of Honingham Hall, near Norwich, Norfolk; only son of William Townshend (ca.1702–38; M.P.); grandson of Charles Townshend (1674–1738; 2d Viscount Townshend); in 1797 created Baron Bayning. Eton, 1742–45; Cambridge from 1747; M.A., 1749. He was known as "Spanish Charles" to distinguish him from his cousin Charles Townshend (1725–67) (*q.v.*), the "Spanish" probably being derived from his first assignment as secretary to the British embassy at Madrid, 1751–56. Originally a supporter of the Pelhams, he voted against the Bute and the Grenville ministries, 1761–65. He supported the Rockingham ministry, 1765–66, and served on the Admiralty Board, 1765–70. He became a trusted supporter of Lord North, and no vote by him against the North ministry is recorded. He served on the Treasury Board, 1770–77; served as a vice treasurer of Ireland, 1777–82; and was privy councillor from 1777. He voted against Shelburne's peace terms, supported the coalition, and voted for Fox's India Bill in 1783, and was treasurer of the navy, April–December, 1783, in the coalition. He went out of office with North, and was not re-elected to Parliament until 1790, when he frequently voted with Pitt. M.P. for Great Yarmouth, 1756–84 and 1790–96.

Townshend, Edward. See **Edward** (formerly **Townshend**) **Lovedon**

Townshend, George. 1724–1807

Of Raynham Hall, near Fakenham, Norfolk; in 1764 succeeded his father, Charles Townshend (1700–64; M.P.), as 4th Viscount Townshend; in 1787 created Marquess Townshend; older brother of Charles Townshend (1725–67) (*q.v.*). Eton, to Cambridge in 1741; M.A., 1749. In 1751 he married (1) Charlotte, daughter of James Compton (5th Earl of Northampton). He fought at Dettingen in 1743, Fontenoy in 1745, Laufelt in 1747, and retired in 1750, when lieutenant colonel, because of a difference with his commanding officer, the Duke of Cumberland. He brought in the militia bill in 1757, returned to the army to serve under Wolfe in Canada as brigadier general, and succeeded Wolfe in 1759 as commanding officer at Quebec. He served in Portugal in 1762; was master general of ordnance, 1763–67; and was lord lieutenant of Ireland from October, 1767 to October, 1772. He was recalled from Ireland because his policies, which were those of the court he represented, had caused great resentment. He was made lieutenant general in 1770 and was again master general of ordnance, 1772–82. He was made general in 1782. He was lord lieutenant of Norfolk in 1792. He supported Pelham and Newcastle until 1755, when he shifted his allegiance to Pitt. In 1762, Newcastle called him "a devoted friend to my Lord Bute," and in 1764 he voted with the Grenville ministry. He later supported the North ministry, in which he was a placeholder. In June, 1780, he was attacked by Gordon rioters and barely escaped serious injury. He was made field marshal in 1796. Horace Walpole called him a man "with much address, some humour, no knowledge, great fickleness, greater want of judgement, and with still more disposition to ridicule." M.P. for Norfolk, 1747–64.

Townshend, George. 1753–1811

Of Raynham Hall, near Fakenham, Norfolk; son of George Townshend (1724–1807) (*q.v.*). In 1774 succeeded through his mother to the title of Baron Ferrers and Compton, and was summoned by writ as Lord Ferrers to the House of Lords; in 1784 created Earl of Leicester; in 1807 succeeded his father as 2d Marquess Townshend. Eton, to Cambridge; M.A., 1773. He entered the army as cornet in 1770 and was lieutenant in 1771 and captain in 1773. He was captain of the gentleman pensioners from 1782. He was master of the mint, 1790–94; joint postmaster general, 1794–99; lord steward of the household, 1799–1802; president of the Society of Antiquaries in 1784; and a trustee of the British Museum. As a young man in the House of Lords during the North ministry, he steadily opposed that ministry and recorded his dissents to at least 10 majority votes. In 1778 he urged that the king be asked to end the war in America. In 1779 he urged a petition to the king to dismiss Sandwich and another petition to ask the king to effect "a total change of System." In that year he also opposed the suspension of the rights of sailors. In 1780 he favored an examination into public expenditures, favored a protest against the dismissal of Pembroke and Carmarthen from their lord lieutenancies, and favored legislation to prevent members of Parliament from holding government contracts. In 1781 he opposed government lotteries and annuities to raise public funds and protested the "ruinous prosecution of the unjust war" against the Americans. In 1782, when he was made privy councillor, he protested the peers' rejection of a bill to prevent abuses in public office. Portrait by J. S. Copley.

Townshend, Henry. ca.1736–62

3d son of Thomas Townshend (1701–80) (*q.v.*); nephew of George

Townshend

Townshend (1724–1807) (*q.v.*); brother of Thomas Townshend (1733–1800) (*q.v.*). Eton, 1748–53. He was ensign in the 2d Foot Guards in 1755, captain in 1758, wounded at Minden in 1759, lieutenant colonel in 1762, and killed in action at Willemstad. In his brief attendance of the House of Commons he represented the interests of his family, which (with the Cornwallis family) controlled the seat for which he had been elected. M.P. for Eye, 1758–60 and 1761–62.

Townshend, John. 1757–1833

Styled Lord John Townshend; 2d son of George Townshend (1724–1807) (*q.v.*). Eton, 1763–71; Cambridge from 1773; Lincoln's Inn from 1774. He became an intimate friend of Charles Fox and in Parliament opposed the North ministry, 1780–82. He voted against the motion to inquire into the recall of Rodney in May, 1782, when he also supported a motion for the reform of parliamentary representation. He was a member of the Admiralty Board in 1782 but resigned with Fox after Rockingham's death and Shelburne's primacy in July, 1782. He voted against Shelburne's peace terms, supported the coalition and Fox's India Bill in 1783, and was again a lord of the Admiralty Board during the coalition. In early 1784 he opposed Pitt and, as a "Fox's martyr," failed of re-election. He was privy councillor from 1806 and joint paymaster general, 1806–1807. M.P. for Cambridge University, 1780–84; Westminster, 1788–90; Knaresborough, 1793–1818.

Townshend, Thomas. 1701–80

Of Frognal, near Chislehurst, Kent; 2d son of Charles Townshend (1674–1738; 2d Viscount Townshend); nephew of Thomas Pelham-Holles (*q.v.*); father of Thomas Townshend (1733–1800) (*q.v.*). Eton from 1718; Cambridge from 1720; M.A., 1727; Lincoln's Inn from 1720. In 1730 he married Albinia, sister of George Augustus Selwyn (*q.v.*). He was a Whig by inheritance but, unlike most other members of his family, had little political ambition. He was an undersecretary of state, 1724–30; teller of the exchequer, 1727–80; and secretary to the Duke of Devonshire when the duke was lord lieutenant of Ireland in 1739. Three speeches by him, all on local matters of interest to his constituents, are recorded in the House of Commons. M.P. for Winchelsea, 1722–27; Cambridge University, 1727–74.

869

Townshend, Thomas. 1733–1800

Of Frognal, near Chislehurst, Kent; oldest son of Thomas Townshend (1701–80) (*q.v.*); grandson of Charles Townshend (1674–1738;
2d Viscount Townshend); in March, 1783, created Baron Sydney; in
1789 created Viscount Sydney. Eton from 1748; Cambridge from
1750; M.A., 1753. He was clerk of the household of the Prince of
Wales, 1756–60; clerk of the Board of the Green Cloth, 1760–62. He
supported Newcastle through 1762, voting against Bute's peace terms
in December. He opposed Grenville's Stamp Act and measures toward Wilkes, 1763–65; supported the Rockingham ministry; served
on the Treasury Board, 1765–67; and was a leading speaker for the
repeal of the Stamp Act. Under the Chatham-Grafton ministry he
was made privy councillor and joint paymaster in 1767, but resigned
in 1768. He was a bitter critic of the North ministry and a close political ally of Lord George (Sackville) Germain until Germain joined
that ministry in late 1775. In February and March, 1782, he voted
against the North ministry in all 5 of the critical divisions reported.
In the Rockingham ministry of 1782 he was secretary at war, and in
the following Shelburne ministry he was home secretary. In December, 1782, he defended Shelburne's peace terms in debate with Fox, and
in February, 1783, he told the House of Commons that Shelburne's
peace terms were the best that could be hoped for. In June, 1783, having just entered the House of Lords, he recorded dissent to the peers'
negation of a bill to curb abuses and mismanagement in public office.
In November, 1783, he allied with Thurlow, Temple, Pitt, and the
king to upset the coalition by defeating Fox's India Bill in the House
of Lords, and was rewarded by Pitt with the post of home secretary
of state, 1784–89. He was president of the Board of Control, 1784–90;
chief justice in Eyre south of Trent, 1789–1800. His daughter Mary
married John Pitt (1756–1835) (*q.v.*). Sydney, Australia, was named
for him. M.P. for Whitchurch, 1754–83.

Townson, John. ca.1725–97

Of Gray's Inn; 2d son of Rev. John Townson (rector of Much Lees,
Essex). He became a London merchant before 1755 and was intermittently a director of the East India Company, 1780–96. He was
allied with John Sawbridge (*q.v.*) and with the London group of
radical reformers, but he was also connected with the Earl of Sand-

wich and supported the North ministry on most issues. He is said to have gained his seat in Parliament in 1780 upon nomination of the government, after having paid that government £3,500 for the seat. In the critical divisions of February and March, 1782, he voted with the North ministry on all 5 that are recorded. He voted against Shelburne's peace terms and for Fox's India Bill in 1783. He supported the Pitt ministry, 1784–87. The records of the House report only one address by him, in 1783, on the East India Company. M.P. for Milbourne Port, 1780–87.

Tracton, 1st Baron. See James Dennis

Tracy, Anthony. See Anthony Keck

Tracy, John. 1722–93

Of Rathcoole, near Dublin; son of Thomas Charles Tracy (1690–1756; 5th Baron Tracy, Irish); in 1792 succeeded his half brother Thomas Charles Tracy (1718–92) as 7th Baron Tracy. Abingdon Grammar School, to Oxford in 1741; B.A., 1745; M.A. and fellow of All Souls' College from 1749; B.D., 1757; D.D., 1761. He was warden of All Souls' College and rector of Didbrook from 1766 until his death.

Tracy, Thomas. ca.1716–80

Of Sandywell Hall, near Cheltenham, Gloucestershire; 4th son of John Tracy (of Stanway, Gloucestershire); younger brother of Anthony Keck (*q.v.*). He became ensign in the 9th Foot in 1737, but retired from military service in 1746, when he married "a great fortune" in the person of Mary, daughter of Sir William Dodwell. In 1763 he won a seat in the House of Commons, where he voted with the opposition on the issues of Wilkes and general warrants, 1763–64. He supported Newcastle and the Rockingham ministry, 1765–66, and voted against Chatham's land tax in 1767. There is no evidence that he ever addressed the House. M.P. for Gloucestershire, 1763–70.

Treby, George Hale. ca.1727–63

Of Plymton Erle, Devon; 2d son of George Treby (of Plympton Erle; M.P.). He was ensign in the 1st Foot Guards in 1745, captain in 1751, and lieutenant colonel in 1758. When he entered the House of Commons in 1761, Bute listed him as "government." There is no evidence that he ever spoke or voted during his brief time in the House. M.P. for Plympton Erle, 1761–63.

Trecothick, Barlow. ca.1719–75

Of Addington, near Croydon, Surrey; son of Captain Mark Trecothick (mariner). Born in Boston, Massachusetts, and lived there until 1741. By 1750 he was well established in London as a merchant trading chiefly with the colonies, but he soon became also part owner of merchant-venture ships to India and elsewhere. He married (1) in 1760 a young woman of Boston and (2) in 1770 Anne, daughter of William Meredith (*q.v.*). He was an alderman of London, 1764–74; sheriff of London in 1766; and lord mayor of London in 1770. He won election to Parliament in 1768 with the help of Rockingham, having already been active and vocal in opposition to the Stamp Act and other repressive measures toward the colonies. He served as agent for the province of New Hampshire, 1766–74. He also held government contracts for remitting funds to America. Though he favored strong action against Wilkes, in January, 1770, he voted against expelling Wilkes from the House of Commons. He spoke some 50 times in House debates, urging conciliation of the colonies, and almost always in opposition to the Grafton and then to the North ministry. He did not stand for re-election in 1774. M.P. for London, 1768–74.

Treise, Christopher. 1728–80

Of Lavethan, near Bodmin, Cornwall; only surviving son of John Treise (of Lavethan). Oxford from 1747. He was sheriff of Cornwall, 1760–61. Though listed as a Tory when he was elected to Parliament in 1762, and again in 1766, he supported Newcastle and was knighted in 1762. He voted against Grenville on Wilkes issues and general warrants, 1763–64, and urged repeal of the cider tax in 1763. M.P. for Bodmin, 1762–68.

Trelawny (or Trelawney), William. ca.1723–72

Of Trelawny (or Trelawney), near Looe, Cornwall; oldest son of William Trelawny (or Trelawney) (navy captain); cousin of Edward Trelawney (1699–1754; governor of Jamaica, 1738–52); in 1762 succeeded his uncle Sir Henry Trelawney (whose daughter Laetitia he had married before 1756) as 6th baronet. Westminster from 1733. He was lieutenant in the navy in 1743 and captain in 1756. He was elected to Parliament in 1757 with the support of Newcastle, whom he supported against Grenville and Bute, voting against general warrants in 1764. In 1765 he supported Rockingham's ministry, and was appointed governor of Jamaica in 1767. He vacated his seat and served in that post until his death in Jamaica. He apparently never addressed the House of Commons. M.P. for West Looe, 1757–67.

Trentham, Viscount. See George Granville Leveson-Gower

Trevanion, John. ca.1740–1810

Of Austin Friars, London; 2d son of Rev. Hugh Trevanion (vicar of West Alvington, Devon). He became a London merchant and an ardent advocate of the Society to Support the Bill of Rights. As its champion he unsuccessfully contested a by-election at Dover in 1769, but in 1774 he won election there. In the House of Commons he regularly opposed the North ministry, voting against approval of the address from the throne in October, 1775, voting for Dunning's resolution of April 6, 1780, and voting against the ministry in all 5 of the critical divisions reported in February and March, 1782. In 1783 he voted for Shelburne's peace terms and against Fox's India Bill. In 1784 he was not re-elected. There is no evidence that he ever addressed the House before 1784. M.P. for Dover, 1774–84 and 1789–1806.

Trevanion, William. 1727–67

Of Caerhayes, near Tregony, Cornwall; son of John Trevanion (M.P.); grandson of 4th Baron Berkeley. He was probably schooled at Eton, and was at Oxford from 1744. He was groom of the bedchamber to the Prince of Wales, 1749–51; auditor of the Duchy of Cornwall, 1751–67. He became a close friend of Edward Eliot (*q.v.*) and probably followed Eliot's lead in support of Newcastle and Rockingham, though his income of £4,000 a year enabled him to profess full independence as a country gentleman. There is no indication that he ever addressed the House of Commons. M.P. for Tregony, 1747–67.

Trevelyan, John. 1735–1828

Of Nettlecombe, near Watchet, Somerset, and Wallington, near Scots

Gap, Northumberland; in 1768 succeeded his father, Sir George Trevelyan (1707–68), as 4th baronet; in 1777 inherited the Northumberland estates of his uncle Walter Blackett (or Calverley-Blackett) (*q.v.*). Oxford from 1753; M.A., 1757. From his election to the House of Commons in 1777, he regularly supported the North ministry until March, 1779, when he opposed it in the Keppel-Palliser controversy. In 1780 he voted for Dunning's resolution of April 6, and in February and March, 1782, he voted against the North ministry in all 5 of the critical divisions reported. In February, 1783, after great hesitation he voted for Shelburne's peace terms. He did not vote on Fox's India Bill in November, 1783. He did, however, support Pitt's proposals for the reform of representation in Parliament in 1783, and from 1784 he supported Pitt's ministry. He was sheriff of Somerset, 1777–78. M.P. for Newcastle-on-Tyne, 1777–80; Somerset, 1780–96.

Trevor, John Hampden. 1749–1824

Born in London, the son of Robert Hampden Trevor (*q.v.*) by his Dutch wife; shortly before his death succeeded his brother Thomas Trevor as 3d Viscount Hampden. Oxford from 1767; B.A., 1770; M.A., 1773. He was minister to Munich in 1780 and minister to Turin, 1783–98.

Trevor, Richard. 1707–71

Of Glynde, near Lewes, Sussex; 2d surviving son of Thomas Trevor (1658–1730; of Bromham, near Bedford, Bedfordshire; M.P.; lord privy seal; 1st Baron Trevor); brother of Robert Hampden Trevor (*q.v.*); cousin of Horace Walpole. Westminster, to Oxford in 1724; B.A., 1727; M.A., 1731; D.C.L., 1731, fellow of All Souls' College from 1727. He was bishop of St. David's, 1744–52; bishop of Durham, 1752–71. Though evangelical Whig, he recorded his dissent in the House of Lords from the vote repealing the Stamp Act in 1766. *DNB* pronounced him "a magnificent patron of merit, a man of considerable learning and exceptional benevolence."

Trevor, Robert Hampden. 1706–83

3d son of Thomas Trevor (1658–1730; of Bromham, near Bedford, Bedfordshire; M.P.; lord privy seal; 1st Baron Trevor); brother of

Richard Trevor (*q.v.*); in 1764 succeeded his half brother John Trevor as 4th Baron Trevor; in 1776 created Viscount Hampden; in 1754 added the surname Hampden upon inheriting the estate of John Hampden (of Great Hampden, Buckinghamshire). Oxford from 1723; B.A., 1725; fellow of All Souls' College from 1725 (2 years before his brother Richard became a fellow). He was clerk to the secretary of state, 1729–34; secretary to the embassy at The Hague, 1734–36; minister to The Hague, 1741–46; commissioner of revenue for Ireland, 1746–59; joint postmaster general, 1759–65. After 1762 he supported the Grenville ministry and opposed repeal of the Stamp Act in 1766. In the House of Lords he recorded dissent to the regulation of dividends and management of the East India Company and to the actions of the House of Commons against Wilkes, 1767–70. He was a fellow of the Royal Society from 1764 and carried on a friendly correspondence with Horace Walpole. He wrote Latin verses which were published in 1792 and gathered a collection of prints and drawings that was called among the finest in England. Portrait, probably by Opie.

Trist, Browse. ca.1698–1777

Of Bowden, near Totnes, Devon; oldest son of Nicholas Trist (of Bowden). Oxford from 1717. In Parliament from 1754, he voted against Bute's peace preliminaries in 1762, but was induced by some *quid pro quo* from Henry Fox to change his mind and vote with Bute in the final division. M.P. for Totnes, 1754–63.

Tryon, William. 1725–88

Of a family which emigrated from the Low Countries to escape the cruelties instigated by the Duke of Alva. He became captain of foot guards in 1751 and lieutenant colonel in 1758. About 1759 he married Miss Wake, a cousin (with a large fortune) of Lord Hillsborough, who thereafter assisted him in his career. He was governor of North Carolina, 1765–70; governor of New York, 1770–78. In 1776 he was forced by the revolutionaries to retire to a British ship in New York's lower harbor, and remain there, "impotent to control the course of events" (*DNB*), until he could re-enter the city with the troops of General Howe in late 1776. He commanded a Surrey regiment which made a successful raid into Connecticut in 1779. He remained in occupied New York as civil governor with only nominal powers until he returned to England in 1780. He was made lieutenant general in 1782.

Tucker, John. ca.1713–79

Of Weymouth, Dorset; oldest son of Edward Tucker (M.P.). Oxford. He was cashier to the treasurer of the navy, 1744–49; paymaster of marines, ca.1757–79; and keeper of the king's private roads, 1770–79. He secured one of the seats in the House of Commons "owned" by Bubb Dodington, and was sometimes called Dodington's "creature." A placeholder continuously, 1757–79, he is not known ever to have voted against the current ministry. He twice addressed the House, briefly and with slight effect. He was mayor of Weymouth 6 times between 1725 and 1773. M.P. for Weymouth and Melcombe Regis, 1735–47 and 1754–78.

Tucker, Josiah. 1712–99

The son of a farmer of Laugharne, Carmarthenshire, and Aberystwyth. He attended Oxford (and was said to have walked back and forth to Oxford from his home in Wales); B.A., 1736; M.A., 1739; D.D., 1755. He was canon and chaplain at Bristol from 1756 and dean of Gloucester Cathedral from 1758. He was vigorous and vocal in expressing his opinions on issues and on some controversial lay figures of the day; his opinions were seldom those of the court, and that fact may account for his failure to receive further advancement in the church. He was, nevertheless, a better-known and more influential figure than many a bishop of his time. In 1763 he published a pamphlet opposing "going to war for the sake of trade"; later he published other pamphlets, including several in favor of free trade, anticipating Adam Smith's arguments against monopolies and restraints on trade. Later he published arguments that the colonies should be allowed completely free trade and, if they wished it, complete independence. In ecclesiastical matters he was sometimes more conservative and insisted on strict interpretation and enforcement of clerical subscription to the 39 articles.

Tuckfield, John. ca.1719–67

Of Little Fulford, near Crediton, Devonshire; son of Roger Tuckfield (of London). In 1761, 1766, and 1767 he was listed as Tory, and while a member of the House of Commons he probably voted mostly against the Old Whig ministries, 1747–61. From 1761, however, he voted with such independence as to be almost unpredictable, and was usually classed as "doubtful" on political lists. He was still frequently in opposition. He did not vote against repeal of the Stamp Act in 1766 but voted against Chatham's land tax in 1767. There is no evidence that he ever addressed the House of Commons in his 20 consecutive years of membership. M.P. for Exeter, 1747–67.

Tudway, Clement. 1734–1815

Oldest son of Charles Tudway (of Wells, Somerset; M.P.); inherited family property in Antigua. Oxford from 1751, Middle Temple from 1752, barrister in 1759. In 1762 he married Elizabeth, daughter of Sir Rowland Hill (1705–83; M.P.; 1st baronet). In 1761 he was listed as Tory, but in 1762 he supported Newcastle against Bute. There is no record of his votes during the Grenville and Rockingham ministries, 1763–66, but he voted against Chatham's land tax in 1767 and supported the Grafton ministry on the Wilkes issues in 1769. In 1772 he voted against the North ministry on the Royal Marriage Bill but in 1774 voted with the ministry in opposition to relief for dissenters and to perpetuation of the Grenville Disputed Elections Act. Thereafter he was in general support of the North ministry until 1780, when he moved openly into opposition. In February and March, 1782, he voted against North in all 5 of the critical recorded divisions. He did not vote on Shelburne's peace terms in February, 1783, but supported Shelburne against the coalition and supported Pitt from January, 1784. He represented the same constituency in the House of Commons for more than 50 consecutive years. M.P. for Wells, 1761–1815.

Tufnell, George Foster. 1723–98

Of Turnham Green, near London, and Chichester, Sussex; 2d son of Samuel Tufnell (1682–1758; of Monkton Hadley, Hertfordshire; M.P.). In the House of Commons he opposed the Grenville administration on Wilkes and on general warrants, 1763–64, and supported the Rockingham ministry, 1765–66. He voted against the North ministry, 1774–80, on most major issues: against approval of the address from the throne in October, 1775, and for Dunning's resolution of

877

April, 1780. When John Glynn (*q.v.*) died in 1780, he declined the request from the forces in opposition to the North ministry that he stand in the 1780 general election for Glynn's seat for Middlesex, and did not return to Parliament. M.P. for Beverley, 1761–68 and 1774–80.

Tufton, Sackville. 1733–86

Styled Lord Tufton from 1734; in 1753 succeeded his father, Sackville Tufton (1688–1753; M.P.), as 8th Earl of Thanet. Westminster, 1741–49. In 1767 he married Mary Sackville, sister of John Frederick Sackville (*q.v.*) and granddaughter of the 1st Earl Gower. That marriage gained public interest because it resulted in Tufton's casting off his mistress, a well-known and popular courtesan named Nelly O'Brien (whose portrait was painted by Reynolds). In the House of Lords he registered dissents from the votes of the peers approving (1) the actions of the House of Commons regarding Wilkes in 1770, (2) the address from the throne in October, 1775, and (3) the address from the throne on continuing the war in America in 1778. He was hereditary sheriff of Westmorland. He died at Nice.

Tunbridge, Viscount. See **William Henry Nassau Zuylestein**

Turberville, Richard. 1707–71

Of Ewenny Abbey, near Bridgend, Glamorganshire; oldest surviving son of Edward Turberville (of Sutton, Glamorganshire). He was elected to the House of Commons merely to hold a seat temporarily in the interest of the Mansel family. He cast no recorded vote and did not reveal his political convictions by addressing the House. M.P. for Glamorganshire, 1767–68.

Turner, Charles. ca.1726–83

Oldest son of William Turner (of Kirkleatham, near Redcar, Yorkshire); created baronet in 1782. Inner Temple from 1744, Cambridge from 1745. He married (1) Elizabeth, daughter of William Wombwell (of Wombwell, near Barnsley, Yorkshire; perhaps a brother of George Wombwell [*q.v.*]). He was sheriff of Yorkshire, 1759–60, and was elected to the House of Commons in 1768 in opposition to the Grafton ministry. He signed the 1769 petition against the ministry's measures in the Wilkes case and in January, 1770, voted against unseating

Wilkes. In 1771 he voted against declaring printers Wheble and Thompson in contempt; in October, 1775, he opposed approval of the address from the throne; in April, 1780, he voted for Dunning's first resolution. In May, 1782, he supported Sawbridge's motion to shorten the duration of Parliaments and Shelburne's plan for a national militia. In March, 1783, he told the House of Commons that North and his fellow ministers should have been impeached long since for bringing about the war with the colonies and then losing it. In May, 1783, he called the coalition unconstitutional and said that he was "for reform" and "against aristocracy." M.P. for York City, 1768–83.

Turner, Edward. 1719–66

Of Ambrosden, near Bicester, Oxfordshire, and Sunbury on Thames, Middlesex; in 1735 succeeded his father, Sir Edward Turner (1691–1735; merchant and director of the East India Company), as 2d baronet. Eton, 1725–32; Oxford from 1735; M.A., 1738; D.C.L., 1740; barrister of Lincoln's Inn in 1745. He inherited and augmented his family's large holdings in government and East India Company stock, and in 1760 inherited from his paternal uncle John Turner a considerable landed estate at Sunbury and some £100,000. He became one of the largest landowners in Oxfordshire and the very pattern of the Whig country gentleman. He contested the hard-fought Oxfordshire election of 1754 and, after the inquiry, secured his seat. Though a Whig, he supported Bute in 1762; supported Grenville, 1763–66; and voted against repeal of the Stamp Act in 1766. M.P. for Great Bedwin, 1741–47; Oxfordshire, 1754–61; Penryn, 1761–66.

Turner, Gregory. 1748–1805

Of Battlesden, near Woburn, Bedfordshire; in 1766 succeeded his father, Edward Turner (*q.v.*), as 3d baronet; added the nurname Page (Page-Turner) in 1775 upon inheriting from his great-uncle Gregory Page. Eton from 1762, Oxford from 1766, Lincoln's Inn from 1765, grand tour. He was high sheriff of Oxfordshire in 1783. He dressed as a dandy, in pink silk suits, and was said to have an income of £24,000 a year, but he was more of a miser than a spendthrift: after his death 30,000 guineas were found in his desk and strongbox. His minor role in politics was played after 1784, when he generally supported Pitt, whom he greatly admired. M.P. for Thirsk, 1784–1805.

Turner, John. 1712–80

Of Warham, near Wells, Norfolk; in 1739 succeeded his father, John Turner (ca.1676–1739; collector of customs), as 3d baronet. Middle Temple from 1729, Cambridge from 1730, barrister in 1736, bencher from 1766, treasurer in 1774. Before 1760 he was considered a Pelham and Newcastle Whig, and he supported Newcastle in 1761. But in that year he also intimated to Bute his readiness to support him if given a place; he was appointed to the Treasury Board in 1762 and held that post until 1765. He then supported the Grenville ministry and voted against repeal of the Stamp Act in 1766. Until he left the House of Commons, he supported the North ministry, but he spoke infrequently and was not influential. M.P. for King's Lynn, 1739–74.

Twiss, William. 1745–1827

Of origins now obscure. He was trained as a military engineer and in 1760 was appointed to serve the Ordnance Office in the Tower of London. In 1762 he was sent to maintain the fortifications at Gibraltar; in 1771 he was recalled to England to improve the defenses of the Portsmouth dockyard. In 1776 he went with Burgoyne to Canada. He was engineer aide to artillery General William Phillips and was with him at Burgoyne's capture of Ticonderoga in 1777. He was made a prisoner of war when Burgoyne surrendered at Saratoga in October, 1777. He was exchanged and later served in Canada until 1783; he then served at Portsmouth and in 1799 was in Holland. He was made major general in 1805, lieutenant general in 1812, and general in 1825.

Twistleton, Thomas. ca.1735–88

2d but 1st surviving son of John Twistleton (1698–1763; of Broughton Castle, near Banbury, Oxfordshire); succeeded his father *de jure* in 1763 and was recognized by the House of Lords in 1781 as *de facto* 7th Baron Saye and Sele. He was ensign in the Scots Guards in 1754, was captain in 1758, and served in Germany until 1762. He was colonel in 1777 and major general in 1782. He played no significant part in the politics of the House of Lords and died by suicide, fearing that the pains in his head were incurable.

Tylney, 2d Earl. See John Child-Tylney

Tylney-Long, James. See James Tylney Long

Tynte, Charles Kemys. 1710–85

Of Halse Well, near Taunton, Somerset, and Kevenmabley, Glamorganshire; 3d son of Sir John Tynte; took the surname Kemys in 1735, upon succeeding his maternal uncle Sir Charles Kemys; in 1740 succeeded his brother as 5th baronet. He was a Somerset country gentleman with Tory instincts. He probably attended Oxford, since in 1759 he was made D.C.L. by Oxford. A colonel in the Somerset militia, he was considered Tory from his first election to the House of Commons in 1745, and in 1761 was listed as Tory. He generally voted in opposition: against the cider tax in 1763, against repeal of the Stamp Act in 1766, and against Chatham's land tax in 1767. He supported Grafton, however, on the Wilkes issues from 1768 and in general supported the North ministry until he withdrew from the House. M.P. for Monmouth Borough, 1745–47; Somerset, 1747–74.

Tyrawley, 2d Baron. See **James O'Hara**

Tyrconnel, 2d Earl. See **George Carpenter**

Tyrone, 2d Earl. See **George Beresford**

Upper Ossory, 1st Baron and 2d Earl. See **John Fitzpatrick**

Upton, Clotworthy. 1721–85

Of Castle Upton, near Templepatrick, County Antrim; 3d son of Lieutenant Colonel John Upton (of Castle Upton); in 1776 created Baron Templetown (Irish). In 1769 he married a sister of Sir Edward Boughton. He was clerk comptroller to the Princess Dowager of Wales, 1761–72. In 1770 he was one of the grantees of the "Upton Patent" of 20,000 acres in Otsego County in upstate New York.

Upton, John. 1718–?

Of Middleton, near Kirkby Lonsdale, Westmorland, and Ingmire Hall, near Sedbergh, Yorkshire; oldest surviving son of John Upton.

Eton from 1730; Cambridge from 1735; fellow, 1740–64; Lincoln's Inn from 1741; barrister in 1746. He was a protégé of James Lowther (1736–1802) (*q.v.*) and regularly followed Lowther's lead in politics. He supported the Grenville ministry, voted against repeal of the Stamp Act in 1766, voted for reduction of the land tax in 1767, and voted against the *Nullum Tempus* Bill in 1768. Only one speech by him before the House of Commons is reported, a minor one in 1762. M.P. for Westmorland, 1761–68.

Usher, St. George. ca.1715–75

Only son of John Usher (of Headford, County Galway; vice admiral of Connaught); in 1734 took the surname St. George from his mother's family; in 1763 created Baron St. George (Irish). He was sheriff of County Roscommon in 1737 and was a member of the Irish Parliament, 1741–63.

Uxbridge, 1st Earl. See Henry Bayly

V

Valentia, 8th Viscount. See Arthur Annesley

Van, Charles. d. 1778

Of Llanwern, near Newport, Monmouthshire; oldest son of Charles Van (of Llanwern). He married into an influential family, the Morgans of Tredegar. Elected to Parliament in 1772, he supported the North ministry on most issues until his death, though he voted against North on the Royal Marriage Bill in 1772 and voted for the extension of the Grenville Disputed Elections Act in 1774. On several occasions he urged the House to adopt strong repressive measures against the recalcitrant Americans. M.P. for Brecon Burgh, 1772–78.

Vane, Frederick. 1732–1801

Of Sellaby, Durham County; 2d son of Henry Vane (3d Baron Barnard of Barnard Castle, Durham County; and 1st Earl of Darlington); brother of Henry Vane (*q.v.*) and Raby Vane (*q.v.*). Westminster, 1740–46; Cambridge from 1750. In 1758 he married (1) Henrietta, sister of William Meredith (*q.v.*). He was a staunch Whig and in the House of Commons opposed Grenville on general warrants in 1764. He supported the Rockingham ministry, 1765–66, but opposed the Grafton and North ministries on the Wilkes and Middlesex election issues. On other matters he supported the North ministry until his retirement. He addressed the House of Commons very seldom. He was deputy treasurer of Chelsea Hospital. M.P. for Durham County, 1761–74.

Vane, Henry. ca.1727–92

Of Barnard Castle, Durham County, and Westminster; in 1758 succeeded his father, Henry Vane (of Barnard Castle), as 2d Earl of Darlington and Viscount Barnard; brother of Frederick Vane (*q.v.*) and Raby Vane (*q.v.*). Westminster, 1736–44; Oxford from 1744; M.A., 1749. In 1757 he married Margaret, sister of James Lowther (1736–1802) (*q.v.*), whose politics he tended to follow. He was ensign in the 1st Foot Guards in 1745, captain in 1747, lieutenant colonel in 1750, and retired from the military in 1758. He was lord lieutenant of Durham County, 1758–92; governor of Carlisle Castle, 1763–92; and master of the jewel office, 1763–82. He supported the Pelham and Newcastle ministries in the House of Commons, and in the House of Lords he took few recorded positions and no extreme ones, confining himself largely to the local interests of his constitutents in the Durham area. He opposed the coalition in 1783 and supported Pitt's Regency Bill in 1788. M.P. for Downton, 1749–53; Durham County, 1753–58.

Vane, Raby. 1736–69

3d son of Henry Vane (of Barnard Castle, Durham County; 1st Earl of Darlington); brother of Henry Vane (*q.v.*) and Frederick Vane (*q.v.*). He was captain in the navy in 1759. In the House of Commons from 1758, he represented the interests of his family and of James Lowther (1736–1802) (*q.v.*). There is no evidence that he ever addressed the House, and he died in his 33d year. M.P. for Durham County, 1758–61; Carlisle, 1761–68.

Vanneck, Gerard (or Gerrard) William. 1743–91

Of Putney and Hevingham Hall, near Norwich, Norfolk; in 1777 succeeded his father, Sir Joshua Vanneck (of London; Dutch by birth; "one of the richest merchants in Europe"), as 2d baronet. Eton, 1755–56. In Parliament from 1768, he opposed the Grafton and North ministries. He voted for Dunning's resolution of April 6, 1780, and in February and March, 1782, he voted against the North ministry in all 5 of the critical divisions recorded. In 1783 he supported Shelburne's peace terms and Pitt's reform proposals, but from 1784 he often opposed the Pitt ministry. There is no record that he ever addressed the House of Commons. M.P. for Dunwich, 1768–90.

Vanneck, Joshua Henry. 1745–1816

Of Hevingham Hall, near Norwich, Norfolk, and Huntingfield, near Halesworth, Suffolk; 2d son of Sir Joshua Vanneck (of London; Dutch by birth; first baronet; "one of the richest merchants in Europe"); younger brother of Gerard (or Gerrard) William Vanneck (*q.v.*), whom he succeeded in 1791 as 3d baronet; in 1796 created Baron Huntingfield (Irish). Eton, 1755–56. He became a partner in the prosperous family merchant-banking business in London. He was regarded as Tory. M.P. for Dunwich, 1790–1816.

Van Sittart, Arthur. 1726–1804

Of Shottesbrook, near Windsor, Berkshire; oldest son of Arthur Van Sittart (of Shottesbrook; wealthy country gentleman who made his fortune as a London merchant); older brother of Henry Van Sittart (*q.v.*) and George Van Sittart (1745–1825; M.P.). Eton from 1742, Oxford from 1744, Middle Temple from 1742. In 1773 he married Anne, daughter of Gabriel Hanger (*q.v.*). He professed political independence, and in 1761 was listed as Tory. He voted against the Grenville ministry on general warrants in 1764 but with Grenville against repeal of the Stamp Act in 1766. In general he supported the Grafton and then the North ministries until he withdrew from the House of Commons, though he voted against Grafton and Chatham's land tax in 1767 and against North on the Middlesex election issues. There is no evidence that he ever addressed the House of Commons. M.P. for Berkshire, 1757–74.

Van Sittart, Henry. 1732–70

Of Foxley, near Malmesbury, Wiltshire; 3d son of Arthur Van Sittart (of Shottesbrook, near Windsor, Berkshire; wealthy country gentleman who made his fortune as a London merchant); brother of Arthur Van Sittart (*q.v.*) and George Van Sittart (1745–1825; M.P.). He went to India with the Company in 1746 and became a friend of Clive at Fort St. David's. He returned to England in 1751, but again went to India and became a member of the council and its president in 1760. He served at the defense of Madras in 1759 and as acting governor of Fort St. George, 1759–60. He had a turbulent administration as governor of Bengal, 1760–64. He returned to England a wealthy man and lived there in lavish style. But he was received with coolness by some of the directors of the Company, and in 1766 he published a pamphlet in defense of his conduct in India. In 1769 he became a director of the Company. In the House of Commons, he voted with the Grafton ministry. He was lost at sea, on his third trip to India, in his 38th year. M.P. for Reading, 1768–70.

Vaughan, Benjamin. 1751–1835

Oldest son of Samuel Vaughan (West Indies planter and merchant; later settled in Mincing Lane, London, and became known as "an honest Whig"); his mother was Sarah, daughter of Benjamin Hallowell (of Boston). He was educated at nonconformist schools and then at Cambridge and Edinburgh. He became a friend and political supporter of Shelburne. He sympathized with the American, and then the French, revolutionaries and the Irish nationalists, and in 1784 he fled to France to avoid imprisonment for his "treasonable opinions." In France he was briefly imprisoned by the Carmelites, and in 1798, disliking the political outlook in both England and France, he emigrated to America. He was active in the literary field: he published the first collected London edition of Benjamin Franklin's works in 1779 and published several political tracts, 1789–96. M.P. for Calne, 1792–96.

Vaughan, Evan Lloyd. ca.1710–91

Of Corsygedol, near Barmouth, Merionethshire; 2d son of Richard Vaughan (of Merioneth; M.P.); brother of William Vaughan (*q.v.*). Eton, 1725–27; Cambridge from 1728. He was constable of Harlech Castle, 1754–91, and sheriff of Denbighshire, 1766–67. In the House of Commons (which he appears never to have addressed), he voted for

Dunning's resolution of April 6, 1780, and in February and March, 1782, voted against the North ministry in all 5 of the recorded critical divisions. He voted for Shelburne's peace terms and did not vote on Fox's India Bill in 1783. In 1785 he supported Pitt's measures for the reform of Parliament but opposed Pitt's ministry on many other measures. M.P. for Merionethshire, 1774–91.

Vaughan, John. ca.1731–95

2d surviving son of Wilmot Vaughan (3d Viscount Lisburne, Irish); half brother of Wilmot Vaughan (*q.v.*). He was ensign in 1746 and captain of dragoons in 1754 and served in Germany. In 1759 he became major and served in America, 1760–67 and 1776–79. He was colonel in 1772 and major general in 1777. He was second-in-command to Clinton in the expedition up the Hudson to relieve Burgoyne in 1777, and was in command at the Leeward Islands, 1779–82, though charged with peculation at the capture of St. Eustacious. In 1782 he was considered for appointment to the command in America, succeeding Clinton, and was made lieutenant general. In politics, when not absent on duty, he supported the North ministry, voting with it in all 5 of the crucial divisions recorded in February and March, 1782. He voted against Shelburne's peace terms and for Fox's India Bill in 1783 and opposed the Pitt ministry, 1784–90. He appears to have addressed the House of Commons only once. He succeeded John Burgoyne as governor of Fort William, 1779–80, and was governor of Berwick Castle, 1780–95, and Knight of the Bath in 1792. He died at Martinique. M.P. for Berwick-on-Tweed, 1774–95.

Vaughan, John. ca.1752–1804

Of Golden Grove, near Llandilo, Carmarthenshire; oldest son of Richard Vaughan (of Golden Grove; large landowner). Lincoln's Inn from 1771. He was lord lieutenant of Carmarthenshire, 1780–1804. He supported the North ministry in the House of Commons from his election in 1779 until February, 1782, when he voted against it in all 5 of the critical divisions reported. He voted for Shelburne's peace terms but did not vote on Fox's India Bill in 1783. There is no indication that he ever addressed the House. M.P. for Carmarthenshire, 1779–84.

Vaughan, William. 1707–75

Of Corsygedol, near Barmouth, Merionethshire; son of Richard Vaughan (of Merioneth; M.P.); brother of Evan Lloyd Vaughan (*q.v.*). Cambridge from 1727. In the 1754 elections he was a country gentleman and an avowed Tory, and in the House of Commons he was in general opposition to the Pelham, Newcastle, and Rockingham ministries, but he did not vote against repeal of the Stamp Act in 1766. He was lord lieutenant of Merionethshire and Cardiganshire from 1762. M.P. for Merionethshire, 1734–68.

Vaughan, Wilmot. ca.1730–1800

Of Crosswood House, near Llanilar, Cardiganshire; in 1776 succeeded his father, Wilmot Vaughan, as 4th Viscount Lisburne (Irish); in 1776 created Earl of Lisburne (Irish); half brother of John Vaughan (ca.1731–95) (*q.v.*). Eton, 1742–45. In 1763 he married (2) Dorothy, sister of Robert Shafto (or Shaftoe) (*q.v.*). He was secretary to the chancellor of the exchequer, 1761–62; lord lieutenant of Cardiganshire, 1762–1800; member of the Board of Trade and Plantations, 1769–70; member of the Admiralty Board, 1770–82; and fellow of the Society of Arts from 1787. As his appointments indicate, he supported the Grafton and North ministries, opposing the Dunning resolution of April 6, 1780. After the fall of the North ministry in 1782 he continued as a North supporter and at the crucial time of November, 1782, extracted from North a written statement of his attitude toward the current political situation and of his own political intentions. He opposed Shelburne's peace terms in February, 1783, but felt "neglected by the Coalition" when not given an English peerage and did not vote on Fox's India Bill in November, 1783. He opposed the Pitt ministry, 1784–90. M.P. for Cardiganshire, 1755–61; Berwick-on-Tweed, 1765–68; Cardiganshire, 1768–96.

Venables-Vernon, George. 1709–80

Of Sudbury Hall, near Uttoxeter, Derbyshire, and Kinderton, near Middlewich, Cheshire; only surviving son of Henry Vernon (of Sudbury, M.P.); added the surname Venables in 1715 upon inheriting from his great-uncle Sir Peter Venables; created in 1762 Baron Vernon. He married (1) in 1733 Mary, daughter of Thomas Howard (6th

Baron Howard of Effingham), (2) in 1741 Anne, daughter of Sir Thomas Lee (1687–1749; 3d baronet; M.P.), and (3) in 1744 Martha, daughter of Simon Harcourt (ca.1661–1727; M.P.; 1st Viscount Harcourt). He entered politics reputed a Tory but from 1754 supported Newcastle and in company with the 3 Cavendishes supported the Duke of Devonshire and opposed Bute in the crucial vote on the peace preliminaries in December, 1762. He opposed the North ministry in the House of Lords and dissented from the vote of that House approving the address from the throne in October, 1775. M.P. for Lichfield, 1731–47; Derby Borough, 1754–62.

Venables-Vernon, George. 1735–1813

Of Briton Ferry, near Swansea, Glamorganshire, and Newick Park, near Lewes, Sussex; grandson of 6th Baron Howard of Effingham; in 1780 succeeded his father, George Venables-Vernon (1709–80) (*q.v.*), as 2d Baron Vernon. Westminster, 1742–45; Cambridge from 1753; M.A., 1755. In 1757 he married Louisa, daughter and heiress of 4th Baron Mansel. He voted against Bute's peace preliminaries in 1762 and with the opposition on the Wilkes issues in 1763. He opposed Chatham's land tax in 1767 and the Grafton and North ministries on Wilkes and on the Middlesex elections. He opposed the North administration's policy and measures toward the Americans and voted for Dunning's resolution of April 6, 1780. His only reported speech in the House of Commons was delivered in 1769, on a point of privilege. M.P. for Weobley, 1757–61; Bramber, 1762–68; Glamorganshire, 1768–80.

Venn, Henry. 1725–97

3d son of Richard Venn (1691–1740; distinguished high churchman). Cambridge from 1742; B.A., 1746; M.A., 1749; ordained deacon, 1747; ordained priest, 1749; fellow at Cambridge from 1749. He was curate of several parishes in Cambridgeshire, London, and Surrey, 1749–59; vicar of Huddersfield, Yorkshire, 1759–71; chaplain to the Countess of Huntingdon until 1781; and rector of Yelling, Huntingdonshire, 1771–97. He became an intimate friend of Charles Whitefield and the Wesley brothers, and made a national reputation with the publication of his *Whole Duty of Man*, as well as of sermons and devotional works.

Verelst, Harry. d. 1785

Grandson of Cornelius Verelst (flower painter). Apparently orphaned at an early age, he was brought up by his uncle William Verelst, a portrait painter. He was with the East India Company in Bengal from 1750 and in 1758 was imprisoned by Suraj. He was in command at Chittagong, 1761–65, and carried out Clive's policies as governor of Bengal, 1767–69. He returned to England in 1770 "with an easy fortune" and purchased Aston Hall, near Sheffield, from Lord Holdernesse. He was attacked in public for corrupt management of affairs in India and, according to *DNB*, was "ruined by litigation raised by corrupt Bengal influences." In 1772 he published his excellently written and reasoned defense in a pamphlet entitled *An Account of English Government in Bengal*. He died at Boulogne.

Vere of Hanworth, 1st and 2d Barons. See **Vere Beauclerk** and **Aubrey Beauclerk**

Verney, John Peyto. 1735–1816

Of Compton Verney, near Kineton, Warwickshire; son of John Verney (master of the rolls, 1738–41); in 1752 succeeded his uncle Richard Verney (1693–1752) as 14th Baron Willoughby deBroke; nephew of the 3d Earl of Oxford; in 1759 added the name Peyto upon inheriting from his cousin Margaret Peyto of Warwickshire. Oxford from 1755; M.A., 1758; D.C.L., 1759. In 1761 he married Louisa (portrait by Romney), daughter of Francis North (*q.v.*) and stepsister of William Legge (*q.v.*) and Lord North, and by her he had 12 children. In 1763 he recorded dissent with a vote in the House of Lords approving the cider tax. He supported the North ministry, and was attacked but not badly hurt by Gordon rioters in 1780. He supported the 1783 coalition, voting for Fox's India Bill in December, 1783, and later supported Pitt. He was neither very active nor very influential in politics but was deeply interested in his home and family; he rebuilt Compton Verney from plans by Robert Adam.

Verney, Ralph. ca.1714–91

Of Claydon House, near Verney, Buckinghamshire; in 1752 succeeded his father, Ralph Verney (1683–1752; M.P.), as 3d Viscount Fermanagh (Irish) and 2d Earl Verney (Irish). Cambridge from

1733; M.A., 1735; Middle Temple from 1729. In 1740 he married Mary, daughter and heiress of Henry Herring (merchant and director of the Bank of England). He was a fellow of the Royal Society from 1758 and a privy councillor from 1765. He and his family were large landholders in Buckinghamshire and a powerful political influence there, largely controlling elections for Wendover. In the House of Commons he was a steady supporter of Rockingham and was a patron of Burke, whom he brought into Parliament for Wendover, to whom he loaned large sums, and whom he involved in speculation in shares of the East India Company—a speculation in which he himself was nearly bankrupted. He signed the Buckinghamshire petition of 1769 against the Grafton ministry for its measures toward Wilkes and voted against unseating Wilkes in January, 1770. He voted against approving the address from the throne in October, 1775; for the Dunning resolution of April 6, 1780; and against the North ministry in all 5 of the critical divisions recorded in February and March, 1782. He did not vote on Shelburne's peace terms in 1783 and supported Fox, as Rockingham's successor, in the coalition. He was, according to the Verney *Memoirs*, a man "of magnificent instincts, great artistic taste and knowledge, and boundless extravagance." M.P. for Wendover, 1753–61; Carmarthen Borough, 1761–68; Buckinghamshire, 1768–84 and 1790–91.

Vernon, Charles. 1719–1810

Of New Forest, Hampshire; 3d son of James Vernon (of Great Thurlow, near Haverhill, Suffolk; M.P.); brother of Francis Vernon (*q.v.*). His military career was sponsored by George Townshend (1724–1807) (*q.v.*). He was ensign in the foot guards in 1737, captain in 1753, colonel in 1761, major general in 1765 for 1762, lieutenant general in 1772, and general in 1783. He was governor of the Tower of London, 1763–1810. His only recorded vote during his 6 years in the House of Commons was against renewing the Grenville Disputed Elections Act in 1774. He was presumably a supporter of the Grafton and North ministries. M.P. for Tamworth, 1768–74.

Vernon, Edward. 1723–94

4th son of Henry Vernon (1663–1732; of Hilton, near Wolverhampton, Staffordshire); older brother of Richard Vernon (*q.v.*). He attended Portsmouth Royal Naval Academy, 1735–39, and became a navy lieutenant in 1743, captain in 1753, rear admiral in 1779, vice admiral in 1787, and admiral in 1794. He was knighted in 1773. He was on almost continuous active duty in and near the Mediterranean, 1739–62, and on harbor duty in British waters, 1763–76. He was in command in East Indies waters, 1776–81, and in 1779 captured Pondichéry from the French. In 1785 he made 2 successful balloon ascents from Tottenham Court Road, London.

Vernon, 1st Baron. See George Venables-Vernon. 1709–80

Vernon, Francis. ca.1715–83

Of Orwell Park, near Ipswich, Suffolk; oldest surviving son of James Vernon (of Great Thurlow, near Haverhill, Suffolk; M.P.; envoy to Denmark, 1702–1706); nephew of Admiral Edward Vernon (1684–1757); brother of Charles Vernon (*q.v.*); in 1762, on the urging of Lord Halifax, created Baron Orwell (Irish); in 1776 created Viscount Orwell (Irish); in 1777 created Earl of Shipbrook (Irish). Westminster from 1725, Cambridge from 1732, Lincoln's Inn from ca.1732, and probably Leyden University in 1737. He came from a Whig family allied to Halifax "but was practically a Tory, though he probably would not so have labeled himself" (*Peerage*). He was clerk to the Privy Council, 1738–62, and commissioner of the victualing office, 1747–62. In 1761 he offered Bute his support in return for "some favour," and was appointed to the Board of Trade and Plantations in 1763 (a post he held until 1765) and given an Irish peerage. He supported the Grenville ministry and voted against repeal of the Stamp Act in 1766 and against Chatham's land tax in 1767. In 1768 he opposed, with the Grafton ministry, Sir George Savile's *Nullum Tempus* Bill. M.P. for Ipswich, 1761–68.

Vernon, Henry. 1718–65

Oldest son of Henry Vernon (of Hilton Park, near Wolverhampton, Staffordshire; M.P.); older brother of Richard Vernon (*q.v.*); related through marriage to Earl Gower. Westminster, 1728–33; Cambridge from 1736; Lincoln's Inn from 1739; and made the grand tour from 1739. In 1743 he married Henrietta, daughter of Thomas Wentworth (3d Earl of Strafford). He sat in the House of Commons "in the interest" of Earl Gower and supported him and the Bedford clique. There is no evidence that he ever addressed the House. He was commissioner of excise, 1762–65. M.P. for Lichfield, 1754 and 1755–61; Newcastle-under-Lyme, 1761–62.

Vernon, Richard. 1726–1800

Of Hilton Park, near Wolverhampton, Staffordshire; 5th son of Henry Vernon (of Hilton Park; M.P.); brother of Henry Vernon (*q.v.*). He was an ensign in the foot guards in 1744, was captain in 1747, and retired from military service in 1757. In 1759 he married Evelyn, daughter of John Leveson-Gower (1st Earl Gower), widow of John Fitzpatrick (1st Earl of Upper Ossory, Irish), and sister of the Duchess of Bedford. He was a staunch supporter of the Bedford-Gower clique, a founder of the Jockey Club, one of the first to train horses at Newmarket, and widely known as "the Father of the Turf." He was clerk and later comptroller of the Board of the Green Cloth, 1764–65, 1768–69, and 1777–82. He supported the North ministry within the limits of the strategy of the Bedford-Gower clique and opposed Dunning's resolution of April 6, 1780, In February, 1782, he paired in 3 of the critical divisions which resulted in the downfall of the North ministry. He voted for Shelburne's peace terms and did not vote on Fox's India Bill in 1783. He generally supported the Pitt ministry, 1784–1790. M.P. for Tavistock, 1754–61; Bedford Borough, 1761–74; Okehampton, 1774–84; Newcastle-under-Lyme, 1784–90.

Verulam, 1st Baron. See James Bucknall Grimston

Villiers, George. 1751–1800

Son of Aland John Mason; grandson of John Villiers (1st Earl Grandison, Irish); took the surname Villiers in 1771 from the family of his mother, who was viscountess in her own right; in 1782 succeeded through her as 2d Earl Grandison (Irish). Eton, 1762–66. In 1772 he married Gertrude, daughter of Francis Seymour Conway (*q.v.*). He was a notoriously spoiled child who developed and retained extravagant tastes, was often on the Continent, and carried no weight in politics. There is no record that he ever spoke or voted in the House of Commons, though his contemporaries referred to him as a supporter of the North ministry. M.P. for Ludlow, 1774–80.

Villiers, George Bussey. 1735–1805

Styled Viscount Villiers from 1742; in 1769, succeeded his father, William Villiers, as 6th Viscount Grandison (Irish) and 4th Earl of Jersey (English); related to Newcastle and a close family friend of the Duke of Grafton, whose political line he followed both as commoner and as peer. He was one of Newcastle's "zealous young men" who formed the Young Whig Club, 1760–63, and was appointed to the Admiralty Board in 1761, but was dismissed from it in December, 1762, for adhering to Newcastle and voting against Bute's peace preliminaries. He returned to office with Rockingham as vice chamberlain of the household, 1765–69, and privy councillor. He was a lord of the bedchamber from 1769, but resigned that office in 1777, when Grafton left the North ministry in protest against its American measures. He returned once more to office with Rockingham, was master of the royal buckhounds, 1782–83, and voted for Fox's India Bill. He was captain of the gentleman pensioners, 1783–90; master of horse to the Prince of Wales, 1795–1800. In the House of Lords he recorded dissent to approval of the address from the throne in October, 1775, and to the peers' refusal to examine into public expenditures in 1780. M.P. for Tamworth, 1756–65; Aldborough, 1765–68; Dover, 1768–69.

Villiers, John Charles. 1757–1838

2d son of Thomas Villiers (1709–86) (*q.v.*); in 1824 succeeded his brother Thomas Villiers (1753–1824) (*q.v.*) as 3d Earl of Clarendon. Eton from 1766; Lincoln's Inn and Cambridge from 1774; M.A., 1776; barrister, 1779; L.L.D., 1833. From entering the House of Commons in 1784, he supported Pitt; his 2 recorded speeches before 1790 were in support of the Pitt ministry. He served as joint king's counsel for the Duchy of Lancaster; as privy councillor from 1787; as chief justice in Eyre north of Trent, 1790–1824; as colonel of yeomanry from 1794; and as ambassador to Portugal, 1807–10. M.P. for Old Sarum, 1784–90; Dartmouth, 1790–1802; Tain and Wick burghs, 1802–1805; Queenborough, 1807–12 and 1820–24.

Villiers, Thomas. 1709–86

Of Hindon House, near Warminster, Wiltshire, and the Grove, near Watford, Hertfordshire; 2d son of William Villiers (2d Earl of Jersey); in 1756 created Baron Hyde of Hindon; in 1776 created Earl of

Clarendon (new creation). Eton from 1725, Cambridge from 1728. In 1752 he married Charlotte, daughter of William Capel (1697–1743; 3d Earl of Essex). He was a regular placeman in government and supported the court in hopes of a peerage. He was not powerful politically but was always hopefully ready to serve. He was envoy to Warsaw in 1738, to Dresden in 1740, to Vienna in 1742, and again to Warsaw in 1744 and was ambassador to Berlin, 1746–48. He served on the Admiralty Board, 1748–56; as privy councillor from 1763; and as joint postmaster general, 1763–65 and in 1786. He was made Baron of the Kingdom of Prussia in 1782. In 1766 he recorded his only known disagreement with a ministry in office when he opposed repeal of the Stamp Act. M.P. for Tamworth, 1747–56.

Villiers, Thomas. 1753–1824

Of The Grove, near Watford, Hertfordshire; styled Lord Hyde from 1776; in 1786 he succeeded his father, Thomas Villiers (1709–86), (*q.v.*), as 2d Earl of Clarendon; brother of John Charles Villiers (*q.v.*). Eton, 1764–70; Cambridge from 1771. He followed his father's expedient politics and usually supported the current ministry. His only reported address to the House of Commons was in 1777, when he moved approval of the address from the throne. He voted against the Dunning resolution of April 6, 1780; he voted first against and then for Shelburne's peace terms in 1783 and against Fox's India Bill. He supported Pitt, 1784–86. M.P. for Christchurch, 1774–79 and 1779–80; Helston, 1781–86.

Vincent, Francis. ca.1718–75

Of Stoke D'Abernon, near Leatherhead, Surrey; in 1757 succeeded his father, Sir Henry Vincent (M.P.), as 7th baronet. Lincoln's Inn from 1734. He married (1) in 1741 Elizabeth, daughter of David Kilmaine (London banker), "who brought him a great fortune," (2) in 1746 Mary, daughter of Lieutenant General Thomas Howard, and (3) in 1761 Arabella, widowed daughter of John Astley (*q.v.*). An independent country Whig, he supported Newcastle against Bute and voted against Bute's peace preliminaries in December, 1762. He voted against Grenville over Wilkes and general warrants, 1763–64. He signed the Surrey petition protesting the Grafton ministry's measures against Wilkes in 1769, and was largely in opposition to the North ministry until he left the House of Commons. In 1779 and 1780 he headed the Wyville Association in Surrey. The records indicate that he addressed the House on 3 occasions. M.P. for Surrey, 1761–75.

Vyner (or Viner), Robert. 1717–99

Son of Robert Vyner (ca.1685–1777; of Gautby, near Horncastle, Lincolnshire; M.P.). Cambridge from 1738, Inner Temple from 1741. In 1754 he was an avowed Tory, and was elected "in the interest" of the Duke of Bedford. He was listed as Tory in 1761, and supported all motions which he believed maintained the rights and powers of Parliament, including those involving Wilkes. He favored the complete subjugation of the rebellious colonies, and opposed the peace commission of 1778. On May 26, 1778, he gave Burgoyne his first chance to state his case before Parliament by "asking him a few questions." Otherwise, he "was almost always with the Government." He voted against Dunning's resolution of April 6, 1780, but supported Burke on his bill to reform civil-list expenditure on June 3, 1780. He went into opposition with North in late 1782 and voted against Shelburne's peace terms and for Fox's India Bill in 1783. Thereafter he usually opposed Pitt. M.P. for Okehampton, 1754–61; Lincoln Borough, 1774–84; Thirsk, 1785–96.

Wake, William. 1742–85

Of Courteenhall, Northamptonshire, and Nazeing, near Ware, Essex; in 1765 succeeded his father, William Wake (of Riddlesworth Hall, Norfolk), as 8th baronet. Eton from 1755; Cambridge from 1760; M.A., 1767; Lincoln's Inn from 1764. He was sheriff of Northamptonshire, 1771–72. An ardent reformer who "piques himself on his independence," he steadily opposed the North ministry upon entering the House of Commons in 1774. He voted against approving the address from the throne in October, 1775; spoke in 1781 against continuing the war in America; and voted against the North ministry in 2 of the critical divisions and did not vote in 2 others in February and March, 1782. In July, 1782, he praised Shelburne to the House, but in 1783 did not vote upon Shelburne's peace terms. He voted against Fox's India Bill later that year, supported Pitt in early 1784, and did not seek re-election. M.P. for Bedford Borough, 1774–84.

Walcot (or Walcott), Charles. 1738–99

Of Walcot (or Walcott) Hall, near Wellington, and Bitterley Court, near Ludlow, Shropshire; oldest son of John Walcot (or Walcott) (M.P.); grandson of Sir Francis Dashwood. Westminster, 1748–54; Oxford from 1756. He was sheriff of Shropshire, 1782–83. In the House of Commons from 1763, he supported the Grenville ministry, 1763–65. He opposed the Rockingham ministry and voted against repeal of the Stamp Act in 1766, when he was listed by Bute as a Tory. In 1767 Newcastle also listed him as Tory, but in that year he voted for Chatham's land tax. There is no evidence that he ever addressed the House. M.P. for Weymouth and Melcombe Regis, 1763–68.

Waldegrave, George. 1751–89

Oldest son of John Waldegrave (*q.v.*); styled Viscount Chewton until 1784, when he succeeded his father as 4th Earl Waldegrave. Eton, 1759–64. In 1782 he married his cousin Elizabeth, daughter of James Waldegrave (*q.v.*). He was ensign in the foot guards in 1768, captain in 1773, and colonel in 1782. He saw active service in America as aide to Cornwallis, 1776–77. He was aide-de-camp to the king in 1782; vice chamberlain of the household, 1782–84; privy councillor from 1784; and master of the horse to the queen, 1784–89. He was elected to the House of Commons in 1774 "in the interest" of his uncle Lord Gower. His only reported speech there was in 1775, and his only recorded vote was in 1779, when he supported the North ministry in the Keppel-Palliser controversy. M.P. for Newcastle-under-Lyme, 1774–80.

Waldegrave, James. 1715–63

Styled Viscount Chewton until 1741, when he succeeded his father, James Waldegrave (1685–1741), as 2d Earl Waldegrave. Eton from ca.1724. In 1759 he married Maria, illegitimate daughter of Edward Walpole (*q.v.*). He was lord of the bedchamber, 1743–52; lord warden of the stanneries, 1751–63; privy councillor from 1752; fellow of the Royal Society from 1749; governor of the Prince of Wales, 1752–56; teller of the exchequer, 1757–63; and Knight of the Garter from 1757.

He was a close confidant of George II, and on June 8, 1757, was nominated first lord of the treasury (a post he held until June 12). He died of smallpox, and his young widow's secret marriage to the Duke of Gloucester was a chief cause of the king's insistence in 1772 on the passage of the Royal Marriage Bill to prevent such disasters in the future. He was, according to Horace Walpole, a man of pleasure but also of strict honor and reasonable sense. His memoirs were published in 1821.

Waldegrave, John. 1718–84

3d but 2d surviving son of James Waldegrave (1685–1741; 1st Earl Waldegrave); brother of James Waldegrave (*q.v.*), whom he succeeded in 1763 as 3d Earl Waldegrave. In 1751 he married Elizabeth, sister of the Duchess of Bedford and Granville Leveson-Gower (*q.v.*). He was ensign of foot guards in 1735, captain in 1743, colonel in 1748, major general in 1757, lieutenant general in 1759, and general in 1772. He was wounded at Fontenoy in 1745, and was present at St. Malo in 1758, at Minden in 1759, and at Warburg in 1760. He was groom of the bedchamber, 1747–63; governor of Plymouth, 1760–84; and master of horse to the queen, 1770–84. From a firm Whig family, he supported the Pelhams and later the Bedford clan, and every administration, 1767–83. Politics was not his chief interest, and he was more respected than influential in Parliament. As a peer he opposed repeal of the Stamp Act in 1766, opposed the coalition, and voted against Fox's India Bill in 1783. "He united much friendliness with a steady attention to his interest," according to Horace Walpole. M.P. for Orford, 1747–54; Newcastle-under-Lyme, 1754–63.

Walden (De Walden), 4th Baron. See John (later Griffin) Whitwell

Wallace, James. 1731–1803

Parentage and boyhood obscure. He entered Portsmouth Naval Academy in 1746 and gave many years of service in the West Indies and in American waters before gaining his commission as lieutenant in 1755. He was commander in 1762, captain in 1771, rear admiral in 1794, and admiral in 1801, having been knighted in 1777. He was with Howe off New York in July, 1778; off Rhode Island in August, 1778;

and with Arbuthnot from June, 1779. Later in 1779 he was captured by D'Estaing but was soon exchanged.

Wallace, James Thomas. 1729–83

Of Carleton Hall, near Carlisle, Cumberland; oldest son of Thomas Wallace (of Asholme, near Haltwhistle, Northumberland; attorney). Lincoln's Inn from 1754, barrister in 1761, bencher of Middle Temple from 1769, reader from 1778, treasurer in 1782. He was king's serjeant of the Duchy of Lancaster in 1768, and attorney general for Lancaster and Durham County. He was a close friend of Alexander Wedderburn and supported the North ministry after Wedderburn joined it. He was solicitor general, 1778–80, and attorney general, 1780–82 and again in May, 1783, when he supported the coalition—following in those offices the expedient footsteps of Wedderburn. On June 25, 1782, he defended Rigby's use as paymaster of interest on government funds under his jurisdiction for his private purposes. In February, 1783, he told the House of Commons that the king would accept Parliament's recognition of American independence, but in the same month he voted against Shelburne's peace terms. M.P. for Horsham, 1770–83.

Waller, Robert. ca.1733–1814

Of Hall Barn, Beaconsfield, Buckinghamshire; 3d son of Edmund Waller (d. 1771; M.P., 1722–54; "a dull, obscure person of great application to figures and the revenue, which knowledge he could never communicate," according to Horace Walpole); a brother of John Waller (ca.1723–57; M.P.) and Edmund Waller (ca.1726–88; M.P.). Eton, 1742–48; Oxford from 1751. He voted against Grenville and general warrants in 1764 but followed Grenville into opposition in 1765 and voted with him against repeal of the Stamp Act in 1766 and against Chatham's land tax in 1767. He voted with the opposition to the Grafton ministry on the Wilkes issues in 1769 but voted with North for expulsion of Wilkes in 1770. He then voted against North for extension of the Grenville Disputed Elections Act in 1774, but thereafter he supported the North ministry on every major issue until its end in late March, 1782, voting against all 5 of the reported crucial motions of February and March, 1782. He voted for Shelburne's peace terms in 1783 and supported Pitt from 1784. He was groom of the bedchamber, 1784–1801. M.P. for Chipping Wycombe, 1761–90.

Wallis, Samuel. 1728–95

3d son of John Wallis (1680–1768; of Fentonwoon, near Camelford, Cornwall). He served in the navy from 1743 and became lieutenant in 1748 and captain in 1757. He sailed around Cape Horn, explored Polynesia in the *Dolphin*, and claimed Tahiti for Britain, returning by way of the Cape of Good Hope after a voyage that took nearly 2 years. He was a member of the Admiralty Board, 1782–83 and 1787–95, and in 1785 published an account of his voyages.

Wallop, Henry. ca.1743–94

2d son of John Wallop (*q.v.*); brother of John Wallop (2d Earl of Portsmouth). He was captain of foot guards in 1762 and groom of the bedchamber, 1767–73. No speech or vote by him is recorded during his 6 years in the House of Commons, but Robinson listed him as "pro" ministry in 1772 and 1774. M.P. for Whitchurch, 1768–74.

Wallop, John. 1690–1762

Of Farley Wallop, Southampton; 3d son of John Wallop (d. 1694); in 1720 created Baron Wallop and Viscount Lymington; in 1743 created Earl of Portsmouth. Eton until 1708; Geneva, 1708–1709. He married (1) in 1716 Bridget, daughter of Charles Bennet (1st Earl of Tankerville), and (2) in 1741 Elizabeth, widowed daughter of James Griffin (2d Baron Griffin of Braybrooke). He was a volunteer officer at Audenaarde in 1708; a member of the Treasury Board, 1717–20; chief justice in Eyre north of Trent, 1732–34; lord lieutenant of Southampton, 1733–42; governor of the Isle of Wight, 1734–42 and 1746–62; D.C.L. of Oxford, 1755. M.P. for Hampshire, 1715–20.

Walpole, Edward. ca.1706–84

Of Frogmore, Windsor, Berkshire; 2d son of Robert Walpole (1st Earl of Orford); brother of Horatio Walpole (1717–97), (*q.v.*). Eton, to Cambridge in 1725; Lincoln's Inn from 1723; barrister in 1727. He took only a fitful interest in politics, preferring his music, his books, his garden, and his mistresses. He attended the House of Commons as an occasional concession to *noblesse oblige*, and there is no indication that he ever addressed it after 1754. He voted with the opposition to Grenville on general warrants in 1764 and, like others of his family, was presumably in condescending support of the Rockingham ministry, 1765–66. He withdrew from the House in 1768. Thanks to the greater energy and shrewdness of his father, his life was well padded by inheritance and by the life sinecures as clerk of the pells and master of pleas in exchequer. In the extravagant energy of his youth he summoned up the fortitude to serve as secretary to the 4th Duke of Devonshire when the duke was lord lieutenant of Ireland, with its further undemanding and unearned increment of Irish councillor, 1755–56. Apparently exhausted by this exacting public service, he thenceforth devoted his chief energies to more congenial pursuits. Unmarried, he left at least 3 illegitimate daughters. They married a bishop, two earls, and a brother of the king. M.P. for Lostwithiel, 1730–34; Great Yarmouth, 1734–68.

Walpole, George. 1730–91

Styled Viscount Walpole from 1745; in 1751 succeeded his father, Sir Robert Walpole (ca.1701–51), as 3d Earl of Orford; in 1781, on the death of his mother, succeeded as Lord Clinton; nephew of Horatio (Horace) Walpole (*q.v.*) and Edward Walpole (*q.v.*). Eton, 1742–47. He was high steward of King's Lynn from 1751, and high steward of Yarmouth, 1751–91; lord of the bedchamber, 1755–82; lord lieutenant of Norfolk, 1757–91; and colonel of Norfolk militia, 1758–91. After 1773 he was intermittently insane. He improved the care and feeding of cattle and practiced the ancient sport of hawking. In 1779 he sold the picture collection at Houghton, his family home, to the Empress of Russia for £40,000.

Walpole, Horatio (or Horace). 1717–97

After 1747 of Strawberry Hill, Twickenham; 3d son of Sir Robert Walpole (1st Earl of Orford); in 1791 succeeded his nephew George Walpole (*q.v.*) as 4th Earl of Orford but never took his seat in the House of Lords; brother of Edward Walpole (*q.v.*) and brother of Robert Walpole (ca.1701–51; 2d Earl of Orford). Eton, 1727–34; Cambridge, 1735–39; Lincoln's Inn from 1739; grand tour with Thomas Gray, 1739–41. He held the sinecure offices, provided by his father, of customs inspector, chief usher of the exchequer, clerk of the escheats, and comptroller of the pipe, 1738–97. He was a fellow of the Royal Society from 1747 and of the Society of Arts from 1753. In 1764 he published *The Castle of Otranto* and began the Gothic literary fashion he had already established in architecture with his mansion at Strawberry Hill. His correspondence and memoirs are invaluable (though not always impartial and accurate), sources for the political and social history of his time. He was a strong Whig, opposed to the North ministry and the war with the Americans. He was a trustee of the Sloane Museum and later the British Museum. For a full account of his career see standard sources. Portrait by Reynolds. M.P. for Callington, 1741–54; Castle Rising, 1754–57; King's Lynn, 1757–68.

Walpole, Horatio. 1723–1809

Of Wolterton, near Aylsham, Norfolk; in 1757 succeeded his father, Horatio Walpole (1678–1757; M.P.), as 2d Baron Walpole; created Earl of Orford in 1806. He was in the House of Commons, 1747–57, and in the House of Lords recorded dissents to the cider tax in 1763 and to restriction of parliamentary privilege in the Wilkes case. Otherwise he took little part in political affairs. M.P. for King's Lynn, 1747–57.

Walpole, Horatio. 1752–1822

Of Wolterton, near Aylsham, Norfolk; oldest son of Horatio Walpole (*q.v.*) whom he succeeded in 1809 as 3d Baron Walpole and 2d Earl of Orford of the new creation. Eton, 1764–70; Cambridge from 1771. He was secretary of Chelsea Hospital from 1783. In the House of Commons from 1780, he voted regularly against the North ministry, including his votes in all 5 of the recorded critical divisions in February and March, 1782. He supported Rockingham and Fox in 1782, voted against Shelburne's peace terms and for Fox's India Bill in 1783, and opposed Pitt in 1784. Later he broke with Fox over the French Revolution. He was but a minor figure in politics. M.P. for Wigan, 1780–84; King's Lynn, 1784–1809.

Walpole, Richard. 1728–98

3d son of Horatio Walpole (1678–1757; M.P.); nephew of Robert Walpole (1676–1745; 1st Earl of Orford; M.P.); brother of Horatio

Walpole (*q.v.*) and Thomas Walpole. In 1757 he married Margaret, daughter of Sir Joshua Vanneck (1st baronet; wealthy London merchant). He was captain of an East Indiaman until 1758, when he became a merchant-banker of London. In the House of Commons from 1768, he voted against approval of the address from the throne in October, 1775, and in general opposed the North ministry: in the 5 crucial divisions recorded in February and March, 1782, he voted against the ministry in all 5. He voted against Shelburne's peace terms and for Fox's India Bill in 1783; opposed Pitt in early 1784, and was not re-elected. M.P. for Great Yarmouth, 1768–84.

Walpole, Thomas. 1727–1803

Of Carshalton, near Sutton, Surrey; 2d son of "Old Horatio" Walpole (1678–1757; M.P.; 1st Baron Walpole); nephew of Robert Walpole (1676–1745, M.P. and 1st Earl of Orford); brother of Richard Walpole (*q.v.*); cousin and correspondent of Horatio (Horace) Walpole (*q.v.*). Eton, to Lincoln's Inn in 1741. In 1750 he married (1) Elizabeth, daughter of his business associate Sir Joshua Vanneck (1st baronet). He became an eminent merchant-banker of London and Paris and profited from government contracts to remit money and goods on a large scale to British forces on the Continent. He was a director of the East India Company, 1753–54. He supported Newcastle and Pitt, 1754–60, and remained faithful to Newcastle against Bute in 1762, voting against Bute's peace preliminaries in December, 1762. As a result, he temporarily lost a government contract to victual Gibraltar. He supported Grafton and then North until 1775, and was a member of North's secret committee on the East India Company in 1772. In 1769 he organized the Walpole Company which petitioned the crown for a grant of 2,400,000 acres in the Ohio Valley for trade and settlement. In that project he had the support of many leading politicians, but was opposed by Hillsborough, then secretary of state for the colonies, who resigned (to prevent dismissal) over the issue. The grant was made, but the project was completely frustrated by the American Revolution. In 1775 he joined Grafton in a turn to the opposition, chiefly because of disagreement with the North's ministry's measures in America. In 1780 he voted for the Dunning resolution of April 6 against the mounting power, so the resolution claimed, of the court. He was abroad and did not vote in any of the critical divisions of February and March, 1782, that led to the fall of the North ministry. He supported the coalition and voted for Fox's India Bill in 1783. He was not re-elected in 1784, and in his later years he fell into serious financial straits. M.P. for Sudbury, 1754–61; Ashburton, 1761–68; Lyme Regis, 1768–84.

Walsh, John. 1726–95

Of Warfield, near Wokingham, Berkshire; son of Joseph Walsh (governor of Fort St. George, India); cousin of Lady Clive. He began his career as a merchant in India, and was secretary to Clive and paymaster to the troops in Madras, 1757–59. He returned to England with the considerable fortune that seemed to accrue to paymasters in India, as in England. There he laid Clive's plans before Pitt and defended Clive's conduct in the House of Commons, to which he had gained election in 1761. He supported Newcastle and voted against Bute's peace preliminaries in 1762. He voted against Grenville on general warrants and on Wilkes issues, 1763–64, and against unseating Wilkes in January, 1770. He was a fellow of the Royal Society from 1770 and a trustee of Clive's will. He opposed the North ministry until 1774 and then supported it in general until 1780, when he voted for the Dunning resolution of April 6. He did not return with the new Parliament in 1780. M.P. for Worcester Borough, 1761–80.

Walsingham, 1st and **2d Barons.** See **William De Grey** and **Thomas De Grey.** 1748–1818

Walter, Edward. 1727–80

Of Stalbridge Park, near Sherborne, Dorset; 2d son of Paget Walter; inherited a fortune of some £300,000. He married Harriet, daughter of George Forrester (5th Lord Forrester, Scottish). He was a country gentleman whose interest in Parliament was primarily confined to local issues and perhaps to protecting his own capital against high taxes. After 1767 he generally supported the Grafton and North ministries until he left the House of Commons, leaving no indication that he had ever addressed the House. M.P. for Milburne Port, 1754–74.

Walter, John Rolle. See **John Rolle-Walter**

Waltham, 1st and **2d Barons.** See **John Olmius** and **Drigue Billiers Olmius**

Warburton, William. 1698–1779

2d and only surviving son of George Warburton (solicitor and town clerk of Newark, Nottinghamshire). He was articled for 5 years to a solicitor at Markham, but managed to secure a master's degree by some special arrangement at Cambridge and then took orders. He won the patronage of Sir Robert Sutton and was rector of Newton Blossomville, Buckinghamshire, 1726–30; vicar of Greasely, Nottinghamshire, 1727–28; and rector of Brant Broughton, near Newark, from 1728, the plurality of those benefices apparently not troubling his religious spirit. With the help of Newcastle he also became vicar of Frisby-cum-Steeping Magna, Lincolnshire, in 1730 and retained that post until 1756. From 1738 he was also chaplain to Frederick, Prince of Wales. He married a niece of Ralph Allen, of Prior Park, and became a friend of William Hurd, bishop of Worcester, and of Pope, whose *Essay on Man* he defended in 1739. In 1747 he published an edition of Shakespeare, and in 1751 an edition of the works of Pope. He was prebendary of Gloucester, 1753–55; prebendary of Durham, 1755–59; dean of Bristol, 1757–58; and bishop of Gloucester, 1759–79. He enhanced his reputation in ecclesiastical circles with his *Divine Legation of Moses*. His church associates were either his strong supporters or his ardent critics, for his personality admitted no moderate reaction. He preached both against the slave trade and against the aims of John Wesley. Though extremely inflexible in his dogma, he was "a very free-and-easy liver." He was robust and dogmatic to the point of overbearing rudeness, and thus naturally a highly controversial figure. Loving argument, he indulged in it with uninhibited vigor of language, attacking freethinkers as "a pestilent herd of Libertine scribblers." In his *Doctrine of Grace* he condemned men as unlike as Bishop William Law, John Wilkes, the Mystics, and the Methodists with equal abandon and ferocity. He attacked all Roman Catholics and all those who suggested that the discriminations against them be somewhat relaxed. He insisted that the existing Church of England was morally and administratively very close to perfection. In his polemics he frequently ignored truth as well as good manners, and because of this indifference to accuracy his scholarship as well as his preaching suffered. He had "the audacity and cunning of a pachyderm" and, in the words of C. R. L. Fletcher, "he was no more

904

exemplary as a bishop than he had been as a scholar." He was the kind of bishop Chancellor Thurlow might have become had he taken orders. Portraits by Charles Phillips and William Hoare.

Ward, John. ca.1700–74

Son and heir of William Ward (of Sedgley Park, Wolverhampton, Staffordshire); grandson of Harry Grey (3d Earl of Stamford); in 1740 succeeded his cousin as 5th Baron Ward; created Viscount Dudley and Ward. After a few years in the House of Commons, he took little part in politics, since he was a Tory and the times did not encourage overt Toryism. After the accession of George III he became more active and more vocal. He appeared ready to support Grenville but in the House of Lords recorded his dissent to the cider tax in 1763. He was with Grenville, however, in opposing repeal of the Stamp Act in 1766 and recorded his dissent to the peers' acceptance of that repeal. He also dissented to the proposed regulation of the dividends and administrative acts of the East India Company, 1767–68. M.P. for Newcastle-under-Lyme, 1727–34.

Ward, John. 1725–88

In 1774 succeeded his father, John Ward (ca.1700–74) (q.v.), as 2d Viscount Dudley and Ward of Worcestershire. Oxford from 1743. When elected to the House of Commons in 1754, he was considered an avowed Tory, and in 1761 he was listed as Tory. He supported the Bute and Grenville ministries and voted against repeal of the Stamp Act in 1766 and against Chatham's land tax in 1767. He regularly supported Grafton and North in the House of Commons until 1774, and then as a peer in the House of Lords. Between 1771 and 1774 he addressed the lower House several times on major issues. M.P. for Marlborough, 1754–61; Worcestershire, 1761–74.

Ward, William. 1750–1823

2d son of John Ward (1700–74) (q.v.); half brother of John Ward (1725–88) (q.v.), whom he succeeded in 1788 as 3d Viscount Dudley and Ward. Eton, 1765–68; Oxford from 1770. From his entrance to the House of Commons he supported the North ministry, voting with it in the 3 critical divisions recorded in February, 1782, and voting on March 15, 1782, against Rous's no-confidence motion. He voted against Shelburne's peace terms in February, 1783, but did not vote on Fox's India Bill in November, 1783. There is no evidence that he ever addressed the House of Commons. M.P. for Worcester Borough, 1780–88.

Ward, William Bernard. 1719–81

Of Bangor, near Belfast, County Down; only surviving son of Michael Ward (1683–1758; judge and member of the Irish Parliament); in 1770 created Baron Bangor (Irish); in 1781 created Viscount Bangor (Irish). In 1747 he married a daughter of the 1st Earl of Darnley (Scottish). He represented County Down in the Irish Parliament, 1745–70.

Waring, Walter. ca.1727–80

Of Groton, near Hadleigh, Suffolk; son of Robert Waring (of Owlbury, Shropshire). Cambridge from 1745. Upon his election to the House of Commons in 1755 he was considered a Tory, but the scarcity of recorded votes by him indicates either illness or lack of interest. His only recorded vote between 1773 and 1775 was with the opposition to the North ministry on the Middlesex election issue. After 1774, however, he does not appear again on any opposition voting list. No speech to the House of Commons is recorded. M.P. for Bishop's Castle, 1755–59; Coventry, 1773–80.

Warkworth, Lord. See Hugh Percy

Warren, George. 1735–1801

Of Stockport, near Manchester, and Poynton, near Macclesfield, Cheshire; only son of Edward Warren (of Poynton); grandson of George Cholmondeley (2d Earl of Cholmondeley). He was ensign in the 3d Foot Guards in 1755 and captain in 1756, but gave up his commission in 1758 after inheriting an income of £16,000 a year. He eloped that year with Jane, wealthy daughter of Thomas Revel (M.P.). In Parliament from 1758, he supported Bute's peace preliminaries in 1762; opposed Grenville over Wilkes and general warrants, 1763–64; supported Newcastle and Rockingham, 1765–66; and then supported Chatham and Grafton. After its first years, he opposed the North ministry in general—because, it was said, he resented not being offered a peerage. He voted with the opposition in the Keppel-

Palliser controversy in 1779; for the Dunning resolution of April 6, 1780; and against North in all 5 of the recorded critical divisions in February and March, 1782. He voted against Shelburne's peace terms but did not vote on Fox's India Bill in 1783. He apparently was abroad during the Fox-North-Pitt debates of early 1784. He was Knight of the Bath from 1761. His daughter married Thomas James Bulkeley (later Warren-Bulkeley) (*q.v.*). M.P. for Lancaster Borough, 1758–80; Beaumaris, 1780–84; Lancaster Borough, 1786–96.

Warren, John. 1730–1800

2d son of Richard Warren (archdeacon of Suffolk, 1745–48). Cambridge from 1747; B.A., 1750; M.A., 1754; ordained priest, 1754; D.D., 1772. He was rector of Leverington in the Isle of Ely from 1754; rector of Teversham, Cambridgeshire, 1761–68; rector of Snailwell, Cambridgeshire from 1768; prebendary of Ely, 1768–69; chaplain to Lord Sondes and vicar of Wisbeck in Cambridgeshire from 1774; rector of Mepal, Cambridgeshire, from 1775; archdeacon of Worcester from ca.1778; bishop of St. David's, 1779–83; and bishop of Bangor, 1783–1800. He published sermons and several tracts, and was considered accurate, hard-working, modest, and honest.

Warrender, John. ca.1686–1772

Of Lochend House, near Dunbar, Haddingtonshire; in 1722 succeeded his father, George Warrender (ca.1658–1722), as 2d baronet. In 1720 he married the daughter of Sir Patrick Johnston, lord provost of Edinburgh. He supported the Hanoverian regime in the Jacobite rising of 1745 and obtained grants of several confiscated estates.

Warrender, Patrick. 1731–99

Of Lochend House, near Dunbar, Haddingtonshire; in 1772 succeeded his father, John Warrender (*q.v.*), as 3d baronet. He was lieutenant of horse guards in 1756, served at Minden in 1759, was captain in 1760, was lieutenant colonel of dragoons in 1764, and retired from military service in 1776. He was first joint and then sole remembrancer in exchequer in Scotland, 1771–91. In Parliament he supported the Grafton and North ministries when present, but no speech by him is recorded. M.P. for Haddington burghs, 1768–74.

Warrington, 1st Earl. See **George Harry Grey**

Warton, Thomas. 1728–90

Younger son of Thomas Warton (vicar of Basingstoke; sometime fellow at Oxford); his brother Joseph Warton (1722–1800) was a literary critic and for nearly 40 years headmaster of Winchester. He went from grammar school at Basingstoke to Oxford in 1744 and remained there the rest of his life: B.A., 1747; M.A., 1750; B.D., 1767; took orders. He was tutor, fellow, and professor of poetry, 1757–65, and was later professor of ancient history. In 1749, at the age of 20, he published *The Triumph of Isis*, and in 1764 *The Oxford Sausage*. He edited Milton's earlier poems and an edition of Theocritus, but was best known for his *History of English Poetry*, which he later revised. He was a friend of Samuel Johnson and his circle. He had a passion for Gothic architecture and a robust contempt for social convention. In 1782 he attacked Chatterton's poems as forgeries. He was poet laureate, 1785–90. Portrait by Reynolds.

Warwick, 1st and 2d Earls. See **Francis Greville** and **George Greville**

Waterford, 1st Marquess: See **George Beresford**

Watson, Brook. 1735–1807

Of East Sheen, near Mortlake, Surrey; only son of John Watson (of Hull); created baronet in 1803. He went to sea at the age of 13 and was commissary at the sieges of Beauséjour, 1755, and Louisburg, 1757–59. From 1759 he was a successful commission merchant in London. He was commissary general to the forces in Canada, 1782–83; agent for New Brunswick, 1786–93; commissary general in Flanders, 1793–95; and commissary general in Britain, 1798–1806. He was alderman of London from 1784; sheriff of London, 1785–86; and lord mayor of London, 1796–97. He was intermittently a director of the Bank of England, 1784–1807, and chairman of Lloyds, 1796–1806. Though he made occasional gestures of political nonpartisanship, he usually supported the current ministry. M.P. for London, 1784–93.

Watson, Lewis Thomas. 1728–95

Of Lee's Court, near Faversham, Kent, and Rockingham Castle, near Market Harborough, Northamptonshire; 2d son of John Monson

(1693–1748; 1st Baron Monson); assumed the surname Watson in 1746 upon succeeding to estates of his first cousin Thomas Watson (3d Earl of Rockingham). Westminster, 1737–45; grand tour. In 1752 he married Grace, daughter of Henry Pelham (ca.1729–1803; M.P.). He was a member of the House of Commons, 1750–60; in 1760 he moved to the House of Lords as 1st Baron Sondes, his great ambition having been a peerage, which he extracted through his uncle the Duke of Newcastle. In the upper House he recorded dissents to Bute's peace preliminaries in 1762, to the cider tax in 1763, and to the ministry's proposals to regulate the dividends and management of the East India Company (as "very injurious to private property and alarming to public credit"). In 1775 he supported Chatham's bill to conciliate the colonies and in general opposed the North ministry. He was joint auditor of the imprest, 1754–95. M.P. for Boroughbridge, 1750–54; Kent, 1754–60.

Watson, Lewis Thomas. 1754–1806

Of Lee's Court, near Faversham, Kent, oldest son of Lewis Thomas Watson (1728–95) (*q.v.*), whom he succeeded in 1795 as 2d Baron Sondes. He was a cousin of Rockingham and gave him political support, opposing the measures of the North ministry in the House of Commons from 1776 and voting for Dunning's first resolution of April, 1780, when he left the House, with no record of having addressed it during his 4 years of membership. M.P. for Heydon, 1776–80.

Watson, Richard. 1737–1816

Younger son of Thomas Watson (1672–1753; clergyman; schoolmaster of Heversham, near Kendal, Westmorland). Cambridge from 1754; B.A., 1757; fellow, 1760; M.A., 1762; D.D., 1771. He became professor of chemistry, without stipend or formal qualifications, at Cambridge in 1764, fellow of the Royal Society in 1769, and regius professor of divinity at Cambridge in 1771. From 1776 he frequently offended the king by his outspoken opposition to the North ministry and its measures and in 1779 and 1780 by his activity in support of Wyvill's reforms and the London Association. He nevertheless was archdeacon of Ely, 1779–82, and bishop of Llandaff, 1782–1816. On May 30, 1783, he spoke long and learnedly in the House of Lords on the bill on church livings, but not lucidly enough to illuminate all the peers about where he stood regarding that bill. He published *Anecdotes of My Own Life,* and in 1776 *An Apology for Christianity,* in reply to attacks in Chapter 15 of Gibbon's *Decline and Fall.* In 1796 he published *An Apology for the Bible* (frequently reprinted in subsequent years) in reply to Thomas Paine. He was ambitious for preferment and flagrantly abused his patronage to that end. He was sympathetic with measures proposed in Parliament in the 1770's for the relief of dissenters from subscription to the 39 articles, so that dissenters might hold certain government offices or study at the 2 universities. While bishop, he lived chiefly on his private estate in Westmorland, where he planted trees, blasted rocks, reclaimed wasteland, and built farmhouses. He was also credited with some scientific ability in his researches into the solutions of salts. Portraits by Reynolds and Romney.

Watson, Thomas. ca.1701–66

Of Grindon Bridge, Durham County; son of Thomas Watson (of Berwick); uncle of Wilmot Vaughan (*q.v.*) and John Vaughan (ca.1731–95; M.P.). He was mayor of Berwick 6 times between 1727 and 1740 and commissary of musters in south Britain in 1732 and for Danish and Hessian mercenary troops in 1741. In 1761, Newcastle listed him as a "sure friend," and at that time he held a secret-service pension, presumably for political services. He voted against the Grenville ministry on Wilkes and general warrants, 1763–64. M.P. for Berwick-on-Tweed, 1740–65.

Watson-Wentworth, Charles. 1730–82

Styled Viscount Higham, 1734–46, and then Earl of Malton until 1750, when (as the 5th but only surviving son) he succeeded his father, Thomas Watson as 2d Marquess of Rockingham; grandson of Daniel Finch (1647–1730; 2d Earl of Nottingham and 6th Earl of Winchilsea); assumed the added surname Wentworth through his mother, Anne (daughter of Thomas Wentworth, 1st Earl of Strafford). Westminster from 1738. In 1752 he married Mary, daughter of Thomas Bright, and £60,000. He was a volunteer under Cumberland against the 1745 Jacobite uprising. He was a country gentleman and sportsman who, from a sense of *noblesse oblige* more than from ambition or talent, became an uncomfortable statesman and first minister but was by no means ignoble in either capacity. He was lord of the bedchamber, 1751–62; lord lieutenant of North and East Ridings, 1751–62; and Knight of the Garter in 1760. In 1762 he was dismissed from court office because he had supported Newcastle against the victorious Bute. He was in opposition until 1765; he then was first lord of the treasury, July 13, 1765–August 2, 1766, during which time he secured repeal of the Stamp Act. He was leader of the "New Whigs," the most numerous opposition party, 1770–82. After the fall of North he formed a ministry with Shelburne, but in about 3 months died suddenly, in July, 1782. Burke denied that he was personally ambitious, but Horace Walpole, given to cynical interpretations of nearly every man's motives but his own, pronounced him "ambitious, with excessive insolence [a phrase in itself illuminating], fond of talking business but dilatory in the execution" and said that his single talent lay in "attracting dependents." His career was largely one of frustration, for though twice first minister he held that post for a total of only about 15 months. His recorded dissents to votes in the House of Lords were many, and included opposition to (1) the East India Company Regulating Bill in 1767, (2) the East India Company dividend restrictions in 1768, and (3) arbitrary adjournment of the House of Lords on January 15, 1770. He also protested (1) the claim of the House of Commons of its right to expel an elected member in 1770, (2) rejection of Chatham's motion to reseat Wilkes in 1770, (3) clearing of the gallery of the House of Lords of all auditors in 1770, (4) acceptance of the Royal Marriage Bill in 1772, (5) restrictions on the East India Company in 1773, (6) regulation of the management of that company in 1773, (7) the Massachusetts Bay Colony Regulating Act in 1774, (8) The Massachusetts Bay Colony Justices Bill in 1774, (9) approval of the address from the throne in October, 1775, and October, 1776, (10) rejection of the address to the king protesting continuance of the American war in 1778, (11) rejection of the motion to protest the continuance of the ministry's policies in 1778, (12) rejection of the motion to ask the king to dismiss Sandwich in 1779, (13) rejection of the motion to ask the king to effect "a total change of System" in 1779, (14) suspension of the rights of sailors in 1779, (15) rejection of the motion to examine into public expenditures in 1779, (16) rejection of the motion to protest the dismissal of Pembroke and Carmarthen in 1780, (17) rejection of the bill to exclude holders of government contracts from membership in Parliament in 1780, (18) war with the United Provinces in 1781, (19) the raising of government revenue by annuities and lotteries in 1781, and (20) approval of the address from the throne of November, 1781. Portraits by Reynolds and Wilson; statue by Nollekens.

Watt, James. 1736–1819

Son of James Watt (1698–1782; carpenter, contractor, shipowning merchant, and chief magistrate of Greenock, near Glasgow). After attending school in Greenock he went to London, where he was apprenticed to an instrument maker of Cornhill. He appears then to have returned to Glasgow and to have spent some time as a student in the university. He was in Birmingham, 1768–1809, where he was long a partner of the leading industrialist, Matthew Boulton. There he invented the steam condenser that revolutionized the use of heat power. He was a fellow of the Royal Society from 1785, L.L.D. of Glasgow University in 1806, and a member of the Institute of France from 1808. For his career, see standard reference works.

Wauchope, Henry. ca.1720–68

Of Kildavannan, near Rothesay, Buteshire; oldest son of Francis Wauchope (of Edinburgh; advocate). He was barrackmaster of Plymouth, 1758–68, and deputy keeper of the privy purse, 1761–68. He was related to the Earl of Bute and acted as confidential secretary to Bute and later to Bute's brother James Stuart-Mackenzie. In 1763 he received a pension of £625 a year for life. His servility to Bute was notorious. After Bute's dismissal he supported Grenville. As a young man he appears to have visited Virginia and thereafter posed as an authority on America and Americans. M.P. for Bute and Caithness, 1762–68.

Way, Benjamin. 1740–1808

Of Denham Place, Buckinghamshire, near Uxbridge; oldest son of Lewis Way. Eton, ca.1753–57; Oxford and Inner Temple from 1758; barrister 1762; bencher from 1797. In 1767 he married Elizabeth Anne, daughter of William Cooke (provost of Kings College, Cambridge). He was elected to Parliament as a "new merchant member" in 1765, and appears to have been a silent supporter of the Rockingham party.

He voted against Chatham's land tax in 1767 and for Savile's *Nullum Tempus* Bill in 1768. He was a director of the South Sea Company from 1763 and its subgovernor, 1794–1807. M.P. for Bridport, 1765–68.

Webb, John. ca.1730–95

Of Norton Court, near Gloucester; son of Nicholas Webb (of Norton Court). He was sheriff of Gloucester, 1761–62; mayor of Gloucester, 1770–71, 1776–77, and 1786–87. He was shipping agent for the East India Company, and was elected to the House of Commons with a pledge to oppose continuance of the war in America. He spoke 4 times against the war, 1780–82, voted for Shelburne's peace terms and for Fox's India Bill in 1783, and opposed Pitt in early 1784. M.P. for Gloucester Borough, 1780–95.

Webb, John Richmond. 1721–66

Of Biddesden, near Ludgershall, Hampshire; oldest son of General John Richmond Webb (M.P.). Lincoln's Inn from 1739, barrister in 1745, bencher from 1762. He was a judge in Wales, 1764–66, and was elected to the House of Commons through the patronage of Bute and Grenville, whose ministries he supported, 1761–65. He spoke supporting the measures taken against Wilkes in 1763. Later he became a close friend of Wedderburn. M.P. for Bossiney, 1761–66.

Webb, Nathaniel. 1725–86

Of Taunton, Somerset; 2d son of Nathaniel Webb (collector of customs at Montserrat, West Indies), from whom he inherited plantations in the West Indies. He was schooled, at least in part, at Eton and was enrolled at Lincoln's Inn from 1742. He was sheriff of Somerset in 1771. He was a silent supporter of the North ministry in the House of Commons throughout its duration, including a vote against the Dunning resolution of April 6, 1780. M.P. for Taunton, 1768–75; Ilchester, 1775–80.

Webb, Philip Carteret. 1700–70

Of Busbridge, near Godalming, Surrey; 2d son of Daniel Webb (of Devizes). Middle Temple from 1727, Lincoln's Inn from 1741, barrister in 1744. He became an authority on constitutional law. He was secretary of bankruptcy in the Court of Chancery, 1745–66, joint solicitor to the treasury, 1756–65. He was a fellow of the Society of Arts from 1747 and of the Royal Society from 1749. In 1762 he declared his allegiance to Bute, played a leading part in the prosecution of Wilkes under Grenville in 1763, and later gave evidence in behalf of Wood in the case of Wilkes v. Wood and Halifax on general warrants. He published pamphlets attacking Wilkes's position, and was later indicted for perjured testimony in that case, but was acquitted. He opposed Rockingham in 1765, voted against repeal of the Stamp Act in 1766, and voted against Chatham's land tax in 1767. M.P. for Haslemere, 1754–68.

Weddell, William. 1736–92

Of Newby Hall, near Ripon, Yorkshire; 2d son of Richard Elcock (later Weddell; of Newby). Cambridge and Gray's Inn from 1753. In 1771 he married Elizabeth, half sister of Lady Rockingham. In the House of Commons from 1766, he naturally supported Rockingham. He signed the 1769 Yorkshire petition against the Grafton ministry for its measures in the Wilkes case; voted against expulsion of Wilkes in January, 1770; voted against approving the address from the throne in October, 1775; voted for Dunning's resolution of April 6, 1780; and voted against the North ministry in all 5 of the critical divisions recorded in February and March, 1782. In 1783 he voted against Shelburne's peace terms, but was prevented by illness from voting on Fox's India Bill. M.P. for Kingston-on-Hull, 1766–74; Malton, 1775–92.

Wedderburn, Alexander. 1733–1805

Oldest son of Peter Wedderburn (of Chesterhill, Haddingtonshire; lord of sessions); in June, 1780, created Baron Loughborough of Leicestershire; in 1801 created Earl of Rosslyn, Midlothian; from good but not affluent Scottish stock and was a brother-in-law of Henry Erskine (ca. 1710–65) (*q.v.*). Schooled at Dalkeith, and Edinburgh University from 1746; Inner Temple from 1753; Scots advocate in 1754; barrister in 1757. In 1782 he married (2) Charlotte, daughter of William Courtenay (*q.v.*), and granddaughter of Heneage Finch (1683–1757; 2d Earl of Aylesford). In 1757, while advocate in an open court case, he made remarks insulting to Lord President Craigie and found it expedient to leave Scotland immediately. In London he was sponsored first by Bute and then by Clive. He entered the House of Commons, listed as a Tory, in 1761, and became king's counsel and bencher of the Inner Temple in 1763. In 1769 he spoke well in support of Wilkes and signed the Yorkshire petition against the Grafton ministry. Rigby wrote to Bedford that Wedderburn's speeches "mixed wit, oratory and abuse to perfection." In 1770 he attacked North on the floor of the House so effectively that North determined to induce him to change sides. In 1771 he altered his previous political professions and joined the North ministry as solicitor general. North, though frequently troubled by Wedderburn's complaints, which were always prefaces to hints or demands for further "favours," was soon convinced that he was indispensable, even if not always dependable, as a defender of the ministry in the House of Commons. Wedderburn, to the king's open disgust, increasingly intrigued with William Eden for further rapid advancement for both men and even threatened to rejoin the opposition if not given additional prompt and lucrative "warrants of the King's confidence." In 1778 he won by this method the attorney generalship and also became chancellor to the queen and shortly thereafter became privy councillor and lord chief justice of the Court of Common Pleas. Disappointed, however, at not gaining a peerage and the lord chancellorship before the North ministry fell, he worked shrewdly with Eden through the remaining months of 1782 to induce North to return to politics in coalition with Charles Fox. They were successful, but Wedderburn was privately bitter about not being given the lord chancellorship. He was successful ten years later, and was lord chancellor, 1793–1801. He was a fellow of the Royal Society and of the Society of Arts from 1787 and a trustee of the British Museum, 1801–1805. His legal talents and rulings suffered from personal and political motivations: he argued with ingenuity, effectiveness, and apparent self-conviction on whichever side of the case seemed to offer the most profit. His desire for high office was voracious and his pursuit of it uninhibited by loyalties, modesties, or common decencies. Junius called him "the wary Wedderburn"; the king had a very low opinion of his integrity; and many thought him the most notorious turncoat of his time. Portrait by Reynolds. M.P. for Ayr burghs, 1761–68; Richmond (Yorkshire), 1768–69; Bishop's Castle, 1770–74; Okehampton, 1774–78; Bishop's Castle, 1778–80.

Wedgwood, Josiah. 1730–95

From a long-established Staffordshire family (his father and grand-father were both potters at Burslem), the 13th child of Thomas Wedgwood. He had little formal schooling. He followed his father into the pottery trade, flourished, and in 1759 opened his own pottery in Staffordshire. Because of the quality of his product he was named potter to the queen in 1762. In 1764 he cemented family unity by marrying Sarah, daughter of Richard Wedgwood and his 3d cousin. In 1769 he enlarged his pottery and built a new works, with an adjacent new village at Etruria to house his workmen and their families. His product made him the greatest contemporary figure in England in the qualitative improvement of the midlands ceramic trade, and he also improved the efficiency of manufacture and reduced the cost of ordinary pottery. He actively supported the notable advances made in the development of inland waterways, especially in the midlands. He was a man of personal charm and fine character and was the grand-father of Charles Darwin. He was a fellow of the Royal Society in 1783 and of the Societies of Art and of Antiquaries in 1786. Portraits by Reynolds and others.

Weir, Charles Hope. See **Charles Hope-Weir**

Wemyss, James. 1726–86

Of Wemyss Castle, Fifeshire; 3d son of James Wemyss (5th Earl Wemyss, Scottish), whose title had been attainted soon after 1745 because his oldest son, James Arthur Wemyss, had supported the Jacobite rising. In 1757 he married his cousin Elizabeth, daughter of William John Gordon (17th Earl of Sutherland, Scottish). He was midshipman in 1741, lieutenant in 1745, and retired from the navy in 1757. In 1759 he inherited Wemyss Castle and estates from his father. Elected to the House of Commons in 1763, he successively supported the Grenville, Grafton, and North ministries, though in 1774 he voted to extend Grenville's Disputed Elections Act. He voted against Dunning's resolution of April 6, 1780; with North in all 5 of the critical divisions recorded in February and March, 1782; and against Shelburne's peace terms in February, 1783. He supported the coalition and followed North into opposition to Pitt in 1784. There is no record of any address by him to the House. M.P. for Fifeshire, 1763–68; Sutherland, 1768–84.

Wenman, Philip. 1742–1800

Of Thame Park, Oxfordshire; in 1760 succeeded his father, Philip
Wenman (1719–60; M.P.), as 4th Viscount Wenman (Irish). Westminster from 1752; Oxford from 1760; M.A., 1762; D.C.L., 1773. In
1766 he married Eleanor, daughter of Willoughby Bertie (3d Earl of
Abingdon). Though of a Tory family, he voted steadily against the
Grafton and North ministries: in January, 1770, against the expulsion
of Wilkes; in October, 1775, against approving the address from the
throne; and in April, 1780, for Dunning's first resolution. He was presumably absent from illness and did not vote in any of the 5 crucial
divisions recorded in the House of Commons in February and March,
1782. He supported the Shelburne ministry in 1782 and voted for Shelburne's peace terms in February, 1783. From early 1784 he supported
Pitt, but there is no indication that, at least before 1790, he ever addressed the House of Commons. M.P. for Oxfordshire, 1768–96.

Wenman, Thomas Francis. 1745–96

2d son of Philip Wenman (1719–60; M.P.; 3d Viscount Wenman,
Irish); younger brother of Philip Wenman (*q.v.*). Westminster, to
Oxford in 1762; Inner Temple from 1764; barrister in 1770. From
1765 he was fellow of All Souls' College, Oxford. He was keeper of
the university archives, 1781–96, and regius professor of civil law,
1789–96. He sat in the House of Commons for 6 years "in the interest"
of the Berties, relations through his brother's marriage. He opposed
the Dunning resolution and, unlike his brother, appears to have supported the North ministry. His only recorded vote against it was in
April, 1777. M.P. for Westbury, 1774–80.

Wentworth, 9th Baron and 1st and 2d Viscounts. See **Edward Noel**   and
   Thomas Noel. 1745–1815

Wentworth, Paul. ?–1793

Of Hammersmith, Middlesex. He was born in America of parents
who were related to John Wentworth (governor of New Hampshire,
1766–76) and to the Marquess of Rockingham, and who owned plantations in Surinam. He went to England as a young man and established
himself as a stockbroker in London. He became a friend of the Earl
of Suffolk and a financial adviser to Lord North, who praised his

judgment and provided him with a pension of £739 a year. He served too briefly in the House of Commons to leave any record there, but was presumably a supporter of the North ministry. M.P. for Saltash, July–September, 1780.

Wesley, Charles. 1707–88

18th child and 3d surviving son of Samuel Wesley (1662–1735; churchman and poet of Epworth Rectory, near Gainsborough, Lincolnshire); younger brother of John Wesley (*q.v.*). Westminster from 1716; Oxford from 1726; B.A., 1730; M.A., 1733; ordained in 1735. While he was an undergraduate at Oxford and his brother, John, was a fellow of Lincoln College, they formed an association of undergraduates which met, at first to study the classics together, but later, led by John Wesley, to pray and conduct religious discussions not always orthodox. They became known, not flatteringly, as "the methodists." With his brother Charles Wesley continued his religious efforts after he left Oxford. He visited and preached in Georgia with his brother, 1735–36, and from 1739 preached itinerantly in England. He was more moderate in his beliefs and words than his brother or Whitefield, the third founder of the Methodist church. He developed no serious differences with the Church of England and in 1784 deplored John Wesley's decision to break with that church by ordaining ministers without its sanction. He wrote some 6,000 hymns, many of which are a familiar part of most English church services and a few of which are among the finest in the English language.

Wesley, John. 1703–91

15th child and 2d surviving son of Samuel Wesley (1662–1735; churchman and poet of Epworth Rectory, near Gainsborough, Lincolnshire); older brother of Charles Wesley (*q.v.*). For an account of his life see standard reference works. He was a deacon of the Church of England from 1725 and a fellow of Oxford from 1726. At Oxford, with his brother, he began the religious movement among undergraduates which developed into the Methodist church. His efforts were known and at that time sanctioned by the then bishop of Oxford. In 1733 he headed a religious mission to the colony of Georgia, and was there much influenced by the religious thinking and methods of the Moravians. In 1736 at Savannah he founded a religious society based on

918

Moravian models, in 1737 he published a hymnal, and in 1738 he began open-air preaching in those towns and villages in England where churches were closed to him. Later, in his most serious break with the Church of England, of which he was still a member, he appointed lay preachers for his movement without the concurrence or ratification of the Established Church. In 1744 he presided over the first Methodist conversion conference in London. Later he traveled widely and tirelessly in England and America, sometimes preaching 5 sermons in a day. His efforts were greatly supported by Selina, Countess of Huntingdon, and by the 2d Earl of Dartmouth. His tract condemning the conduct of the rebellious American colonists, published in 1776, had wide circulation and considerable influence in some British circles. His chief religious doctrine lent itself increasingly to the summary: "Believe, and thou shalt be saved." He was, according to the modern Oxford authority C. R. L. Fletcher, "the last educated believer in witchcraft" in England; and though he preached a system of church government that professed to be democratic, he "had throughout life the autocratic temper of a mediaeval pope." Portraits by Romney, Hone, and others.

West, Benjamin. 1738–1820

Born at Swarthmore, Pennsylvania (where his birthplace still stands on the college campus), the 10th child of John West (Quaker; of Springfield, Chester County, Pennsylvania), from a family of good cultivation and standing. At local schools and in his home he received a solid education in the established essentials, but his paramount interest in the arts was soon evident. Since artistic interest was not encouraged among Quakers of the time, he was at first largely self-taught, but his parents were extremely sympathetic with his hopes and in 1760 allowed him to go to Italy, where he studied painting until 1763. He then went to London, where he first exhibited his historical paintings in 1764. His talent was obvious, and his youthful good looks and charm were appealing to London society to whom a young American of this type was an unexpected *rara avis*. Though he was popular in aristocratic society, he was not carried away from earlier loyalties. In 1765 he married Elizabeth Shewell, Quakeress of Philadelphia. In the same year, he was elected a member of the Incorporated Society of Artists, and from 1767 was much employed by the king, who later gave him £1,000 a year, a stipend which he received until 1811. He was a founding member of the Royal Academy, exhibited at its first exhibition in 1769, and was its president in 1792. His pictures were, like himself, widely popular, and prints from them even more so—especially of *The Death of Wolfe*. He was the first artist to introduce modern costumes into historical paintings. Although his talents were not of the finest order, he was hardworking and determined to make the best of them. Portraits by Lawrence (2), Gainsborough, and Stuart.

West, James. 1704–72

Of Alcott Park, near Cirencester, Gloucestershire; only son of Roland West (of Prior's Marston, near Southam, Warwickshire; of an old Warwickshire family). Oxford from 1719; M.A., 1726; Inner Temple from 1721; barrister in 1728; bencher from 1761; reader from 1767; treasurer in 1768. In 1738 he married Sarah, daughter of Sir Thomas Stevens (timber merchant), and thereby acquired a fortune of £100,000. As a young man he traveled extensively on the Continent, where he collected books, pictures, medals, and manuscripts and became known as an antiquarian and amateur scientist. He was a faithful aide to Henry Pelham for 11 years, and then to Newcastle through 1762. He was secretary to the chancellor of the exchequer, 1743–52; joint secretary to the treasury, 1746–62; recorder of Poole, 1746–72; and recorder of St. Albans, 1759–72. He was a fellow of the Royal Society from 1726; its treasurer, 1736–68; and its president, 1768–72. In 1762 he voted against Bute's peace preliminaries and went into opposition with Newcastle. Although he thought himself shabbily treated by the Rockingham ministry, 1765–66, he supported it for Newcastle's sake. He opposed the Chatham-Grafton and the North ministries and supported movements for the reform of Parliament. In 1762 he made his only recorded speech in the House of Commons, offering a financial resolution. M.P. for St. Albans, 1741–68; Boroughbridge, 1768–72.

West, James. 1742–95

Only son of James West (1704–72) (*q.v.*). Harrow, to Glasgow University in 1760; grand tour in 1763. He served as auditor of land revenues, 1775–95. In his few months in the House of Commons he followed his father in support of the Rockingham-Newcastle Whigs; later, outside of Parliament, he was an active supporter of the Middlesex Association for reform of Parliament. There is no evidence that he ever addressed the House. M.P. for Boroughbridge, 1767–68.

West, John. 1729–77

Of Boldrewood Lodge, New Forest, Hampshire; son of John West (1693–1766), whom he succeeded in 1766 as 2d Earl Delawarr. In 1756 he married Mary, daughter of Lieutenant General John Wynyard. He was ensign in 1746; colonel in 1758; vice chamberlain to Queen Charlotte, 1761–66; master of horse to the queen, 1766–68; major general in 1761; and lieutenant general in 1770. He was a friend and political ally of Edmund Burke but carried little weight in court or in the House of Lords.

Westcote, 1st Baron. See William Henry Lyttelton

Westhall, Lord. See David Dalrymple. 1719–84

Westminster, Earl. See Patrick Murray

Westmorland, 7th, 8th, 9th and 10th Earls. See John Fane. 1685–1762
   Thomas Fane. 1700–71   **John Fane.** 1728–74   and **John Fane.** 1759–
   1841

Westport, 1st Viscount. See John Browne

Weymouth, 3d Viscount. See Thomas Thynne

Whalley (later **Whalley-Smythe-Gardiner**), **John.** 1743–97

Of Tackley Hall, near Woodstock, Oxfordshire, and Roche Court, near Fareham, Hampshire; oldest son of Robert Whalley (of Clerk Hill, near Whalley, Lancashire, and Oxford; physician); added the surname Gardiner in 1779 upon inheriting from his mother's cousin Sir William Gardiner; added the surname Smythe upon receiving another material inheritance in 1787; created baronet in 1783. Oxford from 1760. He was sheriff of Hampshire, 1785–86. In the House of Commons from 1780, he opposed the North ministry, voted for Shelburne's peace terms, voted against Fox's India Bill in 1783, and in January, 1784, supported Pitt, but was not re-elected. He was prominent in hunting and racing circles. M.P. for Westbury, 1780–84.

Whateley, Thomas. ca.1728–72

Of Nonsuch Park, near Sutton, Surrey; oldest son of Thomas Whateloy (of Epsom, Surrey). Middle Temple from 1742, Cambridge from 1745, barrister in 1751. In the House of Commons he supported Bute and then was private secretary in the Treasury to his intimate friend George Grenville, 1763–65, and greatly influenced Grenville in the preparation of tax measures. He also helped draw up the Stamp Act. In 1765 he went with Grenville into opposition and published pamphlets on public finance, 1765–69. In the North ministry he was undersecretary of state to Suffolk, 1771–72, and in 1772 was also a member of the Board of Trade and Plantations and keeper of the king's roads. He died in his 44th year. As a public servant he was loyal, industrious, efficient, and shrewd; as a private citizen he was something of a scholar, writing essays on gardening and on the characters of Shakespeare. M.P. for Ludgershall, 1761–68; Castle Rising, 1768–72.

Whichcot (or Whichcott), Thomas. ca.1700–76

Oldest son of George Whichcot (or Whichcott) (of Harpswell, near Gainsborough, Lincolnshire; M.P.). Cambridge from 1719. He was a member of the House of Commons from 1740 for 34 years. He became a leader of the Old Whigs, and in 1761 Newcastle proposed him as speaker of the new House of Commons. In 1762 he joined the Ancaster family in switching support from Newcastle to Bute. In 1765 he again changed sides and supported the incoming Rockingham ministry. He voted in opposition to the Grafton ministry on the Wilkes issues, and until he left Parliament in 1774 he voted against the North ministry—on Middlesex election issues and on North's settlement with Spain over the Falkland Islands. M.P. for Lincolnshire, 1740–74.

Whitbread, Samuel. 1726–96

Of Cardington, near Bedford, Bedfordshire, and Bedwell Park, near Hatfield, Hertfordshire; 5th son of Henry Whitbread (of Cardington; prosperous "yeomen" and receiver of land taxes for Bedfordshire). He became known as "the eminent brewer of Chiswell Street" of a stout which still bears his name. He amassed a considerable fortune and became by purchase a large landholder in Bedfordshire. He was politically independent but voted fairly steadily with the opposition, 1768–84. He supported several petitions favorable to Wilkes; opposed the unseating of Wilkes in 1770; opposed the seating of Luttrell in place of Wilkes; supported Howe's motion for an increase in the pay of half-pay navy captains in 1773; supported the renewal of Grenville's Disputed Elections Act in 1774; supported Keppel against Palliser in 1779; and voted for the Dunning resolution of April 6, 1780. In February, 1782, however, he voted with the North ministry against both of Conway's motions for an immediate end to the war in America. In March, 1782, he voted against the motion of Cavendish to remove the ministry, but he voted for the motion to censure Sandwich and for Rous's no-confidence motion on March 15, 1782. He voted against Shelburne's peace terms, criticized before the House the terms of the coalition's government loan, but voted for Fox's India Bill in 1783. He frequently addressed the House, usually on financial matters. M.P. for Bedford Borough, 1768–90; Steyning, 1792–96.

White, Gilbert. 1720–93

Born at Selborne, near Alton, Hampshire, the oldest son of 11 children of Thomas John White (1688–1758; barrister); later of Tuxford, near East Retford, Nottinghamshire. Oxford from 1740; B.A., 1743; fellow from 1744; M.A., 1746; proctor of the university and dean of Oriel College from 1752. He took orders and then held several curacies and rectorates. About 1758 he returned to Selborne as curate of nearby Faringdon. Happily settled in the village of his birth, he studied its natural history and social organization and published *Natural History of Selborne*, 1769–89, the importance of which was quickly and widely recognized. It remains an outstanding work of its kind, a model of quiet, thorough research, balanced judgment, charm, and perspective seldom achieved by modern sociologists.

White, John. 1699–1769

Of Wallingwells, near Worksop, Nottinghamshire; oldest son of Thomas White (M.P.). A rugged dissenter and proud independent, he sat in the House of Commons for East Retford for 35 consecutive years and maintained the respect if seldom the concurrence of the majority of his fellow members. In 1760 he urged Newcastle to remain in office and supported him through 1762, voting against Bute's peace preliminaries in December. He opposed Bute and then Grenville, 1762–65, and supported the Rockingham ministry, 1765–66. After 1766 either his health or his hope of achieving his ideals weakened, for his political activity greatly diminished. His opinions were perhaps influenced by his friend Hardwicke. Newcastle pronounced him "a good Whig and a wise man." M.P. for East Retford, 1733–68.

Whitefield, George. 1714–70

Born at the Bell Inn in Gloucester, the 6th son of Thomas Whitefield (d. 1716; wine merchant of Bristol and Gloucester). Oxford from 1732; B.A., 1736. In 1735, while an undergraduate at Oxford, he became a leading member of the group of religious enthusiasts started by John and Charles Wesley, and already called Methodists. He shortly began missionary preaching, in which he displayed great eloquence and gained wide popularity, which rousing strong opposition. From February, 1738, until early 1741 he was largely in America as a missionary preacher in Georgia, and with John Wesley he founded a church and an orphanage in Savannah. He returned to England, and in 1741 married Elizabeth James (of Abergavenny), widowed friend of John Wesley. He soon returned to America and then and on later trips preached in nearly all the American colonies and made many conversions to Methodism. On his returns to England he continued his preaching; he was greatly helped by the friendship and financial support of Selina Hastings (neé Shirley) (*q.v.*), and in 1748 he became her chaplain. He was again in America, 1763–65, and made a final trip to the colonies in 1769, and died at Newburyport, Massachusetts. As a converter to the Methodist faith he was the movement's greatest figure, preaching more than 18,000 sermons in churches, outside churches, and at wayside gatherings. Portraits by Nathaniel Hone and others.

Whitefoord, Caleb. 1734–1810

Illegitimate son of Colonel Charles Whitefoord (d. 1753; active against the Jacobites in 1745); born in Edinburgh. Edinburgh University from 1748. He became a London wine merchant and a London neighbor and friend of Benjamin Franklin in Craven Street. He published witty political squibs critical of the North ministry. In 1782 he was secretary of Shelburne's mission to Paris to arrange a peace. He became a fellow of the Royal Society in 1784. Portrait by Reynolds.

Whitmore, Thomas. ca.1743–95

Of Apley, near Bridgnorth, Shropshire; son of Charles Whitmore (of Southampton; wine merchant); first cousin of William Whitmore (*q.v.*). In 1770 he married his cousin Mary, daughter of Thomas Whitmore (1711–75; M.P.). He was ensign of the 9th Foot in 1759, captain in 1762, major in 1767, and retired in 1773. His family controlled a seat in Parliament for Bridgnorth, which he filled from 1771. In the House of Commons he supported the North ministry until 1774 but thereafter opposed it on many occasions, and in February and March, 1782, he voted against it in all 5 of the crucial divisions recorded. He did not vote on Shelburne's peace terms or on Fox's India Bill in 1783, and from 1784 he supported Fox against the Pitt ministry. There is no evidence that he ever addressed the House, at least before 1790. M.P. for Bridgnorth, 1771–95.

Whitmore, William. 1714–71

Of Lower Slaughter, near Bourton-on-the-Water, Gloucestershire; 3d son of William Whitmore (of Lower Slaughter and Apley, near Bridgnorth, Shropshire; M.P.); cousin of Thomas Whitmore (*q.v.*). He was captain of foot in 1735, colonel in 1751, major general in 1758, and lieutenant general in 1760. He won election to the House of Commons with the support of Lord Powis and like Powis supported Newcastle in 1762, voting against Bute's peace preliminaries in December. He then opposed the Bute and Grenville ministries, 1762–65. He voted with the Rockingham ministry, 1765–66, and opposed Grafton and then North on the various Wilkes issues, 1767–71. He was warden of the mint, 1766–71. M.P. for Bridgnorth, 1741–47 and 1754–71.

Whitshed, James. ca.1718–90

Of Hampton Court, Middlesex; oldest son of James Whitshed (of Dublin); in 1761 succeeded his uncle Richard Whitshed to a large estate in Ireland. Trinity College, Dublin, from 1733. In 1738 he married Frances, daughter of Allen Bathurst (*q.v.*). He supported Leicester House politics, 1754–60, and supported Bute, 1761–62, but voted against Grenville on general warrants in 1764. He supported the Rockingham ministry, 1765–66; he opposed the Chatham-Grafton and the North ministries on Wilkes and Middlesex issues, but on other measures he generally supported North. He voted against Dunning's resolution of April 6, 1780, and with North in all 5 of the critical divisions recorded in February and March, 1782. He voted against Shelburne's peace terms in 1783. There is no record that he ever addressed the House of Commons. He was a member of the Irish Parliament, 1747–60. M.P. for St. Ives, 1754–61; Cirencester, 1761–83.

Whitwell (later Griffin), John. 1719–97

Of Audley End, near Saffron Walden, Essex; oldest son of William Whitwell (of Oundle, near Peterborough, Northamptonshire); descended from the Earls of Suffolk; in 1749 he took the surname Griffin upon inheriting from his uncle Edward Griffin (3d Baron Griffin); in 1784 succeeded as 4th Baron Howard De Walden; in 1788 created Baron Braybrooke. Winchester, 1734–36. He was ensign of foot guards in 1739. He saw military service in the Netherlands and in Germany, 1740–65, being twice wounded. He was made captain in 1743, and served in Flanders under the Duke of Cumberland 1747–48. He was colonel in 1756, major general in 1756, lieutenant general and Knight of the Bath in 1761, general in 1778, and field marshal in 1796. He was elected to Parliament in 1749 "in the interest" of his uncle John Wallop (*q.v.*). He supported Newcastle until late 1762 and then turned to Bute, but he played no consistent role in politics, and on January 11, 1764, he boasted his independence to the House of Commons. In January, 1770, he voted against unseating Wilkes. In February, 1775, he told the House that he had grave doubts regarding North's New England Restraining Bill. In November, 1775, he told the House that although he had hitherto supported the measures of the North ministry he could no longer condone its "pernicious measures" aimed at the colonies. In April, 1780, he voted for Dunning's first resolution, and was thereafter in constant opposition to the North ministry. In 1783 he opposed the coalition. He frequently pressed for a peerage and secured one from Pitt in 1788, after having been unseated in the House of Commons in 1784. M.P. for Andover, 1749–84.

Whitworth, Charles. ca.1718–78

Of Leybourne, near Maidstone, Kent, and Blackford, near Wincanton, Somerset; only son of Francis Whitworth (M.P.); knighted in 1768. Westminster, 1730–38; Lincoln's Inn from 1738. In 1749 he married Martha, niece of John Shelley (*q.v.*) and the Duke of Newcastle. He served briefly with the army, and was lieutenant governor of Gravesend and Tilbury, 1758–78. Newcastle supplied him with £1,000 from secret-service funds for his election expenses in 1754 and later provided him, in lieu of appointive office, with a secret-service pension of £400 a year. Disappointment at his failure to receive a court position made him lukewarm toward Newcastle in the political crisis of December, 1762, when he almost certainly yielded to the bribes of Henry Fox and supported Bute. He was either absent or voted with the unrecorded majorities until 1767, when he voted for Chatham's land tax. He was knighted in 1768, and was a regular supporter of the North ministry from 1770, being chairman of the Ways and Means Committee of the House in 1768 and 1774–78. He compiled several reference works. M.P. for Minehead, 1747–61; Bletchingly, 1761–68; Minehead, 1768–74; East Looe, 1774; Saltash, 1775–78.

Whitworth, Charles. 1752–1825

Son and heir of Charles Whitworth (ca.1718–78) (*q.v.*). He attended school in Tonbridge from 1761. In 1800 created Baron Whitworth (Irish); in 1813 created Viscount Whitworth (English); in 1815 created Earl Whitworth (English). In 1801 he married Arabella, daughter of Sir Charles Cope and widow of his former friend the Duke of Dorset. Thereafter he lived chiefly in the Sackville-Dorset mansion of Knole. He was ensign of foot guards in 1772 and served as captain in America, 1776–77. He was lieutenant colonel in 1781 and retired in 1783. He was minister to Poland, 1786–88; envoy to Russia, 1788–1800; Knight of the Bath in 1793; envoy to Denmark and privy councillor from 1800; ambassador to Russia, 1802–1804; member of the Board of Trade, 1807–17; lord of the bedchamber from 1813; and viceroy of Ireland, 1813–17. Portrait by Lawrence.

Whitworth, Richard. 1734–1811

Of Batchacre, near Eccleshall, Staffordshire; son of Richard Whitworth (of Adbaston, near Eccleshall, Staffordshire); cousin of Charles Whitworth (ca.1718–78) (*q.v.*). Eton, to Cambridge in 1752. He was sheriff of Staffordshire, 1758–59. In the House of Commons from

927

1768, he voted against the expulsion of Wilkes in January, 1770, and against declaring printers Wheble and Thompson in contempt in 1771, and in that year for Howe's motion to increase the pay of half-pay navy officers. In 1774, however, he received a secret-service pension, and from that year until he left Parliament he regularly supported the North ministry. He voted against Dunning's resolution of April 6, 1780, and, despite a gift of £700 toward his election expenses in 1780, was defeated in that election. Between 1768 and 1770 he addressed the House of Commons more than 100 times. M.P. for Stafford Borough, 1768–80.

Wicklow, 1st Viscount. See Ralph Howard

Wigley, James. ca.1701–65

Of Scraptoft Hall, near Leicester; oldest son of Sir Edward Wigley (of Scraptoft). Rugby from 1713, Oxford from 1718. In the 1754 elections he was a declared and active Tory, and in 1761 he was listed as Tory. He voted in opposition to the Whig ministries, 1737–61, but appears to have supported Newcastle and then Bute. M.P. for Leicester Borough, 1737–65.

Wilberforce, William. 1759–1833

Of Hull, Yorkshire, and Wimbledon, Surrey; only son of Robert Wilberforce (merchant of Hull). Cambridge from 1776. He won election to Parliament in 1780. He claimed political independence and voted at first with the North ministry on most issues, opposing at that time the Wyvill Association reform movement. But as he developed a friendship with the younger William Pitt he moved into opposition, and during the last 2 months of the North ministry he voted against it in all 5 of the recorded critical divisions. In February, 1783, he urged drastic and immediate reforms of Parliament, and on February 17 of that year he addressed the House of Commons in strong support of Shelburne's peace terms, for which he voted on the following day. He opposed the coalition and voted against Fox's India Bill in November, 1783. From 1784 he supported Pitt. For his later career, including his reform efforts and opposition to the slave trade, see standard sources. M.P. for Kingston-on-Hull, 1780–84; Yorkshire, 1784–1812; Bramber, 1812–25.

Wilbraham, Randle. 1694–1770

Of Rode Hall, near Congleton, Cheshire; 2d surviving son of Randle Wilbraham (of Nantwich, Cheshire). Oxford and at Lincoln's Inn from 1711, barrister in 1718, bencher from 1743, treasurer in 1754. A Tory of ability, independence, and high reputation in legal matters, he was generally in opposition from his entrance into Parliament in 1740. In 1764 he was prominent in the debates on general warrants, which he pronounced unconstitutional. Though nevertheless thought to be a supporter of Grenville, and classed by Rockingham as adverse in 1765, he did not vote against repeal of the Stamp Act in 1766. He was absent from most of the later votes and did not stand for re-election in 1768. He was vice chamberlain of Chester and deputy steward of Oxford University. M.P. for Newcastle-under-Lyme, 1740–47; Appleby, 1747–54; Newton, 1754–68.

Wilbraham Bootle, Richard. See **Richard Wilbraham Bootle**

Wilkes, John. 1727–97

2d son of Israel Wilkes (prosperous distiller of London) and a very pious mother. Lincoln's Inn from 1742; Leyden University, 1744–46. He was sheriff of Buckinghamshire, 1754–55, and colonel of Buckinghamshire militia, 1762–63. He was regarded by many as a gambler and libertine, and was almost continuously in debt. Soon after his election to the House of Commons in 1757 he took up journalism, and founded with Churchill the *North Briton*. In 1763 the 45th number of that periodical included an article highly critical of the ministry, which the ministry with good reason chose to believe had been written by Wilkes and to be a libel on the king. Wilkes was arrested on a general warrant, but finally, by a legal process upon the propriety of which legal authorities differed, secured a judgment and £1,000 damages from Secretary of State Lord Halifax and his undersecretary Robert Wood, for illegal arrest. Wilkes was further attacked by the Earl of Sandwich, his former crony of the disreputable Medmendham Club, who produced and read in the House of Lords a poem thought both blasphemous and licentious, which he stated had been written by Wilkes. Wilkes was expelled from the House of Commons, declared outlawed, and hurriedly retired to Paris, where he lived largely on funds given him by friends, by Whigs in opposition to the North ministry, and by sincere (whether or not misguided) supporters of the Bill of Rights. He returned to London before the elections of 1768 and was 3 times elected by the constituents of Middlesex to the House of Commons, and 3 times rejected by that House. In 1769 he was elected alderman of London and was the hero of the discontented and the radical reformers. The issues his conduct raised were of far more importance than he was himself, though it is doubtful that he ever thought so. He was sheriff of London, 1771–72; lord mayor of London, 1774–75; and city chamberlain, 1779–97. He was for some years the rallying ground of the defenders of liberty, but he also served as a convenient pawn for less noble purposes and as an excuse for the expression of all sorts of urban, political, and economic dissatisfactions. He supported the case and much of the conduct of the rebellious American colonists, invariably opposed the measures of the North ministry, and voted for Shelburne's peace terms in 1783. He was often called ugly because he was extremely cross-eyed. According to Horace Walpole, himself a Whig in opposition: "Wantonness, rather than ambition or vengeance, guided his hand; and though he became a martyr of the best cause, there was nothing in his principles or morals that led him to care under what government he lived. To laugh and riot and scatter firebrands with him was liberty." M.P. for Aylesbury, 1757–64; Middlesex, 1768 and 1769 (but was refused a seat); Middlesex, 1774–90.

Wilkinson, Andrew. 1697–1784

Son of Charles Wilkinson (of Boroughbridge and Aldborough, Yorkshire). Cambridge from 1715, Middle Temple from 1719. He was a protégé of the Duke of Newcastle and became Newcastle's political agent in Yorkshire. He was receiver of land taxes for West Riding, 1718–34; clerk of deliveries in ordnance, 1741–46; and chief storekeeper of ordnance, 1746–62 and 1765–68. He supported Newcastle against Bute in the vote on Bute's peace preliminaries in December, 1762, and supported the Rockingham ministry in 1765. There is no evidence that he ever addressed the House of Commons. M.P. for Aldborough, 1735–65 and 1768–72.

Wilkinson, Charles. 1725–82

Of Boroughbridge, Yorkshire; oldest son of Andrew Wilkinson

(*q.v.*). Cambridge and Middle Temple from 1742, barrister in 1749. Soon after his election to the House of Commons in 1774 he suffered a mental breakdown and retired in 1777. He would probably have supported the interests of the 2d Duke of Newcastle, to whose father his own father had been political agent. M.P. for Aldborough, 1774–77.

Wilkinson, Jacob. ca.1717–91

Born at Berwick-on-Tweed, of obscure family origins, probably ardently Presbyterian. He became a prosperous London merchant "of good character," according to the *Public Ledger* in 1779, and was a director of the East India Company, 1782–83. From 1759 he subscribed regularly to government loans but often voted with the opposition. He later attached himself to the Rockingham Whig party, and voted against approving the address from the throne in October, 1775; voted for Dunning's resolution of April 6, 1780; and voted against the North ministry in all 5 of the critical recorded divisions of February and March, 1782. In his only reported speech in the House of Commons he supported Fox's India Bill, in which he was named to be an assistant commissioner. M.P. for Berwick-on-Tweed, 1774–80; Honiton, 1781–84.

Wilkinson, Pinckney. ca.1694–1784

Of The Burnhams, near Wells, Norfolk. He became "an eminent merchant in London" and a large holder of government stock—in 1760 estimated to be worth £80,000. He allied with the Pitt family in 1781, when his daughter married Thomas Pitt. He voted regularly in opposition to the North ministry, including a vote for the Dunning resolution of April 6, 1780. In 1782 he suffered a paralytic stroke, which incapacitated him; he did not vote on Shelburne's peace terms or on Fox's India Bill in 1783. There is no evidence that he ever addressed the House of Commons. M.P. for Old Sarum, 1774–84.

Willes, Edward. 1689–1773

Of Newbold Comyn, Warwickshire; 3d son of John Willes (ca.1647–1700; prebendary of Lichfield). Oxford; B.A., 1709; M.A., 1712; D.D., 1726. He was rector of Barton, Bedfordshire, from 1718; prebendary of Westminster from 1724; dean of Lincoln from 1730; bishop of St. David's, 1733–42; and bishop of Bath and Wells, 1743–73.

Willes, Edward. 1723–87

Of Lincoln's Inn Fields; son of Sir John Willes (1685–1761; lord chief justice of common pleas, 1737–61). Oxford from 1738; Lincoln's Inn from 1741; M.A., 1745; barrister in 1747; bencher from 1757. He was king's counsel from 1756; serjeant at law from 1768; solicitor general in the Grafton ministry, 1766–68; and justice of the king's bench, 1768–87. M.P. for Old Sarum, 1747; Aylesbury, 1747–54; Leominster, 1767–68.

William Augustus. 1721–65

3d son of George II, then Prince of Wales, by Caroline, daughter of John Frederick (Margrave of Brandenburg-Anspach); in 1726 created Duke of Cumberland. He was educated for military and naval service, and first served under Sir John Norris (ca.1660–1749) in 1740, when he was also made a Knight of the Garter. He was colonel of the Coldstream Guards in 1740, of the 1st Guards from 1742, and privy councillor from 1742. He was made major general in 1742, and fought at Dettingen in 1743. In 1745 he was captain general of British forces at home and abroad. For his defeat of the Jacobites at Culloden and elsewhere in 1745 and 1746 he received the thanks of Parliament and an income of £25,000 a year for himself and his heirs. He again fought the French on the Continent, not always successfully, 1747–1757, with intermissions in England. In 1757 his father, George II, angrily disavowed the agreements he had made with the French at Kloster-Zeven and forced the duke to resign as commander in chief, an action which Horace Walpole called "a public calamity." The duke's nephew, when he became George III, treated the duke with studied courtesy, and consulted him on political as well as military matters. The duke had a strong political following until his death and played an important part in creating the Rockingham ministry in 1765. Fortescue pronounced him the ablest member of his family over 2 centuries of reign in England.

Williams, George James. 1719–1805

Known as "Gilly" Williams; born at Denton, near Grantham, Lincolnshire, the younger son of William Peere Williams (1664–1736; law reporter and counsel); related by marriage to Lord North. In 1752 he married Diana, daughter of William Coventry (ca.1687–

1751; M.P.; London merchant; 5th Earl of Coventry). He was a wit, an intimate friend and correspondent of George Selwyn, and, to a somewhat less degree, a friend of Horace Walpole. Through Lord North he held the court post of receiver general of excise, 1774–1801. Sir Joshua Reynolds included him in a conversation-group painting with Walpole, Selwyn, and Edgcumbe. He took little or no active part in politics, though he wrote at length to his friends about political affairs.

Williams, Hugh. 1718–94

Of Nant Mill, on River Gorfai, Carnarvonshire, and Caleran, Anglesey; son of Colonel Griffith Williams (of Nant and Ariannws, Anglesey); in 1745 succeeded his cousin Sir Robert Williams (of Marle, Carnarvonshire) as 8th baronet. In 1760 he married Emma, Dowager Duchess Bulkeley of Cashel (Irish). He entered the army in 1739 and was captain in 1744, major in 1756, lieutenant colonel of the 53rd Foot from 1761, and on half pay from 1764. He was constable of Beaumaris Castle, 1761–94. Though he left no record of any speech in the House of Commons and few records of his votes there, he was reported by contemporaries to have opposed the North ministry and to have voted 6 times in opposition on major issues, 1775–80. M.P. for Beaumaris, 1768–80 and 1785–94.

Williams, John. 1736–?

Of Brook Street, London; son of John Williams (of Nevis); according to Horace Walpole, "a West Indian who bribed the Corporation" to win an election to the House of Commons. He was promptly unseated on petition by his rival, Thomas Bradshaw. M.P. for Saltash, May, 1772.

Williams, Watkyn. 1742–1808

Of Penbedw Hall, near Mold, Denbighshire, and Erbistock, on River Dee, Flintshire; son of John Richard Williams (of Penbedw; M.P.). During both his terms in the House of Commons he voted against the North ministry, including a vote for the Dunning resolution of April 6, 1780, and votes against the ministry in all 5 of the critical divisions recorded in February and March, 1782. He voted for Shelburne's peace terms in 1783 and from 1784 supported Pitt. There is no evidence that he addressed the House before 1790. He was lord lieutenant of Merionethshire, 1789–93; lord lieutenant of Denbighshire, 1792–94; and constable of Flint Castle in 1799. M.P. for Montgomeryshire, 1772–74; Flint boroughs, 1777–1806.

Williams, William Peere. ca.1730–61

Of Grey Friars, near Arundel, Sussex; in 1758 succeeded his father, Sir Hutchins Williams (of Chichester, Sussex), as 2d baronet. Winchester, Eton, Cambridge from 1749. He was captain in the 16th Dragoons in 1759, and was killed in the attack on Belleisle on April 27, 1761. He was "exceedingly ambitious," with an enterprising spirit and some talent at parliamentary debate, which he displayed on at least 5 occasions during his 3 years in the House of Commons. M.P. for New Shoreham, 1758–61.

Williams-Wynn (or Williams-Wynne), Watkyn. 1748–89

Of Wynnstay (or Wynnestay), near Ruabon, Denbighshire; in 1749 succeeded his father, Sir Watkyn Williams-Wynn (or Williams-Wynne), as 4th baronet. Westminster, 1764–65; Oxford from 1766. He married (1) in 1769 Henrietta, daughter of Charles Noel Somerset (1709–50; 4th Duke of Beaufort), and (2) in 1771 Charlotte, sister of George Nugent-Temple Grenville (*q.v.*). From a very strong Welsh Tory family, he opposed the North ministry until 1775. He was lord lieutenant of Merionethshire, 1775–89. He supported the North ministry until 1778 and then went again into opposition, and, though sometimes criticized for his poor attendance of the House of Commons, he was present to vote against the North ministry in all 5 of the critical divisions recorded in February and March, 1782. He voted against Shelburne's peace terms and did not vote on Fox's India Bill in 1783. In early 1784 he opposed Pitt, but was re-elected. He was a generous patron of charity schools, an art collector, a musician, and an owner of a private theater at Wynnstay. M.P. for Shropshire, 1772–74; Denbighshire, 1774–89.

Williamson, Adam. 1735–98

Son of Lieutenant General George Williamson (ca.1707–81; active at the captures of Louisburg and Montreal, 1758–60). He became a cadet gunner in 1748, was at Woolwich from 1750, and was a military

934

engineer in 1753. He was with Braddock in America in 1755 and
served as captain in America in 1758 and in the West Indies, 1761–62.
He returned to further military service in America as lieutenant
colonel and colonel, 1775–82. He was lieutenant governor and commanding officer in Jamaica, 1790–92, and established a British pro-
tectorate in Santo Domingo in 1793. He was governor of Jamaica in
1794 and lieutenant general in 1797.

Willis-Fleming, John. 1743–1802

Of Stoneham, near Southampton, Hampshire; 2d son of Thomas
Willis; added the surname Fleming in 1767 upon inheriting from his
half brother Thomas. Eton, 1758–64. He settled down as a country
gentleman of Tory principles and comfortable fortune. In Parliament
from 1774, he supported the North ministry until April, 1780, when
he voted for Dunning's first resolution. In the 1780 election John Robinson suggested that he be replaced, and he was. He returned to the
House of Commons in 1784, after which he appears to have supported
Pitt. M.P. for Southampton Borough, 1774–80 and 1784–90.

Willoughby, Thomas. 1728–81

Of West Leake, near Loughborough, Nottinghamshire; 2d son of
Francis Willoughby (2d Baron Middleton; M.P.); in 1774 succeeded
his brother Francis Willoughby as 4th Baron Middleton. Cambridge
from 1745. From a Tory family, he supported Grenville from 1762
and voted against repeal of the Stamp Act in 1766. He voted against
Chatham's land tax in 1767 and against the expulsion of Wilkes in
January, 1770. Until he left the House of Commons, he opposed the
North ministry in all the votes in which he is on record. M.P. for
Nottinghamshire, 1762–74.

Willoughby De Broke, 14th Baron. See **John Peyto Verney**

Willy, William. 1703–65

Of New Park, Devizes, Wiltshire; son of George Willy (of Devizes;
mercer). He conducted a west-country cloth trade while living mostly
in London, where he was a director of the East India Company, 1746–
54. He was largely in opposition in the House of Commons, 1754–60,
and then supported Newcastle against Bute, voting against Bute's

peace preliminaries in December, 1762. He opposed Grenville on Wilkes and general warrants, 1763–64. There is no evidence that he ever addressed the House. M.P. for Devizes, 1747–65.

Wilmot, Edward. 1693–1786

Of Chaddesden Hall, near Derby, Derbyshire; 2d son of Robert Wilmot (of Chaddesden); created baronet in 1759. Cambridge; B.A. and fellow in 1714; M.A., 1718; M.D., 1725. He was a fellow of the College of Physicians from 1726, fellow of the Royal Society from 1730; and Harveian orator in 1735. He practiced as a physician in London from 1725, became physician to Queen Charlotte in 1731, was physician to the Prince of Wales, and in 1737 was physician to George II. He was physician general to the army in 1740 and physician to George III, 1760–61. In 1761 he retired from active practice. Portrait by Thomas Beach.

Wilmot, John Eardley. 1709–92

Son of Robert Wilmot (of Chaddeston Hall, near Derby, Derbyshire; certainly a relation, if not a brother, of Edward Wilmot (*q.v.*). Westminster from 1724, Cambridge from 1727, barrister of Inner Temple in 1732. In 1743 he married Sarah, daughter of Thomas Rivett (M.P.). He was a fellow of the Society of Arts from 1735, and was knighted and made a judge of the king's bench in 1755. He was commissioner of the great seal, 1756–57; privy councillor and chief justice of the Court of Common Pleas, 1766–71; and a fellow of the Royal Society from 1779. He took an important part in the Wilkes libel proceedings as a government officer. On 3 occasions he declined to be lord chancellor.

Wilmot, John Eardley. 1750–1815

Of Berkswell Hall, near Coventry, Warwickshire; oldest surviving son of Sir John Eardley Wilmot (1709–92; chief justice of the Court of Common Pleas, 1766–71). Westminster, to Oxford in 1766; fellow of All Souls College, Oxford, from 1769; Inner Temple from 1767; barrister in 1773. Elected to Parliament in 1776, in 1778 he published a pamphlet critical of the North ministry, entitled *A Short Defense of the Opposition*. He voted for Dunning's resolution of April 6, 1780, but was nevertheless appointed in 1781 master in chancery, and held

936

that position until 1804. He did not cast a recorded vote in 4 of 5 of the critical divisions in February and March, 1782, but on February 22 he voted for Conway's motion to end the American war. He supported Shelburne's peace preliminaries in a long speech in February, 1783. He did not vote on Fox's India Bill, and from 1784 he supported Pitt. M.P. for Tiverton, 1776–84; Coventry, 1784–96.

Wilson, Richard. 1714–82

Son of the rector of Penegoes, in western Montgomeryshire. He went to London in his 15th year to study portrait painting, and was apprenticed to Thomas Wright, a minor portrait artist. In 1749 he went to Italy, was inspired by the rugged Italian landscape, and gained a reputation for portraits or figures against a romantic landscape. When he returned to England after 6 years, his reputation had preceded him, and his landscapes soon became among the most prized of British works of art of the time. He became a charter member of the Royal Academy in 1768 and its librarian from 1776. Though his reputation continued, he was almost impoverished in his later years. "He hid the structure of Italian scenery behind the bushes and the waters of a greener English countryside." The results were uniquely satisfying, and despite latter-day scorn for "romantic" or "representational" painting, his reputation is currently undergoing another renaissance. Portrait by Mengs.

Wilson, Thomas Spencer. 1727–98

Of Uckfield, near Lewes, Sussex; 2d son of Sir Thomas Wilson (of Eastbourne, Sussex; 4th baronet); in 1760 succeeded his brother Sir Edward Wilson as 6th baronet. He was an army ensign in 1744, lieutenant in 1747, captain in 1755, colonel in 1772, major general in 1777, lieutenant general in 1782, and general in 1796. He was aide to the king, and served in Flanders (where he was twice wounded), in Scotland, in Germany (including Minden in 1759, where he distinguished himself), and in 3 raids on French ports. He appears to have been a soldiers' soldier more than a politicians' soldier, and despite his rapid rise to top ranks, he was not assigned top commands. He was often absent from the House of Commons on duty, and was usually silent when present. His only recorded vote was in 1775, against the North ministry, in support of a motion by Wilkes to expunge certain resolutions regarding him from the records of the House. In 1779 John Robinson classified him as "doubtful." M.P. for Sussex, 1774–80.

Wilson, William. ca.1721–96

Of Keythorpe, near Market Harborough, Leicestershire; 3d son of Rev. William Wilson (rector of Stiffkey, near Wells, Norfolk). Gray's Inn from 1738, Cambridge from 1739. In the House of Commons he supported Grenville on some issues but voted against general warrants in 1764. The Newcastle, Rockingham, and Grafton ministries all listed him as "doubtful." Evidently he never addressed the House. M.P. for Ilchester, 1761–68; Camelford, 1768–74.

Wilton, 1st Earl. See Thomas Egerton

Winchester, 11th Marquess. See Harry Paulet (or Powlett)

Winchilsea, 8th and 9th Earls. See Daniel Finch and George Finch

Windham, William. ca.1705–89

Of Earsham, near Bungay, Norfolk; oldest son of William Windham (of Earsham; M.P.), from whom he inherited a considerable estate in Norfolk. In 1734 he married Mary, widow of Henry Scott (1676–1730; 1st Earl of Deloraine, Scottish). He was subgovernor to the Duke of Cumberland in 1731, and later comptroller of the duke's household until 1765. He supported the ministry currently in office, 1747–61, and supported Newcastle and then Rockingham, 1761–66; but his position was often doubtful and perhaps sometimes equivocal. No speeches or votes by him in the House of Commons are recorded. M.P. for Aldeburgh, 1747–61; Helston, 1766–68.

Windham, William. 1750–1810

Of Felbrigg Hall, near Cromer, Norfolk; oldest son of William Windham (1717–61; of Felbrigg). Eton, 1757–66; Glasgow University in 1766; Oxford from 1767; M.A., 1782; D.C.L., 1793. He became an outstanding scholar and mathematician and a friend of Samuel Johnson, Charles Fox, and Edmund Burke. Horace Walpole called him "full of virtues," and Nathaniel Wraxall said that he was "graceful, elegant and distinguished." He was chief secretary to Lord Northington when Northington was lord lieutenant of Ireland in 1783, until he resigned in July, 1783. He was a member of the court of impeachment of Warren Hastings, 1788–95; privy councillor from 1794; secretary at war, 1794–1801; and secretary for war and colonies, 1806–1807. He helped Cobbett found the *Political Register*. His diary was published in 1866. M.P. for Norwich, 1784–1802; St. Mawes, 1802–1806; New Romney, 1806–1807; Higham Ferrers, 1807–10.

Windsor, 1st Earl. See **John Stuart.** 1744–1814

Windsor, Other Hickman. 1751–99

Of Stanwell, near Staines, Middlesex; styled Lord Windsor until 1771, when he succeeded his father, Other Lewis Windsor (1731–71), as 5th Earl of Plymouth. Eton, 1764–69. In 1788 he married Sarah, his cousin and oldest daughter of his maternal uncle Andrew Archer (2d Baron Archer). He was a fellow of the Royal Society from 1773 and of the Society of Arts from 1790. A Whig, like his father he was in opposition to the North ministry, but he was not a prominent figure in the House of Lords.

Winn, Rowland. 1739–85

Of Nostell Priory, near Pontrefact, Yorkshire; oldest son of Sir Rowland Winn, whom he succeeded in 1765 as 5th baronet. In 1768 he was elected to the House of Commons after a riotous campaign, but was promptly unseated on petition. He declined to stand again until 1784 (the year before his death), when he was defeated. M.P. for Pontrefact for a week in 1768.

Winnington, Edward. 1728–91

Of Stanford Court, near Worcester, Worcestershire; oldest son of Edward Winnington (of Broadway, Worcestershire); created baronet in 1755. Eton from 1742, Oxford from 1746. He was a protégé of Henry Fox, 1748–62; supported Bute and then Grenville; and was Storekeeper of Ordnance, 1762–65. He was briefly secretary to the chancellor of the exchequer, 1765–66, but was dismissed by Rockingham. He did not vote against repeal of the Stamp Act in 1766 but voted against Chatham's land tax in 1767. He supported the Grafton ministry in its measures against Wilkes in 1769, but in January, 1770, he voted against expulsion of Wilkes from the House of Commons, and was therefore regarded by the North ministry as "doubtful." M.P. for Bewdley, 1761–68 and 1769–74.

Winnington, Edward. 1749–1805

Of Stanford Court, near Worcester, Worcestershire; in 1791 succeeded his father, Sir Edward Winnington (1728–91) (*q.v.*), as 2d baronet. Eton, 1763–65; at Oxford from 1767. In 1776 he married Anne, daughter of Thomas Foley (1st Baron Foley). In the House of Commons he was a supporter of Charles Fox and voted steadily against the North ministry. He voted for Dunning's resolution of April 6, 1780, and voted against the North ministry in all 5 crucial divisions reported in February and March, 1782. He opposed Shelburne in 1782 and voted against his peace terms in February, 1783. He supported Fox in the coalition and opposed Pitt in 1784. There is no indication that he addressed the House of Commons before 1790. He was recorded by a contemporary as "a gentleman eminent for his attainments in literature." M.P. for Droitwich, 1777–1805.

Winterton, 1st Baron and 1st Earl. See Edward Tournour Garth-Tournour

Wintringham, Clifton. ca.1712–94

Of Dover Street, London; only son of Clifton Wintringham (of York; physician); created baronet in 1774. He took medical degrees at Cambridge in 1734 and 1749 and joined the army medical service ca. 1735. He became physician to the Duke of Cumberland in 1749, to the forces in 1756 and to George III in 1762. He was a fellow of the College of Physicians from 1763 and censor of the college in 1770. He was fellow of the Royal Society from 1792.

Wodehouse, Armine. 1714–77

Of Kimberley Hall, near Wymondham, Norfolk; in 1754 succeeded his father, Sir John Wodehouse, as 5th baronet; from an old Tory family of Norfolk. Cambridge, 1730–33. About 1740 he married Laetitia, only daughter and heiress of Sir Edmund Bacon (1680–1755; of Norfolk; 4th baronet; M.P.). He was colonel of the East Norfolk militia. He was an avowed Tory in the 1754 elections, and was listed as Tory in 1761 by Bute. He was in steady opposition to

Robert Walpole, Pelham, and Newcastle and supported Bute and voted for his peace preliminaries in December, 1762. He voted with Grenville on general warrants in 1764 and bitterly opposed repeal of the Stamp Act in 1766. He also voted against Chatham's land tax in 1767. M.P. for Norfolk, 1737–68.

Wolcot, John. 1738–1819

Known as "Peter Pindar"; the 4th child of Alexander Wolcot (of Dodbrooke, near Kingsbridge, Devon; country surgeon). At the age of 12 he was taken to France, where he studied languages. In 1762 he studied medicine in London; M.D., of Aberdeen University, 1767. He was physician in Jamaica to William Trelawny (or Trelawney) (*q.v.*), 1767–69; and remained in Jamaica as physician and also as ordained priest until 1773. He returned to England in 1773 and set up a medical practice at Truro and then at Exeter but in 1778 gave up medicine to gratify his literary aspirations and went to London. There he published *Lyric Odes*, 1782–85, and *Farewell Odes*, 1786. From 1785, under the pen name Peter Pindar, he wrote satires on society and on the court which were widely read and enjoyed less by king and court than by the opposition. He was said to have been "a true low comedian of Rhyme ... he caught to the life, and stamped on the mind of the country, the figure and accents of the King."

Wollaston, William. 1731–97

Of Finborough Hall, near Stowmarket, Suffolk; oldest surviving son of William Wollaston (1693–1757; M.P.); grandson of John Francis Fauquier (director of the Bank of England). Cambridge from 1747. In Parliament from 1768, he supported the Grafton ministry on the Wilkes issues, and the North ministry on Wilkes and the Royal Marriage Bill in 1772, but in 1774 he voted for extending Grenville's Disputed Elections Act. He addressed the House of Commons once in 1775, but no speech or vote by him is recorded, 1780–84, when he was reported "abroad." M.P. for Ipswich, 1768–84.

Wolseley, Charles. 1741–1808

2d son of Sir William Wolseley (d. 1779; 5th baronet); connected with the Luttrell family. He was captain in the navy in 1761, rear admiral in 1790, and admiral in 1799. He opposed the American war

941

and the North ministry before 1775, but supported the North ministry in the House of Commons, 1775–80. In 1778 he received a secret-service pension of £600 a year. In his later years he was in financial difficulties and lived chiefly on the Continent. M.P. for Milbourne Port, 1775–80.

Wombwell, George. 1734–80

Of Crutched Friars, London, and Wombwell Hall, near Barnsley, Yorkshire; oldest son of Roger Wombwell (merchant of Barnsley, Yorkshire); created baronet in 1778. In 1765 he married Susanna, daughter of Thomas Rawlinson (*q.v.*). He became a London merchant; was a director of the East India Company intermittently, 1766–80; and was chairman of the Company, 1777–79. In January, 1768, he appeared by invitation before the House of Lords to answer questions on the affairs of the East India Company. In politics he supported the Earl of Sandwich, and consequently the North ministry, in every recorded vote during his 6 years in the House of Commons, 1774–80. The records indicate that he intervened 9 times in debates in the House. In March, 1780, he told House members that the ministry had not acted improperly in its interference in the affairs of the East India Company. In April, 1780, he opposed Dunning's resolutions. With Henniker and Desvaynes, he held a contract to victual 12,000 troops in America and from time to time held or shared other lucrative contracts. M.P. for Huntingdon Borough, 1774–80.

Wood, Robert. 1714–71

Of Putney, Surrey; oldest son of James Wood (of Summerhill, County Meath). Glasgow University from 1732, Middle Temple from 1736. He traveled in the Near East, 1750–51, and in 1753 published *The Ruins of Palmyra*. Later he traveled farther and extensively on the Continent, exploring Palmyra again and also Baalbeck, and becoming a distinguished Homeric scholar. He served under Egremont as undersecretary of state, 1756–63, and supported his chief's politics until Egremont died. As undersecretary of state to Halifax, 1768–70, he was one of those sued by Wilkes on the charge that the general warrant issued by him (on orders from Halifax) for Wilkes' arrest was illegal. He was ultimately fined £1,000 as scapegoat for the ministry. He then supported the measures of the Bedford clique and with its members voted against repeal of the Stamp Act in 1766. He was again undersecretary of state under Weymouth in 1770 and resigned with Weymouth in disagreement with North's "soft" measures toward Spain over the Falkland Islands. He was groom porter at the court, 1764–66. M.P. for Brackley, 1761–71.

Wood, Thomas. 1708–99

Of Littleton House, near Staines, Middlesex; 7th son of Edward Wood. Eton, 1718–25; Oxford from 1725; Inner Temple from 1729; barrister in 1735; bencher from 1766. He was a fellow of All Souls College from 1732. He was a Wilkite candidate in the Middlesex by-election, opposed the North ministry, and voted for the Dunning resolution of April 6, 1780. M.P. for Middlesex, 1779–80.

Woodfall, Henry Sampson. 1739–1805

Son of Henry Woodfall (printer of the *Public Advertiser* in London); brother of William Woodfall (*q.v.*). St. Paul's School from 1751. In 1754 he was apprenticed to his father. He became not only an expert printer but also a journalist and manager of the *Public Advertiser* and in 1797 master of the Stationers' Company. With his brother he was involved in controversies with the House of Commons over their journalistic publications, especially in their reports of the proceedings of the House, and was summoned before it and reproved for printing letters of "Junius" that were said to be libelous.

Woodfall, William. 1746–1803

Younger son of Henry Woodfall (printer of the *Public Advertiser* in London); brother of Henry Sampson Woodfall (*q.v.*). He was editor-publisher of the *London Packet*, 1772–74, and was on the staff of the *Morning Chronicle*, 1774–89, and of *The Diary*. He was called before the House of Commons and reproved for printing full reports of the debates in the House of Commons in violation of the traditional rules of that House.

Woodhouse, Armine. See **Armine Wodehouse**

Woodley, William. 1728–93

Oldest son of William Woodley (of St. Kitts), from whom he inherited plantations in Nevis and St. Kitts. Oxford University. In

943

1761 he gained a seat in the House of Commons, where he voted against Bute's peace preliminaries in December, 1762; opposed the Grenville ministry, 1763–65; and supported the Rockingham ministry, 1765–66. He was governor of the Leeward Islands, 1766–71. In 1780 he again sat in the House of Commons. He left no record of any vote against the North ministry, but in 1781 Robinson wrote that "he seldom attends and seldomer votes." He was absent during all 5 of the critical votes which were recorded in February and March, 1782, immediately before the fall of the North ministry. It is reasonable to suppose that he continued his support of Rockingham's party until Rockingham's death in July, 1782. He voted for Shelburne's peace terms but did not vote on Fox's India Bill in 1783. He was again governor of the Leeward Islands, 1791–93. M.P. for Great Bedwin, 1761–66; Marlborough, 1780–84.

Worge, Richard Alchorne. 1707–74

Of Bedford Row, London; 2d son of Thomas Worge (of Eastbourne, Sussex). He was lieutenant in the 1st Foot Guards in 1732, captain in 1738, colonel in 1762, and major general in 1770. He was severely wounded at Fontenoy, distinguished himself at Culloden in 1745, and was governor of Senegal, 1758–68. In 1767 he was among those who solicited and received a large royal grant of land on St. John's Island in maritime Canada. In 1770 he voted against unseating Wilkes, his only recorded vote, 1770–72. M.P. for Stockbridge, 1768–72.

Worsley, Edward Meux. 1747–82

Of Gatcombe, Isle of Wight, Hampshire; oldest son of Sir Edward Worsley (of Gatcombe). Oxford from 1764. He became a member of the House of Commons in 1774. No vote is recorded in his name, 1774–80 (which may mean only that he voted steadily in the affirmative). He voted against the Dunning resolution of April 6, 1780, and supported the North ministry in every crucial division in the first 3 months of 1782. There is no indication that he ever addressed the House. M.P. for Yarmouth (Isle of Wight), 1774–75; Stockbridge, 1775–80; Newtown, 1780–82.

Worsley, James. 1725–87

Of Stembury, Isle of Wight; oldest son of David Worsley (of Stembury); probably a 2d cousin of Edward Meux Worsley (*q.v.*). During the first term of his service in the House of Commons he supported the North ministry, 1775–80, apparently without ever addressing the House, and voted against Dunning's resolution of April 6, 1780. M.P. for Yarmouth (Isle of Wight), 1775–80; Newtown, 1784.

Worsley, Richard. 1751–1805

Of Appuldurcombe, Isle of Wight; in 1768 succeeded his father, Thomas Worsley, as 7th baronet. Winchester, to Oxford in 1768; grand tour. In 1775 he married Dorothy, daughter of Sir John Fleming (1st baronet). After entering the House of Commons in 1774, he regularly supported the North ministry and according to the records addressed the House twice, in 1779 and in 1780, in defense of the North ministry. He was clerk comptroller of the Board of the Green Cloth, 1777–79; clerk of the Privy Council, privy councillor, and comptroller of the king's household in 1779; and vice admiral of the Isle of Wight, 1780–82. He was absent from a crucial vote in the House of Commons on February 22, 1782, because his presence was required at court in his divorce charge of adultery against his wife. (North commented: "If all my cuckolds desert me, I shall be beaten indeed!") But he voted with North in the other 4 critical divisions recorded for February and early March, 1782. He voted against Shelburne's peace terms in 1783; traveled extensively in the Near East, 1783–88; and was minister to Venice, 1793–97. A well-known antiquary, he collected art treasures and wrote about them; in 1781 he also published *A History of the Isle of Wight.* He was a fellow of the Royal Society. M.P. for Newport (Isle of Wight), 1774–84; Newtown, 1790–93 and 1796–1801.

Worsley, Thomas. 1710–78

Oldest son of Thomas Worsley (1686–1750; of Havingham Hall, Yorkshire; M.P.). Eton, 1725–28; Westminster; grand tour, 1735–37. He was a gentleman of the bedchamber, 1730–48; equerry to the king, 1743–60; and surveyor general of the Board of Works, 1760–78. He was apparently little interested in politics except as might be necessary to a career, and there is no indication that he ever addressed the House of Commons in the 13 years he was a member. He was a friend of Bute and supported him. He then voted with Grenville in 1763 and against repeal of the Stamp Act in 1766. He voted for Chatham's land tax in 1767 and in general supported the Grafton ministry and then the North ministry on Wilkes issues until his retirement in 1774. Namier pronounced him "a harmless gentleman of over fifty who never made any mark in politics." M.P. for Orford, 1761–68; Callington, 1768–74.

Wortley-Montagu, Edward. 1713–76

Of Wortley Hall, near Penistone; Wharncliffe, near Sheffield, Yorkshire; and Borehamwood, near Elstree, Hertfordshire; only son of Edward Wortley-Montagu (ca.1678–1761; M.P.). Westminster, to Leyden University in 1741, where he married "Sally, an industrious washerwoman." He was cornet of dragoons in 1743 and captain in the 1st Foot Guards in 1745, but resigned from military service in 1748 to become secretary at the Congress of Aix-la-Chapelle. Although he was a member of the House of Commons for 20 years, he appears never to have spoken there; records of his attendance are scanty, and he took no significant part. He left England in 1762 and spent most of the rest of his life in Italy, Egypt, and Asia Minor. He was talented but wildly eccentric—so much so that his extremely wealthy father left him only a pittance in 1761. He had none of the standard ambitions of the society into which he had been born. M.P. for Huntingdonshire, 1747–54; Bossiney, 1754–68.

Wraxall, Nathaniel William. 1751–1831

Of Laleham, near Staines, Middlesex; only son of Nathaniel Wraxall (merchant of Bristol); created baronet in 1813. In 1769, in his 18th year, he took ship to Bombay to become a writer for the East India Company. He served as judge advocate and paymaster of troops on the Guzerat and Baroche expeditions, 1771–72, and then returned to England. In 1774 he conducted negotiations between George III and the Danish court regarding Queen Mathilda, sister of George III, whom her husband had imprisoned for adultery with his first minister. In 1775 he published *Cursory Remarks Made on a Tour Through Northern Europe*, and in 1777 *Memoirs of the Kings of France*. Elected to the House of Commons in 1780, he voted with the North ministry, including all 5 of the critical divisions recorded in February and March, 1782. He made several long speeches. In May, 1782, he condemned the recall of Admiral Rodney by the Rockingham ministry, and in

December, 1782, he praised the naval measures the North ministry had taken before its fall. He voted against Shelburne's peace terms in 1783. In 1815 he published the first installments of his important, though not always accurate, *Historical Memoirs of My Own Times*. M.P. for Hindon, 1780–84; Ludgershall, 1784–90; Wallingford, 1790–94.

Wray, Cecil. 1734–1805

Of Fillingham, Lindsey, Lincolnshire; in 1752 succeeded his father, Sir John Wray (of St. Nicholas, Richmond, Yorkshire), as 13th baronet. Westminster from 1745, Cambridge from 1749. He was cornet of dragoons in 1755 but retired from military service in 1757, though he became captain of Lincolnshire militia in 1778. He was a Whig of strong traditions and reform inclinations and a founder of the Society of Supporters of the Bill of Rights in 1769. Entering the House of Commons in 1768, he defended Wilkes and voted against unseating him in January, 1770, against finding printers Wheble and Thompson in contempt of the House, and in general against the North ministry. He ardently supported the Wyvill Association movement from 1779, and voted for Dunning's first resolution in April, 1780. In 1782 he was a member of the Westminster Association Committee for the reform of Parliament, and on June 21, 1782 he spoke supporting, though with reservations, Stanhope's bill on bribery at elections. In February, 1783, he told the House of Commons that he would not support any ministry that included Lord North and decried North's "high prerogative principles and continued involvement in the American war." In that month he also urged the members of the House to show less partisanship, having recently shown much himself. He criticized Shelburne's peace terms but in the event supported them. In March, 1783, he deplored the desire to make, at all hazards, insistence on retaining Gibraltar the determining issue in judging the peace terms. In April, 1783, he criticized the management of the East India Company but later voted against Fox's India Bill, being strongly opposed to the coalition. In early 1784 he supported Pitt, but failed of re-election in a triangular contest for Westminster against Charles Fox and Admiral Hood. M.P. for East Retford, 1768–80; Westminster, 1782–84.

Wright (or Wrighte), George. ca.1705–66

Of Gayhurst, on River Ouse, Buckinghamshire, and Brooksby Hall, on River Wreak, near Leicester; oldest surviving son of George Wright (or Wrighte) (of Brooksby); grandson of Sir Nathaniel Wright (or Wrighte) (lord keeper of the great seal, 1700–1705); cousin of Harry Grey (1715–68; M.P.; 4th Earl of Stamford). Cambridge from 1724, at Inner Temple from 1725. In 1733 he married Barbara, daughter of Sir Thomas Clarges (2d baronet; M.P.). He was a demonstrated Tory in the 1754 elections and was listed as Tory in 1761, but his name appears in none of the opposition lists, 1763–65, and he presumably supported Grenville. M.P. for Leicester Borough, 1727–66.

Wright, James. 1716–85

4th son of Robert Wright (of Durham County; and chief justice of South Carolina); created baronet in 1772. In 1740, at Charleston, South Carolina, he married Sarah, only daughter of Captain James Maidman and a considerable heiress. He was a barrister of Grey's Inn from 1741, attorney general of South Carolina ca. 1742, and governor of Georgia, 1761–66. In 1765–66 he urged passage and then retention of the Stamp Act and became highly unpopular in the colonies. He had become a friend of Bute and corresponded with him regularly after Bute's enforced retirement in 1763. He returned to England in 1771 but again went to the colonies in 1773. In 1776 he was forced to leave hastily because of the rancor against him. In 1779 he was sent to Georgia to reorganize its government after it had been temporarily subdued by Sir Archibald Campbell (1739–91) (q.v.), but he received orders to abandon that effort in 1782, returned to England, and died shortly afterward.

Wrottesley, John. 1744–87

Of Wrottesley Hall, near Wolverhampton, Staffordshire; in 1769 succeeded his father, Sir Richard Wrottesley (1721–69; M.P.), as 8th baronet; his sister married Augustus Henry Fitzroy (q.v.); he was a nephew of Granville Leveson-Gower (q.v.). He was schooled at Westminster. In 1770 he married Frances, daughter of William Courtenay (q.v.). He was ensign in the 2d Foot Guards in 1761, captain in 1762, colonel in 1779, major general in 1782, and sometime master of horse to the Duke of York. In the House of Commons he voted with the administration, 1768–74, and during those years made 12 relatively unimportant speeches in the House. He served with his regiment in America, 1775–78. On his return to England he opposed continuing the war in America and thereafter voted with the opposition. He voted for Dunning's resolution of April 6, 1780; for Conway's 2 motions in February, 1782, to end the American war immediately; and for Sir John Rous's no-confidence motion of March 15, 1782. On April 1, 1782, he spoke in criticism of the new Rockingham ministry for lack of "candour and fairness" in its management of the select committee on East Indian affairs. He voted for Shelburne's peace terms in 1783 and supported Pitt, 1784–87. M.P. for Newcastle-under-Lyme, 1768; Staffordshire, 1768–87.

Wycombe, 2d Baron. See **William Fitzmaurice Petty**

Wyldbore, Matthew. ca.1716–81

Of Peterborough, Northamptonshire; only surviving son of John Wyldbore (of Peterborough). Cambridge from 1733, Inner Temple from 1735. Elected to the House of Commons in 1768, in 1774 he voted to continue the Grenville Election Act but almost invariably supported the North ministry until he left the House in 1780, just after voting against Dunning's resolution of April 6. One speech by him in the House is recorded, in 1779 on the militia. M.P. for Peterborough, 1768–80.

Wyndham, Charles. See **Charles Wyndham Edwin**

Wyndham, Charles. 1710–63

Of Orchard Wyndham, near Frome, Somerset; son of Sir William Wyndham (ca.1687–1740; of Orchard Wyndham; 3d baronet; M.P.; Tory leader), whom he succeeded in 1740 as 4th baronet; in 1750 succeeded his maternal uncle Algernon Seymour (1684–1750; 7th Duke of Somerset, 1st Earl of Egremont) as 2d Earl of Egremont. Westminster, to Oxford in 1725. In 1751 he married Alicia, sister of George Carpenter (1723–62; M.P.; 1st Earl of Tyrconnel, Irish). He came from an old Tory family long in Somerset and in 1754 demonstrated his Tory affiliation in the general elections but later co-operated with the Whig ministries. He was lord lieutenant of Cumberland, 1751–59; lord lieutenant of Sussex, 1762–63; and vice admiral of Cumberland, 1755–63. He was envoy to the proposed congress at Augsburg in 1761, which never officially convened. After 1760 he usually supported the policies of the court; but as secretary of state, southern department, 1761–63, his peace negotiations with France and Spain were not wholly satisfactory to Bute and Bedford. He was associated with Lord Halifax in the prosecution of Wilkes by general warrant in 1763. Horace Walpole called him "a composite of pride, ill-nature, avarice, and strict good-breeding ... he had no humour, and did not want sense, but he had neither knowledge of business, nor the smallest share of parliamentary abilities." M.P. for Bridgwater, 1735–41; Appleby, 1742–47; Taunton, 1747–50.

Wyndham, George O'Brien. 1752–1837

Styled Lord Cockermouth until 1763, when he succeeded his father, Charles Wyndham (*q.v.*), as 3d Earl of Egremont. Westminster, Eton, and Oxford from 1767. He became a successful stockbroker and was a patron of the turf, the arts, and smart society. He sponsored Flaxman, Hayden, Nollekens, and Turner, and gave away some £1,200,000 to charities and friends. In his earlier years he acted with the Whig opposition to the North ministry, but later he inclined to the Tory policies traditional in his family. In the House of Lords he voted for Fox's India Bill in 1783 and for some time afterward opposed Pitt but ended by supporting him. He was lord lieutenant of Sussex, 1819–35; vice admiral of Sussex, 1820–31; fellow of the Royal Society from 1797 and of the Society of Arts from 1800. Charles Greville called him "that fine old fellow."

Wyndham, Percy Charles. 1757–1833

2d son of Charles Wyndham (*q.v.*). Westminster from 1765. He secured the sinecure appointments of chancery registrar for Jamaica, and of prothonotary for the court in Barbados. He was elected to the House of Commons on March 11, 1782, just in time to cast his vote for Sir John Rous's motion of no confidence in the North ministry on March 15. He voted against Shelburne's peace terms in 1783 and then supported the coalition, but there is no indication that before 1790 he ever addressed the House of Commons. M.P. for Chichester, 1782–84; Midhurst, 1790–96.

Wyndham-O'Brien, Percy. ca.1723–74

2d son of Sir William Wyndham (ca.1687–1740; 3d baronet; M.P.);

younger brother of Charles Wyndham (*q.v.*); grandson of Charles Seymour (1662–1748; 6th Duke of Somerset); in 1741 added the surname O'Brien upon inheriting large estates under the will of his maternal uncle Henry O'Brien (7th Earl of Thomond, Irish); in 1756 created Earl of Thomond (Irish, new creation). Winchester, 1737–40; Oxford from 1740; grand tour. In the House of Commons from 1745, he supported the Egremont interests and, though reputed to have Tory leanings, supported the Whig ministries, 1745–66. He was a member of the Treasury Board, 1755–66; member of the Privy Council from 1757; treasurer of the king's household, 1757–61; cofferer, 1761–65; and lord lieutenant of Somerset, 1764–73. He went into opposition with Grenville in 1765 and voted against repeal of the Stamp Act in 1766 and against Chatham's land tax in 1767. He voted against the Grafton ministry, 1769–70, and in January, 1770, opposed the unseating of Wilkes. He opposed the North ministry in 1774 when he voted for extension of the Grenville Disputed Elections Act. He was recorder of Taunton in 1765. M.P. for Taunton, 1745–47; Minehead, 1747–54; Cockermouth, 1754–61; Minehead, 1761–68; Winchelsea, 1768–74.

Wynn, Glynn. ca.1737–93

Of Carnarvon; 2d surviving son of John Wynn (*q.v.*); younger brother of Thomas Wynn (*q.v.*). He entered the army in 1755 and was captain in 1759, lieutenant colonel in 1763, and retired in 1773. He was clerk of the crown for Carnarvonshire and Merionethshire, 1762–93; and in 1781 was appointed receiver general of the king's quit-rents in North Wales. A member of the House of Commons from 1768, he voted with the North ministry until March, 1777, when he joined the opposition, and in 1780 he voted for the Dunning resolution of April 6. But when given a court appointment in 1781 he reverted to support of the North ministry and voted with it in all 5 of the critical divisions in February and March, 1782. He supported Shelburne but did not vote on Shelburne's peace terms or on Fox's India Bill in 1783. From 1784 he voted irregularly. M.P. for Carnarvon boroughs, 1768–90.

Wynn, John. 1701–73

Of Bodvean, near Nevin, and Glynnllivon Castle, near Carnarvon;

951

in 1749 succeeded his father, Sir Thomas Wynn (ca.1678–1749; of Bodvean), as 2d baronet. Cambridge from 1720. He was constable of Carnarvon Castle, 1727–61; sheriff of Carnarvonshire, 1732–33; deputy cofferer of the king's household from 1743; deputy treasurer of Chelsea Hospital, 1744–54; and surveyor of the king's mines in Wales, 1754–61. In the House of Commons from 1740, he supported Pelham and Newcastle until 1762; George Grenville, 1763–65; and Chatham, 1767–68. M.P. for Carnarvonshire, 1740–41; Denbigh boroughs, 1741–47; Carnarvonshire, 1754–61; Carnarvon boroughs, 1761–68.

Wynn, Thomas. 1736–1807

Of Glynnllivon Castle, near Carnarvon; in 1773 succeeded his father, John Wynn (*q.v.*), as 3d baronet; in 1776 created Baron Newborough (Irish). Cambridge from 1754; grand tour, 1758–60. He married (1) in 1776 Catherine, daughter of John Perceval (*q.v.*), (2) in 1786 Maria Stella, aged 13, daughter of Lorenzo Chiappini (Italian innkeeper and sometime jailor of Modigliana, Italy. He was auditor of land revenues in Wales, 1756–81; constable of Carnarvon Castle (succeeding his father), 1761–81; and lord lieutenant of Carnarvonshire, 1761–81. He was colonel by brevet and was fellow of the Society of Arts from 1774. In the House of Commons from 1761, he voted with his father until 1768 in support of Grenville. Later he spoke and wrote against the war with the colonies but generally supported the North ministry and voted against the Dunning resolution of April 6, 1780, after which he left Parliament, to return 16 years later. In 1778 he raised militia against a French invasion and did so again in 1799. In 1769 he petitioned for a royal grant of 20,000 acres in Florida. M.P. for Carnarvonshire, 1761–74; St. Ives, 1775–80; Beaumaris, 1796–1807.

Wyvill, Christopher. 1740–1822

Of Constable Burton, near Leyburn, Yorkshire; born at Edinburgh, the son of Edward Wyvill (d. 1791; supervisor of excise at Edinburgh). Cambridge and took orders; L.L.D., 1764. In 1773 he married his cousin Elizabeth Wyvill, and through her inherited large estates in Berkshire. In 1779, as a comfortably endowed cleric of Black Notley, in Essex, who also held a living in Yorkshire, he conceived and to a great extent organized and directed the Yorkshire Association movement and its petitions for the reform of Parliament. He was also active in organizing similar associations elsewhere in England. The movement was inevitably an attack on the North ministry, and it was to some extent all too possessively embraced by the Whig opposition, and particularly its largest organized group, the Rockingham party. In 1794–95 he published an account of his activities in behalf of reform, a document of some historical importance. For details of his life see standard sources.

Yarborough, 1st Baron. See **Charles Anderson** (later **Pelham**)

Yarmouth, 1st Earl. See **Francis Seymour Conway**

Yelverton, Barry. 1736–1805

Oldest son of Francis Yelverton (d. 1746; of Blackwater and Kanturk, near Mallow, County Cork; weaver); in 1795 created Baron Yelverton (Irish); in 1800 created Viscount Avonmore (Irish) and Baron Avonmore (English). Trinity College, Dublin, from 1753; B.A., 1757; L.L.B., 1761; L.L.D., 1774; Middle Temple from 1759; bencher from 1772. In 1761 he married Mary, daughter of William Nugent (of County Westmeath), and the modest fortune she brought him greatly relieved his near poverty. He was king's counsel from 1772; attorney general for Ireland and privy councillor for Ireland, 1782; and chief baron of the Irish exchequer, 1783–1805. He was long a member of the Irish Parliament and "a zealous partisan for the claims of Ireland." "Few men possessed so much talent, so much heart, or so much weakness." His extravagance brought him heavily into debt, and his character broke down at the sight of the poverty of his family.

Yelverton, Henry. 1728–99

2d son of Talbot Yelverton (1690–1731; in 1717 created Earl of Sussex); in 1758 succeeded his brother George Augustus Yelverton (1727–58) as 3d (and 17th) Earl of Sussex. Westminster from 1738, Oxford from 1745. He was cornet of dragoons in 1752, lieutenant in 1755, captain in 1756, and colonel of Northamptonshire militia, 1763–84. In the House of Lords he voted for Fox's India Bill in 1783 and for Pitt's

Regency Bill in 1788, but had very little influence in politics of the period.

Yeo, Edward Roe. 1742–82

Of Normanton, near Grantham, Leicestershire, and North Huish, near Totnes, Devon; only son of George Yeo (of Huish). Eton, 1758–60; at Oxford and Middle Temple from 1761. Elected to the House of Commons in 1774, he voted with the opposition on the Wilkes issues in 1775 but supported the North ministry to its end, voting with it in all 5 of the crucial divisions recorded in February and March, 1782. There is no evidence that he ever addressed the House. In April, 1782, he supported Rockingham's proposals for Ireland, but he opposed the receipt tax, in deference, he said, to opposition opinion among his constituents. M.P. for Coventry, 1774–80 and 1781–82.

Yonge, George. 1731–1812

Of Colyton, near Seaton, and Escott, near Ottery St. Mary, Devon; in 1755 succeeded his father, Sir William Yonge (ca.1693–1755; M.P.), as 5th baronet. Eton, 1742–45; and Leipzig. In 1765 he married Anne Cleve, wealthy heiress of a London merchant. He was a member of the Admiralty Board, 1766–70; a vice treasurer of Ireland in 1782; and secretary at war and privy councillor in the Shelburne ministry, 1782–83, and in the Pitt ministry, 1783–94. He was made Knight of the Bath in 1788; was master of the mint, 1794–99; and was governor of the Cape of Good Hope from 1799. In January, 1770, he voted against unseating Wilkes; in October, 1775, he voted against approving the address from the throne; in 1780 he voted for Dunning's resolution of April 6; in February and March, 1782, he voted against the North ministry in all 5 of the critical divisions recorded. On behalf of Scotland he opposed North's proposal to increase the tax on barley; opposed North's wish to appoint commissioners of accounts from among others than members of Parliament; opposed Clerke's contractors' bill as too loosely drawn; and in March, 1781, supported the demands from the opposition for an investigation of navy and dockyard costs. M.P. for Honiton, 1754–61 and 1763–96; Old Sarum, 1799–1801.

Yonge, Philip. 1708–83

Son of Francis Yonge (merchant in Portugal). Westminster, to Cambridge in 1728; M.A., 1735; fellow from 1734; D.D., 1750. He was public orator of Cambridge University, 1746–52; master of Jesus College, 1752–58; and vice chancellor, 1752–54. He was vicar of Barrington in Cambridgeshire concurrently, 1748–50; vicar of Over in Cambridgeshire and prebendary of Westminster concurrently from 1750; rector of Loughton in Buckinghamshire concurrently from 1752; canon of St. Paul's largely concurrently, 1754–61; and rector of Therfield in Hertfordshire, 1757–62. He was bishop of Bristol, 1758–61; and bishop of Norwich, 1761–83. In the House of Lords from 1759, he recorded dissent to the vote approving the cider tax in 1763.

York, Duke of. See **Edward Augustus, Duke of York**

Yorke, Charles. 1722–70

Of Tittenhanger Park, near St. Albans, Hertfordshire; 2d son of Philip Yorke (1690–1764) (*q.v.*); brother of Philip Yorke (1720–90) (*q.v.*), James Yorke (*q.v.*), John Yorke (*q.v.*), and Joseph Yorke (*q.v.*); created 1st Baron Morden in 1770. Middle Temple from 1735, Cambridge from 1739, Lincoln's Inn from 1742, barrister in 1746, bencher from 1754. He was joint clerk of the crown in chancery, 1747–70; counsel for the East India Company from 1751; king's counsel from 1754; solicitor general to the Prince of Wales, 1754–56; solicitor general, 1756–61; and attorney general, 1762–63. He left Pitt's party for Rockingham's in 1763, and was proposed by Rockingham for the lord chancellorship in 1766, was rejected, but served again as attorney general, 1765–67. He helped draft the constitution for the province of Quebec, and in January, 1770, was offered the lord chancellorship by Grafton. He was eager for the post but hesitated in deference to his family's strong objection. He finally accepted, and was, in anticipation, created Lord Morden. But almost immediately afterward, after a difficult evening with a brother, he committed suicide, an event which played its emotional part in the almost immediate resignation of Grafton. Walpole, with something less than charity or justice, wrote of him: "His conduct was timid, irresolute, often influenced by his profession, oftener by his interest. He sacrificed his character to his ambition for the Great Seal, and his life to his repentance of having attained it." M.P. for Reigate, 1747–68; Cambridge University, 1768–70.

Yorke, James. ca.1730–1808

5th son of Philip Yorke (1690–1764) (*q.v.*); brother of Charles Yorke (*q.v.*), Philip Yorke (1720–90) (*q.v.*), John Yorke (*q.v.*), and Joseph Yorke (*q.v.*). He was prebendary of Rochester Cathedral in 1754; canon of Windsor in 1756; prebendary of Lincoln Cathedral and dean at Lincoln in 1762; bishop of St. David's, 1774–79; bishop of Gloucester, 1779–81; and bishop of Ely, 1781–1808.

Yorke, John. 1728–1801

Of Sonning, near Reading, Berkshire; 4th son of Philip Yorke (1690–1764) (*q.v.*); brother of Philip Yorke (1720–90) (*q.v.*), Charles Yorke (*q.v.*), Joseph Yorke (*q.v.*), and James Yorke (*q.v.*) Cambridge and Lincoln's Inn from 1746, barrister in 1754. He was clerk in chancery, 1746–1801; member of the Board of Trade and Plantations, 1761–63 and 1765; member of the Admiralty Board, 1765–66; and clerk of the crown from 1774. In 1762 he left Newcastle to support Bute. He lost his chief court appointment when the Grenville ministry came into office, but regained it under Rockingham in 1765. He voted with his family but appears to have been only lukewarm in his support of the North ministry. He nevertheless voted against Rous's no-confidence motion on March 15, 1782. Few other votes by him were recorded. M.P. for Higham Ferrers, 1753–68; Reigate, 1768–84.

Yorke, Joseph. 1724–92

3d son of Philip Yorke (1690–1764) (*q.v.*); brother of John Yorke (*q.v.*), Philip Yorke (1720–90) (*q.v.*), Charles Yorke (*q.v.*), and James Yorke (*q.v.*). He was created Baron Dover in 1788. He was ensign of foot guards in 1741; lieutenant colonel of guards at Fontenoy and in Scotland, 1744–46; aide to the Duke of Cumberland and then to the king, 1745–48; colonel in 1749; major general in 1758; lieutenant general in 1760; and general in 1777. He was secretary to the embassy at Paris, 1749–51; minister at The Hague, 1751–61; and ambassador to The Hague, 1761–80. He was Knight of the Bath from 1761 and privy councillor from 1768. In 1778 Eden and Wedderburn urged North to appoint him secretary of state. North approached Yorke, but he declined, because, Wedderburn claimed, North's offer had been half-hearted. In general he supported the current ministry. M.P. for East Grinstead, 1751–61; Dover, 1761–74; Grampound, 1774–80.

Yorke, Philip. 1690–1764

Born at Dover, the only son of Philip Yorke (of Dover; attorney); in

1733 created Baron Hardwicke of Worcestershire; in 1754 created Viscount Royston and Earl of Hardwicke; father of Philip Yorke (1720–90) (*q.v.*); Charles Yorke (*q.v.*), James Yorke (*q.v.*), John Yorke (*q.v.*), and Joseph Yorke (*q.v.*). He worked in the office of a London solicitor, 1706–1708. In 1708 he enrolled at Middle Temple and became a barrister. Later he joined Lincoln's Inn and was a bencher there from 1724. His legal talents were nearly as evident as his ambition, and he rose rapidly. He was solicitor general, 1720–24; privy councillor from 1733; chief justice of the king's bench, 1733–37; speaker of the House of Lords in 1734 and 1736; and lord chancellor, 1736–56. He did much to transform the laws of equity from a chaos of precedents to an orderly system and had considerable political influence during the Pelham and Newcastle regimes. The Earl of Chesterfield said of him: "He valued himself more for being a great Minister of State, which he certainly was not, than upon being a great Chancellor, which he certainly was." In the House of Lords, in 1763 he recorded dissents from majority votes approving (1) Bute's peace preliminaries, (2) the cider tax, and (3) restrictions on parliamentary privilege in the Wilkes case. M.P. for Lewes, 1719–22; Seaford, 1722–34.

Yorke, Philip. 1720–90

Styled Viscount Royston from 1754; in 1764 succeeded his father, Philip Yorke (1690–1764) (*q.v.*), as 2d Earl of Hardwicke; brother of Charles Yorke (*q.v.*), John Yorke (*q.v.*), James Yorke (*q.v.*), and Joseph Yorke (*q.v.*). Cambridge from 1737; L.L.D., 1749. In 1740 he married Jemima, daughter of John Campbell (1696–1782) (*q.v.*). He was teller of the exchequer, 1738–90; fellow of the Royal Society from 1741; fellow of the Society of Arts from 1744; a trustee of the British Museum, 1753–90; lord lieutenant of Cambridgeshire, 1757–90; privy councillor from 1760; and high steward of Cambridge University, 1764–90. He was a member of the cabinet without portfolio with the Rockingham ministry in 1766. In the House of Lords he voted for Fox's India Bill in 1783, despite the king's statement of his bitter opposition to that bill. M.P. for Reigate, 1741–47; Cambridgeshire, 1747–64.

Yorke, Philip. ca.1743–1804

Of Erthig, near Wrexham, Denbighshire; only son of Simon Yorke

957

(of Erthig; cousin of Philip Yorke [1690–1764] [*q.v.*]). Eton, 1759–60; Cambridge from 1762; Lincoln's Inn from 1762; barrister in 1767. In 1770 he married Elizabeth, daughter of Sir John Cust (*q.v.*). He generally supported the North ministry from his election to the House of Commons in 1775, except that he supported some of the reform measures which North opposed. He was sheriff of Denbighshire, 1786–87. M.P. for Helston, 1775–81; Grantham, 1792.

Yorke, Philip. 1757–1834

Oldest son of Charles Yorke (*q.v.*); in 1790 succeeded his uncle Philip Yorke (1720–90) (*q.v.*) as 3d Earl of Hardwicke. Harrow, 1770–71; Cambridge, 1775–76; grand tour. In 1782 he married Elizabeth, sister of Alexander Lindsay (*q.v.*). He was lord lieutenant of Cambridgeshire, 1790–1834; privy councillor from 1801; lord lieutenant of Ireland, 1801–1806; a trustee of the British Museum, 1802–34; and high steward of Cambridge University, 1806–34. He supported the North ministry, with reservations, from his election to the House of Commons in 1780. He voted for Shelburne's peace terms in February, 1783, and opposed the coalition. On one occasion in 1783 he accused North and Fox before the House of Commons with attempts to bribe a member of the House, but his charge was deflated and laughed out of court. He was made Knight of the Garter in 1803. M.P. for Cambridgeshire, 1780–90.

Young, Arthur. 1741–1820

Younger son of Arthur Young (1693–1759; rector of Bradfield, near Bury St. Edmunds, Suffolk; prebendary of Canterbury). In 1758 he was apprenticed to Robertson of Lynn to learn finance for a career in banking, but soon yielded to the heady temptation to write and publish political pamphlets. From that experience he moved to the more placid one of farming and soon gained the practical experience in agriculture evident in his writing. He then made traveling surveys of agricultural conditions and methods, which became the basis for his immediately successful *Farmer's Letters*, 1767; for *The State of the Waste Lands of Great Britain*, 1773, which enhanced his reputation; for *Political Arithmetic*, 1774, which was probably even more widely read; for *Annals of Agriculture*, 1784–1809; and for his final classic, *Travels in France*, 1792, which is still widely read.

Young, James. d. 1789

His origins are now obscure. He probably entered the navy in 1737. He was a lieutenant in 1739 and captain in 1743. He served in the Mediterranean area, 1737–48, and was successively captain of the *Jason* in 1752; the *Intrepid* in 1755, under Admiral John Byng at Minorca; the *Burford* in 1757, under Hawke in the Bay of Biscay; and the *Mars* in 1759, off Brest. He commanded a squadron off Havre in 1761, was rear admiral in 1762, vice admiral in 1770, and in command of the Leeward Islands station in 1778.

Young, William. d. 1788

Of Charlton, by Dover, Kent, and Delaford, near Iver, Buckinghamshire; created baronet in 1769. He was born in the West Indies, where his father had gone after participating in the Jacobite uprising in 1715. He was lieutenant governor of Dominica, 1763–70, and governor, 1770–74. In 1775 he went to Paris with Robert Melville to seek indulgence for British settled on the then French island of Tobago. He died at St. Vincent's.

Z

Zoffany (or **Zoffanji** or **Zaffanii**), **John** (or **Johann**). 1733–1810

Born at Ratisbon; his father, of a Bohemian family, was architect to the Prince of Tours and Taxis. He studied painting at Rome until 1758, when he went to England and first worked for Stephen Rimbault, famous clockmaker, and then for Benjamin Wilson as a painter of drapery. He also painted portraits which attracted notice, and he became a member of the Society of Artists in 1762. He painted Garrick and other notables with a fine dramatic flair and became a member of the Royal Academy in 1769. He was in Italy, 1772–79, and then in India, 1783–90, in both places painting for lucrative commissions. His skill lay chiefly in conversation pieces with dramatic backgrounds, the latter sometimes painted by his assistants. His portrait of George III is striking and handsomer than the subject; so, perhaps, is his self-portrait.

959

Zuylestein, William Henry Nassau. 1717–81

Of St. Osyth Priory, near Colchester, Essex; styled Viscount Tunbridge until 1738, when he succeeded his father, Frederick Nassau Zuylestein (1683–1738), as 4th Earl of Rochford. Eton, 1725–32. He was lord of the bedchamber (at £1,000 a year), 1738–55, vice admiral of Essex in 1748; a member of Whites Club from 1749; envoy to Turin and to the king of Sardinia, 1749–55; 1st lord of the bedchamber and groom of the stole, 1755–60; privy councillor from 1755; and lord lieutenant of Essex, 1756–81. He was ambassador to Spain, 1763–66. In 1766 his personal extravagance had been so great that to escape from his debts when leaving Madrid he had to pawn his silver plate and jewels for £6,000. He was ambassador to France, 1766–68; secretary of state, northern department, October 21, 1768–December 19, 1770; secretary of state, southern department, 1770–November 10, 1775. He was made Knight of the Garter in 1778. He favored a firm line with the American colonists, opposed the repeal of taxes and duties on the colonists, and in 1775 resigned partly on the American issue. Horace Walpole wrote that he had little ability or knowledge but "meant honestly, behaved plausibly," and was pliant and inoffensive.